Algorithmic Trading & DMA

An introduction to direct access trading strategies.

By Barry Johnson

In memory of my mother.

To my father.

Contents

Preface

Trading is still very much an art rather than a science.

The fundamentals of trading have not changed for decades (if not millennia). However, the modern trading environment bears very little resemblance to that of the 1980s, or even the early 1990s. Electronic trading has transformed the markets, making them more accessible than ever before. Tools like Direct Market Access (DMA) and algorithmic trading give investors a lot more control over how their strategies are executed. For instance, DMA enables investors to send orders to exchanges, using their broker's infrastructure.

Accessibility is great, but good traders are a special breed; they have a lot of experience and detailed market knowledge. Algorithmic trading distils some of this knowledge into pre-packaged rule-sets, or algorithms. A computerised system is responsible for executing orders by strictly following these rules, offering an efficient alternative to manual trading.

In order to get the maximum benefit from technologies like algorithmic trading and DMA it is vital to have a thorough understanding of them. Hopefully, by reading this book you should end up with a good fundamental knowledge of both of these topics, as well as trading and markets in general.

Who should read this book?

Algorithmic trading encompasses trading, quantitative analysis and computer programming. Hence, this book is targeted towards all three areas. It should serve as a good introduction for any investors, traders, salespeople, analysts, quantitative analysts (quants), or software developers who are new to this field.

The aim is to take the reader from the ground up, so very little knowledge of the markets or trading is assumed. There are also no requirements for any programming knowledge. We will review trading algorithms in some detail, but tables and diagrams will be used to illustrate their function rather than snippets of code. Similarly, whilst there is some mathematics in this book, it is not a mathematical text, so formulas are provided only where relevant. Examples are used to keep the math in context. References are given for those who might want to find the actual proofs.

Another aim of this book is to try to help bridge some of the gaps between the practice of trading and the theory. A phenomenal amount of research has been carried out into trading and markets. Digitisation has meant that huge amounts of data are now available for study. The fields of econophysics and "phynance" are also busily applying advanced techniques from physics to analyse the markets. Some of these studies are highly theoretical; however, there is also a large amount of empirical research, based on data from the world's major markets. Throughout this book there are sections providing reviews of relevant research and showing how this might be applied in practice. References to key academic papers are given, so it is also a good starting point for more advanced research.

A wide range of financial assets may be traded on the world's markets. One of the most interesting things about algorithmic trading and DMA is their potential to span across asset classes, catering for anything from stocks and bonds to derivatives. Hence, this book provides coverage for all the major types of asset, together with a thorough overview of the world's markets. Obviously, there is a slight bias towards equities, since these continue to lead the way in terms of adoption. Even so, there is a lot to be learned from other asset classes. So throughout this book examples will refer to asset XYZ, only discussing equities, bonds or derivatives when there are distinct differences.

An outline of the book

The book is divided into four main parts. The first two parts offer a general overview of trading and markets followed by a more detailed review of algorithmic trading and DMA. The last two parts offer an in-depth look at the implementation of these trading strategies together with a summary of some advanced trading techniques. Experienced users may prefer to skim over the first parts, whilst readers who just want an introduction should focus on parts I and II and perhaps part IV.

Part I: An overview of trading and markets

These chapters set the scene with a broad overview of the world's major asset classes and a summary of their respective markets. Market microstructure is also introduced to help highlight the main structural differences between the world's markets.

Chapter 1 introduces algorithmic trading and direct market access, highlighting their roles as core execution methods for institutional trading. After a brief review of each of these mechanisms, they are compared in terms of their efficiency, usability and performance. Some of the fears and myths, which have gathered around the use of algorithmic trading, are also addressed.

Chapter 2 introduces the theory of market microstructure, which focuses solely on the mechanics of trading, unlike economics or asset pricing. A basic grounding in this underlying theory is useful, allowing us to take advantage of the empirical research that has been carried out, and to appreciate the fundamental differences between the world's markets. The key components of market structure and design are discussed, before analysing the trading process in more detail. The principles behind transaction cost analysis are also introduced.

Chapter 3 rounds off the introduction by reviewing the world's major asset classes and their respective markets. Trading has been divided by asset class for decades. Still, over the last few years institutions have increasingly started to break down the walls, bringing them closer together. This is not a case of "one size fits all"; there are still huge differences between many of the world's markets, but there many common trends as well. There are also important lessons that they can learn from each other.

Part II: Algorithmic trading and DMA strategies

The second part of the book concentrates on the specifics of algorithmic trading and DMA. This starts with orders since these are the basic building block for all trading strategies. Next, trading algorithms are reviewed in more detail. Transaction cost analysis is then revisited, leading on to consider how to find the optimal trading strategy.

Chapter 4 focuses on orders. These may simply represent trade instructions, but there are a huge variety of different order types beyond the standard market and limit orders. Optional conditions allow control over factors such as how and when the orders become active and for how long. With markets increasingly comprising of multiple venues, the rules for order routing are also a key consideration. A detailed understanding of the mechanism and variety of order types and conditions is vital for both DMA and algorithmic trading.

Chapter 5 covers the various types of trading algorithm in more detail. They are classified using three main types, namely impact-driven (e.g. Volume Weighted Average Price (VWAP)), cost-driven (e.g. implementation shortfall) and opportunistic (e.g. liquidity seeking). For each algorithm, we examine their basic mechanism and discuss common variations. To enable comparison, a standard example order is used throughout. This, combined with charts showing the potential trading patterns, highlights the differences (and similarities) between the various algorithms.

Chapter 6 concentrates on the importance of transaction cost analysis. Costs have a significant effect on investment returns; therefore, both pre and post-trade analysis are vital. An example trade is used to decompose the transaction costs into their key components, such as market impact and timing risk. To put this in perspective, some comparisons of costs across the world's markets are provided.

Chapter 7 goes on to consider how the optimal trading strategy might be selected. A framework for trading decisions is examined; this assesses orders in terms of their difficulty. The impact of investment decisions/requirements, such as benchmarks or risk aversion, is also considered. The "trader's dilemma" of balancing the trade-off between cost and risk is visualised using the efficient trading frontier. This is then applied to the selection of trading algorithms. The effect of both requirements and asset-specific factors, such as liquidity and volatility, are then reviewed. A potential decision tree for algorithm selection is then proposed.

Part III: Implementing trading strategies

The third part of the book focuses on the specifics of implementing algorithmic trading and DMA strategies. The decisions related to order placement are discussed, as well as the common tactics that may be used to achieve the goals of algorithms. Methods for enhancing the performance of these strategies are then reviewed. The technological aspects of implementing these strategies are also considered.

Chapter 8 considers the intricacies of order placement. A considerable amount of market microstructure research has analysed how market conditions affect order placement decisions and execution probability.

Chapter 9 discusses execution tactics. These provide common order placement mechanisms to achieve the goals of trading algorithms. Based on the theory of order placement, common tactics/mechanisms are then described together with a summary of how they might be used by trading algorithms.

Chapter 10 considers some of the ways in which the performance of trading algorithms may be enhanced. To help make these strategies more proactive, short-term forecasting models for key market conditions, such as price, volume and volatility, are considered. There is also a review of cost estimation models for more cost-driven algorithms. Another potential area for improvement is the handling of specific events such as witching days or trading halts. Empirical market microstructure studies are reviewed to give an insight into how predictable the reactions to such events might be.

Chapter 11 reviews the main considerations for actually implementing trading strategies, with a focus on the required technology. Clearly, order management is a key component, so the mechanics of order entry and routing are described. The requirements for developing platforms for electronic trading strategies are then reviewed. The implementation and testing of trading rules is also discussed.

Part IV: Advanced trading strategies

The final part of the book focuses on techniques that are closer to the cutting edge, in terms of algorithmic trading, such as portfolio and multi-asset trading, handling news and artificial intelligence. All of these subjects are being tackled at present in one form or another; it is only a matter of time before they become as common as VWAP or implementation shortfall.

Chapter 12 highlights the potential for portfolio trading. Portfolio risk and diversification are discussed in more detail, together with a review of some common portfolio risk measures, such as beta and tracking error. Next, some additional goals for optimal portfolio trading, e.g. hedging and cash balancing, are examined. Based on this, the use of standard algorithms is considered, followed by a review of how best to tailor trading algorithms for portfolio trading.

Chapter 13 considers the potential for multi-asset trading. This ranges from straightforward approaches, such as incorporating cross currency execution, to more complex hedging and arbitrage. Hedging provides a mechanism for offsetting risk, generally via derivatives. Arbitrage extracts profits from mispricing between assets, and relies on hedging to stay risk-free. After looking at some examples, the chapter ends with a summary of additional considerations for multi-asset trading algorithms.

Chapter 14 examines the potential for incorporating news into trading algorithms. The main issue with this is the difficulty of accurately interpreting news. Complex artificial intelligence and natural language processing techniques are being employed for this. The impact of news and information flow has also been a key topic for microstructure research. Therefore, a summary of market reactions to news in terms of market conditions, such as price, volume and volatility, is provided. These may be used to enhance existing algorithms' performance when news breaks; more news-centric algorithms are also discussed.

Chapter 15 shifts the focus to data mining and artificial intelligence (AI). These techniques may be used to search for relationships between assets, often by analysing historical time series data for prices, volume etc. Potentially, they offer a means of short-term forecasting that may give better results than purely statistical measures, even in volatile markets. They may also be used for testing trading strategies and their associated parameters.

Appendices: A review of world markets by asset class

The appendices provide an overview of each of the major asset classes and their main markets. The focus is on their adoption of electronic trading and the provision of algorithmic trading and DMA. The regional differences between the Americas, Europe and Asia are also examined.

About the author

My background is software development, having spent more than twelve years working in major investment banks. Most of my experience is in electronic trading and risk analysis, spanning platforms for algorithmic and portfolio trading, as well as some for proprietary trading. The main focus has been equities, although listed derivatives, foreign exchange and fixed income have also played a part. The book evolved out of my desire to understand how market microstructure could be applied to create more efficient trading algorithms.

Acknowledgements

This book is based on a wide range of sources. It would not have been possible without all the information which other researchers and firms have made available through their own endeavours. In particular, thanks must go to all the researchers, firms and publishers who have given permission to use figures from their publications, as well as all the individuals who gave feedback on the various drafts. This project is also indebted to services such as the Social Science Research Network (SSRN) and Google Scholar, which made finding research so much easier.

Part I

An overview of trading and markets

This first part of the book sets the scene with a general overview of algorithmic and direct access trading. It also provides a brief review of the world's major asset classes and their respective markets.

- Chapter 1 covers the core execution methods that are used in institutional trading and details how and why algorithmic and direct access trading developed.

- Chapter 2 introduces market microstructure, the theory for the mechanics of trading. This highlights some of the fundamental differences between the world's markets.

- Chapter 3 offers a brief overview of all the world's major asset classes and their markets. More detailed reviews are provided for each asset class in the appendices.

Hopefully, by the end of these three chapters you should have a broad appreciation of the world's markets and trading in general. You should also have a clearer view of algorithmic and direct access trading and their use in the world's markets.

Chapter 1

Overview

Algorithmic trading is simply a computerised rule-based system responsible for executing orders to buy or sell a given asset.

Direct Market Access (DMA) enables clients to send orders to exchanges by using their broker's membership.

1.1 Introduction

Algorithmic trading and Direct Market Access (DMA) are important tools for the electronic trading of financial assets.

Nowadays, a bewildering array of assets can be traded electronically. Stocks and bonds, cash, certificates and a variety of derivatives contracts may all be bought and sold just at the push of a button. The technology to achieve this is still relatively new, but the fundamental market mechanics of buying and selling remain the same. Put simply, sellers need to find buyers (and vice-versa) as quickly and efficiently as possible. Corporations and governments issue assets in order to raise the cash (or capital) required to meet their needs. Likewise, investors and speculators must be able to easily buy and sell assets in order to see a return from their capital.

Over time, the world's markets have evolved to accommodate the differing requirements of both the issuers of financial assets and those who invest in them. The ease with which such trading takes place is commonly referred to as liquidity: Highly liquid markets (or assets) are more active and so usually much easier and cheaper to trade in. To improve liquidity, dedicated trading venues, such as exchanges, have often been established. However, there may not always be a natural buyer or seller to trade with, so markets also rely on intermediaries to "grease the wheels": Specialised traders, or dealers, trade for a set price with the aim of making a short-term profit. Brokers act as agents to place their clients' orders with the dealers, or match them with other clients' orders. Since both brokers and dealers facilitate the issuance and selling of assets they are often referred to as the "sell-side". In turn, institutional investors are often called the "buy-side".

To illustrate the trading process, Figure 1-1 shows some example trade flows from the point of view of an investor. Traditionally, a buy-side initiated trade is placed as an order with a broker's salesperson who must then communicate the order to a trader (or dealer). In turn, the trader would then either quote a price to trade against their own inventory or alternatively work the order on an exchange. This is shown as the pathway labelled A in Figure 1-1. Electronic trading simply offers a means of issuing such orders via computers.

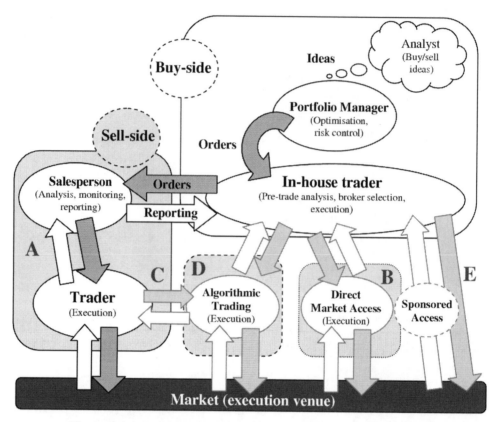

Figure 1-1 A comparison of the different order execution methods

Direct Market Access (DMA) is where brokers allow clients access to their order routing infrastructure, as shown by pathway B. This allows the buy-side to issue their electronic orders almost directly to the exchanges, effectively giving them much the same level of control over an order's execution as a sell-side trader has. Sponsored access takes this to the next level, for clients whose high-frequency trading strategies need ultra-low latency connections. Essentially, this allows clients to connect directly to the market, as shown in pathway E, using the broker's trading identifier, but their own infrastructure. Alternatively, the buy-side can organise membership of the specific market and so have native access.

Algorithmic trading takes a slightly different approach to DMA: A computerised system is responsible for executing the orders to buy or sell a given asset, rather than being worked manually by a trader. So a computer program follows preset rules to determine how each order should be executed. Based on these rules, it splits off portions (or child orders) to send to the market, often tracking market conditions and events. Initially, such trading algorithms were used as a labour-saving device for busy sell-side traders, labelled pathway C in Figure 1-1. As these algorithms became more established, brokers started to offer their buy-side clients direct access to them, shown by pathway D. Together with DMA, allowing clients access to trade on markets in this way is also known as Direct Access Trading.

It is important to note that all of the labelled pathways in Figure 1-1 are only concerned with executing a given order. The actual investment decision is a completely separate process. In this case, it is shown as an idea from a buy-side analyst; it is this idea that leads to the decision to trade. This is then analysed and approved by the portfolio manager before being translated into an actual order to buy (or sell) a set quantity of asset XYZ. The order is then usually passed on to an in-house trader who decides on the most appropriate approach and on which broker/s to use. Alternatively, for more quantitative investment funds the order may well be generated by an automated system. Either way, algorithmic trading, DMA and the sell-side trader are all just a means to execute this order; hence, we can also refer to them as core execution methods.

In some ways, the term algorithmic trading is an unfortunate choice, particularly for such use by institutional investors. Trading tends to make people think of dealers buying low and selling high. Whereas the algorithmic trading systems, which are offered by the major brokers, only execute the orders they are given, as Figure 1-1 tries to show. Perhaps a more representative name for this process is "algorithmic execution".

Clearly, there are exceptions to every rule; there are no major technical reasons why trading algorithms could not also incorporate investment decisions. Indeed, as the buy-side starts to develop their own algorithms this may well become more commonplace. However, the main aim of this book is focus on how algorithms and DMA may be used to enhance order execution.

Over the last few years, algorithmic trading has become a hot topic. New reports keep predicting an increasing global market share, which is expanding from equities to foreign exchange, futures and options and even bonds. There has also been bad press; some headlines have foretold the end of trading, as we know it. Whilst the start of the sub-prime crisis in the summer of 2007, saw "algorithmic trading" blamed for both market volatility and some firms realising huge losses. Volatility is certainly higher; in part, this is due to the increase in speed achieved by electronic and algorithmic trading. However, any losses that firms have made are generally due to their investment strategy. If this is not suitable for the market conditions then losses will be realised. Algorithmic trading is the bullet, not the finger on the trigger. In section 1.10, some of the common fears and myths surrounding algorithmic trading will also be examined (and hopefully debunked).

Before we move on to consider each of these core execution methods in more detail, let's briefly review some fundamentals, such as risk, return and costs, from the perspective of both an investor and a trader.

1.2 Fundamentals

Investment theory tries to maximize profits and minimize risk by carefully choosing different assets. Arguably, the best known approach is modern portfolio theory (MPT) pioneered by Harry Markowitz (1952).

Modern portfolio theory models profits from the returns (or price changes) in a portfolio of financial assets. Volatility is often used as a proxy for the overall risk; this represents the standard deviation of the returns. Assets with higher returns are generally riskier. Portfolios can be made up of an almost infinite set of compositions, using a range of assets with various weightings. Plotting the risk-return characteristics of these allows an efficient frontier to be constructed, as shown in Figure 1-2 (a). This is the upper edge of the shaded region; it represents the portfolios with the highest returns for a given amount of risk. Consequently, an investor must focus on the overall makeup of their portfolio, as much as the risk and returns for individual assets.

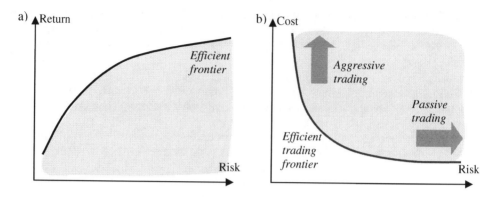

Figure 1-2 A difference in perspective

In order to build up this optimal portfolio we need to buy or sell the specific assets, and so send order/s to broker/dealers or direct to the markets, as we saw in Figure 1-1. Risk (or volatility) is again important, since it shows how much each asset's price might change by. However, returns are somewhat less important, since we are now focussed on executing the given order/s, often in the next second/s, minute/s or hour/s. Instead, cost becomes more important, as shown in Figure 1-2 (b). Executing each order has an associated cost, from the impact it has on the asset's price to broker and exchange fees. Trading faster with large or aggressively priced orders will generally have more impact and so cost more, although the speed of execution reduces the risk. Whereas trading more slowly or passively costs less but exposes us to risk from the asset's price volatility. This is what Robert Kissell and Morton Glantz (2003) refer to as the trader's dilemma. Striking the right balance between cost and risk is a question of taking into account the investor's priorities, as we will see in Chapter 7; it can be the key to achieving optimal execution.

1.3   Core execution methods

Institutional trading can broadly be classified as either agency or principal trading. In agency trading, the broker acts as a conduit to the market, as we saw in Figure 1-1. The client may also give trading instructions, such as to execute throughout the day or target a specific benchmark price or a certain percentage of the market volume. With principal trading, the broker/dealer agrees an up-front price for the asset, which they will fulfil either from their own inventory or by executing on the markets. Since principal trading is carried out with a specific dealer, rather than at an exchange, this is also referred to as "over-the-counter" (OTC) trading.

In terms of risk, the client is exposed to the market with agency trading. The price may move favourably (or not), there is also the possibility that the order may fail to be completed. The broker will strive to achieve best execution for the client, but at the end of the day they are acting as an agent for the client, they do not take on any of the risk. In comparison, with principal trades the risk is transferred immediately to the broker/dealer. Consequently, principal trading is more expensive because the dealer tries to offset this by incorporating it in the negotiated price. The investor must decide whether the up-front costs are worthwhile compared to the potential market risk.

In general, both types of trading are supported for most equities and for the standardised (or listed) futures and options contracts, which are traded on exchanges. The bond and foreign exchange markets have tended to be based more on dealers (or market makers), and so principal or OTC trading is more common (although agency trading is sometimes available for the more liquid assets).

Hence, the final destination for orders in Figure 1-1 also depends on the asset being traded. Algorithmic trading and DMA are generally only viable options when there is a well-established secondary market, such as an exchange. So direct access trading has historically centred on stocks and futures. Although algorithmic trading and DMA are rapidly spreading to most of the major asset classes, as we shall see in Chapter 3.

Agency trading may also be classified based on the execution method used to achieve it. "High-touch" trading is where orders are worked manually by a trader. Algorithmic trading is sometimes referred to as "Low-touch" trading, since it requires little or no handling by actual traders and so can be offered as a lower cost agency service. The final piece of the puzzle is DMA, which is also referred to as "Zero-touch". With DMA the broker's own electronic access to markets is extended out to their clients. The sell-side traders have nothing to do with the order; instead, the execution is handled manually by the client.

The increasing focus on transaction costs by the buy-side has meant a decline in the more traditional "High-touch" trading. Still, all these methods are in fact complementary, since they are trying to meet the same objectives, as Figure 1-3 tries to show.

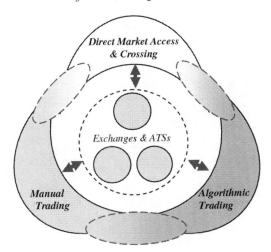

Figure 1-3 The range of core execution methods

Both buy (and sell-side) traders now have a wider choice of execution method than ever before. They can take complete control of the execution by using DMA (or native access), or they can delegate it to an algorithmic trading system. Vendors are even working on systems that allow traders to "pick and mix". For instance, Neovest's AlgoGenetics allows "meta-algorithms" to be created which can combine algorithms from a range of brokers together with DMA orders.

Continual evolution and the adoption of similar tactics mean that the boundaries between these methods are constantly blurring. For example, increasingly complex DMA order types, such as iceberg orders and smart order routing, are making it more difficult to differentiate between pure DMA and algorithmic trading.

Another example of the constant evolution of trading strategies is crossing. Block trading is a specialisation for handling large orders of single assets. The advent of platforms such as ITG's POSIT allowed investors to participate in electronic crossing, rather than use brokers' block trading desks for such orders. This trend has continued with the success of the so-called "dark pools" of liquidity offered by the hidden crossings of Alternative Trading Systems (ATS). Although the probability of execution is lower than a broker-mediated block trade, these approaches offer the potential of getting a better price. As with DMA, it is the client's responsibility to manage these orders. Therefore, crossing is shown together with DMA in Figure 1-3. Sourcing liquidity via these "dark pools" has also become extremely important for algorithmic trading.

1.4   Institutional trading types

In the previous section, we focussed on the methods used to actually execute orders. The orders themselves are invariably sourced from the buy-side, in other words institutional or hedge fund investors, as part of their overall trading strategy. Figure 1-4 shows the broader range of trading types, which are widely adopted by different kinds of investors.

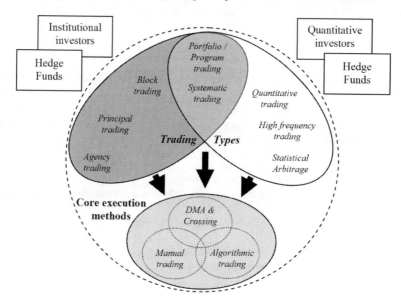

Figure 1-4 Different trading types

Traditionally, institutional investors, such as investment and pension funds, maintain large portfolios with specific investment criteria. Orders are generated when they need to change the make-up of their portfolios. For single assets, they may choose to trade in either an agency or a principal fashion, whilst block trading may be used for larger orders.

Quantitative investment funds adopt more highly automated strategies, as do some hedge funds. For those targeting short-term arbitrage opportunities or generating revenue by market making, this means much higher trading frequencies. So they are even more focussed on low-cost execution methods, such as algorithmic trading and DMA.

Portfolio trading is sometimes referred to as basket or **program trading**. It provides investors with a cost-effective means of trading multiple assets, rather than having to trade them individually. Typically, this is used when they need to adjust or rebalance their portfolios. The trading list represents the assets that must be bought or sold to transform the investor's current portfolio to their desired target. Portfolio trading is a broker provided service, which allows for economies of scale, and so it generally offers a cheaper alternative for handling such transitions. As with single stock institutional trading, the investor may choose to negotiate a principal trade with a broker/dealer, or have a broker trade the list in an agency fashion. We will revisit this topic in more detail in Chapter 12.

Systematic, black-box, quantitative and high frequency trading are terms which all sound like references to algorithmic trading, and are sometimes mistakenly used as such. However, they have as much to do with the style of investment as the actual trading. In fact, they are all forms of systematic trading (or investment), and are sometimes referred to as **Automated trading**. Predominantly, these strategies are adopted by either quantitative investors or proprietary trading desks.

Systematic trading, as its name suggests, is all about consistently adopting the same approach for trading. This may be used to dictate points for trade entry and exit, for instance by comparing market prices with boundary conditions, e.g. Bollinger bands. Alternatively, it may require an intricate set of rules, which accommodate a wide range of intraday conditions such as price, volume or volatility.

Quantitative trading (sometimes referred to as "Black-box" trading) is often confused with algorithmic trading. Here the trading rules are enforced by adopting proprietary quantitative models. [1] The difference is fairly subtle, but quantitative trading systems instigate trades whereas algorithmic trading systems merely execute them. Therefore, quantitative trading systems need to focus on a wider range of goals in addition to the actual execution strategies. These may range from tracking indicators to determine trade initiation and closeout, to monitoring the overall portfolio risk.

High frequency trading aims to take advantage of opportunities intraday. The time scales involved range from hours down to seconds or even fractions of a second. Effectively, it is a specialised form of black-box/quantitative trading focussed on exploiting short-term gains. Some high frequency strategies adopt a style similar to a market maker, trying to keep a relatively neutral position except to take advantage of any price discrepancies. For such strategies, monitoring the overall position/inventory risk and incorporating this information into the pricing/trading decisions is vital.

Statistical arbitrage represents a systematic investment/trading approach, which is based on a fusion of real-time and historical data analysis. The main difference from high frequency trading is that strategies may span over longer timeframes. Other than this, the goals are generally the same, both try to take advantage of mispricing whilst minimising the overall exposure to risk. Strategies try to find trends or indicators from previous data (intraday and/or historical) and then use these to gain an edge. Time series analysis, data mining and even artificial intelligence are employed to try to isolate useful information from the mass of data that is available.

---

[1] Such models have sometimes been termed "black-boxes", since their actual mechanisms are closely guarded, although obviously their creators have a clear understanding of how they work.

Regardless of which of these trading types are actually chosen, each of them may be implemented using one or more of the core execution methods, as shown in Figure 1-4.

1.5   Electronic trading

In their time, the invention of the telegraph and telephone revolutionised trading, allowing prices and orders to be communicated remotely. Still, it was the advent of the computer that has most affected trading. Before we go into any more detail on algorithmic trading and DMA techniques, it is worth briefly reviewing the development of electronic trading. Some of the more notable milestones in this journey are shown in Table 1-1.

Year	Event
1969	Instinet's "Institutional Networks" started, allowing electronic block-trading.
1971	NASDAQ electronic bulletin board started, allowing OTC trading of stocks.
1972	Cantor establish first electronic marketplace for U.S. Government securities.
1976	NYSE's Designated Order Turnaround (DOT) system routes small orders.
1978	U.S. Intermarket Trading System (ITS) established, providing an electronic link between NYSE and the other U.S. stock exchanges.
1980	Instinet introduces PSE Scorex, enabling DMA to U.S. exchanges.
1981	Reuters pioneered electronic monitor dealing service for FX.
1982	Tokyo Stock Exchange introduces its Computer-assisted Order Routing & Execution System (CORES).
1986	London Stock Exchange's "The Big Bang" shifts to screen trading. Paris Bourse introduced an electronic trading system.
1987	ITG POSIT offers scheduled block crossings for stocks.
1988	MTS platform created electronic secondary market for Italian government bonds.
1992	CME launches first version of GLOBEX electronic futures platform.
1993	EBS (Electronic Brokers System) adds competition for spot FX.
1997	U.S. SEC order handling rules change results in the creation of Arca, Brut, Island and Bloomberg Tradebook ECNs.
1998	Eurex offers the first fully electronic exchange for futures.
1999	EuroMTS launched for European government bond trading. eSpeed available for client bond trading.
2000	ICAP's BrokerTec bond trading platform launches.
2001	Liquidnet ATS created, allowing "dark pool" buy-side crossing for equities.
2006	NYSE starts moving equity trading to its Hybrid platform.
2007	U.S. Regulation NMS, European MiFID regulations come in force.

Table 1-1 Some of the key milestones in the adoption of electronic trading

In the 1960s, computer networks were used to route prices to computer terminals, effectively making ticker-tape machines obsolete. Soon afterwards, computers were used to start transmitting orders and trades. Systems supporting fully electronic trading began to appear in the 1960-70s. Suddenly, traders could issue orders remotely; there was no longer a technical need for them to be physically based on an exchange floor.

Early on, electronic trading was mainly focussed on handling relatively small orders. The bulk of trading was still carried out over the phone or in person on exchanges. However, by the mid 1990s many of the world's major stock exchanges were trading a considerable proportion of their volume electronically. Since then the shift to fully electronic trading has become almost inevitable.

The equities markets have clearly led the way in electronic trading. In the early stages, the New York Stock Exchange (NYSE) and NASDAQ (National Association of Securities Dealers Automated Quotations) were undoubtedly at the forefront. By the 1990s, though, the focus had shifted to Europe where trading floors started closing as exchanges shifted to fully electronic order books. Then in 1997, the U.S. saw a major shake-up with the Securities and Exchange Commission (SEC) order handling rules, which allowed new competition in the form of Electronic Communication Networks (ECNs). These new venues saw a huge expansion around the millennium, followed by a fierce round of takeovers and consolidations. Over the last few years, innovation has still continued at a rapid pace, particularly in terms of new variants of the block crossing Alternative Trading Systems (ATSs), such as Liquidnet. Two of the major ECNs, namely BATS and Direct Edge have even become exchanges in their own right (or are in the process of doing so). Further changes are likely as the full effects of the U.S. Regulation-NMS (National Market System) and Europe's Markets in Financial Instruments Directive (MiFID) take effect. In fact, Multilateral Trading Facilities (MTFs), Europe's equivalent to ECNs, are starting to become significant competition for the major European exchanges.

The bond markets have been slower to adopt electronic trading, in part due to them being centred more on market makers rather than exchanges. Europe has again played an important part in the evolution of electronic bond trading, most notably with Italy's MTS (Mercato Telematico dei Titoli di Stato), which has become Europe's leading centre for government bond trading. In the U.S., a mass of electronic systems appeared around the millennium; however, since then the consolidations and closeouts have been brutal. The electronic market for bonds is now dominated by a handful of major players.

Foreign exchange has also shifted towards electronic trading. ECNs are well established and even "dark pool" ATSs have started to appear.

The derivatives marketplace is more complex. The majority of trading is still carried out over the counter (OTC). Still, there is also a sizeable market for exchange-listed derivatives. The Chicago Mercantile Exchange (CME) launched the first version of its GLOBEX platform back in 1992; though, initially this was primarily for after-hours trading. Six years later Eurex became the first fully electronic exchange for futures. Electronic trading is now commonplace for most of the world's major future and options exchanges.

Overall, the rapid proliferation of electronic trading has made the world markets accessible to a much wider range of users. Without this innovation, algorithmic trading, DMA and automated crossing simply would not exist. Note that we will cover the individual markets in more detail in Chapter 3, and the appendices.

1.6 Algorithmic trading

An algorithm [2] is a set of instructions for accomplishing a given task. So a trading algorithm is just a computerised model that incorporates the steps required to trade an order in a specific way. Admittedly, for the algorithm to react to ever changing market conditions these rules can become quite complex. Hence, in this book we shall break them down and consider these decisions in isolation as well as showing how they may then be grouped together to build actual trading algorithms.

For example, given an order to buy 20,000 of asset XYZ the rules might dictate placing

---

[2] The word algorithm derives from the term algorism, which was used by the 9th century Persian mathematician Abu Abdullah Muhammad ibn Musa al-Khwarizmi in referring to the rules of arithmetic.

the whole quantity as a limit order at the current best market price. Alternatively, they might work the order over the day, splitting it into segments. The rules determine the type, price and quantity for each of these child orders, often based on a mixture of historical and live market data. A computerised system is responsible for handling the algorithm's instructions, so the execution is fully automated. The system ensures that each corresponding child order is split and placed on the market. It then monitors these child orders, adjusting or cancelling them, as and when it becomes necessary.

Let's consider a very simple trading algorithm that aims to achieve an average market price. It does this by dividing each order into uniform slices, which are traded sequentially. Given an order to buy 10,000 of asset ABC over the next five hours, our simple algorithm will trade 1,000 ABC every half hour, by sending a market order to the exchange. Figure 1-5 shows the resultant trading pattern for these child orders.

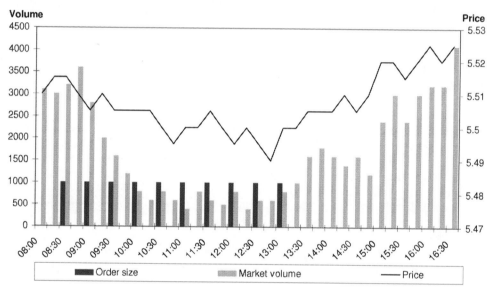

Figure 1-5 A simple example algorithm

Table 1-2 shows another way of viewing our algorithm, as a trading schedule with the target quantity specified for each time period.

Time	08:30	09:00	09:30	10:00	10:30	11:00	11:30	12:00	12:30	13:00
Trade	1000	1000	1000	1000	1000	1000	1000	1000	1000	1000
Total	1000	2000	3000	4000	5000	6000	7000	8000	9000	10000

Table 1-2 A simplified trading schedule

Clearly, our example algorithm is far from perfect; it is predictable and it takes no account of either market prices or volumes. Modern trading algorithms have evolved from this simplistic order slicing strategy to the point where their trading patterns are unrecognisable in comparison. Complex algorithms must be expertly defined and implemented. So the actual trading rules upon which these algorithms are based are defined by experienced traders and quantitative analysts. They are designed to target the best execution, given the specified objectives.

Types of trading algorithms

At present, there are literally hundreds of different trading algorithms available. Each broker or vendor provides their own range of trading algorithms, catering for specific goals. Unsurprisingly, the driving forces for many of these algorithms are price, volume or liquidity. Some algorithms rigidly adhere to a given trading schedule whilst others may be more dynamic, adapting in real-time to ever changing market conditions. Obviously, it is vital for the objectives to be clearly defined for an algorithm to have a chance of achieving its goals.

If we ignore the various names that are used we can start to distil the existing algorithms into a handful of basic types. Table 1-3 shows a summary of the more commonly adopted trading algorithms, which are presently in widespread use.

Key driver		Algorithms
Schedule	Time	Time Weighted Average Price (TWAP)
	Volume	Volume Weighted Average Price (VWAP)
Predetermined benchmark	Volume	Percentage Of Volume (POV)
	Price	Implementation Shortfall (IS)
	Ratio	Pairs / Spread trading
Dynamic Benchmark	Price	Price Inline
		Market On Close (MOC)
Liquidity		Liquidity-based algorithms Smart order routing

Table 1-3 A summary of common trading algorithms

Often, trading algorithms are designed to meet (or beat) specific benchmarks, such as the Volume Weighted Average Price (VWAP) or the market closing price. Others try to minimise overall transaction costs whilst some try to trade more opportunistically. There are also algorithms that are driven by liquidity, spanning multiple execution venues or "dark pools" to seek additional liquidity. In Chapter 5, we will cover the whole range of trading algorithms in more detail.

The evolution of trading algorithms

The origins of algorithmic trading may be traced back to electronic trading systems developed as efficiency aids for sell-side traders. Around the millennium, brokers started to realise that these tools could also be offered to clients. Within a few years, every major brokerage was offering algorithmic trading services, and client uptake has steadily increased. Vendors are also starting to create frameworks that make it easier for the buy-side to create their own trading algorithms.

The first generation of trading algorithms were natural evolutions of simple order slicing. They focussed on meeting specific benchmarks, starting with a Time Weighted Average Price (TWAP) and progressing on to the ubiquitous Volume Weighted Average Price

(VWAP). The simplicity of calculating a VWAP and its more accurate reflection of daily price moves meant that for several years VWAP reigned supreme.

Both the early TWAP and VWAP algorithms tended to be statically driven. So as soon as an order was received a specific trading schedule was determined, which then drove the trading algorithm. For VWAP, this schedule would be based on a historical volume profile, essentially this is a representation of how trading volume progresses through an average day. Though, using statically created trading schedules increasingly proved vulnerable, since other market participants could easily spot and take advantage of such regular trading patterns. To combat predatory trading, algorithms started to incorporate more randomisation. Consequently, there was a natural progression from purely schedule driven algorithms to more dynamic strategies. For example, the Percentage of Volume (POV) algorithm bases its execution in response to the live market volume instead of trading based on a historical volume profile.

The second generation of trading algorithms were created in response to the application of transaction cost analysis (TCA). This analysis breaks down all the various costs associated with trading. TCA highlighted that the effect an order has on the asset's price (its market impact) was not the only significant cost. Indeed, other factors, such as timing risk and opportunity cost, could actually outweigh the market impact. André Perold (1988) coined the term implementation shortfall to represent the actual costs of trading. Essentially, this reflects the difference between the market price when the investment decision was actually made (the decision price) and the actual executed price. The increasing popularity of TCA meant investors started to re-examine their use of benchmarks. In fact, VWAP began to be replaced by decision price. In general, the first generation trading algorithms were not designed to be price or risk sensitive; they were more focussed on reducing the overall market impact. Hence, brokers needed to develop algorithms that were more price- and cost-centric, the most notable of which being the Implementation Shortfall (IS) based algorithms. These new algorithms tried to tackle what Robert Kissell and Morton Glantz (2003) termed the trader's dilemma: trading too fast brings high market impact costs whilst trading too slowly exposes us to considerable risk. Suddenly, algorithms started incorporating complex market models to estimate potential transaction costs, as they attempted to determine the optimum trading strategy for each order.

The third generation of algorithms have resulted from the ongoing search for liquidity, triggered by the rapid proliferation of Electronic Crossing Networks (ECNs) and Alternative Trading Systems (ATSs) in the U.S. equity market. Having so many potential execution venues meant a raft of simple order routing systems were created. Another important factor has been the increasing order book transparency as markets have transitioned to electronic trading. Many of the first generation algorithms focussed solely on the best bid and offer quotes, often because that was all that was available. As order book data becomes increasingly available, more and more algorithms are taking advantage of this for their order placement decisions. The combination of multiple venues and increasing transparency has helped transform simple order routing systems into complex liquidity-based algorithms. These constantly examine the order books of different venues to decide where best to place orders.

Off-market trading has also shifted to new electronic venues, in particular the "dark pools" or ATSs that have proven so successful for U.S. equities. Algorithms now routinely interact with these "dark pools" to find additional liquidity at set price points, trying to achieve best execution. At first, this started with dedicated liquidity-seeking algorithms, but increasingly this behaviour is also being incorporated in other algorithms, such as Implementation

Shortfall or even VWAP. Thus, new hybrid strategies are starting to evolve.

In parallel with the search for liquidity, another shift in algorithm behaviour is taking place. Customisation and adaptability are becoming key focuses for algorithms, allowing brokers to more easily offer client-centric trading algorithms.

Exactly what the next generation of trading algorithms will offer is hard to predict, but it is certain that they will keep evolving.

1.7   Direct Access Trading

Direct access trading represents the shift in access and control of execution to the buy-side. Investors and buy-side traders can now get direct access allowing them to place orders on many of the world's financial marketplaces. Originally, direct access trading was synonymous with DMA; however, the introduction of crossing and algorithmic trading has meant institutions now have an even broader choice of execution methods.

Direct Market Access

Direct Market Access (DMA) extends the principle of remote access to a broker's clients. Its roots trace back to the 1980s with vendors such as Instinet. Although used by some institutional clients, many of the early adopters of DMA were retail users. Certainly, vendors targeted the retail market with their DMA systems. This gave day traders, or SOES bandits (named after NASDAQ's Small Order Execution System), an unprecedented level of access and control over their orders.

Institutional users became interested in the prospect of DMA in the 1990s. In particular, this was led by hedge funds and statistical arbitrageurs. Many of the initial DMA offerings were provided by software houses and small agency brokerages. However, after the millennium the larger brokers started investing in DMA in a big way. In 2000, Goldman Sachs acquired REDIPlus whilst in 2004 Bank of America Securities bought Direct Access Financial Corp., Sonic Trading Management went to Bank of New York and Lava Trading became part of Citigroup. Suddenly, the DMA marketplace was dominated by major brokers; DMA had become a key selling point for institutional use.

With DMA, the client can take advantage of the broker's infrastructure to send their orders to the exchange, much like the broker's own orders. Hence the moniker "Zero touch", since the order execution is controlled by the client. This requires the client traders to have access to an Order Management System (OMS) or Execution Management System (EMS), which is linked to the broker. Prime brokerage agreements are often established to organise the clearing and settlement of any executions, and any other custodial or financing requirements.

Clearly, information leakage is a key concern for institutional users. Therefore DMA services are generally run by brokers as a separate entity to protect the client orders from being viewed by the rest of the broker's traders, and in particular their proprietary desks.

Sponsored access

Sponsored access caters for buy-side clients with high-frequency trading strategies. This allows the client to connect to the market using use their broker's unique market identifier (or MPID), but without having to go through their entire infrastructure. Although the markets generally require the broker to monitor the trading, ensuring that no excessive risks are taken. The monitoring may be carried out pre-trade, either with a fast, dedicated system or by using a solution from a third-party vendor, such as FTEN. Whilst this adds some overhead, the client should still get faster access than normal DMA.

Alternatively, some sponsored access may rely on post-trade monitoring. This has been termed "naked access", since this does not allow the broker to prevent erroneous trading. Given the increased regulatory attention, the future for such "naked access" is uncertain.

Crossing

Institutions often need to trade in large sizes, but large block orders can expose them to substantial price risk. Traditionally, these large orders were handled by brokers off the trading floor. This is sometimes referred to as the "upstairs market" since historically such negotiations took place upstairs in broker's offices, well away from the exchange floor.

Often block trading is undertaken on a principal basis, although agency trading is also catered for. In a principal trade, the broker/dealer assumes all the risk by taking the required position onto their inventory. To work such large block orders they may need to find new counterparties who require the asset, or they may split the order into smaller quantities and work them on the market.

Crossing systems provide an electronic mechanism allowing investors to carry out their own block trading anonymously. These systems aggregate orders and then match them at set points throughout the day. For instance, ITG's POSIT matches orders at over a dozen set times daily. In comparison, Alternative Trading Systems (ATS), such as Liquidnet, generally provide continuous electronic order matching. These anonymous trading venues ensure the order details (size and sometimes price) are hidden; hence, they have often been referred to as "dark pools" of liquidity. Effectively, they offer the buy-side the chance to cut out the broker as an intermediary and trade anonymously with each other. Due to the size of the orders involved, they have become significant sources of liquidity.

Note that it is important to remember that orders placed on crossing systems or ATSs are not guaranteed to execute. Instead, the focus is on achieving a better price and minimising information leakage. In fact, the probability of execution can be much lower than on the main exchanges, depending on the liquidity of the asset and the size of the block order. Consequently, such orders tend to require some monitoring. In order to guarantee execution other trading methods, such as algorithmic trading or DMA, may be used in tandem. For example, we could place an order to buy a million shares of XYZ on a crossing system in the morning. As the day progresses if it still has not executed we could reduce the quantity by 10 or 20% every hour and work this separately. This allows us to hold out for the best price from crossing, whilst still ensuring that the order is executed. Indeed, there are now trading algorithms that offer this kind of approach.

Direct Liquidity Access

Managing an order on a crossing network or ATS is essentially the same as DMA. This similarity has meant that vendors now offer solutions that enable access to both mechanisms. To reflect this some brokers/vendors have started using the term Direct Liquidity Access (DLA) for their services.

DLA type services are not necessarily just a combination of DMA and crossing provision. They may also incorporate features such as liquidity aggregation, where smart order routing or custom trading algorithms are used to seek out sufficient liquidity at the desired price.

Direct Strategy Access

Client access for trading algorithms was initially handled over the phone. Nowadays, more and more OMSs and EMSs can handle algorithmic trading. So clients now have direct access to algorithms, much as they have direct access to orders via DMA. In fact, some brokers, such as UBS, have started using the term Direct Strategy Access (DSA).

1.8   Comparing execution methods

Although all the core execution methods are complimentary, there are still some significant differences between them. To illustrate this Table 1-4 shows two simple example orders. The first order is simply a limit order to buy asset ABC within a fixed price limit, whilst the second order targets the daily VWAP as a benchmark.

Order	Trading method		
	Manual	DMA/Crossing	Algorithmic
1.	"Buy 10,000 ABC with a limit of 53"	Buy limit order 10,000 ABC at 53	No direct equivalent
2.	"Buy 100,000 ABC Trade VWAP over the day Don't go above 53"	No direct equivalent	Buy 100,000 ABC Algorithm: VWAP Start time: Now End time: Close Price limit: 53

Table 1-4 Different trading methods for some example orders

Manual trading can deal with any type of order. The instructions are simple and easy to understand. It is also popular because it allows the client to discuss the order with the broker. This gives them an opportunity to gain new market information and analysis (or "colour") which may even lead them to alter their trading strategy. Such information can be vital to clients, and is one of the main reasons why manual trading is still so widespread.

DMA is perfect for simple order types such the first order in Table 1-4. It allows clients complete control over how and when orders are placed. However, there is not usually a single equivalent order that can handle something like the example daily VWAP trade. DMA caters solely for low-level access. So instead, the client must try to reproduce the strategy that a trader might adopt manually. Therefore, to achieve best execution a client will need considerable market experience, as well as having the time to analyse and decide how best to place each child order. Whilst this may suit some clients, clearly this is a more time consuming approach. That is why, for many clients, either manual or algorithmic trading offer a more practical alternative.

Likewise, order crossing can easily handle simple limit orders, but not more complicated order types. Again, it is up to the client to monitor the order's status, possibly cancelling and re-routing it if executions are not forthcoming on the ATS. Since such crossing networks tend to deal with larger order sizes, a client may actually prefer a dual trading strategy, whereby most of the order is left on the ATS for potential crossing whilst a smaller portion is traded on the exchange to try to ensure execution. Such strategies are starting to be offered by new liquidity-based trading algorithms.

Algorithmic trading is intended to cope with more complex trading strategies, so the example VWAP order in Table 1-4 poses no problems. Upon receiving the order, a VWAP trading algorithm will then decide how it should be handled. Some algorithms adopt a static approach, splitting orders based purely on information from historical data. Alternatively, ones that are more dynamic incorporate a mixture of historical and live market data in their decisions. As required, the algorithm will then send child orders to the market, selecting the most appropriate order type/price and size; then continually monitor their progress. Essentially, this is no different to what happens for traders working such orders manually or via DMA, except that the trading algorithm provides a fully automated process. Clearly, in order for the execution to meet the client's objectives it is vital that any requirements such as limit prices, benchmarks etc. are fully specified. As we can see from Table 1-4, the algorithm parameters (the start and end times and the limit price) are similar to how we might ask a trader to work the order. Admittedly, this is a more constrained approach than just talking to a trader over the phone. However, brokers are constantly introducing new algorithms and refining their parameters to try and make it easier to issue appropriate orders and to cope with any required customisations. They have even started introducing algorithms that look at the order details and decide the most appropriate trading strategy/algorithm for it.

Another way of comparing execution methods is to try to rate them in terms of factors such as:

- Efficiency
- Usability
- Performance/Cost

These are broken down in more detail in Table 1-5.

Factors		Manual	Direct Access		
			DMA	Crossing	Algorithmic
Efficiency	Capacity	★	★	★	★ ★ ★
	Speed	★	★	★	★ ★ ★
Usability	Control	★	★ ★ ★	★	★
	Transparency	★	★ ★ ★	★	★
	Anonymity	★ ★	★ ★	★ ★ ★	★ ★
	Market conditions	★	★	★	★ ★
	Market knowledge	★ ★ ★	★	★ ★	★ ★ ★
	Asset knowledge	★ ★ ★	★	★ ★	★ ★ ★
Performance/ Cost	Performance	★ ★	★ ★	★ ★	★ ★
	Commission	★	★ ★ ★	★	★ ★
	Risk/Cost control	★ ★	★	★	★ ★
Other	Regulations	★ ★	★	★	★ ★

Graded from weakest (★) to strongest (★ ★ ★)

Table 1-5 Comparing the core methods for trading

Efficiency

Efficiency has been one of the key drivers for the sell-side; a skilled trader is a valuable commodity, anything that helps make them more productive is clearly beneficial. For some segments of the buy-side, typically hedge funds, speed is becoming ever more important. Low latency trading mechanisms allow them to capitalise on opportunities as soon as they see them.

In terms of capacity, algorithmic trading is clearly the winner; computers can easily handle thousands of orders simultaneously. Additional capacity can often be added by setting up another computer server, provided the underlying infrastructure (networks, links to exchanges etc.) is good enough. In comparison, manual trading is quite an expensive option.

Traders are inherently good at multi-tasking; however, there is still a limit to how many orders a person can handle at any one time, beyond this level the quality of execution may suffer. DMA has similar capacity issues since all that has really happened is a shift of the manual trading from the broker to the buy-side. Capacity is less of an issue when using crossing systems since this tends to be a more passive trading style. Though, the orders still need to be monitored, and if they have not crossed after some time, alternative trading methods may need to be used.

With respect to speed, algorithmic trading is again the best option. Computerised systems are perfect for monitoring and analysing thousands of variables in fractions of a second. Exchanges used to have latencies of around 300 milliseconds, at present they are now competing to offer services with latencies below 10 milliseconds. To put this in perspective a blink takes between 100-150 milliseconds (as noted by David Burr (2005)). Even complex analytics for determining the most appropriate reaction can be calculated in fractions of a second. In other words, a trading algorithm can spot an opportunity and send an appropriate order to the exchange before we even notice the quote flickering on our monitor. Speed has become such a key issue that some exchanges and ATSs now offer co-location services, essentially allowing member's computer servers to be placed in their machine rooms to virtually eradicate any network delays.

Usability

Usability is obviously a major issue for most users. A convoluted trading method is unlikely to be popular, even if it gets good results.

Direct control over how their orders are handled has significantly improved for the buy-side. DMA allows them to place and manage orders as if they were a broker/dealer. In comparison, both manual and algorithmic trading represent a slight loss of control, since the client can only issue general trade instructions or select an appropriate trading algorithm. Clearly, it is often easier to communicate such instructions to a person, but trading algorithms are continually evolving to try to be as intuitive as possible. They are also becoming highly customisable, catering for an ever-expanding range of trading requirements.

Transparency is closely related to control. If we cannot dictate exactly how something is done, we would at least like to be able to monitor it closely to ensure that it is doing what we want. Competitive advantage means that brokers cannot divulge the exact inner workings of their algorithms, but they should be still be able to explain the behaviour for specific orders. It is also important to get a broad understanding of how each trading algorithm works, so as to be able choose the most appropriate one for our orders.

Anonymity is important as well, since information leakage is one of the key concerns for many investors. Over the last few years, the anonymity offered by crossing networks has helped these systems gain a substantial market share, particularly in the U.S. DMA and algorithmic trading can also provide anonymity, since most brokers segregate the trading for their prime brokerages to ensure client privacy.

Another factor that affects usability is changing market conditions, in part triggered by electronic and algorithmic trading and by the competition between venues. Across many of the world's markets average order sizes have significantly decreased whilst trading volumes have rocketed. So orders, which might have immediately filled five years ago, must now be split to prevent market impact. Similarly, having multiple execution venues fragments the available liquidity, making it harder to trade. Algorithmic trading is the best suited to handling such conditions; computer capacity means it can closely monitor each venue and decide where best to trade, for thousands of orders. Neither DMA, nor manual trading can match this.

Market and asset specific knowledge are also key to achieving best execution. This can be as simple as knowing when markets are open and understanding the supported order types. Alternatively, it might mean having in-depth experience of how each asset trades. For manual or algorithmic trading, the orders are being handled by a dedicated expert or system, so orders can be easily delegated to these methods. It does not matter whether the order is for U.S. bonds or Japanese equities they will handle the complexities of each market and asset type. Whereas for DMA, and to a lesser extent crossing, there is less inbuilt guidance, it is up to the client to determine how best to trade. That said, many OMSs and EMSs often have built-in rules to prevent simple errors such as selecting an unsupported order type.

Performance / Cost

Execution methods have to deliver in terms of both performance and cost. Performance may be measured by comparing the average execution price to a specific benchmark. Note that it is also important to consider the variability, or volatility, of these averages. For any specific order, manual trading should generally be able to beat the performance of an algorithm, since traders can often infer much more subtle signals from the market. However, the rule based nature of algorithms means that they should provide more consistent results, since they do not get tired or distracted. Therefore, in terms of overall performance algorithms and manual trading are relatively evenly matched. Admittedly, traders probably still have the edge, but algorithms are improving all the time.

It is also important to get the balance right between performance and efficiency. An experienced trader should generally be able to outperform most trading algorithms; however, this may consume a large proportion of their time. Overall, better performance might be achieved by having the trader manually work the more difficult orders whilst delegating the others to trading algorithms.

When examining performance, the investment goals should be considered as well. For instance, trading passively may save the bid offer spread and so result in a good average price, but this may be at the expense of fully completing the order. If, the next day, the asset price shifts then completing the order may be more expensive than if we had traded more aggressively the day before. Transaction cost analysis (TCA) has played a key role in making traders and investors examine such costs more thoroughly.

For markets where brokers still charge commissions, e.g. equities, this is clearly a very visible cost of trading. Until the 2007-09 financial crisis, overall commissions have been steadily declining. Figure 1-6 charts their progression over the last few years, in terms of $/share. It also highlights the differences between DMA, algorithmic and manual (high touch) trading. From a broker's point of view, the low touch services (DMA and algorithmic trading) have relatively low labour costs hence the lower charges. The costs for high touch / manual trading also reflect the fact that traders can offer additional information to clients, such as market colour or sentiment.

Overall, TCA has highlighted the fact that hidden costs, such as market impact and timing risk, are more significant than visible costs, such as commissions. Most algorithms are adept at reducing overall market impact, by splitting the order into smaller sizes.

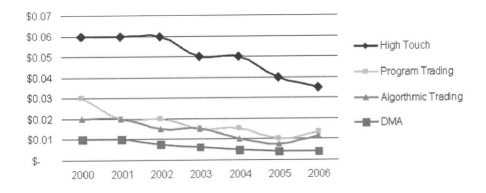

Figure 1-6 U.S. equity average commissions

Similarly, crossing is an equally efficient, if not better, means of reducing market impact. Minimising timing risk and opportunity costs is more complex. The second generation of algorithms introduced cost-centric models, typified by Implementation Shortfall, which are better suited to this. We shall cover this in more detail in Chapters 5 and 6.

Other reasons

Market regulation, such as Regulation NMS in the U.S. and MiFID in Europe, means that brokers and investors must be able to demonstrate that they achieved best execution. Electronic trading has made this somewhat easier, since detailed audit trails are relatively simple to maintain. Therefore, algorithmic trading is arguably one of the best choices to cater for such regulations, since its rule based nature provides consistent and easily auditable trading decisions, as well as coping well with fragmented marketplaces.

1.9   How much are these execution methods used?

The sell-side brokerages have had electronic trading for years. Internally, almost all their trading is electronic, except for the few markets where there is still considerable floor-based activity. Similarly, automated trading systems and trading algorithms have long been established. Hence, most studies focus on the uptake of these technologies with the buy-side institutions. For example, Figure 1-7 shows estimates from the Aite Group consultancy for the breakdown of trading methods adopted by U.S. institutions.

The growth trends for algorithmic trading and DMA are clearly visible, as is the decline in "High touch" (and higher cost) manual trading. A report by the TABB Group (2008) estimates that by 2007 algorithmic trading, DMA, crossing and program trading together accounted for 63% of the U.S. institutional equities trades. Still, in 2008 they also note that the market crisis led to a slight shift in the trends. Algorithmic trading continued to increase, reaching 24% of buy-side flow, up 2% from the year before. However, high touch trading via sales traders also increased, recovering to 44% (back from 37% in 2007), as institutions sought to cope with the heightened levels of volatility.

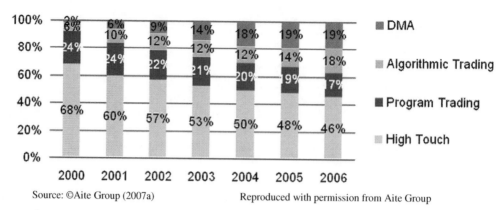

Source: ©Aite Group (2007a)   Reproduced with permission from Aite Group

Figure 1-7 Estimates for the use of different trading methods by U.S. institutions

1.10 Fears and myths

Algorithmic trading has attracted a lot of publicity; there has also been a lot of marketing and hype. So in this section let's examine some of the common fears and myths that have attached themselves to this topic. Broadly speaking, these may be categorised into three main issues, namely safety, performance and usefulness.

Safety of algorithmic trading

Some of the commonest concerns about algorithmic trading are that:
- Algorithms are fundamentally changing the market
- Algorithms will replace traders
- Algorithms can leak alpha to proprietary traders

There can be no doubt that electronic trading has transformed the world markets. Marketplaces are seeing waves of fragmentation and consolidation as competition for market share drives the creation of new execution venues whilst existing ones are bought, merge or fail. The emergence of crossing systems is a perfect example of this cycle. Order sizes are shrinking, so off-exchange crossing becomes increasingly popular. In response, the exchanges introduce new mechanisms to try to regain liquidity from the crossing networks, and the cycle begins again. All the while, these market shifts offer opportunities for astute investors and traders who are ahead of the market. Coping with this constant change is clearly difficult. Nevertheless, Pandora's Box has already been opened, for better or worse, so we may as well look inside and find ways to deal with the new market reality.

Algorithmic trading is a natural evolution from electronic trading. Computers are ideally suited to working in complex multi-venue markets, since they can easily monitor the order books of a range of execution venues. If everyone used VWAP algorithms for their trading then clearly some self-reinforcement of trading patterns would occur, much like if everyone used the same technical analysis. However, people's views differ: Indeed, the very reason that the world's markets function is because investors and traders have a diverse range of opinions. Therefore, they target different prices and use a range of alternative trading strategies. There is no reason why algorithmic trading should alter this diversity.

Job security is also an issue. Eye-catching news headlines have proclaimed the end of the trader, but then we're all going to be replaced with robots in 2075 aren't we? It is important to remember that electronic and algorithmic trading are simply tools. Certainly, job roles are evolving, for example, salespeople are becoming sales traders. Sell-side desks are now covering multiple asset classes. Not long ago, it was predicted that principal or risk trading would become more commonly used than agency trading. The 2007-09 financial crisis and the transformation of the financial sector have given a new lease of life to agency trading. In fact, during this crisis principal trading looked far more endangered. In such markets, traders and investors need to be flexible to take advantage of any tools that help give them an edge and drive profits.

An article in the CFA Magazine (2006) titled 'Hype and Algorithms' poses a good counterpoint to the fear that algorithms will take over the world. In the article, Joe Gawronski, COO of Rosenblatt Securities, highlights the fact that:

"Algorithms can't react in the true sense of how I define a reaction. Everything they do is based on a rule that's been provided, whereas traders can change their mind on the fly. There's no way to incorporate into algorithms the random facts and observation that may give a trader a "feel" for the market."

Artificial Intelligence (AI) may offer a solution to this; however, this is still some way off. AI first took of in the 1950s, but it was not until 1997 that IBM's Deep Blue computer could beat the world chess champion. In the same CFA article James Finnegan, editor of the Financial Engineering News, points out:

"People equate black-box algorithms with super computers developed to play chess and mistakenly assume there will one day be an algorithm that is so smart, quick, and innovative that even the best traders in the world won't stand a chance. However, the difference is that although there are billions and billions of permutations with chess, there is a defined board and a very strict set of rules, so a computer with enough memory can learn every move. That's not the case with markets."

Beyond all the hype, algorithmic trading will certainly have a major impact. For instance, good algorithms may be just as efficiently used by a salesperson as a sales trader. It should also open up new avenues for trading, expanding the potential of multi-region and multi-asset trading.

Another concern for investors is information leakage. There is still some suspicion that brokers can garner information from client order flow and use this for their own proprietary trading. That said, the buy-side has more power and control than it has ever had. Off-exchange crossing networks even allow the buy-side to completely bypass brokers. Given that commissions are declining, it is vital for brokers to retain order flow. Reputation is paramount. Brokers have to ensure that their proprietary trading desks are truly isolated from the brokerage operations. This holds true for all the major brokers, whose prime brokerage units are often segregated, located on separate floors or even buildings.

Performance of algorithmic trading

Another common fear is that trading algorithms have now become commoditised and there is little differentiation between them. There is some truth to this, in that there are only so many ways of implementing an algorithm that targets a benchmark like VWAP. However, being commoditised is not altogether a bad thing; it is important to have a certain level of standardisation. We just have to look at the markets to see how standardised products have better liquidity and so lower trading costs. Similarly, standardised algorithms, at least in terms of their parameters and basic functions, would allow clients to swap between brokers more easily, thus encouraging more competition.

Commoditisation is less of an issue for the more complex cost driven and opportunistic algorithms. Here the performance is dependent on the quality of their quantitative models, so brokers can add significant value. Indeed, there can be considerable variation in the performance of these algorithms between brokers.

Algorithm choice is also an important factor: If an unsuitable type of algorithm is chosen then performance is bound to suffer. This can be addressed by a combination of education and improving the available pre-trade analytics. Another solution is the increasing provision of systems that can automatically suggest the most suitable algorithm for a specific order. Post-trade analysis is vital to check the actual performance. Note that both the mean and standard deviation of performance need to be considered.

There is also the feeling that brokers hold back the best performing algorithms for themselves. Fundamentally, proprietary desks, particularly those employing high frequency trading or statistical arbitrage adopt different strategies to investors. They are usually keen to stay market neutral and so strategies tend not to build up large positions, instead acting more like sophisticated day traders. Thus, any algorithms they use tend to be highly specialised, often based on market making. That's not to say brokers don't run different algorithms. Newer versions of algorithms need extensive testing, so these will be used internally before being made available to clients. In general, algorithms are a valuable marketing resource which brokers are keen to make available as soon as they are ready.

Finally, it is important to remember that algorithmic trading is just a tool, not a panacea. It is not designed to generate profits (or alpha), simply to help control costs and provide best execution.

Usefulness of algorithmic trading

The success of algorithmic trading means that less people are still questioning its usefulness. Although there are still a few issues rooted from the early days of algorithmic trading, namely that:

- Algorithms are complicated to use
- They only really work for liquid assets or small orders

Algorithms sometimes have a reputation of being complicated, but as we saw in the example in Table 1-4, they require parameters that look very similar to the instructions we might give to a trader. Most algorithms will have sanity checks, so if an order is unusually large, or the price limit is miles away from the actual market price then the order may be rejected, just to be safe. Nevertheless, as with any computer program, it is important to bear in mind the "Garbage In Garbage Out" maxim, and assume that it will not be as forgiving with any typos.

Algorithm selection from the hundreds available may seem like an ominous task. That said, any one broker probably offers a maximum of a dozen trading algorithms. Therefore, it is simply a case of using pre-trade analytics to estimate the potential impact and risk of an order. Increasingly, brokers are rationalising their suites of algorithms to make selection even easier. They are also starting to provide more client-focussed solutions that cater for specific requirements. Some brokers even provide services that suggest the most appropriate algorithm, based on the order size and the asset's liquidity and volatility.

In terms of algorithms only being able to cope with liquid assets or small orders, this may have been true for the first generation of algorithms. Modern algorithms are much more versatile. In particular, the introduction of cost-centric and liquidity seeking algorithms means they can now support a much broader set of requirements.

Illiquid assets pose a specific problem, namely signalling risk. This represents the information leakage to other market participants from our trading strategy. Imagine using the simplistic algorithm we saw in Figure 1-5 for an illiquid asset. The regular large buy orders would scream, "We have a buyer", whereas for a more heavily traded asset they would not stand out as much. Consequently, it is often necessary to hide our actual intentions as much as possible, by using special order types and by seeking liquidity from alternative sources such as crossing networks. We shall cover this in more detail in Chapters 8 and 9. Interestingly, these techniques are increasingly being applied to more liquid assets.

One area where algorithms do need more work is coping with unexpected events or news. Human traders can often deal with this much more effectively. That said, the next generation of algorithms are already starting to look at how best to incorporate additional information to deal with such situations. We will look at this in more depth in Chapters 10 and 14.

1.11 Summary

- Direct Market Access (DMA) enables clients to send orders to exchanges by using a proxy for their broker's membership, giving them a similar level of control for an order's execution to a sell-side trader.

- Algorithmic trading is a computerised rule-based system responsible for executing orders to buy or sell a given asset. A computer program follows preset rules to determine how each order should be executed. Algorithmic execution is perhaps a more representative name.

- Systematic, black-box, quantitative and high frequency or automated trading are terms that are sometimes mistakenly used as references to algorithmic trading. In fact, they are more to do with the style of investment than the execution.

- So far, there have been three main generations in the evolution of trading algorithms:
    - The first algorithms were natural evolutions of simple order slicing, focussing on specific benchmarks, such as TWAP or VWAP. Initially, these were schedule driven, often based on historical data. Later, more dynamic versions incorporated market conditions, leading to tracking algorithms, such as percentage of volume.
    - The second generation of trading algorithms were created in response to the application of transaction cost analysis. Implementation shortfall algorithms strive to minimise cost by balancing both market impact and risk.
    - The third generation of algorithms are focussed more on liquidity, resulting from the fragmentation of major markets and the arrival of "dark pools".
    - Continual evolution and the adoption of similar tactics mean that the boundaries between these methods are constantly blurring. Increasingly, complex DMA order types are making it difficult to differentiate between them and trading algorithms.

- Comparing algorithmic trading and DMA with manual trading:
  - In terms of speed and capacity, algorithmic trading is clearly the winner; computers can handle thousands of orders simultaneously, responding in fractions of a second.
  - In terms of performance, experienced traders still have the edge over algorithms since they can infer more subtle signals from the market. Though, as algorithms continue to evolve, the gap is closing. Algorithms also offer the prospect of more consistent results. Note that selecting the appropriate algorithm is vital.

Chapter 2

Market microstructure

Market microstructure focuses on the key mechanisms involved in trading. It also helps explain many of the costs that arise.

2.1 Introduction

Economics tends to abstract itself from the underlying mechanics of trading. Similarly, asset-pricing theory focuses solely on the fundamental values of assets. Whereas the field of market microstructure [1] concentrates on the actual trading process, analysing how specific mechanisms affect both observed prices and traded volumes. Market microstructure helps explain many of the costs that prevent assets from achieving their fundamental values.

Interest in market microstructure has grown rapidly over the last two decades, alongside the rapid changes in the structure and technology of the world markets. Structural shifts have arisen due to globalization, the demutualization of many exchanges (to become profit-based enterprises) and increasing intra-market competition. Regulation has also played its part. For example, in the U.S., Securities and Exchange Commission (SEC) governance led to the creation of ECNs (Electronic Communications Networks), which have aggressively competed with exchanges for market share. The pace of technological change has also helped, as tools like DMA and algorithmic trading open up markets, lowering the barriers for entry and altering the balance between investors, brokers and dealers.

What topics does market microstructure actually cover? We can break down the theory into three key areas:
- Market structure and design
- Trading mechanism research
- Transaction cost measurement and analysis

The purpose of this overview is to provide a basic introduction to these key areas. For further reading, a concise practitioner's guide is given by Ananth Madhavan (2002). Whilst comprehensive reviews of the academic literature are provided by Bruno Biais, Larry Glosten and Chester Spatt (2005), Hans Stoll (2001) and an earlier work by Madhavan (2000). A more detailed conceptual review of trading and markets in general may be found in Larry Harris's (1999) book 'Trading and Exchanges'.

---

[1] Mark Garman (1976) first used the term "market microstructure" in an article on market making. However, published market microstructure research dates back to the 17th Century, when Joseph De la Vega (1688) was analysing trading practices and pricing on the Amsterdam stock exchange.

2.2 Fundamentals

Before covering the key concepts of market microstructure in more detail, let's first address some of the fundamental features of trading and markets.

Markets exist to accommodate trade. A marketplace is intended to bring different participants together, allowing them to trade. Since supply and demand are not always evenly balanced, most markets also rely on intermediaries, such as brokers or dealers, to facilitate trading.

Liquidity characterizes the ease of trading on a given market or for a specific asset. Trading in highly liquid markets is much easier, and more efficient, than trading in illiquid ones. Given the importance of trade, and particularly given its increasingly global nature, it is useful to be able to compare markets in terms of their efficiency. The cost of an asset is not necessarily a fair measure since many other economic factors, such as currencies, interest rates or inflation, may affect this. Therefore, measures based on liquidity are often used instead.

Market function

The fundamental purpose of a market is to bring buyers and sellers together. Broadly speaking, the capital markets may be categorised into primary and secondary markets, based on the two stages of an asset's lifecycle. [2] The primary market deals with the issuance of new assets/securities. Subsequent trading of these assets takes place on the secondary markets.

New government bonds are generally issued via specialised auctions. For equities, the primary market is concerned with initial public offerings (IPOs), follow-on offerings and rights issues. Similarly, new corporate debt is generally placed using underwriters (usually a syndicate of banks).

Historically, the secondary market for bonds has often been "over the counter" (OTC), although there are now also substantial inter-dealer and dealer-to-customer markets. The situation is similar for the trading of foreign exchange and many derivative assets. Whilst for equities the main marketplaces are exchanges, although increasingly these must now compete with other venues such as ECNs and Alternative Trading Systems (ATSs).

The secondary markets are vital since investors will be more willing to provide capital if they know the assets may readily be traded. This flexibility allows them to withdraw capital when needed and to switch between assets. Thus, market microstructure research has mainly focussed on the efficiency of the secondary markets. In particular, examining the diverse range of market structures and trading mechanisms, as we will see in sections 2.3 and 2.4.

Participants

Conventionally, market roles have been defined by trading needs. The "buy-side" corresponds to the traditional customers, namely institutional and individual investors. Whilst the "sell-side" represents the brokers, dealers and other financial intermediaries who service customer needs. Brokers act as agents to facilitate the actual trading, whilst dealers (or market makers) trade on their own behalf trying to profit from offering liquidity. Speculators act independently, trading for themselves.

In comparison, the market microstructure models in academic literature tend to classify the participants based on the information they possess:

---

[2] Note this distinction is less meaningful for foreign exchange and derivatives.

- "Informed traders" are assumed to have private information, which enables them to accurately determine an asset's true value.

- "Liquidity traders" must trade in order to fulfil certain requirements, such as to release capital or to adjust the balance of a portfolio.

The models also often incorporate the style of trading: Active traders are classified as those who demand immediate execution of their orders (immediacy) and push prices in the direction of their trading, whereas passive traders effectively supply immediacy and so stabilize prices. Unsurprisingly, microstructure models have shown that over the long-run liquidity traders generally lose if they trade with informed traders. Likewise, passive traders tend to profit from active traders. Still, informed traders do not have it all their own way; they are vulnerable to information-leakage. Consequently, informed traders try to minimise this by seeking to trade anonymously or even altering their trading patterns to look more like a liquidity trader.

Microstructure model trader types		Actual participants
Informed		Investors
Liquidity	Active	Investors Speculators
	Passive	Dealers Investors

Table 2-1 Microstructure model participants

Table 2-1 tries to map the model participants to their real world counterparts. The clearest link is for dealers. They act as passive liquidity traders, benefiting from offering liquidity to active traders, but at risk of losing to more informed ones; hence, their pricing tries to balance this information risk: The gains made from active traders should offset any potential losses. Conversely, speculators tend to take a more active, or aggressive, trading style. They often take advantage of short-term price moves, which may be contrary to longer-term expectations. For investors, the mapping is less clearly defined, since for any particular situation some investors will have more relevant, or valuable, information than others will. Hence, sometimes investors may actually be acting as liquidity traders, compared to other better-informed investors. The only way to tell is their ultimate profit (or loss).

Liquidity

Trading generally means converting an asset into cash or vice versa. How much this conversion actually costs may be represented by the liquidity of the asset, or the market it was traded on. This view of liquidity dates back to Harold Demsetz (1968). He expressed liquidity in terms of immediacy, which reflects the ability to trade immediately by executing at the best available price.

An asset's price is closely linked to its liquidity. For example, newly issued U.S. treasury bonds often have higher prices than older issues (termed "off-the-run") for the same maturity. This liquidity premium reflects the value of being able to readily convert the asset back to cash.

A liquid market or asset should have a lower cost for immediacy, i.e. trading costs. Liquid markets or assets will also usually have higher trading volumes. For instance, the stock market is generally more liquid than the real estate market.

Overall, we can characterise a market's liquidity [3] in terms of three main features:

- Depth
- Tightness
- Resiliency

Depth indicates the total quantity of buy and sell orders that are available for the asset, around the equilibrium price. Thus, a deep market enables us to trade large volumes without causing sizeable price movements (or impacts). Conversely, a shallow market means it is much harder to trade; often we will have to alter our price to attract buyers or sellers.

Tightness refers to the bid offer spread. That is to say, it is the difference between the prices to buy and sell an asset. A tight spread means that the trading costs are low (for average quantities) and so it is relatively easy to trade in and out of a position.

Resiliency determines how quickly the market recovers from a shock. A resilient market will suffer less price discrepancies from trading. So changes in price do not affect the overall level of trading, or availability of orders.

These three factors are closely related: deeper markets generally have narrower bid offer spreads (so are tighter) since they are easier to trade in, and so less risky. This also makes them more likely to be resilient.

Another potential factor, *Diversity*, is suggested by Avinash Persaud (2001). His study of market crises, titled 'Liquidity Black Holes', highlighted the importance of a diverse range of market views amongst investors and traders. Without such diversity, everyone wants to buy or sell at the same time or price, so liquidity is bound to disappear. Fortunately, for most markets, there is generally a great deal of diversity in opinions. Though, as Persaud points out, periodically a convergence of market sentiment helps trigger crises, such as the 1987 stock market crash or the 2007-09 financial crisis.

2.3 Market structure and design

For markets to work well, their design must accommodate the needs of institutional (or individual) investors, dealers and speculators. Therefore, a successful market allows investors to trade when they want, and minimizes the costs of trading orders whilst still making it worthwhile for dealers and speculators.

The key characteristics of market architecture [4] may be defined as:

- Market type
- Order types
- Trading protocols
- Transparency
- Off-market trading

These characteristics can significantly influence factors such as liquidity and the speed of

---

[3] As outlined by Fisher Black (1971) and Albert Kyle (1985) in their papers on continuous auction markets.
[4] Based on a list by Madhavan (2002).

price discovery, which in turn can affect the overall cost of trading. However, no two markets are the same, even if they are based on the same design, since local regulations may differ, as will the universe of traded assets.

Types of markets

Historically, the two most important properties for classifying markets are their trading mechanism and the actual frequency of trading:

Trading mechanism

Markets are generally thought of as being either quote-driven, order-driven or a mix (or hybrid) of the two. A purely quote-driven market means traders must transact with a dealer (or market maker) who quotes prices at which they will buy and sell a given quantity. Order-driven markets allow all traders to participate equally, placing orders on an order book that are then matched using a consistent set of rules. Figure 2-1 tries to highlight these differences.

	Quote-driven	*Order-driven*
	Market maker's two-way quote:	**Best bid and offer orders:**

	Potential actions

Quote-driven — Market maker's two-way quote:

Bid size	Bid	Offer	Off size
500	52.0	53.5	1,000

Order-driven — Best bid and offer orders:

Bid size	Bid	Offer	Off size
500	52.0	53.5	1,000

Quote-driven potential actions:

1. "Take the offer"

Bid size	Bid	Offer	Off size
500	52.0	**53.5**	**1,000**

2. "Hit the bid"

Bid size	Bid	Offer	Off size
500	**52.0**	53.5	1,000

3. Negotiate, or leave limit order

Order-driven potential actions:

1. Place buy market order, or buy limit order matching best offer

2. Place sell market order, or sell limit order matching best bid

3a. Place passive sell order

Bid size	Bid	Offer	Off size
500	52.0	53.5	1,000
		54.0	**1,000**

3b. Set market with new sell order

Bid size	Bid	Offer	Off size
500	52.0	**53.0**	**1,000**
		53.5	1,000

Figure 2-1 Comparing quote-driven and order-driven trading mechanisms

For a quote-driven market, when faced with a two-way quote we can choose to "take the offer", "hit the bid", renegotiate or just leave it. Choosing to "take the offer" results in a buy execution priced at their offer, whilst hitting the bid results in a sell. The market maker's two-way quote provides a guaranteed execution at that price, for a set size.

With an order-driven market, the prices are established by actual orders. The best bid price represents the highest priced buy order, whilst the best offer is set by the lowest priced sell order. A trade may only occur when a buy order matches (or betters) the current best offer price, whilst for a sell order the best bid price is the target. So instead of responding to the market maker's two-way quote we react to the available liquidity on the order book. The outcome also depends on the type of order used. A market order tries to guarantee execution regardless of price, whilst a limit order sticks to a strict price limit but sacrifices execution certainty. The equivalent to "taking the offer" is to place either a market order, or a limit order priced to match the best offer. Its size should be equal to or less than the available offer size. Conversely, we can "hit the bid" by placing a sell market order, or a limit order priced to match the best bid. Note that there are no guarantees, since at any moment many other traders will also be issuing new orders, updating existing ones and cancelling stale ones. By the time we react and place an order, it is quite possible that another order has already matched with the current best bid or offer. Hence, a buy (sell) market order may execute but potentially at a higher (lower) price than the currently displayed best offer. Alternatively, a limit order may fail to execute, in which case it will stay on the order book until it matches with another order or is cancelled. Therefore, for order-driven markets the best bid and offer prices are indicative rather than guaranteed like a dealer's firm two-way quote.

Whilst the immediacy of the two-way quote is useful, the persistence of orders within order-driven systems is also beneficial since they provide visible liquidity, which enhances price discovery. Order-driven markets also offer more control over order choice. Orders may be placed for any preferred price and size without the need for negotiation. For example, believing that the price will rise, we may choose to issue a more passive sell order priced just above the current best offer. Effectively, this will join the queue behind the best sell order, as shown in panel 3a. Alternatively, we may choose to set a new market level, at a price slightly lower than the best offer, shown in panel 3b.

Negotiation is a key difference between order-driven and quote-driven markets. Many quote-driven markets, even electronic ones, provide a mechanism that allows both counterparties to negotiate the size and/or price. The creation of new crossing systems and ATSs, such as Liquidnet, which also incorporate negotiation mechanisms mean that this is no longer limited to purely dealer-based markets. However, there is no direct equivalent to this mechanism for purely order-driven markets. The closest approximation is to place an order for our desired size and price, and then closely monitor and update it to try to ensure it is executed. But this is still far from entering into a bilateral negotiation. In fact, this difference is so fundamental that it can be used as a key factor in the categorisation of trading mechanisms.

Despite these differences, Figure 2-1 also highlights some clear similarities between a dealer's two-way quotes and using orders. A market where dealers must provide continuous firm quotes effectively forces them to constantly offer limit orders. In many ways, this may be thought of as a hybrid market. Indeed, markets such as NASDAQ, which used to be purely quote-driven, have since shifted to become truly hybrid markets, incorporating much of the same functionality as order-driven markets. In comparison, a market where the dealers' quotes are only indicative remains a purely quote-driven market, since we must still request a separate firm quote.

Trading frequency

The frequency of trading is the other main classifier for the structure of markets, since this determines when requirement matches (whether they are from quotes or orders) are actually turned into executions. Generally, markets provide one or more of the following types:

- Continuous trading
- Periodic trading
- Request-driven trading

Continuous trading provides a convenient and efficient means of execution. Although such immediacy can lead to price volatility, particularly when there is an imbalance between supply and demand. Periodic trading is generally scheduled for specific time/s in the day. The time period beforehand permits more considered price formation, it also allows liquidity to accumulate. Request-driven trading means requesting a quote from a market maker, whilst it may be convenient it is not necessarily as efficient in terms of the price achieved.

Classifying major market types

Based on these two key properties, a wide range of market types is possible; some examples are highlighted in Table 2-2.

		Mechanism		
		Order-driven	Hybrid		Negotiation-based
Frequency	Continuous	• CDA • Cont. blind crosses/ATS Instinet CBX LeveL • Internal crossing	• CDA w/LP CME • Continuous advertised crosses/ATS Pipeline ITG POSIT Alert	• Cont. dealer (firm quote) MTS • RFS	• Cont. dealer (indicative quote) • Cont. negotiated crosses/ATS Liquidnet
	Continuous with call	• CDA Tokyo SE	• CDA w/LP Euronext, LSE, Eurex	• Hybrid dealer/ order book NYSE, NASDAQ, ICAP BrokerTec EBS	
	Scheduled Call	• Call auction Euronext illiquid • Crossing sys ITG POSIT, Instinet crosses			
	Request	• Dealer limit order			• Dealer RFQ • "Upstairs" trading

Table 2-2 Market types organised by their mechanism and trading frequency

The corners of this table correspond to the extremes, whilst the centre shows the more hybrid "mix 'n match" approach. Notice that the trading mechanism classification actually uses "negotiation-based" which encompasses the quote-driven approach. Before we move on to consider other factors in market design, it is worth briefly reviewing some of the key market types shown in Table 2-2:

CDA stands for Continuous Double Auction; this is simply an order-driven continuous auction market. Its name is derived from the fact that it supports simultaneous buy and sell auctions. The CDA mechanism is synonymous with Central Limit Order books (CLO) which form the basis for most order-driven markets. As each new order arrives, is updated or cancelled the matching process checks the order book for any orders that match.

Continuous dealer markets ensure that the market makers constantly update two-way quotes to reflect their latest prices. They may be subdivided into those where the dealers provide either firm or indicative quotes. Markets based on firm quotes, including Request-for-streaming (RFS) mechanisms, effectively force the dealers to constantly maintain limit orders. This corresponds to a more hybrid mechanism, which may even be able to cater for anonymous trading. As mentioned earlier, venues where indicative quotes are used represent a more negotiation-based (or quote-driven) approach.

At the other end of the spectrum are request-driven mechanisms such as single dealer Request-for-quote (RFQ) platforms. Likewise, the traditional "upstairs" trading for large block orders is purely request-driven. Whilst requesting a limit order from a dealer effectively places an order on their private order book.

Scheduled, or periodic, call auctions are generally set for specific time/s in the day. The period before the auction allows orders (and so liquidity) to accumulate. The auction process then matches buy and sell orders, usually by attempting to find a single clearing price that maximizes the amount executed. By forcing trading interest to wait, orders may accumulate ready for the auction call, helping to reduce volatility. The successful pooling of liquidity also means they are often used for less liquid assets.

Hybrid markets offer elements of both order-driven and negotiation-based markets. Notice that in Table 2-2 the hybrid mechanism column is actually sub-divided. This loosely represents the markets that were originally based on either an order-driven or a negotiation-based approach. Hence, CDA markets, such as Euronext, which have become hybrid by allowing dedicated Liquidity Providers (w/LP) to improve their overall liquidity, are shown on the left hand side. In comparison, NASDAQ effectively converted itself from a quote-driven market into a hybrid order book by extending its multiple dealer platform to support displayed limit orders. So, NASDAQ is shown on the right hand side of this column.

Many markets now incorporate both continuous and call auctions. Combining these two mechanisms types offers the convenience of continuous execution with the stabilising effect of the call. Therefore, many continuous auction markets now use call auctions for their most volatile periods, namely the open and close, and after trading halts for liquidity or price suspensions. Some markets even incorporate additional intraday call auctions.

The scheme shown in Table 2-2 may also be used to categorise the various types of "dark pool" Alternative Trading Systems (ATSs). Essentially, this follows the approach outlined by Jeromee Johnson from the TABB Group (2006), which classifies crossings as scheduled or continuous and either blind, negotiated, advertised or internal. Scheduled crosses, such as ITG's POSIT, are similar to scheduled call auctions, except the liquidity is hidden. Continuous blind crosses, such as Instinet's CBX, are effectively a CDA where the order book remains completely opaque. A similar mechanism is adopted for brokers' internal crossing systems. Continuous negotiated crossing platforms constantly search for potential matches notifying each participant when one is found. This then allows them to enter into an anonymous bilateral negotiation for both the size and price. Continuous advertised crossing systems, such as Pipeline, highlight when liquidity is present, without giving away the size.

This allows participants to place firm orders to execute with it.

In general, the trend for market design seems to be towards the centre of Table 2-2. In other words, continuous trading based on hybrid mechanisms, often with additional call auctions to help start and/or close the market. This approach is increasingly being adopted by the world's leading market venues. That said, notable innovations are also occurring in other areas, mainly due to the advent of crossing systems and ATSs. Exactly what the markets of the future will look like is still far from certain.

Order types

Orders also play an important role in market structure. An order is simply an instruction to buy or sell a specific quantity of a given asset. Market microstructure tends to differentiate orders both by their liquidity-effect and by their associated risks. The two main types are:

- Market orders - these are directions to trade immediately at the best price available. Hence, they demand liquidity and risk execution price uncertainty.

- Limit orders - these have an inbuilt price limit that must not be breached, a maximum price for buys and a minimum price for sell orders. Thus, limit orders can help provide liquidity but risk failing to execute.

Note that markets may also differ in terms of the behaviour of these order types. For instance, a limit order placed with a dealer may be kept hidden until the market conditions are right, in which case it does not provide visible liquidity. Whereas in a pure order-driven market such a limit order immediately goes on the central order book and is visible, provided that the order book is sufficiently transparent.

A wide range of conditions may also be applied to each order. These allow control over when each order becomes active, their duration and whether they may be partially filled. Conditions may even be set which direct the order to specific dealers or venues.

Using these conditions and incorporating additional special behaviours has enabled venues to offer a wide range of order types. For example, hybrid orders such as market-to-limit orders actually have some of the properties of both market orders and limit orders. Whilst conditional orders allow orders to become active, only once a specific condition is true. For instance, stop orders are activated when the market price exceeds their internal stop limit. Hidden and iceberg orders are also becoming increasingly important, as traders try to achieve the best price for their orders without disclosing all the associated liquidity.

Each market supports a diverse set of conditions and order types. In Chapter 4, we shall cover these in much more detail.

Trading Protocols

Markets need to provide a "fair and orderly" trading environment. They achieve this by defining suitable trading rules or protocols and then applying them rigorously. The rules cover everything from:
- order precedence
- requirements for trade sizes
- pricing increments
- specifying how the market actually opens and closes
- mandating how it reacts to asset and market-wide events

So they can have a considerable effect on the efficiency of trading on a given market.

Order precedence: These rules specify how incoming orders execute with existing orders or dealer quotes. Generally, markets give most priority to orders with the best price, with secondary priority based on the time of order entry. Alternatively, some give secondary priority based on order size.

Minimum trade quantities: Also known as lot-sizes, these limits can vary from a single unit to a thousand or more. Retail investors prefer the flexibility of smaller lot sizes, so markets can use lot-size rules to help control the mix of institutional and retail investors.

Minimum price increments: Also known as tick-sizes, these limits affect the spread between the bid and offer prices. Larger increments increase the spread and so make it more profitable to provide liquidity (both for dealers and for users of limit orders). But if the tick size is too small then time-based order priority can become meaningless, as noted by Larry Harris (1991). Setting a new market price is cheap for small ticks, so the temptation is to step in front of other orders in order to maintain priority. In the U.S., this is often referred to as "pennying".

Opening/closing procedures: The specifics of how (and when) the market opens and closes, and what constitutes the official opening and closing prices. Microstructure research has shown that price discovery can be made more efficient by batching orders in periodic call auctions. Many types of markets now use call auctions to open and/or close the market.

Trading halts and circuit-breakers: A trading halt may be called for regulatory reasons, for example, just before a company makes an announcement that may significantly affect its stock price. Alternatively, it may also be triggered by a large price move. Halting the trading allows the market time to assess the new information, and may reduce the impact when trading restarts. Alternatively, trading may be switched temporarily to a special call auction to reduce the volatility of trading. Circuit-breakers concern market-wide events, they are designed to protect against mass selling during large market declines. For example, the NYSE has breakers set at thresholds for 10, 20 and 30% of the Dow Jones Industrial Average (DJIA). If these are reached, the market may halt for 1-2 hours or even completely close.

Transparency

Transparency represents the amount of market information that is available before and after a trade has occurred. Pre-trade information corresponds to the prices and sizes of quotes or orders. Post-trade information relates to actual trade execution details, namely the time, size and price.

Quote-driven markets tend to be less transparent than order-driven ones since they only ever show a broker's best bid and offer. The bilateral nature of quote-driven trading means that both parties usually know who they are dealing with. Multi-broker markets improve visibility slightly by making it easier to compare quotes from a range of market makers. If the market makers provide firm quotes then there is also the possibility of anonymous trading.

Order-driven markets tend to offer much higher visibility. Certainly, the most transparent market is a fully displayed order book, which shows the owners of each order and with no hidden order volume, where trades are reported promptly and publicly. Still, such complete transparency is not appealing to all users. In particular, institutional traders generally need to reduce the potential impact of large orders, which is difficult if each of their orders is clearly identifiable. A common solution is to make the order book anonymous. Increasingly, markets are also allowing hidden orders, providing traders control over the visibility of their total order volume.

Venues which specialise in handling large block orders, such as the "dark pool" ATSs, tend to be opaque. This allows traders to place large orders without fear of signalling their intentions to other market participants. Obviously, it is much more difficult to discover the market price for an asset when limited information is available. Therefore, these opaque venues tend to be most successful when there is also a large and highly visible market from which fair market prices may be determined. Hence, ATSs have so far seen the most success in the U.S. equity marketplace, although they are rapidly spreading globally.

In general, the trend across most markets, and asset classes, appears to be increasing transparency but with anonymity. In fact, several markets, which had fully disclosed broker identities, have now moved back to voluntary identification or completely anonymous trading. Nevertheless, the success of ATSs means that there will also continue to be a large and growing number of completely opaque markets.

After-hours and off-market trading

The globalisation of investment and trading means that there is an increasing demand for access to trade 24x7. So the provision of after-hours and off-market trading is another key differentiator for markets.

After-hours trading can be particularly useful for cross-border trading, helping to compensate for time zone differences. Large block traders also sometimes take advantage of the extra trading opportunities. Though, a different trading approach may be required, since out-of-hours liquidity may be substantially lower. Price changes during after-hours trading can also act as an indicator for the next days open.

Off-market trading takes two main forms, the same assets can be traded on a range of venues in the same country, alternatively new assets may be created to permit dual listing in foreign markets. For instance, taking the US equities market as an example, stocks may be listed on exchanges, such as NYSE and NASDAQ. Links between the venues allow trading most NYSE stocks on the other exchanges as well as across a range of ECNs and ATSs. The same applies for NASDAQ listed stocks. For non-U.S. companies depository receipts allow their stocks to be effectively traded on US venues.

Having such a wide range of possible execution venues has led the US equity market to be described as fragmented. Hans Stoll (2001) provides a valuable discussion of the issues between market centralisation and fragmentation. Essentially, centralisation benefits from two factors, economies of scale and network externalities. Both of these factors offer the most advantage to the "first-mover"; hence, well-established primary markets tend to benefit most. For example, high trade volumes allow a venue to reduce its average cost per trade due to economies of scale. Similarly, the trade volume and number of participants affect the probability of trading. Again, this makes established markets more attractive to traders since they offer a higher likelihood of successful execution.

On the other hand, market fragmentation benefits from a range of closely related factors:

- Market transparency
- Technological changes
- Regulatory policy

As we saw in the previous section, market transparency enables venues (such as ATSs) to reliably guarantee to match the main market best prices. Without this, traders must participate on the main market just to discover the price. Likewise, technological improvements have made it easier to distribute prices and orders between venues. Many regulatory bodies are also mandating transparency in order to encourage competition. In the U.S. equities markets, regulation has also encouraged markets to link together, allowing other venues to compete directly with the main markets. Thus, traders can participate with a range of venues either directly or indirectly.

To capture order flow from more established markets the competing venues often have to offer additional functionality, such as anonymity or better handling for block orders. Some even offer inducements, either through reduced costs for liquidity providers (giving rebates for orders which supply liquidity) or via direct payments to brokers to capture order flow (which has been criticised since the payment does not go to the customer).

As Stoll (2001) points out, so long as markets are linked then the consequences of market fragmentation can be relatively minor. One of the main issues is that fragmented markets are only really capable of supporting price priority. Though, this can be broken when a large order "walks the book" and trades through a range of prices at one venue. Secondary priorities, such as time, are not fully supportable across multiple linked markets at present. Note that liquidity-driven trading algorithms and smart order routing can be used to cope with this.

Most markets are in a state of constant flux; new trading venues keep appearing whilst fierce competition has resulted in many either merging or failing. The only certainty is that existing markets will have to keep adapting to cope with these changes.

Other important market design features

Although the trading mechanism and frequency are the main determinants of market structure, other market features can still have a marked effect, namely:

Means of price discovery: Most markets have an inbuilt price discovery mechanism. For instance, a market maker's two-way quote or the best buy and sell orders on an order-driven market, which reflect the current best bid and offer prices. However, some markets do not have a dedicated pricing mechanism; instead, they take reference prices from another market (generally from the principal market). This approach tends to be more suitable for block trading.

Intraday breaks: Some markets remain closed around lunchtime, such as the Hong Kong, Singapore and Tokyo stock exchanges.

Automation: A high level of automation helps reduce the distinction between market makers and other traders. Less automated or manually handled markets offer delays, which give dealers opportunities to become more informed (either from new information, new orders or new trades).

Segmentation: A "one size fits all" approach does not generally work well for all assets. Thus, many markets now employ a more segmented approach, using a continuous order-driven mechanism for the most liquid assets and a periodic call auction for the least liquid.

Market design is constantly evolving, driven by competition, regulation and technology. In the future, other market design features may well become more important. For instance, complex order books are able to deal with linked orders between assets; these allow derivative and even multi-asset trading strategies to be adopted.

2.4   Trading mechanism research

The trading process can be broken down into three key stages:

1.   Price formation
2.   Price discovery / trade execution
3.   Reporting, clearing & settlement

In other words, we first need to decide on the price we are willing to trade at, referred to as price formation. Secondly, for a trade to occur we need to find a counterparty that is prepared to trade with us at this price, also termed price discovery or trade execution. Finally, the trades are reported and the clearing and settlement processes handle the required cash flows and transfers of ownership.

Most research has focussed on the first two phases, trying to determine the relationships between market structure, trading volume, prices and trading costs.

Price formation

Investors tend to have different views on the future value of an asset; in part, this is because they have varying levels of information. Consequently, their valuations target diverse prices. Therefore, price formation for an asset is usually based on supply and demand conditions. It is also affected by the fundamental market mechanism, i.e. quote-driven or order-driven. Market microstructure researchers have used a wide range of models to investigate this process; Chapter 8 provides a more detailed review of these.

Quote-driven markets are a perfect starting point for analysis into price formation since the very nature of market makers is to quote prices. Information-based models assume that some participants have a definite information advantage over others. The bid offer spread represents the cost for which market makers are prepared to trade. Essentially, this spread should generate enough returns to cover their costs and any losses from trading with more informed traders. Inventory-based models derive the dealer's quote based on their inventory (or position). This just needs to be sufficient to service any incoming orders. So the market maker's bid offer spread often tends to increase as their position moves further from their ideal inventory.

For order-driven markets, price formation is more complex since there are many more participants, each with their own opinion. Order-driven markets are generally based around a central limit order book, which contains every live order for the asset. The screenshot shown in Figure 2-2 displays a typical order book trading screen. Orders are arranged by their limit price with the best prices at the top. The top buy order has the highest buy limit price, in this case 336.00, whilst the top sell order has the lowest sell limit price, at 336.75.

Note that the best bids and offers shown in Figure 2-2 are actually aggregated totals, designed to quickly show the quantity available at each price point. The outermost column shows the number of orders in each total; it may also show any specific owner identifiers, such as FIRM, CMPY. So the 10,800 available to sell at 337.25 is actually composed of two separate orders. Figure 2-3 shows an alternate view of this order book, expanding it to illustrate each of the underlying orders (in this case S6 and S8) which make up these totals.

Clearly, the transparency of the order book has a marked effect on the price formation. If only the best bid and offer quotes are displayed, as shaded in Figure 2-3, then effectively the order book is reduced to being like a market maker's two-way quote. This adds a degree of uncertainty since traders cannot tell what other liquidity might be available. This additional risk could lead to orders being priced more aggressively than is necessary.

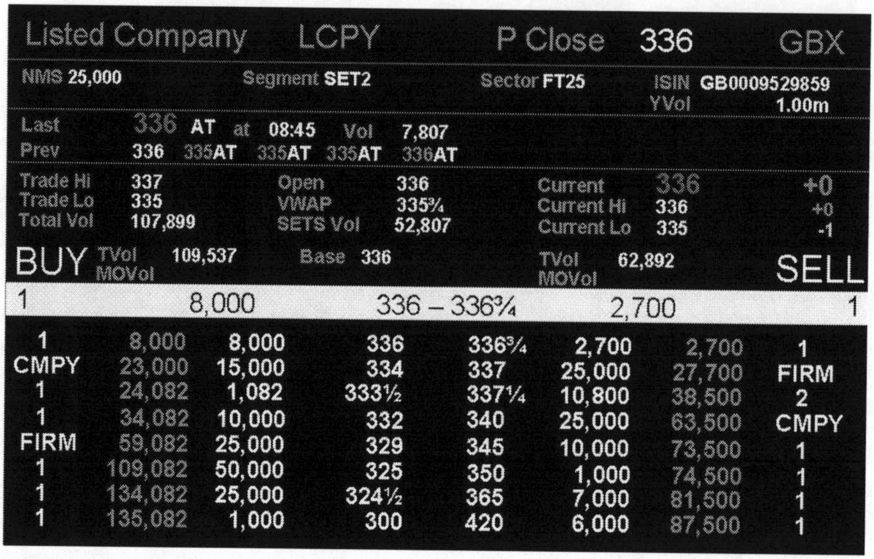

Source: © LSE (2006a)   Reproduced with permission from London Stock Exchange PLC

Figure 2-2 A typical order book trading screen

Buys				Sells			
Id	Time	Size	Price	Price	Size	Time	Id
B8	8:25:00	8,000	336.0	336.75	2,700	8:25:00	S7
B1	8:20:25	15,000	334.0	337.0	25,000	8:25:30	S9
B5	8:23:25	1,082	333.5	337.25	4,000	8:23:00	S6
B7	8:24:09	10,000	332.0	337.25	6,800	8:25:25	S8
B3	8:20:25	25,000	329.0	340.0	25,000	8:20:25	S2
B4	8:21:00	50,000	325.0	345.0	10,000	8:20:42	S3
B6	8:24:05	25,000	324.5	350.0	1,000	8:21:50	S4
B2	8:20:40	1,000	300.0	365.0	7,000	8:22:20	S5
				420.0	6,000	8:20:00	S1

Figure 2-3 A simplified representation of an order book

On the other hand, if the entire order book is visible, or even just the best five orders, traders can immediately see the range of available prices and volumes. By using the visible liquidity, they can then adjust their valuations to determine their own price for the asset.

Note that sometimes the best bid and offer price might temporarily be the same, in which case the market is said to be "locked". If the best offer price is below the best bid, it is termed "crossed". These situations can arise in some markets where the prices are based on multiple dealers, or take feeds from other venues. Each market will have its own way of dealing with this, getting the order book back to normal as quickly as possible.

Price discovery / trade execution

Price discovery is synonymous with trade execution, it occurs when supply and demand requirements cross. The actual price at which this happens is determined by the mechanism. There are three main types of discovery mechanism:

- Bilateral trading
- Continuous auction
- Call auction

Bilateral trading is mainly used for quote-driven and negotiation-based trading, whereas order-driven and hybrid markets adopt more multilateral auction-based mechanisms. The main difference between the two types of auction is the frequency. Unlike continuous auctions, call based auctions allow orders to accumulate for some time before the actual discovery (or matching) takes place.

Note that some markets do not have an independent price discovery mechanism: An auction takes place, but the execution price is derived externally (often from the primary market). As an example, we will see how a mid-point match works for continuous auctions.

Bilateral trading

As its name suggests, bilateral trading represents one-to-one trading mechanisms. Therefore, it is mainly used for quote-driven and negotiation-based trading, although some hybrid markets also support this method.

A market maker's two-way quote states both the prices and quantities that they are willing to trade at. The bid price represents what they will pay to buy an asset whilst the offer is what they will sell it for. As we saw in Figure 2-1, price discovery only occurs if a client is prepared to deal at these prices. In which case, they may then "hit the bid" (sell) or "take the offer" (buy). Alternatively, they can try to renegotiate a new price, often for a different quantity, or simply walk away.

The one-to-one nature of bilateral trading means that each party generally knows the other's identity. This allows the market maker to tailor their quote based on the client. In particular, they can estimate the risk of adverse selection and incorporate this into their quote. Note that some protection is given to clients by the two-way quote, since they do not have to immediately disclose whether they are buyers or sellers, which could prejudice the market maker's price.

Multi-dealer systems do not change the fundamentals of a bilateral trading mechanism, but they can help speed it up. As Figure 2-4 shows, by aggregating the market maker quotes a customer can easily see the available prices and sizes without having to contact them individually. For simplicity, each broker is shown on a separate row, together with a shaded row for the best bid and offer quotes. Although many systems allow this view to be sorted by price, so that it looks like an order book.

Id	Bid size	Bid	Offer	Offer size	Id
BrokerC	700	52.1	53.4	900	BrokerD
BrokerA	500	52.0	53.5	800	BrokerA
BrokerB	1,000	52.0	53.5	1,000	BrokerB
BrokerC	700	52.1	53.6	500	BrokerC
BrokerD	800	52.0	53.4	900	BrokerD
BrokerE	1,000	51.9	53.5	700	BrokerE

Figure 2-4 An example multi-dealer quote view

Price formation is still done by the dealers, although in a multi-dealer environment they will often need to provide continuous updates. This gives us a better idea of their prices, without even having to contact dealers, and so give away our interest. For markets where they are obliged to make firm quotes, such as NASDAQ, we can then immediately hit or lift a quote to trade. Some hybrid markets also support special order types that allow clients to direct orders to specific market makers. For example, NASDAQ used to provide a directed non-liability order that could be routed to a specific market maker. They were then allowed to choose whether they accepted the order. The market maker could also opt to accept part of the order, try to renegotiate a deal or just decline the order, all within a fixed time limit (5s).

For some multi-dealer systems, the price quotes are merely indicative, so we must click on a broker to issue a "request for quote" (RFQ). This will then signal our interest to the market maker, who will then give a quote, as shown in Figure 2-5.

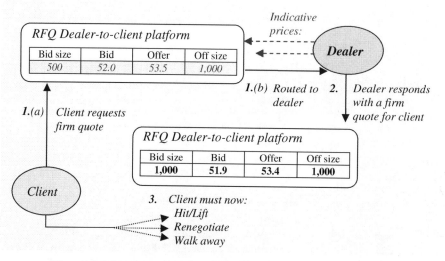

Figure 2-5 An example Request For Quote (RFQ) mechanism

Note that Figure 2-5 depicts a two-way quote, but many RFQ systems only support one-way quoting, so the client must also state whether they wish to buy or sell the asset.

Streaming quotes via "request for stream" (RFS) is another alternative. With RFS, we are actually requesting a stream of updates rather than a single one-off quote, as shown in Figure 2-6. Since each new update is a firm quote, we can decide whether to trade with the dealer by hitting or lifting. Alternatively, we can opt to wait and see whether the price improves for subsequent updates. Whilst it is still not quite the same as trading on a continuous order book, this is a much more dynamic approach than RFQ-based trading, since the onus has now shifted to the dealer to provide a continuously updating stream of firm quotes.

Typically, these request-driven approaches are used in the fixed income (mainly RFQ) and foreign exchange (both RFQ and RFS) markets.

Anonymous bilateral mechanisms have also been introduced, most notably Liquidnet's crossing service. Requirements for buys or sells are entered anonymously. If the system finds a potential match, it then creates a negotiation session between the two parties. Each counterparty can see a scorecard for the other. This summarises their history of previously successful negotiations, allowing them to gauge the validity of each other. They can then negotiate the quantity, whilst the price is often set by the primary market, such as the U.S. National Best Bid and Offer (NBBO). Only after successful execution may their actual identities become known.

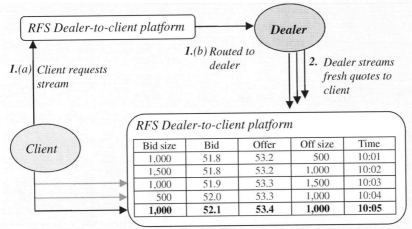

3. For each new quote client must decide whether to hit/lift or ignore

Figure 2-6 An example Request For Stream (RFS) mechanism

Continuous auction

The continuous auction mechanism consistently applies the matching rules each time an order is added, updated or cancelled. This is a multilateral process with many different traders all placing and amending orders. Therefore, a queuing system is needed to ensure that each order is processed in turn, as shown in Figure 2-7.

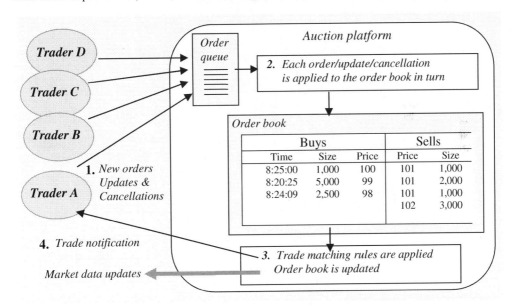

Figure 2-7 An example continuous auction mechanism

For each order, the following steps are applied:

- The order instruction is added to the internal order book
- Trade matching rules are then used to see if any matches are now possible
- The order book is updated to reflect any changes
- Execution notifications are sent for any resultant matches

Then the cycle simply starts all over again for the next order instruction in the queue.

In terms of the actual trade matching, strictly defined rules are consistently applied. Typically, markets give the highest priority to orders based on price, but a variety of approaches is used for the secondary priority. The two most common are time and pro-rata, some markets also give priority to the first order at a set price point whilst others may even give priority to specific users.

Price/time based trade matching is common in most equities markets. The highest priced buy orders and the lowest priced sells are rewarded with the highest probabilities of execution. For orders at the same price, the time they were placed is then used to distinguish between them, thus favouring earlier orders.

Price/pro-rata trade matching is more common in futures markets. Again, the best priced buy and sell orders take priority, but allocation between orders at the same price point is done on a pro-rata basis. So each order is allocated based on its proportion of the total volume of orders at that price. Thus, rewarding larger orders rather than those placed earlier.

For example, let's look at how a market order to buy 1,000 EEE might be handled for the order book shown in Figure 2-8. Adopting a price/time based priority, we can see that the orders are already arranged in terms of their price and time. The earlier sell order S1 takes priority over the similarly priced S2 and S3 and the higher priced S4.

Id	Buys			Sells			
	Time	Size	Price	Price	Size	Time	Id
	8:20:00	500	100	101	750	8:21:00	S1
	8:20:25	1,000	100	101	250	8:21:25	S2
	8:21:09	400	99	101	1,000	8:22:05	S3
	8:20:04	200	99	102	800	8:19:09	S4

(a) Before

Price/time

	Sells		
	Price	Size	Id
.	~~101~~	~~750~~	~~S1~~
.	~~101~~	~~250~~	~~S2~~
.	101	1,000	S3
.	102	800	S4

Price/pro-rata

	Sells			Alloc
	Price	Size	Id	
.	101	**375**	S1	375
.	101	**125**	S2	125
.	101	**500**	S3	500
.	102	800	S4	

(b) After

Figure 2-8 An example buy order matched with different priorities

Based on the size of the incoming market order, we can see that order S1 will be filled completely, as will the next order S2. Afterwards, order S3 now has both price and time priority for any new incoming buy orders.

In comparison, using a price/pro-rata based approach the allocation (labelled Alloc) is based on order size, since orders S1, S2 and S3 all have the same price priority. The proportions allocated are based on each order's size divided by the total amount available at that price. So order S3 will be allocated (1,000 / 2,000) = 50% of the incoming order. Order

S1 will get (750 / 2000) = 37.5%, leaving the remaining 12.5% for order S2. The net result is that all three orders receive partial execution and remain on the order book ready for the next execution. The residual amounts are highlighted in Figure 2-8(b), confirming that this approach rewards size nearly as much as price.

Some continuous markets do not have an independent price discovery mechanism. Instead, the execution price is derived externally (usually from the primary market). Often this is the midpoint of the external best bid and offer prices. If market orders are supported, they execute at the mid-point whenever there is sufficient volume available on the other side of the order book. Limit orders will only match when the mid-point price is better than their limit. So the limit prices shown in Figure 2-9 actually refer to this mid-point.

	Buys				Sells		
Id	Time	Size	Price	Price	Size	Time	Id
B1	8:25:00	1,000		*101*	1,000	8:25:00	S1
B2	8:20:25	5,000	99	*102*	3,000	8:20:25	S2
B3	8:24:09	2,500	98	*102*	1,500	8:24:09	S3

(a) before, external mid-point is 100

	Buys				Sells		
Id	Time	Size	Price	Price	Size	Time	Id
~~B1~~	~~8:25:00~~	~~1,000~~	*~~101~~*	*~~101~~*	~~1,000~~	~~8:25:00~~	~~S1~~
B2	8:20:25	5,000	99	*102*	3,000	8:20:25	S2
B3	8:24:09	2,500	98	*102*	1,500	8:24:09	S3

(b) after mid-point becomes 101

Figure 2-9 An example mid-point match

On a normal continuous auction, the market order B1 would simply have crossed with order S1. But it is unable to do so because the external best bid and offer is 99-101, which is below the mid-point limit of 101 for order S1. As soon as the external mid-point shifts to 101, B1 can cross with order S1 since the mid-point is now sufficient. Note that both orders achieve the mid-point price, so unlike a normal market order B1 has not had to pay half the spread; though, it has sacrificed immediacy for this price improvement. This mechanism is generally used to support continuous crossing for block-size orders, hence the order book shown in Figure 2-9 would be completely opaque.

Clearly, a wide variety of continuous trade matching mechanisms are in use. In Chapter 8, we will review some of these in more detail.

Call auction

A call auction may occur as little as once a day or as frequently as every 10 to 15 minutes throughout the trading day. Essentially, the process is similar to Figure 2-7 in that orders are queued up and applied to the auction order book. Still, trade matching is not instantaneous; it is carried out at a set auction time. The goal is to ensure that the maximum possible volume of orders is crossed at the auction price. Hence, orders accumulate before the auction takes place, allowing longer for price formation. This can be particularly useful when there is more uncertainty about what the price should actually be. In fact, many markets that use continuous auctions often choose to open and close the market with a separate call auction in an effort to reduce price volatility.

Before the crossing begins, the venue may also publish information about the overall imbalance between the buy and sell orders. They may even offer an indicative auction price to help traders to decide on pricing for their auction orders.

The auction crossing begins by checking that the order book is crossed; in other words, either the book contains market orders (MO) or there are buy orders with limit prices higher than some of the sell orders. It will then try to determine the best price for the auction. For the example order book shown in Figure 2-10(a), the best crossing price is 104.

Buys			Sells		
Time	Size	Price	Price	Size	Time
7:25:00	7,000	MO	MO	2,000	7:25:00
7:20:25	3,000	105	101	3,000	7:25:00
7:24:09	1,000	104	102	5,000	7:20:25
7:20:25	2,000	102	104	1,000	7:20:25
7:21:00	1,000	101	105	5,000	7:24:09

(a) order book crossing

Buys			Sells		
Time	Size	Price	Price	Size	Time
7:20:25	2,000	102	105	5,000	7:24:09
7:21:00	1,000	101			

(b) once crossing completed

Figure 2-10 An example call auction crossing

Note that this auction price is generally determined independently, although for some crossing systems it may actually be derived from another market. Alternatively, if a single best price cannot be found then the price will be based on a reference price; generally, this is the last traded price (so last night's close for an opening auction or the last trade for a closing auction). We shall cover the specific criteria for determining the auction price in more detail in Chapter 8.

Once an auction price is determined, the order book is then processed to match any orders that will execute within this price limit. These rows are shaded in the example order book shown in Figure 2-10(a). Note that many venues use time as a secondary priority, this rewards the early entry of auction orders.

Having completed the auction, the order book is then updated for the matched orders and trade notifications are sent out. Note that if this was the opening auction for a continuous double auction market, then Figure 2-10(b) shows the order book as it will be when the market officially opens for continuous trading. Alternatively, if this was for the close or an intraday/batch call auction then the orders will either be cancelled or left for the next auction crossing (although this depends on the market).

Reporting, clearing and settlement

The final stages of the trading mechanism are reporting, clearing and settlement. Once a trade has been executed, detailed confirmations of the deal must be reported to the associated counterparties, the market authorities may also need to be informed.

The next stage of the process is clearing, which is basically a preparatory step before actual settlement. Clearing involves validating the trade and settlement details, as well as ensuring that the buyer and seller have the required assets/funds to be able to proceed. Often, a specific clearing agent will be mandated for trades at regulated venues such as exchanges.

The settlement process represents the actual exchange of assets and funds. The details for the buyer and seller are matched; a payment is made from the buyer's account and the asset's ownership is reassigned. Nowadays, most financial assets are dematerialised, so this literally means updating a book entry to reflect the change in ownership. However, for some assets, such as commodities, it can still involve a physical delivery. Generally, this process is handled by security depositories or dedicated custodians, financial institutions that specialise in the safekeeping of assets. Custodians also manage any associated interest or dividend payments, and even handle corporate actions for the holdings. Many security depositories and custodians have now become international, catering for a wide range of markets and allowing cross border trading.

The clearing and settlement process has become increasingly automated to keep up with electronic trading. Straight-through-processing (STP) offers the prospect of a fully electronic trading, clearing and settlement pathway. Gradually, more and more markets are migrating to support electronic clearing and settlement. Settlement dates used to commonly be five working days after the actual execution, denoted as T+5. This is gradually shifting to T+1, and ultimately towards T+0.

Increasingly, execution venues are adopting a central counterparty (CCP) approach for their clearing and settlement. This effectively splits each deal into two parts; each half is then transacted versus the CCP. So the buyer actually pays the CCP in return for the asset, whilst the seller must deliver the asset to the CCP in return for payment. This helps reduce counterparty risk as well, since the central counterparty now bears the risk of default. The CCP mechanism also allows for fully anonymous trading, since each party will only need to deal with the CCP. The buyer and seller just need to provide sufficient collateral to cover their trades. This also means clearing can be netted across all a participant's trades for an asset, resulting in a single net trade versus the CCP. Clearly, such netting means much less transfers and settlements and so can lead to substantial cost savings. It can also help reduce the required margin (or collateral) commitments needed to cover credit risk. Many central counterparties support margining across different assets, so the margin for a futures position may be reduced by a corresponding holding in the underlying asset. This can help reduce the costs of funding/position management.

For more information on the clearing and settlement processes, the review by Marco Pagano and Jorge Padilla (2005) is a good starting point.

2.5 Transaction cost measurement and analysis

Transaction costs are the last key area for market microstructure research. They are unavoidable, and are incurred each time an asset is bought or sold. Costs can have a considerable effect on investment returns and so affect market efficiency. Increased costs mean that investors must seek higher returns, and so they reduce the number of potential trading opportunities. In turn, this means that investors may hold positions for longer periods, helping to reduce trading volumes and so decreasing overall market liquidity. Electronic trading has helped increase market access to a wider range of participants. In so doing, it has improved market efficiency and led to a reduction in overall transaction costs.

By carefully measuring and analysing transaction costs, we can try to minimise them. Hence understanding how and why they occur has become a key factor in achieving significant investment returns. Clearly, the first stage is accurately measuring the overall costs. Post-trade analysis has also proved important for performance analysis, enabling comparison of both trading styles and individual brokers/traders.

Further research has broken down transaction costs into separate components, such as market impact and timing risk. A combination of theoretical models and empirical analysis has allowed accurate cost models to be created. These can be used for pre-trade analysis to estimate the potential cost, and so may be used to choose the most appropriate trading strategy.

Cost measurement

Cost measurement has focussed predominantly on spreads and benchmark prices. Both measures are easy to calculate and can give meaningful insights.

Using spreads

Spreads have long been a popular measure for cost measurement, in part due to the simplicity of determining them. They have also been used as a measure of overall market efficiency. Many academic studies have compared the average spreads for various market types. Table 2-3 shows the key spreads which are commonly used:

Type	Measures	From:
Quoted spread	Market quality	Difference between best bid and offer price
Effective spread	Execution cost	Signed difference between trade price and quote midpoint when order was received
Realized spread	Trading intermediary profits	Signed difference between trade price and quote midpoint 5 minutes after the trade

Table 2-3 The different types of spreads

As we have already seen, the bid offer spread can be attributed to a range of factors. Market makers use it to compensate themselves for the fixed costs incurred by trading, as well as to protect themselves from the risk of adverse selection. Similarly, spreads arise in purely order-driven markets as a function of the available supply and demand.

The effective spread represents the difference between the achieved trade price and the mid point between the bid and offer when the order was first received. It measures the actual cost our order incurred by executing in the market.

The realized spread compares the difference between the trade price and the mid price five minutes later. It is sometimes used as a measure of the potential profits that may be made by trading intermediaries, i.e. market makers, dealers, brokers.

Note that to compare effective and realized spreads with the quoted spread the cost differences need to be doubled, since they are both calculated using the mid price.

Using benchmarks

Price benchmarks are extensively used to monitor the performance of trades. They have also become a key factor in measuring transaction costs. Performance is often measured in basis points (bps), which are hundredths of a percent.

A wide variety of benchmarks may be used, ranging from opening and closing prices to averages such as the Volume Weighted Average Price (VWAP). One way of choosing between them is based on when they may be determined. Post-trade benchmarks will not be available until after the close of trading. Likewise, intraday benchmarks that span the whole trading day will not have a definitive value until the close. Nevertheless, interim values may be calculated throughout the day. Pre-trade benchmarks are available before the main trading session starts. Table 2-4 summarises the different benchmarks based on this categorisation:

Type	*Name*
Post-Trade	Close
	Future Close
Intraday	Open-High-Low-Close (OHLC)
	Time Weighted Average Price (TWAP)
	Volume Weighted Average Price (VWAP)
Pre-Trade	Previous Close
	Opening Price
	Decision Price
	Arrival Price

Table 2-4 Classifying benchmark types

Post-trade benchmarks are generally closing prices. Most commonly, the current day's closing price (or close) is taken, although other future prices may also be used. Closing prices have long been a popular benchmark, in particular because they are often used as a milestone for marking to market and for profit and loss (P&L) calculations.

Intraday benchmarks use an average price to more accurately reflect market conditions. This is because markets tend to be more active at the close, so the closing price will not necessarily reflect the actual conditions throughout the day. One of the first popular intraday benchmarks was the Open High Low Close (OHLC) average. More accurate averages have also been adopted, as tick-by-tick price and volume market data has become more widely available. For instance, the Time Weighted Average Price (TWAP) applies an equal weighting to all the day's trade prices. Alternatively, the Volume Weighted Average Price (VWAP) weights each trade price by its corresponding size, so the average will most reflect the largest trades. This ability to accurately reflect intraday market conditions has made VWAP an extremely popular benchmark.

Pre-trade benchmarks are also useful since they are both easily determined and readily available. As the use of transaction cost analysis has become more widespread implementation shortfall is increasingly used as a measure of performance. Effectively, this represents the difference between the average price achieved in execution, and the market price when the investor's decision was first made (the decision price). Pre-trade benchmarks correspond well to the decision price, hence their popularity.

Analysing the components of transaction costs

Transaction costs incorporate much more than just broker commissions and the bid offer spread. The market trend to un-bundle research fees has helped make it much easier to quantify the actual transaction costs.

The different cost components are commonly termed as either explicit or implicit. Likewise, they represent fixed overheads or a variable amount that will differ based on the asset, the order, market conditions and the trading strategy.

The explicit costs are clearly identifiable and easily measured. They are commissions, fees and taxes. Often, these will be quoted in advance of trading as percentages of the traded value or as basis points. They may be reduced to a certain extent, based on negotiation between the investor and the brokers. The rates offered will usually depend on the client's trading volumes and the level of service they require.

The implicit costs are generally associated with the actual trading process, and are harder to quantify, since they are less directly observable. They tend to be more variable, but often have a greater impact on the overall performance. Indeed, they are often represented as the hidden part of an iceberg (9/10^{ths} below the surface). Wayne Wagner and Mark Edwards (1993) proposed separating the implicit trading costs into the following components:

- Timing cost (due to price trends and timing risk)
- Delay cost
- Impact
- Opportunity cost

All of these are price related and correspond to decisions that the investor and trader must make, based on knowledge of the order and current market conditions. Figure 2-11 provides a view of these costs based on the relative visibility of each component. Note that the size of each cost component will vary based on the asset, order size and trading style so Figure 2-11 is not drawn to any particular scale.

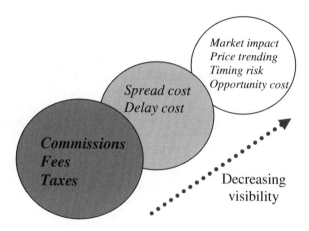

Figure 2-11 Transaction cost components

Starting from the most visible components, we have:

Commissions: This is most obvious cost component, representing the broker's compensation for providing the trading service. In particular, this should cover both their capital and labour costs.

Fees: Charges may be levied by floor brokers and exchanges as well as any costs associated with clearing and settlement. Note that fees are often rolled into the overall commission charge.

Taxes: Generally, taxes are an investment cost, applied to any realized profits from capital gains. However, some markets also apply additional duties for trading. For example, the U.K. stock market applies a 0.5% stamp duty on share purchases.

Spread cost: The bid offer spread compensates traders for providing liquidity. The spread usually reflects the liquidity of an asset. There are noticeable differences in average spreads across the capital markets. For instance, decimalisation in the U.S. equity market has resulted in considerably lower average spreads than in either Europe or Asia. Spread may be classed as a visible cost, although it is not always as easily measurable as fees or commissions. For single executions, it is obviously straightforward to measure, but for trades that are split up and worked over the day we must track the spread for each child order.

Delay cost: This reflects any price change from when the initial decision to invest is made and when an order is actually sent for execution. This may be because the decision was made before the market open; alternatively, time may be spent identifying the best way to trade the order. Delay cost can be a substantial proportion of overall costs, particularly for assets which are volatile or whose price is trending unfavourably. Therefore, to monitor this cost it is important for investors to record the market mid-price when the initial decision is made and when an order is dispatched.

Market impact: This represents how much effect the order has on the asset's price. Larger orders result in a larger impact compared to smaller ones; however, the effect decreases significantly with asset liquidity. Market impact consists of both a temporary effect and a permanent one. The temporary market impact reflects the overall cost incurred by demanding immediacy (when combined with the spread cost). Whereas the permanent impact signifies the long-term information cost of the trade, based on how it affects the asset's overall order buy/sell imbalance.

Price trend: Asset prices may sometimes exhibit broadly consistent trends. An upward trend implies that costs will increase when buying an asset, whilst savings will be accrued if selling, whereas the opposite is true for a downward price trend.

Timing risk: This cost reflects uncertainty, in particular for volatility in both the asset's price and its liquidity. The more volatile an asset then the more likely its price will move away and so increase the transaction costs. Similarly, if liquidity suddenly falls then market impact costs will rise. Timing risk may be considerable, especially for volatile assets and for orders that have a long trading horizon.

Opportunity cost: Orders are not always fully completed, maybe due to passive trading or unfavourable market conditions. This cost represents the missed opportunity, since the next day prices may move even further away.

Clearly, there is a lot more to transaction costs than just the explicit costs. In Chapter 6, we will cover this topic in much more detail using worked examples to provide in-depth post-trade analysis of sample orders. We will also cover the increasingly important field of pre-trade transaction cost analysis, which is used to compare potential trading strategies.

2.6 Summary

- Market microstructure concentrates on the actual trading process, analysing how specific designs or mechanisms affect both observed prices and traded volumes as well as helping to explain the associated costs.

- Liquidity represents the cost for converting an asset into cash or vice versa.

- Markets may be classified in terms of two main mechanisms:
  - Purely quote-driven markets, where traders must transact with a dealer (or market maker), who quotes prices at which they will buy and sell a given quantity.
  - Purely order-driven markets, where traders participate equally, by placing orders. These are then matched on the order book using a consistent set of rules.
  - Increasingly markets are actually hybrids of these two approaches.

- Trading may be broken down into three main stages:
  - Price formation
  - Price discovery / trade execution
  - Reporting, clearing & settlement

- There are three key methods for trade execution:
  - Bilateral trading, which is a one-to-one negotiation often with a market maker.
  - Continuous auctions, where matching rules are applied each time an order is added, updated or cancelled to determine whether there is a resultant execution.
  - Call auctions, where orders are allowed to accumulate for a set time before the matching rules are applied, and so helping to reduce price volatility.

- Transaction costs are unavoidable, they are incurred each time an asset is bought or sold. Cost measurement has focussed predominantly on spreads and benchmark prices. Costs may be broken down into two main classes:
  - Explicit costs, such as commissions, fees and taxes, are clearly identifiable and easily measured.
  - Implicit costs, such as market impact and timing risk, are generally associated with the actual trading process and are harder to identify and measure.

Chapter 3
World markets

Investors, traders and trading systems are increasingly covering multiple markets and asset classes. Therefore, it is important to have a basic grounding in all the major world markets.

3.1 Introduction

The world's financial markets are vast, in terms of both their sheer size and the diversity of products they incorporate. Broadly speaking, we can break them down into several main categories, namely the:

- Capital markets
- Foreign exchange markets
- Money markets
- Derivative markets

The capital markets provide medium and long-term financing via stocks and fixed income assets, whilst the foreign exchange market enables the transfer of money across currencies. Short-term financing is provided in the money markets, which are closely linked to both fixed income and foreign exchange. The derivatives markets provide a means of trading financial contracts, which are in turn based on underlying assets. The underliers may include stocks, bonds, currencies, commodities or even other derivatives. In fact, so much commodity trading is handled via derivatives the commodity market has effectively been subsumed into the derivatives market.

Each market has its own strong identity. Even though many of the same players (brokers and investors) are involved in them, they are still often treated separately. In part, this is due to their different market structures. Conventionally, trading for equities and listed derivatives has centred on exchanges, whilst for many of the other asset classes over the counter (OTC) trading has predominated.

In the following sections, we will briefly cover the main asset class types and how they are traded. We shall then consider some of the major trends that are affecting the world's major markets. Finally, to try to put things in context we will compare the main world markets in terms of their overall sizes, trading volumes and the uptake of electronic and algorithmic trading.

Note that Appendices A-F provide more detailed reviews of each of the major markets. For even more in-depth analysis the reports compiled by consultancies such as the Aite Group, Celent, Greenwich Associates and the TABB Group are invaluable.

3.2 Asset classes

Financial assets generally provide their issuers with a means of financing themselves, and investors with an opportunity to earn income. For example, stocks represent a share in the firm that issued them, whereas fixed income assets correspond to loans. Foreign exchange is a transfer of cash deposits in different currencies. Derivatives offer a way of trading on the future price of assets, providing both a means of insurance and an opportunity for speculation.

Equity

Stocks allow companies to finance themselves by actually making their ownership public; each share represents a portion of the firm's inherent value, or equity. This value represents what the corporation's remaining assets are worth once all the liabilities have been deducted. A finite number of shares are issued by public corporations, although they may also choose to issue new ones or buy back some of the outstanding shares. Firms may also make periodic dividend payments to shareholders.

Shares are forward looking investments, since they represent a portion of the firm's total equity. Investors expect the value of their shares to increase or dividends to be paid in order to compensate them for the risk of bankruptcy.

Determining the fair value for equities is non-trivial. Present value theory states that the value of an asset corresponds to a discounted sum of its future payments. This may be based on the present value of their future dividend payments. In turn, this depends on future earnings, which can be difficult to predict. Firms may also choose to reinvest some of their income rather than increasing dividend payouts. Consequently, there are countless different valuation methods that may be applied to companies, each trying to tackle the range of possibilities.

A detailed review of equities and the associated markets may be found in Appendix A.

Fixed income

Fixed income assets, such as bonds, allow both governments and corporations to publicly issue debt for periods of up to 30 years, or even perpetually. The issuer is obliged to repay the holder a specific amount (the principal) at a set date in the future (the maturity date). Many names are given to these assets, but for the purposes of this chapter, we will just use the term bond. The issuer of a bond will usually pay interest (the coupon) to the holder at a given frequency for the lifetime of the loan, e.g. every 6 months. Alternatively, zero coupon bonds make no such payments; instead, their price is discounted by an equivalent amount.

These debts can be issued by governments, other agencies and by companies. They may also be issued based on pools of loans, which is the essence of asset-backed securities. Similarly, mortgage-backed securities are the equivalent for real estate debt. The effective interest rate, which the issuer must pay, depends on the maturity date of the contract as well as their credit rating and the current market rates. Bonds will sometimes have additional collateralization or protection to reduce their credit risk. They may also be differentiated in terms of their seniority when it comes to bankruptcy hearings. An indenture for each contract specifies any additional conditions. All of these features mean that bonds are much more bespoke assets than equities. In fact, there are more than three million different bonds in the U.S alone, which is two hundred times more than the number of equities available globally. This diversity can pose serious liquidity problems, since for many assets it will be difficult to find sufficient depth to support a continuous market.

In general, bonds are more straightforward to price than equities. Essentially, the fair price of a bond is the present value of all its future interest and principal payments. The present value incorporates a discount for the market rate of return, which in turn depends on the bond's characteristics. The risk of default has a considerable impact on the price of bonds, macroeconomic factors, such as inflation expectations, can also have a significant effect.

A more detailed review of bonds and the associated markets may be found in Appendix B.

Foreign exchange

Foreign exchange (FX) represents the trading of currencies, essentially by transferring the ownership of deposits. Generally, what we first think of as foreign exchange is spot trading. FX spot transactions lock-in the current exchange rate for cash settlement, usually within two days. So a U.S. dollar / Japanese yen trade consists of selling U.S. dollars to another counterparty in exchange for a specific amount of yen.

There are also FX derivative contracts, namely forwards, options and swaps. FX forwards (or outrights) may be used to arrange transfers for months or even years in the future. They are based on binding contracts with a forward rate, which will then be used for an exchange at a specified date in the future. This rate reflects the expected future exchange rate, and so incorporates the volatility of the two currencies. Hence, they offer a means of locking-in an exchange rate. FX options are similar, although they give the purchaser the right to buy or sell, rather than an obligation. An FX swap is slightly more complex since it consists of two legs: a standard spot FX transaction linked with a simultaneous FX forward trade. Initially, the two currencies are exchanged, and when the outright matures, they are swapped back again, at the pre-agreed rate. They are often used for much longer-term exchanges than FX forwards (years rather than months).

Pricing foreign exchange rates can be quite difficult, since they are affected by a wide range of economic factors, such as changes in economic growth, inflation, interest rates or budget/trade balances. Traditional exchange rate determination models based solely on macroeconomic factors have failed to explain and forecast fluctuations in exchange rates. Alternative models have adopted market microstructure based approaches to analyse order flow with some success.

A more detailed review of FX and the associated markets may be found in Appendix C.

Money markets

The money markets are key to the provision of short-term financing for banks, institutions and corporations. This may range from overnight to around a month, although it can be for as much as a year. Typical money market assets are short-term debt, deposits, repos and stock lending. Therefore, the money markets are also closely linked to both fixed income and foreign exchange.

Short-term debt encompasses a range of types, from traditional fixed income contracts to tradable loans/deposits and commercial paper. Government bonds, such as U.S. Treasury bills, provide a comparatively risk-free investment, particularly over the short term. Inter-bank lending is also an important source of short-term liquidity for banks, particularly overnight. In the U.S., this corresponds to the "Fed funds" depository accounts held with the Federal Reserve, whilst in Europe it is Eurodollar deposits. There are also secondary markets for negotiable (or tradable) cash deposits and banker's acceptances (or money drafts). Commercial paper is traded as well; this represents unsecured promissory notes issued by corporations as an alternative (and cheaper) means of funding. Although the 2007-09 financial crisis and resultant market turmoil has had a considerable impact on the short-term debt markets.

A repo is the common name for a sale and repurchase agreement. Essentially, this is a secured loan. The seller provides securities in return for cash, but they also commit to repurchase them back on a specified date at a set price. At the agreed maturity date, the seller repays the cash loan together with an interest payment, whilst the securities are returned to them. The interest paid is based on a pre negotiated repo rate, which will often be offset from a benchmark, such as the Fed funds rate. There are two main types of repo: Specific repos are for a certain security. General collateral repos allow the security to be fungible so any acceptable security that meets the set requirements may be used. This flexibility is reflected in a lower lending rate.

Securities (or stock) lending is like a repo without the loan; the securities are simply lent for a fee. As with repos, the type of lending may be classified into general and specific. General lending offers a security that is equivalent to a repo with general collateral, so it just needs to match a set of criteria. Again, the fees for lending depend on the scarcity of the security, so general lending costs significantly less.

A more detailed review of the money markets may be found in Appendix D.

Derivatives

As their name suggests, derivative contracts are derived from other assets, referred to as the underlying assets. Purely financial derivatives were first created in the 1970s. These allowed the underlying assets to expand beyond commodities to also include stocks and stock indices, bonds, currencies or even other derivatives.

The main types of derivative contract are forwards and futures, options, swaps and credit derivatives. They may be classified as either "listed" (or exchange-traded) or over the counter (OTC). Listed derivatives are standardised contracts that may be traded much like stocks; typically, these are futures and options contracts. OTC contracts are bespoke, so they may represent more complex or exotic derivatives contracts.

Futures and options

A forward contract is an agreement to buy (or sell) a fixed quantity of a given asset at a certain price at a specific date in the future, e.g. a contract to buy 5,000 bushels of grain in July for $3. When the maturity date is reached, the contract expires and the transaction must then be settled. A futures contract is just a forward with standardised terms (e.g. amounts, prices, dates) which is traded on an exchange.

Option contracts are similar to forwards and futures in that they allow a price to be struck to trade a set quantity of a given asset at a specific future date. The settlement price is called the strike price of the option. The premium represents the actual price paid for the option contract. An option to buy is called a call, whilst a contract to sell is a put. Options may also be classified as European or American style. This refers to when they may actually be exercised. American style options may be exercised at any time prior to the expiry date, whereas European style options may only be exercised at maturity.

The main difference between futures (or forwards) and options is that the owner of an option is not obliged to trade. So if the market price is more favourable they may choose not to exercise their option contract (hence its name). Whereas the creator (writer) of the option contract is obliged to trade, should the purchaser wish to do so. Therefore, whilst there may be plenty of investors who want to buy calls or puts much fewer may be prepared to sell them. Hence, specialised broker/dealers often play a vital role as liquidity providers and market makers.

Pricing these derivatives can be complex. They are obviously based on the price of their underlying asset/s. For instance, a futures contract reflects the expected future value of its underlier discounted to give a present value. Other factors may also need to be considered, such as the interest rate and any additional costs related to storage or transfer (typically for commodity-based contracts), or any potential incomes (e.g. from dividends).

Options are more complex to price than futures, although many standard pricing models exist, such as the ubiquitous Black Scholes equation created by Fisher Black and Merton Scholes (1973). These can compute the fair value of an option based on factors such as the contract's strike price, the underlying asset's market price and its volatility, the time left to expiry and the risk-free interest rate.

Swaps

A swap is essentially an agreement between two counterparties to exchange cash streams. These may be linked to fixed/floating interest rates, currencies, or even dividend payments. Thus, they offer a flexible means of controlling cash flows, which goes some of the way to explaining their popularity. The commonest type of swap is a straightforward Interest Rate Swap (IRS). A vanilla interest rate swap consists of one leg based on a floating rate of interest whilst the other has a fixed rate. Note that the principal (or notional) amount is not actually exchanged; only the associated interest payments are swapped. A wide range of other swaps may also be traded. For example, basis swaps have both legs based on floating rates. Currency swaps allow firms to borrow in the currency where they can obtain the best interest rate then convert this to the currency they actually need. Total return swaps exchange interest payments for the total return of an asset or basket of assets whilst asset swaps represent the combination of an interest rate swap with a fixed rate bond. There are also many models for pricing swaps, but they are beyond the scope of this book.

Credit derivatives

Credit derivatives act as financial guarantees, which may be used to provide protection against a variety of credit events, but most typically default or bankruptcy. A credit default swap (CDS) is a contract that transfers the credit risk for a notional amount of debt issued by an entity. The purchaser gains protection from this credit risk, whilst the seller is paid regular premiums for the lifetime of the contract. If a credit event occurs then the seller must compensate the purchaser and the contract expires. The typical maturity for a CDS contract is five years. CDS indices expand the scope by covering multiple entities, often encompassing more than a hundred separate companies. They have proven to be incredibly popular, since they allow investors to make much broader macro trades for credit risk. Leading exchanges have also started to offer futures and options based on underlying CDS indices. Again, there are many models for pricing credit derivatives, but they are beyond the scope of this book.

A more detailed review of derivatives and their markets may be found in Appendix E.

Other asset classes

A few types of financial asset do not quite fit in the main categories. Most notably depositary receipts and exchange traded funds. Both asset classes have seen substantial growth over the last few years.

Depositary receipts (DRs) represent shares in a foreign company. They provide an alternative to cross-border trading, as well as being an important means of accessing the major financial markets for foreign companies. DRs essentially act as proxies for foreign shares that may be traded locally, either at exchanges, other execution venues or OTC. They are issued by a domestic bank or brokerage against their own inventory of the foreign stock. Any dividends are generally paid in the local currency, and for a fee the depositary bank will convert the receipts back into the underlying stock. So, in many respects, these behave much like domestic stocks. Although to gain voting rights, the DR must be part of a sponsored program, since the depositary bank must organise the proxy votes. The two most common types are American Depositary Receipts (ADRs) and global depositary receipts (GDRs). ADRs are traded OTC or on the major U.S. exchanges, whilst GDRs allow trading in more than one country. Pricing these assets is based on the current market price of this underlier, adjusted by the current market exchange rates and any associated fees.

Exchange traded funds (ETFs) are a tradable share in an investment fund. Since they represent baskets of assets, they are an extremely efficient means of gaining exposure to whole sectors or markets, much like index futures. ETFs are generally classified as either being index or optimised. Index funds passively track, or replicate, a specific benchmark whilst optimised funds try to beat the benchmark and so adopt similar techniques to active investors. Note that ETFs are not just restricted to equities; they may also be created based on portfolios of bonds or even commodities. In terms of valuation, the net asset value (NAV) of a fund is essentially the total value of all the assets in the fund divided by the number of shares issued. Because of their inherent transparency, the NAV is easily calculated, although for funds holding foreign assets differences in time zones and FX rates can lead to discrepancies between the market price and the NAV.

A more detailed review of the markets for these asset types may be found in Appendix F.

3.3   Market structure

In Chapter 2, we covered the basic trading mechanisms, specifically quote-driven and order-driven execution. Initially, most markets begin with quote-driven trading. For instance, imagine an exotic new class of asset: To start off the market is so specialised that there may only be a single dealer prepared to "make a market" for this. Any trading is invariably a one-to-one process between the dealer and each client (investor), as shown in Figure 3-1(a).

Gradually the number of investors (or potential clients) will increase and so more dealers will get involved. This enables clients to check prices with several dealers before deciding to trade, as shown in Figure 3-1(b). Trading is still bilateral and quote-driven, but at least there is more choice. This type of structure is the basis for much of the "over the counter" (OTC) trading which takes place for a wide range of assets, from stocks to bonds and derivatives.

Eventually the marketplace may become so large that there is enough trading (and participants) to warrant dedicated execution venues, as shown in Figure 3-1(c). Historically, inter-dealer networks started out as organised exchanges, whilst dealer-to-client communications were handled by brokers. Over time, these have increasingly shifted to phone-based and/or screen-based electronic trading platforms.

Trading for many of the world's assets is now based on market structures similar to Figure 3-1(c). For highly standardised assets, such as equities, trading has continued to develop around exchanges, whilst for less standardised ones, such as bonds or complex derivatives, much of the trading is carried out OTC or via specialised inter-dealer brokers (IDBs).

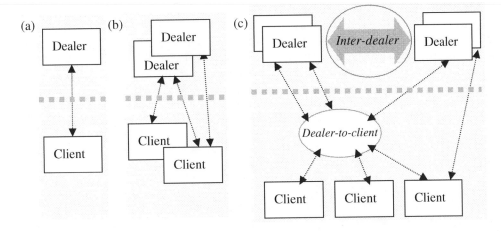

Figure 3-1 Three phases of marketplace development

Table 3-1 tries to provide a broad summary of these market structures for the major asset classes, although inevitably there are some isolated exceptions. [1]

Asset class	Inter-dealer	Dealer-to-client	Alternative
Equities	Exchange	Single/Multi broker, DMA	ECN/MTF, ATS
Derivative (Listed)			
Other (ADR, ETF)			
Fixed income	OTC/IDB	Single/Multi broker	ECN, ATS
Foreign exchange			
Money markets			
Derivative (OTC)	OTC	OTC	

Table 3-1 Market structure across asset classes

Over the last few years, the strict segmentation between the dealer and client markets, visible in Figure 3-1, has started to blur. Alternative trading venues (accessed by both dealers and clients) have become increasingly important. They are the Electronic Communication Networks (ECNs) or Multilateral Trading Facilities (MTFs) and "dark pool" Alternative Trading Systems (ATSs) which have started to spread across the world's markets. These further complicate the market structure, to the point where clients may even use certain venues to bypass dealers altogether. We shall consider the impact of these alternatives in some more detail after a brief review of the inter-dealer and dealer-to-client markets.

Inter-dealer markets

A strong inter-dealer market is vital for liquidity. Otherwise, dealers may be less willing to trade beyond their current inventory. Having a market where they can easily trade with other dealers enables them to control their positions and so meet their clients' requirements.

---

[1] For instance, some exchanges provide trading platforms for bonds and repos.

Many of the differences between the world's inter-dealer markets are historical. Exchange-based trading was originally based on open outcry auctions, and so the mechanism was order-based. In comparison, OTC trading is often bilateral and so quote-driven. However, the advent of electronic trading has resulted in many of the exchanges and inter-dealer brokers moving to platforms based on electronic order books. In fact, nowadays there are a lot more similarities between inter-dealer markets.

Exchanges

Exchanges are probably the best-known venue for trading. The world's oldest exchanges mainly date back to the 17th or 18th centuries, although organised exchanges may be traced back as far as the 13th century.

Trading on exchanges is carried out by its members, who are primarily specialised dealing houses or broker/dealer firms. Historically, regulation and the costs of maintaining a presence on trading floors have ensured that exchanges remained the domain of dealers and brokers. Increasingly, though, brokers are offering their clients DMA access to exchanges. Likewise, memberships are not limited to dealers; so large investors, who can justify the cost, can gain access by buying a membership. That is why the market segmentation is not quite as black and white as suggested by Figure 3-1(c).

As we saw in Table 3-1, exchange-based trading is generally adopted for more standardised assets. The largest markets are for equities and listed futures and options, but exchanges are also used to trade fixed income, money market and other types of asset. Table 3-2 gives some examples for the various asset classes and regions.

Asset class	Venues
Equities	U.S.: New York Stock Exchange (NYSE), NASDAQ Europe: London Stock Exchange (LSE), Euronext Asia: Tokyo Stock Exchange (TSE)
Futures/options	U.S.: Chicago Mercantile Exchange (CME), Chicago Board of Trade (CBOT), Chicago Board Options Exchange (CBOE) Europe: Eurex, London International Futures Exchange (Liffe)
Money markets	Europe (Debt/repos): Eurex Bonds
Fixed income	Europe: LSE, BME Spanish exchanges, Eurex Bonds Asia: Korea exchange
Other	DRs, ETFs: NYSE, LSE

Table 3-2 Example exchanges by asset class

Traditionally, the world's exchanges have been centred on floor-based open-outcry auctions. Some venues still feature this; however, over the last few years electronic order books have now become the norm for most of the major trading centres. In terms of the actual trading mechanism, exchanges' electronic trading platforms are generally based on central limit order books, often allowing anonymous trading. For liquid assets, this means continuous auctions, as we saw in Chapter 2. Call auctions are used for less liquid assets, and are often adopted for the opening and closing periods to reduce volatility. Conventionally, stock markets have tended to adopt a price/time based priority for their trade matching, whilst listed derivatives exchanges have often used a price/pro-rata based approach. That said, such distinctions are becoming increasingly blurred. For instance, in the U.S. the NYSE and NASDAQ stock markets have both launched their own dedicated equity options exchanges based on a price/time priority.

Stock exchanges have generally focussed on domestic trading, in part due to the higher level of regulation associated with equities. Still, over the last few years demutualization has seen many of the world's major exchanges become standalone corporations. In order to survive in the increasingly competitive markets, there has been wave after wave of global mergers and consolidations. Most notably, the mergers between the New York Stock Exchange (NYSE) and Euronext, and NASDAQ and the OMX, have created two massive entities competing for both U.S. and European volume. Global competition is likely to continue to increase over the coming years. Local competition has also been triggered by regulation. In the U.S., the Securities and Exchange Commission (SEC) introduced NASDAQ order handling rules in 1997, which helped spur new execution venues (the ECNs). 2007 saw Regulation NMS, which was introduced to improve competition; offering order protection at the National Best Bid and Offer (NBBO) for orders on the major U.S. stock exchanges and ECNs. Although competition has increased, the available liquidity has become more fragmented. Likewise, in Europe, the Markets in Financial Instruments Directive (MiFID) regulations introduced in 2007 sought to encourage competition (and to regulate) off-exchange trading in the form of Multilateral Trading Facilities (MTFs), which are broadly similar to ECNs. Although some time behind the U.S., the European markets are also starting to become fragmented, as competition takes liquidity away from the major exchanges. A more detailed review is provided in Appendix A.

In comparison, the exchanges for listed derivatives have faced global competition for some time. U.S. and European exchanges have often launched rival contracts to try to grab liquidity from each other. Computerisation has also helped turn this into virtually a 24-hour marketplace. The U.S. equity option marketplace has become one of the most competitive market places in the world, where options may be traded on any one of seven exchanges. Certainly, the U.S. equity options marketplace has seen some of the highest levels of growth of any of the world's listed derivatives markets. This highlights the benefits of a common clearing mechanism and assets that are readily transferable.

Exchange-based trading is also important for other assets, particularly ADRs and ETFs. They may not have their own dedicated exchanges, but they contribute considerable flow to the world's stock exchanges. In fact, in the U.S. leading ETFs such as the SPDR are often the most traded assets on the major exchanges. Fixed income bonds are also traded on some stock and listed derivative exchanges.

Exchanges are facing increased competition; however, the safety offered by centralised clearing and settlement means that other asset classes will no doubt continue to consider exchange or exchange-like market structures in the future.

OTC/Inter-dealer broker networks

For assets that are generally traded over the counter (OTC), the inter-dealer networks have often developed in a less centralised fashion than exchange-based markets. Instead of being based around physical locations, they have evolved from phone-based trading between dealers and specialised inter-dealer brokers (IDBs). Over time, phone (or voice) based trading has been augmented by dedicated electronic trading platforms, particularly for the more liquid assets. Table 3-3 gives some examples for the various asset classes and regions.

A range of mechanisms is used for inter-dealer trading. Many platforms start out by aggregating dealers' quotes. Since a firm quote is effectively a limit order, some have evolved to offer full order book based-functionality. Several IDBs have even started to

Asset class	Platforms
Fixed income	U.S. (Treasuries): ICAP BrokerTec, BGC eSpeed Europe: MTS
Foreign exchange	EBS, Reuters
Money markets	U.S. (Debt/repos): ICAP BrokerTec, BGC eSpeed U.S. (Fed funds): ICAP i-Feds Europe (Debt/repos): MTS, Eurex Bonds, ICAP Europe (Deposits) e-MID
Swaps	ICAP i-Swap, CME Swapstream, EuroMTS
Credit default swaps	Creditex RealTime, GFI CreditMatch, ICAP BrokerTec

Table 3-3 Example inter-dealer trading platforms by asset class

incorporate this with their voice-based OTC liquidity to create hybrid trading systems.

In fixed income, government bonds generally have the highest liquidity since they tend to be more standardised and often have the highest demand. The best example of this is the U.S. Treasury market. Inter-dealer brokers such as ICAP and BGC offer both phone-based and electronic trading platforms for Treasuries, together with a wide range of other fixed income assets. Indeed, as Larry Tabb (2004) points out, IDBs have effectively taken the place of exchanges for many U.S. bonds. In Europe, a considerable proportion of government bonds are traded over the MTS (Mercato Telematico dei Titoli di Stato) and Euro MTS platforms, which aggregate quotes from all the major dealers. Competition from dedicated IDBs has been somewhat less in Europe. In part, this is because primary dealerships have often been awarded based on trading on local platforms. So there has been less incentive for dealers to use alternatives. That said, treasury agencies have started to formally recognise alternatives, such as BGC's European Government platform, so competition in this space may well increase over the next few years.

Foreign exchange also has a well-established electronic inter-dealer marketplace. Reuters first introduced a monitor-based dealing service back in 1981. Over time, this has evolved into a hybrid order book based trading platform. It was joined by EBS in 1993, which was launched by a consortium of banks, and is now part of ICAP. Between them, these two platforms cater for much of the inter-dealer trading in the FX marketplace.

Unsurprisingly, the major players in fixed income and FX also provide platforms for money market trading. ICAP's BrokerTec and BGC's eSpeed platforms cater for short-term debt and repos in the U.S., whilst MTS and ICAP are important for European debt and repos. For the overnight Fed funds market, ICAP also offers the i-Feds platform. In Europe e-MID offers a platform for trading deposits.

OTC derivatives are catered for as well. For example, ICAP brokerage's i-Swap provides a platform for electronic swap trading, as does the CME's Swapstream. EuroMTS has also launched a dedicated swap market for trading overnight interest rate swaps (EONIAs). Credit default swaps are starting to see dedicated trading platforms as well. For example, Creditex's RealTime, GFI's CreditMatch and ICAP's BrokerTec all cater for CDSs.

Dealer-to-client markets

Traditionally, bridging the gap between dealers and clients has been the domain of brokers. Nowadays dealer-to-client (D2C) markets are represented by a mix of phone-based trading, single and multi-broker/dealer electronic trading platforms, provided by a range of brokers and third-party vendors. Table 3-4 shows some examples.

Asset class	Platforms
Equities, Listed futures/options, DRs/ETFs	Broker or vendor OMSs
Fixed income	Tradeweb, Bloomberg BondTrader, Reuters RTFI, MarketAxess
Foreign exchange	Bank platforms, FXAll, State Street FX Connect, Currenex
Money market	Tradeweb, Bloomberg BondTrader, State Street FX Connect
Swaps	Tradeweb, Bloomberg SwapTrader, CME sPro
Credit default swaps	Tradeweb, MarketAxess

Table 3-4 Example dealer-to-client trading platforms by asset class

The mechanism for these trading platforms depends on the underlying inter-dealer market. With exchange-based markets, they are generally order-based. Whilst on OTC markets, the D2C platforms are quote-based, and so they tend to adopt the request for quote (RFQ) or request for stream (RFS) mechanisms we saw in Chapter 2.

For equities, listed futures and options, depositary receipts and ETFs, broker and/or vendor Order Management Systems (OMSs) are the mainstay for providing D2C trading. These offer a suite of appropriate tools for pre- and post-trade handling. The broker may provide DMA as well. They may also cater for OTC trading of these assets.

Fixed income platforms, such as Tradeweb, Bloomberg's BondTrader and Reuter's RTFI trading system, offer electronic trading via RFQ. Further competition should have arrived in the form of LiquidityHub, which was to provide clients with a stream-based trading mechanism for government bonds, aggregating the liquidity from a consortium of over a dozen banks. Unfortunately, the 2007-09 financial crisis put an end to this venture.

In foreign exchange, the large multi-national banks provide their own client trading platforms. There are also important multi-broker platforms, such as FXAll and State Street's FX Connect and Currenex. Generally, these systems all either provide access via RFQ or RFS. Currenex actually uses a hybrid mechanism that also supports limit orders, although there is no visible order book.

Again, the major fixed income platforms, such as Tradeweb and Bloomberg, also support money markets trading. Similarly, foreign exchange platforms, such as FXAll and Currenex, have expanded to incorporate money market trading.

For OTC derivatives, there is a mix of single and multi-dealer platforms. Swap trading is supported by Tradeweb, Bloomberg's SwapTrader and Reuters Matching for Interest Rates. The Chicago Mercantile Exchange (CME) is also introducing sPro, a dealer-to-client version of Swapstream. Credit default swaps are supported by MarketAxess and Tradeweb.

Alternative markets

Alternative trading venues have become more and more important over the last few years. Many of these venues serve both the buy and sell-side, so they effectively straddle the strict segmentation we saw back in Figure 3-1. Hence, market structures are becoming increasingly complex, as we can see in Figure 3-2.

Broker/dealers have started to provide DMA access to exchanges and other execution venues (shown as the grey dashed line). Clients can also get direct access to many of the ECNs and ATSs; so they are no longer restricted to dealer-to-client platforms.

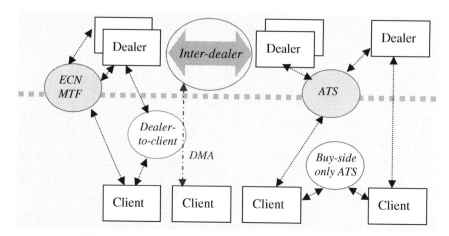

Figure 3-2 Marketplace interconnections for alternative venues

In fact, some ATSs are buy-side only, completely bypassing the broker/dealers. Effectively, these are client-to-client trading networks. In section 3.4 we will revisit this increased accessibility, but first let's briefly review the different types of alternative execution venue.

ECNs/MTFs

Electronic Communication Networks (ECNs) are probably the best-known off-exchange trading venues. They started in the U.S. equity marketplace; however, they have since spread to many of the world's markets. Table 3-5 gives some examples.

Asset class	Venues
Equities	U.S.: Bloomberg Tradebook Europe: Chi-X, Turquoise
Foreign exchange	Hotspot FXi, LavaFX, Bloomberg Tradebook FX, FXAll Accelor
Money market	Securities lending: SecFinex

Table 3-5 Example ECNs/MTFs by asset class

In terms of their mechanism, ECNs are generally based on central limit order books, with continuous auctions that usually allow anonymous trading. So they are very similar to exchanges.

ECNs came about through the quote ruling introduced in 1997 by the Securities and Exchange Commission (SEC). Previously, dealers had been able to use private inter-dealer systems to trade at better prices than on NASDAQ; the new ruling meant that these prices should also be available to the public. In effect, this opened a window for external execution venues, and suddenly a series of new ECNs were created. By the millennium, there were over a dozen ECNs, all vying for market share in U.S. equities. Since then, the competition has increased, but there has been a lot of consolidation. Indeed, of the original four ECNs founded, only Bloomberg Tradebook remains as such. Two of the main ECNs, BATS and Direct Edge, have either become exchanges in their own right or are in the process of doing so.

Europe is starting to see the same level of intense competition as experienced in the U.S. In the past, pan European execution venues had mixed success; though, some have flourished, such as Chi-X. The introduction of the Markets in Financial Instruments Directive (MiFID), in 2007, aimed to encourage competition between trading venues, improve pre and post-trade transparency and enforce "best execution" requirements. Its immediate effect was the creation of a range of new venues. These are classified as Systematic Internalisers (SIs), for single-broker platforms, or as multi-broker Multilateral Trading Facilities (MTFs), such as Turquoise. Hence, the major exchanges now have to compete for liquidity, although this has led to the marketplace becoming more fragmented.

ECNs have also become established in the FX marketplace, the first was Hotspot FXi. Based around visible, but anonymous, central limit order books, these systems are targeting hedge funds, a rapidly growing portion of the marketplace. Hotspot was joined by Lava Trading's LavaFX in 2006. FXAll have also released their Accelor ECN, whilst Bloomberg have launched Tradebook FX.

Centralised order-driven markets are also starting to appear for other asset classes, such as securities lending and OTC DR trading.

"Dark pool" ATSs

As their moniker suggests, Alternative Trading Systems (ATSs) provide opaque order-driven trading platforms that help to aggregate pools of liquidity. They have proved popular because they allow buy and/or sell-side traders to place large orders without them being seen by other market participants, and so reducing market impact costs.

ATSs actually cover quite a diverse range of market types. Table 3-6 provides a summary of these. As we saw in Chapter 2, markets may be classified in terms of whether trade matching is scheduled or is continuous. ATSs may also be distinguished in terms of their crossing. They either adopt a standard auction or use negotiated, advertised or internal crossing mechanisms. Constant market evolution means hybrids of these crossing types are also developing.

Frequency	Crossing Mechanism
Scheduled	Auction
Continuous	Blind auction
	Negotiated
	Advertised
	Internal

Table 3-6 ATS classifications

The mechanics of price discovery vary for each type of ATS as well. Some do not incorporate their own mechanism; instead, orders are matched at the mid-point price taken from the main market, e.g. the U.S. NBBO. Others contain full order book functionality and so determine their own prices when matching.

Scheduled crosses are in effect equivalent to scheduled anonymous call auctions. For instance, for U.S. equities ITG's POSIT offers a dozen separate intraday crosses together with two after the close. Each cross is a call auction priced at the midpoint of the NBBO.

Continuous blind crosses, such as Instinet's CBX, offer trading on a completely opaque electronic order book. Effectively, it is like trading on an exchange where all the orders are hidden. Some of these venues also offer "pass through" orders that first try to match with the liquidity available within the ATS before being routed on to their intended destination, whether that is a primary/regional exchange, ECN or another ATS. These have proven to be an important additional source of liquidity.

Negotiated crossing platforms constantly search for potential matches notifying each participant when one is found. This then allows them to enter into an anonymous bilateral negotiation for both the size and price. Liquidnet is probably the best-known example, it employs a scorecard (like eBay's ratings) to reflect each users history of successful crossings.

Advertised crossing systems highlight when liquidity is present, although they do not give away sizes. For example, Pipeline maintains a block-board of stocks, which are highlighted in orange when liquidity is present. Block price ranges are available as a guideline and no sizes are displayed. Users may then place firm orders to execute with this liquidity.

Brokers' own crossing networks generally adopt a similar mechanism to the continuous blind crossing platforms. Originally, these were just internal crossing networks, allowing them to save the fees from executing on exchanges. However, they have rapidly become a considerable force in terms of "dark pool" liquidity.

Although ATSs started in the U.S. equities markets, most of the major operators are now also present in the European and Asian markets. ATSs are also starting to appear for other asset classes, Table 3-7 shows some examples.

Asset class	Venues
Equities	ITG POSIT (Scheduled), Instinet CBX (Blind), Liquidnet (Negotiated), Pipeline (Advertised), Credit Suisse CrossFinder (Internal)
Foreign exchange	Instinet FX Cross (Scheduled), Flextrade MilanFX (Advertised)
Options	U.S.: Archangel ATS (Blind), Ballista (Hybrid/negotiation)

Table 3-7 Example ATSs by asset class

For foreign exchange, Instinet's FX Cross, a joint venture with Citigroup, provides three anonymous crossing sessions a day in 17 currencies. Flextrade also offer MilanFX, a continuous block-trading venue for FX. Similarly, U.S. listed options are also getting their own ATSs: Pipeline Archangel provides a blind auction for listed options, similarly Ballista offer a hybrid option ATS combining auctions with electronic negotiations. LiquidityPort has also announced plans to offer an electronic block-trading platform for both futures and options contracts.

3.4 Global market trends

There are certainly differences amongst the world's major markets; however, there are also many similarities. A focus on costs, by both the buy- and sell-sides, and the onward march of technology mean that the markets for each asset class are exhibiting many of the same trends, albeit at different rates. Notably, many of the markets are seeing increases in:

- Electronic trading
- Transparency
- Accessibility

Electronic trading is already widespread; indeed, for many markets it is now the norm. Transparency is also improving, for both pre- and post-trade information. Accessibility has also become a key issue as buy-side traders seek to gain access to the same venues as their sell-side counterparts.

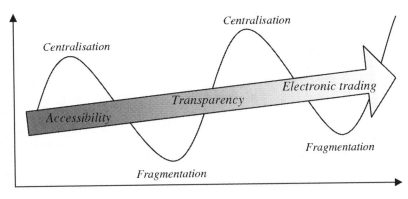

Figure 3-3 Common global market trends

Running alongside these trends is a seemingly endless cycle of centralisation and fragmentation, as shown in Figure 3-3. New venues keep appearing, attracting order flow and fragmenting the available liquidity. Then within a few years, consolidation means the market starts to centralise again.

Electronic trading

Electronic trading is now commonplace for most asset classes, in particular for more standardised assets. A large number of electronic platforms exist, providing inter-dealer and dealer-to-client trading for both exchange-based and OTC markets.

Technology has substantially lowered the barriers to market entry. New entrants such as the ECNs and ATSs have had a huge impact, particularly in the U.S. equities market. Capturing liquidity from established market centres can be extremely difficult and expensive. Still, electronic trading has proven to be a powerful tool in achieving this. For instance, in early in 1997 the DTB (now Eurex) had around a quarter of the market with its Euro-Bund futures contract. A new electronic trading platform helped it win back market leadership from Liffe, by the end of the year its market share had reached 90%.

Competition has forced dealers and exchanges to shift to electronic platforms in order to achieve cost reductions and to increase the capacity for trading volume. In the exchange-based markets, there has been a considerable migration from floor-based to electronic trading. Even the most successful trading floors, such as the NYSE and the CME, have now fully embraced electronic trading.

The advent of electronic trading has also led to irrevocable changes in the global markets. Most notably in terms of:

- Speed/Latency
- Order size
- Growth in volumes

Order placement and execution times are now measured in fractions of a second. In comparison, the old U.S. equity inter-market system (ITS) allowed dealers up to 30 seconds. We are currently in the midst of a race between venues to provide the fastest platforms. A few years ago, a latency, or delay, of 300 milliseconds (10^{-3}s) used to be perfectly reasonable. Nowadays cutting-edge venues are targeting latencies in microseconds (10^{-6}s). In the light of this, co-location services are becoming increasingly popular. These allow market participants to host their computerised trading systems in the same machine rooms as the execution venue, thus minimising any transmission-related delays.

Average order sizes have seen considerable shifts as well. In some markets, such as FX and U.S. listed options, order sizes are actually increasing, in order to cope with the huge increases in trading these markets are experiencing. However, the longer-term effect of electronic trading is probably best illustrated by the equity markets. Over the last ten years, there has been a steady decline in average order sizes on electronic trading platforms for equities. For example, in the late 1980s the average order size on NYSE was nearly 2,500 whereas now it hovers at around 300. A noticeable decline occurred with the introduction of decimalisation in 2001, as shown in Figure 3-4, based on data for the average trade sizes from the U.S. Government Accountability Office (GAO). This trend becomes self-perpetuating as traders progressively adopt order slicing and algorithmic trading strategies in order to minimise market impact. A similar decline is taking place in order sizes for the listed futures markets; in fact single contract orders are becoming commonplace.

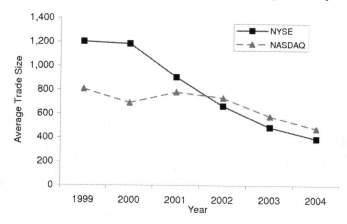

Source: GAO (2005) based on data from NYSE and NASDAQ

Figure 3-4 Average trade sizes for U.S. equities

Trading volumes have also rocketed over the last few years, in part due to the easy access and lower costs afforded by electronic trading. Much of this is due to the influx of trading from hedge funds. Although investment firms across the board are adopting a much wider range of assets, particularly derivatives.

The ratio of orders to executions has also changed, with electronic platforms having to cope with a much higher level of order placements, modifications and cancellations than ever before.

Pandora's Box has been opened. Markets will continue to evolve in order to adapt to the changes which electronic trading brings. Algorithmic trading is a key tool to help cope with these changes.

Transparency

Transparency plays an important part in improving execution quality. It is also a key factor in reflecting the accessibility of markets. Pre- and post-trade information is vital for effective trading. Venues need to provide timely data on the size and price of orders/quotes/trades, as well as the time of executions. Historically, quote-driven or OTC markets have tended to be much less transparent than order-driven ones.

Post-trade transparency is well established for exchange-based markets. But it is also improving for OTC markets. For instance, in the U.S., the Trade Reporting and Compliance Engine (TRACE) initiative has mandated reporting of trade prices for corporate debt since 2001. This may well expand to include primary market, government agency and debt from the Federal National Mortgage Association (Fannie Mae) and Federal Home Loan Mortgage Corporation (Freddie Mac). In Europe, MiFID has mandated reporting for OTC equity trades. This may also spread to encompass other European asset classes, such as bonds and OTC derivatives.

Pre-trade transparency poses more issues, since for OTC markets only the broker/dealers' best bid and offer are available. Multi-broker platforms/markets improve this slightly by making it easier to discover and to compare quotes from a range of market makers. In comparison, exchanges and other execution venues based on electronic order books are capable of much more transparency. They may allow the best five bids and offers or even the entire order book to be viewed.

Conversely, there is also a global trend for more pre-trade anonymity. Whilst transparency is important to see the currently available prices and liquidity, it can also pose problems for participants who need to trade larger quantities. Signalling risk represents the information that may be given away by such large orders. Pre-trade anonymity helps reduce the signalling risk, as can the adoption of order splitting or algorithmic strategies. Anonymity is generally only offered by order-driven venues and a few multi-broker platforms. This is because prime-brokerage type agreements and central counterparties are available, which help to reduce the potential credit and settlement risk. So for most OTC trading the only client protection is still the two-way quote.

A justification for these seemingly opposing trends in transparency and anonymity is provided by Robert Schwartz and Michael Pagano (2005). They point out that whilst transparency is required for price discovery, opacity is required for quantity discovery. This explains the popularity of "dark pool" ATSs which allow participants to anonymously trade in size. Ironically, some of the success of the "dark pools" is due to the transparency of the primary exchanges. Since, in general, they match based on size, using prices discovered from the primary exchange. Thus, dark pools have so far been concentrated in markets where prices are readily available, such as the equities markets. They are also starting to be introduced for the FX and listed derivatives markets. Negotiation based "dark pools" could be established for other asset classes, albeit with the additional burden of price discovery.

Accessibility

Traditionally, the marketplaces for most assets have been split into two, between dealers and clients, as we saw in section 3.3. Electronic trading has blurred these boundaries, creating much more open marketplaces. Screen trading has helped lower the cost of access to the inter-dealer network: Once an electronic trading platform is established, accessibility is no longer about being able to support a physical presence on a trading floor. Suddenly, there is a lot less difference between the buy-side and the sell-side. Remote access has also meant that location and time-zones start to become less important.

The advent of hedge funds has seen a concerted push by the buy-side to gain access to trade on the exchanges and dedicated inter-dealer networks. For large investment firms, the costs of electronic membership to exchanges can be worthwhile as a means of reducing broker/dealer commissions. Alternatively, many brokers have extended their agency-based trading to support DMA, providing clients with a low-cost means of sending orders to the exchanges. Even some of the dedicated inter-dealer platforms for bonds and FX have started to provide access for hedge funds and other investment firms.

Many new venues, such as ECNs and ATSs, cater for dealers and clients alike, as shown in Figure 3-2. Broker/dealers have also started to group together to create new venues, which are competing head-to-head with exchanges. So the segmentation between dealers and clients is weakening, although admittedly it is happening a lot slower for the traditionally OTC markets.

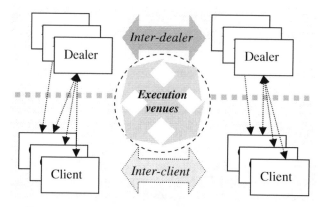

Figure 3-5 Potential marketplace inter-connections

Figure 3-5 tries to illustrate this more fluid market structure. Note the term execution venue is used to represent the whole range of exchanges, ECNs, ATSs and other platforms that now span the gap between dealers and clients.

Final proof that competition has improved accessibility is the establishment of inter-client networks, such as the buy-side only ATSs, which allow much larger trades than are possible on the open market. This is because the clients are trading with each other in an opaque venue, so signalling risk is less of an issue. Prior to this, such orders would have been handled by specialised block trading dealers in the "upstairs" market. Consequently, the advent of buy-side only "dark pools" has improved accessibility for this hidden liquidity.

Centralisation versus fragmentation

Constant competition means that markets often wax and wane between centralisation and fragmentation, as we saw in Figure 3-3. Although gauging exactly where a market lies between these two extremes is still more of a qualitative exercise than a quantitative one.

Fragmentation makes price discovery more difficult, so it is hard to be sure whether best execution has been achieved. Conversely, the lack of competition in a monopoly can also lead to increased costs. So the middle-ground is likely to provide the fairest solution. Though, as Figure 3-6 tries to show, it is still unclear exactly what form this should take.

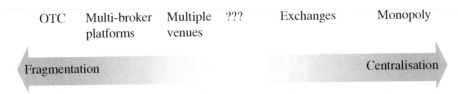

OTC   Multi-broker   Multiple   ???   Exchanges   Monopoly
       platforms   venues

Fragmentation   Centralisation

Figure 3-6 Centralisation versus fragmentation

By its very nature, OTC based trading is much more fragmented than exchange-based trading. The ideal marketplace is probably some sort of hybrid of these two, capturing the best features of both. It should be able to support both principal and agency-based trading, as well as allowing both direct execution and negotiation for clients.

Centralisation

Trading is easier, and usually cheaper, in liquid markets. This leads to a "network effect" which means venues with sufficient liquidity tend to retain and even attract new trade flow. There is a natural tendency for markets to centralise, as market liquidity tends to be "sticky". Hence, the success of the world's major exchanges. Even OTC markets are focussed around a number of major broker/dealers who have demonstrated they can provide sufficient liquidity.

Centralisation may arise from regulation. For example, in 1963, the SEC recommended restructuring OTC stock trading; this led to the creation of NASDAQ. In Europe concentration regulations were used (by France, Spain and Italy) to prevent significant off-exchange trading, until the introduction of MiFID. Indeed, for many countries the main national exchange often handles most of the trading for shares in domestic firms. Therefore, the stock exchange is still often viewed as the embodiment of centralisation.

Competition can also lead to centralisation. Over the last ten years, the average cost of trading has substantially decreased (except during the 2007-09 financial crisis). Reduced margins for broker/dealers mean that cost reductions from economies of scale are vital. Thus, consolidation tends to occur; the successful broker/dealers get larger and the rest either try to compete with innovations and incentives, or shift their focus to other markets. Key inter-dealer brokers, such as ICAP and BGC, dominate electronic trading in U.S. fixed income. Whilst in Europe the MTS and Euro MTS platforms handle a considerable proportion of government bond trading. In the FX market, the top ten banks now account for nearly 80% of the trading. [2]

Demutualization and global competition have led to a wave of exchange mergers and alliances. For instance, Euronext merged with NYSE, although previously there had been talk of a link with the Deutsche Börse. Similarly, NASDAQ bought the OMX, although they were previously focussed on the London Stock Exchange (LSE). The LSE in turn was busy planning a takeover of the Borsa Italiana. So there are now two massive entities competing for both U.S. and European volume, namely NYSE Euronext and NASDAQ OMX. Whilst in the derivatives markets, the CME and CBOT have also merged in order to maintain their global position versus other exchanges, such as Eurex and Liffe. Global competition is likely to continue to increase over the coming years, particularly as more pan-European (and even pan-Asian) execution venues are established.

Note that centralisation does not just apply to execution venues, clearance and settlement

---

[2] As reported in the 2008 Euromoney FX poll (Euromoney (2008)).

procedures should be considered as well. Having a single depository, such as the U.S. Depository Trust & Clearing Corp. (DTCC), makes settlement much more straightforward. Centralisation has also proved successful for FX, based on the CLS settlement system. However, this is a more complex issue for the OTC markets. The 2007-09 financial crisis showed how vulnerable they could be. Over the next few years, it is likely that regulation will mandate more centralisation for these. Streamlining the clearing and settlement processes could realise meaningful cost savings and help improve liquidity. Adopting central counterparties reduces counterparty risk. Still, this is only viable if the risk is readily quantifiable, otherwise the clearinghouses may be over exposed. Valuation is much less certain for more complex and less liquid assets. Therefore, a degree of standardisation might also be required. In fact, this process has already begun for CDSs, with several exchanges setting up clearing houses for them. If the OTC markets yield to the pressure to change then their liquidity may well improve. These measures could lead to lower transaction costs. Centralised clearing would allow participants more flexibility in managing collateral, by netting their exposures. Prime brokerage type arrangements could be established to help control credit risk. All these measures are the precursors to pre-trade anonymity, and so they might even lead to new electronic trading venues for OTC assets.

Fragmentation

Fragmentation is often referred to with sinister undertones. That said, it is an important part of the cycle of competition. Too little would mean the markets become huge monopolies, with no opposition to help reduce fees. On the other hand, too much fragmentation and we have a free-for-all that would make even the OTC markets seem centralised.

Regulation can also encourage fragmentation, by aiming to reduce costs with increased competition. For example, the SEC's 1997 NASDAQ quote ruling helped launch the ECN as a competitor. By the millennium, there were over a dozen ECNs trading U.S. equities. Similarly, 2007 saw the introduction of MiFID in Europe, leading to the creation of ECN-like MTFs and Systematic Internalisers. Indeed, pan European execution venues are starting to flourish, directly competing with the major stock exchanges. Still, Europe is inherently more fragmented than the U.S. since there are not yet regulations for a European-wide Best Bid and Offer (EBBO) or Regulation NMS style order routing requirements. Clearing and settlement is also more complicated in Europe.

To attract liquidity, new market entrants obviously need to offer something special. For ECNs, it was the electronic order book and the possibility of trading at a better price than the major markets. ATSs offer the ability of anonymous crossing large orders with minimal impact. Continued survival means retaining this liquidity and attracting more. Hence, innovation is not always enough, price incentives may also be required. For example, BATS captured a significant share of NASDAQ volume by offering a series of price rebates.

Fragmentation is also affecting other asset classes, such as foreign exchange. ICAP's EBS and Reuters still dominate the inter-dealer market. However, the last few years have seen fresh competition from ECNs such as Hotspot FXi, LavaFX, Bloomberg Tradebook FX and Accelor. "Dark pool" ATSs, such as MilanFX, have also started to appear.

The listed derivative markets are affected as well. Since most of these contracts are not transferable (or fungible) between venues, fragmentation means multiple venues offering similar contracts for the same underlying. Often this competition has been global, such as between the CME, Eurex and Liffe. However, local competition has also arrived, particularly in the U.S. with venues such as NYSE Liffe U.S. and the Electronic Liquidity Exchange (ELX). An important exception is the U.S. equity options market, which has a common clearing mechanism. This may be traced back to changes in market regulation (in 1994) ensuring that these could be traded at any of the market centres rather than concentrated at specific venues. Trading for U.S. equity options is now spread amongst more than half a dozen venues. Given that this market has seen some of the highest levels of growth of any of the world's listed derivatives it would seem to have been a success.

Venues are also starting to cater for multiple asset classes, leading to inter-market fragmentation. For instance, both NYSE and NASDAQ have expanded into equity options. NYSE has also renewed its corporate bond market. Initially, these may just be additional venues competing in the different asset marketplaces. Though, in the future multi-asset strategies may start to bind the various asset classes more closely.

Again, fragmentation does not only apply to execution venues, clearance and settlement procedures must also be considered. In Europe, there is a range of depositories for equities; hence, the price of a stock is not necessarily the only factor, since each of these depositories levy different charges.

Having praised fragmentation for increasing competition, it is important to note that there are also associated costs. By reducing liquidity at any one venue, it increases the complexity of trading. This is difficult to accurately quantify, but may be significant. Despite this, computerised trading systems have made it easier to cope with fragmented liquidity. Order routing tends to focus on matching the best price. Trading algorithms can offer even more sophisticated approaches: tracking both visible and hidden liquidity across multiple venues and taking advantage of opportunities within a fraction of a second. As trading systems become more sophisticated, the effects of market fragmentation may be noticeably reduced.

Repeating cycles

Waves of fragmentation are generally followed by periods of centralisation (or consolidation), as Figure 3-3 tried to show. Note that the periods involved generally span years, or even decades.

The "network effect" means there is a strong centralising force for liquidity to centralise around established market centres. New market entrants must offer significant innovation, or cost incentives, to attract liquidity away from these centres. Such competition often fragments the marketplace. Nevertheless, the more successful centres will continue to grow, consolidating their position by acquiring or merging with other venues. Thus, centralisation starts to take hold again, until the next cycle.

The U.S. equities market is probably the best example of these waves of centralisation and fragmentation. Clear marker periods for centralisation are the founding of the major exchanges, NYSE in 1792 with the "Buttonwood agreement" and NASDAQ in 1973. Whilst fragmentation may be linked to the 1997 quote ruling which led over a dozen ECNs, all vying for market share. By the millennium, the market for U.S. equities was clearly fragmented. Following this, a series of mergers and consolidations occurred, swinging back towards centralisation. Many of the acquisitions were by the major exchanges, helping to consolidate their market share. Suddenly, only a handful of independent ECNs remained. Also, two of the main remaining ECNs, BATS and Direct Edge, have either become exchanges in their own right or are in the process of doing so.

Another wave of new market entrants arrived in the U.S. stock market since the millennium, namely the "dark pool" ATSs. There are now around 40 venues where shares may be traded. Clearly, the ATSs have made the situation more complex, and have increased fragmentation. On the other hand, they are playing a key role in making additional liquidity accessible. Orders which might previously been traded in the "upstairs" market are now available on these ATSs, giving other participants the opportunity to trade in size. The cycle is also showing some signs of starting again, as mergers and consolidations have begun between some of the ATSs and other venues.

It is likely that we shall see these cycles repeated in the other major asset classes. For instance, the millennium saw a flood of electronic bond trading platforms in the U.S. fixed income market. In fact, over 80 were created, but a wave of consolidation has left only a handful. So we might say that this portion of the market is more centralised than it was. Nevertheless, this is still a fragmented marketplace since a considerable amount of bond trading is carried out OTC.

Note that there are no guarantees that the cycle of consolidation and fragmentation will always maintain a steady equilibrium. Over the last few years, demutualization has changed the dynamics between broker/dealers and exchanges. Many broker/dealers have bought shares in regional exchanges, ECNs and ATSs. They have even started directly competing with the exchanges, as opposed to merely pressing for fee reductions. By launching their own ATS platforms, they can handle their own internalised order flow. This also saves them from paying fees to the exchanges/ECNs and allows them to offer price improvement to their clients whilst still capturing part of the bid offer spread. The profitability of such operations means they are less likely to consolidate or disappear. Meanwhile, many exchanges have shifted from mutual organisations to becoming public companies. Suddenly, exchanges are now competing with their historical owners, as Larry Harris points out in an article for Securities Industry News (SIN) (2006a). If they do not get the balance right, liquidity will shift to alternate venues. This could become a real issue since the primary exchanges still provide much of the price discovery for these markets.

3.5 Global market comparison

So far, we have covered the various asset classes and seen how they are traded. It is also important to try to view these markets in context. One way of doing this is to compare them in terms of their overall size or value. Average daily turnovers also give an idea of their relative significance. Finally, we will look at some estimates for their levels of adoption of electronic and algorithmic trading.

Overall size

The global outstanding debt is split between equity, fixed income debt, commercial bank assets (deposits/loans) and derivatives. In 2006, the global outstanding debt was around $208 trillion, according to the Securities Industry and Financial Markets Association (SIFMA).

Figure 3-7 shows the breakdown of debt for these four asset classes over the last few years. The market capitalisation of the world's public companies accounts for 26% of this total, whilst another 32% is from bonds issued by corporations, governments and their agencies. However, the majority, 36%, of the debt is actually provided by commercial banks.

Derivatives are based on separate underlying assets, so their actual contribution is slightly more complex to measure. Multiple derivative contracts may cover the same underlying physical asset. Therefore, notional amounts for derivatives are not comparable to other asset classes. Based on figures from the 2007 triennial BIS (2007c) OTC derivatives survey, the total notional amount outstanding for all derivatives is actually $613 trillion.

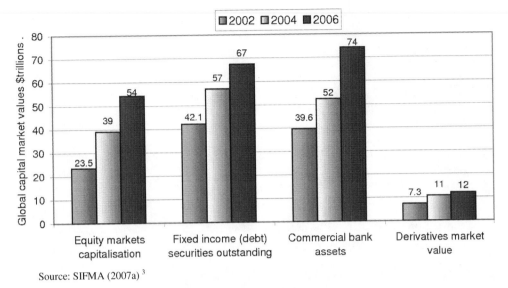

Source: SIFMA (2007a) [3]

Figure 3-7 Global market values

In order to quantify the size of debt associated with derivatives an alternative measure is often used, namely their gross market value. This corresponds to the cost of replacing all open derivative contracts, based on current market prices. The SIFMA (2007a) gross market value estimate for all derivatives (exchange traded and OTC) is $12 trillion; hence, they only contribute to 6% of the debt shown in Figure 3-7.

Average daily turnover

In general, equities are traded much more frequently than bonds; similarly, listed (exchange traded) derivatives have much higher turnovers than OTC contracts. Although this does not take into account the actual value of each trade. For example, the average value for equity trades is generally much lower than for bonds.

Figure 3-8 shows estimates of the average daily turnovers, in billions of U.S. dollars, for each of the major asset classes. Clearly, exchange traded (ET) derivatives dominate the world markets, in terms of turnover. Similarly, although levels of fixed income trading may be lower than for equities, the actual value traded is an order of magnitude greater. Also note the foreign exchange market, which as a cash-flow based market does not appear as a separate category in Figure 3-7.

Another way of viewing this data is to break it down by region, as shown in Figure 3-9. The equity, fixed income and exchange traded derivatives markets all follow a similar trend. Most of the volume occurs in the Americas, primarily the U.S., whilst the level of trading in the EMEA (Europe, Middle East and Africa) region is nearly half as much, and in turn trading in Asia is around half the EMEA levels. The two notable exceptions to this trend are foreign exchange and OTC derivatives where Europe has by far the highest trading volumes.

---

[3] Based on data from the International Monetary Fund, the Bank for International Settlements, Standard and Poor's, MSCI-Barra and the World Federation of Exchanges.

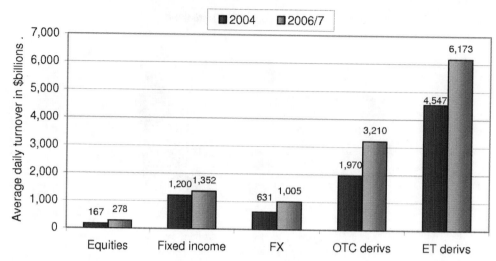

Source: Equities WFE (2007a), FX/Derivatives [4] BIS (2007b), Fixed income Authors own estimates using SIFMA (2007a, 2008) [5]

Figure 3-8 Average daily turnover in the global markets

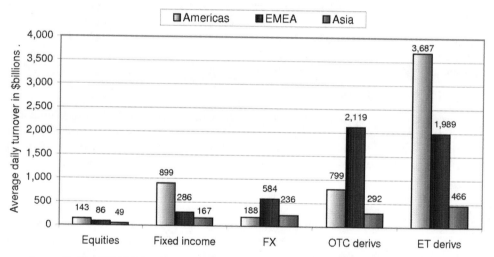

Source: Equities WFE (2007a), Fixed income SIFMA (2007a), FX/derivs BIS (2007b)

Figure 3-9 Regional daily turnover in the global markets

Also, the level of FX trading in Asia is noticeably higher than in the Americas.

---

[4] Note for the purposes of this chart FX outrights and swaps are classified as OTC derivatives
[5] Based on data from the Federal Reserve Bank of New York, Municipal Securities Rulemaking Board, NASD TRACE, Asian Bonds Online, UK Debt Management Office, and local central banks.

Adoption of electronic and algorithmic trading

Electronic trading is now commonplace for most asset classes, in particular for more standardised assets. Figure 3-10 shows estimates from the Aite Group (2008) consultancy for the levels of adoption in the major asset classes.

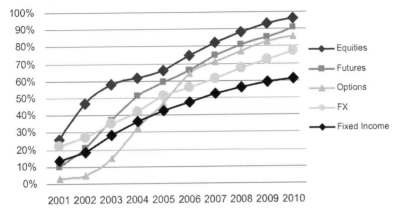

Source: ©Aite Group (2008)   Reproduced with permission from Aite Group

Figure 3-10 Estimates for the adoption of electronic trading in the major asset classes

The equities markets still lead foreign exchange and fixed income by a substantial margin, with around 80% adoption. If the current increases continue we might expect foreign exchange to reach this level by around 2009-10. Fixed income might be a few years behind this. Though, it is harder to see a wholesale shift occurring in some of the OTC markets.

The growth of electronic trading for futures, options and FX has been even more rapid than that seen in the equity markets. This is possibly due to reuse of existing technology and a faster learning curve, benefiting from past experience. Market conditions are also a vital factor. In fact, the proportion of electronic trading dipped slightly in many markets in 2008 due to the massive volatility from the financial crisis. Though, in the mid to long term the levels of adoption of electronic trading should stay pretty much on course.

The world's markets will continue to evolve in order to adapt to the changes which electronic trading brings. Algorithmic trading is increasingly being used by market participants in order to cope with these changes. Figure 3-11 plots the Aite Group (2008) estimates for the uptake of algorithmic trading, primarily for the U.S. Again, algorithmic trading has its strongest hold over the equities market, closely followed by listed futures, whilst fixed income lags behind. Still, by 2010, algorithmic trading could well be handling considerable trading volumes in all the major asset classes.

Overall, the equities market is still some way ahead of any of the other markets, in terms of levels of electronic and algorithmic trading. Although if we look back to Figure 3-8, the huge turnovers for FX and exchange traded derivatives highlight the importance of the progress being made in these markets. The OTC derivative market also represents a sizeable opportunity, although the bespoke nature of many of the contracts means this is by far the most complex market to tackle. Therefore, it is likely that for the foreseeable future progress will continue to be focussed on exchange traded derivatives and FX, whilst consolidating the efforts made in equities and fixed income.

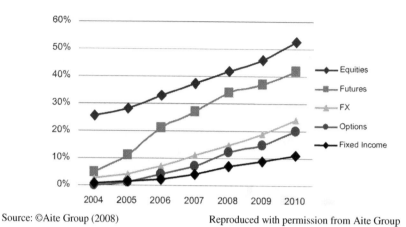

Figure 3-11 Estimates for the adoption of algorithmic trading in the major asset classes

Similarly, looking back at Figure 3-9 we can see that, in terms of capturing turnover for the U.S., by far the biggest opportunity for electronic and algorithmic trading is exchange-traded derivatives, followed by fixed income. Whilst for Europe and Asia the most major markets are FX and exchange traded derivatives.

Future investment in electronic and algorithmic trading will probably continue to differ across both asset classes and regions. This will depend on a mix of factors, namely market conditions, demand from institutions and investors, and the relative sizes of each market.

3.6 Summary

- A basic grounding in the world markets is important as investors, traders and platforms increasingly have to cope with globalisation and a range of different asset classes.

- There are still huge differences between many of the world's markets, but an increased focus on costs (by both the buy- and sell-sides) and the pace of technological change mean that many of them are exhibiting similar trends, albeit at different rates:
    - Electronic trading is widespread, for many markets it is now the norm.
    - Transparency is increasing, both for pre- and post-trade information.
    - Crossing for block orders is shifting to electronic "dark pool" ATSs.
    - Accessibility is improving for the buy-side.
    - Central counterparties for clearing and settlement are becoming more widespread.

- Counter to these trends is a seemingly endless cycle of centralisation and fragmentation.
    - Centralisation occurs because it is easier for established venues to retain liquidity.
    - Fragmentation due to competition from new market entrants helps prevent monopolies. This adds complexity to trading decisions, although as trading systems become more sophisticated such problems may be significantly reduced.

- Electronic trading is leading to irrevocable changes in the global markets, in particular:
  - Increased speed of trading
  - Massive growth in trading volume
  - Long-term decrease in order sizes

- Algorithmic trading is being used more and more by market participants in order to cope with today's markets. Equities are still at the forefront, but by 2010, it could well be handling considerable trading volumes in all the major asset classes.

- Based on their daily turnovers, the FX and exchange-traded derivatives markets stand out as important opportunities for algorithmic trading and DMA. Levels of electronic trading are also gradually increasing for fixed income and the money markets. The OTC derivative market also represents a sizeable opportunity, although this is by far the most complex market to tackle.

Part II

Algorithmic trading and DMA strategies

This is the main part of the book; it details the specifics of algorithmic trading and DMA, starting with orders, the basic building block for all trading strategies.

- Chapter 4 covers the wide range of different order types and conditions, which are available on the world's markets, together with examples.

- Chapter 5 reviews the different types of trading algorithm, from impact and cost-driven to more opportunistic strategies. Charts are used to show the trading patterns and highlight the differences (and similarities) between the various algorithms.

- Chapter 6 concentrates on transaction cost analysis. An example trade is used to decompose the transaction costs into their key components.

- Chapter 7 considers how the optimal trading strategy may be found by assessing orders in terms of their relative difficulty. This is then applied to the selection of trading algorithms.

Hopefully, by the end of these four chapters you should have a good understanding of the principles of algorithmic trading and DMA, together with how they may be applied to achieve "best execution".

$$\boxed{\begin{array}{c} \textit{Chapter 4} \\[1mm] \textbf{\huge Orders} \end{array}}$$

Orders are the fundamental building block for any trading strategy.

4.1   Introduction

Orders represent execution instructions. They allow investors and traders to communicate their requirements, both from the type of order chosen as well as with a range of additional conditions and directions. This chapter focuses on the basic mechanics of these various order types and conditions.

The two main order types are market orders and limit orders. In terms of liquidity provision, these are complete opposites. Market orders demand liquidity; they require immediate trading at the best price available. Whereas limit orders provide liquidity, they act as standing orders with inbuilt price limits, which must not be breached (a maximum price for buys and a minimum price for sells).

The conditions that may be applied to each order allow the trader to control many features of the execution, for example:

- Both how and when it becomes active
- Its lifetime/duration
- Whether it may be partially filled
- Whether it should be routed to other venues or linked to other orders

A wide range of trading styles can be achieved just by combining these conditions with limit and market orders. Indeed, many venues have gone on to support an even broader spectrum of orders, all essentially derived from basic market and limit orders. These include:

- Hybrid orders, such as market-to-limit
- Conditional orders, such as stops and trailing stops
- Hidden and iceberg orders
- Discretional orders, such as pegged orders
- Routed orders, such as pass-through orders

New order types are continuing to evolve. Some venues even offer orders that behave like algorithms, such as targeting the VWAP or participating in a set percentage of the market volume. Indeed, the line between them and trading algorithms is becoming increasingly blurred. Dynamic order types are very similar to trading algorithms, since they both alter based on market conditions. One way of differentiating between the two is that dynamic orders generally only focus on one specific variable, often the current market price (e.g. stop orders, pegging orders). Whereas trading algorithms base their decisions on a range of conditions, from volume to volatility. For the purposes of this text, we shall adopt this classification, so trading strategies such as VWAP and volume participation will be discussed further in Chapter 5. We shall also discuss how orders are actually used to implement algorithms and trading strategies in Chapter 9.

The examples in this chapter are broadly based on examples from the major exchanges. Some venues, notably the London Stock Exchange (LSE) (2006) and the Chicago Mercantile Exchange (CME) (2006), provide excellent materials with detailed examples for their order types. So it is always worth checking for such documentation. Another useful guide to the various types of orders is Larry Harris's (1999) book 'Trading and Exchanges'.

Finally, before we start covering the different order types and conditions in more detail, it is worth noting a few of the key assumptions made in the examples for this chapter. Firstly, they are all based around order books. Fundamentally, all trading involves order books, whether it is a phone-based OTC transaction or electronic trading via DMA, RFQ or a trading algorithm. The only real difference is that for quote-driven markets the order book is completely private and belongs to the market maker, whereas for order-driven markets the order book is usually centralised and much more transparent. Secondly, the examples generally cater for continuous trading periods, although some separate ones are highlighted for call auctions. This is simply because for most of these order types continuous trading is the most relevant period. Also for convenience, we usually assume that an execution will occur when we place an order that matches. Obviously, in real markets hundreds of participants can be issuing orders at the same time so regardless of a match our orders will sometimes be beaten to it. Lastly, the examples generally assume that the marketplace adopts a price/time priority, though for some cases the effect of different priorities is also highlighted.

So let's start by reviewing the mechanism of market and limit orders in more detail.

4.2 Market orders

The market order is an instruction to trade a given quantity at the best price possible. The focus is on completing the order with no specific price limit, so the main risk is the uncertainty of the ultimate execution price.

Market orders demand liquidity, a buy market order will try to execute at the offer price, whilst a sell order will try to execute at the bid price. The immediate cost of this is half the bid offer spread. We can see this using the sample order book shown in Figure 4-1.

Buys				Sells			
Id	Time	Size	Price	Price	Size	Time	Id
B1	8:25:00	1,000	100	101	1,000	8:25:00	S1
B2	8:20:20	1,500	99	102	800	8:20:25	S2
B3	8:24:00	900	98	102	1,200	8:24:09	S3

Figure 4-1 An example order book

A market order to buy 1,000 ABC can cross with sell order (S1) achieving a price of 101. We should then be able to immediately close out this position with an equivalent order to sell, which crosses with the buy order (B1) at 100. Hence the overall cost of both our market orders has been (101 – 100) which equals the spread, or half the spread each way.

For orders that are larger than the current best bid or offer size, most venues allow market orders to "walk the book". If they cannot fill completely from the top level of the order book, they then progress deeper into the book (increasing the price for buys, or decreasing for sells) until the order is completed. If the order still cannot be completed some venues will cancel it, such as the LSE, whilst others may leave the residual market order on the order book, e.g. Euronext.

Thus, the execution price achieved depends on both the current market liquidity and the size of the market order. For example, if we issue a market order to buy 2,000 ABC, the order book in Figure 4-2(a) shows that this can potentially cross with the sell orders S1 and S2. Receiving fills of 1,000 at 101 from order S1, and 1,000 at 102 from S2 gives an average execution price of 101.5. The resultant order book (b) shows that order S1 has been completed and S2 now only has 500 on offer (the buy side is unchanged and so is omitted).

Buys		Sells					Sells			
Size	Price	Price	Size	Time	Id		Price	Size	Time	Id
1,000	100	101	1,000	8:25:00	S1	.	~~101~~	~~1,000~~	~~8:25:00~~	~~S1~~
800	99	102	1,500	8:20:25	S2	.	~~102~~	~~1,000~~	~~8:20:25~~	~~S2~~
1,500	98	104	2,000	8:19:09	S3	.	102	**500**	8:20:25	S2
		106	3,000	8:15:00	S4	.	104	2,000	8:19:09	S3
						.	106	3,000	8:15:00	S4

(a) before   (b) after

Figure 4-2 The effect of a market order on the order book

In this example, as well as paying half the spread there is an additional cost that corresponds to the price jump from 101 to 102, resulting in a higher average execution price. This additional cost represents the market impact of our order. It is dependent on both the size of the order and the current market conditions, particularly the liquidity. For instance, if the example had been for an order of 5,000 we can see from Figure 4-2(a) that it would require crossing with orders S1 to S4, resulting in an average execution price of 103. Consequently, large orders often have a greater market impact than smaller ones.

Market conditions can also change rapidly. Again using the example from Figure 4-2 let's assume the owner of order S2 suddenly cancelled just before our market order to buy 2,000 hit the order book. In which case, our market order must now cross with order S3, the fill of 1,000 at 104 raises the average execution price to 102.5.

Sometimes market orders can actually achieve better prices than expected. This price improvement could be because the market order executed against a hidden order, such as an iceberg order, so a better price may be possible than the order book suggests. We will cover these order types later on in this chapter.

With no price limit, the performance of market orders is clearly dependent on current market conditions. Similarly, large market orders can have significant market impact, so it may be worth splitting such orders into smaller ones. If performance is more important than the speed (and certainty) of execution then a limit order may be a better choice.

4.3   Limit orders

A limit order is an instruction to buy or sell a given quantity at a specified price or better. A buy limit order must execute at or below this limit price, whereas a sell order must execute at or above it.

Limit orders will try to fill as much of the order as they can, without breaking the price limit. If there are no orders that match at an acceptable price then the order is left in place on the order book until it expires or is cancelled. If the order is partially executed then any residual quantity will remain on the order book. This helps provide liquidity since other traders can see we are willing to trade at a given price and quantity.

This persistence makes limit orders quite versatile. They may be used with an aggressive limit price, in which case they act like a market order demanding liquidity. The firm price limit gives added price protection compared to a market order, although there is the risk of failing to execute. Alternatively, limit orders may be issued with more passive limits, such as when trying to capture gains from future price trends or reversions, as shown in Figure 4-3.

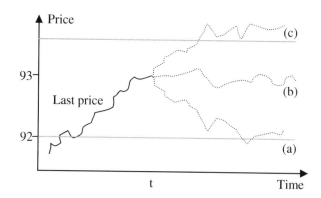

Figure 4-3 Limit orders intended to gain from future price trends

For example, by placing a limit order to sell at 93.5, at time t, when the last traded price was 93 we are hoping that the price does not suddenly drop, otherwise our order will expire unexecuted. Alternatively, we might place a buy order with a limit of 92, just in case the price reverts as shown in pathway (a). Note that even if the price reaches our limit there is still no guarantee of execution, since other orders may have priority over ours.

Let's consider a more detailed example: If we issue a buy limit order for 1,000 ABC at 100, as shown in Figure 4-4, there is no order that can immediately be crossed with this.

Buys				Sells			Buys			
Id	Time	Size	Price	Price	Size		Id	Time	Size	Price
B1	8:25:00	500	100	101	1,000		B1	8:25:00	500	100
B2	8:20:25	1,500	99	102	800		B4	8:28:00	1,000	100
B3	8:24:09	2,000	98	102	1,500		B2	8:20:25	1,500	99
							B3	8:24:09	2,000	98

(a) before   (b) after

Figure 4-4 The effect of a limit order on the order book

Thus, our order is left on the order book as B4. Note its position, it is placed after order B1 since it has less time priority, but is placed ahead of order B2 because it has price priority. So any incoming sell orders that would cross at a price of 100 will first match with order B1, then with B4 (unless pro-rata based matching is used).

To see how limit orders differ from market orders lets do a similar trade to the example in Figure 4-2, using instead a limit order to buy 2,000 ABC at the current best offer (i.e. 101).

This is shown in Figure 4-5.

Buys				Sells			
Id	Time	Size	Price	Price	Size	Time	Id
B1	8:25:01	1,000	100	101	1,000	8:25:00	S1
B2	8:20:02	800	99	102	1,500	8:20:25	S2
B3	8:24:09	1,500	98	104	2,000	8:19:09	S3

(a) before

Buys				Sells			
Id	Time	Size	Price	Price	Size	Time	Id
B4	8:28:00	**1,000**	101	~~101~~	~~1,000~~	~~8:25:00~~	~~S1~~
B1	8:25:01	1,000	100	102	1,500	8:20:25	S2
B2	8:20:02	800	99	104	2,000	8:19:09	S3
B3	8:24:09	1,500	98				

(b) after

Figure 4-5 A partially executed limit order

We can see from this that order S1 can be immediately crossed with our buy order. However, we cannot cross with sell order S2 because its price of 102 breaks our limit condition. The remaining 1,000 will be left on the order book as a buy at 101, shown as order B4. Due to price priority, our order is placed at the top of the order book, resulting in shifting the spread to 101-102, up from 100-101.

If the owner of order S1 suddenly cancelled just before our order hit the order book then since we cannot cross with order S2 the whole 2,000 would have been left on the order book as order B4 to buy at 101.

In comparison with the market order, we have sacrificed complete execution to ensure our price, so instead of filling 2,000 at 101.5 we have achieved 1,000 at exactly 101. Whilst if we had changed our limit price to be 102 we could have matched with the sell order S2, giving the same average price as the market order.

So the main risk with limit orders is this lack of execution certainty. The market price may never reach our limit or even if it does, it may still not be executed since other orders may have time priority. This emphasises the need to make a careful choice between the requirements for immediacy and price.

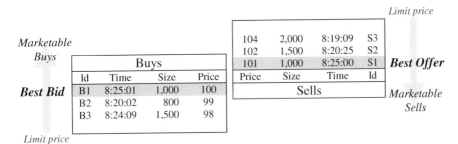

Figure 4-6 Viewing the order book in terms of price

The limit price is also an important means of classifying limit orders, since it reflects their probability of immediate execution. Figure 4-6 tries to show this by twisting the order book from Figure 4-5(a) to align all the orders by increasing limit price. Limit orders with the highest probability of execution are often termed marketable orders, since their limit prices are such that they can potentially cross immediately with an order on the other side of the book. Hence, a marketable buy order has a limit equal to or greater than the current best offer price, whilst a marketable sell order has a limit price greater than or equal to the best bid.

Orders that are placed "at the market" correspond to buys with a limit of the best bid or sells with a limit at the best offer. The traders who placed these orders are said to be making the market. Whilst the most passively priced limit orders are termed "behind the market". Their prices mean that they are likely to remain on the order book as standing limit orders until the best bid or offer price moves closer to them.

4.4 Optional order instructions

Order instructions are conditions that cater for the various requirements for a wide range of trading styles. As we can see in the summary in Table 4-1, they allow control over how and when orders become active, how they are filled and can even specify where (or to whom) they are sent to.

Type	*Example Instructions*
Duration	Good for the day, Good 'til date, Good 'til cancel, Good after time/date
Auction/Crossing session	On-open, On-close, Next-auction
Fill	Immediate-or-cancel, Fill-or-kill, All-or-none, Minimum-volume, Must-be-filled
Preferencing	Preferenced, Directed
Routing	Do-not-route, Directed-routing, Inter-market sweeps, Flashing
Linking	One-cancels-other, One-triggers-other
Miscellaneous	Identity, Short sales, Odd lots, Settlement

Table 4-1 Order instruction conditions

In the following sub-sections, we will see how each of these instruction types may be used.

Duration instructions

Generally, orders are assumed to be valid from their creation until they are completely filled or cancelled, or it reaches the end of the current trading day. These are known as day orders or "good for the day" (GFD) orders.

Specific instructions may be used to alter this duration, such as:
- "good 'til date" (GTD):
- "good 'til cancel" (GTC)
- "good after time/date" (GAT)

As the names suggest, a "good 'til date" order will remain active until the end of trading on the given date. Some venues even support variants such as "good this week" (GTW) and "good this month" (GTM).

A "good 'til cancel" instruction means the associated order should stay active until the user specifically cancels it, or until the instrument expires. Some exchanges also offer a "good 'til expiration" type for these instruments, e.g. futures.

The "good after time/date" instruction is somewhat less common. Clearly, it allows control over when the order actually becomes active. This instruction is more often used for broker systems where clients may choose to spread orders throughout the day, rather than for actual exchange orders. Most trading algorithms support similar behaviour by using a start time parameter.

Auction/Crossing session instructions

Auction/session instructions are used to mark an order for participation in a specific auction, or trading either at the open, close or intraday. They can also be used for the intraday crosses, which some exchanges have started introducing to compete with external crossing networks and ATSs.

Like normal market orders, auction market orders are intended to maximise the probability of execution, since in the auction matching they will always have price priority. Whereas auction limit orders will only be executed if the auction price equals or is better than their limit price, as we saw in Chapter 2.

On-open orders may be submitted during the pre-open period for participation in the opening auction. If the matching volume is sufficient then market-on-open (MOO) orders will execute at the auction price. For any unfilled MOO orders, some venues convert them to a limit order at the auction price, whilst others simply cancel them. Whereas limit-on-open (LOO) orders will only execute if there is sufficient volume and the auction price is equal to or better than their price limit.

On-close orders may be submitted during the pre-close period. Market-on-close (MOC) orders will execute at the closing price, given sufficient matching volume. Any unfilled orders will be cancelled. Again limit-on-close (LOC) orders will only fill given sufficient matching volume and an auction price equal to or better than their specific limit.

Venues with intraday auctions generally support an intraday auction or a "next auction" type. This is able to roll to the next valid auction, whether that is an intraday, open or close. A similar approach is often adopted for daily crossings or "mid point" matches.

In addition to the session instructions, NASDAQ also provides "imbalance-only" opening and closing orders. These are intended to allow liquidity providers to add orders to offset the extant on-open and on-close orders without adding to the overall imbalance.

Fill instructions

Traditionally, fill instructions were used to try to minimize the clearance and settlement costs for trades. But they are now more commonly used as part of liquidity seeking strategies. Instructions such as immediate-or-cancel enable orders to demand liquidity without leaving an obvious footprint on the order book.

Table 4-2 summarises the range of fill instructions that are available, most markets support a subset of these.

Immediate-or-cancel

This instruction means any portion of the order that cannot execute immediately against existing orders will be cancelled. Any limit price will be enforced, so it will execute as much of the required quantity as is available within the specified limit. This can result in only partially filling the order.

Instruction	Partial execution allowed	Unexecuted part added to the book?	Expires
Immediate-or-cancel	Yes	No	Immediately after submission
Fill-or-kill	No	No	Immediately after submission
All-or-none	No	No	End of day
Minimum-volume	Yes	Yes	End of day
Must-be-filled	No	N/A	After submission

Table 4-2 Order fill instruction types

Immediate or cancel (IOC) order instructions are also sometimes referred to as execute and eliminate, fill and kill, good on sight, immediate liquidity access and accept orders, across a range of execution venues. Such a variety of naming standards is clearly confusing; it is always worth carefully checking the documentation to confirm the exact behaviour. Note that for some venues immediate may actually correspond to being within a set time period (up to a few seconds); so again, it is vital to check the specifications.

As an example, if we issue an IOC limit order to buy 1,500 ABC at 101, we can see from the order book in Figure 4-7 that this can immediately cross with the sell orders S1 and S2. Order S3 is priced at 102 so no more of the order may be filled within the price limit. Therefore our buy order is now immediately cancelled, although 500 remains unfilled. We have obtained 1,000 ABC at 101 and left no residual order on the book.

Buys		Sells			
Size	Price	Price	Size	Time	Id
1,000	100	101	400	8:20:00	S1
800	99	101	600	8:22:25	S2
2,500	98	102	1,200	8:24:09	S3

(a) before

Sells			
Price	Size	Time	Id
~~101~~	~~400~~	~~8:20:00~~	~~S1~~
~~101~~	~~600~~	~~8:22:25~~	~~S2~~
102	1,200	8:24:09	S3

(b) after

Figure 4-7 The effect of an IOC order on the order book

Orders using this type of instruction have also been termed "Immediate Liquidity Access", which is an appropriate name since that is exactly what it has done. The IOC instruction makes an order grab available liquidity; unlike a market order, it also maintains our price limit. Thus, the IOC instruction is often used by algorithms when probing for liquidity.

NYSE's Arca offers a novel twist on the concept of immediate-or-cancel orders. Their "NOW" order instruction means that if an order cannot be immediately executed then it will be routed to a dedicated liquidity provider.

Fill-or-kill

A fill-or-kill (FOK) instruction ensures that the order either executes immediately in full or not at all. Effectively, it is an IOC instruction combined with a 100% completion requirement. Any limit price takes precedence, so if it cannot fill the order within the given limit then it will cancel it. This instruction is also sometimes referred to as a complete volume (CV) order. Note that some venues use the term fill-and-kill, but, as always, it is important to check their documentation since this may actually refer to an immediate-or-cancel style behaviour.

Figure 4-8 shows an example FOK limit order to buy 1,000 ABC at 101. Again, we can see from the order book in that this can immediately cross this with the sell order S1. Also note that just like IOC orders, the fill-or-kill instruction makes an order non-persistent, so if someone else managed to cross with sell order S1 first then our order would be cancelled, since we cannot cross with order S2 because of its price.

Buys		Sells					Sells			
Size	Price	Price	Size	Time	Id		Price	Size	Time	Id
1,000	100	101	1,000	8:25:00	S1	.	~~101~~	~~1,000~~	~~8:25:00~~	~~S1~~
1,200	99	102	900	8:20:25	S2	.	102	900	8:20:25	S2
2,000	98	102	1,800	8:24:00	S3	.	102	1,800	8:24:00	S3

(a) before   (b) after

Figure 4-8 The effect of an FOK order on the order book

All-or-none

The all-or-none (AON) instruction enforces a 100% completion requirement on an order. Unlike the fill-or-kill instruction there is no requirement for immediacy, so all-or-none orders may persist for some time. This can pose a problem for order book based systems, since the asset could well end up trading below the price of an AON buy order, or above the price of an AON sell, particularly if the AON order is large. Thus, AON orders are given a lower priority for execution, and are often handled by storing them on a separate conditional order book. This additional complexity has meant that many of the markets which once supported all-or-none instructions, such as NYSE, Euronext and the ASX, have switched to using IOC or fill-or-kill orders instead.

Minimum-volume

This is also sometimes referred to as a minimum fill or minimum acceptable quantity instruction. A minimum-volume ensures that the order will only match if the quantity is sufficient. As we saw with AON orders, this constraint could mean that minimum volume orders are left behind by the market. Hence, some markets, such as Euronext, cancel the order if it cannot immediately fill for the minimum quantity.

Minimum-volume constraints are also supported for call auctions in some markets, for example, NASDAQ. Figure 4-9 shows a simplified call auction for asset ABC where several of the sell orders have minimum quantity instructions.

Buys			Sells				Weight	Alloc
Time	Size	Price	Price	Size	Notes	Id		
7:25:00	15,000	MO	MO	3,000	Min 1,000	S1	1,500	2,100
			MO	5,000	Min 1,000	S2	2,500	3,500
			MO	9,000	Min 5,000	S3	4,500	0
			MO	13,000		S4	6,500	9,400
			MO	5,000				
			107	7,000				

Figure 4-9 An example call auction with minimum volume instructions

The "Weight" column shows how the allocations might have been assigned. Note that sell order S3 has a minimum volume constraint of 5,000. This is more than the assigned weighting of 4,500, so order S3 is excluded from the crossing. Consequently, the allocations we actually see in the "Alloc" column are quite different, since the 4,500 is redistributed amongst the other sell orders.

Note that in this example lot sizes of 100 are applied so there is a residual of 200. When assigning any residual amounts some auctions will favour orders with the lowest minimum quantity, so in this case the allocation for order S4 is increased to 9,400.

Must-be-filled

Unlike some of the other fill instructions, failure to fully execute is really not an option for must-be-filled (MBF) orders. Indeed, on Euronext they used to trigger a volatility interruption, a sudden intraday halt followed by a call auction, if they were not filled.

Nowadays must-be-filled orders are generally associated with trading to fulfil expiring futures or option contracts. A separate trading session is established on the day before expiration, so for options this is often the third Thursday of each month. Traders may place orders to offset their expiring positions. For instance, an uncovered option writer for an in-the-money call must buy the underlying in readiness for its exercise the next day. MBF orders are effectively treated as market orders, although they are exempted from any short sale regulations. They will then be crossed as part of the following morning's opening auction. Some exchanges publish an MBF imbalance to ensure liquidity providers place sufficient orders for the MBF orders to complete.

Preferencing and directed instructions

Order preferencing and directed instructions permit bilateral trading, since they direct orders to a specific broker or dealer. One controversy with both directed and preferenced orders is the fact that they bypass any execution priority rules. So other orders which may have time priority will lose out to the directed market maker.

Preferenced orders prioritise a specific market maker; generally, they are handled alongside normal order flow. On some venues, such as NASDAQ, preferenced orders behave more like a directed fill-or-kill order, since they are cancelled if the chosen market maker is not quoting at the best price.

Directed orders are routed to a specified market maker or dealer who may accept or reject them. On both the International Securities Exchange (ISE) and the Boston Options Exchange (BOX), market makers can offer price improvement for directed orders. The ISE has a dedicated price improvement mechanism, which is a special one-second auction.

Note that NASDAQ used to offer directed orders via SelectNet, but retired this in 2005. Directed non-liability orders allowed the market maker five seconds to accept, partially accept, decline or issue a counter offer for the order. Now when NASDAQ refers to directed orders it is in terms of routing instructions for specific venues.

Routing instructions

Execution venues have often catered for additional routing instructions for orders. Thus providing a gateway service that allows orders to be routed to other venues as well as handling them locally.

In the U.S. equities market, the introduction of Regulation-NMS has made routing instructions even more important. In particular, the Order Protection Rule means that brokers and venues are now responsible for protecting orders to ensure they achieve the best price.

So if an order might "trade-through" the best price available at another venue, the host venue should either reject the order or forward it on to the venue where it can achieve the better price. However, such automated order routing is not always appropriate, especially for traders or systems that are simultaneously executing across a range of venues. Therefore, instructions such as do-not-route and inter-market sweep allow better control over the order routing. Clearly, when using such instructions it becomes the trader's or system's responsibility to ensure it is still complying with Regulation-NMS.

In section 4.5, we will cover some additional order types that cater for even more complex routing strategies.

Do-not-route

This instruction ensures that the execution venue will handle the order locally and not route it to another venue. They are also referred to as do-not-ship instructions on NYSE and post-no-preference orders on NYSE Arca.

In terms of Regulation-NMS, this means that if an order is placed at a venue, but a better price is available elsewhere then it should be rejected. In all other respects, orders with this instruction behave as normal.

Directed-routing

Directed-routing provides an associated destination for where the order should be routed to. Effectively, the host venue acts as a gateway to route such orders on to their chosen destination. The advantage of this approach is that orders may be routed to venues for which we do not have a membership, although the host venue will levy routing fees for such orders.

Inter-market sweeps

Under Regulation-NMS, flagging an order as an inter-market sweep allows the order to sweep, or walk down, the order book at a single venue. It means the broker/trader must ensure that the order protection and best execution requirements are met. So an inter-market sweep order will generally be part of a group of orders, issued simultaneously, to a range of execution venues (hence the name).

For example, let's consider the consolidated market order book for asset ABC shown in Figure 4-10. For simplicity, the market has only two venues, exchange Exch-1 and ECN-1.

Buys			Sells		
Venue	Size	Price	Price	Size	Venue
ECN-1	800	50.00	50.01	1,500	Exch-1
Exch-1	1,500	50.00	50.01	500	ECN-1
ECN-1	1,000	49.99	50.02	1,200	Exch-1
Exch-1	700	49.99	50.02	800	ECN-1
ECN-1	1,200	49.98	50.03	2,200	Exch-1

Figure 4-10 An example market consolidated order book

We could send a buy order for 3,000 at 50.03 to the exchange and leave it to decide whether any of the order needs to be routed to alternate venues. Alternatively, if we also have access to ECN-1 we could save routing fees by sending a buy for 2,000 at 50.02 to Exch-1 and a buy for 1,000 at 50.02 to ECN-1.

If we use standard orders for this, each venue will apply their own logic to ensure that any matches do not "trade through" better prices at other venues. For example, let's assume the order book for Exch-1 looks like Figure 4-11(a). Our order to buy 2,000 can immediately

Exch-1	Sells	
Price	Size	Id
50.01	500	S1
50.01	1,000	S2
50.02	500	S3
50.02	700	S4
(a) Before		

Exch-1	Sells	
Price	Size	Id
~~50.01~~	~~500~~	~~S1~~
~~50.01~~	~~1,000~~	~~S2~~
50.02	500	S3
50.02	700	S4
(b) Exchange routing		

Exch-1	Sells	
Price	Size	Id
~~50.01~~	~~500~~	~~S1~~
~~50.01~~	~~1,000~~	~~S2~~
~~50.02~~	~~500~~	~~S3~~
50.02	700	S4
(c) Inter-market sweep		

Figure 4-11 Example execution for an inter-market sweep

cross with orders S1 and S2 since they are priced at 50.01, which is the best price available across all the market venues. For the remaining amount, there are no more orders on the exchange at this price level.

Before matching at a new price level, the exchange needs to check whether any orders at 50.01 are quoted at other venues. Based on the consolidated order book the exchange would need to route the remaining 500 to ECN-1. So the resultant order book for Exch-1 is shown in Figure 4-11(b).

Given that we know we have already routed a separate order to ECN-1, we clearly do not want the exchange to try to route part of our order to ECN-1. Instead, we just want to sweep the book at Exch-1 for all 2,000. So we must flag our order to Exch-1 as an inter-market sweep. Consequently, it will no longer seek to route the order and just fill versus orders S1 to S3, as shown in Figure 4-11(c).

By using an inter-market sweep, we get better control over exactly how and where our orders are placed, something that becomes vital when systems are working different orders simultaneously across many venues. It also allows us to save any additional routing charges that venues may apply.

Flashing

As their name suggests, flash orders are displayed on the source venue for an instant before either being routed on to another destination. The timescales involved are often around 25-30 milliseconds, although some variants may last for up to half a second.

In the U.S equities market, the Regulation-NMS order protection rule means orders must be routed to the venue displaying the best bid price, although routing charges may be applied. There may also be fees for taking liquidity from the destination venue. So the intention of flash orders was to offer traders the potential for achieving the best market price, in this case, the national best bid and offer (NBBO), without having to pay any extra charges. Similarly, for execution venues, they provide the chance to fill orders locally instead of routing them to a competitor.

This was achievable because each venue provides their own market data feed/s in addition to the national quotation system. During the flash period, market participants with the right data feeds could see and potentially trade with these orders, before they were routed on or cancelled. This has made them controversial, with much talk of creating a "two-tiered" market; despite the fact that venues offering flash orders made their data feeds readily available. In fact, many of the U.S. equity venues have now withdrawn their flash orders.

In part, this controversy simply reflects the pace of change of technology: The old inter-market system (ITS), which was replaced by the order protection rule, allowed a 30-second time window for an order to be acted on. Only time will tell whether flash orders become more widely accepted (for equities or any other asset classes).

Linking Instructions

Linking instructions provide a means of introducing dependencies between orders.

A one-cancels-other (OCO) instruction may be used to make two orders mutually exclusive, often this is used to close out of a position. For instance, to capitalise from any gains on a long position we could place a sell order at a high price. If the market moves against us, it makes sense to also have a separate stop order at a lower price. Clearly, we do not want both orders to execute since this would not only flatten our position but could actually reverse it, leading to a short position. By linking the two sells with an OCO instruction, we can ensure that if either of the sell orders executes then the other will immediately be cancelled. Note that if one of the OCO orders is cancelled the other remains unaffected.

A One-triggers-other (OTO) instruction links a supplementary order that will only be created upon the successful execution of the main order. For example, a successful buy order could automatically spawn a stop order as protection from any losses. The secondary order is contingent on the main order, and so is sometimes referred to as an if-done order. Note that if the primary order is cancelled then the secondary order will also be cancelled; however, this linkage does not work the other way around.

Some venues even allow orders to be grouped. For example, the SAXESS trading platform supports both linked and combination orders. Linked orders effectively provide an "OR" logic, so for a given amount we can buy assets ABC, DEF or XYZ. As an order fills for one asset, the other orders all reduce their sizes proportionally. Combination orders provide "AND" logic linking both the prices and sizes for two distinct orders, effectively allowing spread trading. We shall go through these order-contingent types in more detail in section 4.5.

Miscellaneous instructions

So far, we have focussed on the instructions that are commonly adopted across most execution venues. There are also more specialised options, which tend to be more venue specific. As always, it is worth carefully checking each venue's documentation to see exactly what additional instructions are supported. Some of the more common miscellaneous instructions are:

Identity details: Many venues offer anonymity by default. Although some others still allow anonymous identifiers to be used, for instance, using the SIZE identifier on NASDAQ.

Short-sales: This flag must be set for markets that enforce short sales regulations. This is used to enforce tick-sensitive trading, i.e. selling only on an uptick or even tick.

Odd-lots: Some venues incorporate odd-lot trading together with the normal trading mechanism. This instruction allows round lot orders to be matched with odd-lots.

Settlement instructions: Generally, non-standard settlement instructions require negotiation, and depending on the conditions may incur higher broker fees or may not even be possible. However, some reasonably common non-standard instructions are supported, such as foreign currency settlement. Cash settlement is the most common alternative for equities. This is often used to achieve same day settlement, rather than T+1 or T+3. Typically, cash settlement is needed in order to become the shareholder of record before dividends, rights issues or stock splits, as Larry Harris (1999) points out. Clearly, though, this benefit will attract additional costs, to compensate the provider.

4.5   Other order types

In addition to the default market and limit order types, there are a wide range of other orders available across the various execution venues. Table 4-3 summarises these, classified by function:

Class	Order types
Standard	Market, Limit
Hybrid	Market-to-limit, Market-with-protection
Conditional	Stop, Trailing stop, Contingent, Tick sensitive
Hidden	Hidden, Iceberg / reserve
Discretional	Not-held, Discretionary, Pegged
Routed	Pass-through, Routing-strategy
Crossing	Uncommitted, Negotiated, Alerted
Order-contingent	Linked-alternatives, Contingent, Implied

Table 4-3 Order type classifications

The hybrid, conditional, hidden and discretional order types are common across many venues. Regulation and the proliferation of new venues means that routed order types are also becoming more common. The success of "dark pools" has also led many exchanges to offer more specialised crossing orders, in order to compete. Finally, order contingent orders are less common and tend to be reasonably venue specific. In the following sections, we will go through each class in turn, examining the associated order types in more detail.

Hybrid order types

In many ways, market orders and limit orders represent different ends of the spectrum. Market orders offer immediacy but cannot guarantee the execution price, whilst limit orders offer price control but their execution is uncertain. Hybrid orders use a variety of mechanisms to try to offer the best of both limit and market orders.

Market-to-limit orders

Market-to-limit orders are indeed a hybrid: a market order with a strong implicit price limit. When the order first arrives, it behaves like a market order, seeking liquidity at the best available price, which then becomes its price limit. Unlike a traditional market order, it will not just sweep the order book, instead if there is insufficient liquidity available at the best price it will convert into a standing limit order for the residual amount.

For example, if we issue a market-to-limit order to buy 2,000 ABC, as shown in Figure 4-12, the initial market order will immediately cross with the order S1. This price now becomes the order's price limit; therefore, it is unable to cross with order S2. Thus, a partial fill of 1,000 at 101 is achieved and the order now converts to a limit order at this last executed price, as shown in Figure 4-12(c) as order B4.

Buys				Sells			
Id	Time	Size	Price	Price	Size	Time	Id
B1	8:25:10	1,200	100	101	1,000	8:25:00	S1
B2	8:20:15	800	99	102	1,500	8:20:25	S2
B3	8:24:10	2,100	98	103	700	8:24:09	S3

(a) before

Sells		
Price	Size	Id
~~101~~	~~1,000~~	~~S1~~
102	1,500	S2
103	700	S3

(b) MO crosses

Buys				Sells			
Id	Time	Size	Price	Price	Size	Time	Id
B4	8:28:00	1,000	101	~~101~~	~~1,000~~	~~8:25:00~~	~~S1~~
B1	8:25:10	1,200	100	102	1,500	8:20:25	S2
B2	8:20:15	800	99	103	700	8:24:09	S3
B3	8:24:10	2,100	98				

(c) after

Figure 4-12 The effect of a market to limit order on the order book

Admittedly, a marketable limit order priced at 101 would have achieved the same thing. But what if the owner of order S1 suddenly cancelled their order just before our market to limit order was processed?

Using a marketable limit order at 101 we would fail to match with order S2, and so remain in full on the order book. Conversely, a market order would have executed with both orders S2 and S3 completing with an average price of 102.25. In comparison, our market-to-limit order would have crossed with order S2 resulting in executing 1,500 at 102 and leaving the residual 500 as a limit order to buy at 102.

Hence, market-to-limit orders offer a middle ground between market orders and marketable fill orders. Their initial market order behaviour means that they offer more certainty of execution than a marketable limit order, but slightly less certainty of the execution price.

Market-with-protection orders

A market-with-protection order offers the immediacy of a market order together with the protection of an inbuilt price limit. Effectively, it is an extension of the market-to-limit order with a limit price further away from the last execution price.

For example, let's issue a market-with-protection order to buy 3,500 ABC as shown in Figure 4-13. We will assume the price limit equates to 103, so our market order can cross with orders S1, S2 and S3. Since order S4 is priced at 104 we are unable to cross and so the residual 500 is left on the order book as limit order B1 with a limit price of 103.

Market-with-protection orders help to ensure that execution is not achieved at any cost. Provided that a reasonable protection limit is set, they strike a balance between certainty of execution and certainty of price.

Note for the CME all market orders are actually implemented as market-with-protection orders. The price limit is calculated for buy orders by adding predefined protection points to the best offer, whilst for sells they are subtracted from the best bid. The protection points are equal to half of the asset's "no-bust range". [1]

---

[1] The no-bust range is a limit intended to protect market participants, within this range orders may not be cancelled.

Buys				Sells			
Id	Time	Size	Price	Price	Size	Time	Id
	8:25:00	1,000	100	101	1,000	8:25:00	S1
	8:20:25	900	100	102	1,500	8:09:25	S2
	8:21:00	2,000	99	103	500	8:14:09	S3
	8:22:00	1,500	99	104	1,000	8:16:00	S4
	8:14:00	800	98	105	1,300	8:13:00	S5

(a) before

Sells		
Price	Size	Id
~~101~~	~~1,000~~	~~S1~~
~~102~~	~~1,500~~	~~S2~~
~~103~~	~~500~~	~~S3~~
104	1,000	S4
105	1,300	S5

(b) MO crosses

Buys				Sells			
Id	Time	Size	Price	Price	Size	Time	Id
B1	8:28:00	500	103	104	1,000	8:16:00	S4
	8:25:00	1,000	100	105	1,300	8:13:00	S5
	8:20:25	900	100				
	8:21:00	2,000	99				

(c) after

Figure 4-13 The effect of a market-with-protection order on the order book

Conditional order types

Conditional orders base their validity on a set condition, often the market price. Only when the condition is met will it result in an actual order being placed. Thus, stops and contingent orders only become active when a threshold price is breached. Trailing stop orders are similar, although they use a dynamic threshold. Finally, tick-sensitive orders base their validity by comparing the current best price with the last traded price.

Stop orders

Stop orders are contingent on an activation (or stop) price. Once the market price reaches or passes this point, they are transformed into active market orders. In continuous trading, the price being tracked is generally the last traded price, [2] whilst in an auction it is usually the clearing price. Activation occurs for buys when the market price hits the stop price or moves above, whilst for sells it is when the market price hits or moves below the stop.

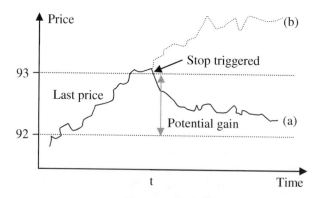

Figure 4-14 An example sell stop order

---

[2] On some exchanges, e.g. the CME, the stop price tracks the market bid and offer as well as the last traded price.

Stops are sometimes also referred to as stop-loss orders. Since as sells (buys) they are generally used as a safety net to protect profits, by closing out long (short) positions should the market move against us, as we can see in Figure 4-14. So, for example, let's assume a long position was initiated at 92; once the price reaches 93 a stop sell order is placed (at 93) as protection. If the price trend reverts at time t, as shown in pathway (a), then the stop will be triggered. Alternatively, if the price continues to trend favourably (b) the stop will remain inactive.

Note that the market order generated by a stop gives no guarantees on the price achieved. This is important since the very nature of stops means that they are only activated when the market price becomes unfavourable. They offer the lesser of two evils; a poor price may be achieved, but if the market does not revert, the alternative is even worse.

Stop limit orders replace the market order with a limit order. The stop price activates the order, whilst the limit price controls the triggered order. Although this offers some price protection by controlling the price of the triggered order, it also introduces a risk of failing to execute. Unfortunately, fast market conditions often heighten this risk.

The market-with-protection order type acts as a halfway house between market orders and a limit orders. Stop orders with protection use this order type to increase the probability of execution whilst still having a limit for some price control. The limit price is based on the stop price and the specified protection limit. Nevertheless, it is still fundamentally a limit order, so if the price shifts are severe enough to breach the protection limit then the position will remain exposed.

Therefore, if closing out of a position is a must then there is no real choice other than by using a pure stop order. It may also be worth considering other means of hedging the position, such as with options or futures.

Whilst stop orders are a useful tool, they can also have considerable market impact, in particular when the market is at its most vulnerable. Upon activation, all stop orders tend to accelerate the price trend that triggered them. For instance, a sell stop order is trying to sell when there has already been a significant fall in the price. Such a drop is most likely due to an imbalance between the order book volume to buy and sell. The stop order is effectively looking for liquidity when it has already decreased. If it manages to execute then the imbalance will be even greater.

Trailing stop orders

A stop order uses an absolute stop price, whereas for a trailing stop order the stop price follows (or pegs) favourable moves in the market price. A trailing offset is either specified as

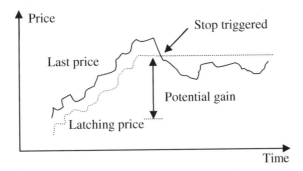

Figure 4-15 The price latching behaviour of a trailing stop order

an actual amount or sometimes as a percentage change. For a sell order, as the market price rises the trailing stop price will rise by a similar amount. However, when the market price falls the stop price does not change, as shown in Figure 4-15. Once the market price becomes less favourable, the stop price remains fixed until the market price actually reaches the stop and triggers it. The order then behaves exactly like a stop order or a stop limit order. This price latching mechanism allows profits to be locked-in without having to try to predict the best price level to set the stop at.

Contingent / if-touched orders

Contingent, or if-touched, orders are effectively the opposite of stops. For foreign exchange, they are sometimes called entry orders since they are generally used to establish positions.

As with stops, there are two main types, a market if-touched order and a limit if-touched. Note that a limit if-touched order is similar to a standing limit order, except that is hidden from the order book until activated.

Their operation is extremely similar to stops; both remain hidden until the market price moves sufficiently to activate them, whereupon they create a corresponding order. But the activation logic is the reverse of that for stops. So a buy if-touched order is triggered when the market price hits the target price or moves below, whilst a sell triggers when the market price hits the target or moves above.

Some venues even allow if-touched orders that are contingent on the price of a completely different asset, such as a stock index.

Tick sensitive orders

Tick-sensitive instructions introduce a validity condition based on the last traded price. If the current price is the same as the last trade it is referred to as a zero tick, above it is an up tick and below is a downtick. (Note zero ticks may be further classified as zero up and downticks by comparing with the last different trade price).

Thus, a buy downtick order may only be crossed on a downtick or zero downtick price. Likewise, a sell up tick order may only be crossed on an up tick or a zero uptick. Larry Harris (1999) points out that tick sensitive orders are essentially limit orders with dynamically adjusting limit prices. Tick sensitive orders employ a similar price latching mechanism to trailing stops; a downtick order will raise its dynamic limit price only when the price increases, whilst an uptick order will only decrease its limit when the price falls.

Tick sensitive orders have no immediate market impact. The tick dependency means that immediacy is sacrificed in order to obtain a price one tick better. Harris observes that they are therefore most useful when the tick size is large. In fact, the decimalisation of the U.S. stock markets in 2000 actually reduced the appeal of tick dependency, since it meant that for most stocks the tick size decreased from a sixteenth to just 1 cent.

Tick dependent orders exist mainly because of regulation, in part to try to curb the downward price momentum due to hidden stop orders being triggered. Consequently, some venues enforce a rule that short sales must be on an uptick. In other words, an uncovered sale is only allowed when the current price is above the last traded price.

Hidden order types

Efficient markets need to satisfy the needs of a range of users. Whilst transparency allows traders to easily see the available supply and demand, it poses problems for large orders. Many markets and venues provide hidden order types that allow traders to work larger orders without attracting undue attention. This ensures that liquidity remains available at the execution venue, rather than shifting to an alternative liquidity pool or crossing network.

A few years ago, completely hidden orders had all but been phased out. Hidden orders were viewed to increase the uncertainty of execution, and so affect the quality of price formation. They were also thought to act as a disincentive for placing limit orders, possibly leading to increased spreads. Transparency was viewed as being more important, and so venues, such as Euronext and the ASX, switched to providing iceberg orders instead. These offer a reasonable compromise, since a portion of the order is still visible. Still, the success of ATS venues providing "dark pools" of liquidity has led to resurgence in the popularity of hidden orders. Indeed exchanges, such as NASDAQ, AMEX and NYSE's Arca, are now introducing hidden orders in order to retain their liquidity and to compete with the ATSs.

Hidden orders

Hidden, undisclosed or non-displayed orders allow traders to participate without giving away their position. For example, Figure 4-16(a) shows the order book before a market order to buy 1,000 ABC arrives. Afterwards we can see that the order book has not changed as much as we might have expected. From the subsequent trade reports, we can see that 1,000 filled at 101, but on the order book we can only see order S1 filled and there were no new incoming orders, so where did the other 500 come from?

Buys				Sells					Sells		
Id	Time	Size	Price	Price	Size	Time	Id		Price	Size	Id
	8:25:00	1,000	100	101	500	8:20:00	S1		~~101~~	~~500~~	~~S1~~
	8:20:25	900	99	102	1,000	8:22:25	S2		102	1,000	S2
	8:24:09	1,400	98	102	800	8:24:09	S3		102	800	S3
	8:24:20	2,000	97	102	1,500	8:25:00	S4		102	1,500	S4
(a) before									(b) after		

Figure 4-16 A hidden order?

There may be hidden volume available at 101, or it may have all been consumed. The only way to know is to see the result of the next buy order. Hence the popularity of "liquidity pinging" using IOC orders. By issuing an IOC limit order to buy 1,000 at 101 we can try to cross with any hidden orders. That said, other participants are likely to have the same idea, so it is a question of speed of response.

One important consideration when using hidden orders is that they are usually given lower priority than visible orders. Otherwise, everyone would simply use hidden orders, making it much harder to determine the market price.

As hidden orders become more popular again there will doubtless be new variations. For instance, the London stock exchange is planning on supporting minimum order sizes, which should offer some protection from small liquidity-seeking orders.

Iceberg / reserve orders

As its name suggests, an iceberg order comprises of a small visible peak and a significantly larger hidden volume. The peak (or display) size is configurable, although some venues stipulate a minimum, often a percentage of the normal market size (NMS). The visible portion of the order is indistinguishable from any other limit order. Each time this displayed order is fully executed the venue's trading system splits a new order from the hidden volume, until the whole iceberg order is completed. Therefore, each displayed order has normal time priority within the order book whilst the hidden volume just has price priority.

Iceberg orders are also sometimes called reserve orders or drip orders.

For example, if we look at Figure 4-17(a), we can see sell order S1 for 1,000 at 101. This is actually the display size of the iceberg order H1 that has another 9,000 hidden volume. Obviously, the hidden volume is not actually visible on the order book, but just for these examples it shown (in light grey) to emphasize that it still has price priority in the order book. Thus, order S3 will not manage to cross with any other orders until our hidden volume H1 is exhausted.

Buys		Sells			
Size	Price	Price	Size	Time	Id
1,000	100	101	**1,000**	8:20:00	**S1**
900	99	101	1,000	8:21:25	S2
1,500	98	*101*	*9,000*	*8:10:09*	*H1*
		102	1,500	8:24:09	S3

(a) before

	Sells			
	Price	Size	Time	Id
.	~~101~~	~~1,000~~	~~8:20:00~~	~~S1~~
.	~~101~~	~~500~~	~~8:21:25~~	~~S2~~
.	101	**500**	8:21:25	S2
.	101	1,000	8:27:00	S4
.	*101*	*8,000*	*8:10:09*	*H1*
.	102	1,500	8:24:09	S3

(b) after

Figure 4-17 Crossing with the display portion of an iceberg order

When a market order to buy 1,500 ABC hits the order book:
- Our iceberg's displayed order S1 immediately crosses with it for 1,000
- Next, the remaining 500 is filled by partially crossing with order S2.
- Since our displayed order is completed, a new order is split from the hidden quantity as sell S4.

Continuing this example with a second market order to buy another 2,200 ABC, is shown in Figure 4-18.

Buys		Sells			
Size	Price	Price	Size	Time	Id
1,000	100	101	500	8:21:25	S2
900	99	101	1,000	8:27:00	S4
1,500	98	*101*	*8,000*	*8:10:09*	*H1*
		102	1,500	8:24:09	S3

(a) before

	Sells			
	Price	Size	Time	Id
.	~~101~~	~~500~~	~~8:21:25~~	~~S2~~
.	~~101~~	~~1,000~~	~~8:27:00~~	~~S4~~
.	~~101~~	~~700~~	~~8:28:09~~	~~S5~~
.	101	300	8:28:09	S5
.	*101*	*7,000*	*8:10:09*	*H1*
.	102	1,500	8:24:09	S3

(b) after

Figure 4-18 Another crossing with the iceberg order

So we can see that:
- The remaining 500 of order S2 is immediately executed.
- The 1,000 from our iceberg's order S4 is also filled.
- A new order S5 for another 1,000 is split from our hidden volume H1.
- The remaining 700 of the market order is filled from the newly created order S5 that has price priority over order S3.

The mechanism is just the same if we have multiple iceberg orders on the order book. For instance, let's consider the order book shown in Figure 4-19 which has two iceberg orders.

Buys		Sells			
Size	Price	Price	Size	Time	Id
1,000	100	101	**1,000**	8:20:25	**S1**
900	99	101	500	8:21:25	S2
1,200	98	101	**1,500**	8:23:00	**S3**
		101	*6,000*	*8:20:09*	*H1*
		101	*9,000*	*8:23:00*	*H2*
		102	1,800	8:24:10	S4

Sells			
Price	Size	Time	Id
~~101~~	~~1,000~~	~~8:20:25~~	~~S1~~
~~101~~	~~500~~	~~8:21:25~~	~~S2~~
~~101~~	~~1,500~~	~~8:23:00~~	~~S3~~
~~101~~	~~200~~	~~8:25:02~~	~~S5~~
101	**800**	8:25:02	S5
101	1,500	8:25:02	S6
101	*5,000*	*8:20:09*	*H1*
101	*7,500*	*8:23:00*	*H2*
102	1,800	8:24:10	S4

(a) before   (b) after

Figure 4-19 Crossing with multiple iceberg orders

The first iceberg is currently displaying sell order S1 with a hidden volume H1 of 6,000, whilst the second has a greater hidden volume of 9,000, but it also uses a greater display size of 1,500 for its order S3. So when a market order to buy 3,200 arrives:

- The first iceberg's order S1 will be completely filled.
- As will standing limit order S2.
- The second iceberg's displayed order S3 is also filled, leaving 200 remaining on the market order.
- New orders S5 and S6 will then be split for each iceberg.
- The last 200 of the market order will be crossed with the first iceberg's newly split order S5, since this iceberg has time priority.

This also highlights the importance of the iceberg's display size. Even though the second iceberg H2 has lower time priority, each time it splits a new order it is for 1,500, so it will fill quicker than H1.

These examples have all shown how the hidden volume on the order book participates in the order matching mechanism. This is the key difference between native exchange based iceberg orders and an external order-slicing mechanism, where the hidden volume resides outside the order book. External mechanisms are reliant on receiving execution confirmations to show that the previous order has completed, only then will a new order be created. This may occur some time after the order book crossing has finished, so an external mechanism will not be able to respond in time. Hence, in order to fill the market order the order book will instead cross with other standing limit orders, such as S4 in Figure 4-19. This means that order-slicing approaches may take longer to execute than native iceberg orders. However, it also enables them to have more scope for price improvement; we shall go through this in more detail in Chapter 9.

Discretional order types

Traditionally, discretional order types afforded the trader more freedom in how a particular order should be worked, since they are the expert. This is perhaps best typified by the Not-held instruction that basically gives the trader *carte blanche*. Computerisation has resulted in the evolution of more rules-based approaches, such as pegged and discretionary orders. These offer more quantifiable steps, compared to the rather vague "do the best you can".

Not-held orders

A not-held order gives complete discretion to the trader about how the order is worked.

Generally, these are used for floor traders since in less transparent markets they will have the best knowledge of market conditions. The quality of execution relies on them choosing the best time to trade.

Discretionary orders

A discretionary order is a limit order with a slightly more flexible limit price. The limit that is displayed on the order book may be augmented by an additional amount when conditions are appropriate. For a buy order, the real price limit is actually the limit price plus this discretionary amount, whilst for a sell it is the limit price minus the discretionary. The true limit is taken into account only when a matching order comes within the discretionary range. Therefore, the order may execute at any price between the displayed limit and the true limit. Note that any visible orders will still have priority over the discretionary order.

For example, let's issue a buy limit order for ABC at with a limit of 100 and a discretionary range of 1, as shown by buy B1 in Figure 4-20(a).

	Buys			Sells			
Id	Time	Size	Price	Price	Size	Time	Id
B1	8:25:01	1,000	100	102	1,000	8:25:00	S1
	8:20:05	800	99	103	2,000	8:20:25	S2
	8:24:00	1,200	98	104	900	8:24:09	

(a) before

	Buys			Sells			
Id	Time	Size	Price	Price	Size	Time	Id
~~B1~~	~~8:25:01~~	~~500~~	~~101~~	~~101~~	~~-500~~	~~8:28:00~~	~~S4~~
B1	8:29:00	500	100	102	1,000	8:25:00	S1
	8:20:05	800	99	103	2,000	8:20:25	S2
	8:24:00	1,200	98	104	900	8:24:09	S3

(b) after

Figure 4-20 The effect of a discretionary order on the order book

Initially, there is no order that can immediately be crossed, so order B1 simply rests on the order book with a visible limit price of 100. When sell order S4 is added at a price of 101, this is now within our discretionary range. So we can match this. The remaining 500 for order B1 remains on the order book, still with a visible limit of 100.

Some venues, such as NASDAQ and NYSE Arca, support a minimum quantity as well, so that the discretionary order will only stretch its price limit for orders above this size.

Pegged orders

Pegged orders provide a dynamic limit price; therefore, they can help reduce the inherent miss-pricing risk of standing limit orders. A pegged order's limit price may track the best bid, offer or even mid price, applying an additional offset amount. For instance, Figure 4-21 shows the trajectory of a pegged limit order tracking the best bid price. A firm price limit may still be applied which will prevent the order pegging beyond this limit.

For example, let's issue a buy limit order for ABC pegging from the best bid with an offset of 1. Initially, our order B2 will be placed with a limit of 99, 1 away from the current best bid, as shown in Figure 4-22(a). When a new order B4 joins the book, the best bid moves up to 101, so in response our order is updated with a new limit of 100 to keep pace

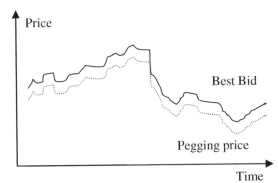

Figure 4-21 Pegging the best bid price

Buys				Sells	
Id	Time	Size	Price	Price	Size
B1	8:20:00	1,000	100	102	900
B2	8:25:25	1,200	99	103	1,000
B3	8:24:09	800	98	104	1,500

(a) before

Buys				
Id	Time	Size	Price	
B4	8:27:00	500	101	.
B1	8:20:00	1,000	100	.
B2	8:25:25	1,200	99	.
B3	8:24:09	800	98	.

(b) spread narrows

Buys				Sells			
Id	Time	Size	Price	Price	Size	Time	Id
B4	8:27:00	500	101	102	900	8:28:00	
B1	8:20:00	1,000	100	103	1,000	8:25:00	
B2	8:27:25	1,200	100	104	1,500	8:20:25	
B3	8:24:09	800	98				

(c) after

Figure 4-22 The effect of a pegged order on the order book

with the best bid.

As for discretionary orders, some venues, such as NYSE, support a minimum quantity, so that pegging is not triggered by small orders. Instinet even offers pegged order types that can have an associated display size, just like an iceberg order.

Scale orders

These may be used to layer child orders throughout the order book at a range of price levels.

Buys				Sells			
Id	Time	Size	Price	Price	Size	Time	Id
B5	8:25:00	900	100	101	1,000	8:24:20	S3
B2	8:20:25	1,500	99	101	800	8:25:00	S5
B4	8:24:09	2,000	98	102	1,200	8:24:25	S4
B1	8:20:25	1,200	97	102	2,000	8:24:20	S2
B3	8:24:00	700	97	103	1,000	8:24:20	S1

Figure 4-23 An example set of scale orders

For instance, we might specify a sell order for 4,000 ABC, scaled with 25% at 101, 50% at 102 and 25% at 103, as shown in Figure 4-23. Alternatively, set amounts may be specified for the various price levels. In a fast moving market, this approach has the advantage that our orders are already in place, and so receive time priority. But if the price keeps trending favourably, better prices might be achieved by waiting. We will revisit these layering tactics in Chapter 9.

Routed order types

Routed order types are becoming more and more common; they can be an important means of seeking additional liquidity in today's increasingly fragmented markets.

As we have already seen, there are order instructions that cater for routing, allowing orders to be sent to specific venues or to stay at a single venue. The natural progression is increasingly complex order routing strategies, leading to "smart order routing". The simplest of which is represented by pass-through orders. These allow liquidity to be accessed from two venues. There is also a range of strategies allowing routing back and forth between venues, and even participating in special sessions such as the opening auction. As these continue to evolve, the line between them and trading algorithms is becoming increasingly blurred.

Pass-through orders

As their name suggests, pass-through orders allow an order to initially pass-through the hosting venue on the way to their ultimate destination, often the primary exchange. Effectively, they act like two sequential orders, an IOC order at the initial host venue followed by an order for the remainder sent to the destination venue.

This allows an order to consume liquidity from the hosted order book before routing any residual to the chosen destination. In comparison, a standard limit order that sweeps the order book will just leave any remainder as a standing order. Therefore, they are typically provided by crossing networks or venues seeking to attract additional liquidity.

For example, let's consider an order to sell 1,500 of asset ABC at 100. Figure 4-24 shows the order books for both the ECN (ECN-1) and the primary exchange (Exch-1).

ECN-1

Buys		Sells		
Size	Price	Price	Size	Id
500	100	101	1,200	S1
1,000	99	102	900	S2
800	98	102	1,500	S3

ECN-1

Buys		Sells		
Size	Price	Price	Size	Id
~~500~~	~~100~~	101	1,200	S1
1,000	99	102	900	S2
800	98	102	1,500	S3

Exch-1

Buys		Sells		
Size	Price	Price	Size	Id
1,000	99	101	800	S1
900	99	102	1,500	S2
1,400	98	102	2,000	S3

Exch-1

Buys		Sells		
Size	Price	Price	Size	Id
1,000	99	100	1,000	S4
900	99	101	800	S1
1,400	98	102	1,500	S2
		102	2,000	S3

(a) before   (b) after

Figure 4-24 An example pass-through order

We can see from Figure 4-24(a) that there are 500 available at ECN-1. Hence, we can issue a pass-through order, which will try to cross with the liquidity available at ECN-1 before routing to the primary exchange, Exch-1. Having consumed the available liquidity at 100, our order will now become a standing limit order S4 at Exch-1.

Although Figure 4-24 shows an example of routing between two visible order books, it does not take a huge leap of imagination to replace ECN-1 with a "dark pool" ATS. When placing our sell order we can no longer see what liquidity is available, but we know it will try to cross before routing to the primary exchange, Exch-1. This is quite a convenient way of providing additional liquidity for the ATS. Typically, ATSs have been keen to have brokers route retail flow through in this way since there is less chance of information leakage.

Routing-strategy orders

Routing-strategy orders extend the straightforward concept of pass-through orders to allow more complex routing instructions. These may enable orders to participate in auctions, or be routed to additional venues before reaching their final destination. For example, Table 4-4 shows some of the routing strategies offered by NASDAQ.

Name	Strategy
MOPP	Route to all protected quotes for display size only Post any residual on NASDAQ
DOTI	Sweep NASDAQ for NBBO or better Route any residual to NYSE or AMEX
SKIP	Sweep NASDAQ for NBBO or better Route to Reg NMS protected venues Post any residual on NASDAQ
SCAN	Sweep NASDAQ for NBBO or better Route to alternate execution venues Post any residual on NASDAQ
STGY	As SCAN Residual will route if NASDAQ subsequently locked or crossed

Source: NASDAQ (2008a)

Table 4-4 Example NASDAQ routing strategies

The MOPP strategy takes advantage of liquidity visible at other venues by routing to access the Regulation NMS (Reg NMS) protected quotes for their displayed size. Any residual amount is then posted on the NASDAQ order book.

In comparison, the DOTI strategy first sweeps the NASDAQ order book, trying to beat or match the national best bid and offer (NBBO). It then routes the any residual amount on to either NYSE or AMEX. Note that once the order reaches its final destination, it will remain there until it is completely filled or cancelled.

The SKIP strategy extends the DOTI approach by being able to route the residual to any of the venues that offer Reg NMS protected quotes. After this routing, the SKIP strategy finally posts any remainder on NASDAQ.

The SCAN strategy takes a similar approach to SKIP, first sweeping NASDAQ then routing the residual. The list of possible destinations for the residual is even wider than for SKIP since it also includes a range of alternative venues. The STGY strategy is based on similar rules to SCAN; although, it will re-route the residual order if the NASDAQ order book subsequently becomes locked or crossed.

More strategies are also based on these. For instance, DOTM behaves similarly to STGY; although it requires orders to be non-attributable and accepts on-open and on-close orders.

Other venues have their own specific order routing strategies, but the above examples give an idea of what is commonly offered. No doubt, other innovative strategies will develop over time.

Crossing order types

Many venues already provide orders allowing traders to report off order book crosses. New order types are also being introduced to allow crossing to actually take place on the order book. These have become increasingly important as venues compete for "dark pool" liquidity. A nice summary of the order types and flows is provided by Gabriel Butler's (2007) review of crossing networks. He classifies the available order types as:

- Committed orders, firm orders available for immediate execution
- Uncommitted orders, requiring confirmation before execution
- Negotiated orders
- Pass-through orders, routed on their way to another venue

As we saw in Chapters 2 and 3, crossing networks vary widely in their actual mechanisms. These types are not supported by every venue; however, they encompass most of the various kinds of mechanism that are available.

Committed orders are essentially just standard market or limit orders. Uncommitted orders are similar to indications of interest (IOIs), whilst negotiated orders provide a bilateral trading mechanism. As we have already seen, pass-through orders act as a means of providing additional liquidity for crossing. Note an indication of interest (IOI) is a non-binding interest in buying (or selling) an asset. These may be sent between the buy-side and sell-side to discover interested counterparties.

There is one additional order type worth mentioning, that is the alerted order. Venues may also use indications to advertise the availability of liquidity. Some even provide separate order types, allowing traders and investors to choose whether they wish to use this mechanism.

Uncommitted orders

Uncommitted orders are similar to indications of interest (IOIs) combined with a mechanism which enables them to convert to firm orders. They are also sometimes referred to as conditional orders, such as on BIDS.

Uncommitted orders can cross with each other or with firm orders. If a potential cross is discovered, the owner will be sent a notification, at which point they can then decide whether to convert them to a firm order. This allows investors/traders to leave an uncommitted order on the crossing network whilst they try to work the same order on other venues, knowing that they will not get any unexpected fills.

Some venues also allow additional sensitivity parameters, which may be used to specify discretionary price/volume limits at which we may be prepared to trade. These are incorporated into the matching logic, so when a notification is received for a potential match a structured negotiation can take place.

When firm orders are being matched with uncommitted ones, it is important to also provide some protection for the owner of the firm order. To ensure fairness, and prevent predatory trading, a reasonably large minimum order size is often required for uncommitted orders. BIDS also uses its scorecard mechanism to ensure that both participants have a sufficient success rate from prior crossings. Otherwise, predatory traders could simply "ping" for liquidity using uncommitted orders.

Negotiated orders

Negotiated orders are used by venues to provide a structured negotiation environment. Essentially, they provide a bilateral trading mechanism, as we saw in Chapter 2. Each counterparty has an idea of the price and size they are prepared to trade at, so they must simply alter these until they both agree a deal. Alternatively, they can just walk away since there is no obligation to trade.

One of the interesting things about crossing networks is that the negotiation is anonymous. Both participants may be investors, or one may be a liquidity provider. A common solution is to allow the participants to be able to gauge each other, by providing them with a scorecard that shows the historical success rate of their previous crossings.

Alerted orders

These orders use indications, or alerts, to try to improve the probability of execution by broadcasting a message that notifies other market participants of interest in a particular asset. This is particularly important for "dark pool" crossing networks where the order book is completely invisible.

For example, the Millennium ATS has an opt-in Plus order type which triggers an alert to their Liquidity Partners (PLPs). These represent a mix of buy-side institutions, other "dark pool" ATSs and broker internalization engines. Note that this process is fully automated, so the alerts are not visible to traders. The PLPs must therefore use automated systems to respond to any alerts, detailing their available liquidity to Millennium, which then looks for any matches. If a match is found, the corresponding PLP must then reply with a firm order.

The ISE also provides an advertised order, which it calls a Solicitation of Interest. This activates a block trading mechanism that notifies the exchange members of the asset's ticker symbol. They may then enter responses that detail the price and size at which they are willing to trade with a block order. At the end of this period (10 seconds), any orders that are priced better than the block execution price will execute. Priority is given first to orders on the exchange, then member responses and non-customer orders.

Order-contingent order types

Orders can easily be linked together, as we saw using linking instructions. Venues often use these to allow orders to either cancel or even trigger another order. Order-contingent orders extend this concept by allowing orders to adjust their price and/or size, based on other orders. In the case of linked-alternative orders, they adjust their size based on how much the other alternative orders have filled. Contingent and implied orders vary their price and size based on the best market quotes and a predetermined spread. Contingent orders also enforce an execution dependency to make certain they are all fully executed.

Linked-alternative orders

This relatively uncommon order type allows a list of alternative orders to be linked so that if one order receives fills then the other orders will be reduced by an equivalent amount. Effectively, it enables simultaneous trading of assets ABC or DEF or HIJ, so this order type is sometimes referred to as linked or "OR" orders. Obviously, one of the main precautions when handling such orders is to ensure that several of the grouped orders do not simultaneously fill, potentially causing an over-fill.

For example, in Figure 4-25(a) a sample set of linked orders is shown. When we receive a fill of 500 for our KLM buy we have effectively 50% completed our order.

Asset	Side	Original Size	Extant size	Filled		Extant size	Filled
KLM	Buy	1,000	1,000	0		500	500
NOP	Buy	3,000	3,000	0		1,500	0
QRS	Buy	800	800	0		400	0
TUV	Buy	2,000	2,000	0		1,000	0

(a) before   (b) after

Figure 4-25 An example set of linked alternative orders

Hence, the extant order sizes for the other linked orders are all reduced to 50%, as we can see in Figure 4-25(b). The SAXESS platform, used by some of the Nordic exchanges, can link up to 8 orders in this way.

Contingent orders

Some venues allow even more dynamic linking between orders spanning multiple assets. Such contingent orders ensure that a match is only possible when all the other dependent orders may also be matched. Typically, this functionality is offered by futures exchanges to support spread trading, whereby simultaneous long and short positions are traded to try to profit from any price differences between two assets. It may also be employed to cater for more complex, multi-leg derivatives trading strategies.

For example, in Figure 4-26(a) we can see the order books for assets JKL and XYZ. Let's assume we wish to buy the spread, and so buy 1,000 JKL whilst selling 1,000 XYZ, but only when the spread reaches -0.2. So we could place a combined order to buy 1,000 JKL and sell 1,000 XYZ with a spread of -0.2.

At present the spread is actually -0.5, since the best offer buy for JKL is 50.8 and the best bid of XYZ is 50.3. So we must use more passively priced limit orders and wait for the spread to narrow, as we can see in Figure 4-26(b). In terms of pricing, our buy order B4 is dependent on the sell order S4, and vice-versa. The price of B4 is based on the best bid for XYZ and the spread, i.e. (50.3 - -0.2) = 50.5.

JKL

Id	Time	Size	Price	Price	Size		Id	Time	Size	Price	
	Buys			**Sells**				**Buys**			
B1	8:24:00	1,000	50.6	50.8	1,500		B1	8:24:00	1,000	50.6	.
B2	8:22:25	800	50.6	50.9	900		B2	8:22:25	800	50.6	.
B3	8:23:09	1,200	50.5	50.9	2,000		B3	8:23:09	1,200	50.5	.
							B4	8:26:00	1,000	50.5	.

XYZ

Size	Price	Price	Size	Time	Id		Price	Size	Time	Id
Buys		**Sells**					**Sells**			
1,000	50.3	50.5	1,000	8:25:40	S1	.	50.5	1,000	8:25:40	S1
600	50.3	50.6	1,200	8:21:05	S2	.	50.6	1,200	8:21:05	S2
1,500	50.2	50.6	700	8:22:49	S3	.	50.6	700	8:22:49	S3
						.	50.6	1,000	8:26:00	S4

(a) before   (b) after

Figure 4-26 An example pair of combined orders

Similarly, our sell order S4 is based on the best offer price for JKL, i.e. (50.8 + -0.2) = 50.6. If one of our orders is matched then the other order will immediately change its price in order to ensure it is filled. So, if B4 can be filled then order S4 will simultaneously re-price to 50.3 in order to complete.

Clearly, our orders need to update to adjust to new market prices and sizes to ensure the required spread is maintained. If there is insufficient volume available for one of the assets then the size of the other order must be reduced by a corresponding amount. For example, if the order to buy 1,000 XYZ at 50.3 was suddenly cancelled we would need to change the size for our orders. For more sophisticated handling of such spread orders, we could use pairs trading algorithms, which we shall discuss in more detail in Chapter 5.

Implied orders

As we saw in the previous section, one way of handling combined orders is to use the current market prices and the desired spread to imply their current price and size. Therefore, real orders are dynamically adjusted to ensure they keep in line with the required spread.

Implied orders represent the next evolution of this approach. Spread trading is so commonplace for futures that many venues allow them to be traded as standalone orders. So we can buy a JUN-SEP spread, just as we might buy or sell the June or September futures contracts. This is usually handled by having separate order books dedicated to spread trading or handling complex strategies. However, over the last few years more and more venues have started to link their standard order books with these complex books. This has allowed the creation of implied orders, which are able to span both types of order book. An implied spread may be derived from the combination of outright orders for different contracts, whilst implied orders may be derived from the combination of spread orders and outright orders.

The importance of such implied trading in futures markets is highlighted in a nice piece by John Blank (2007): In relatively new markets, such as NYMEX energy, up to 44.6% of the trades are achieved via implied trading. Even in mature markets, such as the CME Eurodollars, around 16% of the trading is attributable to implied orders (11.5% of the volume). Consequently, implied orders are an important source of additional liquidity.

Figure 4-27 shows an example of how an implied IN order is created. For simplicity only the orders which create the implied order are shown, namely the buy for the June futures contract (B1) and the sell order for the equivalent September future (S1). Hence, we can sell a June futures contract at 96.5 and buy a September future for 96.0, in other words we can sell the spread for (96.5 – 96.0) = 0.5. This implies there is a bid of 0.5 available to buy the spread. The size is determined by whichever order is smallest (between orders B1 and S1) and so is 10. As we can see in Figure 4-27, these two orders result in the implied order I1.

	Id	Bid size	Bid	Offer	Offer Size	Id
JUN future	B1	10	96.50			

	Id	Bid size	Bid	Offer	Offer Size	Id
SEP future				96.00	15	S1

	Id	Bid size	Bid	Offer	Offer Size	Id
JUN-SEP	I1	10	0.50			

Figure 4-27 Creating an implied IN order

Conversely, a sell order for the June contract will combine with a buy order for the September future to create a JUN-SEP spread offer price and size.

Likewise, by deconstructing a firm spread order into its constituents we can create an implied OUT order. For example, in Figure 4-28 we can see S2, a firm order to sell the SEP-DEC spread at 0.6. By combining this with the firm buy order B1 for the September contract, we can imply the price of a December future. In other words, there must be an equivalent buy order for the December future at (95.7-0.6) = 95.1, shown as implied order I2.

SEP future

Id	Bid size	Bid	Offer	Offer Size	Id
B1	10	95.70			

DEC future

Id	Bid size	Bid	Offer	Offer Size	Id
B2	10	95.10			
I2	5	95.10			

SEP-DEC

Id	Bid size	Bid	Offer	Offer Size	Id
			0.60	5	S2

Figure 4-28 Creating an implied OUT order

Also notice that there is already a bid (B2) at this price. When matching trades, most venues will assign priority to actual orders, any residual is then matched with the implied orders.

Implied orders may also be combined with actual orders to create second-generation implied orders. So the implied orders I1 and I2 may in turn be used to create other implied spreads or orders.

Butterfly spreads may also be used to create implied orders. These are effectively pairs of spread trades. For example, selling the JUN-SEP-DEC butterfly means selling a JUN-SEP spread and buying a SEP-DEC one. In effect, this results in buying two September contracts and selling both a June and a December one. Again, there is a separate order book dedicated to handling these butterfly spreads, which may in turn be combined with standard orders to create more implied orders. Although complex, this is clearly an effective way of increasing liquidity on the main order book.

4.6 Summary

- Orders are the fundamental building block for any trading strategy.

- Orders represent execution instructions. There are two main types:
  - Market orders buy or sell a given quantity at the best price possible. They focus on completing the order with no specific price limit, and so demand liquidity.
  - Limit orders buy or sell a given quantity at a specified price or better. The price limit must not be breached, even at the risk of failing to execute. They persist until executed or cancelled and so provide liquidity.

- A range of optional conditions allow control over factors such as:
  - How and when the order becomes active.
  - Its lifetime/duration.
  - Whether it may be partially filled.
  - Participation in auction/crossing sessions.
  - Whether it should be directed to specific venues or even market makers.
  - Linking with other orders.
  - Miscellaneous factors, such as odd lots and settlement handling.

- More specialised order types (derived from both market and limit orders) offer:
  - Hybrid orders, such as market-to-limit, which try to offer the best of both limit and market orders.
  - Conditional orders, such as stops, which base their validity on a set condition. Only when the condition is met will it result in an actual order being placed.
  - Hidden orders try to reduce signalling risk for large orders.
  - Discretional orders offer more dynamic handling of limit prices.
  - Routed orders allow more complex routing logic than possible via conditions.
  - Order-contingent orders, which offer more complex linking relationships.

- New order types are continuing to evolve. Some venues even offer orders that behave like algorithms, such as targeting the VWAP or participating in a set percentage of the market volume. Indeed, the line between them and trading algorithms is becoming increasingly blurred.

Chapter 5

Algorithm overview

Trading algorithms are predefined sets of rules for execution, each targeting a specific goal, whether it is matching the VWAP or seeking liquidity.

5.1 Introduction

An algorithm is basically a set of instructions for accomplishing a given task. Therefore, a trading algorithm simply defines the steps required to execute an order in a specific way. Brokers/vendors provide a range of trading algorithms, each with distinct goals. Some strive to match or beat a specific benchmark, or try to minimise overall transaction costs whilst others seek to trade more opportunistically. To achieve these goals, some approaches rigidly adhere to a given trading schedule whilst others are more dynamic, adapting to ever-changing market conditions.

Although the individual rules may be quite straightforward, the wide array of different events and possibilities that must be catered for mean algorithms can rapidly become quite complex. A common way of tackling this complexity has been to split the problem in two. For instance, Vladimir Kazakov (2003) decomposes VWAP trading into determining the optimum trading strategy and then realising this with optimal execution. The strategy concentrates on the trading schedule and benchmark, whilst the execution focuses on choosing appropriate orders to achieve this. Similarly, Robert Kissell and Roberto Malamut (2005) propose breaking algorithmic trading down into macro and micro level decisions. Again, the macro level makes strategic choices, based on the overall objectives. The micro level considers more tactical details, such as the specifics of order submission.

As an example, let's take a simple order to buy 6,000 of asset ABC over the next hour and time-slice its execution so that we trade 1,000 every ten minutes. We can represent this task with some pseudo-code:

```
for timer = 1 to 6
        quantity = 1000
        trade(quantity)
        sleep(10 minutes)
```

This code will not win any awards, but it does highlight that we are following a specific trading schedule until the order is completed. Obviously, we can make the trading algorithm more sophisticated by incorporating historical data or live market conditions. For instance, the quantity could be based on the best bid or offer size rather than just setting it to 1,000.

Exactly how we trade is a separate decision, for which the `trade()` function simply acts as a placeholder. A variety of approaches might be adopted, so the `trade()` function could:

- always place market orders
- always place limit orders
- dynamically choose the optimal order type based on market conditions

By separating the execution logic from the trading pattern in this way, we can create a common set of functions, which we will refer to as execution tactics. These are then available for all trading algorithms, and may be used interchangeably. This makes it much easier to customise our trading strategies. For example, we might default to a more passive execution style, but then change to use a more aggressive one when we get behind target or when conditions become more favourable.

So trading algorithms deal with the big picture, they primarily focus on how best to break up the order for execution. At the micro level are the actual mechanisms for managing order submission. We shall cover such execution tactics in more detail in Chapter 9.

5.2   Categorising algorithms

Although there are a wide variety of trading algorithms out there, if we strip off the customisations, we can start to see a small set of core strategies that are commonly provided by most brokers/vendors.

One way of classifying these algorithms is based on the benchmarks that they use. For example, the benchmark for implementation shortfall algorithms is predetermined, whilst for VWAP it is dynamic, and Market-on-Close seeks to match a future closing price.

Another way of classifying algorithms is based on their fundamental mechanisms. Ian Domowitz and Henry Yegerman (2005a) describe these as a continuum, which ranges from unstructured strategies, such as liquidity seeking algorithms, to highly structured approaches, such as a VWAP algorithm. Jian Yang and Brett Jiu (2006) go on to extend this approach by splitting this continuum into three main categories, namely:

- Schedule-driven
- Evaluative
- Opportunistic

Purely schedule-driven algorithms follow a strictly defined trading trajectory, generally created statically from historical data. For instance, historical volume profiles have often been used to implement VWAP algorithms; they represent intra-day historical volume averages. These profiles may then be used as a template for how the order should be split over time.

At the other end of the spectrum, opportunistic algorithms are completely dynamic. They react to favourable market conditions, trading more aggressively to take advantage of them. Then as conditions become less favourable, they trade more passively, if at all. Hence, liquidity-seeking algorithms are a good fit for this category.

Evaluative algorithms represent the middle ground between these two extremes. Often they combine aspects of each approach. Indeed, Yang and Jiu (2006) suggest that at the macro level they may behave in a more schedule-driven fashion whilst at the micro-level they focus on balancing the trade-off between cost and risk. Algorithms targeting implementation shortfall are good fit for the evaluative category.

This mechanistic style of classification focuses more on how algorithms are implemented, whereas a trader or investor makes their decisions based on set objectives or goals. To better reflect these we can adopt a slightly modified scheme using three main types, namely:

- Impact-driven
- Cost-driven
- Opportunistic

Table 5-1 shows some common trading algorithms grouped using these categories. It also shows some of the specific factors which trading algorithms are most affected by, or are sensitive to.

| Type | Key focus | Algorithms | Benchmark | | Sensitivity | |
			Dynamic	Pre-determine	Price	Volume
Impact-driven	Time	Time Weighted Average Price	✓			
	Volume	Volume Weighted Average Price	✓			
		Percentage Of Volume		✓		●
	Impact	Minimal impact	✓		○	○
Cost-driven	Price/ Risk	Implementation Shortfall		✓	○	○
		Adaptive Shortfall		✓	●	○
		Market On Close	✓		○	○
Opportunistic	Price	Price Inline		✓	●	○
	Liquidity	Liquidity-driven		✓	○	○
	Ratio/ Spread	Pair / Spread trading		✓	●	

● often ○ sometimes

Table 5-1 Algorithm classification

Impact-driven algorithms aim to minimise the overall market impact. In other words, they try to reduce the effect trading has on the asset's price. Therefore, large orders will often be split into much smaller ones, trading them over a longer period. This is best typified by the VWAP algorithm.

Cost-driven algorithms try to reduce the overall trading costs. Therefore, they need to take account of market impact, timing risk, and even factors such as price trends. Implementation shortfall is therefore an important performance benchmark for these. Consequently, this has become the name of the most commonly used cost-driven algorithm.

Opportunistic algorithms, as with Yang and Jiu (2006), take advantage whenever the market conditions are favourable. So these algorithms are generally price or liquidity-driven or involve pair/spread trading.

Clearly, Table 5-1 is not a definitive list of every possible trading algorithm. To see a summary of the algorithms each broker offers both the A-Team Group (2009) and Advanced Trading [1] publish directories, which are readily available. Still, Table 5-1 covers most of the

---

[1] Advanced Trading directories are available at www.advancedtrading.com/directories

basic different types of functionality. Generally speaking, more exotic algorithms may be constructed by using one (or more) of these core strategies as the basis. For example, pair trading may act as the core for some multi-asset class trading, which we will cover in more detail in Chapter 13.

Note that this chapter focuses on trading algorithms that might be used by institutions and investors. We shall also cover some of the potential arbitrage strategies in Chapter 13. However, in general, algorithms that are predominantly used for market making or high-frequency trading / statistical arbitrage are beyond the scope of this book.

Before we go through each of these classes of algorithm in more detail, the following section outlines some features that are common to all algorithms.

5.3   Common features of algorithms

Algorithmic trading is evolving in a similar fashion to electronic trading. Initially, each broker offered standalone solutions, adopting their own style of naming and controls. Gradually, these have started to become more standardised as they have been integrated into Execution Management Systems (EMS) and Order Management Systems (OMS). This allows investors and traders to switch between vendors more easily. However, the constant evolution of new algorithms and the increasing need for customisation means that there will be a continual cycle of innovation and consolidation.

Despite their different goals, there is still a significant amount of commonality between trading algorithms. In particular, this may be seen for their parameters, which are their equivalents of the optional instructions we saw for orders.

Algorithm parameters

Trading algorithms may be controlled by a range of parameters. These provide the algorithms with limits or guidelines; they can be algorithm specific or generic.

Specific parameters may be used to specify how much a VWAP algorithm may deviate from the historical volume profile, or the participation required for a percent of volume algorithm.

Generic parameters represent common details, such as when to start and stop and whether to enforce a limit price etc. The following list summarises most of the parameters that are commonly supported, although various names may be used:

Start/End Times: Algorithms generally accept specific start and end times, instead of conditions such as "good for the day". Some algorithms, mainly the cost-based ones, may derive their own optimal trading horizons, although the start and end times should still act as hard limits. Certain algorithms might require a minimum amount of time to trade, so orders with too short a horizon may be rejected. Note that when start or end times are undefined, defaults are usually applied: For end time, the default is usually the market close, whilst the start time will be now (or the market open). Also, remember that when using times it is important to check that they are transmitted and interpreted correctly, particularly for foreign time zones. For algorithms that support multi-day trading, the end date becomes equally important.

Duration: Some vendors may actually forgo end times, instead using a duration parameter.

Must-be-filled: Generally, trading algorithms aim for complete execution, excluding the more opportunistic ones. Market conditions may mean that this goal cannot always be achieved. Hence, a must-be-filled parameter will ensure that the algorithm trades any residual amounts. Often this will invoke specialised finish up logic, which takes quite an aggressive approach to ensure completion. This may affect the overall cost/performance.

Execution style: Usually, this represents passive, aggressive or neutral trading. Aggressiveness is a function of both size and price, so an aggressive algorithm will often execute more quickly, but at a higher impact cost than a passive one.

Limit price: A hard price limit offers price protection just as it would for a limit order. This is particularly useful for algorithms that do not have an inbuilt sensitivity to price.

Volume limit (maximum): This prevents an algorithm from trading more than a certain percent of the actual market volume. If this is being used to prevent signalling risk, it may be better to use a minimal impact or a liquidity-driven algorithm.

Volume limit (minimum): Care needs to be taken when enforcing minimum levels of trading since it could have a substantial effect on market impact costs.

Volume limit (child): Some algorithms may even support limits on the size of any child orders that are split off, or even the number of orders that can be extant at any one time. Again, if this is being used to reduce signalling risk it may be better to switch to a minimal impact or a liquidity-driven algorithm.

Auctions: This flag may be used to specify whether the order may participate in opening, closing and any intraday auctions. There may even be parameters to state this as a percentage of the order size.

As algorithms develop, there will doubtless be new common parameters, but the above list gives an idea of their scope. In the following sections, each of the different classes of algorithm will be reviewed in more depth, as well as detailing any specific parameters. For consistency, we will generally use the same sample order, to buy 10,000 of a reasonably liquid asset ABC, for each algorithm. [2] This approach should make it easier to compare the trading algorithms.

5.4   Impact-driven algorithms

Impact-driven algorithms evolved from simple order slicing strategies. By splitting larger orders into smaller child orders, they try to reduce the effect trading has on the asset's price, and so minimise the overall market impact costs.

The average price based algorithms, namely TWAP and VWAP, represent the first generation of impact-driven algorithms. Although intended to minimise impact costs, their main focus is their respective benchmarks. These are predominantly schedule-based algorithms, and so they usually track statically created trajectories with little or no sensitivity to conditions such as price or volume. Their aim is to completely execute the order within the given timeframe, irrespective of market conditions.

The natural progression from these static approaches has been the adoption of more dynamic methods. This has also resulted in a gradual shift towards more opportunistic

---

[2] Obviously, trading volumes are significantly different between asset classes. So an overall order size of 10,000 is small for most equities but quite large for some futures or bonds. However, the same principles apply regardless.

trading. Percentage-of-volume (POV) algorithms are based on the actual market volume rather than relying on statically created schedules. These have further evolved into minimal impact algorithms, which take a more stealthy approach, aiming for zero market impact.

Time Weighted Average Price (TWAP)

The Time Weighted Average Price (TWAP) benchmark is an average price, which reflects how the asset's market price has changed over time. Therefore, trading algorithms that attempt to match this benchmark are usually based on a uniform time-based schedule. They are unaffected by any other factors, such as market price or volume. TWAP algorithms are the natural extension of the earliest time slicing based approaches.

Basic Mechanism

The simplest version of a TWAP algorithm is based on time slicing. Figure 5-1 shows two such orders, each to buy 10,000 of asset ABC. Order 1 issues child orders for 500 every fifteen-minute period for 5 hours, whilst order 2 trades double that over half the time.

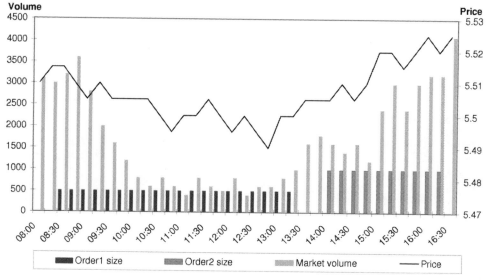

Figure 5-1 Two example TWAP orders

Clearly, both trading patterns are extremely uniform, and independent of both market volume and price. Unsurprisingly, the idealised completion rate charts for both orders are straight lines, as shown in Figure 5-2.

Trading in such a predictable way can lead to considerable signalling risk. Indeed, the only thing the other market participants do not know is the total size of the order. Even if other participants do not "game" this strategy it can still suffer poor execution quality due to its rigid adherence to the time schedule, in particular when prices become unfavourable or the available liquidity suddenly drops.

Alternatively, we can use the linear nature of the target completion profile to adopt a more flexible trading approach. At any given time, we can determine the target quantity the order should have achieved just by looking up the corresponding value on the completion rate chart. For instance, a 2-hour TWAP should have 25% of the order executed after half an hour. So instead of following the strict time slicing pattern we could adopt a slightly more random approach. By constantly comparing our progress with the ideal target quantity, we can then see how far behind (or ahead of) the schedule we are. Thus, we may now vary both the frequency and size of trading whilst still tracking the same target completion profile. This enables us to trade with a much less obvious trading pattern.

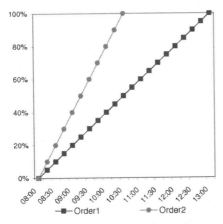

Figure 5-2 Completion rate for sample TWAP orders

For example, Figure 5-3 shows a randomised TWAP order to buy 10,000 ABC:

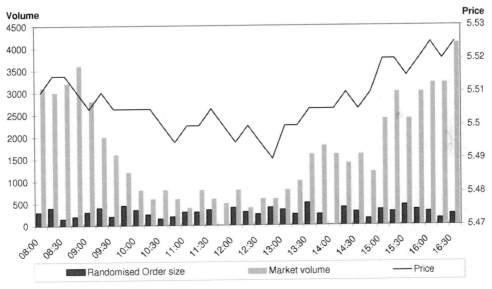

Figure 5-3 A more randomised TWAP order

The child orders are split randomly throughout the day, with some periods not even issuing an order. Table 5-2 shows how the traded quantities for each 15-minute period compare with the idealised targets. Sometimes the trading lags behind the target quantities, although it can also get slightly ahead of schedule, for instance at 8:15 and 9:45.

This may be seen more clearly in a comparison of the completion rate charts, as shown in Figure 5-4. Evidently, the randomised order still tracks the linear target completion rate quite closely, which gives it a good chance of matching the TWAP benchmark.

Time	08:00	08:15	08:30	08:45	09:00	09:15	09:30	09:45	..
Trade	300	400	150	200	300	400	200	450	..
Total	300	700	850	1050	1350	1750	1950	2400	..
Target total	290	570	860	1140	1430	1710	2000	2290	..
Difference	10	130	-10	-90	-80	40	-50	110	..

Table 5-2 The trading pattern for a more randomised TWAP order

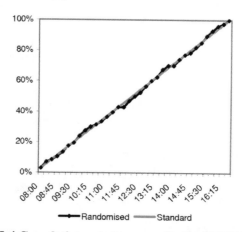

Figure 5-4 Completion rate for a randomised TWAP order

This slightly randomised approach also allows more flexibility in the trading strategy, although it can increase the risk of missing the TWAP benchmark. It also enables a more dynamic approach, for example, we could adjust the order aggressiveness based on how far ahead or behind schedule we are. Hence, a more passive order placement strategy is possible, allowing for some degree of price improvement. In addition, this approach allows us to ignore unfavourable market conditions (small best bid/offer sizes, large price jumps), or even spurious ones which might correspond to gaming attempts. That said, such enhancements mean we are now trying to beat the TWAP benchmark rather than match it.

Common variations

Some versions may allow an additional factor to be applied to the trading schedule, which tilts it and so making it trade either more aggressively or more passively, as shown in Figure 5-5. A more aggressive stance will issue more orders early on, helping reduce timing risk, whilst a more passive approach should result in lower market impact costs.

A price adaptive TWAP algorithm might even adjust its schedule dynamically based on the market price (although arguably this makes it a simple price inline algorithm).

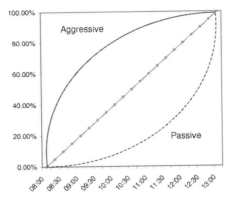

Figure 5-5 Completion rates for a "tilted" TWAP

Special Parameters:

Tracking: Some variants may have custom parameters that allow control over how closely they track the target completion profile. This might just be an on/off switch or actual limits for how far it may go ahead (or behind) schedule (either as a percentage or possibly a cash value). This could even be inferred from an execution style parameter.

Interval frequency: Some versions may allow control over how frequently it trades and whether it uses randomisations to vary the intervals.

Volume Weighted Average Price (VWAP)

The VWAP (volume weighted average price) benchmark for a given time span is the total traded value divided by the total traded quantity. As a benchmark, it rapidly became ubiquitous since it gives a fair reflection of market conditions throughout the day and is simple to calculate. This led to algorithms that tracked the VWAP benchmark becoming extremely popular.

Basic Mechanism

As its name suggests, VWAP is a volume-weighted average, it corresponds to the overall turnover divided by the total volume. Given n trades in a day, each with a specific price p_n and size v_n we can express the daily VWAP as:

$$VWAP = \frac{\sum_n v_n p_n}{\sum_n v_n}$$

Thus, large trades will have more impact on the benchmark price than small ones. Whereas approximating the TWAP was simply a matter of trading regularly throughout the day, for VWAP we will also need to trade in the correct proportions. Though, since these are based on the day's trading volume we do not know beforehand what these proportions should be.

A common solution to this problem has been to use historical volume profiles. These are averages of historical traded volume for fixed time intervals throughout the day. If the day is broken down into j periods then the daily VWAP may be expressed as:

$$VWAP = \sum_j u_j \bar{p}_j$$

where u_j is the percentage of daily volume traded and $\bar{p}_j$ is the average price in each period. Robert Kissell and Morton Glantz (2003) show that the optimal trading schedule to meet the VWAP benchmark may be based on this percentage. In other words, the target quantity x_j for each period j is:

$$x_j = u_j X \tag{5-1}$$

where X is the total size of the order. Hence, we can use this equation to predetermine our ideal trading pattern. This approach has formed the basis for most VWAP algorithms. Note that it clearly assumes that the day's trading volume follows a similar pattern to the historical profile. Provided that the historical profile is based on sufficient data this is a reasonable assumption for many liquid assets. In Chapter 10, we shall discuss historical volume profiles in more detail.

Continuing with our example order to buy 10,000 ABC, Figure 5-6 shows a sample daily VWAP trading pattern. Notice that in this example the trading is dependent on the historical volume profile. It is not affected by the actual market volume or by price changes.

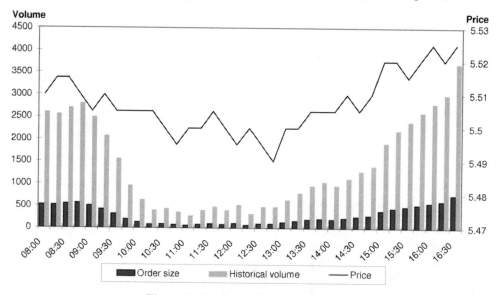

Figure 5-6 An example VWAP order

To see how the trading pattern was determined, Table 5-3 shows the historical volume profile for each fifteen-minute period, together with the target size based on it. For example, from 8:00 to 8:15 the historical volume profile shows an average volume of 2,600, out of a total of 49,780. This corresponds to 5.2%, so using equation 5-1 and given that we are trading for the entire day then our target size for this time period is 520.

Time	08:00	08:15	08:30	08:45	09:00	09:15	09:30	09:45	10:00
Hist Volm	2600	2560	2700	2800	2500	2080	1560	960	640
% of day	5.2	10.4	15.8	21.4	26.4	30.6	33.7	35.7	37.0
Target	520	510	540	560	500	420	310	190	130
Time	10:15	10:30	10:45	11:00	11:15	11:30	11:45	12:00	12:15
Hist Volm	400	440	360	280	400	480	400	520	320
% of day	37.8	38.7	39.4	39.9	40.7	41.7	42.5	43.6	44.2
Target	80	90	70	60	80	100	80	100	60
Time	12:30	12:45	13:00	13:15	13:30	13:45	14:00	14:15	14:30
Hist Volm	480	480	640	800	960	1040	960	1120	1280
% of day	45.2	46.1	47.4	49.0	50.9	53.0	55.0	57.2	59.8
Target	100	100	130	160	190	210	190	220	260
Time	14:45	15:00	15:15	15:30	15:45	16:00	16:15	16:30	
Hist Volm	1400	1920	2200	2400	2600	2800	3000	3700	
% of day	62.6	66.5	70.9	75.7	80.9	86.5	92.6	100.0	
Target	280	390	440	480	520	560	600	740	

Table 5-3 Volume profile data for an example VWAP order

Throughout the day, the trading algorithm then just needs to place sufficient orders in each interval to keep up with this target execution profile. Assuming this is achieved, the resultant chart of percentage completion is shown in Figure 5-7.

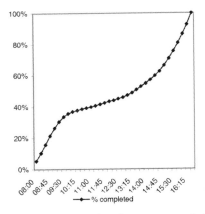

Figure 5-7 Percentage completion for an example VWAP order

Modern VWAP algorithms often incorporate complex logic to determine whether they may get ahead of their schedule, and how best to catch up if they are behind their target. Overall, their performance is based on how well they track the target, but also on how well they predict market volume. Therefore, the way the historical volume profiles are compiled can also have a marked effect. Note for fragmented markets aggregated data may be used.

Broadly speaking, for this example the historical and actual market volumes are reasonably similar, so our trading pattern should be a fair approximation for the day's VWAP (without accounting for market impact and other such slippage costs). Obviously, if the market volume is significantly different to the historical volume profile then performance may well suffer.

Another way of visualising this is to group the day's market volume by its price. For instance, using the same data from our example trade to buy 10,000 ABC, Table 5-4 shows the total market (and historical) volumes grouped by the average price for each hour of the trading day. From this, we can calculate an approximate VWAP for the whole trading day,

$$VWAP = Total\ Value\ /\ Quantity = 332360\ /\ 60300 = 5.5118$$

Instead of using the actual market volumes, we can also calculate a theoretical VWAP based purely on the volumes from the historical profile. This gives a $VWAP_{hist} = 274400\ /\ 49780 = 5.5123$. Hence, in this example our historical volume profile is indeed an acceptable fit, using it to guide our trading patterns results in an average price within one basis point of the daily VWAP.

Price	5.49	5.495	5.5	5.505	5.51	5.515	5.52	5.525	Σ
Mkt Volm	600	2000	4700	14200	11300	8600	11600	7300	60300
Hist Volm	480	1360	3280	10780	10000	7660	9720	6500	49780
Ideal Trade	100	330	780	2350	1870	1430	1920	1210	10000
Hist Trade	100	270	660	2170	2010	1540	1950	1310	10000

Table 5-4 Market and historical volumes from example trade

Common variations

The dependence on historical data means that VWAP algorithms can be vulnerable to sudden shifts in trading volume or liquidity. These can cause considerable deviations from VWAP. Therefore, some versions may also monitor current market conditions. Effectively, this makes them a hybrid between a static VWAP algorithm and the more dynamic volume participation approach.

Some variants may offer a more adaptive approach that tracks short-term price and volume trends and dynamically adjusts their target execution profile accordingly. Though, such customisations mean they are not really true VWAP algorithms anymore.

Special Parameters:

Tracking: Some VWAP algorithms allow control over how closely they track the target completion profile. Usually, this is via custom parameters or just inferred from an execution style parameter.

Start time/End time: These can be specified to trade the VWAP for a specific interval; otherwise most algorithms will default to trading over the whole day.

Trending/Tilting: Generally, VWAP is an acceptable benchmark to trade towards if we have no specific view on the asset's price. But if we expect the price to trend throughout the day then this could prove to be an expensive option. Some versions may provide parameters that let the target execution profile be tilted towards either the start or the end of the day. A more detailed example is given in Kissell and Glantz (2003). Note that it may also be worth considering an alternative algorithm in such cases.

Percent of Volume (POV)

Percent of volume (POV) algorithms "go along" with the market volume; hence, they are also sometimes called volume inline, participation, target volume or follow algorithms. Ideally, the net result should be that if a million shares of XYZ trade in a day then a POV algorithm tracking a 20% participation rate should have executed 200,000 of those.

Basic Mechanism

Unlike algorithms, such as TWAP and VWAP, where a trading schedule may be predetermined, for POV algorithms the trading schedule is dynamically determined. The algorithm tries to participate in the market at a given rate, in proportion with the market volume. For example, Figure 5-8 shows our example order to buy 10,000 ABC using a POV algorithm with a 20% participation rate. Notice that there is no relationship between the trading pattern and the market price. As Table 5-5 shows, the target trade size is driven solely by the observed market volume.

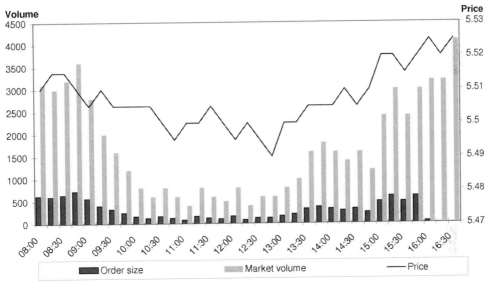

Figure 5-8 An example POV order

Time	08:00	08:15	08:30	08:45	09:00	09:15	09:30	09:45	..
Mkt Volm	3100	3000	3200	3600	2800	2000	1600	1200	..
Target	620	600	640	720	560	400	320	240	..

Table 5-5 Market volume data for the example POV order

Also, notice that the order completes by 4pm. The POV algorithm completes as soon as the market volume allows, or at its specified end time (whichever is sooner). The percentage completion profile is shown in Figure 5-9. In comparison, a VWAP order will spread itself out to take all the available time. Broadly speaking, though, the POV trading pattern still looks fairly similar to the example VWAP order we saw in Figure 5-6. This is because the order represents around a fifth of the day's historical volume, and the historical and market volume profiles are fairly similar. So the example VWAP order from Figure 5-6 is almost a proxy for 20% participation.

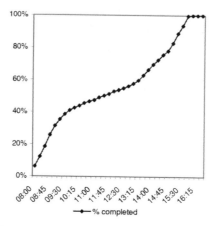

Figure 5-9 Percentage completion for an example POV order

It is important to note that although POV algorithms are dynamic, they still cannot predict market volume. They react to reported trades to keep in line with the observed volume. For instance, Table 5-6 shows a more detailed breakdown of the market trades for our example order, for the 8:15-8:30 time interval, with our executions highlighted.

Time	Trade price	Trade size	Accum. market volume	Target position	Quantity behind
08:16:02	5.56	500	500	100	100
08:19:24	5.56	1000	1500	300	300
08:23:09	5.57	200	1700	340	340
08:25:15	5.55	400	2100	420	20
08:27:06	5.56	300	2400	480	80
08:28:26	5.56	400	2800	560	160
08:29:21	5.56	200	3000	600	0

Table 5-6 A breakdown of the market trades for the example POV order

As we saw in Table 5-5, for this period the market volume is 3,000, of which we would like to be 600. Therefore, by 08:23 when 1,700 of ABC has already traded we would like to have seen 20% of this, or 340. Though, rather than respond to each individual trade we can set trigger points, for instance, we catch up at 08:25 by filling an order for 400. Note that since we are reacting to executed volume, when calculating our actual order sizes we need to adjust our participation rate slightly to account for our own trading. This is because when we see 1,000 has executed, if we then trade another 200, we have changed the overall volume, and so this will not actually be 20% participation any more:

Participation rate = 200 / (1000 + 200) = 16.667%

Therefore, we can approximate the required trade size by using the adjustment factor $1/(1-p)$, where p is our participation rate. In the case of our example order, we actually need $1/(1-0.2) = 25\%$ of each observed new trade (excluding our own trades). For example, when a trade of 1000 has executed, splitting a child order for another 250 gives:

Participation rate = 250 / (1000 + 250) = 20%

This highlights a common concern about POV algorithms: If several are competing for an illiquid asset, they could start driving each other on, like two bidders in an auction desperate to buy the last lot. Potentially, this could lead to significant market impact. To try to protect from such situations firm price limits may be applied to POV orders, since the algorithm itself has no inbuilt price sensitivity. This will at least control the execution price, although it might well lead to the order failing to execute fully.

Another consideration is how the POV algorithm actually responds to reported volume. If it simply splits a new child order each time there is a trade then the resultant trading pattern is nearly as predictable as simple order slicing, as Tom Middleton (2005) highlights. To prevent such signalling risk we can keep track of the target volume and trade more periodically, as we do in the example shown in Table 5-6. Trading in this fashion allows us to vary the order placement, and adjust the aggressiveness of our execution tactics based on how far behind we are.

Similarly, although it is based on real-time data, POV can still be quite a reactive approach. Sudden volume surges are difficult to predict so even if the algorithm has been keeping ahead of the target participation rate, a sharp increase in volume will inevitably put it behind target. If the increase was due to a few large trades, it may well be too late to participate. Hence, most POV algorithms use a variety of safeguards to prevent themselves from chasing volume spikes, such as comparing the target trade size with the currently available volume on the order book. Some versions may allow control over the market volume calculations, either to exclude block prints or to set a maximum permissible trade size. Fragmented markets also complicate things, since there are multiple volumes to track.

As with VWAP algorithms, the performance of POV algorithms depends on the techniques they employ to track their targets. It must be remembered that one of the key goals is to minimise overall market impact. In practice, POV algorithms may well take account of other factors, such as liquidity, to help determine how best they should trade.

Common variations

Some POV algorithms may incorporate forecasting to try and better anticipate the upcoming trading volume. Generally, such approaches are based on a mixture of historical volume profiles, current observed volume and quantitative analytics.

Price adaptive versions of POV algorithms are also starting to appear. These adjust the participation rate based on how the current market price compares to a benchmark. Some variants can even adapt to the relative price changes for other assets, such as sector or market indices or even ETFs.

Corporate buyback programs in the U.S. often use the "safe harbour" provision granted by the SEC's Rule 10b-18, which protects issuers against liability for market manipulation. This mandates strict timing, price and volume conditions, designed to minimise the market impact of repurchases. Some brokers/vendors provide dedicated corporate buyback algorithms that adhere to these requirements. Often these are in fact based on modified POV algorithms. One of the key changes is to add a price condition that ensures the algorithm does not issue orders that end up making the market, so they do not allow their child orders to be priced more than the last trade or the current best bid.

Special Parameters:

Participation rate: Clearly, this percentage is the key parameter for POV algorithms.

Tracking: Some POV algorithms allow control over how closely they track the target participation rate. It may even be possible to dictate how far ahead and behind it can get, so we might allow it plenty of leeway for being ahead, but almost none should it fall behind. Effectively, this becomes a tilting mechanism for the target participation rate. Also for variants that allow a more dynamic adjustment of the participation rate there will need to be additional parameters, which allow us to specify what the benchmark is and exactly how the participation rate should change in relation to this.

Volume filters: These help prevent the algorithm needlessly chasing volume. Some versions allow block trades to be excluded; alternatively maximum trade size limits may be set. In the U.S., some vendors even allow control over whether the volume being tracked is from the primary exchange or a composite volume total for all the common execution venues.

Start time: Note that POV algorithms only track market volume while they are active, they will not try to catch up with volume traded since the open.

End time: Since POV algorithms are driven by market volume not by a schedule, their actual end time is variable. The end time just acts as a firm limit, although there is no guarantee that the order will be completed by then. Conversely, if the market volume spikes then the order could complete sooner than expected.

Must-be-filled: As we saw for end time, the variable nature of POV means that we need to flag if 100% completion is required. This allows the algorithm to change its trading style when it is running out of time.

Limit price: POV algorithms have no intrinsic price dependency; therefore, a firm price limit may be used. Note that although POV algorithms normally track all trading volume when a limit price is applied it should ignore any trades that are out of range of this limit. Otherwise, every time that the price moves back within the limit it will behave as if there had been a sudden volume spike.

Execution style: Some POV algorithms may support an execution-style parameter, which allows fine-tuning of its trading behaviour. A more passive approach may be used to try to achieve price improvement, whereas an aggressive style will track the participation rate more closely. Essentially, this is another form of the tracking parameter. This choice may also be dictated by the asset's liquidity, for instance, for illiquid assets more aggressive trading may be necessary to prevent getting behind its targets.

Minimal impact

Minimal impact algorithms represent the next logical progression from VWAP and POV algorithms. Rather than seeking to track a market-driven benchmark they focus solely on minimising market impact.

Signalling risk is an important consideration for these algorithms. This represents the potential losses due to information that our trading pattern relays to the other market participants. It is dependent on both our order size and the asset's liquidity. Thus, algorithms focus on taking advantage of the facilities offered by "dark pool" ATSs and broker's internal crossing networks as well as using hidden order types to reduce this risk.

Basic Mechanism

The simplest version of a minimal impact algorithm is to route the entire order to a "dark pool" ATS and just leave it there. Although the actual hit ratios on some ATSs can be quite low, so many algorithms may also work a small portion of the order separately to ensure a reasonable level of execution. For example, we might leave 80% on the ATS and trade the remainder using a passive VWAP or POV algorithm, or even a liquidity-driven one. Alternatively, some variants may dynamically adjust the total size available on the ATS each time the algorithm decides to split of another child order. Note that for ATSs, which support conditional orders or IOIs, an indication could be left for the entire order whilst in parallel child orders could be worked in the markets. Therefore, the overall trading pattern is very much dependent on fills from the ATS. Hence, this is much more variable than some of the other algorithms we have already seen, so Figure 5-10 is just one possibility:

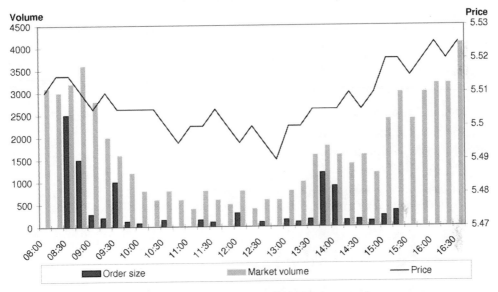

Figure 5-10 An example minimal impact order

The sizable fills in Figure 5-10 correspond to successful crossings on the ATS, which are generally done at the mid price for the main market. The remaining fills correspond to trading on the main market and other venues.

Overall, the completion rate chart for this example looks fairly similar to the ones for the VWAP and POV algorithms, as Figure 5-11 shows. Note that for this example 80% of the order was filled from the ATS. If these fills had not occurred, the algorithm would have had to make up as much as it could on the other venues whilst still trying to minimise impact costs. Thus, it is possible that the order would only have partially completed.

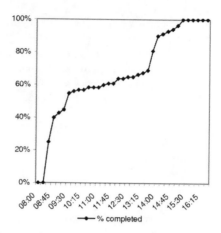

Figure 5-11 Completion rate for sample minimal impact order

Common variations

Some versions may incorporate models to estimate the probability of being filled on the ATS, using this to determine how much of the order should be left there. Likewise, impact cost models may be used to forecast the overall potential cost, which may then be used as a target benchmark. In many ways, there is a lot of crossover between these algorithms and those of the more cost-based ones, which we will review in the next section. Similarly, the stealth-based approaches used to reduce impact mean they share a lot of the same logic as the liquidity-driven algorithms, which we shall see in more detail in section 5.6.

Special Parameters:

Visibility: How much of the order may actually be displayed at execution venues. No visibility implies the order is only worked in "dark pool" ATSs whilst low visibility ensures that only hidden order types or IOC orders are used at other venues.

Must-be-filled: The minimal impact algorithm is focussed solely on reducing this cost at the risk of failing to fully execute, much like a limit order. If there is a requirement to fully fill the order, it may be more appropriate to use a cost-based algorithm instead.

5.5 Cost-driven algorithms

Cost-driven algorithms seek to reduce the overall transaction costs. As we saw in Chapter 2, these are much more than just commissions and spreads. Implicit costs such as market impact and timing risk are important components of the overall cost.

We have already seen that market impact may be minimised by splitting the trading over a long period of time. However, this exposes orders to a much greater timing risk, particularly for volatile assets. Therefore, cost-driven algorithms need to somehow reduce timing risk as well. Figure 5-12 highlights these differing requirements by plotting how the various costs change over time. Clearly, time has an opposite effect on market impact and timing risk.

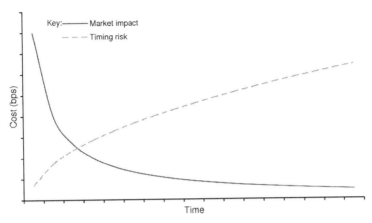

Figure 5-12 Trading strategy costs

In order to minimise the overall transaction costs we need to somehow strike a balance between market impact and the overall exposure to timing risk. As we saw in Chapter 1, this is what Kissell and Glantz (2003) refer to as the trader's dilemma: Trading too aggressively may result in considerable market impact, whilst trading too passively incurs timing risk. In order to strike the right balance we must also take into account the investor's level of urgency, or risk aversion.

Early cost-driven algorithms evolved from impact-driven ones by incorporating factors such as timing risk. Increasingly, though, cost-driven algorithms have been built from scratch using complex market models to estimate potential transaction costs and so determine the optimum trading strategy for each order.

Implementation shortfall represents a purely cost-driven algorithm. It seeks to minimise the shortfall between the average trade price and the assigned benchmark, which should reflect the investor's decision price.

Adaptive shortfall algorithms are just more opportunistic derivatives of implementation shortfall. In general, they are more price sensitive, although liquidity-driven variants are also starting to appear.

Market-on-close algorithms strive to beat an undetermined benchmark, namely the future closing price. Unlike TWAP or VWAP where the average evolves through the day, it is harder to predict where the closing price will actually be. Again, the key goal for this algorithm is to strike a balance between impact cost and timing risk. Effectively, it is the reverse of implementation shortfall: Instead of determining an optimal end time, we need to calculate the optimal starting time.

In the following sections, we will see how each of these handles our example order.

Implementation Shortfall (IS)

Implementation shortfall represents the difference between the price at which the investor decides to trade and the average execution price that is actually achieved. Their decision price acts as the benchmark, although often it is not specified so instead the mid price when the order reaches the broker is used as a default.

Basic Mechanism

The aim of implementation shortfall algorithms is to achieve an average execution price that minimises the shortfall when compared with the decision price. As we saw in Figure 5-12, the key to accomplishing this is to strike the right balance between market impact and timing risk. Often, this means the algorithms tend to take only as long as is necessary to prevent significant market impact.

Since achieving this goal is more complicated, there is a lot more variety in how brokers/vendors tackle implementation shortfall compared to simpler algorithms. As Middleton (2005) reports, some of these algorithms are essentially enhanced versions of VWAP or POV algorithms. These use cost models to determine an optimal trading horizon, which is incorporated as either a model determined end time or an optimal participation rate. Modern versions have often been built from the ground up, to react more opportunistically to price and liquidity.

For simplicity, we shall focus on examples based on an optimal trading horizon. These may be split into two main approaches; one based on statically created trading schedules whilst the other adopts a more dynamic mechanism reacting to market volume.

The first step is to actually determine the optimal trade horizon, which needs to account for factors such as the order size and the time available for trading. It must also incorporate asset specific information such as its liquidity and volatility. In addition, we must also take account of the investor's urgency, or risk aversion. Quantitative models will then be used to take all these factors and derive the optimal trade horizon. Generally, a shorter trade horizon is due to:

- Assets with high volatility, also those with low bid offer spreads
- High risk aversion
- Smaller order size, so less potential impact

We will cover the effects of these factors in more detail in Chapter 7. For the purposes of this section, we shall assume that our example asset ABC is liquid with a moderate volatility resulting in an optimal end time of 14:30 for an order to buy 10,000.

Having calculated the trade horizon our example static version will then determine the trading schedule, whilst the dynamic one will determine the most appropriate participation rate. Since their benchmark is predetermined, both approaches tend to favour trading more at the beginning of an order, while the price is closest to the benchmark, as Tracy Black and Owain Self (2005) note. Hence, a tilt factor may be used to try to shift the trading to the beginning, aiming to reduce the timing risk without causing excessive market impact.

Let's start first with the static version. Broadly speaking, this is similar to a tilted VWAP algorithm. Figure 5-13 shows the resultant trading pattern for an example order to buy 10,000 ABC.

The historical volume profile is used with the optimal end time to determine a basic trading profile. For our example, the historical volume information from 8:00 to 14:30 is used to generate new target percentages for this time window. These are shown for each interval in Table 5-7, labelled as "% of window". With fewer intervals, these targets are all higher, so whilst for the full day VWAP the interval from 8:45 to 9:00 accounted for 5.8% of the total historical volume, now it accounts for 9.4%.

Next, a tilt factor is applied to further increase trading at the start of order. For simplicity, we will use a factor that ranges from 1.3 down to 0.7 and decreases by 0.1 each hour.

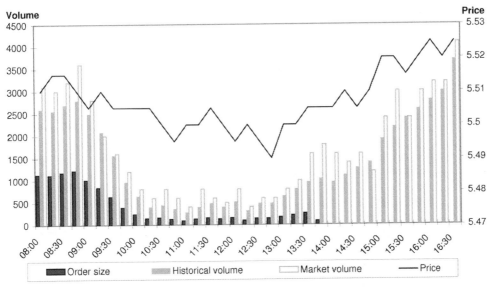

Figure 5-13 An example statically determined IS order

Time	08:00	08:15	08:30	08:45	09:00	09:15	09:30	09:45	10:00
Hist Volm	2600	2560	2700	2800	2500	2080	1560	960	640
% of window	8.7	8.6	9.1	9.4	8.4	7.0	5.2	3.2	2.2
Tilt	1.3	1.3	1.3	1.3	1.2	1.2	1.2	1.2	1.1
Target Volm	1140	1120	1180	1220	1010	840	630	390	240
Time	10:15	10:30	10:45	11:00	11:15	11:30	11:45	12:00	12:15
Hist Volm	400	440	360	280	400	480	400	520	320
% of window	1.3	1.5	1.2	0.9	1.3	1.6	1.3	1.7	1.1
Tilt	1.1	1.1	1.1	1	1	1	1	0.9	0.9
Target Volm	150	160	130	90	130	160	130	160	100

Table 5-7 Trading schedule extract for a static implementation shortfall

Although simplistic, it still gives a reasonable trading profile, as we can see from Figure 5-13, finishing just ahead of the optimal end time. Trading is more aggressive, especially for the first hour, and then it gradually tails off as market volumes decrease around midday.

For a more dynamic approach, the trading pattern may be based on inline participation with the market volume, as we saw for POV algorithms. In fact, an implementation shortfall algorithm using a dynamic mechanism may be likened to a tilted POV algorithm. Figure 5-14 shows an example IS trading pattern generated by a dynamic mechanism. Using the end time of 14:30 the historical volume profile suggests that usually around 30,000 has traded by then. Given our order size of 10,000, this implies an optimal participation rate of 33.33%.

Again, we can apply a simplified tilt factor to this, starting with +3% and decreasing by a percent each hour. Table 5-8 shows some of the resultant targets. The target participation rate is also shown in Figure 5-15.

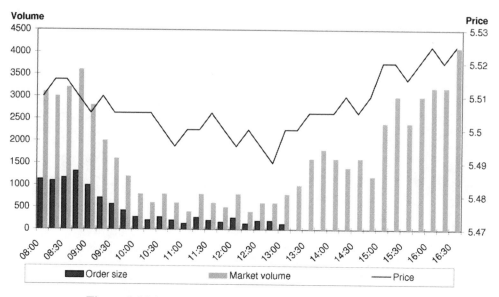

Figure 5-14 An example dynamically determined IS order

Time	08:00	08:15	08:30	08:45	09:00	09:15	09:30	09:45	10:00
Mkt Volm	3100	3000	3200	3600	2800	2000	1600	1200	800
% particip	36	36	36	36	35	35	35	35	34
Target Volm	1130	1090	1160	1310	990	710	570	420	270
Time	10:15	10:30	10:45	11:00	11:15	11:30	11:45	12:00	12:15
Mkt Volm	600	800	600	400	800	600	500	800	400
% particip	34	34	34	33	33	33	33	32	32
Target Volm	210	270	210	130	270	200	170	260	130

Table 5-8 Trading schedule extract for a dynamic implementation shortfall

Note that the high participation rates are chosen to try to magnify the visual effect for this example. In reality, lower rates might often be used; otherwise, there could be considerable signalling risk and market impact. Spreading the order amongst multiple venues would also help.

Because the historical profile is a relatively good fit for the example asset's market volume, both the static and dynamic approaches give similar trading patterns, as can be seen by the similarity between Figure 5-13 and Figure 5-14. However, the dynamic version is more adaptable to changes in market conditions, and as we can see in Figure 5-15 it finishes earlier. This was because the actual market volume was higher than the estimate from the historical volume profile.

Admittedly, these examples use simplistic tilting mechanisms. Still, they both give reasonable approximations for how implementation shortfall algorithms work. Modern versions may employ much more complex logic; incorporating factors such as the asset's volatility or spread and the investor's risk aversion.

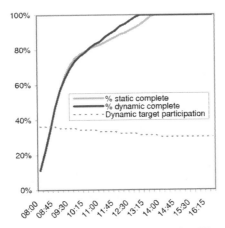

Figure 5-15 Percentage completion for IS orders

To cope with changing market conditions, the trading horizon may be dynamically re-optimised if specific constraints, such as a limit price, are reached, as Middleton (2005a) suggests. The quality of the cost model is also a key determinant for the performance of any given version. In Chapter 10, we shall cover cost models in more detail.

Many of the newer generation of implementation shortfall (IS) algorithms were designed from the ground up, built around intricate market models, which can be used to predict transaction costs. Some may be based on optimal participation rates, although these are constantly adjusted based on market conditions and cost estimates. Other versions achieve the optimal trading strategy by constantly monitoring market conditions, and performing detailed cost analysis before each and every order is placed, as Niall McIntyre (2006) suggests. These more advanced versions cope much better with unexpected conditions. [3] However, under general conditions their resultant trading patterns will probably still be reasonably similar to Figure 5-14.

Common variations

Adapting to market conditions, such as liquidity or price has become a key focus for many algorithms. Price adaptive implementation shortfall algorithms have become sufficiently important that the following sub-section is dedicated to them. IS algorithms which have access to "dark pools" of liquidity are also available.

Volatility is another key factor for IS algorithms. Some versions actually adjust to changes in short-term price volatility; when the volatility falls, they can afford to trade more passively. Other variants may also use alternative estimates for volatility. For example, Instinet's Wizard algorithm uses the implied volatility from the options markets as a more accurate gauge of intraday volatility.

Special Parameters:

Benchmark price: This allows the investor to specify their decision price; otherwise, this generally defaults to the arrival price (midpoint) when the order was received.

---

[3] In Chapter 10, we will see how short-term forecasts may be made for market conditions, such as price and volume.

Risk aversion: This represents an investor's level of urgency. A high-risk aversion suggests that the position is more subject to price risk, so the algorithm will use a shorter time horizon, adopting more aggressive execution tactics. Some versions may only support passive, aggressive or neutral, whilst others may allow a finer grained setting (say from 1-10).

Execution style: Essentially, this is replaced by Risk aversion, although for some variants it may actually provide the risk aversion setting.

End time: This acts as an absolute deadline. Though, as we have seen, many IS algorithms are driven by determining an optimal trading horizon. Note that it is important to check with pre-trade analytics/models that the specified end time is not actually before the optimal time, otherwise performance may suffer.

Limit prices: These are supported, but it is important to note that implementation shortfall algorithms are optimised to work towards their benchmark, which is the arrival price.

Volume limits: In order to minimise timing risk, IS algorithms often start by trading fairly aggressively. Their internal models are trying to balance potential market impact versus this risk. Placing too stringent a volume limit may actually affect the performance of the algorithm. If the volume limit is being used to reduce signalling risk then a minimal impact or liquidity-driven algorithm may be a better choice.

Adaptive Shortfall (AS)

Adaptive shortfall represents a new subclass of algorithms derived from implementation shortfall. The adaptive moniker refers to the addition of adaptive behaviour; predominantly this is a reaction to the market price. Effectively, this means price adaptive shortfall algorithms behave more opportunistically.

A useful naming scheme for price adaptive algorithms was suggested by Robert Kissell, Andrew Freyre-Sanders and Carl Carrie (2005). This is based on the concept of price 'moneyness', taken from options nomenclature.

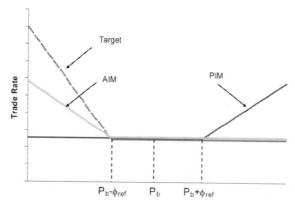

Source: Kissell and Malamut (2005b)   Reproduced with permission from Institutional Investor

Figure 5-16 Comparison of price adaptation trading rates

Figure 5-16 illustrates this by plotting the target trading rate versus the market price for an example buy order. An aggressive in-the-money (AIM) strategy trades more aggressively with favourable prices and less when they become adverse. For a buy order, favourable conditions correspond to when the market price drops below the benchmark, with the opposite for a sell. So in Figure 5-16 its trading rate only increases when the market price falls significantly below the benchmark price (P_b). Whereas a passive in-the-money (PIM) tactic is the opposite, it becomes more passive when prices are favourable. Hence, in Figure 5-16 its trading rate only increases when the price rises significantly above the benchmark.

Note the Target strategy shown in Figure 5-16 is similar to a price-inline algorithm, since it does not account for timing risk, we will cover this further in section 5.6.

Another way of looking at price adaptive strategies is based on how they handle overall price trends. An AIM strategy assumes that trends are short-lived and will soon revert, whereas a PIM approach relies on the trend persisting. Thus, AIM trading will immediately try to take advantage of any favourable prices, and hope that unfavourable prices will revert. Conversely, PIM trading will react aggressively to stem any potential losses from an unfavourable trend, but it will be passive during favourable trends, hoping to achieve further price improvement.

Basic Mechanism

Essentially, this is still an implementation shortfall algorithm, so the basic behaviour will follow an IS approach. But in addition, the algorithm dynamically adapts to market conditions. Effectively, this is like having a tilt function that adjusts in real-time based on the current market conditions.

Initially, a baseline target for volume participation may be determined, based on the estimated optimal trade horizon. During trading, the adaptive portion is then used to modify this rate. The results for an example trade to buy 10,000 ABC using both AIM and PIM approaches is shown in Figure 5-17.

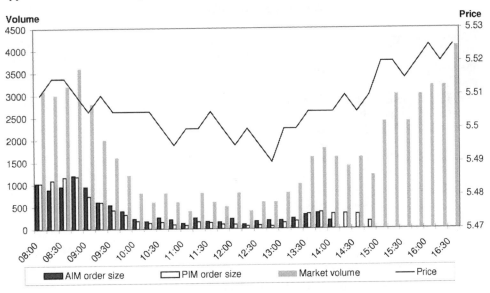

Figure 5-17 Example price adaptive shortfall orders

With an AIM strategy, a favourable price trend will result in additional participation. Some variants may also apply a tilt to encourage earlier trading. For this example, the baseline participation was set as 30%, with the first hour raised to 35%. A short-term momentum indicator was used to vary this by up to 10%, dependent on the price and the trading strategy. Again, these participation rates are chosen to magnify the difference between the two approaches for this example. In reality, these would often be lower and the adjustment would probably depend on the asset's volatility. The effect this has on the target participation rate is shown in Figure 5-18. Clearly, as the price becomes increasingly favourable, from around 10:00, the AIM capitalises on this by increasing its participation rate, whilst the PIM strategy does the opposite. Then, from 11:00 to 12:00 when the price starts to rise again, the reverse happens. Finally, as both orders reach completion the participation rates tail off towards zero.

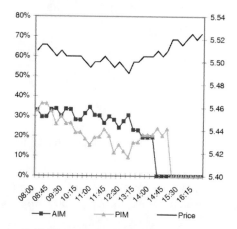

Figure 5-18 Target participation rate adaptations

The overall completion rates may be seen in Figure 5-19. For this example, the market price showed more mean reverting behaviour rather than a consistent trend. Therefore, the aggressive in-the-money approach benefited from this, completing before the passive in-the-money strategy. Had this been a sell order we would have seen the opposite.

Overall, Kissell, Freyre-Sanders and Carrie (2005) found that the AIM strategy achieves better prices, but at a slightly higher risk. The PIM strategy is quicker to cut losses short so achieves a slightly lower risk, but may achieve poorer prices than AIM.

Common variations

Just as these algorithms react to the market price, we could also add behaviour that reacts to changes in the order book depth or overall liquidity measures. Increasingly, they are also accessing liquidity from "dark pool" ATSs.

Special Parameters:

In general, adaptive shortfall algorithms will have the same parameters as implementation shortfall. Obviously, there is one key addition:

Adaptation type: Either aggressive in-the-money (AIM) or passive in-the-money (PIM).

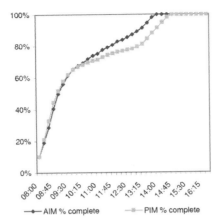

100%
80%
60%
40%
20%
0%

08:00 08:45 09:30 10:15 11:00 11:45 12:30 13:15 14:00 14:45 15:30 16:15

AIM % complete   PIM % complete

Figure 5-19 Percent completion for price adaptive shortfall orders

Note that unlike price inline algorithms there generally is not much provision for parameters to control exactly how much it reacts to actual price moves. This is because fundamentally it is based on an implementation shortfall algorithm. Even though it adapts to market prices, the optimal trading rate is still a function of its balancing market impact with timing risk.

Market Close (MC)

The close price is often used for marking to market, and calculating net asset values and daily returns/profit and loss. Hence, many institutions are still interested in the close price as a benchmark. Though, trading at the close can be costly. David Cushing and Ananth Madhavan (2001) found prices are more sensitive to order flows at the close. They also noted price reversals after days with significant auction imbalances. Whilst call auctions have helped reduce the end of day volatility, the liquidity premium can still be considerable around the close.

Basic Mechanism

Clearly, the main issue for a market close algorithm is the fact that the benchmark is unknown until the end of the trading day. Unlike for VWAP or TWAP it is not an average based on the days trading, so we cannot simply slice the order into portions in an attempt to match the benchmark. If we start trading too early, we could be exposed to a substantial amount of timing risk, due to variability in the closing price. Whereas trading too late may cause significant market impact.

Many market close algorithms determine an optimal trading horizon using quantitative models, which incorporate estimates of an asset's volatility, and trading volume. So just as implementation shortfall algorithms determine an optimal end time market close algorithms can calculate an optimal start time, as Middleton (2005) points out. Figure 5-20 shows the resultant trading pattern for our example market close order.

Assuming a target participation rate of 30%, we therefore need 33,333 of ABC to trade. By working backwards our modified historical model shows that to meet this requirement we should start trading at 11:45, as we can see in Figure 5-20.

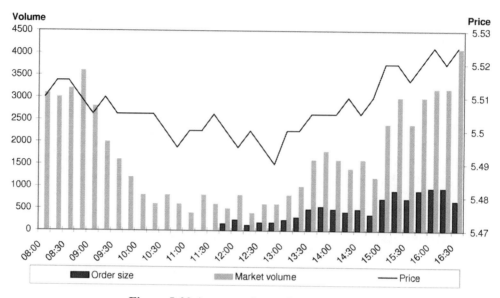

Figure 5-20 An example market close order

Since market close orders are often submitted during trading hours this also enables us to see how today's market volume actually compares with the historical volume profile. For instance, from our example data the opening market volumes appear to be around 15% more than the historical values. Assuming this trend continues we can adjust our historical volume profile accordingly.

For this simple example, adjusting the historical volume profile by 15% gives a good match for the actual market volumes. By targeting a 30% participation rate our order comfortably completes, as shown in Figure 5-21.

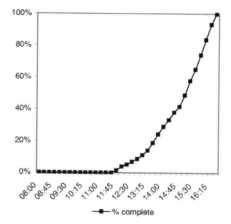

Figure 5-21 Percent completion for a market close order

In reality, we would need to constantly monitor the market volume and adjust the participation rate accordingly. In this example, the price trend is in our favour so there is no real need to tilt the participation rate. Clearly, this will not always be the case so we need to regularly estimate the impact of current market price trends and adjust our participation accordingly. Effectively, this is similar to what a passive in-the-money adaptive shortfall algorithm would do.

Common variations

Some algorithms are now being termed departure price algorithms. These provide a more generic mechanism which will trade to any given end time, rather than just the market close. For example, should we want to ensure a position is achieved by midday we could set the end time accordingly and leave the algorithm to find the optimal start time.

Special Parameters:

In general, market close algorithms will have similar parameters to implementation shortfall, although there are some obvious differences:

Risk aversion: A high risk aversion signifies that the trade is more subject to price risk and so should be traded more quickly. Still, in terms of a market close algorithm, this generally means an optimal start time closer to the market close. Therefore, if there is genuine price risk for an asset it may make more sense to use a shortfall algorithm rather than a market close one.

End time: As noted in the common variations, some versions allow control over the end time, giving a much more flexible approach.

Auction participation: There may also be parameters to specify the minimum and/or maximum order size allowed to participate in the close auction.

5.6   Opportunistic algorithms

Opportunistic algorithms have evolved from a range of trading strategies. They all take advantage of favourable market conditions, whether this is based on price, liquidity or another factor.

Price inline algorithms are essentially based on an underlying impact-driven strategy such as VWAP or POV. What they add is price sensitivity, which enables them to modify their trading style based on whether the current market price is favourable or not. So a focus on market impact has given way to a more opportunistic approach.

Similarly, liquidity-driven algorithms are an evolution of simpler rule-based order routing strategies. The trading is driven by the available liquidity, although cost is also a factor. Whilst pair trading is effectively a market neutral strategy, so risk is less of a concern. Instead, the key driver is when the spread or ratio between the assets is favourable.

Note that for each of these algorithms price is still an important factor. Target benchmarks provide a baseline that allows them to gauge whether the market conditions are favourable or not. Since they are so dynamic, opportunistic algorithms tend to be much more closely aligned to their underlying execution tactics than other algorithms, as we will see in Chapter 9. In the following sections, we shall examine each of the opportunistic algorithms in some more depth.

Price inline (PI)

A price inline algorithm adapts its trading to the market price in a similar way to how POV algorithms adjust to market volume. A benchmark price is defined and trading is then altered based on how the market price compares to this. Note that if no benchmark is specified then the mid price when the order arrives is generally used instead. Clearly, a favourable price for a buy order means the market price is less than the benchmark, with the opposite for sells.

To describe its price-adaptation mechanism, we will reuse the price 'moneyness' naming scheme from Kissell, Freyre-Sanders and Carrie (2005). So, as we saw for Adaptive Shortfall algorithms, aggressive in-the-money (AIM) strategies trade more aggressively with favourable prices whilst passive in-the-money (PIM) tactics behave in the opposite manner. Note that usually when people refer to price inline algorithms they mean an AIM approach, but increasingly there are versions offering both types.

Basic Mechanism

A price inline algorithm consists of a basic trading mechanism combined with the price adaptive functionality. Hence, it could be based on a static VWAP algorithm or a more dynamic percent of volume approach. The actual price adaptation may directly track the difference between the market price and the benchmark, or it might even include other factors such as momentum.

Figure 5-22 shows a simple price inline algorithm, based on an underlying percent of volume strategy. The price adaptation is a straightforward adjustment to the participation rate based on the difference between the market price and the benchmark.

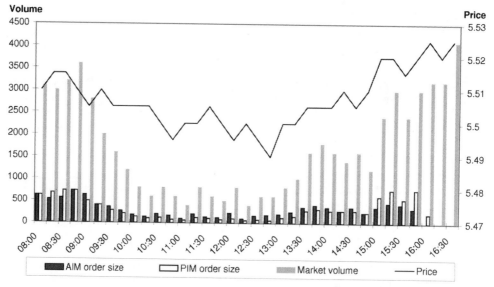

Figure 5-22 Example price inline orders

The reverting price favours early completion by the AIM approach. We can see how the price changes affect the participation rate more clearly in Figure 5-23. As the price becomes increasingly favourable, from around 10:00, the AIM increases its participation rate, whilst the PIM strategy does the opposite.

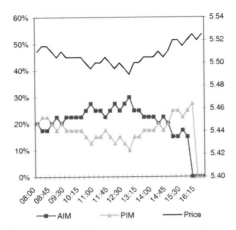

Figure 5-23 Target participation rate changes with price

These continue to oscillate inline with the price changes. Finally, as the AIM strategy reaches completion, its participation rate tails off to nothing. Figure 5-24 shows how this affects the overall completion rates.

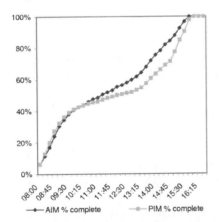

Figure 5-24 Percent completion for example price inline orders

As with the other algorithms, modern variants will differ in terms of they how they respond to being behind their target, and whether they permit going ahead of the target.

Common variations

Some versions may even allow the price adaptation to be based on the price of other assets, sectors, market indices or even ETFs.

Special Parameters:

Adaptation type: Either aggressive in-the-money (AIM) or passive in-the-money (PIM).

Benchmark price: If the benchmark is related to another asset, index or ETF then details will also need to be provided for this to allow the algorithm to make a real-time price subscription for this.

Participation rate: For algorithms based on a dynamic POV type mechanism, a baseline participation rate will be needed.

Participation adjustment: This specifies how much to alter the participation rate by for a given price move, for instance, 5% every $0.50. Note some versions may allow these to be asymmetrical, e.g. +5% for favourable prices, but only -2% for unfavourable ones.

Price levels: These specify the size of price moves for the participation adjustments, e.g. every $0.50 or even every 20 basis points (bps). Again, some variants may allow these to be set separately for favourable and adverse conditions.

Liquidity-driven

Liquidity represents the ease of trading a specific asset, so it has a considerable effect on overall transaction costs. Highly liquid assets tend to trade in greater volume, and so often will have lower spreads and more depth available. Whereas for illiquid assets, activity is much lower, the spread higher and order book may have little visible depth. So finding liquidity is an important means of reducing costs, particularly for illiquid assets.

Originally, liquidity-based trading simply meant making decisions based on the available order book depth, rather than just the best bid and offer. In today's fragmented markets liquidity-seeking has become more complicated. For example, the U.S. equity market has dozens of possible execution venues, with the number continuing to increase. In such an environment, visualising the available liquidity becomes non-trivial. If a trading strategy focuses on just one execution venue, there is a danger that it will miss opportunities on the other venues and so achieve a poorer execution price. Hence, for fragmented markets liquidity aggregation has become an important tool. Essentially, just as multi-broker systems pooled dealer quotes, we gather as much order book data as possible from every venue and aggregate these into a virtual order book. Figure 5-25 shows an example that pools the orders from the primary exchange (Exch-1) and several electronic crossing networks (ECNs) and "dark pool" alternative trading systems (ATSs).

Liquidity aggregation can be as simple as summing the available orders at each price point across all the different venues. For assets such as futures or options, this might also mean accounting for liquidity "implied" from more complex spread strategies. However, as we saw in Chapter 4, venues are increasingly adopting implied order types to make such liquidity more easily available. Still, there are some further complications such as fees and latencies. Venues have their own fee structures, so the algorithm needs to consider this when comparing prices. Latency is also an issue, since any time lag between our orders being sent and processed could significantly reduce the probability of execution.

Given that execution is not guaranteed, it is also important to deal with execution probability when choosing between venues. Notice that in Figure 5-25 the time field has been replaced by a percentage. This represents the overall probability of execution for that volume. For order E1, on ECN-1, we estimate a 70% chance of crossing with this order if we now dispatched an order to sell at 100. This percentage is based on a range of factors, including the probability of cancellation, latency and historical results.

Hidden liquidity is another important consideration. For hidden orders (shaded in Figure 5-25), the probability is primarily based on the likelihood of there being hidden volume at that price. Thus on ATS-1 order H3 corresponds to a 15% probability that this "dark pool"

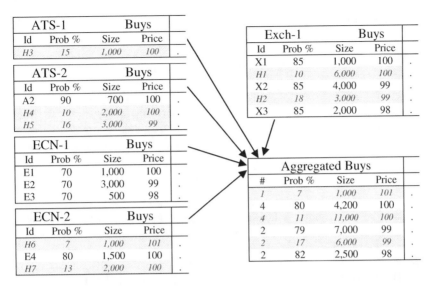

Figure 5-25 Aggregating order data from multiple venues

ATS has a hidden buy order for at least 1,000 ABC at 100. These are all then aggregated into a virtual order book, where the priority is based on price then probability (rather than time). Clearly, when placing orders, preference will be given to venues with the best price and the highest probability of execution.

Finding hidden volume is a case of continually tracking reported trades and matching these to the order book state. When trades are reported with a better price than the order book suggests, this may be due to hidden liquidity. For instance, Figure 5-26 shows the visible order book before and after trades for 2,000 ABC at 100 are reported.

Buys				Sells	
Id	Time	Size	Price	Price	Volume
B3	8:25:00	1,000	100	101	800
B4	8:25:25	500	100	102	1,500
B1	8:20:25	2,000	99		
B2	8:24:09	1,500	98		

(a) before

Buys			
Id	Time	Size	Price
B3	8:25:00	1,000	100
B4	8:25:25	500	100
B5	**8:26:05**	**1,000**	**100**
B1	8:20:25	2,000	99

(b) after

Figure 5-26 Order book before and after trade reports for ABC

The buy orders B3 and B4 only account for 1,500 of the trade; so unless a new order suddenly arrived, 500 was potentially filled from a hidden order. Also, the new order B5 may be the display size for an iceberg order, or it may just be a new standalone limit order. Only by tracking the order book over a long period of time can we start to estimate which possibility is more likely. With more historical data, we can even start to predict what the hidden size might be, hence giving the sort of estimates we saw in Figure 5-25.

So by using historical data and closely monitoring the order book, we can create models for the estimation of hidden liquidity. We can then tailor our order placement strategy to try to take advantage of this. Usually, this is with immediate-or-cancel or fill-or-kill limit orders, so no standing orders are left on the limit book. Sometimes this is referred to as pinging for liquidity, much like a radar or sonar signal. We will go into the mechanics of hidden order placement and seeking in more detail in Chapters 8 and 9.

The last main consideration for liquidity-based algorithms is signalling risk. For illiquid assets, even a small order can result in the price shifting away as other traders try to second-guess our requirements. To counter this, we can adopt a similar strategy of using immediate-or-cancel style (IOC) orders. So when liquidity becomes available an aggressive order is used to cross with it, sometimes referred to as sniping. In order to leave the best price unaffected, some strategies only take a portion of the available size. Alternatively, hidden orders may be used, either iceberg orders or discretionary orders, although these will leave a certain display size on the order book. Again, we will cover this in more detail in Chapter 9.

Basic Mechanism

Liquidity is closely related to market depth and price. Therefore, a liquidity-seeking algorithm will react strongest when there is plenty of market depth and the price is favourable. This is reasonably similar to the aggressive in-the-money style trading we saw for price inline and adaptive shortfall algorithms.

Instead of making the algorithm react to traded volume, we will create a market depth measure that reflects the volume available at a favourable price point. Figure 5-27 shows an example order to buy 10,000 ABC with a liquidity-seeking algorithm using this metric.

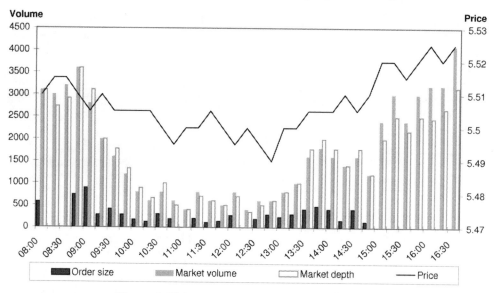

Figure 5-27 An example liquidity seeking order

Therefore, when the price and market depth are favourable, the algorithm trades aggressively to consume liquidity, as may be seen by the participation spikes shown in Figure 5-28. One of the benefits of fragmented markets is that a higher level of participation may be achieved by spreading the execution across a wide range of venues.

Note that this example shows a purely liquidity-driven approach, so when market conditions are unfavourable it then does not trade at all. Hence, the participation falls to zero several times in the middle of the day as the liquidity falls to low levels. It is also zero when

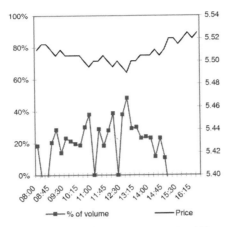

Figure 5-28 Target participation rate for a liquidity seeking order

the price becomes unfavourable, such as towards the close. Though, this could be avoided by setting a looser price limit or target benchmark. Other versions may simply reduce their participation when the price becomes unfavourable, much like a price inline algorithm.

A side effect of this purely opportunistic approach is that in this example the order does not fully complete, as shown in Figure 5-29. In this case, it was due to the price becoming unfavourable, since there was sufficient liquidity. In practice, brokers may well offer versions that support a base level of participation or finish-up logic to help ensure the order executes fully.

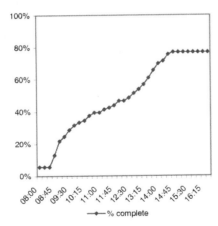

Figure 5-29 Percent completion for a liquidity seeking order

Although liquidity seeking algorithms may be used for any asset, they were originally intended for more illiquid assets and fragmented markets. The example in Figure 5-27 was for a reasonably liquid asset. In comparison, Figure 5-30 shows an example order to buy 10,000 NOP, a much less liquid asset. Again, we can see a similar pattern of comparatively aggressive trading as soon as the price and depth are favourable. With illiquid assets, signalling risk is an even more important concern and more of the liquidity is hidden. Hence,

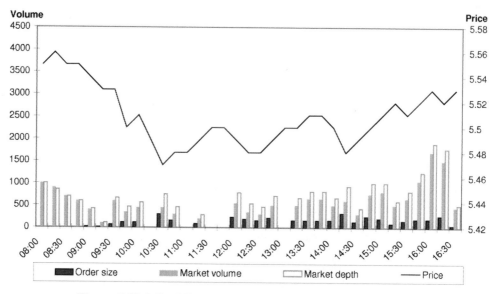

Figure 5-30 A liquidity seeking order for a more illiquid asset

tactics such as seeking and sniping using IOC type orders become important, as we will see in Chapter 9. Also, note that these examples merely give a flavour of how this problem might be tackled. As with implementation shortfall, the complexity of successfully seeking liquidity means there is a lot of variety in how they achieve their goals.

Common variations

Liquidity-driven algorithms are often used in fragmented markets. Clients may want their orders to only participate at specific venues, such as only certain "dark pool" ATSs. In addition, they may (or not) want their orders to be included in the broker's internalisation stream. Brokers/vendors often tailor versions for each client's specific requirements.

Special Parameters:

Visibility: This specifies how much of the order may actually be displayed at execution venues. Low visibility implies hidden order types or IOC orders should be used, alternatively it might mean that the order is only worked in "dark pool" ATSs. Higher visibility may be used to leave orders exposed, trying to encourage trading for illiquid assets.

Benchmark price: This may be used to decide whether the price is favourable enough to warrant participation.

Pair trading

Pair trading involves buying one asset whilst simultaneously selling another. Therefore, this is a market neutral strategy; the risks from each asset should hedge or offset each other. This makes the trading less affected by market-wide moves, provided that the asset prices are sufficiently correlated. The ideal situation is that the asset we bought increases in price, whilst the one we sold falls. Although so long as the profit on one side of the trade outweighs any loss on the other side, we should still come out ahead. The profits may then be locked in by trading the reverse pair to flatten our positions. Note that the timescales involved here could be anything from minutes to days, weeks, months or even longer.

There are two main types of pair trading, namely statistical arbitrage and risk (or merger) arbitrage. Statistical arbitrage is based on relative asset valuations whilst risk arbitrage is more equity specific, it revolves around the probability of a merger happening. A common approach for statistical arbitrage is based on the expectation of mean-reversion. This assumes that the spread or ratio for the prices of two highly correlated assets will generally oscillate around its mean.

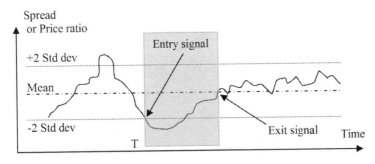

Figure 5-31 An example statistical arbitrage pair trading strategy

As Figure 5-31 shows, when the spread significantly diverts from the mean this signifies a trading opportunity. A typical trade entry signal occurs when we expect the spread to return to the mean; in this case, the band is based on two standard deviations above and below the mean. If the spread continues in this fashion, we can then exit the position at the mean. On the other hand, if it fails to revert and continues to diverge then we stand to make losses. This may be because the assets are not as correlated as we thought, or the relationship between them may have fundamentally changed.

The quantitative methods for identifying pairs for statistical arbitrage are beyond the scope of this book, since algorithmic trading kicks in once the pairs have already been found. For those interested in this topic the book 'Pairs Trading: Quantitative Methods and Analysis' by Ganapathy Vidyamurthy (2004) is a good place to start.

Basic Mechanism

Pair trading algorithms focus on trading for a pre-determined benchmark, which is either the spread between two assets or the ratio of their prices.

The simplest example of a pair trade is based on the spread between two asset prices. When the difference in prices between the two assets exceeds a specified threshold, trading is activated. This may be based on the mid prices, or the bid price for the asset to be bought and the offer price for the asset to be sold, or even all possible combinations.

For example, let's assume that historical data has shown assets XYZ and EFG to be highly correlated, following the trend we saw in Figure 5-31. Sometime after time T, we expect the two standard deviation bands to be breached and the spread and ratio to start to return to their historical means, this breach will be our trigger. Figure 5-32 shows the intraday prices, spread and ratio. Note that the spread shown in Figure 5-32 is an absolute value, it is just the mid price of XYZ minus the mid price of EFG.

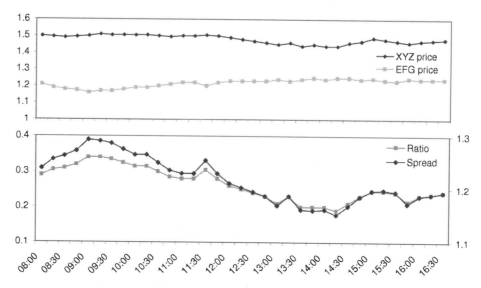

Figure 5-32 Pair spread and ratio for XYZ and EFG

Based on historical data, the trigger spread is 0.24 (mean minus two standard deviations). So we will place a pair trade to buy 10,000 XYZ and sell 12,000 EFG with a spread less than or equal to 0.24. This is shown in Figure 5-33.

Note that the ratio of quantities for our trade is 1.2; this is sometimes referred to as the execution ratio. For this example, it was set based on the current price ratio, but any reasonable value may be used.

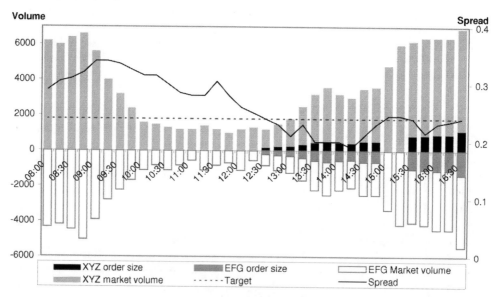

Figure 5-33 An example spread based pair trade

Initially, the spread continues to widen (a separate pair trade may already be taking advantage of this (selling XYZ and buying EFG)). However, just after midday the spread crosses the two standard deviation band, presumably on its way back towards the historical mean. Hence, the pair trade starts executing. Though, notice the blip around 3pm when the spread temporarily increases again, causing the pair trade to pause.

An alternative way of specifying the trade is to use a price ratio as the trigger. Again based on historical data we shall set the ratio trigger as 1.2. Figure 5-34 shows an example order to buy 10,000 XYZ and sell EFG when the ratio is less than or equal to 1.2.

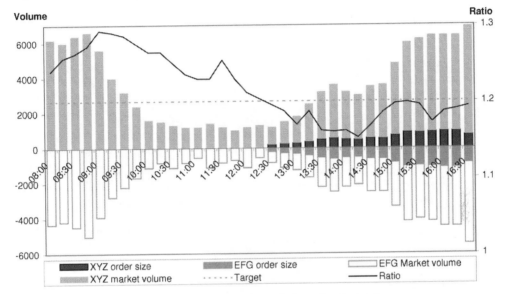

Figure 5-34 An example ratio based pair trade

This time the ratio dips under 1.2 at 12:30 and just stays at or under this for the rest of the day, so there is no interruption to the algorithm. Another difference is that this ratio order is cash balanced, so no execution ratio is used. Instead, each leg of the pair trade is balanced in terms of their value, Table 5-9 shows this more clearly. Note that generally it is more common to specify cash balanced trades in terms of their value, i.e. buy $500,000 XYZ and sell EFG. As its name suggests, the cash balanced order keeps the trade more market neutral than the non-balanced one.

For both these examples, we have kept the trading of each asset closely linked. In practice, this constraint may be loosened, so that each asset may be traded slightly more autonomously. Clearly, it is important for the algorithm to incorporate the liquidity of each asset, since there could be a substantial difference between the two. In such cases, the algorithm will need to make the trading more dependent on the less liquid asset.

Common variations

Risk arbitrage pairs can generally use the same approach as the statistical arbitrage ones. The trading strategy is to sell the shares of the bidding company and buy those of the target company. If the merger happens, the position may then be unwound. The profit is from the difference in spreads; generally the spread is wider before the merger then tightens as the

Time	Spread based trade				Cash balanced ratio trade			
	XYZ		EFG		XYZ		EFG	
	Trade	Value	Trade	Value	Trade	Value	Trade	Value
12:30	180	260	-220	-270	180	260	-220	-270
12:45	230	340	-280	-340	240	350	-280	-340
13:00	260	380	-310	-380	270	390	-320	-400
13:15	350	510	-420	-520	350	510	-420	-520
13:30	470	680	-560	-690	480	690	-560	-690
13:45	530	770	-640	-800	540	780	-630	-790
14:00	470	680	-560	-690	480	690	-560	-690
14:15	440	630	-530	-660	460	660	-530	-660
14:30	530	770	-640	-800	540	790	-630	-790
14:45	530	780	-640	-790	530	780	-630	-780
15:00	0	0	0	0	700	1040	-840	-1050
15:15	0	0	0	0	880	1300	-1050	-1300
15:30	850	1250	-1020	-1250	850	1250	-1020	-1250
15:45	880	1280	-1060	-1320	900	1310	-1060	-1320
16:00	930	1370	-1120	-1390	940	1380	-1120	-1390
16:15	930	1370	-1120	-1390	940	1390	-1120	-1390
16:30	1140	1690	-1350	-1670	720	1070	-860	-1070
Totals	8720	12760	-10470	-12990	10000	14660	-11850	-14700

Table 5-9 Comparison of execution values for example pair trades

deal reaches completion.

Some versions may also support a cash adjustment, which may be applied before the ratio, or spread is calculated.

Special Parameters:

Spread/Ratio: Clearly, this acts as the benchmark for the relationship. Note it is often necessary to specify how it is based, so whether it is an A-B spread or A/B ratio, or B-A or B/A. This can be a useful sanity check to ensure the target is correctly defined.

Order identifier: It may be that each leg of the pair needs to be sent separately, in which case some sort of common identifier is necessary to link the two leg orders.

Legging: This allows control over how autonomously each leg may be traded. A small value will constrain the trading, but will also protect us from exposure to price risk.

Volume limit: In these examples, the participation rate was capped at 25%. Some variants may allow specific volume constraints for each side of the pair trade.

5.7 Other trading algorithms

So far, all the algorithms we have considered are relatively generic, within reason they could be applied to any asset class. Still, there are also some algorithms based on the unique properties of certain asset classes. For example, we have already seen how some brokers/vendors provide algorithms for handling corporate buyback programs (SEC's Rule 10b-18) for U.S. equities, based on modified POV algorithms.

As algorithmic trading continues to expand outside of the equities markets, it must address the common trading problems found in each new market. There will undoubtedly be more asset-class specialisations in the future. Ultimately, these may even take advantage of the fungible nature of some of these assets. For instance, an algorithm might select the optimal bond to trade based on its yield to maturity, or an option based on specific risk factors.

In the near-term some of the areas in which further development is most likely are:

- Multi-leg trading
- Volatility driven trading
- Targeting new benchmarks

Algorithms often mimic existing trading strategies. For bonds and derivatives, this means multi-leg trading strategies such as barbells, butterflies or condors. The fundamental drivers can also vary across different asset classes. Most of the algorithms we have seen so far have focussed on factors such as price, volume or liquidity; but other factors can also be important. For example, derivatives are affected by the price of their underlying assets, as well as interest rates, and volatility estimates. Price shifts may occur even when there does not appear to be a significant change in the levels of liquidity, supply and demand. Trading algorithms must take this into account if they are to maintain best execution. Therefore, algorithms may need to be completely rethought for trading some of these assets. Hence, some options algorithms may be driven by implied volatility levels rather than price. Similarly, new benchmarks, such as the GWAP (gamma weighted average price) may be more appropriate.

Multi-leg

Trading strategies for bonds, futures and options often involve multiple legs. Each leg represents an order for a specific asset. These might be as simple as a two-way spread trade, although they may have three or four legs or be even more complex. However complex they might be, these are still usually relative value trades, seeking to take advantage of differences in pricing between assets. Overall, they go long the currently under valued asset/s, hoping that in the future the prices will rebalance netting us a profit. Essentially, they are much the same as pairs (or spread) trading, although they may consist of baskets (or portfolios) of trades.

For instance, Table 5-10 shows some example trading strategies for bonds. Although these examples have 2-3 legs each, we can view them simply in terms of the overall buys and sells.

Type	*Side A (buys)*	*Side B (sells)*
Coupon Rolls, On/Off the-run	New issue	Current issue
Barbell	Long maturity Short maturity	
Butterfly (Bullet-barbell)	Long maturity Short maturity	Intermediate maturity

Table 5-10 Multi-leg bond-based strategies

Bond positions may be rolled when new issues occur as investors might decide to swap (or roll) their investments into them. In which case they may need to buy the new issue and sell their current position. Investors may also adopt a barbell strategy, by buying both short-term and long-term bonds. Alternatively, they may take a view on interest rates based on the yield curve. For instance, the butterfly strategy shown in Table 5-10 is structured to take advantage of a future increase in curvature. If rates for intermediate maturity bonds rise, the price of our intermediate bonds will fall giving our short position a profit. Conversely, if the yield curve is expected to flatten the opposite positions may be taken.

For futures, spread trading is so well established that most exchanges support dedicated order books just for spreads. In a sense, the spreads are almost treated as assets in their own right. Table 5-11 shows some of the types of multi-leg strategy which may be used with futures contracts.

Type	Side A (buys)	Side B (sells)
Spread (bull)	Nearby contract e.g. JAN09	Deferred contract e.g. MAR09
Butterfly spread (long)	Nearby contract e.g. JAN09 Deferred contract e.g. MAY09	Next contract (x2) e.g. MAR09
Condor spread (long)	Nearby contract e.g. JAN09 Deferred contract e.g. JUL09	Next two contracts e.g. MAR09, MAY09

Table 5-11 Multi-leg futures-based strategies

Spread trades may be calendar-based, such as the example in Table 5-11. They may also be traded between contracts for different underliers, or even contracts from other venues. A bull spread tries to take advantage of increasing prices for the near contract in a typically bullish market. Butterfly spreads are essentially two calendar spreads combined, trading the spread between spreads. In the given example, a JAN-MAR bull spread is combined with a MAR-MAY bear spread. The strategy will benefit if the spread between these widens or becomes more positive. A condor is an extension of this approach with a wider body. From the example in Table 5-11 we now sell two different dated contracts. Again this strategy benefits if the spread widens; conversely, for a short condor the positions would be reversed and it would gain from the spread narrowing. More examples of futures spread trading may be found in a nice overview by the CME (2006a).

Options add extra degrees of complexity since we can buy or sell both calls and puts. In addition, each contract has a specific strike price and maturity. Some example strategies are shown in Table 5-12.

Option spreads may also be strike-based (vertical) as well as calendar spreads. For example, the butterfly and condor long call strategies shown in Table 5-12 are based on calls all with the same expiry, but different strike prices. The payoff for these examples is dependent on the price of the underlying asset staying around the middle strike price. One-sided strategies are also possible since we can buy a put rather than risk writing a call. So the long straddle example will benefit if a marked price shift occurs (in either direction), essentially profiting from volatility. A strangle benefits in a similar way, although this is for prices outside a set range since the put and the call have different strike prices. Options strategies could easily fill a book in their own right. Sheldon Natenberg's (1994) book 'Option volatility and pricing' provides a more detailed review of these trading strategies.

In terms of executing these multi-leg strategies, we could tackle each leg separately. Still, this can expose us to considerable legging risk. For example, we might end up with the desired long position, but only half of the target shorts. Therefore, linking the legs and trading them simultaneously is often a safer option. In some cases this might be as simple as using the linked order types we saw in Chapter 4.

Type	Side A (buys)	Side B (sells)
Call spread (bull)	Call (x1) e.g. Aug 50	Call (x1) at higher strike e.g. Aug 55
Put spread (bear)	Put (x1)	Put (x1) at higher strike
Call ratio spread	Call (x1)	Call (x2) at higher strike
Calendar spread	Call (x1) e.g. Mar 50	Call (x1) at later expiration e.g. Jul 50
Collar	Put (x1)	Call (x1) at higher strike
Butterfly (long) call	Call (x1) at lower strike e.g. Sep 50 Call (x1) at higher strike e.g. Sep 60	Call (x2) e.g. Sep 55
Condor (long) call	Call (x1) at lowest strike e.g. Aug 45 Call (x1) at highest strike e.g. Aug 60	Call (x1) at lower strike e.g. Aug 50 Call (x1) at higher strike e.g. Aug 55
Straddle (long)	Call (x1) Put (x1) at same strike	
Strangle (long)	Call (x1) Put (x1) at lower strike	

Table 5-12 Multi-leg options-based strategies

Alternatively, a dedicated algorithm could offer more sophisticated handling, varying the legging based on both risk and the current market conditions. These multi-leg trading examples may also be viewed as one or two-sided portfolio trades. In Chapter 12, we shall address some of these considerations in more detail when we consider portfolio trading.

Multi-leg trading can also span across asset classes. In Chapter 13, we will review some of these strategies, including both hedging (beta, delta, gamma and duration) and arbitrage (dividend, ADR, indices, futures and options).

Volatility-driven

The algorithms we have considered so far have generally been driven by market conditions for the required asset, whether this is the price, volume or liquidity. However, derivatives are contracts based on an underlying asset, so price moves in the underlying are an important factor. Some brokers/vendors have started to take this into account offering algorithms that can effectively peg to the underlying price.

The prices of options contracts are usually generated by models, which may be based on pricing formulas such as the Black Scholes (1973) model. For instance, a call option's price (C) may be defined as a function of the price of its underlying asset (S) and the time left to expiry (T):

$$C(S,T) = SN(d_1) - Ke^{-rT} N(d_2) \qquad (5\text{-}2)$$

where K is the option's strike price, r is the interest rate and N() is the standard normal cumulative distribution function. The factors d_1 and d_2 are defined by:

$$d_1 = \frac{\ln(S/K) + (r + \sigma^2/2)T}{\sigma\sqrt{T}} \qquad d_2 = d_1 - \sigma\sqrt{T}$$

where σ is the asset's price volatility. Thus, the option's price is dependent on the underlying asset, its time to maturity and interest rates. Note that this is its theoretical price, or fair value. Just as with any other type of asset, the market price will be slightly different from this. These differences reflect the views (and inventories) of the other market participants (dealers). Given that the time to maturity and interest rates are pretty much fixed, this leaves volatility as the main variable. Hence, an alternative way of viewing these price differences is to treat them as differing estimates for the volatility of the underlying asset. By reversing the pricing logic, we can therefore determine implied volatilities based on these market prices. For example, Figure 5-35 shows an order book with September 09 call options for asset EFG with a strike price of 50. The current price of EFG is 47.

Buys		Sells			
Size	Price	Price	Size	Time	Id
50	3.78	3.93	10	9:02:00	S1
		3.98	25	9:02:05	S2
		4.03	20	9:02:19	S3

(a) Prices

	Sells			
	Implied Vol.	Size	Time	Id
.	**25.00%**	10	9:02:00	S1
.	**25.25%**	25	9:02:05	S2
.	**25.50%**	20	9:02:19	S3
.				

(b) Implied vols

Figure 5-35 A sample option order book together with a view of the implied volatilities

Figure 5-35(b) shows how the market prices have been converted back to their implied volatilities. Now let's consider the situation nearly an hour later.

Buys		Sells			
Size	Price	Price	Size	Time	Id
20	3.95	4.09	15	9:51:00	S4
		4.20	5	9:51:45	S5
		4.23	30	9:52:19	S6

(a) Prices

	Sells			
	Implied Vol.	Size	Time	Id
.	**24.50%**	15	9:51:00	S4
.	**25.10%**	5	9:51:45	S5
.	**25.25%**	30	9:52:19	S6
.				

(b) Implied vols

Figure 5-36 A later snapshot of the order book from Figure 5-35

The price of EFG has risen to 47.5, hence the call option prices have also increased. Though, based on implied volatility we can see that order S4 now actually has a slightly lower value. In effect, this order may be viewed as being "cheaper" in terms of volatility. We can explain this by plugging this volatility into the option price calculation together with the original underlying price of 47. This gives an option a price of 3.84, which is considerably less than any of the prices available an hour before in Figure 5-35.

When comparing option prices it is important to remember that they are being driven by a lot of factors. Consequently, traders may prefer to base their decisions on implied volatility rather than just the current price. In turn, brokers and vendors are starting to offer trading algorithms that adopt a similar approach, effectively driving the algorithm from a modified order book, as shown in Figure 5-35(b).

This approach may also be extended to trading option spreads. Effectively, this is similar to what we discussed for pair trading and multi-leg algorithms, just replacing prices with implied volatilities. Note that it is somewhat more complicated than simple pair trading since other risk factors such as time decay will also need to be taken into account.

Basing the trading decisions on volatility also makes it possible to consider trading different contracts. Given that there can be hundreds (or even thousands) of contracts for a specific asset, each of these will have much lower liquidity. By viewing them in terms of their implied volatility, we can potentially fulfil our requirements with other contracts. For instance, in the previous example we might have also traded some August contracts, or some with another strike price. That said, this approach can add further complications, since different contracts can bring exposure to other risks. Therefore if a portfolio of options contracts is being generated it is important to consider the risk factors (or "Greeks") to make sure that there are no surprises in terms of risk exposure.

As algorithms expand further into the derivatives markets, incorporating these risk factors into trading algorithms is likely to become a much more common requirement. In Chapter 13 we will briefly review how some risk factors (such as delta and gamma) may be hedged.

Gamma Weighted Average Price (GWAP)

Implementation shortfall has become ubiquitous in the equities markets, although there is still a large contingent of traders and investors who also track benchmarks such as VWAP. Still, VWAP is not necessarily a universal benchmark, particularly for fragmented markets or illiquid assets. The Gamma Weighted Average Price (GWAP) is an alternative benchmark outlined by Scott Larison (2008). It is designed to tackle some of the shortcomings of VWAP for the options markets: A single asset may have thousands of related options contracts, so the liquidity of any one contract will generally be significantly lower than that of the underlying asset. As Larison points out, this lower trading activity makes benchmarks like VWAP less meaningful for options. A further complication is the fact that complex multi-leg strategies represent a considerable volume in the options markets. Thus, prices may also be influenced by those of other contracts. So the GWAP benchmark also takes into account the VWAP of the underlying asset. It may be represented as:

$$G_{wap}(call) = P + [\Delta' * \lambda_{roc}] \qquad G_{wap}(put) = P - [\Delta' * \lambda_{roc}]$$

where P is the option price, Δ' is the adjusted delta and λ_{roc} is the rate of change price. In turn, the rate of change price (λ_{roc}) is based on the VWAP of the underlying asset:

$$\lambda_{roc} = S_{vwap} - S_0$$

where S_0 is the reference price of the underlying asset, for example, the arrival price or the previous close, and S_{vwap} is the VWAP average for the specified interval.

The delta is one of the "Greeks"; it is a measure that represents the risk in terms of price moves by the underlying asset. [4] A delta of 1.0 means that for every rise (fall) of $1 in the underlying asset the option's price will also rise (fall) by $1. Conversely, a negative delta means that the option's price moves in the opposite direction. In the GWAP calculation, the adjusted delta (Δ') is based on the option's implied delta (Δ) and gamma (γ) from when the order was entered:

$$\Delta'_{(call)} = \Delta + (\lambda_{roc} * \gamma) \qquad \Delta'_{(put)} = \Delta - (\lambda_{roc} * \gamma)$$

Gamma is a second derivative risk measure. It quantifies how much the delta will change when the underlying asset's price moves by one unit, e.g. $1. For example, let's consider a call option priced at $6 with a delta 0.5 and a gamma of 0.1. When the underlying asset price increases by $1, the delta means the call option will increase to $6.5, whilst its delta will increase to 0.6 because of the gamma. We shall cover both of these in more detail in Chapter 13 in the review of delta and gamma hedging strategies.

Larison (2008) goes on to give an example of how the GWAP may be calculated. Based

---

[4] The delta for a call is actually $N(d_1)$ from equation 5-2.

on this, let's assume that the underlying asset ABC starts with a benchmark price (S_0) of $45.0. Throughout the day from 9:30 to 4:00pm, it achieves a VWAP of $46.00. The price of a September 09 call option with a strike of 50 starts out at $2.15, with an implied delta of 38% and a gamma of 4%.

Therefore the rate of change of price: $\lambda_{roc} = 46.0 - 45.0 = 1.0$.

The adjusted delta: $\Delta' = 38\% + (1.0 * 4\%) = 42\ \%$.

Giving a GWAP for our call option: $G_{wap} = \$2.15 + [38\ \% * 1.0] = \$2.53$.

Consequently, the target benchmark is based on the price moves in the underlying asset rather than those from the option market.

The CBOE have partnered with Pipeline to provide a benchmark crossing based on the GWAP. If this proves successful we may well start to see option algorithms trying to track the GWAP in real-time.

As algorithms continue to spread to more markets we may well see other new benchmarks being adopted.

5.8   Summary

- A trading algorithm is simply a set of instructions used to execute an order.

- Trading algorithms may be broadly categorised into three main groups based on the target objectives. These are impact-driven, cost-driven or opportunistic.

- Impact-driven algorithms seek to minimise the overall market impact costs, usually by splitting larger orders into smaller child orders.
    - TWAP (time weighted average price) is often driven by a time-based schedule.
    - VWAP (volume weighted average price) often uses historical volumes as a guide.
    - Percent of volume (POV) algorithms "go along" with the market volume.
    - Minimal impact algorithms use ATSs and "dark pools" to reduce signalling risk.

- Cost-driven algorithms aim to reduce the overall trading costs.
    - Implementation shortfall (IS) seeks to achieve a balance between cost and risk.
    - Adaptive shortfall algorithms extend this, adapting to the market price (or liquidity).
    - Market-on-close algorithms target the future closing price.

- Opportunistic algorithms strive to take best advantage of favourable market conditions.
    - Price inline algorithms are price-sensitive variants of impact-driven algorithms.
    - Liquidity-driven algorithms are an evolution of simpler rule-based order routing.
    - Pair trading is a market neutral strategy driven by a favourable spread or ratio.

- Most of these algorithms will work across asset classes. Still, the unique features of some asset classes mean that completely new types may also be needed. For instance:
    - Multi-leg trading for bonds and derivatives
    - Algorithms driven by factors such as interest rates or volatility
    - Handling fungible assets, so specification-based trading rather than explicit assets
    - Targeting new more appropriate benchmarks

Chapter 6 ————

Transaction costs

Transaction costs can have a significant effect on investment returns. Therefore, it is important to both measure and analyse them if "best execution" is to be achieved.

6.1 Introduction

Each time an asset is bought or sold transaction costs are incurred. In economic terms, Robert Kissell (2006) describes them as costs paid by buyers, but not received by the sellers. They can have a considerable effect on investment returns, for instance, Ed Nicoll (2004) estimated total annual transaction costs of approximately $120 billion for the $12 trillion U.S. equity market. This is based on costs per order ranging from 20 basis points (bps) up to 200 (or 2%) of the value. The wide range is partly due to the different characteristics of each asset and order, but is also due to the different ways transaction costs may be assigned.

One of the most common ways to examine transaction costs has been to compare the actual performance of a portfolio with its "paper" equivalent. A paper portfolio is simply a virtual portfolio traded at benchmark prices, but without accounting for any costs.

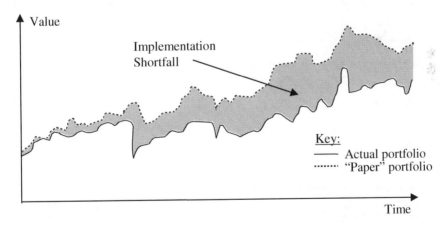

Figure 6-1 Comparing the performance of a portfolio

The difference in performance between a portfolio and its theoretical "paper" equivalent was termed the "implementation shortfall" by André Perold (1988), as shown in Figure 6-1. Alternatively, this is sometimes referred to as "slippage".

A specific example of the impact of transaction costs is given by David Leinweber (2002) for the returns of a fund based on the Value Line portfolio. The Value Line Investment Survey is a weekly stock analysis newsletter focussed on the U.S. Between 1979 and 1991 the paper portfolio achieved an annualized return of 26.2%, whereas the actual fund actually managed 16.1%. Much of this difference is directly attributable to transaction costs, since the fund made the same trades as recommended in the newsletter. [1]

Whilst transaction costs are inevitable, they can be minimised. Therefore, in order to maximise investment returns it is important to accurately measure transaction costs and to analyse them to understand how and why they occur.

6.2 The investment process

Transaction costs span the entire investment process. They may be tracked from the initial decision to buy/sell an asset through to the actual orders and executions that achieve it.

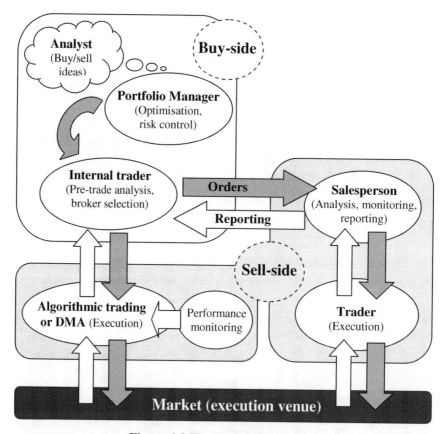

Figure 6-2 The investment process

---

[1] Leinweber notes that some of the shortfall was due to enforced delays before trading, ensuring that the fund did not front-run the newsletter subscribers.

Figure 6-2 shows a simplified view of the process, covering both traditional broker trading as well as algorithmic / DMA execution: The initial source of each order lies on the buy-side, with an investment buy or sell idea. The potential impact on the investment portfolio is then modelled by the portfolio manager, who will use optimisation techniques and risk analysis to determine the set of target positions. An internal trader must then identify the best way to trade these orders. [2] This is achieved by estimating the potential transaction costs, as well as considering historical broker performance. Having decided on the most appropriate means of trading, the orders are then routed for execution. Most commonly, this will mean sending them to a sell-side institution, from where they will be sent out to the market. This may be achieved via a salesperson/trader or by an algorithmic trading/DMA process. [3] Finally, executions from the market will complete the order and trade reports will be sent back to the buy-side.

An alternative way of viewing this process is to consider the whole investment cycle, as highlighted by Ananth Madhavan (2002). Rather than focussing on the individuals involved, it emphasises the cyclical nature of the investment process, shown in Figure 6-3. Trade execution is driven by the investment strategy, but it also gives important feedback, which may affect future investment decisions.

Source: Madhavan (2002b)   Reproduced with permission from ITG Inc. and Institutional Investor

Figure 6-3 The investment cycle

Clearly, transaction cost analysis is an important part of the investment process:

- Pre-trade analysis concentrates on estimating potential transaction costs. Hence it is a key input into the choice of trading strategy and can have a substantial effect on the overall execution (and so investment) performance. Liquidity analysis may also be used to identify the best strategies and venues for trading.

- Post-trade analysis focuses on execution performance and measurement of transaction costs. It is essential for understanding the effectiveness of both the investment ideas and their implementation. In turn, this performance is an

---

[2] Note that some of these different roles may be adopted the same person depending on the size of the organisation.
[3] Salespeople are increasingly becoming sales/traders, able to route orders directly to trading algorithms.

important consideration when new investment strategies are formulated. For example, an investment opportunity worth 30 basis points may not be worth following up if previous transaction costs for similar orders have been around this level.

Historically, most of the early research on transaction costs focussed on post-trade analysis. Though, over the last few years pre-trade analysis has become ever more important. In particular, algorithmic trading is often reliant on pre-trade models in order to achieve more cost efficient execution.

In order to compare the various components of transaction costs, throughout this chapter we will use the following example trade.

Example 6-1: A decision to buy 50,000 of asset XYZ, its mid-price and our executions are all shown in Figure 6-4.

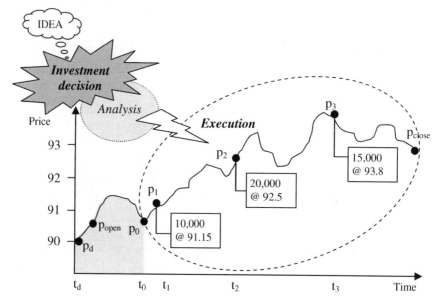

Figure 6-4 A plot of trading price and executions for the order in Example 6-1

As we can see in Figure 6-4, the investment decision to buy XYZ is made when the price is at p_d, which happens to coincide with the previous day's closing price of 90. After analysis, an order to buy 50,000 is dispatched to a broker at time t_0, which (for simplicity) is filled by three separate child orders. The child orders execute at times t_1, t_2 and t_3. The first two executions are for 10,000 at an average price of 91.15 followed by 20,000 at 92.5, and are reasonably close to the best market price at those times. The third order, of 15,000, caused more impact and so achieved a poorer price of 93.8. Note that these example executions are just intended to help highlight the various types of transaction costs; they are not linked to any specific type of trading strategy or algorithm.

Immediately from Figure 6-4 we can see two distinct phases, the pre-trade period and the actual execution. The pre-trade period lasts from t_d to t_0 when the order is dispatched to a broker, whilst the execution phase lasts from t_0 to the order's completion, or in this case, the day's close since the order is not fully executed. The strong price trend is also obvious, rising steadily, from opening at 90.5 to finally closing at 93.0.

The following sections provide a more comprehensive description of both pre and post-trade analysis, together with a detailed breakdown of how transaction costs are formed, using this example trade. For even more detailed coverage of transaction cost analysis it is well worth referring to 'Optimal Trading Strategies' by Robert Kissell and Morton Glantz (2003).

6.3   Pre-trade analysis

Pre-trade analysis is important to ensure that best execution is achieved. These analytics help investors or traders make informed decisions about how best to execute a given order.

Most brokers/vendors provide a considerable amount of general reference information. This may be as simple as the associated country and currency, or it may be more asset specific. For instance, for equities they may provide fundamental information such as the market capitalisation and the various investment ratios (e.g. price to earnings (P/E), price to book (P/B)), together with any relevant sector and index data. Similarly, for bonds, they may provide the bond's yield and duration, as well as details of its credit rating, issue size and any relevant terms and conditions.

Table 6-1 outlines the data that is key to trading strategy selection. Essentially, this consists of prices, liquidity measures and data for risk analysis and cost estimates.

Type	Data
Prices	Market prices, Price ranges, Trends/momentum
Liquidity	Percentage of ADV, Volume profile, Trading stability
Risk	Volatility, Beta, Risk exposure
Cost estimates	Market impact, Timing risk

Table 6-1 A summary of key pre-trade analytics data

The liquidity and risk estimates highlight the expected difficulty of trading. The cost estimates give a reasonable indication of what might be achieved. This is particularly important for algorithmic trading, since it gives us an idea of how suitable the order is for a given strategy. Prohibitive risk or cost estimates mean that it is worth discussing the order directly with a broker or trader since manual execution may be the best option. In Chapter 7, we shall see how we can use these cost and risk estimates to try to select the optimal trading strategy for a specific order.

Price data

A wide range of price data is useful for pre-trade analytics. The current market bid and offer prices, or a recent snapshot, act as a baseline for what we might achieve. The last traded price is also useful, particularly for illiquid assets, since this may be significantly different from the current quotes. The bid offer spread provides an estimate for the cost of immediacy. Historical average spreads allow us to gauge whether the current spread is unusual.

Price ranges, such as the difference between today's high and low prices, give an indication of the current price volatility. Likewise, benchmarks such as today's opening price or last night's close are also useful. Trends may be reflected by daily, weekly or even monthly percentage changes.

Liquidity data

Liquidity is closely related to transaction costs. Trading volume offers a simple way to rate the liquidity of a given asset. The average daily volume (ADV) is often calculated for the last 30 or 90 days. The percentage of ADV represents our order size as a fraction of this volume. Hence, we can gauge how difficult it may be to work any given order. For instance, anything less than 20-25% should be achievable within a day; however, anything over this could have a more significant effect on the market.

An estimate of the required trading horizon may be based on the ADV, together with a factor (α) which represents our desired trading rate:

$$\text{Horizon} = \text{Size} / (\text{ADV} * \alpha)$$

For example, given an order size of 50,000 with an ADV of 1,000,000, if we do not want to participate in more than 10% of the market volume then the required time is:

$$\text{Horizon} = 50,000 / (1,000,000 * 0.1) = 0.5 \text{ days.}$$

At 10% participation, it could take us half a day to complete the order, whilst if we are only prepared to be 5% it could take the entire day.

Clearly, for such estimates to be reliable it is important that the actual trading volume closely matches the historical volume profile. Kissell and Glantz (2003) quantify this by adopting a coefficient of variation (CV), which is based on the standard deviation σ (ADV):

$$\text{CV} = \sigma(\text{ADV}) / \text{ADV}$$

The trading stability is inversely related to this coefficient, so a high value of CV implies that sizeable variation from the historical average is possible.

Provided the trading activity is reasonably stable we can estimate what today's trading volume might be just by comparing the volume so far with the historical profile. If the market has only been open an hour and the days volume is 50% higher than the historical average then this may well continue for the rest of the day, in which case we need to resize the volume profile. Obviously, in such cases it is also important to check whether there is any news that may be driving this additional volume.

As we will see in Chapter 10, a range of factors can have an impact on the expected volumes. For instance, Kissell and Glantz (2003) note the importance of the day of the week for U.S. equities: Mondays generally see below average volumes whilst Wednesday and Thursdays see slightly above average ones.

The average trade size can also sometimes be useful, particularly if the order is to be worked manually. This acts as a simple guide to prevent signalling risk; if the order is significantly larger than the average trade size then it is worth splitting it or using hidden orders.

Risk data

Volatility is a key variable for estimating how much risk we may be exposed to. It is based on the standard deviation of price returns, often for the last 3 or 6 months. As we have already seen, a high volatility implies a considerable amount of timing risk. Therefore, more aggressive trading strategies will generally be used to counteract this.

Market risk may be measured using an asset's beta, which is a measure of its sensitivity to market returns. A positive value means that the asset price moves in the same direction as the market whilst a negative one means it behaves in a contrarian fashion. [4] A beta of 1 means that the asset price moves in line with the market, so if the market as a whole drops 10% then the asset price will do the same. A beta of greater than 1 means the price response is magnified, so a beta of 2 would drop 20%, whilst a beta of 0.5 would only drop 5%. Note we shall cover other portfolio risk metrics in more detail in Chapter 12.

Transaction cost estimates

Transaction cost models generally provide an estimate for the overall cost as well as detailing the major cost components such as market impact and timing risk. These are detailed in section 6.5.

The basis for many transaction cost models is a framework suggested by Robert Almgren and Neil Chriss (2000). This uses a random walk model to estimate the current market price in terms of permanent market impact, price trending and volatility. Chapter 10 provides a more in-depth review of these cost-estimation models.

In terms of asset selection, given two assets with similar expected returns it is logical to trade the one that has the lower expected transaction costs. Exactly the same may be said for comparing various types of trading strategy, whether it is using a crossing system, a trading algorithm or DMA. Detailed pre-trade analysis is still required (to ensure the latest market information is incorporated in any decisions); however, historical cost data may certainly also be used to guide the selection decision.

Cost estimates are an important guide to the difficulty of an order. For instance, if the timing risk estimate is significantly larger than the market impact forecast then it is worth considering a more aggressive trading strategy. Conversely, a larger market impact may suggest adopting a more passive style. In Chapter 7, we will see how these decisions affect algorithm choice.

6.4   Post-trade analysis

The historical results of post trade analysis act as a measure of broker/trader performance; they may also inform both investment and execution decisions.

Clearly, there is a lot more to transaction costs than fees and commissions. Past performance is therefore an important tool for comparing the quality of execution of both brokers and individual traders. Unbundling research fees has also made it easier for investors to link costs to the execution, and so use post-trade analysis to accurately compare broker performance.

Breaking the costs down into their components allows us to see where and how the costs (or slippage) actually occurred. Detailed measurement helps to ensure that future efforts for cost reduction are focussed on the correct stage of the investment process. It may also be used to guide the execution method selection. For example, high timing risk and/or opportunity cost suggests that the trading may have been too passive.

Performance analysis

How can we tell if a broker/trader is skilful or lucky? Similarly, how can we know whether a certain broker's VWAP algorithm performs better than another's? Performance analysis is an important tool for post-trade comparison of broker/trader/algorithm results.

Benchmark comparison is probably the most widespread tool used for performance

---

[4] Note it can sometimes be hard to find assets with a negative beta (except over a short time period).

analysis. This simply means selecting an appropriate benchmark and then comparing the average execution price with it. In theory a good performer should, on average, match (or beat) the benchmark.

Still, benchmarks are not perfect; in particular, difficulties can arise when using them to compare performance across assets and over time. So after a brief review of the major benchmarks we shall also consider an alternative metric proposed by Robert Kissell (1998). This is the Relative Performance Measure (RPM), which assigns each trade a percentile ranking compared to the rest of the market. This makes it much easier to compare performance across a range of assets as well as over time. It can also allow for price trends and other market conditions.

Benchmarks

A good benchmark should be easy to track and readily verifiable, it should also provide an accurate performance measurement. Table 6-2 shows the various benchmarks grouped in terms of when they may be determined.

Benchmark		Results for Example 6-1	
Type	Name	Benchmark Price	Relative performance (bps)
Post-Trade	Close	93.00	37
	Future Close (next day)	94.00	137
Intraday	OHLC	92.00	-63
	TWAP	92.20	-43
	VWAP	92.40	-23
Pre-Trade	Previous Close	90.00	-263
	Opening Price	90.50	-213
	Decision Price	90.00	-263
	Arrival Price	90.65	-198
Average execution price		92.63	n/a

Table 6-2 Types of benchmark

Post-trade benchmarks, such as the day's close, will not be known until after the trading has been completed. In comparison, pre-trade benchmarks, such as the previous close or the opening price, are known before the day's trading even commences. Intraday benchmarks, such as VWAP, need to be recalculated as the day progresses. For those that span the whole trading day, the definitive value will not in fact be known until trading has completed. Hence, trading with an intraday or post-trade benchmark usually requires some extra work. An interim value for the benchmark (intraday) or prediction (post-trade) will need to be maintained so that intraday performance may be monitored.

To allow comparison, the benchmark prices and performances from Example 6-1 are quoted separately in Table 6-2. For example, if we compare the average execution price to the closing price for our execution:

Close price   = (92.63 - 93) * 45,000 = $16,500
                = (16,500/4,500,000) = 0.37% or 37 bps (basis points)

To convert into basis points we can divide by the value of our overall order. Note that this was for 50,000 XYZ based on a decision price of 90 (rather than the 45,000 we executed).

These values may be viewed in turn to evaluate the performance of the example trade. Positive relative performances are good, therefore the example appears to have done well compared to the post-trade benchmarks. Conversely, it seems to have fared less well in terms of the intraday and pre-trade benchmarks. The following sub-sections outline each of the benchmarks in more detail.

Note that Example 6-1 has been specifically designed to highlight the different potential costs; hence, it has missed some of the benchmarks by over 200 basis points (bps). In section 6.6 we shall look at actual reported transaction costs from some of the world's markets.

Post-trade benchmarks

Generally, these are based on closing prices, whether they are for the current trading day or for some time in the near future. Their popularity as a benchmark is due to the fact that the closing price is often used as a milestone for marking to market and for profit and loss (P&L) calculations. Future close prices may be used to retrospectively analyse performance. They provide a benchmark that is easy to determine and widely used. Though, in terms of a performance measure, they merely act as a milestone.

Markets tend to be more active at the close so prices are less reflective of actual market conditions throughout the day. In particular, if the asset's price is trending then orders completed earlier in the day will be compared with a benchmark price that is substantially different to that at the time of execution. Thus, an unfavourable price trend may make buy or sell orders look to have performed well; conversely, a favourable trend may make them appear to have performed poorly.

Post-trade benchmarks also tend to encourage trading closer to the end of the trading day. Unfortunately, the closing period is exactly when asset prices may be most sensitive to order flow, as demonstrated by Cushing and Madhavan (2001). This can expose an order to unnecessary timing risk and also to more volatile conditions. Whilst call auctions can reduce end of day volatility there can still be a considerable premium for traders requiring liquidity at the close.

For a trader or algorithm trying to track a post-trade benchmark, generally the goal will be to achieve (or beat) the closing price. Therefore, unless the trading strategy is simply to participate in the closing auction they will need to use a predicted price as a guideline. This price will need to be regularly updated, for instance, notice how the price trails off towards the close in Figure 6-4.

In terms of our example order, the price trend makes it appear to have performed well. The average price achieved for Example 6-1 is 92.63, beating the close by 37 basis points. Assuming the trend continues for the next day, to close at 94, means it performs even better versus this future close price. However, even better performance could have been achieved by tilting the execution towards the beginning of the day, when prices were lower. In terms of benchmarks, this only becomes evident by looking at the previous close price of 90. So although closing prices might be a popular benchmark, in isolation they are not the best means of performance analysis.

Intraday benchmarks

These use average prices to try and more accurately reflect the intraday market conditions.

The OHLC (Open High Low Close) average has often been used as a proxy for the mean market price. Though, its popularity has waned as improved access to time and sales data has allowed more accurate calculations. Clearly, as an average of only four data points it may be easily distorted by extreme values.

The TWAP (Time Weighted Average Price) benchmark is an average of all the observed trade prices over a set period. Equal weighting is given to all trades, so small trades at extreme prices can have a large effect on it. Generally, TWAP is used where trade volume data is not available.

The VWAP (Volume Weighted Average Price) benchmark arguably gives the fairest indication of how the market price has moved over the time span. This average weights each trade price by its corresponding size. The VWAP for a given period is the total traded value divided by the total traded quantity. Consequently, small trades at extreme prices will have much less effect; instead, the average will be dominated by the largest trades.

A trader or algorithm trying to track the TWAP or VWAP will need to frequently recalculate the benchmark price to incorporate new market information. Since post trade information has become more widely available VWAP has become one of the most popular benchmarks, due to the accuracy of its intraday performance.

The VWAP benchmark is not perfect, though, particularly for large orders. Institutional investors frequently need to trade large quantities, for example, consider trading an order equal to the average daily volume (ADV) of asset XYZ. The order would represent so much of the day's trading that the VWAP has practically no meaning in terms of performance. In fact, the same may be argued for anything over 30% of the ADV. Tracking the VWAP also tends to encourage trading to be spread out over time, reducing the overall market impact, but exposing the order to considerable price risk. For instance, let's assume half an order is worked throughout the first day, achieving an average price close to the current VWAP. Based on the benchmark, the performance so far is good, so the temptation is to leave the rest of the order for the next day. However, in terms of overall costs it may have been more advantageous to fully execute the order on the first day, despite any additional market impact. For assets which are volatile or for which there is a strong adverse price trend tracking the VWAP may even lead to poorer overall performance. Likewise, for small orders, it may not be appropriate to spread the execution out over a long time.

In terms of the performance for Example 6-1, the following table shows an aggregated view of the trading volumes throughout the day grouped by execution price.

Price	90.50	91.00	91.50	92.00	92.50	93.00	93.50	94.00		Σ
Size	25,000	20,000	15,000	10,000	30,000	50,000	40,000	10,000	200,000	
# Trades	5	3	2	2	4	5	4	2	27	
Value $k	2,262.5	1,820.0	1,372.5	920.0	2,775.0	4,650.0	3,740.0	940.0	18,480.0	

Table 6-3 Aggregated price and volume data for Example 6-1

Using this data the intraday benchmarks may be calculated as:

$$\text{OHLC} = (90.5+94+90.5+93)/4 \qquad = 92.00$$
$$\text{TWAP} = (5*90.50 + 3*91.00 + 2*91.50.....)/27 \qquad = 92.20$$
$$\text{VWAP} = (18{,}480{,}000/200{,}000) \qquad = 92.40$$

In comparison with the others, the VWAP benchmark best represents the average market conditions throughout the day. Its higher price corresponds to the greater impact from the increased trading volumes at 93 and 93.5. It is also lower than the closing price of 93, and so reflects the volume that was traded earlier in the day at lower prices.

In comparison to the post-trade benchmarks, the example order seems to have performed less well versus the intraday ones. The example order has missed the VWAP by 23 basis points. This is not that surprising given that the order was filled in three executions;

especially since more was filled later in the day when the price had risen. Given the trending price, it seems that more of the order should have been executed earlier in the day. Hence, the VWAP does indeed act as a reasonable performance benchmark.

Pre-trade benchmarks

These are an immediately available milestone, which may be used to directly measure performance. The previous close and the opening price may both be used to determine trading costs. Although, just as for the post-trade benchmarks, the trading at these times may be more volatile and so they are not necessarily reflective of the actual market conditions throughout the day. A substantial price shift can also make the benchmark less meaningful for any subsequently entered orders, since they will be comparing to a price they could never have achieved.

The decision price represents the price at which the choice to invest was actually made, which ties in with Perold's concept of implementation shortfall. Arrival price is used in a similar fashion to the decision price, it represents the time at which the order could actually be traded. In the case of a broker, it is the time when the order arrives from the investor. This may then be used to measure what has sometimes been termed the execution shortfall, since unlike implementation shortfall it only tracks the trading-related costs.

Pre-trade benchmarks are appealing since they are both easily determined and immediately available for comparison. Whilst they do not reflect actual market conditions throughout the day, this may also be used as an advantage since it means there is no way to influence or "game" the benchmark. Another advantage is that they are just as appropriate for all order sizes.

Note that the decision and arrival prices are not always recorded by investors, so previous close and opening prices may be used as corresponding proxies for them. This will clearly affect the accuracy of the transaction cost measurement. In particular, it will affect the investment-related costs, often meaning these are underestimated.

The trade from Example 6-1 appears to have performed extremely poorly compared to the pre-trade benchmarks. This is caused by the noticeable price trend throughout the day. Lower transaction costs could have been achieved by completing more of the order earlier in the day.

Relative Performance Measure

Kissell's (1998) Relative Performance Measure (RPM) is an alternative to price-based benchmarks. It is based on a comparison of what the trade achieved in relation to the rest of the market. In terms of volume, the RPM represents the ratio of the volume traded at a less favourable price to the total market volume:

$$\text{RPM(volume)} = \frac{\text{Total volume at price less favourable than execution}}{\text{Total market volume}}$$

$$\text{RPM(trades)} = \frac{\text{Number of trades at price less favourable than execution}}{\text{Total number of trades}}$$

Transaction cost is dependent on many factors: the asset's characteristics (liquidity, volatility), market conditions (price trends, momentum), trading strategy etc. Therefore, when comparing the performance of two separate orders we need to take these various factors into account. Simply comparing how many basis points each order beat the VWAP by does not give a fair comparison.

One of the main advantages of the RPM metric is the fact that its results are already normalised, since the percentage rates the trade's performance compared to the rest of the market. Thus, a trade that achieves a 90% RPM has performed significantly better than one achieving 60%. This makes the RPM a useful tool for comparing the relative performance across a variety of both orders and assets, as well as over time.

Kissell proposes a range of adjustments for RPM to make it suitable for a wide range of trading strategies. Such as using time filtering to deal better with short trades, or adding weightings to incorporate the aggressiveness of the trading strategy. More details about the RPM may be found in Kissell and Glantz (2003).

Using the aggregated volume data from Table 6-3, the RPM's for Example 6-1 may be determined:

$$RPM(volume) = (50,000 + 40,000 + 10,000) / 200,000 = 50\%$$
$$RPM(trades) = (5 + 4 + 2) / 27 = 41\%$$
$$Average\ RPM = 45\%$$

In other words, 50% of traded volume performed as well or better than the example order, whilst the remainder achieved a worse average price. This confirms that the example trade's performance is average at best.

Post-trade transaction costs

The total transaction costs of a trade may be determined using Perold's implementation shortfall measure. This is the difference in value between the idealised paper portfolio and the actually traded one:

$$IS = Returns_{Paper} - Returns_{Real}$$

The theoretical (or paper) returns depend on the price when the decision to invest was made (p_d), the final market price (p_N) and the size of the intended investment (X). The real returns depend on the actual transaction costs. So if x_j represent the sizes of the individual executions and p_j are the achieved prices:

$$IS = \underbrace{X(p_N - p_d)}_{Returns_{Paper}} - \underbrace{(Xp_N - \sum x_j p_j - fixed)}_{Returns_{Real}} = \sum x_j p_j - Xp_d + fixed$$

Note that this assumes that the order is fully executed. To take account of this Robert Kissell and Morton Glantz (2003) introduced an opportunity cost factor, since not every order will be fully executed:

$$IS = \underbrace{\sum x_j p_j - (\sum x_j) p_d}_{Execution\ Cost} + \underbrace{(X - \sum x_j)(p_N - p_d)}_{Opportunity\ Cost} + fixed$$

where ($X - \Sigma x_j$) corresponds to the size of the unexecuted position.

So for Example 6-1:

Execution cost $= (10,000*91.15 + 20,000*92.5 + 93.8*15,000) - (45,000*90.0)$
$= \$118,500$

Opportunity cost $= (50,000 - 45,000) * (93.0 - 90.0)$
$= \$15,000$

Order value $= 50,000 * 90.0 = \$4,500,000$

Implementation shortfall (IS) = \$133,500 + fixed costs
$$= (133{,}500/4{,}500{,}000) = 297 \text{ bps} + \text{fixed costs}$$

Wayne Wagner and Steven Glass (2001) also showed that transaction costs incorporate a delay factor. This corresponds to the effect of a price move from when the initial investment decision is made to when the order is actually sent for execution. So it may be shown that the overall costs consist of:

$$Transaction\ costs = \underbrace{X(p_0 - p_d)}_{Investment\ related} + \underbrace{\sum x_j p_j - (\sum x_j) p_0}_{Trading\ related} + \underbrace{(X - \sum x_j)(p_N - p_0)}_{Opportunity\ Cost} + fixed \qquad (6\text{-}1)$$

where the price p_0 is the market price when the order was dispatched, commonly known as the arrival price. Notice that the trading-related and opportunity costs now account for the change from this arrival price rather than the decision price.

Kissell and Glantz (2003) incorporated this into a measure they called the expanded implementation shortfall. This manages to not only account for transaction costs, but also helps to identify where the costs actually occurred. The following section shows how these costs may be broken down into factors such as spreads, market impact and timing risk.

6.5 Breaking down transaction costs

There has been a considerable amount of research focussed on trading costs. Most notable amongst these is a study by Wayne Wagner and Mark Edwards (1993) which split out the trading costs into specific components, namely timing, delay, impact and opportunity costs.

There are several different ways of classifying the constituents of transaction costs, as shown in Table 6-4.

Cost type		Classification				Focus for:	
		Explicit	*Implicit*	*Fixed*	*Variable*	*Algorithms*	*Execution Tactics*
Investment	Taxes	✓			✓		
	Delay Cost	✓ [5]			✓		
Trading	Commission	✓		✓			
	Fees	✓		✓		○	○
	Spreads		✓ [6]		✓		●
	Market Impact		✓		✓	●	○
	Price Trend		✓		✓	●	
	Timing Risk		✓		✓	●	○
	Opportunity Cost		✓		✓	○	

● often ○ sometimes

Table 6-4 Transaction cost constituents

---

[5] Note that if the investment decision price (p_d) and the arrival price (p_0) are known then delay cost is explicit, but since one or both of these prices are often not recorded then it becomes a more implicit cost.

[6] Although bid offer spreads are easily viewable, they must be recorded each time an order is split in order to determine the spread cost. So measuring it is similar to monitoring a price trends or market impact.

Differentiating between investment and trading related costs is useful since it helps identify who best can control them. Looking back at the trading example in Figure 6-4, the investment-related costs may be classed as everything which occurs before t_0 (when the order is placed with the broker/trader) whilst the trading-related costs account for the rest.

Transaction costs are also commonly termed as either explicit or implicit. Explicit costs are clearly identifiable and easily measured, whereas implicit costs are less directly observable and so harder to quantify. Fixed costs are set regardless of the trading strategy whilst variable ones depend on the asset, the order, market conditions and the trading strategy. Another way of viewing these different cost types is shown in Figure 6-5. Note that although this is not drawn to scale, it does try to emphasise the relative importance of each type.

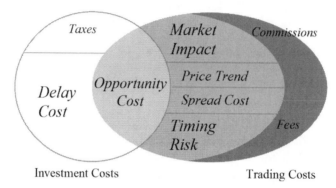

Figure 6-5 Categorising transaction cost types

Pre-trade analysis tools allow both investors and traders to estimate these various transaction costs. This also helps make trading-related costs more transparent, and allows investors much more control over them. Investors should set clear targets for acceptable levels of cost and risk. Then by modelling a range of diverse trading strategies/algorithms, they may select the most appropriate approach. This is also a good way of reducing opportunity cost, since the analysis will highlight orders that may be too large. If an order does not appear to be viable, the investor may choose to consider other assets that are more liquid. Alternatively, if the order is not price sensitive then spreading it over several days may work. Note that most pre-trade analysis is based on historical data, so discussing with a trader can confirm current market conditions.

Clearly, the main aim is to achieve a reduction in the total transaction costs. The fixed commissions and fees may be reduced by negotiation. However, in terms of reducing overall cost, the most potential lies with the implicit and variable costs. The most important of which are trading-related, in particular market impact and timing risk. Generally, these are dependent on the asset, market conditions, the order and the trading strategy. By taking advantage of pre-trade analysis and algorithmic trading, investors can select trading strategies that are much more suitable for their overall investment goals. By choosing an appropriate trading strategy, the overall cost and risk should be considerably reduced.

A nice illustration of an in-depth transaction cost breakdown is provided by Instinet (2005). In order to compare the relative effects of the components Figure 6-6 shows a more detailed breakdown of the costs associated with Example 6-1. The following sub-sections provide more detailed descriptions for each of the individual cost components.

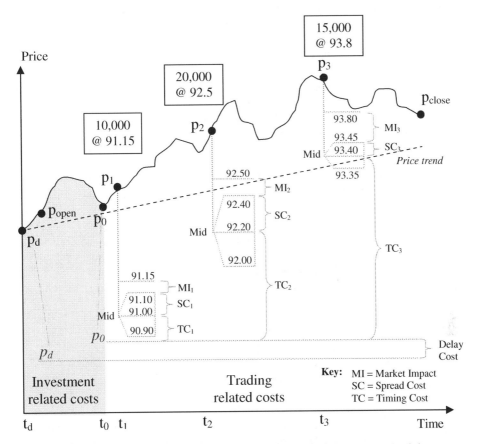

Figure 6-6 Detailed transaction cost breakdown for Example 6-1

Investment-related costs

Investment-related costs can be a significant proportion of the overall transaction costs. They primarily consist of a delay cost with taxes making up the rest. The delay reflects the time from the investment decision being made (t_d) to when an order is actually dispatched (t_0). This is shown as the shaded region in Figure 6-6.

Taxes

Taxes must be incorporated into the investment strategy. Generally, they are applied based on capital gains; however, some markets such as the U.K. stock market have an additional stamp duty on share purchases.

Delay Cost

The delay cost is caused by any price change from the initial decision to invest to when an order has actually been received by a broker. This may be specified as:

$$\text{Delay Cost} = X * (p_0 - p_d)$$

where X is the order size, p_d is the mid price when the investment decision was made (time

t_d) and p_0 is the mid price at t_0 when the order was received by the broker.

For Example 6-1:   Delay Cost   = 50,000 * (90.65 – 90.00)
                                       = \$32,500
                                       = 72 bps

Using the decision price benchmark, the example trade's performance was -293 bps. Therefore, for this example a quarter of the transaction costs are due to delay cost.

Such costs are clearly more important for assets whose price is trending away (i.e. up for buys and down for sells). Similarly, more volatile assets may also suffer.

Delay cost may be caused by a simple lag between the investment decision and issuing the order. Sometimes it may be inevitable, for instance, when the decision is made out of market hours. Time may also be spent on pre-trade analysis and choosing the most suitable broker, particularly for more illiquid assets and markets. Alternatively, if the buy-side trader has a strong view on the market this may cause them to wait for an optimal time. Nevertheless, if this judgement proves incorrect it will incur a delay cost.

The increasing availability of tools and systems for pre-trade analysis could help reduce this cost. Especially as they become more tightly integrated with order and execution management systems (OMSs and EMSs). Note there is no reason why the delay cost could not be broken down further. For example, market prices could be recorded at each stage of the process from the initial strategy and research through to portfolio formation.

Trading-related costs

The explicit trading-related costs comprise of commissions and fees. Often these will be quoted in advance of trading as percentages of the traded value. Obviously, these may be reduced to a certain extent, based on negotiation between the investor and the brokers. The rates offered will usually depend on the client's volume of trading and the level of service they require.

The most significant costs are the implicit trading-related costs, primarily market impact and timing risk, but also spread, price trend and opportunity cost. Figure 6-6 shows the breakdown of these costs for our example buy order.

Market impact represents a payment for liquidity (or immediacy) and a cost due to the information content of the order. The price trend cost represents the added burden caused by a trending market. Timing risk is primarily associated with the volatility of an asset's price, as well as its liquidity. Spread cost is also included here since although being visible it is not always as easily measurable as fees or commissions. Finally, opportunity cost represents the risk from not fully executing the order, possibly because the trading strategy was too passive.

Note that for convenience the time related costs are grouped together as an overall timing cost in Figure 6-6, where:

$$\text{Timing Cost} = \text{Price Trend} + \text{Timing Risk} \qquad (6\text{-}2)$$

Whilst these trading costs may not be eliminated, they may be controlled by selecting suitable trading strategies. Market impact costs are higher for aggressive trading whereas timing risk is higher for passive trading. Consequently, the trader needs to find the appropriate balance between impact cost and risk, and adjust the trading strategy accordingly. This selection also needs to take into account the specifics of each order together with the current market conditions and the investor's goal's and level of risk aversion. In Chapter 7, we will cover these decisions in more detail.

In terms of trading algorithms, Table 6-4 showed which cost components are generally focussed on. Clearly, market impact is a prime focus, but some algorithms will also closely monitor timing risk (e.g. implementation shortfall) and price trends. Execution tactics generally concentrate on spread costs, although some may also monitor price trends. Smart order routing systems and liquidity algorithms will also incorporate fees into their calculations when deciding the best venue to route orders to.

Commission

Brokers charge commission for agency trading to compensate them for the costs (particularly labour and capital) incurred in handling orders, executing trades and performing clearing and settlement. Commission is generally quoted in basis points (bps). Though, in the U.S. equity markets quoting in cents per share (cps) is common.

Commissions have been steadily decreasing over time. Certainly, over a longer period commissions have fallen significantly. For instance, Hans Stoll (2001) noted that back in 1970 commissions for 500 shares of a $40 stock were $270, or 135 bps (54 cps). Whilst this was for a retail investor, even institutional investors paid around 65 bps (26 cps) on a 5000 share trade. Nowadays, in the U.S., commissions are often below ten basis points, particularly for DMA. Similarly, in the European equities marketplace a full service brokerage will probably charge around 20 bps, with algorithmic trading services costing around 10 bps and basic DMA even less than this.

Clearly, one way of reducing this cost is to compare the commissions for a wide range of brokers. Bear in mind, though, that commission is only one part of the transaction costs. A detailed comparison of all the associated costs is required to properly compare brokers.

Fees

Fees represent the actual charges from trading. These may be from floor brokers, exchange fees, or clearing and settlement costs. Often brokers incorporate these into their commission charge. Note that some exchanges and ECNs assign costs only to aggressively priced orders in order to encourage liquidity provision. For instance, Table 6-5 highlights charges from BATS for September 2008.

Fees ($/share)	Tape A (NYSE)	Tape B (Regional)	Tape C (NASDAQ)
Adding liquidity	-0.0024	-0.0030	0.0024
Removing liquidity	0.0025	0.0025	0.0025
Routing out	0.0029	0.0029	0.0029

Source: BATS (2008)

Table 6-5 Sample Fees for using BATS (Sept 2008)

Notice how the charges for taking liquidity (i.e. aggressive orders) may be almost nullified by rebates offered for providing liquidity (i.e. passive orders). Some markets even provide multiple venues with different pricing schemes. For example, the Direct-Edge ECN provides EDGA where all orders pay a set fee, whilst EDGX offers the rebate style pricing where liquidity providers are compensated at the expense of liquidity takers.

Algorithms and execution tactics which deal with multiple execution venues are the most likely to track broker and exchange fees. They need this information when deciding between routing destinations to ensure they make a fair comparison of the real price.

Spreads

Spread cost represents the difference between the best bid and offer prices at any given time. The spread compensates those who provide liquidity. Clearly, aggressive trading styles will result in a higher spread cost than passive ones.

The overall spread cost may be determined by summing the bid offer spreads for each execution. (A factor of 0.5 is used since we only pay half the spread for each trade):

$$\text{Spread Cost} = \Sigma\left(x_j * (0.5 * s_j)\right)$$

where x_j is the size of each execution and s_j is the bid offer spread at that time. Note that this is the quoted spread at the time of each execution, rather than the effective spread, which also incorporates the immediate market impact.

In Example 6-1: Spread Cost $= (10{,}000 * (91.1\text{-}91)) + (20{,}000* (92.4\text{-}92.2))$
$\qquad\qquad\qquad\qquad\qquad + (15{,}000 * (93.45\text{-}93.4))$
$\qquad\qquad\qquad\qquad = \$ 5{,}750$
$\qquad\qquad\qquad\qquad = 13 \text{ bps}$

Spread costs vary considerably across both markets and assets. For some assets/markets, the spread can be a major cost factor. In the U.S. equity market, decimalisation sharply reduced spread cost to around 5 bps, although during the 2007-09 financial crisis spreads nearly doubled. In Europe and Japan spreads may be much higher, ranging from 10-50 bps or even more. Unsurprisingly, large-cap and liquid stocks have lower spreads. More volatile stocks tend to have higher spreads.

The simplest way to lower spread costs is to trade more passively, using limit orders which are priced at the market or just behind it. Algorithms may not always directly consider spread cost, although it may affect their choice of execution tactics (passive or aggressive). Most price-based execution tactics will closely monitor the spread in order to use an appropriate level of aggression when placing and updating orders.

Market impact

Market impact represents the price change caused by a specific trade or order. Generally, it has an adverse affect, for instance, helping drive prices up when we are trying to buy.

The exact market impact cost is the difference between the actual price chart and the hypothetical one that would have occurred if our order had not been created. Though, this makes market impact difficult to measure and estimate accurately, as Kissell and Glantz (2003) observe. Figure 6-7 tries to show this effect for the order from Example 6-1; the hypothetical price chart is labelled as the "paper" one (borrowing from Perold's implementation shortfall nomenclature).

Market impact is usually broken down into temporary and permanent impacts:

$$\text{Market Impact} = \text{Temporary Impact} + \text{Permanent Impact} \qquad (6\text{-}3)$$

The temporary impact reflects the cost of demanding liquidity. For instance, an order that "walks the book" will usually achieve a poorer price than if it had just taken the quantity available at the best bid or offer.

Permanent impact corresponds to the long-term effect of our order, representing the information content that it has exposed to the market. Clearly, if the market detects a large buyer or seller this acts as a strong signal and will affect the price accordingly. A single, large order might have a larger temporary impact than a series of smaller orders. However,

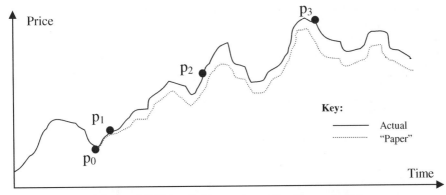

Figure 6-7 Potential impact cost for Example 6-1

netting the permanent impacts of the smaller orders will give a similar result to the signal given by the large order.

An approximate measure for market impact is to sum the total impacts for each order. The impact may be determined as the difference in price between our execution and the best bid or offer at that time (bid for sells and offer for buys):

$$\text{Market Impact} = \Sigma \left(x_j * (p_j - p_b) \right) \qquad (6\text{-}4)$$

where x_j is the size of each execution and p_j is the price achieved for each execution and p_b is the best bid or offer at that time.

For example, let's consider one of the individual trades from Example 6-1 in more detail. Figure 6-8 shows a before and after view of the order book for the second execution at t_2.

	Buys				Sells		
Id	Time	Size	Price	Price	Size	Time	Id
B1	1:05:00	1,000	92.0	92.4	10,000	1:05:00	S1
B2	1:00:25	3,000	91.9	92.5	7,000	1:00:25	S2
B3	1:04:09	4,000	91.8	92.8	2,000	1:04:09	S3
				92.9	3,000	1:05:00	S4

(a) before

	Sells		
	Price	Size	Time	Id
.	92.4	10,000	1:05:00	S1
.	92.5	7,000	1:00:25	S2
.	92.8	2,000	1:04:09	S3
.	92.9	1,000	1:05:00	S4
.	92.9	**2,000**	1:05:00	S4

(b) immediately after

	Buys				Sells		
Id	Time	Size	Price	Price	Size	Time	Id
B6	1:07:00	1,000	92.1	92.5	5,000	1:08:00	S5
B5	1:08:00	2,000	92.1	92.6	4,000	1:09:00	S6
B1	1:05:00	1,000	92.0	92.9	2,000	1:09:10	S7
B2	1:00:25	3,000	91.9	92.9	5,000	1:08:00	S8

(c) 5 minutes later

Figure 6-8 A view of the order book for trade t_2 from Example 6-1

By issuing a market order to buy 20,000 XYZ, we can see that this will "walk the book", crossing with sell orders S1, S2, S3 and S4. So we receive fills of 10,000 at 92.4, 7,000 at

92.5, 2,000 at 92.8 and 2,000 at 92.9, achieving an average price of 92.5. The temporary effect of the trade has been to shift the offer price up to 92.9. Though, within a few minutes new orders arrive which stabilise the offer price back to 92.5. The permanent impact, caused by our trade, helped shift the offer price from 92.4 to 92.5. Our order acted as an indication that the asset was undervalued and so helped raise the price permanently, as we can see in Figure 6-9.

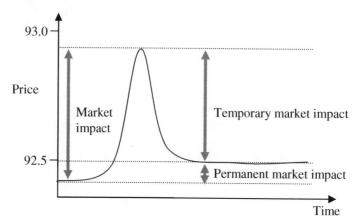

Figure 6-9 The components of market impact

The overall impact for Example 6-1, using equation 6-4:

Market impact = $(10,000 * (91.15\text{-}91.1)) + (20,000* (92.5\text{-}92.4))$
             $+ (15,000 * (93.8\text{-}93.45))$
             = $ 7,750
             = 17 bps

Breaking this down into its temporary and permanent components is a bit more difficult. Some cost estimation models actually set the permanent impact as zero, assuming that the trade will not have a significant overall effect. Still, we can make an approximation by using the estimation model from Kissell and Glantz (2003). [7] First, the instantaneous impact cost $I_\$$ is determined by rearranging their estimation equation as follows:

$$MI_\$ = \underbrace{0.95 I_\$ \cdot \eta^{-1}}_{\text{Temporary impact}} + \underbrace{0.05 I_\$}_{\text{Permanent impact}} \quad \Rightarrow \quad I_\$ = \frac{MI_\$}{(0.95\eta^{-1} + 0.05)} \qquad (6\text{-}5)$$

where $\eta = (X + 0.5 * Q) / X$, and X is the order size, Q is the ADV.

Hence η = $(45,000 + (0.5 * 200,000)) / 45,000 = 3.22$

             $I_\$$ = $ 7,750 / ((0.95 / 3.22) + 0.05)$
                      = $ 22,475
                      = 50 bps

---

[7] Note the Kissell and Glantz (2003) market impact estimation model is discussed in more detail in Chapter 10.

This instantaneous impact cost may then be fed back into the first part of equation 6-5 to determine both the temporary and permanent impact costs:

Temporary Impact = (0.95 * $ 22,475) / 3.22
                   = $ 6,626
                   = 15 bps

Permanent Impact = 0.05 * $ 22,475
                   = $ 1,124
                   = 2 bps

Overall market impact is dependent on the order/trade size, but most importantly on the market liquidity. Generally, larger orders incur a higher market impact compared to smaller ones. Though, this effect is considerably reduced for more liquid assets.

As we saw in Chapter 5, reducing market impact cost has been one of the primary aims of algorithms since the earliest order slicing approaches. By taking a large order and splitting it into smaller ones, which are traded over a period of time, we should achieve a much lower overall impact cost. Many of the currently available algorithms directly incorporate this factor into their decisions of how and when to place orders. The aggressiveness of execution tactics also has an effect on the market impact costs. Issuing market orders or aggressive limit orders will incur higher costs. Some tactics may actually use limit order models to decide on the appropriate level of aggression.

Price trending

Asset prices sometimes exhibit broadly consistent trends. This price drift, or momentum, is also known as short-term alpha. An upward trend implies that costs will increase when buying an asset, whilst savings will be made if selling. Conversely, the opposite is true for a downward price trend.

The price trend cost may be determined based on the difference between this trend price and the arrival price:

$$\text{Price Trend Cost} = \Sigma \left(x_j * (p^*_j - p_0) \right)$$

where x_j is the size of each execution, p^*_j is the expected price based on the price trend and p_0 is again the mid price at t_0 when the order was received by the broker.

For simplicity, in Example 6-1 the trend line has been set to cross between the previous close and the days OHLC average. This is shown on as the dashed line on Figure 6-6. Interpolation gives the following trend prices:

Trade	t_1	t_2	t_3
Mid price	91.00	92.20	93.40
Trend price	90.50	91.00	91.60

Table 6-6 Trend prices for Example 6-1

So: Price Trend Cost = (10,000 * (90.5-90.65)) + (20,000* (91-90.65))
                       + (15,000 * (91.6-90.65))
                     = $ 19,750
                     = 44 bps

Note this simplistic trend may have given a higher trend cost measurement; however, this will not affect the overall transaction cost measurement. Since timing cost is the sum of trend cost and timing risk, if the trend cost is overestimated then the timing risk will be underestimated by an equivalent amount.

For our example, the timing cost may be determined from the difference between the mid price (m_j) and the arrival price (p_0).

$$\text{Timing Cost} = \Sigma\left(x_j * (m_j - p_0)\right)$$

Reducing trend cost may really only be achieved by shortening the trading horizon and so increasing market impact costs. For large orders, which may span multiple days, investors must use pre-trade analysis to find the optimal trading approach to balance both these costs.

Price trending is a focus for the price-sensitive algorithms, such as implementation shortfall and market on close. In particular, the adaptive shortfall and price inline algorithms actively respond to trends either aggressively or passively. That said, schedule based algorithms may also be modified to cope with price trends. Some variants of TWAP and VWAP allow parameters to specify how to tilt their schedules based on which way the trader thinks the price may trend. Some execution tactics may also become more or less aggressive if they detect short-term market trends.

Timing risk

Kissell and Glantz (2003) use timing risk to represent the uncertainty of the transaction cost estimate. The two main sources of uncertainty are volatility of both the asset's price and of the traded volume, although other factors such as spread risk could also be considered. For the purposes of this book, timing risk will simply be reduced to the sum of these two main risks together with a generic error factor (ε):

$$\text{Timing Risk} = \text{Volatility Risk} + \text{Liquidity Risk} + \varepsilon$$

Price volatility is arguably the most important risk. The more volatile an asset then the more likely its price will move away and so increase the transaction costs. The liquidity risk represents the uncertainty with respect to the market impact cost. Generally, market impact costs are estimated based on historical volumes, so if the actual trading volumes differ significantly this may result in a shift in the market impact. For instance, if the market volume is higher then the market impact costs will tend to be less.

Based on the calculation for timing cost shown in the previous sub-section, timing risk is effectively the residual cost once the price trend has been accounted for. Hence, timing risk may be measured using:

$$\text{Timing Risk} = \Sigma\left(x_j * (m_j - p_j^*)\right)$$

where x_j is the size of each execution, m_j is the mid price at this time and p_j^* is the expected price based on the price trend.

For Example 6-1, using the mid and trend prices from Table 6-6:

Timing Risk   = (10,000 * (91-90.5)) + (20,000* (92.2-91))
                     + (15,000 * (93.4-91.6))
                     = \$ 56,000
                     = 124 bps

Clearly, this order has been considerably affected by timing risk. Shortening the trading horizon should reduce the effect. So investors must find an appropriate balance between market impact costs and timing risk.

Timing risk is a focus for the risk based algorithms, namely implementation and adaptive shortfall as well as market on close. Most execution tactics do not directly incorporate timing risk, although some may become more aggressive as time goes on, to try to complete any extant orders. Similarly, when an aggressive execution style is set by an algorithm this will somewhat reduce timing risk by preventing the algorithm from lagging behind their trading targets. Though, this only ensures completion of the dispatched child orders. An aggressive VWAP algorithm will still schedule its orders based on a historic volume profile, so orders will still be spaced out over time.

Opportunity cost

Opportunity cost reflects the cost of not fully executing an order. This may be because the asset's price went beyond a client's price limit or could just be due to insufficient liquidity. Either way, it represents a missed opportunity, since the next day prices may move even further away.

The overall cost may be determined as the product of the remaining order size and the price difference between the final price (p_N) and the arrival price:

$$OC = (X - \sum x_j)(p_N - p_0)$$

Unlike the other cost components, opportunity cost represents a virtual loss rather than a physical one. The loss is only realised when a new order makes up the remainder at a less favourable price.

So for Example 6-1:   Opportunity Cost $= (50,000 - 45,000) * (93.0 - 90.65)$
$= \$11,750$
$= 26 \text{ bps}$

If the price trend reverts tomorrow then it should be easy to purchase the remaining 5,000 XYZ at less than 93.0. If the trend continues then an opportunity cost of at least 26 bps will be realised.

Reducing opportunity cost may really only be achieved by using pre-trade analysis to confirm orders are sized correctly for current market conditions. For large orders, the investor must decide whether to risk market impact, or spread the trade over several days, risking exposure to a price move. Setting price limits effectively signifies that opportunity cost is acceptable (so long as it is due to the market moving to an unfavourable price). For such orders sudden price shifts can stop the order from being executable. Good communication between the investor and traders is vital to allow modification of the trading strategy if necessary.

Some algorithms may directly consider opportunity cost; typically, this is the cost-based ones such as implementation shortfall. Still, it is important to use pre-trade analytics to ensure the asset's liquidity is sufficient for the proposed order. Opportunity cost is also addressed indirectly by the optional finish-up logic provided by brokers/vendors for some algorithms. This is primarily intended to complete orders that may have an odd lot remainder.

Summary

The previous sections have outlined each of these individual transaction cost components in some detail. Figure 6-6 gave a visual breakdown of the constituent costs for Example 6-1. These are summarised in the following table.

Type	Cost $	Cost bps	% of costs
Taxes [8]	0	0	0
Delay cost	32,500	72	24
Commission/Fees	4,500	10	3
Spread cost	5,750	13	4
Market impact	7,750	17	6
Price trend	19,750	44	14
Timing risk	56,000	124	41
Opportunity cost	11,750	26	9
Total	138,000	307	100

Table 6-7 Cost Estimate for Example 6-1

Thus, the overall cost is 10 bps more than the 297 bps implementation shortfall we calculated earlier. This is because the initial implementation shortfall calculation did not take into account commissions/fees (or taxes).

Note it is also different from the 263 bps underperformance we saw back in Table 6-2 using the decision price benchmark. This is because the benchmark only shows the performance for the executed trades, and not the 5,000 which did not execute. So it does not include the opportunity cost. This is why implementation shortfall is an important (and accurate) tool for post-trade analysis, and can be more useful than benchmarks.

In terms of individual cost components, clearly delay cost and timing risk are important cost factors in this example. Market impact cost is also significant. Our estimate for the instantaneous impact cost was 50bps. For this order, market impact has been reduced by splitting into several smaller orders. Though, with hindsight, much better performance could have been achieved by trading more aggressively at the start of day. Admittedly, the market impact costs would have been higher, but the timing risk and price trend cost would have been much less.

It is important to remember that Example 6-1 was specifically designed to highlight the various potential costs. Obviously, the trading strategy was sub-optimal. In Chapter 7, we shall address the selection of optimal trading strategies in more detail. For more realistic costs, the following section shows figures reported for some of the world's major markets.

6.6   Transaction costs across world markets

Having gone through a worked example to illustrate each of the main components of transaction costs it is worth seeing how these actually differ across the world's markets. A few vendors provide transaction cost analysis (TCA) which is truly global in scope. In general, these have been focussed on the equities markets, although they are also starting to cover other asset classes. Table 6-8 shows average transaction costs for global equity trading taken from quarterly cost reviews carried out by ITG Inc. for both 2007 and 2008.

---

[8] For simplicity taxes are assumed to be zero (we will assume it is a charitable account).

Region	Average Cost in Q4 2008 /bps			Average Cost in Q2 2007 /bps			
	Shortfall	Comm	Total	Delay	Impact	Comm	Total
U.S. (Combined)	76	9	85	20	11	7	38
U.S. (Large Cap)	54	8	62	19	10	6	35
U.S. (Small Cap)	124	12	136	27	13	10	51
U.K.	73	12	84	31	4	11	46
Europe ex U.K. (Austria, Belgium, Denmark, Finland, France, Germany, Greece, Ireland, Italy, Luxembourg, Netherlands, Norway, Portugal, Spain, Sweden, Switzerland)	66	11	77	37	6	11	54
Japan	111	9	120	39	16	8	63
Developed Asia (Australia, Hong Kong, Malaysia, New Zealand, Singapore)	113	15	128	95	16	14	125
All Emerging (Argentina, Brazil, Chile, Chile, China, Colombia, Cyprus, Czech Republic, Egypt, Hungary, India, Indonesia, Israel, Jordan, Mexico, Morocco, Pakistan, Peru, Philippines, Poland, Russia, S. Korea, South Africa, Sri Lanka, Taiwan, Thailand, Turkey)	128	21	148	80	12	20	112

Source: ITG (2009, 2008)

Table 6-8 Average transaction costs for global equities

Unsurprisingly, the costs are closely related to market liquidity, so the lowest costs are for U.S. large cap firms, followed by Europe and Japan. Comparing the differences between 2007 and 2008, it is clear that during the market turmoil costs rose sharply, particularly in the more developed markets. In fact, Table 6-8 shows that transaction costs doubled from Q2 2007 to Q4 2008 for the ITG U.S. combined figures, mainly due to a massive increase in costs for small cap equities. Similarly, the U.K. and Japan saw cost increases of over 50%, whilst European markets saw around a 22% increase.

Table 6-8 also shows a breakdown of these costs. For 2007 the delay cost, market impact and commissions (labelled *Comm*) are shown, whilst for 2008 the shortfall cost represents the sum of the delay and market impact. Again, market impact costs are generally lower in the largest and most developed markets. The delay cost seems to be most important for the Asian markets. Commissions tend to be lowest in the US and Japan, followed by Europe then the rest of Asia.

Transaction cost analysis has seen a slower uptake for other asset classes. A lack of transparency has been one of the key difficulties with dealer driven markets like fixed income. Clearly, for transaction cost analysis to be useful we need access to price data in order to accurately determine market impact, spread and delay costs. Still, the situation is gradually improving with the increasing adoption of electronic trading for these asset classes.

In the fixed income marketplace, several TCA vendors now offer global cost reports. For example, Table 6-9 shows some average costs from reviews by Elkins/McSherry for 2007/8. Fixed income markets also saw significant cost increases during the 2007-09 financial crisis. Note the sample costs shown in Table 6-9 do not give a breakdown into their individual

Country	Average cost / bps Q4-Q1 2007-8
Greece	~9.1
UK	~5.3
Netherlands	~9.5
Japan	~5.5
Hong Kong	~11.1
Singapore	~12.0
Malaysia	~14.0
Mexico	~7.2
Turkey	~16.0

U.S. bonds	Average cost / bps 2007
Treasury	5.87
Agency	6.73
Municipal	11.32
Mortgage	5.23
Corporate	6.97

Source: Elkins McSherry (2008, a)

Table 6-9 Average transaction costs for global bond trading

components, although they are noticeably lower than the figures reported for equities. However, there can also be a substantial cost associated with volatility, as shown in a proof of concept study of over 25,000 State Street bond portfolios reported in Pensions & Investments (2003). A volatility cost of 22 bps was found for trading in Japanese bonds, 47 bps for German ones, 53 bps in the U.S. and up to 62 bps in the U.K. This additional cost brings the figures more in line with equities, and may be seen as delay costs or timing risk.

For foreign exchange, the sums involved mean a few basis points can mean millions, so transaction cost analysis could bring considerable benefits to investors and traders. A review of FX specific transaction cost analysis by Michael DuCharme (2007) notes an average cost of around 9 bps, based on a study of FX trading by the Russell Investment Group. The dataset consisted of more than 36,000 trades for both developed and emerging currencies, worth around $15 billion. One interesting problem they faced was a lack of time stamps for their data. Simple omissions like this can pose real problems for TCA. Outside of the major systems from Reuters and EBS, some vendors are starting to provide multi-broker aggregated price feeds, helping tackle the issue of sourcing sufficient price data. Although daily price fixings still provide a key benchmark for many users.

There are also signs of TCA spreading into listed derivatives. Hopefully, the adoption of TCA will continue to grow, allowing us to monitor the efficiency of these markets.

6.7 Summary

- Transaction costs can have a significant effect on investment returns; therefore, it is important to both measure and analyse them if "best execution" is to be achieved.

- Implementation shortfall, or "slippage", is the difference in performance between an actual portfolio and its theoretical "paper" equivalent.

- Pre-trade analysis concentrates on estimating the:
  - Expected difficulty of trading, using forecasts from liquidity and risk models.

     −   Potential transaction cost. This helps show how suitable a given trading strategy is.

- Post-trade analysis focuses on execution performance and cost measurement.
  - Benchmark comparison is still one of the most common tools:
    - Closing price benchmarks are popular since they are used for P&L calculations.
    - Intraday benchmarks, such as VWAP, reflect the market conditions.
    - The decision price gives the closest estimate for implementation shortfall.
  - Alternative metrics, such as Kissell's RPM, may be used to compare performance across a range of assets as well as over time.

- Transaction costs may be decomposed into a wide range of different components:
  - Commissions, fees and taxes represent charges levied by floor brokers and exchanges as well as any costs associated with clearing and settlement.
  - Spread cost represents the compensation traders require for providing liquidity.
  - Delay cost reflects any price changes between the initial decision to invest and when an order is actually sent for execution.
  - Market impact represents the effect the order has on the asset's price (both temporary and permanent).
  - Timing risk reflects volatility in both the asset's price and its liquidity.
  - Opportunity cost represents the missed opportunity if an order is not completed.

- Transaction cost analysis is spreading across asset classes. Costs are closely related to market liquidity and volatility, so it is often cheaper to trade in the U.S. followed by Europe and Asia.

Chapter 7

Optimal trading strategies

Selecting the best trading strategy for any given order is a case of carefully balancing the investment objectives with market conditions.

7.1 Introduction

Best execution has become an increasingly commonplace term of late. Market regulators are trying to put in force rules and guidelines to ensure that client orders are executed with the most favourable terms, based on their objectives and on market conditions. Clearly, the overall transaction cost is a key component to best execution. Therefore, it is important to note that the speed of execution (reflecting timing risk) and its completeness (reflecting opportunity cost) can have as much significance as price.

Unfortunately, there are no hard and fast rules for how to achieve best execution. The judgement depends on factors such as the choice of benchmark and the investor's level of risk aversion, as well as their overall goals.

So how do we go about determining the optimal trading strategy for a given order? We will start by examining an example trading decision framework, as described by Wayne Wagner (2006) and shown in Figure 7-1. This framework illustrates the process from the point of view of a buy-side trader:

Step

1.   A portfolio manager initially notifies them of the order.

2.   If there are any specific restrictions then the trader must use the designated broker.

3.   Otherwise, the trader must assess how difficult the order will be to trade.

3.1   For orders that will provide much needed liquidity to the markets, the trader should strive for the optimal price.

3.2   Similarly, for orders that are judged easy, the trader has a lot of leeway in how best to deal with them.

3.3   Tough orders may be sub-categorised based on whether:
- They are a large percentage of the average daily volume (ADV).
- The asset is exhibiting significant trading momentum.
- The investor has flagged the order as urgent.

Depending on the perceived difficulty, the trader then must select the most appropriate method of trading. This may mean using trading algorithms, DMA, trying to cross the order, or negotiating a principal transaction with a dealer.

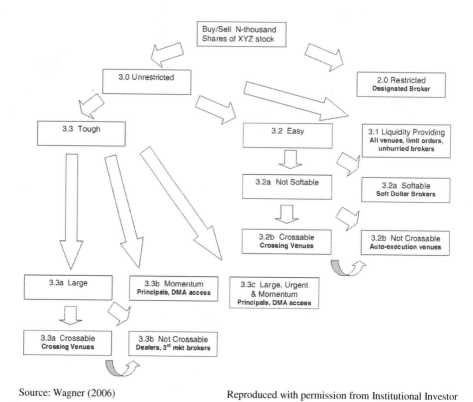

Figure 7-1 A hierarchy of trading decisions

7.2   Assessing the difficulty of orders

Determining how difficult an order will be depends on a range of properties. Wagner (2006) points out three such factors, namely large orders (relative to the ADV), unfavourable price momentum and urgency. Conversely, the key feature that makes trading easy is liquidity. Other asset specific properties such as volatility can also have a substantial effect.

One way of quantifying the potential order difficulty is based on historical results from transaction cost analysis (TCA). For example, Figure 7-2 shows the results of a proprietary liquidity and impact cost analysis performed by Jacqueline King and Yan Yaroshevsky (2005) at Abel/Noser. They studied the realized costs for a sample of 1,500 equities across a range of different order sizes (shown as a percentage of the ADV). Let's examine each of these key factors in turn:

Order size:

A large order executed immediately will generally cause significant market impact. Anything over 20-25% of the ADV is a large trade and so is more difficult, whilst anything less than 1% is a small trade. Still, as we can see in Figure 7-2 the effect of order size is closely linked to the asset's liquidity. A large order for a highly liquid asset will tend to cause much less market impact than for an illiquid one.

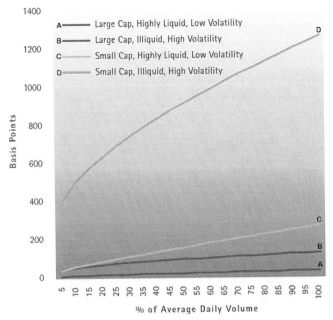

Source: King and Yaroshevsky (2005)   ©Abel/Noser 2005
Reproduced with permission from Abel/Noser

Figure 7-2 Realized costs for different asset groups

Liquidity:

An asset's liquidity can also have a considerable effect on transaction costs, as Figure 7-2 shows. A lower bid offer spread is commonly associated with liquid assets, so the expected spread cost should be lower for these. For equities, the company's market capitalisation and turnover may be used as a proxy for liquidity. In the Abel/Noser study, the market capitalisation ranged from $100 million to $100 billion. A large-cap stock has a value of greater than $10 billion, a small-cap is below $1 billion and a micro-cap has a value under $100 million. Likewise, a higher relative turnover means the stock is more liquid, so again we would expect lower impact costs.

Volatility:

An asset's volatility affects both its expected cost and timing risk. When combined with liquidity it can have a massive effect on the overall costs. For instance, in Figure 7-2 there is a huge jump in costs for equities which were illiquid with a high volatility (from around 400-1200 bps) when compared to those which were highly liquid with a low volatility (from around 10-40 bps).

Price momentum:

A persistent and favourable price trend also makes trades easier. Still, the key to reducing costs is trading more passively so as to take advantage of the trend. Conversely, a persistently adverse trend favours aggressive trading, so any delay will simply result in even worse executions.

Urgency:

Trading aggressively over a small time horizon will often cause significant market impact. The key is to determine whether this is outweighed by factors such as price momentum or volatility. Either way, aggressive trading will probably be required to meet the trading goals.

Trading horizon:

The trade horizon is closely linked with the urgency. Comparing the order size to the ADV assumes that the trade horizon is for the entire trading day. So a shorter trading horizon can make executing the order more difficult. For instance, an order for 10% of the ADV received two hours before the close is much more difficult to trade than its order size alone might suggest.

Other factors can also have an effect. For example, Scott Lyden (2007) reported on the importance of the time of day, noting that market impact for U.S. stocks was higher for trading in the first half hour after the open.

7.3   Selecting the optimal trading strategy

Having gauged the difficulty of the order, we now need to determine the best way to execute it. Since the concept of best execution revolves around achieving the investor's objectives, it is vital that these are considered. Therefore, we also need to know the:

- intended benchmark
- level of risk aversion
- desired trading goals

These will have a significant impact on our choice of strategy. Though, before we cover each of these factors in more detail, we must first explain a concept known as the efficient trading frontier. This provides the basis for comparing the expected costs and risks associated with different trading strategies, and so is a key part of the decision process.

The efficient trading frontier

In Chapter 1, we saw the efficient frontier for portfolios proposed by Harry Markowitz (1952). This plots the optimal portfolio in terms of returns for different levels of risk (or volatility). However, trading strategies are generally more focussed on cost, so Robert Almgren and Neil Chriss (2000) proposed the efficient trading frontier. They reasoned that rational traders would always seek to minimize expected costs for a certain level of risk. Hence, an optimal trading strategy was defined as one for which there were no alternatives with lower expected costs for the same degree of risk. The set of optimal solutions were termed the efficient trading frontier, consisting of a single solution for every possible level of risk. In order to determine this frontier they sought to solve the following unconstrained optimization for the expected cost $E(x)$:

$$\min_{x}(E(x) + \lambda V(x)) \tag{7-1}$$

where $V(x)$ corresponds to the expected risk and λ is a Lagrange multiplier introduced to relate to the various levels of risk. By plotting the optimal solutions on a chart of expected cost (or loss) against its corresponding variance (as a proxy for risk), as shown in Figure 7-3, the convex nature of the efficient trading frontier may clearly be seen.

The shaded region in Figure 7-3 represents the set of all possible strategies, whilst the solid curve shows the actual efficient trading frontier. Each point on this curve represents an optimal solution for a specific value of λ. In terms of cost, strategy B has the lowest expected value, although focussing on minimising this has resulted in the highest risk of any of the optimal strategies. Note that the dashed curve highlights strategies for which there is an optimal alternative with both lower expected cost and risk, namely strategy B.

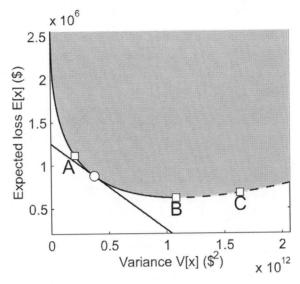

Source: Almgren and Chriss (2000)
Reprinted with kind permission from The Journal of Risk, Incisive Media

Figure 7-3 An efficient trading frontier

Based on equation 7-1 the gradient of the curve in Figure 7-3 corresponds to $-\lambda$, so the tangent shows the optimal strategy for λ with a value of around 10^{-6} (marked with a circle). In financial terms, the risk multiplier λ corresponds to the level of risk aversion. A higher value signifies less willingness to accept possible variance and so infers a higher expected cost. In other words, a higher risk aversion implies more aggressive trading. Conversely, a lower value of λ means less risk aversion; more passive trading results in lower expected costs, but with a higher variance. Thus in Figure 7-3 strategy A corresponds to a more aggressive strategy, whilst strategy B is the most passive optimal strategy.

Note that although variance is used in Figure 7-3 other risk measures may also be adopted. For instance, Almgren and Chriss (2000) also created a version for Value at Risk (VaR) whilst Robert Kissell and Roberto Malamut (2005b) normalised the frontier by plotting both cost and risk in terms of basis points.

Although the efficient trading frontier is an extremely useful theoretical concept, creating them can be time consuming since it requires the solution of the optimisation shown in equation 7-1 for every reasonable value of λ. To make things easier, Robert Kissell and Morton Glantz proposed an approximation by fitting an exponential decay curve to just a few specific strategies. More details may be found in Kissell and Glantz (2003).

Choosing the benchmark

As we saw in Chapter 6, the benchmark can have a substantial effect on the accuracy of performance measures. A similar result may be observed for the efficient trading frontiers, as highlighted in a study by Kissell and Malamut (2005b), shown in Figure 7-4. The expected costs and risks for each of these benchmarks are given in Table 7-1. We will cover the actual cost estimation models in more detail in Chapter 10.

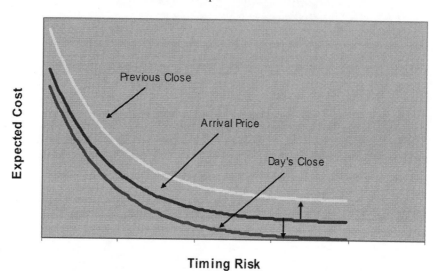

Source: Kissell and Malamut (2005b)   Reproduced with permission from Institutional Investor

Figure 7-4 The efficient trading frontier for a range of different benchmarks

Bench-mark	Cost	Risk
Previous Closing/ Opening Price	$Cost(\alpha) = h(X,\alpha) + g(X) + (p_0 - p_d) + \varepsilon$	$\Re(\alpha) = \sqrt{\sigma^2(\varepsilon(\alpha)) + \sigma^2(p_0 - p_d)}$
Arrival Price	$Cost(\alpha) = h(X,\alpha) + g(X) + \varepsilon$	$\Re(\alpha) = \sigma(\varepsilon(\alpha))$
Future Closing Price	$Cost(\alpha) = h(X,\alpha) + \varepsilon$	$\Re(\alpha) = \sigma(\varepsilon(\alpha))$

Source: Kissell and Malamut (2005 and 2005b)

Table 7-1 Benchmark expected costs and risks

An arrival price benchmark (p_0) gives the same expected cost and risk as we saw in Chapter 6. The cost consists of both temporary and permanent impact. The permanent impact $g()$ is based on the order size (X) whilst the temporary impact cost function $h()$ also depends on the trade rate (α). The timing risk principally consists of the price volatility $\sigma()$, which in turn is based on an error factor (ε), this just represents random noise. [1]

Using a pre-trade benchmark (p_d) earlier than the arrival price means an additional price change ($p_0 - p_d$) must be considered. This corresponds to the delay cost. Therefore, benchmarks based on previous closing or opening prices must incorporate this into their expected costs and risks. In terms of expected cost, the efficient trading frontier will be shifted by this amount. The direction depends on whether the order is a buy or a sell. For instance, assuming a buy order then a price rise will shift the frontier upwards, with the opposite effect for a sell order. Similarly, the additional timing risk factor is reflected as $\sigma^2(p_0 - p_d)$. This increased risk helps shift the frontier to the right in Figure 7-4.

In comparison, using a post-trade benchmark based on a future closing price will reduce the expected cost. This is because the permanent market impact is already accounted for in the future benchmark price. Hence, the estimated cost is just the temporary market impact (assuming no real price trend). Thus, the efficient trading frontier is shifted downwards by an amount equal to the permanent market impact. Though, in terms of timing risk, it will be just like the arrival price benchmark (since the time periods are the same).

Note that intraday benchmarks behave somewhat differently, since they are based on prices throughout the day so they incorporate both temporary and permanent impact cost. Therefore, for a VWAP benchmark it is possible to minimise both cost and timing risk by participating evenly with the day's volume.

The benchmark choice can clearly affect the efficient trading frontier, and so it can alter the optimal choice of trading strategy. For instance, Figure 7-5(a) shows the two frontiers depending on whether the arrival price or the previous close is used as the benchmark. Given the same target cost C_1, the shifted efficient trading frontier for the previous close benchmark results in an optimal strategy (X_2), which has a higher risk (R_2) than the corresponding optimal strategy (X_1) for an arrival price benchmark.

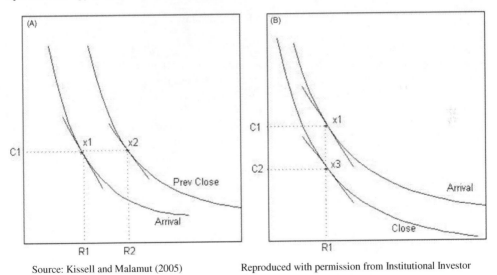

Source: Kissell and Malamut (2005)   Reproduced with permission from Institutional Investor

Figure 7-5 The effect of benchmarks on implementation goals

---

[1] For simplicity these examples assume there is no real price trend and liquidity volatility is excluded from the timing risk.

Conversely, given the same timing risk (R_1), Figure 7-5(b) shows how using the day's close price as a benchmark will have a lower expected cost (C_2) when compared to using the arrival price (C_1), due to the closing price incorporating permanent market impact.

Determining the level of risk aversion

Risk aversion directly affects the aggressiveness of a trading strategy. A high level indicates that timing risk is not acceptable and so the strategy should be more aggressive to try to complete faster. This increases the expected cost due to market impact. Alternatively, a low level suggests that minimising market impact is more important.

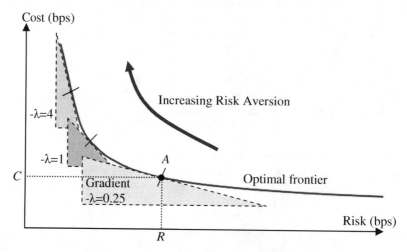

Figure 7-6 Risk aversion

Kissell and Malamut (2005b) highlighted this relationship between the risk aversion parameter (λ) and trading style by plotting a normalised efficient trading frontier. As Figure 7-6 shows, both the cost and timing risk axes are expressed in terms of basis points. Hence, the values of λ are much clearer, ranging from 0 to 3, rather than 10^{-6} to 10^{-7}. They observed an approximately linear relationship between the risk aversion parameter (λ) and an investor's level of concern about risk relative to cost. For example, a value of $\lambda = 1$ in Figure 7-6 represents an investor who is equally concerned about both risk and expected cost, whereas for $\lambda = 0.5$ the investor is only half as concerned about risk. The gradient λ also corresponds to the total trading time. A higher value of λ suggests more urgency and so a shorter horizon, whilst lower values suggest a more patient approach.

Choosing a trading goal

Having specified both a benchmark and the level of risk aversion, we can now start to focus on finding the optimal trading strategy. Robert Kissell, Morton Glantz, and Roberto Malamut (2004) outline three distinct trading objectives, namely to:
- Minimize the expected cost for a given level of risk
- Achieve price improvement over a given level of cost
- Balance the trade-off between expected cost and risk

Different types of investors may prefer specific goals; those driven by exposure will often choose to fix their expected risk, whilst information-driven investors may select price improvement to maximize the short-term returns.

Minimize cost

The efficient trading frontier represents the set of optimal trading strategies; they offer the lowest expected cost for each specific level of risk. Therefore, for a given level of risk we can find the optimal strategy simply by finding the corresponding point on the frontier. The optimal strategy A lies on the frontier with an estimated cost C and risk R, as Figure 7-6 shows. In comparison, sub-optimal strategies lie above the frontier, and so achieve the same level of risk, but with a much higher expected cost.

Price improvement

Roberto Malamut proved that the optimal price improvement strategy to beat a specific cost (C) could be found from the tangent of a line drawn from (0, C) to the efficient trading frontier.

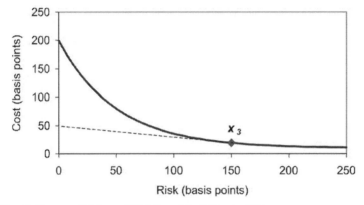

Figure 7-7 Maximising the likelihood of price improvement

This is shown as strategy X_3 in Figure 7-7, with a timing risk of 150 bps it offers the most chance of beating the expected cost of 50 bps.

Balancing the trade-off between cost and risk

Minimising the overall cost of trading is made more difficult by the fact that its two main components move in opposite directions. Impact cost may be reduced by more passive trading, whilst timing risk may be lowered by trading more aggressively. Kissell and Glantz (2003) term this optimisation problem the trader's dilemma. As we saw in Figure 7-6, each level of risk aversion λ has a corresponding optimal strategy. At this point, the slope of a line tangent to the efficient trading frontier equals $-\lambda$. We can use this fact to determine the optimal cost profile for a given λ, simply by sliding a line with a slope of $-\lambda$ until it becomes a tangent with the frontier curve. Thus, in Figure 7-8 the optimal strategy where $\lambda=1$ is X_2, which has an expected cost of 62 bps and a risk of 65 bps.

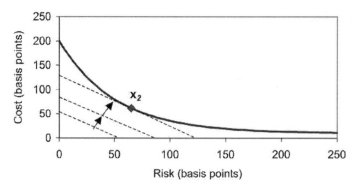

Figure 7-8 Balancing the trade-off between cost and risk

Determining the optimal trading horizon

Understanding the optimal trading horizon can be very useful, even for orders which are intended to be traded VWAP over the day (if only to confirm they are viable to trade over a single day). Figure 7-9 shows the various costs/risks for an example strategy as they vary over time. We can construct the total cost curve by summing the market impact and timing risk for different levels of risk aversion (λ) based on equation 7-1.

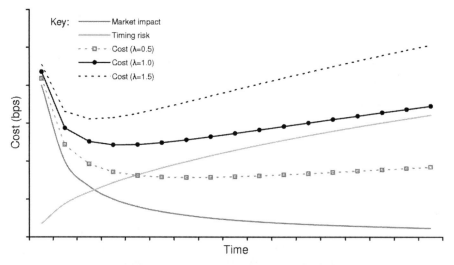

Figure 7-9 Trading strategy optimisation

From this, we can then determine the trading horizon that achieves the minimum overall cost. This time span could be used to guide an implementation shortfall algorithm, or converted into a target volume participation rate, based on the historical volume profile or ADV. Kissell and Malamut (2005b) go on to derive a solution for the minimum cost in terms of the optimal trading rate.

7.4   Choosing between trading algorithms

So far, we have seen how various factors can affect strategy choice, but how does this actually translate to selecting different trading algorithms?

Firstly, we shall map the trading algorithms onto an example efficient trading frontier. This will allow us to compare the suitability of specific algorithms for set objectives. To choose the optimal algorithm for a given order, we would need to create an efficient trading frontier tailored for its specific details. This will incorporate the factors we saw in section 7.2 when assessing the difficulty of orders. Hence, we will examine how these conditions affect both the efficient trading frontier and our ultimate choice of the optimal strategy. We will also consider some of the essential requirements for trading algorithms, and see how factors such as data availability and market structure limit our choice.

Mapping algorithms to the efficient trading frontier

As we have seen, the efficient trading frontier allows traders and investors to see the potential costs and risks of a wide range of trading strategies, from which they may then select their preferred approach.

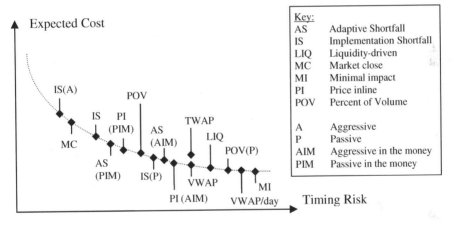

Figure 7-10 Differentiating algorithms using an efficient trading frontier

In order to map trading algorithms onto this, we would need to determine estimates for each of their expected costs and timing risks and then overlay these on an efficient trading frontier for the prospective order. Figure 7-10 tries to illustrate this for an example order. Note that this is merely an illustration, to highlight the relative differences between algorithm types. Clearly, specific instances may perform differently. Also not all algorithms may even be on the efficient frontier, since there may be better alternatives.

Notice that for some algorithms Figure 7-10 also includes aggressive (A), passive (P) and neutral versions. As we have seen, more aggressive trading generally implies higher expected costs, although interestingly the price adaptive mechanisms (e.g. aggressive-in-the-money (AIM)) actually have the opposite effect.

Impact-driven algorithms tend to appear towards the right hand side of the efficient trading frontier, exhibiting lower expected cost but higher risk, as we might expect.

VWAP:

The VWAP algorithm concentrates on minimizing market impact, by splitting the order into quantities based on the historical volume profile. Although for smaller orders this may unnecessarily prolong trading, causing additional risk exposure. So, a VWAP order left to trade through the whole day has one of the highest associated risks. This may be used as a reference point on the efficient trading frontier, labelled as VWAP/day in Figure 7-10. Simply by reducing the trading time to one appropriate for the order size, the risk may be considerably reduced (labelled VWAP). Notice that the cost does not significantly increase to achieve this.

TWAP:

In Figure 7-10, TWAP is shown as the only algorithm not to be actually on the efficient trading frontier. This is because when a TWAP algorithm splits an order it does not take into account market conditions. So it may incur additional market impact compared to other algorithms (except for small orders or very liquid assets). Still, in terms of risk it is similar to VWAP, either spread over the whole trading day or for a shorter period. Thus, TWAP is shown directly above VWAP on the efficient trading frontier. (Note that for venues where volume information is not available TWAP is a viable alternative to VWAP.)

Percent of volume (POV):

POV algorithms have a similar goal to VWAP, namely minimization of market impact. The only real difference between the two approaches is that the trading trajectory for a POV algorithm is generated dynamically, based on a fixed proportion of the actual market volume. Since its participation is based on the current market volume, each order is more likely to complete in a timescale appropriate for its size. Consequently, the timing risk should be reduced compared to VWAP, although the market impact cost may be slightly higher to achieve this. So, on the efficient trading frontier, POV algorithms are positioned to the just left of VWAP, whilst still exhibiting more risk than implementation shortfall algorithms. Note that the aggressiveness of a POV algorithm may be inferred from its participation rate, <5% is relatively passive, so this appears to the right of VWAP on the frontier.

Minimal impact:

By focusing solely on minimising the overall market impact cost, these algorithms take on a higher level of timing risk. Consequently, they appear on the right hand side of the efficient trading frontier.

Cost-driven algorithms attempt to balance both cost and risk. Therefore, they will tend to be more in the centre of the efficient trading frontier. Although aggressive versions will be closer to the left hand side, achieving lower risk, but at a higher expected cost.

Implementation Shortfall (IS):

These algorithms seek to minimize both market impact and risk, often by determining the optimal rate of trading. They tend to trade more quickly than VWAP or POV algorithms, resulting in a lower timing risk. Though, this reduced risk is achieved at a slightly higher expected cost. Thus IS trading algorithms using aggressive (A) or neutral trading styles appear to the left of POV on the efficient trading frontier shown in Figure 7-10. Only the passive (P) style exhibits lower cost, although this still has lower timing risk than VWAP.

Market close (MC):

These algorithms aim to match or better the future closing price. Whereas an implementation shortfall algorithm calculates an optimal trade duration, MC algorithms reverse this process to determine an optimal start time. Since their target price is subject to the same timing risk, this offsets some of their risk. However, the closing period is often more volatile and so MC algorithms will often incur higher costs. As a result, they are positioned just to the left of implementation shortfall on the efficient frontier, with lower risk, but higher expected costs.

Adaptive Shortfall:

An aggressive in-the-money (AIM) adaptive shortfall algorithm becomes more aggressive with favourable prices. As Kissell and Malamut (2005b) highlighted this results in a skewed distribution of returns between rising and falling markets. In comparison, algorithms with a low sensitivity to price movements (such as POV) have a more symmetrical distribution of returns. We can clearly see this in Figure 7-11 (a) taken from their study, where the AIM adaptive shortfall algorithm is compared with a constant trade rate (POV) algorithm. Since the AIM price adaptation takes advantage of better market conditions, it achieves a lower expected cost (C3). The downside is that this approach will be increasingly exposed to risk in adverse conditions, since it will be more passive as the price becomes unfavourable. This also helps explain the skewed cost distribution. Therefore, in terms of the efficient trading frontier the AIM adaptive shortfall (AS) algorithm will be to the right of the POV algorithm.

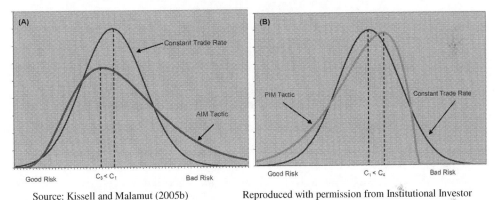

Source: Kissell and Malamut (2005b)   Reproduced with permission from Institutional Investor

Figure 7-11 Cost distribution of adaptation tactics

Conversely, the passive in-the-money (PIM) version becomes more passive with favourable prices, again shown in Figure 7-11 (b). Therefore, it has a higher expected cost (C4) but a lower overall risk; so it is sited to the left of POV on the frontier.

Note that since adaptive shortfall algorithms are sensitive to timing risk their rate of trading does not change pace quite as rapidly as a purely price inline algorithm. The net result is that whilst the effective cost of an AIM adaptive shortfall algorithm is still lower than a POV algorithm it is slightly more than that of an aggressive price inline algorithm. So it sits between these two algorithms on the efficient trading frontier.

The opportunistic algorithms are slightly more difficult to place on the efficient trading frontier. They can aggressively take advantage of favourable conditions, although this can lead to substantial impact costs. They are also prepared to wait passively until the market conditions become favourable, exposing them to timing risk.

Price Inline:

As we have already seen for the adaptive shortfall algorithm, an AIM price inline algorithm has a skewed cost distribution. We can see this most clearly when compared with a POV algorithm as shown in Figure 7-12, again taken from the study by Kissell and Malamut (2005b). Note the price inline algorithm is labelled as "Target". Thus, the AIM price adaptation takes advantage of better market conditions, achieving a lower expected cost (C2), but exposing it to higher overall risk. Therefore, on the efficient trading frontier the aggressive PI(AIM) algorithm will be to the right of the POV algorithm. On the other hand, the reversed behaviour of the passive in-the-money (PIM) version is effectively a mirror image resulting in a lower overall risk (but higher cost) and so is sited to the left of POV on the efficient frontier.

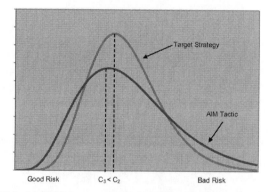

Source: Kissell and Malamut (2005b)   Reproduced with permission from Institutional Investor

Figure 7-12 Cost distribution of an AIM price inline algorithm

Liquidity-driven:

A liquidity-driven algorithm will trade fairly aggressively when there is liquidity, but at other times it simply will not trade. Some controls on the permitted level of participation will prevent the market impact being too high. However, the algorithms do not generally account for timing risk. So in Figure 7-10 the optimal liquidity-seeking algorithm is positioned just to the right of the price adaptive AIM based strategies. Though, it is arguable that different versions of the algorithm might be placed anywhere on the frontier between VWAP/day and implementation shortfall.

Pairs:

A pair trading algorithm has a degree of inbuilt hedging, provided the relationship between the two asset prices behaves as we expect. So gains (or losses) on asset B should hopefully offset any losses (or gains) on asset A. Still, if the relationship breaks down the strategy may expose us to more risk. There is also an issue if there is a sizable difference in liquidity between the two assets; significant legging will mean a higher exposure to risk. Therefore, it is hard to place pair trading algorithms on Figure 7-10. Given a suitable pair, the optimal pair trading algorithm could achieve a similar expected cost to VWAP, but with less risk. Whilst a sub-optimal pair may require much more aggressive trading in order to try to minimise the risk.

Again note that these summaries merely give an indication of how the various trading algorithms might be positioned on an efficient trading frontier, actual versions may perform slightly differently.

Factors affecting algorithm choice

When seeking the optimal trading strategy it is vital to balance the investor's objectives with the factors that dictate the overall difficulty of trading. Consequently, the choice of algorithm/strategy is dictated by factors such as:

- Investor requirements (e.g. benchmark, risk aversion and trading goals)
- Order specific properties (e.g. size)
- Asset specific properties (e.g. liquidity, volatility and price trends)

Each of these can have a considerable effect on the overall cost. For instance, Figure 7-13 shows how both order size and asset volatility increase the overall cost for a percent of volume (POV) algorithm.

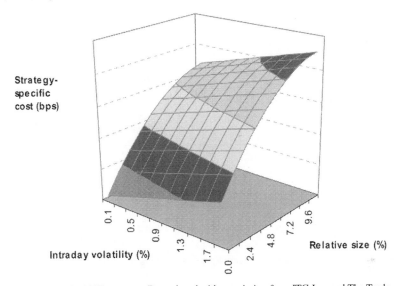

Source: Brandes *et al.* (2007)   Reproduced with permission from ITG Inc. and The Trade

Figure 7-13 Relating cost to order size and volatility

This cost estimate is based on performance data from ITG Inc., reported in a study by Yossi Brandes *et al.* (2007). We can therefore use such historical performance data to guide our choice. If the projected cost is too high then we can repeat the process for other types of algorithm until we find the one that is closest to matching our requirements. In the following sub-sections, we shall examine the effect of each of these factors.

Investor requirements

The investor's requirements are clearly also a key determinant in the choice of trading algorithm, in much the same way as we saw for the optimal strategy selection.

Benchmark

The choice of benchmark affects the efficient trading frontier, as we saw in Figure 7-4. If the benchmark is the arrival or decision price then implementation shortfall is probably the most appropriate algorithm. If it is VWAP then a VWAP algorithm makes most sense.

Risk aversion

A high risk aversion suggests an aggressive trading style, whereas a low aversion means more passive algorithms may be used. For example, Figure 7-14 shows the relationship between cost and risk aversion for an opportunistic algorithm (ITG Active) and a more aggressive implementation shortfall based approach (ITG ACE), based on a review by Jian Yang and Brett Jiu (2006). At low levels of risk aversion, the more opportunistic algorithm proves cost effective, whilst at higher levels the implementation shortfall algorithm performs best. A similar effect might be seen if we replaced the opportunistic algorithm with an impact driven one, such as VWAP. In terms of the efficient trading frontier, a high risk aversion suggests a shift towards more aggressive algorithms on the left hand side of the frontier, whilst a low aversion implies a shift to the right.

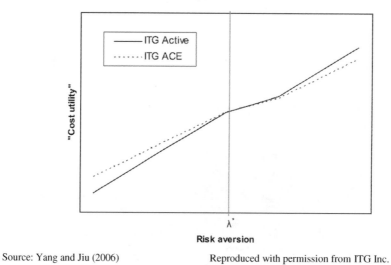

Source: Yang and Jiu (2006)   Reproduced with permission from ITG Inc.

Figure 7-14 Relating cost to risk aversion

Trading goals

If the goal is to minimise the expected cost, then we can achieve that by finding the algorithm whose projected risk is the closest match for the required level. Whereas if the goal is to achieve a balance between expected cost and risk then cost-driven algorithms such as implementation shortfall may be the most appropriate choice. Alternatively, if price improvement is the main focus then perhaps an opportunistic liquidity-driven algorithm or a passively priced impact-driven algorithm is more suitable.

Order specific factors

From section 7.2, we have already seen the effect order-specific properties, such as size and trading horizon, can have on the difficulty of an order. Hence, this can also affect our choice of algorithm, based on the expected cost and risk.

Order size

Larger order sizes generally mean increased transaction costs. Trying to execute a large order immediately will cause significant market impact. Conversely, splitting it into smaller child orders and working these over time will expose it to timing risk. Therefore, most algorithms exhibit increased costs as order size increases. However, the magnitude of these increases can vary markedly across different algorithms. Figure 7-15 highlights this for a range of algorithms trading low volatility stocks, taken from a study by ITG Inc.

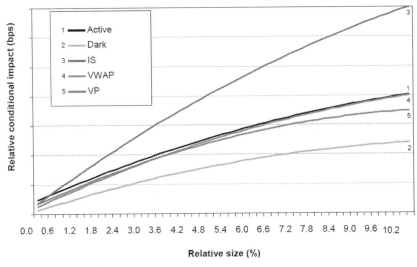

Source: Brandes *et al.* (2007)   Reproduced with permission from ITG Inc. and The Trade

Figure 7-15 Relating impact cost to order size for a range of algorithms

Clearly, the opportunistic stealth-driven algorithm (labelled "Dark") performs the best. In part, this is due to its successful minimisation of signalling risk by using IOC orders and hidden trading at "dark pool" ATSs. The impact-driven algorithms perform reasonably well, with VWAP outperforming POV at the highest order sizes. Though, the implementation shortfall (IS) algorithm fares the worst for large orders. The size of difference between this and VWAP is interesting, suggesting that they may have been executed more aggressively, resulting in higher market impact.

If the order size is sufficiently large, then it may be worth considering trading over multiple days, depending on price trends and volatility. In comparison, the choice of algorithm has much less effect for small orders. An order for <1% ADV will probably attain similar results with either VWAP or implementation shortfall.

In terms of the efficient trading frontier, the potential cost of large orders tends to shift the selection to the more passive (but riskier) algorithms on the right hand side of Figure 7-10. In other words, a participation or VWAP algorithm may be preferable to implementation shortfall for large orders.

Trade horizon
The trade horizon is usually specified by the order's start and end-time parameters. This is also related to the order size, since we can determine an estimate for the optimal horizon based on the ADV and the desired trading rate.

Clearly, a trade horizon that is shorter than the optimal one is more aggressive, although meeting this requirement can lead to excessive market impact costs. Whereas, if the horizon is much longer than optimal then there can be substantial timing risk. For instance, a small order worked throughout the entire trading day is exposed to unnecessary risk since it could have easily been completed much earlier. As we saw for order size, there will tend to be less difference in performance for short horizons compared to longer ones.

So in terms of algorithm selection, shorter horizons will therefore favour a more aggressive trading, such as a percent of volume or even an implementation shortfall algorithm. Longer horizons favour more passive, impact-driven algorithms, such as an all-day VWAP.

Asset specific factors

Asset-specific factors, such as liquidity and volatility, also affect algorithm choice since they reflect the difficulty of an order, as we saw in the trading costs back in Figure 7-2.

Liquidity

Liquidity can have a considerable effect on market impact. In fact, it can counteract some of the effects of order size, since a large order for a highly liquid asset will tend to cause less impact than for an illiquid one. Signalling risk can also be an issue for less liquid assets, even for quite small orders.

Since a liquid asset will be easier (and so cost less) to trade than an illiquid one this tends to widen the potential choice of optimal algorithms. Conversely, an illiquid asset limits the choice to more specialised algorithms, such as liquidity-driven ones.

Volatility

An asset's volatility affects both its expected cost and timing risk. So for volatile assets it is generally better to select an algorithm that is risk sensitive. In other words, algorithms that achieve lower timing risk such as implementation or adaptive shortfall algorithms.

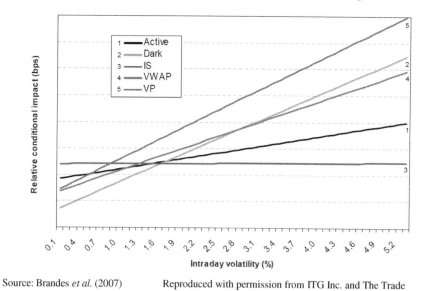

Source: Brandes *et al.* (2007)   Reproduced with permission from ITG Inc. and The Trade

Figure 7-16 Relating impact cost to volatility for a range of algorithms

We can clearly see this in Figure 7-16, which shows the results of the study by Brandes *et al.* (2007). As the intraday volatility increases, the cost barely changes for the implementation shortfall (IS) algorithms. The impact driven VWAP and percent of volume (labelled VP) algorithms fare less well, both suffering increased costs as volatility increases. This is hardly surprising since they have no inbuilt price sensitivity. Certainly, the percent of volume algorithm is the most affected; Brandes *et al.* reason that this is due to the fluctuation of market volume in reaction to price movements. The opportunistic algorithms are also affected, but somewhat less than the impact-driven ones. For example, ITG Active, a liquidity seeking algorithm which uses dynamic pegging, seems to cope with short term price moves nearly as well as an implementation shortfall algorithm.

For lower volatility assets, timing risk is less of an issue and so the potential reduced costs of volume participation make impact-driven or even opportunistic algorithms more suitable.

Price trends

A persistent and favourable price trend allows us to reduce costs by trading more passively. Whilst an unfavourable trend requires more aggressive trading, since any delay will simply result in even worse executions. Therefore, if we are confident of a price trend persisting then we should consider using algorithms from the appropriate side of the efficient trading frontier in order to benefit most. For instance, a more passively traded VWAP algorithm may perform better for favourable price trends. Alternatively, an implementation shortfall algorithm is more appropriate to prevent losses from an unfavourable price trend. Note that the level of aggressiveness needs to be appropriate for the size of the expected price trend; otherwise, the increased market impact costs will counteract any gains/savings.

Price adaptive algorithms, such as price inline or adaptive shortfall may also be used to take advantage of trends. As we have seen these give a more skewed distribution of expected costs, with aggressive in-the-money (AIM) strategies achieving a lower cost but higher risk, whilst passive in-the-money (PIM) versions do the opposite. If the price trend is short-lived or mean reverts then an aggressive (AIM) approach may be more appropriate. Though, if the trend persists then the passive in-the-money approach may offer the best results.

So in terms of the efficient trading frontier favourable and persistent trends shift the selection to the more passive (but riskier) algorithms on the right hand side of Figure 7-10, whereas unfavourable trends shift it to the left.

Summary

The efficient trading frontier can also be used to summarise the effect these factors have, as

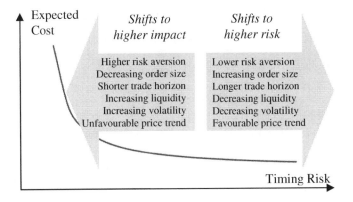

Figure 7-17 Factors which influence trading choice

Figure 7-17 shows. Unsurprisingly, urgency, risk aversion, and volatility all tend to bias the strategy selection towards more aggressive trading with lower risk, but potentially higher impact costs. Conversely, larger orders and favourable price trends tend to encourage a more passive approach with lower impact costs, but potentially higher risk.

Other requirements for trading algorithms

So far, we have focussed on the theory of algorithm selection. In the real world, basic requirements such as market structure and data availability also limit our choices. Obviously, algorithms need electronic access to make requests or place orders. Market data is another key requirement for trading algorithms, without it they are blind. Hence, the availability of pre- and post-trade market data is vital for most strategies.

Market structure also plays its part. In a single dealer environment there is little point in splitting up an order (unless it is huge and even then it is debatable). Instead, it makes more sense to discuss with the dealer how best to work the whole order. Therefore, to even consider using trading algorithms the market should have multiple dealers/market makers. Conversely, markets that are very fragmented are more difficult to trade in than centralised ones, so this will also affect algorithm choice.

Asset specific factors such as liquidity and trade frequency may also be broadly generalised by asset class. For instance, equities tend to be more liquid than most bonds. Thus, characteristics of the asset class can also affect algorithm choice.

Data requirements

Trading algorithms rely on market data in order to function. Although market transparency is increasing, there are still marked differences between the world's markets, both for pre- and post-trade information.

Pre-trade prices can be delivered in streams, either from a market data vendor, direct from the execution venue or via a request for stream (RFS) type mechanism. They may also be gathered via a request for quote (RFQ) mechanism. Although the considerable latency associated with an RFQ-based approach means that it is only really viable for strategies that will not be generating a lot of small child orders.

Post-trade data needs to provide accurate information on trade prices, sizes and times (and if possible any counterparty information). For some markets, such information simply has not been available. For example, in the early days of adoption in the FX markets some venues only provided traded prices but not sizes.

Many algorithms track the traded volume, so if this is not available the choice will be severely restricted. Likewise, if the data is available but only after a considerable delay then it is of little use to algorithms such as percent of volume. Post-trade data is also needed to create historical volume profiles, as well as for many of the models that algorithms use to estimate execution probability or costs.

Order book data is necessary for any strategies that are based on the available liquidity. Clearly, this must be available in real-time for any algorithm which actively tracks liquidity. Historical order book data may also be required for limit order and cost models.

Even the most basic trading algorithms need access to real-time best bid and offer prices, otherwise they risk placing orders significantly away from the market. The alternative is to only ever issue market orders. More complex trading algorithms obviously have more stringent requirements, as outlined in Table 7-2.

Algorithm	Real-time			Historical
	Prices	*Trades*	*Order book*	*Trades*
TWAP	●			
VWAP	●	○		●
Percent of Volume	●	●	○	○
Implementation shortfall	●	○	○	○
Liquidity-based	●	○	●	○

● Required ○ Often needed

Table 7-2 Basic data requirements for common trading algorithms

As we saw in Chapter 5, some of the earlier statically-driven algorithms can survive based on historical data. So for markets with the bare minimum of electronic access and multiple dealers the only really viable trading algorithm is simple order slicing or TWAP. Consequently, they are available for most types of market or asset class.

VWAP algorithms require detailed trade information in order to construct their volume profiles. Likewise, percent of volume (POV) algorithms need trade reports in real-time in order to track the market volume. In fragmented markets, some brokers/vendors have also started to create their own proprietary measures, based on aggregated data.

Implementation shortfall (IS) algorithms need to carefully track the current price and the potential risk in order to minimise the overall cost. Therefore, these algorithms need as much help as they can get, otherwise their performance will suffer. Although we might possibly be able to get a shortfall-based algorithm to work for an RFQ based market, it is debatable whether this approach is worthwhile.

Similarly, liquidity-driven algorithms need readily available order book information. If this is limited then algorithms will have to rely more on estimates, which may substantially reduce their efficiency. Signalling risk is obviously a key concern, so again the market needs to support anonymous trading. Given the opportunistic nature of such algorithms, latency can also be a key consideration for them.

Other information such as fees for routing and/or clearing/settlement may also need to taken into account; otherwise, unexpected costs may be incurred.

Market structure

Each of the world's major markets has their own specific characteristics, as we saw in Chapter 3. Equities and listed derivatives are traded at centralised venues, although admittedly there is considerable fragmentation in some of these markets. In comparison, OTC trading is still the norm for a lot of fixed income trading. Although clearly there are exceptions, such as the U.S. Treasury market which is so large that its inter-dealer market is not that different from the major U.S. exchanges.

Given their well-established central markets with a range of highly liquid assets, the equities markets were the perfect starting place for algorithmic trading. As we have already seen, the algorithms have progressed from simple order slicing to VWAP, implementation shortfall and liquidity-based algorithms. However, not all algorithms are equal; some are more applicable across a range of asset classes than others, as Table 7-3 tries to show.

Simple order slicing or TWAP algorithms are a basic starting point for every asset class, since they have the least requirements.

Volume-driven algorithms, such as VWAP, make most sense for centralised markets. This is because there only needs to be one set of trade reports, so it is easy to track the market

Algorithm	Equities	Bonds	FX	Futures	Options	ETFs
TWAP	○	○	○	○	○	○
VWAP	●	○		●		
Percent of Volume	●	○	○	●		
Implementation shortfall	●	●	●	●	●	●
Liquidity-based	●	●	●	●	●	

● High ○ Medium

Table 7-3 Applicability of current trading algorithms across different asset classes

volume. As markets become more fragmented, the volumes for each venue need to be tracked. In order to give meaningful results these algorithms really need to track the total market volume. For instance, if the main market only has around 50% of the total trading volume then VWAP or POV algorithms, which only consider the volume traded here are missing half the picture. Thus, aggregated market data feeds have become increasingly important. If there is a unified source of pre- and post-trade information, this is straightforward; otherwise, we will have to create our own. This also makes transaction cost analysis and performance monitoring more difficult.

Hence, going forward the two most applicable types of algorithm are the implementation shortfall and liquidity-based approaches.

Asset-class specific factors

There are considerable differences between asset classes in terms of the:
- Number of assets available
- Liquidity
- Frequency of trading / average trade size

The FX market has easily the lowest number of tradable assets; hence, these are highly liquid. Conversely, there are hundreds of thousands of distinct bonds and options, so any one generally has much less liquidity than a corresponding equity.

Trading activity is linked to liquidity and the number of available assets. It is also affected by investors' objectives. For instance, bonds are often bought and held, so after an initial flurry on their first issuance the trading activity quickly subsides. It is not uncommon for corporate bonds to trade less than once a day, on average. In comparison, equities are often held for shorter periods, hence their much higher levels of trading. Volume-driven algorithms need a substantial amount of trading activity for them to be useful; they are just not as meaningful for illiquid assets. So, whilst a VWAP algorithm may be viable for some U.S. Treasuries, it will not be for certain corporate bonds or options.

Trade size and costs also differ amongst the asset classes. For example, bonds generally trade in larger sizes than equities. Bonds also realise lower costs for larger trades, so impact costs will be very different to those for equities.

Other properties associated with asset classes can also affect algorithm choice. For instance, price is not always a key driver for assets. As we saw in Chapter 5, implied volatility can be more important than the actual price for some options algorithms.

Likewise, trading volume is not as vital for some assets. Open-ended ETFs are not subject to a fixed fund size, an in-kind creation and redemption process allows specialised dealers to react to the demands of the secondary market. Therefore, supply and demand have less impact on the price of such ETFs than for equities. Thus, trading volume is a less important indicator for these. So, volume driven approaches, such as VWAP or POV, may be less appropriate.

As algorithmic trading continues to spread, algorithms will probably evolve to be even more tailored for specific asset-classes. In the future, we may well see a new breed of algorithms evolve which treat assets in a more fungible way. Algorithms tailored for bond trading might select between a set of assets, if the investor is happy to consider an alternative with similar characteristics. Similarly, for options, trading based on the risk characteristics (or the "Greeks") may become more important than finding a match for a specific contract.

7.5   To cross or not to cross?

The additional liquidity offered by "dark pool" ATSs means that crossing is another important consideration when seeking the optimal trading strategy. They offer the potential for substantial cost reduction by trading in size without incurring significant market impact. Therefore, it is important to also consider the possibility of using crossing as part of the optimal trading strategy.

Although crossing has obvious advantages, execution is not always guaranteed. Also, whenever trading in size signalling risk is always a concern, even for venues that are intended to be completely opaque. So the optimal approach may well involve a combination of crossing and trading algorithms.

The benefits of crossing networks and "dark pools"

Using crossing networks or trading via "dark pools" can realise considerable cost savings. Table 7-4 shows a breakdown of these from a study by the Quantitative Services Group LLC (QSG). They compared the performance of trades on the Millennium ATS (between December 2007 and March 2008) with those from a wide range of other execution venues. Overall, they found that "dark pool" execution reduced the market impact of trades by 62%, giving a saving of 6.6 bps. The market impact savings appear to be fairly consistent, regardless of market capitalisation, although the higher costs associated with trading less liquid stocks mean significantly larger savings for the small and micro-cap stocks in terms of basis points/share.

Category	Decrease in market impact	Savings (in bps/share)
Micro-cap	66%	21.53
Small-cap	63%	13.43
Mid-cap	59%	8.08
Large-cap	62%	5.18
Weighted Average	62%	6.61

Source: QSG (2008)

Table 7-4 Comparative cost savings achieved on the Millennium ATS

An interesting comparison of the performance between traditional crossing networks and "dark pool" algorithms was carried out in a detailed study for ITG Inc. by Ian Domowitz, Ilya Finkelshteyn and Henry Yegerman (2008). They found that using crossing networks achieved significant cost savings regardless of the market conditions, as shown in Table 7-5.

Conditions	Cost saving versus benchmark (bps)			
	Periodic crossing (POSIT)	Continuous crossing (POSIT Now)	"Dark pool" algorithms (ITG Dark)	Peer universe
Low volatility	+3	+1	-2	-11
High volatility	+4	-1	-8	-18
Overall	+4	0	-4	-12

Source: Domowitz, Finkelshteyn and Yegerman (2008)

Table 7-5 A comparison of the costs of different crossing mechanisms by ITG Inc.

From their data, crossing via POSIT realised savings of 3-4 bps in both low and high volatility regimes. Continuous crossing via POSIT Now and "dark pool" algorithms (ITG Dark) were also found to achieve lower costs than a universe of peer trades, whose average cost was 12 bps, reaching 18 bps during periods of high volatility.

Their study considered over 20 million orders, of which around 12.6 million were entered during 2007 using a range of mechanisms, including both periodic and continuous crossing and liquidity aggregation. A further 8 million orders were taken from a complementary transaction cost database. So as well as covering the ITG crossing networks the study also encompassed "dark pools" from a variety of vendors/brokers.

Domowitz, Finkelshteyn and Yegerman also analysed the distribution of transaction costs between these different mechanisms. For orders completed within thirty minutes of submission, they found that the probability of achieving a cost between -20 and +20 bps was highest for periodic crossing (POSIT) at 88%. Continuous crossing via POSIT Now had a 77% probability of meeting this cost band whilst trading via a liquidity aggregator was found to only have a 61% chance. They found that the risk of incurring higher transaction costs was significantly lower for the dedicated crossing mechanisms. For periodic crossing, the probability of incurring a cost of more than 20 bps was only 4% whilst for continuous crossing it was 10%, reaching 20% for the "dark pool" algorithms based on liquidity aggregation.

The effect of execution duration was analysed as well. They found a consistent degradation in performance with increasing time. For example, the periodic crossing for POSIT realised healthy savings for up to the first hour of execution, but after 2.5 hours this became a cost of 6 bps. In comparison, they found this effect to be even greater for other "dark pools", realising losses of up to 25 bps after 2.5 hours.

Overall, Domowitz, Finkelshteyn and Yegerman (2008) concluded that execution using "dark pools" is beneficial; though, they found no improvement using "dark pool" algorithms compared to periodic crossing. They reason that this is probably due to information leakage: whilst each venue may be dark, the more orders are routed between them the more chance there is of leakage. Hence, algorithms that route orders between different "dark pools" may not necessarily perform as well as simply routing the order to a single venue.

Clearly, substantial cost savings can be realised by crossing, but it is also worth comparing the various mechanisms. Using a periodic crossing may well prove to be a more cost efficient approach than using some of the dedicated "dark pool" liquidity algorithms.

7.6   Market conditions during the 2007-09 financial crisis

Up until this point, the focus has been on general principles. Still, it is impossible to ignore the conditions during the 2007-09 financial crisis, particularly in the stock markets. Major stock indices saw ten year lows, with daily falls (and rises) of 3-5%, or even more.

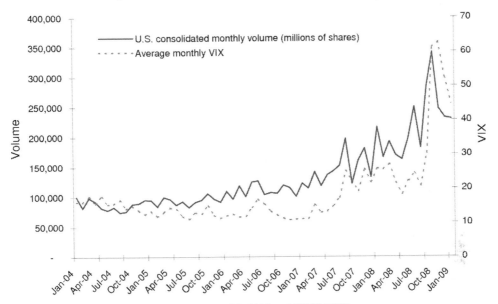

Source: Authors own calculations based on CBOE (2009) and NYSE (2009)

Figure 7-18 Changing market conditions

Market volatility and trading volumes surged, as shown in Figure 7-18, the volatility spikes are easy to see. Indeed, the CBOE's VIX volatility index reached an unprecedented high of 89 in October 2008. Market volumes also surged, as investors sought to convert their positions to cash, as well as the unwinding of positions in funds that had failed.

In contrast to this, many of the key indicators of market liquidity actually declined: Spreads increased whilst the displayed depth on many order books was significantly reduced. In such an unpredictable trading environment, there is clearly a benefit to getting additional market "colour" and discussing orders with a trader. In fact, a TABB Group (2008) review of U.S. institutional trading found that sales traders' captured 44% of buy-side flow in 2008, up from 37% the year before. Interestingly, though, this seems mainly to have been at the expense of DMA and crossing networks or "dark pools". They found that algorithmic trading usage actually increased to 24%, from 22% in 2007. Despite the harshest of trading conditions, algorithms appear to have proved themselves.

The partial decline in usage of DMA and crossing networks is understandable given the extreme market conditions: When markets move so rapidly it is difficult to handle a large number of orders directly. Similarly, leaving an order for a long time in a "dark pool" is a much riskier proposition since the market prices could rapidly change. In both cases, it is easier to leave orders to be handled by a sales trader or an algorithm.

The market crisis also led banks to reduce the amount of principal and proprietary trading.

Trading large block orders became more difficult, since the "upstairs" market was a shadow of its former self. Hence the value of crossing networks and "dark pools". In fact, a survey of U.S. "dark pools" carried out by Rosenblatt Securities (2008a) found that their market share actually increased in November 2008, to 8.57%, after falls in September and October. They also note that the volatility seemed to have most impact on the venues focussed on large block orders.

Transaction costs also saw considerable increases due to the market volatility. The most visible change was in spread costs. Dealers and market makers need to incorporate the higher level of risk in their quoted prices. Thus, bid offer spreads nearly doubled, even for some blue-chip stocks. Less liquid firms saw even higher increases. Spreads saw similar increases across Europe and even larger ones in Asia. Although spread cost is not the only concern, since the reduced liquidity also led to higher market impact costs. In fact, in their study of 2008 ITG client execution data Hitesh Mittal and James Wong (2008) found that there was 37% less displayed liquidity during the high volatility regime. Overall, they estimated that selecting the optimal trading algorithm led to savings of 60 bps for their clients, compared to 20 bps during lower volatility periods.

As we have already seen, volatility tends to lead to more aggressive trading strategies seeking to minimise the risk at the cost of higher potential impact. Consequently, the market crisis resulted in a shift in the type of algorithms being used. Implementation or adaptive shortfall algorithms became much more important. Lower levels of visible liquidity and the desire to minimise signalling risk also meant that liquidity-based algorithms became more widely used. Overall, Mittal and Wong (2008) found the best performance was from dynamic/opportunistic algorithms, which took advantage of market conditions but also tracked implementation shortfall costs. So it is important for trading algorithms to:

- Track cost and risk
- Take advantage of all available liquidity
- Minimise signalling risk / information leakage

Clearly, a first generation static schedule-driven VWAP algorithm is going to struggle compared to more sophisticated algorithms that dynamically adapt to conditions. Note, this is not to say VWAP trading does not still have a place. As we saw in the previous section, in high volatility it can actually realise lower costs than POV algorithms since it is less prone to chasing the market. Again, it is all down to doing the pre-trade analysis and selecting the most appropriate algorithm for a given order based on the investor's requirements and the market conditions.

Volatile markets also pose a significant problem for the models which trading algorithms use to determine potential costs or to determine a trading horizon. In turbulent markets, historical data often does not act as a good indicator for future conditions. Short-term forecasting models may be used, adjusting the historical estimates based on current market conditions. In Chapter 10, we will cover these forecast models for conditions, such as price, volatility and volume, in more detail. Also in Chapter 15, we will see how techniques such as data mining and artificial intelligence may be used to improve their accuracy.

7.7 A decision tree for strategy selection

We started this chapter with Wayne Wagner's (2006) example trading decision framework, shown back in Figure 7-1. The first key decision was to determine the difficulty of the order. As we saw in section 7.2, three of the main factors for this are liquidity, volatility and order size. These also tie in with the trends shown back in Figure 7-17.

A potential decision tree for algorithm selection for difficult orders is shown in Figure 7-19. The main choice is whether the order is urgent or large. An order may be urgent because the investor's risk aversion is high or the asset is volatile, whilst a large order might be anything over 20% of the ADV.

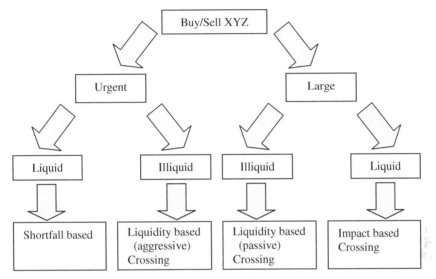

Figure 7-19 An algorithm selection decision tree for difficult orders

Volatile assets can have considerable timing risk, so they need to be traded more urgently. Larger orders can cause substantial market impact, so they require more careful handling. Bear in mind that order size is relative. For instance, a million shares might be very little for a blue-chip stock whilst ten thousand might be a massive amount for an illiquid firm. So liquidity can be incorporated, to an extent, in the relative order size. Hence, liquidity is treated as a secondary factor, which makes our trading easier. Thus, urgent or large orders for liquid assets pose much less of a problem than for illiquid ones.

The choice of trading algorithm follows the trends we saw in Figure 7-17, which also ties in with the algorithm mapping from the efficient frontier in Figure 7-10. Urgent trades for liquid assets will tend to use the cost-driven implementation (or adaptive) shortfall based algorithms, whilst large trades for liquid assets will use the more impact-driven VWAP or POV algorithms. With illiquid assets there is much less choice, in order to achieve best execution we shall have to rely on liquidity based algorithm. For urgent orders, the timing risk means the trading will need to be reasonably aggressive, whilst for large orders a more passive approach is worthwhile.

Crossing is another key consideration. Trading algorithms are increasingly interacting with crossing networks. Though, this may simply mean passing orders through crossing venues. The risk of overfilling means it is often not viable to leave an entire order at a crossing venue whilst trading it in parallel via an algorithm or DMA. Therefore, some liquidity-based algorithms may well leave a sizeable proportion of the order at a crossing venue, whilst splitting off slices to trade on the markets. This approach will generally be adopted for illiquid assets or larger orders, since the lower probability of execution makes it less appealing for urgent orders.

Figure 7-19 does not show any choices for easy orders. This is because these have no real constraints. Similar results could be achieved with any of the trading algorithms. So, it comes down to the investor/trader's preferences. Clearly, the decision tree shown in Figure 7-19 is only one example of how we might perform algorithm selection.

Going one step further, Neovest has actually created an algorithmic management system called AlgoGenetics; a screenshot is shown in Figure 7-20. This provides a drag-and-drop interface allowing traders to establish the exact conditions for algorithm or DMA order selection. It also caters for algorithms from a wide range of brokers/vendors. Thus, rules may be set to select the "best of breed". Traders can also specify their own customised behaviours effectively creating their own "meta-algorithms". For instance, an order might initially be configured to participate in the opening auction. The remainder could then be split between a range of different algorithms: baseline participation might be achieved with a POV algorithm whilst in parallel it might seek further price improvement from a more price adaptive or liquidity-seeking algorithm.

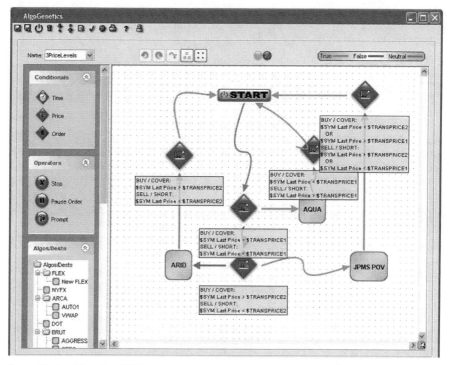

Source: Traders Magazine (2007b)   Reproduced with permission of Neovest, Inc. and Traders Magazine

Figure 7-20 Creating rules for algorithm choice with AlgoGenetics

Such flexibility clearly gives traders a powerful tool for algorithm selection. Note that selecting the optimal trading algorithm from the many hundreds versions which are available will always be a difficult choice. Still, it is important to stay focused on the overall investment objectives. As usual, the choice will often mean striking the right balance between cost and risk.

7.8 Summary

- There are no hard and fast rules for how to achieve best execution. The judgement depends on the investor's objectives, so key factors are the:
  - Target benchmark
  - Level of risk aversion
  - Specific trading goals, such as to:
    - Minimize the expected cost.
    - Achieve price improvement.
    - Balance the trade-off between expected cost and risk.

- Trading decision frameworks often start by gauging the difficulty of the order, which is determined by the following properties:
  - Order size (relative to the ADV)
  - Price momentum
  - Volatility
  - Urgency and/or the trading horizon
  - Liquidity

- Based on this difficulty, the trader then must select the most appropriate methods, whether this means manual, DMA, crossing, using trading algorithms or a mixture of these.

- The efficient trading frontier represents the set of optimal trading strategies. Each one of these has the lowest expected cost for a given level of risk. Algorithms and other strategies may be mapped to this frontier, allowing comparison between them.

- A wide range of factors affects the choice of trading algorithm.
  - Urgency, risk aversion and volatility tend to bias towards more aggressive trading.
  - Larger orders and favourable price trends tend to encourage a more passive style.
  - Fundamental issues, such as the availability of market data and market structure also restrict the choice of strategy.

Part III

Implementing trading strategies

This part of the book delves further into the nitty-gritty of implementing trading strategies; it also shows how they may be enhanced and looks at the infrastructure required to make them work.

- Chapter 8 covers order placement, using empirical market microstructure research to analyse how market conditions affect execution probability.

- Chapter 9 focuses on execution tactics, which provide common mechanisms to achieve the goals of trading algorithms.

- Chapter 10 considers ways to enhance the performance of trading algorithms, using models for short-term forecasting and cost estimation, as well as handling special events.

- Chapter 11 reviews the infrastructure requirements associated with algorithmic trading and DMA, such as order management and the design of trading platforms.

Hopefully, by the end of these four chapters you should have a deeper understanding of the technical issues required to actually implement algorithmic trading strategies.

Chapter 8

Order placement

Order placement decisions are important to the success of any trading strategy.

8.1 Introduction

Order placement decisions are a key part of trading. Executing too aggressively could result in significant market impact; it also broadcasts our intentions to other market participants. Whereas trading too passively may result in us failing to complete the order, which could lead to a sizeable opportunity cost. Therefore we need to find the right balance which best achieves our objectives.

Based on these requirements, we need to select each order's size and price, and any special order types or conditions (if appropriate). Increasingly, marketplaces consist of multiple competing execution venues. So, for multi-venue markets we also need to choose the best destination. The possibility of hidden liquidity must also be taken into account. Hence, order placement decisions are affected by a wide range of factors, such as:

- current market conditions (price, volatility and liquidity)
- projected future trends
- historical results

Another way of looking at order placement is in terms of execution probability. Factors such as liquidity and price trends help us to estimate the likelihood of an order executing. Therefore, we can adjust orders to try to maximise their chance of being filled. This provides a more quantitative basis for actual order selection, and enables us to choose between execution venues.

To make best use of orders it is vital to understand the actual mechanisms that are involved in order matching. As we saw in Chapter 2, trading consists of three main stages:

1. Price formation
2. Price discovery / trade execution
3. Reporting, clearing & settlement

Consequently, order placement decisions are closely linked to both price formation and price discovery (or execution). So we shall start this chapter by reviewing these two fundamental mechanisms in some more detail, before moving on to consider the specifics of order placement and execution probability.

8.2   Price formation

Price formation is a multi-stage process. The fair value of an asset reflects its actual value whereas the market price reflects what people are prepared to pay. The market price may also reflect their expectations for the future value. If demand is high and supply is limited, assets will often trade at a premium to their fair value. Conversely, if demand is low then discounting may occur.

This division is also reflected in price analysis. Fundamental analysts tackle the problem by striving to determine the fair (or present) value of the asset. So the actual market price will be the key determinant of whether it is worth trading or not. Conversely, technical analysts tend to base their pricing solely from trends in the market price and volume.

Given the importance of the market price, market transparency also plays a key part in price discovery. A market maker's two-way quote only gives one view on pricing. Similarly, if only the best bid and offer quotes are displayed from an order book then effectively this is the same as a two-way quote. This adds a degree of uncertainty since traders cannot tell what other liquidity might be available. This additional risk could lead to orders being priced more aggressively than is necessary. On the other hand, if quotes are sought from multiple dealers or more of the order book is visible then traders can see the range of available prices and sizes. By using such visible liquidity, they can then adjust their own valuations to determine their own target price for the asset.

Valuation

The value of an asset is clearly a fundamental component of its price. Many books have been dedicated to this subject alone. Though, for the purposes of this chapter, the discounted cash flow model will suffice as our pricing model: Present value theory states that the present value of an asset corresponds to a discounted sum of its future payments. The discount rate takes account of the time value of money as well as other factors such as risk. Thus, asset prices will be higher for larger cash flows and lower when the discount rate increases.

Fixed income assets, such as bonds, offer fixed levels of interest for a given period of time and so have very clearly defined future payment streams, or cash flows. Present value theory lends itself well to the pricing of these assets.

Valuation for assets such as equity shares in a company is more complex, since the cash flows are less predictable. Nevertheless, present value theory has also been applied to stocks, dating back to work by Robert Wiese (1930) and John Williams (1938). Discounted cash flow models make valuations based on the present value of future dividend payments, which in turn depend on future earnings. Though, there are further complications when valuing stocks. For example, companies with high returns on capital will often reinvest income rather than increasing dividend payouts. Also, unlike bonds, companies could last forever (in theory), perpetually issuing dividend payments. Thus, Myron Gordon (1962) developed his growth model, where valuations are based on the current stock price and dividend, together with the expected rate of dividend growth and a discount rate. Other models have gone on to incorporate multiple growth periods, or finite horizons.

Other assets can also be complex to price, as we saw in Chapter 3. Foreign exchange is affected by both macroeconomic information, such as interest rates, and order flow. Derivatives reflect the price of their underlying assets combined with estimates for factors such as volatility and interest rates. Thus, appropriate adjustments must be made for their corresponding pricing models.

Regardless of how these valuations are actually determined, the amount of information and data required means that investors will invariably achieve different prices for assets (even if only slightly). The resultant diversity is crucial to keep markets flowing.

Models of price formation

Market microstructure researchers have used a wide array of models to investigate the price formation mechanism. Investors tend to have different views on assets, so supply and demand often affects price formation.

Inventory-based models take the dealer's point of view, focussing on how their position affects the prices they offer. Essentially, the bid offer spread represents the cost for which market makers are prepared to offer immediacy. Information-based models take the point of view that traders have differing levels of information, which in turn affects their pricing. Likewise, visible order books are themselves are a source of information. Thus, a range of studies has focussed on how this affects price formation. Various combinations of these models have also been used to try to explain this process.

Inventory-based models

A market maker is not an investor; they are not trying to establish a position in a given asset. Their inventory, or position, simply needs to be sufficient to service any incoming orders. In order to achieve this, they adjust their quoted prices to encourage orders that take them closer to their preferred inventory size. So the market maker's bid offer spread often tends to increase as their position moves further from their ideal inventory. The strength of this reaction tends to reflect their allowed capital; smaller brokers will generally exhibit a more noticeable effect.

For instance, Figure 8-1 shows how an example market maker's bid and offer quotes can change for a range of different inventories. The centre of each circle represents their quoted bid or offer price and the diameter corresponds to their quoted size. For simplicity we will assume that their optimal inventory is zero, in other words to be "flat".

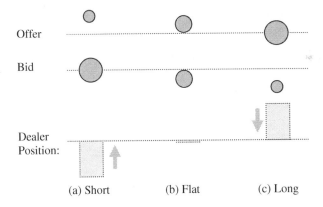

Figure 8-1 How inventory can affect market maker quotes

Therefore, in Figure 8-1 (a), when the market maker's position is too low they may raise their bid quote to try to encourage sellers to sell to them, and so reduce the deficit. They can also discourage any further buy orders by setting a high offer price. The opposite holds true when the inventory is too high. So in (c) the market maker may quote a lower offer price than in (a) to encourage buy orders and so reduce their surplus. Likewise, the bid price may be set lower to discourage any further sell orders.

Regulation means that market maker's must often quote within a given range of the best bid and offer. So an alternative to adjusting the price is just to alter the size for the quotes, a low bid size will discourage sells, whilst a high offer size will encourage buy orders.

Note that in multi-broker markets the inventory effects will be distinct for each market maker, reflecting their differing inventories. So at any one time different brokers will be keen to set the best bid or offer. Hence, competition means that the market's overall spread tends to be narrower than any given market maker's spread.

The inventory-based model is also able to account for other market features. For example, liquid assets tend to have lower spreads than illiquid ones. Since market makers are able to turnover their positions more quickly for liquid assets they demand less compensation and so quote tighter spreads. Conversely, David Cushing and Ananth Madhavan (2001) observed substantial increases in costs towards the market close. This may be attributed to market makers being less keen to carry overnight positions and so pricing accordingly.

Information-based models

The value of information was nicely outlined by Hirotaka Inoue (1999) in a study of the price formation and discovery process: For assets such as government bonds, where the cash flow is well established, prices are mainly affected by public information. Macroeconomic announcements can affect the discount rate, and so alter the present value. Whereas assets like stocks are much more affected by private information, since the future cash flows are less certain.

Information-based models attempt to account for the information asymmetry that is an important factor in real markets. Some traders will have a definite information advantage over others. When trading with such an informed trader we are likely to lose, due to the resultant price reaction when the information becomes public. This is sometimes referred to as the adverse selection effect.

A study by Thomas Copeland and Dan Galai (1983) found that to protect against adverse selection a market maker's bid offer spread should generate enough returns to cover this cost. They characterised the cost of supplying quotes as writing a put and a call option. Copeland and Galai concluded that the bid offer spread is positively related to the price and volatility and negatively related to market activity and depth. They also found the spread to be negatively correlated with the degree of competition faced by market makers. Likewise, an empirical study of NYSE specialists by Charles Lee, Belinda Mucklow and Mark Ready (1993) found that they are sensitive to information asymmetry, using both spread and quoted depth to manage their risk. Their study tracked the reactions of specialists to earnings announcements, after which they observed a widening of the spreads.

Information-based models for order-driven markets are slightly different; this is because the bid offer spread arises due to market conditions. A wide range of studies has used models of limit order markets to analyse how this affects trading. A purely valuation-based approach was adopted by Thierry Foucault (1999), using a game theoretic model of price formation for a dynamic limit order market. Trading occurred due to inherent differences in valuation; there was no private information.

Foucault's model was extended to incorporate asymmetric information by Puneet Handa, Robert Schwartz and Ashish Tiwari (2003). Using empirical data from France's main stock index, the CAC40, they showed that the size of the spread is based on differences in valuation among the traders as well as the risk of adverse selection. These effects were further quantified in a study by Ming-Chang Wang, Lon-Ping Zu and Chau-Jung Kuo

(2006). Using empirical data from the Taiwan Stock Exchange they found that around 25% of the spread was attributable to valuation differences. The remaining 75% was a premium to offset the risk of adverse selection (split evenly for buyers and sellers).

Wang, Zu and Kuo (2006) also found that the average adverse selection cost varied significantly over time; the largest cost was at the open whilst the smallest was at lunchtime. This is consistent with studies by Ken Nyholm (2002), and Harrison Hong and Jiang Wang (2000) who showed that the probability of informed trading is larger in the morning than in the afternoon. So spreads tend to be wider in the morning compared to later in the day.

Order book data models

Many order-driven markets have visible order books, which in themselves are a source of information. Hence, a range of studies has focussed on how order book information affects the price formation process.

The interaction between the order book and the supply and demand of liquidity was analysed for stocks on the Paris Bourse by Bruno Biais, Pierre Hillion and Chester Spatt (1995). They found that when there were few limit orders on the order book incoming orders were often priced less aggressively than the corresponding best bid or offer. Therefore, instead of resulting in an execution such orders would stay on the order book, gradually increasing liquidity by adding to the available depth. Conversely, when the order book was sufficiently deep they found that new orders were often priced more aggressively, to take advantage of this liquidity, and so resulting in executions. A similar analysis was applied to the Swiss Stock Exchange by Angelo Ranaldo (2004). He tracked how the available depth on each side of the order book affected new order placement. His analysis showed that traders tended to place more aggressively priced orders when the same side of the order book was deeper, or when the opposite side was thinner.

In terms of the bid offer spread, Ranaldo (2004) found that less aggressively priced orders were placed as the spread widens. A similar result was found by Yue-Cheong Chan (2005). Chan also analysed the impact of short-term price movements and found that traders place more aggressively priced orders after previously positive returns.

Combined models

A hybrid model incorporating both inventory and asymmetric information effects was developed by Ananth Madhavan and Seymour Smidt (1993). In this model, the market maker also actively invested by dynamically modifying their target inventory levels according to the market conditions. Using data from NYSE specialists, they found that inventories exhibited a slow mean reversion with a half-life of around seven days.

In another study Wang, Zu and Kuo (2008) extended the Handa, Schwartz and Tiwari (2003) information-based model to include risk-averse traders. They also studied the effect of order book information, again using empirical data from the Taiwan Stock Exchange. The following information acted as indicators for the traders' order strategies:

- order imbalance
- prior order aggressiveness
- short-term volatility
- short-term price momentum
- relative spread
- timeframe

Sellers were found to be more concerned about non-execution risk; they followed the order aggressiveness of both prior buy and sell orders. Whereas buyers were more concerned about orders becoming mispriced and so "picked-off"; hence, orders were more dependent on the aggressiveness of prior buys. A favourable signal tended to make buyers more aggressive and sellers more patient whilst the opposite applied for unfavourable information. They concluded that price formation continually reflected the changes in expectation of picking-off risk and non-execution risk for buyers and sellers.

8.3   Price discovery/Order matching

Price discovery is trade execution, it occurs when the supply and demand requirements from orders are matched. The price at which this happens is determined by the mechanism. As we saw in Chapter 2, there are three main types of discovery mechanism:

- Bilateral trading
- Continuous auction
- Call auction

Bilateral trading represents one-to-one quote-driven and negotiation-based mechanisms. The matching process is just a matter of whether their quoted prices are acceptable or not. The multilateral auction-based mechanisms are used for order-driven and hybrid markets. Specific rules are applied to determine whether executions occur. The main difference between these two types of auction is simply the frequency. Unlike continuous auctions, call-based auctions allow orders to accumulate for some time before the actual discovery (or matching) takes place.

Continuous matching

The continuous auction mechanism consistently applies the matching rules each time an order is added, updated or cancelled. Any matches result in corresponding executions. Typically, markets give price the most priority. A variety of approaches is used for the secondary priority, which is used to differentiate between orders with the same ranking in terms of the primary condition (e.g. the same price). Two of the most common are time and pro-rata, so orders are often either ranked based on when they were first received, or their size. There are also several common derivations of these two main types. In the following sections we will consider some worked examples for each of these. Note that some venues do not have their own internal pricing mechanism; instead, the mid-point prices from the primary exchange are often used, so we shall also look at an example for a mid-point match.

Price/Time priority

Trade matching using price/time based priority is common in most equities markets. The highest priced buy orders and the lowest priced sells have the highest probabilities of execution. For orders at the same price, the time they were placed is then used to distinguish between them, thus rewarding earlier orders.

For example, let's look at how a market order to buy 2,500 EEE will be handled for the order book shown in Figure 8-2. The order book shows the orders arranged in terms of their execution priority, so the earlier sell order S1 takes priority over the similarly priced S2 and S3 and the higher priced S4. Now, in order to cross with the incoming market order we can see that order S1 will be filled completely, as will the next order S2. The last 300 will result from a partial execution with order S3, leaving 2,200 remaining on the book. Afterwards, order S3 now has both price and time priority for any new incoming buy orders.

Buys			Sells					Sells		
Id	Time	Size	Price	Price	Size	Time	Id	Price	Size	Id
	8:25:00	1,000	100	101	1,000	8:20:00	S1	. ~~101~~	~~1,000~~	~~S1~~
	8:20:25	700	99	101	1,200	8:20:25	S2	. ~~101~~	~~1,200~~	~~S2~~
	8:24:00	1,500	98	101	2,500	8:21:09	S3	. ~~101~~	~~300~~	~~S3~~
				102	900	8:15:00	S4	. 101	**2,200**	S3
								. 102	900	S4

(a) before   (b) after

Figure 8-2 An example buy order matched using price/time priority

Price/Pro-rata priority

Trade matching using price/pro-rata based priority is more common in futures markets. Again, the best priced buy and sell orders take priority, but allocation between orders at the same price point is done on a pro-rata basis. That is to say, each order is allocated based on its proportion of the total volume of orders at that price, thus rewarding larger orders.

For example, let's see how a market order to buy 1,000 EEE will be handled for the order book shown in Figure 8-3. Since orders S1, S2 and S3 all have the same price priority, the allocation is based on their size. Hence, sell S1 gets (750 / 2000) = 37.5% of the allocation (labelled Alloc), or 375, whilst the larger order S3 gets 50%, despite being placed later than either order S1 or S2. The net result is that all three orders receive partial execution and remain on the order book ready for the next execution. Clearly, this approach rewards size nearly as much as price.

Buys		Sells					Sells			Alloc
Size	Price	Price	Size	Time	Id		Price	Size	Id	
500	100	101	750	8:21:00	S1	.	101	**375**	S1	375
1,000	100	101	250	8:21:25	S2	.	101	**125**	S2	125
400	99	101	1,000	8:22:05	S3	.	101	**500**	S3	500
200	99	102	800	8:19:09	S4	.	102	800	S4	

(a) before   (b) after

Figure 8-3 An example buy order matched using price/pro-rata priority

A common addition is to grant special priority to the first order at each new price point, in order to encourage traders to place more aggressively priced orders. Taking the same example as before and applying this additional criterion, we shall assume that order S1 was the first order at 101 and so has special priority over the others.

Buys		Sells					Sells			Alloc
Size	Price	Price	Size	Time	Id		Price	Size	Id	
500	100	101	750	8:21:00	S1	.	~~101~~	~~750~~	~~S1~~	750
1,000	100	101	250	8:21:25	S2	.	101	**200**	S2	50
400	99	101	1,000	8:22:05	S3	.	101	**800**	S3	200
200	99	102	800	8:19:09	S4	.	102	1,000	S4	

(a) before   (b) after

Figure 8-4 An example buy order using price/pro-rata priority matched with preference for the first order

Therefore, as we can see in Figure 8-4 the market order to buy 1,000 EEE now is handled somewhat differently. This time, order S1 is completely filled and the remainder is allocated pro-rata between orders S2 and S3. Note that neither orders S2, nor S3 have the special priority so when a new buy order hits the order book the matching will go back to using the original pro-rata method.

Other variants of this approach apply volume caps to prevent traders from entering large orders at a new price, thus gaining special priority privileges for a significant volume. Conversely, minimum volume requirements may also be adopted to ensure that traders do not simply place a small order at a new price in order to obtain special priority.

Another alternative aimed at helping pro-rata allocations for smaller orders is adopted by the CME for its Eurodollar futures. The allocation is split into two stages. The first stage is a pro-rata based method; however, it rounds down all the allocations, and assigns zero to any orders that end up with less than two units. The remaining quantity is then distributed on a time-based priority, so earlier orders will get additional allocation. For example, let's look at how a market order to buy 100 EFG will be handled for the order book shown in Figure 8-5.

Buys		Sells					Sells			Alloc
Size	Price	Price	Size	Time	Id		Price	Size	Id	
500	100	101	50	8:21:00	S1	.	~~101~~	~~50~~	~~S1~~	50
1,000	100	101	25	8:21:20	S2	.	101	21	S2	0+4
1,000	100	101	50	8:21:25	S3	.	101	47	S3	3+0
400	99	101	500	8:21:35	S4	.	101	462	S4	38+0
400	99	101	75	8:22:05	S5	.	101	70	S5	5+0
200	99	102	200	8:19:09	S6	.	102	200	S6	
(a) before							(b) after			

Figure 8-5 An example buy order using price/pro-rata priority, with first order preference and secondary time priority

Order S1 had special priority so it is completely filled, the remaining 50 is then allocated amongst orders S2 to S5 (for simplicity we will assume the lot size is 1). Initially, the small order S2 gets nothing based on this allocation. The remaining 4 units are then assigned based on time priority, so these are allocated to the earliest order, which in this case is order S2.

Priority, Parity, Yielding

The Priority, Parity, Yielding (PPY) trade matching mechanism represents another noteworthy modification. Historically, NYSE's trading mechanism was based on this approach, although they have since moved to a more standard price/pro-rata mechanism. Still, it has some interesting features, so it is worth examining in more detail.

The priority refers to the fact that priority is assigned to the first order at a new price point, like some futures exchanges. Parity simply refers to its pro-rata nature, since after the order with priority is filled orders are then assigned based on their size. Though, there is one important difference from the price/pro-rata mechanisms, namely yielding. Traditionally, NYSE specialists acted as sole market makers for each asset. To protect client orders yielding meant that the specialist's quotes were required to give priority to client orders, i.e. those on the Designated Order Turnaround (DOT) system.

For example, let's focus on the sells for asset NLO as shown in Figure 8-6. The order book is formatted slightly differently, based on examples from NYSE (2006), because it actually comprises of orders from several sources.

Offer	Size	DOT	e-Quote	s-Quote
7.01	9,200	6,200	2,000	1,000
7.02	7,000	4,000	2,000	1,000

(a) before

Offer	Size	DOT	e-Quote	s-Quote
7.01	**4,200**	**2,400**	**800**	1,000
7.02	7,000	4,000	2,000	1,000

(b) after

Figure 8-6 An example buy order matched with price, parity, yielding

The DOT orders are also competing with electronic quotes from other floor brokers (e-Quotes) and the specialist (s-Quotes). Figure 8-7 shows this in the more familiar order book style, orders with price priority are shaded in light grey whilst the specialist's quote (SQ) is highlighted in dark grey. The DOT orders have identifiers beginning with D, the e-Quotes start with E.

Buys		Sells			
Size	Price	Price	Size	Time	ID
500	7.00	7.01	200	9:41:00	D1
800	7.00	7.01	2,000	9:41:20	D2
400	7.00	7.01	800	9:41:25	E1
300	6.99	7.01	4,000	9:41:35	D3
100	6.99	7.01	1,200	9:42:05	E2
100	6.99	7.01	1,000	9:41:09	SQ
200	6.98	7.02	1,000	9:41:45	D4

(a) before

Sells			Alloc
Price	Size	ID	
~~7.01~~	~~200~~	~~D1~~	200
7.01	800	D2	1,200
7.01	320	E1	480
7.01	1,600	D3	2,400
7.01	480	E2	720
7.01	1,000	SQ	0
7.02	1,000	D4	

(b) after

Figure 8-7 An order level view of the example using price, parity, yielding

When a market order to buy 5,000 NLO hits the order book, the priority is given to the earliest order at 7.01, which happens to be for a quantity of 200. The remaining 4,800 is then assigned at parity amongst the DOT orders and the floor brokers' e-Quotes. Given the extant order sizes have ratio of 3:1 between DOT and e-Quotes, 3600 will cross with DOT orders, whilst 1,200 will match with e-Quotes. The specialist's s-Quote is not involved since it yields to the extant DOT orders.

Hence, in Figure 8-7 the DOT order D1 is completely filled, whilst orders D2 and D3 and the e-Quotes E1 and E2 are all partially filled from the remaining 4,800, based on their size. The specialist's quote SQ remains unchanged. The residuals are shown in Figure 8-7(b).

If another market order to buy 5,000 NLO now hits the exchange, the specialist's s-Quote may then participate, once the extant DOT orders at 7.01 have been filled. Since there are only 4,200 available in total at 7.01, all these orders will be filled. For the remaining 800, DOT order D4 at 7.02 has priority, so this will cross with the market order leaving a total remainder of 3,200 at 7.02 on DOT. We can see this summarised in Figure 8-8:

Price	Offer	DOT	e-Quote	s-Quote
7.01	4,200	2,400	800	1,000
7.02	7,000	4,000	2,000	1,000

(a) before

Price	Offer	DOT	e-Quote	s-Quote
7.02	**6,200**	**3,200**	2,000	1,000

(b) after

Figure 8-8 A subsequent buy order handled with price, parity, yielding

This mechanism allowed the specialists to provide additional liquidity without taking priority over client orders.

Mid-point matches

Matching orders based on the mid-point price from the primary exchange is becoming a popular mechanism for continuous crossing systems. As we saw in Chapter 2, market orders will execute at the mid-point whenever there is sufficient volume available on the other side of the order book. Limit orders will only match when the mid-point price is better than their limit; hence, the limit prices in Figure 8-9 are greyed out.

For example, if the order book shown in Figure 8-9 applied a normal continuous auction we would expect orders B1 and S1 to have matched already since their prices cross.

	Buys			Sells			
Id	Time	Size	Price	Price	Size	Time	Id
B1	8:25:00	1,500	*101*	*100*	1,500	8:25:00	S1
B2	8:21:25	3,000	*100*	*102*	2,000	8:20:20	S2
B3	8:23:00	2,500	*99*	*103*	1,800	8:24:09	S3

(a) before, external mid-point is 102

	Buys			Sells			
Id	Time	Size	Price	Price	Size	Time	Id
~~B1~~	~~8:25:00~~	~~1,500~~	~~*101*~~	~~*100*~~	~~1,500~~	~~8:25:00~~	~~S1~~
B2	8:21:25	3,000	*100*	*102*	2,000	8:20:20	S2
B3	8:23:00	2,500	*99*	*103*	1,800	8:24:09	S3

(b) after mid-point becomes 101

Figure 8-9 An example mid-point match

However, on the primary exchange the best bid and offer is 101-103, so the external mid-point price is 102. Therefore, the limit price on buy order B1 prevents it from being matched. Only when the external best bid and offer changes to 100-102 (so the mid-point becomes 101) can it participate. Since sell order S1 has a mid-point limit of 100, this can therefore cross with order B1. Note that both orders execute at the mid-point, so order S1 actually sees a price improvement over its original limit price of 100.

This mechanism is generally used to support continuous crossing for block-size orders, hence the order book shown in Figure 8-9 would be completely opaque. Some venues also support minimum acceptable quantities (or minimum volumes), as we saw for call auctions in Chapter 4.

Other types

Most of the common mechanisms for trade matching have already been covered in the previous sub-sections. Though, there will invariably be venues that use slightly different rules. It is always worth carefully reading the documentation and regulations for each market venue to confirm exactly how matching is carried out.

Catering for some custom order types may also require modifications to the trade matching mechanism. These can be reasonably straightforward, requiring a few extensions to the order matching logic, such as for handling hidden orders or discretionary price limits. However, some custom order types can pose more substantial problems. For instance, supporting contingent orders may require a separate order book.

In terms of pure matching, hidden orders are still limit orders. Though, to ensure fairness for other market participants most venues assign them a lower priority than visible orders at the same price. Otherwise, there would be little incentive to post visible liquidity.

Similarly, iceberg orders have a portion that is visible and a reserve, which is hidden. A key feature of iceberg orders is that when the visible portion is filled, it will be replaced with an equivalent order by reducing the size of the hidden reserve. Again, the trading mechanism will need to be modified to manage this process.

Discretionary orders actually have two price limits, a public one and a private one. Just as iceberg orders hide their true size, discretionary orders hide their true price limit. Therefore, when handling discretionary orders the trade matching mechanism needs to also check whether any orders match on the discretionary price limit.

Contingent orders are more complex because they introduce additional dependencies. They allow links between orders, often for different assets. Normally, the order books for each asset are completely separate, so conditional orders introduce linkages between them. Suddenly, the trade matching mechanisms for several assets need to interact with each other to determine whether a trade can occur. For this reason, markets that support contingent orders have tended to handle them in dedicated order books. Hence, spread orders between futures contracts and some complex option strategies may be handled completely separately. That said, as trade-matching engines become increasingly sophisticated some venues are now actually starting to use "implied orders" to integrate these complex orders back into the main order books. The aim of this is to improve the overall liquidity, although it does add a considerable level of complexity for the matching engines.

Researchers are also constantly looking into ways of improving the existing trade matching mechanisms. An important area of study is finding a way of balancing the requirement for visibility (for price discovery) with the need to hide large orders (to prevent information leakage). An interesting proposal by Peter Gomber, Miroslav Budimir and Uwe Schweickert (2006) introduces a new custom order type, the volume order. Essentially, this is a cross between an iceberg order and a discretionary one: The discretionary price is linked to a minimum volume requirement, so if there are corresponding orders which can fill this required volume and they are within the price limit then a match may occur. Alternatively, Leslie Boni and Chris Leach (2004) investigate the "expandable" limit order, which has been used in the inter-dealer market for U.S. Treasuries. Effectively, it gives the trader whose limit order had just executed the right of first refusal to trade additional volume with the same dealer. Whilst they note that this is useful for trading large block orders, the time taken for negotiation can be disruptive, since they are essentially pushing in front of other orders on the order book. Boni and Leach propose some potential work-arounds, based on strict time limits for the option to refuse, only granting this right to the first order at a new price level, or even handling them on a separate order book. Hopefully, more research will continue to look into alternative methods for trade matching, since this could well provide innovative new mechanisms that will help bridge the gap that currently exists between exchanges and crossing systems.

Call-based matching

A call auction may be carried out as little as once a day, or as frequently as every 10 to 15 minutes throughout the trading day. Rather than continuously matching each order as it arrives, orders are just queued up and applied to the auction order book. The actual trade matching only occurs at the set auction time. So, orders accumulate before the auction takes place. This allows longer for price formation and so can help when there is more uncertainty about what the price should actually be. Consequently, many markets often choose to open and close with a separate call auction in an effort to reduce price volatility.

When the auction starts, a crossing algorithm tries to ensure that the maximum possible volume of orders is crossed at the auction price. A typical approach is as follows:

- Check that the order book is crossed, i.e. either the book contains market orders or there are buy orders with limit prices higher than some of the sell orders.

- Apply the following criteria step-wise until a single price match which achieves them is found:
  1. A maximum executable volume
  2. As above & a minimum order surplus
  3. As above & a consistent market pressure

- If a single price cannot be found then determine a price based on the reference price. Generally, this will be the last traded price, so last night's close for an opening auction or the last trade for a closing auction.

- Once a price is found, the auction order book is then processed to match any orders that will execute within this price limit. Many venues use time as a secondary priority, this rewards the early entry of auction orders.

This forms the basis for many of the equity market call auctions, e.g. the Deutsche Börse and the London, Australian, Hong Kong and Singapore stock exchanges. A more in-depth review for a wide range of markets is provided by Carole Comerton-Forde and James Rydge (2004).

Some venues may also publish information about the overall imbalance between the buy and sell orders before the crossing begins. The aim is to encourage new buyers/sellers to address the imbalance and so maximise the potential auction volume. They may also offer an indicative auction price to help traders to decide on pricing for their auction orders.

As an example, let's consider the auction order book shown in Figure 8-10.

Buys			Sells		
Time	Size	Price	Price	Size	Time
7:25:00	12,000	MO	MO	2,000	7:25:00
7:20:25	2,000	105	MO	3,000	7:25:00
7:24:09	5,000	104	102	4,000	7:20:25
7:20:25	10,000	102	102	1,000	7:20:25
7:24:09	6,000	101	103	5,000	7:24:09
7:24:09	4,000	101	105	12,000	7:20:25
			106	15,000	7:24:09

Figure 8-10 An example call auction

From this, we can construct Table 8-1 which shows the calculated executable volumes, surpluses and pressures.

Cumulative buy/sell side pressures: These represent the total volume available for crossing at any given limit price. They are calculated by summing the order quantities from the highest priority, so this will start with any market orders and then sum from the highest priced limit order for buys, or the lowest for sells.

Pooled buy orders at limit	Price	Pooled sell orders at limit	Cumulative pressure		Executable volume	Order surplus	Market pressure
			Buy	Sell			
12,000	MO	5,000					
0	106	15,000	12,000	42,000	12,000	-30,000	–
2,000	105	12,000	14,000	27,000	14,000	-13,000	–
5,000	**104**	**0**	**19,000**	**15,000**	**15,000**	**4,000**	**+**
0	103	5,000	19,000	15,000	15,000	4,000	+
10,000	102	5,000	29,000	10,000	10,000	19,000	+
10,000	101	0	39,000	5,000	5,000	34,000	+

Table 8-1 Call auction calculation data

Executable volume: For each price, this volume is simply the minimum of the buy and sell pressures for that limit. This is because the total volume we can cross is limited by the buy and sell pressures, since it does not matter how much buy pressure there is if no-one wants to sell.

Order surplus: This represents the amount of buy or sell pressure that remains unexecuted due to lack of orders on the opposite side of the order book.

Market pressure: This is just the sign of the order surplus. Positive pressure reflects a surplus of buy orders whilst negative shows a surplus of sells.

We can now use this example order book and the data from Table 8-1 to apply the outlined auction-crossing algorithm:

1. The light grey shading in Figure 8-10 shows the orders that cross, so we can continue.
2. Two prices achieve the maximum executable volume of 15,000, so we should next use the order surpluses to try to isolate a single price match.
3. Both of these prices result in the same order surplus of 4,000, so we must now consider the market pressure.
4. The market pressure is consistent; it is positive for both 103 and 104. Since the surpluses are for buys, this implies the prices are more likely to increase after the auction; therefore, the higher of the two prices is used for the auction price.
5. Hence, 104 will be used as the auction price, so we do not need to look at the reference price.

Having now assigned an auction-crossing price of 104, we can see the effect on the actual auction order book in Figure 8-11 (a) as the crossings take place and (b) once the auction is finally completed.

If this was the opening auction for a continuous double auction market, then Figure 8-11 (b) shows the order book as it will be when the market officially opens for continuous trading. Alternatively, if this was a batch call auction or a closing auction then, depending on the market, these remaining orders will either be cancelled or left for the next auction.

Some crossing systems derive their auction price from another market. However, in all other respects the auction crossing mechanism is the same as shown in Figure 8-11.

Buys			Sells		
Time	Size	Price	Price	Size	Time
~~7:25:00~~	~~12,000~~	~~MO~~	~~MO~~	~~2,000~~	~~7:25:00~~
~~7:20:25~~	~~2,000~~	~~105~~	~~MO~~	~~3,000~~	~~7:25:00~~
~~7:24:09~~	~~1,000~~	~~104~~	~~102~~	~~4,000~~	~~7:20:25~~
7:24:09	4,000	104	~~102~~	~~1,000~~	~~7:20:25~~
7:20:25	10,000	102	~~103~~	~~5,000~~	~~7:24:09~~
7:24:09	6,000	101	105	12,000	7:20:25
7:24:09	4,000	101	106	15,000	7:24:09

(a) order book crossing

Buys			Sells		
Time	Size	Price	Price	Size	Time
7:24:09	4,000	104	105	12,000	7:20:25
7:20:25	10,000	102	106	15,000	7:24:09
7:24:09	6,000	101			
7:24:09	4,000	101			

(b) once crossing completed

Figure 8-11 A call auction crossing

8.4 Order placement decisions

When making decisions about order placement we need to balance the required objectives with the current market conditions. Essentially, we are trying to find the best price with an acceptable probability of execution and risk. That used to simply mean choosing a target price and deciding when and how best to split an order for execution.

In today's increasingly fragmented marketplaces, choosing where to place an order can be as important a factor as the price or size. The small average order size now common in many markets (best typified by equities and listed futures) also means that signalling risk is now a significant concern. So to strive for optimal execution we must decide where we are prepared to trade and how (which order types we will use) as well as how aggressively we will price and size our order.

Signalling risk

Signalling risk represents the information leakage to other market participants from our trading strategy. Placing an order on an open order book provides a valuable trading option that other traders may freely execute against. Our trading pattern also relays information to the other market participants, such as whether we are a large buyer or seller.

Armed with this information the other participants may then adjust their trading strategies. For example, in seeing a large buy order sellers may become less aggressive in their pricing, since they know there is a buyer. Often, it is necessary to hide our actual intentions as much as possible, by seeking liquidity from alternative sources such as crossing networks or "dark pool" ATSs, or by using special order types.

Note that signalling risk is dependent on both the order size and the asset's liquidity. For instance, with an illiquid asset even a small order can result can result in signalling risk, since there may be very little displayed order book depth. Whereas for liquid assets the increased trade activity and deeper order books means that signalling risk is less severe.

Venue choice

Assets may often be traded on multiple exchanges, ECNs (MTFs), ATSs, or even over the counter, so there is a wide range of choice, as Figure 8-12 tries to show.

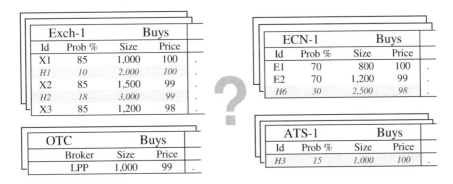

Figure 8-12 Venue choice

In terms of visibility, venues range from fully transparent ones that do not support any hidden order types, to completely opaque ones where the whole order book is hidden. Investors or traders wishing to reduce their signalling risk will opt for venues which either support hidden order types, or are opaque, such as the "dark pool" ATSs. In fact, nowadays completely transparent venues are a rarity, since most exchanges or ECNs offer some type of hidden/iceberg order.

Execution probability is another important factor when choosing between venues. The execution of our order may not be guaranteed, since there might be many other participants, sending different orders at the same time. Hence, in Figure 8-12 the order books are also shown with a percentage that reflects this probability. This may be based on a range of factors, including the probability of cancellation, latency and historical results. In section 8.6, we will consider this in some more detail. Hidden liquidity is another important consideration; we will cover this in more detail in section 8.5.

Using "dark pool" ATSs

As their name implies, "dark pool" ATSs are intended to be opaque, hiding all orders so that their participants can trade in size without significant signalling risk. Though, the wide range of different mechanisms employed by ATSs and the increasing provision of hidden order types by exchanges has made it difficult to gauge just how opaque each venue is. Some of the key concerns for investors are that their large orders are *not*:

- gamed by other participants
- providing information for proprietary trading desks

Gaming refers to manipulating the market price for profit. We have already seen how IOC orders may be used to seek hidden liquidity without leaving a standing order on the order book. Normally, this should be used to try to cross in size with such liquidity, to the mutual benefit of both parties. In comparison, gaming implies taking a more cynical approach by issuing orders to drive the market price up (or down) before the final hit, when a large order is issued to cross with the hidden liquidity at this new price. This is a particular risk when the crossing is based on the main market's best bid and offer (e.g. the U.S. NBBO).

There is also concern that information about large orders is spotted by (or even made available to) proprietary trading desks. This would give them the advantage, allowing them to game or "front-run" the orders. [1] To prevent this most major broker/dealers enforce strict "Chinese walls" between their operations. This is not a question of technology - it is one of trust.

Toxic order flow is another term that is sometimes used. This is when orders interact with flow driven by participants, or quantitative systems, that are actively trying to seek liquidity, solely to profit from short-term movements.

Many venues employ monitoring to spot when suspicious situations arise, gamers or front-runners may then be excluded from the venue. They may also set their pricing structures to make small orders prohibitively expensive for high-frequency use. Enforcing large minimum trade sizes is another commonly used deterrent, since this prevents the initial liquidity seeking (or "pinging"). Though, as Gabriel Butler (2007) points out, these have the downside of limiting the potential for aggregating liquidity since they prevent genuinely small orders.

Hitesh Mittal (2008) provides a nice review of some of the main concerns about these issues. In essence the main questions investors need to consider before using an ATS are:

- Who has access?
  - Is it buy-side only?
  - Are liquidity providers used?
  - Are proprietary desks allowed?
- What happens to my orders?
  - Are they advertised?
- How/where are trades reported?

Clearly, buy-side only venues should be the "safest", since all participants should solely be focussed on finding matches for their liquidity requirements. Still, it must also be remembered that liquidity providers and proprietary desks are useful sources of additional liquidity. It just needs to be clear that they are active at the venue and that there is monitoring to protect all participants.

Indications of interest (IOIs) are another common concern. Advertisement-based ATSs generally restrict the information that is passed via these. Hence, the adverts or indications are either sent to potential matches, or if they are broadcast to all participants then only a subset of the information is distributed, usually the asset and maybe the side and/or price. Some venues even allow the sender to control what information is publicised. Again, it is important to know these specifics.

It is also important to remember that even though a "dark pool" may keep its order book hidden the trades must still be reported. If the trade report does not include the ATS name traders may still be able to narrow it down to a number of venues based on where it is reported. For crossings, Mittal (2008) points out that most firms advertise the completed crosses with services such as Autex or Bloomberg. So there is always the potential for some signalling risk. This must also be factored in when deciding how best to take advantage of "dark pool" liquidity.

---

[1] Front running is a malpractice. It is where a broker receives an order but before placing this uses the information to trade on their own account, benefiting from the subsequent client order.

Order choice

In terms of risk, standing limit orders supply liquidity and so large orders have considerable signalling risk. Therefore, to reduce signalling risk it is important to hide our intentions. As we saw in Chapter 4, there is a wide range of order types that the trader may choose from, together with an array of optional instructions. Most exchanges and ECNs now support a mix of discretionary, iceberg or fully hidden orders. Figure 8-13 highlights these various types and shows how different order choices take us from highly visible trading patterns through to more hidden ones.

	Transparent			*Opaque*
Liquidity suppliers	Limit orders	Discretionary orders	Iceberg orders	Hidden orders
Liquidity demanders	Limit orders Market orders	Discretionary IOC orders Market orders	Iceberg orders Fill-or-kill orders Market orders	Hidden orders Fill-or-kill orders Market orders

Figure 8-13 Order types grouped by visibility

Starting with limit orders we then progress on to discretionary ones (hiding our true price limit) then to iceberg orders (hiding a portion of our order size), finally ending with completely hidden orders. The orders are still providing liquidity, but with less and less visibility. Similarly, immediate-or-cancel and fill-or-kill instructions help hide marketable limit orders when they demand liquidity, since they prevent a residual order from staying on the order book.

Order size is a key factor for order choice. Bessembinder, Panayides and Venkataraman (2008) found that on Euronext for large orders (>€50,000) more than 70% of orders were hidden, whilst for small orders (<€5,000) only 5% were hidden. D'Hondt, De Winne and Francois-Heude (2005) also confirmed that an order was more likely to be hidden when its size was greater than the currently displayed order book depth.

Due to their size, hidden orders can account for a considerable proportion of the available market volume. For instance, Bessembinder, Panayides and Venkataraman (2008) found that 18% of the orders for their sample of Euronext Paris were hidden, these accounted for 44% of the total order volume.

Order aggressiveness

Aggressiveness is reflected by order choice, price and size.

Market orders are generally the most aggressive type of order, since they have no price constraint. They strive to achieve immediate execution at the best price available. At the very least we shall probably have to pay half the bid offer spread, or even more if the order needs to sweep the order book in order to complete. So the aggressiveness of a market order is based on its size, since large orders are more likely to have to sweep the book.

Limit orders allow more control since we can choose how to set their inbuilt price limit.

Although this offers some price protection, it means they face the risk of failing to execute completely. Thus, the aggressiveness of a limit order is a function of both its limit price and its size.

In order to be able to compare the aggressiveness of different orders many of the microstructure studies have created classification schemes based on both price and size. One of the best-known schemes is shown in Table 8-2, based on a study by Bruno Biais, Pierre Hillion and Chester Spatt (1995). They assigned six categories, ranked in order of aggressiveness. The three most aggressive levels are immediately executable and correspond to market orders or marketable limit orders, so order size is key to determining their impact.

Category	Price	Size
1	Better than the best opposite price	Larger than the best opposite size
2	At the best opposite price	
3	At or better than the best opposite price	Less than or equal to the best opposite size
4	Within the best bid and offer	Any
5	At the best price (same side)	Any
6	Below the best price (same side)	Any

Table 8-2 A classification scheme for order aggressiveness

The most aggressive category (1) represents orders that are priced better than the best opposite price (either market orders or marketable limit orders) and are larger than the best opposite size. Next are orders that have a similar size, but are limited to the best opposite price, so a residual will be left on the book at that price. The third category consists of smaller orders, these are less than or equal to the best opposite size and are priced so that they may immediately execute. The remaining types are all standing limit orders that help provide liquidity; they are priced between, at or below the best price.

Market factors affecting order placement decisions

A substantial amount of microstructure research has examined how market conditions affect order choice and aggressiveness. The studies are based on trading across a wide variety of execution venues, and help show how traders react to various market conditions. Some of these reactions are common sense, but some of the research offers an insight into subtler responses.

To briefly summarise these, the main determinants for order choice are generally the:
- Spread
- Order book depth/height
- Volatility
- Time of day

Broadly speaking we can categorise these factors into three main types, based on liquidity, price and time. In the following sub-sections, we shall review the effect of each of these in turn.

Liquidity-based factors

The importance of liquidity-based factors such as spread and order book depth is hardly surprising. Liquidity is obviously a key driver for order placement decisions.

Spread

A wider bid offer spread directly increases the cost of a market order. The price for immediacy is half the spread plus any additional market impact. Unsurprisingly, traders are more willing to supply liquidity when the reward is higher. Wider spreads tend to encourage the placement of limit orders over market orders. They also often decrease overall order aggressiveness.

Empirical support for this has been demonstrated for a range of stock exchanges, notably for the Paris Bourse by Biais, Hillion and Spatt (1995). It was also observed on the Stockholm Stock Exchange by Burton Hollifield, Robert Miller and Patrik Sandås (2004). Similarly, Angelo Ranaldo (2004) observed this for the Swiss Stock Exchange, whilst Joachim Grammig, Andreas Heinen and Erick Rengifo (2004) reported it for the Xetra trading system. Interestingly, a study of the NYSE by Alessandro Beber and Cecilia Caglio (2005) found that this effect seems to be stronger for buyers than sellers.

Hidden orders also seem to be adopted more when spreads are narrower. This negative relationship with spread size was observed for NYSE Arca by Steve Bongiovanni, Milan Borkovec and Robert Sinclair (2006). It was also noted for trading on Euronext by Catherine D'Hondt, Rudy De Winne and Alain Francois-Heude (2005). They concluded that since narrow spreads encourage more aggressive orders, traders place more hidden orders to take advantage of this increased execution probability.

In terms of overall aggressiveness, a study of the NYSE by Andrew Ellul *et al.* (2003) reported that marketable limit orders were more sensitive to spread than market orders. Whilst for the Spanish Stock Exchange Roberto Pascual and David Veredas (2008) concluded that the high immediacy costs of wider spreads discouraged traders from issuing small market orders.

Order book information

The order book is an important source of information since it highlights the available liquidity. Order book depth represents the amount actually available for trading, whilst the imbalance corresponds to the difference between quantities available to buy and sell. The order book height indicates the maximum potential price impact for a market order walking up the order book.

So far, we have generally viewed order books in a tabular fashion, Figure 8-14 shows another way of representing this liquidity, based on the total available depth. From this chart, we can clearly see the different order book heights for buy and sell orders whilst the different gradients highlight the buy/sell imbalance.

The order book height affects the potential market impact. Charles Cao, Oliver Hansch and Xiaoxin Wang (2008a) showed that for the same side of the order book aggressiveness increases with book height, whilst for the opposite side it decreases.

Order book depth is important because so much of the available liquidity often lies outside the current best bid and offer, as we can clearly see in Figure 8-14. Mike Aitken *et al.* (2007) found on the ASX that institutional traders tended to offer more sell volume at one price step above the best offer, with over 60% of the total volume up to three price steps away. Likewise, Hollifield, Miller, and Sandås (2004) noted that much more depth was available on the Stockholm Stock Exchange, for Ericsson, away from the current best bid and offer.

Buys		Sells	
Size	Price	Price	Size
500	96	97	900
1,200	94	97	1,500
2,000	93.5	97	2,500
4,000	92	100	5,000
2,500	89	105	2,500
3,000	85	110	4,500
4,000	84.5	115	2,000
2,000	75	120	2,500

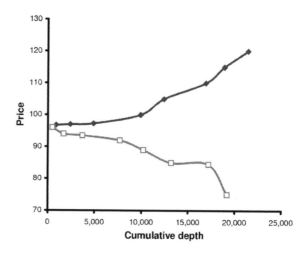

Figure 8-14 Viewing the cumulative depth for an example order book

Empirically Jón Daníelsson and Richard Payne (2002) showed that limit orders became more common when order book depth was visibly low, for FX trading on Reuters Dealing-2000. A similar result was found for orders on the Hong Kong Stock Exchange by Hee-Joon Ahn, Kee-Hong Bae and Kalok Chan (2001).

The different depths on each side of the order book can also have a major impact on the overall aggressiveness of orders. For instance, Mark Griffiths *et al.* (2000), Pascual and Veredas (2008) and Ranaldo (2004) all observed that traders placed more aggressively priced orders when their own side of the order book was deeper. Conversely, they became less aggressive when the opposite side of the order book was deeper. This is not that surprising for execution venues that enforce strict price/time priority trade matching. In an already crowded order book, the other orders will have time priority, therefore changing to use a market order or a more aggressive price limit is the most effective way of increasing the execution probability. Hence, traders tend to place more aggressive orders when the execution probability of a limit order is low. On the other hand traders placing orders on the opposite side will often tend to be more passive, relying on aggressive pricing by traders on the crowded side of the book. This is less of an issue for venues based on price/pro-rata based trade matching.

Another way of viewing this is in terms of the overall order imbalance. A large imbalance of sells acts as an unfavourable signal, encouraging sellers to be more aggressive and buyers to be more passive.

Just as with spreads, Beber and Caglio (2005) observed some asymmetry in the behaviour of buyers and sellers with respect to depth on the opposite side. Sellers are considered to be more liquidity-driven and so become more aggressive when the buy side of the order book is deeper. Failing to sell as the market moves downwards can result in a realised loss, whereas failing to buy as the market moves upwards means a reduced profit. Interestingly, Pascual and Veredas (2008) studied these relationships for both the best bid and offer as well as across the best five bids and offers for the Spanish Stock Exchange. They found that whilst liquidity providers seemed to base their decisions on information from the whole order book, market order traders focussed solely on the data from the best bid and offer.

The available depth can also have an important effect on the pricing of hidden orders. A study of hidden order placement on Euronext by D'Hondt, De Winne and Francois-Heude (2004) found that hidden orders were priced more aggressively if there was sufficient depth already available on the same side of the order book. Conversely, they noted that the displayed depth on the opposite side had limited effect on hidden order placement.

Trade flow

There are two key indicators for trade flow, namely volume and frequency. Beber and Caglio (2005) found that for the NYSE, transacted volume had more impact on order aggressiveness than the trading frequency, particularly for sell orders.

Trading volume has traditionally been seen as a proxy for market information, notably from work by David Easley and Maureen O'Hara (1987). Indeed Beber and Caglio (2005) concluded that the increased aggressiveness they observed for buy orders was consistent with information being revealed by large trading volumes. They also noted that volume could confirm information about price trends. For most of their sample, there was a positive price trend, but even accounting for momentum effects they found that higher volumes generally led to an increase in demand. Thus, buy orders became even more aggressive and sell orders more passive. For sell orders the increased picking-off risk helps explain the shift to more passive pricing.

In terms of trading frequency, Beber and Caglio (2005) linked higher frequencies to less aggressive buy and more aggressive sell orders. They concluded that these results were consistent with liquidity-based trading clustering on the sell side.

Note that the increasing adoption of algorithmic trading and falling order sizes means that trade flow is significantly increasing. So in terms of information, there is now more noise in the markets; trade flow is not quite the indicator it once was.

Other liquidity-based factors

Other asset-specific attributes may also be used as a proxy for liquidity. Most notably for equities, we can use the market capitalisation of firms as a rough guide. Likewise, credit ratings might also be used to help differentiate between the liquidity of bonds.

For firms traded on NYSE Arca, Bongiovanni, Borkovec and Sinclair (2006) found that hidden orders were used more for smaller cap firms, as shown in Table 8-3.

	Large cap > $10 billion	Mid cap	Small cap <$1.5 billion
# of stocks	26	43	260
# of trades	207,000	87,800	72,000
Average visible size of trade	370	300	200
Average hidden size	550	450	320
% of trade hidden	21	23	28
% fleeting/cancelled orders	11	9	13

Source: Bongiovanni, Borkovec and Sinclair (2006)

Table 8-3 Results for trading on NYSE Arca

Similarly, Pardo and Pascual (2006) noticed that hidden orders were more common for the less frequently traded Spanish index constituents. Whilst for Euronext Paris, Bessembinder, Panayides and Venkataraman (2008) found that up to 50% of orders for the least liquid stocks were hidden, compared to 30% for the most liquid firms. Again, this makes sense, since we might expect hidden orders to be more prevalent for more illiquid assets, where signalling risk is greater. Rudy De Winne and Catherine D'Hondt (2005) also found hidden liquidity to be negatively related to both trading volume and market capitalization.

Price-based factors

Again, it is no great surprise that price factors such as volatility and short-term trends have a considerable impact on order selection. In particular, they affect order aggressiveness, as traders try to either catch up with the market or take advantage of favourable prices.

Volatility

The execution probability of limit orders is clearly price dependent: The closer the price limit is to the current market price then the more chance it has to be filled. Higher volatility means the observed price range is likely to be wider and so increases the likelihood of execution for limit orders. However, it also increases the risk of adverse selection since orders are more likely to become mispriced. In seeking compensation for the raised adverse selection risk, traders may place less aggressively priced orders. This in turn causes spreads to widen, making market orders more expensive.

Several studies have confirmed that traders place less aggressive limit orders as volatility increases; for instance, Ahn, Bae, and Chan (2001), Daníelsson and Payne (2002), Ranaldo (2004) and Beber and Caglio (2005). These studies also noted a reduction in the use of market orders. However, both Ellul et al. (2003) and Anthony Hall and Nikolaus Hautsch (2006) noted an increase in both limit and market order trading as volatility increased. Whilst Joel Hasbrouck and Gideon Saar (2002) found that limit orders were less likely to be submitted as volatility increased.

Price volatility may be measured over a wide range of timescales, ranging from intra-day to those based on months of historical data. Some of the differences in these empirical observations may be explained by these different types of volatility. Short-term, or transient, volatility tends to closely reflect the asset's liquidity whilst fundamental volatility is more long-term and is often information-driven. For transient volatility, Puneet Handa and Robert Schwartz (1996) showed that the gains from supplying liquidity outweighed the adverse selection risk. Whilst in a later work, Handa, Schwartz and Tiwari, (2003) also found that higher fundamental volatility makes limit orders less attractive due to their increased option value. For such assets, they concluded that risk averse and informed traders tend to prefer the certainty of market orders.

Empirical studies have also positively linked the use of hidden orders to volatility. Hidden orders were found to be more commonly used for volatile stocks in trading on NYSE Arca by Bongiovanni, Borkovec and Sinclair (2006). Comparable results were observed for the Australian Stock Exchange by Michael Aitken, Henk Berkman and Derek Mak (2001). Likewise, Michael Fleming and Bruce Mizrach (2008) found that price volatility increased the usage of iceberg orders for U.S. Treasuries on ICAP's BrokerTec.

Interestingly, analysis of Euronext's hidden orders found that liquidity-driven price volatility affected the order book asymmetrically. A study by D'Hondt, De Winne and Francois-Heude (2004) found that liquidity-driven volatility arising from the bid side encouraged placement of hidden buy orders. Whilst sell side volatility triggered more hidden sell orders. They concluded that traders adopted hidden orders when the risk of order exposure increases.

Price Momentum

Trends in the market price are something that many traders closely follow. Consequently, price momentum can affect their decisions on both order choice and aggressiveness. Ellul *et al.* (2003) analysed short-term momentum trading on the NYSE. They found a positive dependency between the frequency of buy orders and the return from the last five minutes, whilst a negative correlation was noted for sells. In a similar study, Beber and Caglio (2005) used a momentum indicator based on the ratio between the price and an exponential moving average (EMA):

$$MOM_t = \frac{P_t}{EMA_t(P_i)} = \frac{P_t}{\lambda EMA_{t-1}(P_i) + (1-\lambda)P_t}$$

where P_t is the current price and the decay factor $\lambda=0.95$. They observed that as price momentum increased, buy orders became more aggressively priced whilst sell orders became less aggressive. Risk of non-execution is clearly an issue for limit orders, particularly when the price is trending away. Beber and Caglio (2005) concluded that traders expect positive price trends to reduce the probability of execution of passive buy orders, whilst increasing the probability for sell limit orders. Conversely, the opposite holds for downward price momentum. A similar relationship was also noted by Yue-cheong Chan (2005) for the Hong Kong Stock Exchange.

The opposite effect was observed for the ASX by Hall and Hautsch (2006). They found a decrease in buy order aggressiveness for positive price trends, based on five-minute returns. One possible explanation for these differences is that in the ASX study more traders may have been expecting a reversion rather than a prolonged price trend. So any relationship between momentum and order pricing should also incorporate trader expectations.

Hidden order placement may also be affected by recent returns. Pardo and Pascual (2006) noticed a positive dependency between the proportion of hidden orders and intraday stock returns. They concluded that traders using hidden orders were often following the prevailing price trend.

Tick-size

The tick-size represents the minimum allowed price increment. Therefore, it is closely aligned with the bid offer spread. Larger tick sizes will generally cause the bid offer spread to increase. They also make it more expensive to jump in front of an order, making "pennying" less attractive and helping to offset some of the signalling risk. So, in theory, hidden orders should be more common for assets with lower tick-sizes. Larry Harris (1996) studied the relationship between tick-size and order exposure for the trading of both French and Canadian stocks. He found that larger ticks did encourage more order exposure. This was also confirmed in an empirical study of the French segment of the Euro NM by D'Hondt, De Winne and Francois-Heude (2001) and by analysis of the Australian Stock Exchange by Aitken, Berkman and Mak (2001).

Time-based factors

Time also has a marked effect on order placement, whether it is the time of day or the recent trading history. Often, markets are more volatile around their opening and closing, hence the adoption of call auctions.

Time of day

Market conditions change throughout the day; therefore, traders adjust their order placement decisions accordingly. Figure 8-15 shows how the average spread, depth, volume and volatility changed for stocks on the Spanish stock market in 2002, taken from a study by

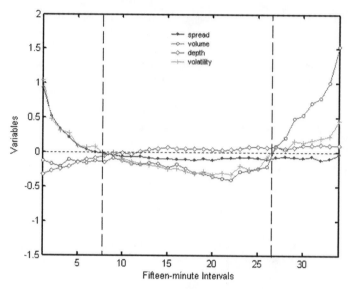

Figure 8-15 Intraday patterns of liquidity/activity in the Spanish stock market in 2002

David Abad, Sonia Sanabria and José Yagüe (2005). The dashed lines highlight three distinct phases throughout the trading day. At the open, a period of lower liquidity lasted for around two hours, with higher spreads and relatively low quoted depths. This corresponds to the uncertainty that traders face each morning. The next phase was an intermediate period where liquidity improved and volatility decreased. This may be explained by the fact that the trading patterns help relay information, thus decreasing some of the uncertainty for traders. Finally, the last period, from around 3:30 pm, coincided with the U.S. open, hence there was a substantial increase in trading volume. Though, there was only a slight improvement in overall liquidity.

Similar trends may be found in most markets. For example, a comparable change in the average relative spread combined with an increase in the cumulative depth is noted for a study of Xetra stocks by Alexander Kempf and Daniel Mayston (2008).

Clearly, the natural evolution of market conditions throughout the day has a significant impact on order placement decisions. Simply knowing that the market will soon be closing can force some trader's hands. Indeed, it seems to polarise traders' behaviour; some become considerably more aggressive, whilst others will place more passive orders just before the close. Figure 8-16 shows how the type of order can vary over time, again taken from the Abad, Sanabria and Yagüe (2005) study. In this case, limit orders were more heavily used in the uncertain morning period whilst market orders dominated as the day reached a close. Similarly, several studies of the NYSE have found that traders tend to place more aggressive orders as the day progresses. Beber and Caglio (2005) observed this for both buy and sell orders, whilst Ellul et al. (2003) found that towards the close, limit orders were more likely to be priced at or inside the quote. They also found that traders placed less aggressively priced limit orders earlier in the day.

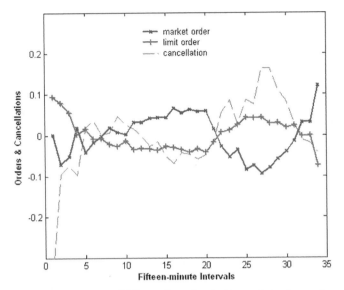

Source: © Abad, Sanabria and Yagüe (2005)   Reproduced with permission from authors

Figure 8-16 Intraday patterns of orders in the Spanish stock market in 2002

This reaction seems to vary based on the execution venue. For instance, Figure 8-17 shows order placement decisions throughout the day on NYSE Arca, from a study by Bongiovanni, Borkovec and Sinclair (2006). They found that towards the close orders were more likely to be passive, priced away from the market. At the beginning of the day, the

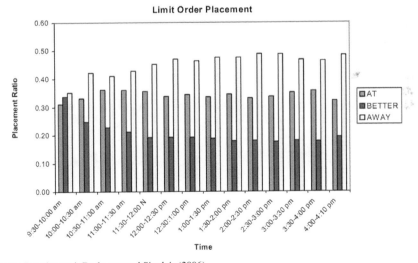

Source: Bongiovanni, Borkovec and Sinclair (2006)
Reproduced with permission from ITG Inc. and Institutional Investor

Figure 8-17 Order placement probabilities on NYSE Arca based on the time of the day

placement decisions were fairly evenly split between pricing at, better or away from the current best price. Then, as the day progressed, the proportion of aggressively priced orders steadily declined. They observed that the order placement pattern mimicked the spread curve; so much of the change in order placement choice may be attributed to this. Some of this difference may also be due to the fact that NYSE Arca is effectively an ECN so traders may adopt slightly different strategies on the primary exchange.

The time of day can also affect the decision to place hidden orders. Studies have shown that the proportion of hidden orders tends to increase towards the end of the day. A possible reason for this increase was proposed by D'Hondt, De Winne and Francois-Heude (2001). They reasoned that the informational value of orders increases before a call auction. Therefore, before the closing auction orders suffer higher levels of exposure risk, making hidden orders more attractive.

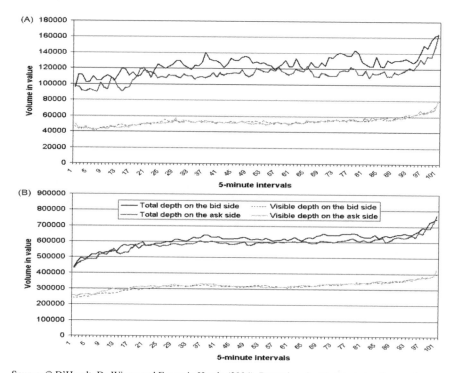

Source: © D'Hondt, De Winne and Francois-Heude (2004) Reproduced with permission from authors

Figure 8-18 Depth behaviour at the (a) best (b) five best limits of the order book

Figure 8-18 shows charts for both the total and visible order book depth for stocks in the CAC40, throughout the trading day. This is from analysis by D'Hondt, De Winne and Francois-Heude (2004). As we can see, the visible depth is fairly stable and increases gradually throughout the day, both at the best limit and at the best five limits. However, note the volatile total depth for the best limit in Figure 8-18(a). This is due to sizeable fluctuations in hidden liquidity throughout the day, whereas across the best five limit prices the hidden depth seems to be a lot more stable.

Hendrik Bessembinder, Marios Panayides and Kumar Venkataraman (2008) found a similar increase in hidden order usage on Euronext. Likewise, Ángel Pardo and Roberto Pascual (2006) reported the same trend for hidden orders on the Spanish Stock Exchange.

Note that so far all of this analysis has been for equities. For U.S. Treasuries, Fleming and Mizrach (2008) found that the proportion of hidden depth was much higher outside New York trading hours; in fact, it was at its lowest between 08:00 and 11:00. Hence, different behaviour may well apply for other asset classes.

Last event

Trading activity is often clustered, so any event is likely to increase the probability of another one happening soon after, whether they are new orders, modifications or cancellations.

In their empirical analysis of the Paris Bourse Bias, Hillion, and Spatt (1995) found a positive serial correlation for the arrival of order types. In other words, a buy order will often be followed by another buy. A similar result was found in a study of the NYSE by Andrew Ellul *et al.* (2003). Note that this effect is not limited to stock markets, for instance, Daníelsson and Payne (2002) discovered a serial correlation for order placement on Reuters' Dealing 2000 FX broking system.

Hans Degryse *et al.* (2005) found a similar correlation in their study of French stocks. Though, they also found that there was a high probability that an aggressively priced order was followed by a more passively priced one, for both buy and sell orders. They attributed this to traders reacting to the change in spread after aggressive orders. Similarly, Ellul *et al.* (2003) found that after a marketable order had consumed liquidity, limit orders were more likely to arrive on the opposite side of the order book, rather than replacing the lost depth on the same side.

Research is continuing to look into why such serial correlation occurs. In fact, the empirical evidence is still at odds with some of the theoretical models. For example, a model created by Christine Parlour (1998) predicted a negative serial correlation, since sequential buys or sells reduce the probability of execution. The positive correlation is most likely due to a combination of factors, based on traders' order placement strategies and their reaction to short-term price trends. In fact, a study of NYSE data by Wee Yong Yeo (2008) ascribes over two thirds of the correlation as being due to order splitting strategies and price undercutting.

8.5   Dealing with hidden liquidity

A range of studies has examined the impact of hidden liquidity, whether this is from fully hidden orders or the hidden portion of icebergs. The hidden liquidity is either inferred from order book data or by analysing private exchange data. Primarily, these studies have focussed on the equity markets. Table 8-4 shows estimates for the proportion of hidden orders used at the major U.S. venues, based on analysis by Rosenblatt Securities (2009). Clearly, a significant proportion of order flow at these venues is now hidden.

Academic studies have found similar results, for instance, Laura Tuttle (2003) found that up to 20% of the inside depth for NASDAQ 100 stocks was hidden. In Europe, D'Hondt, De Winne and Francois-Heude (2004) reported that for France's CAC 40 stocks around 35% of the order volume at the five best limits was hidden. [2] Likewise, Bessembinder, Panayides and Venkataraman (2008) found that around 45% of the order volume was hidden for a

---

[2] D'Hondt (2008) used execution improvement statistics for Euronext to track hidden volume. She found that 37% of the eligible marketable orders received execution improvement, and so had traded with hidden orders.

Venue	Hidden ADV (April 2009) in millions of shares	% of venue's volume
NASDAQ	243.2	10.4
BATS	88.2	4.8
Direct Edge	65.2	4.6
NYSE Arca	63.1	3.4

Source: Rosenblatt Securities (2009)

Table 8-4 Hidden volume estimates for the order books of major U.S. equities venues

sample of 100 stocks traded on Euronext Paris. Whilst Pardo and Pascual (2006) found that for their sample of trades on the Spanish Stock Exchange around 18% involved hidden volume.

So far, there has been less analysis of the usage of hidden liquidity for other asset classes. For U.S. Treasuries the use of iceberg orders on ICAP's BrokerTec platform was analysed by Michael Fleming and Bruce Mizrach (2008). They found that usage was fairly low on average (around 3.3% for the 2-year note); although when there was hidden depth, it was substantial.

Fully hidden orders have become popular once more, in part due to the success of the "dark pool" ATSs. Exchanges had been switching to the partially visible iceberg orders, but have now started to offer purely visible orders again. A study by Amber Anand and Daniel Weaver (2004) found that the total visible depth for Canadian stocks did not change whether hidden orders were allowed or not. However, the actual market depth increased with their reintroduction. They concluded that hidden orders increased the use of the limit order book and provided liquidity that would not have otherwise been available. Tuttle (2003) reported similar findings for hidden volume on NASDAQ.

Spotting hidden liquidity

Hidden orders and "dark pool" ATSs represent an important source of additional liquidity. Spotting or predicting where any such liquidity may be available can give a significant edge.

Whilst hidden orders may be used to reduce signalling risk it is important to remember that they are not always truly invisible. For instance, on venues with visible order books the other market participants can try to track hidden orders by following changes on the order book and comparing these with the reported trades (provided they are reported in real-time). This is harder for completely opaque venues, such as some "dark pool" ATSs, but some participants may still try to find such liquidity.

To search for hidden liquidity we must compare the size and price of each trade with the order book. Any discrepancies may signify additional liquidity, or they might be due to a delay between the price and trade feeds.

For example, Figure 8-19 shows the order book before and after a trade for 500 ABC at 101. Given the trade price and the fact that the buy side of the order book remains unchanged, presumably the trade was triggered by a buy market order for 500 or a marketable limit order with a limit of 101, possibly with an IOC or fill-or-kill instruction.

On the sell side, notice the new order S4 for 1,000 at 101. This may just be a new limit order; alternatively, it may correspond to another tranche of an iceberg order. Without being able to identify the owner of each order, it is difficult to tell. Only by tracking the order book

Buys				Sells			
Id	Time	Size	Price	Price	Size	Time	Id
	8:25:00	1,000	100	101	500	8:20:00	S1
	8:20:20	700	99	101	700	8:22:25	S2
	8:24:00	1,500	98	102	1,500	8:24:09	S3

Sells		
Price	Size	Id
~~101~~	~~500~~	~~S1~~
101	700	S2
101	1,000	S4
102	1,500	S3

(a) before   (b) after

Figure 8-19 Order book before and after a trade for ABC

continually may we start to identify regular patterns. For example, if the order S1 had originally been for 1,000 and 500 had previously executed, there might possibly be an iceberg order with a display size of 1,000 at 101.

Continuing our example from Figure 8-19, another order triggers trades of 2,200 at 101, leaving the order book as shown in Figure 8-20(b). The new sell order S5 could just be a coincidence, but it could also be a 1,000 display size for an iceberg at 101, which just crossed 500 with the last buy order.

Buys				Sells			
Id	Time	Size	Price	Price	Size	Time	Id
	8:25:00	1,000	100	101	700	8:22:25	S2
	8:20:20	700	99	101	1,000	8:25:30	S4
	8:24:00	1,500	98	102	1,500	8:24:09	S3

Sells		
Price	Size	Id
~~101~~	~~700~~	~~S2~~
~~101~~	~~1,000~~	~~S4~~
~~101~~	~~500~~	
101	500	S5
102	1,500	S3

(a) before   (b) after

Figure 8-20 Order book before and after further trades for ABC

A regular display size can make iceberg orders easier to spot, though the actual hidden liquidity may still only be estimated. If the iceberg display sizes are randomized or fully hidden orders are used then things become even more difficult.

Often it is easier to spot hidden liquidity once it has been consumed. For example, Figure 8-21 shows the order book before and after trades for 2,000 ADE are reported at 110.

Buys				Sells	
Id	Time	Size	Price	Price	Size
B3	8:25:00	1,000	110	111	1,200
B4	8:25:25	500	110	112	2,500
B1	8:20:25	1,200	109		
B2	8:24:09	2,000	108		

Buys				
Id	Time	Size	Price	
~~B3~~	~~8:25:00~~	~~1,000~~	~~110~~	.
~~B4~~	~~8:25:25~~	~~500~~	~~110~~	.
B1	8:20:25	1,200	109	.
B2	8:24:09	2,000	108	.

(a) before   (b) after

Figure 8-21 Order book before and after trades for ADE

The sell side of the order book remained unchanged, so the incoming order crossed with buy orders and completed. However, buy orders B3 and B4 can only account for 1,500 of the traded volume, therefore 500 was potentially filled from a hidden order. Since no new order has appeared on the buy side and the best bid is now 109, the hidden liquidity at 110 may well have been exhausted. The only way to find out will be to send an order at 110 and see if it is filled.

When traders do discover hidden liquidity, unsurprisingly, they tend to place more aggressive orders in an attempt to benefit from execution improvement. Thus discovering hidden depth on the buy side will result in more aggressive sell orders. Pardo and Pascual (2006) found empirical evidence for this on the Spanish Stock Exchange, as did D'Hondt, De Winne and Francois-Heude (2004) for Euronext Paris.

Still, even if the hidden liquidity is exhausted by the time our orders reach the venue, there is always the chance for more. As Bongiovanni, Borkovec and Sinclair (2006) point out, once hidden liquidity has been discovered there is a good chance that more will return in the near future.

Estimating the probability of hidden liquidity

As we have already seen, the proportion of hidden orders is dependent on market conditions such as the spread, price volatility and momentum, as well as factors such as the time of day. The aggressiveness of hidden orders may be related to the order book depth on the same side. Therefore, models to estimate the size and location of hidden liquidity must incorporate these various conditions.

Another important factor for the availability of hidden liquidity is the type of orders that are provided by the venue. A fully hidden order may exist anywhere on the order book as a standing limit order, although it must give priority to displayed orders. For some markets that support fully hidden orders, liquidity may even exist between the current best bid and offer. Alternatively, iceberg orders only hide a portion of their total order size. An aggressively priced iceberg order will make the market, thus becoming the new best bid or offer. So using these orders liquidity may only be hidden at, or behind, the best bid or offer.

A nice example of predicting the placement of fully hidden orders is provided by a study of trading on NYSE Arca by Steve Bongiovanni, Milan Borkovec, and Robert Sinclair (2006) from ITG Inc. They used models to estimate the size and location of hidden orders based on a mixture of live and historical market conditions. Firstly, they identified all the trades that executed with hidden orders and extracted the associated market conditions, mapping them using a probability regression model. Thus, for any given set of market conditions working backwards gave the historical average for the size of hidden orders. Next, they used a separate model to estimate the probabilities for where this volume might be hidden, again based on current market conditions such as spread and volatility.

As an example, they used the NASDAQ listed stock AGII (Argonaut Group Inc.): In the last five minutes, 1,000 shares traded, of which 30% were classified as hidden. They also note that the current effective spread was one standard deviation less than its historical average, whilst the current volatility was half a deviation higher than the norm. Both these factors suggest that more hidden liquidity is likely to be placed. Using these conditions, their model expected around 60 shares to be instantly available between the best bid and offer, whilst in five minutes this should increase to nearly 300 shares. Similarly, their placement model estimated that nearly three quarters of this hidden sell liquidity would be priced at the best offer price. By multiplying these probabilities by the expected quantities, we can create a breakdown that shows the hidden sizes expected at each price level, shown in Table 8-5.

Figure 8-22 shows how our order book model might look once these estimates have been incorporated. This should help improve our order placement decisions for the next five minutes.

Price $	Estimated hidden quantity available:			Probability %
	Instantaneous	2 minutes	5 minutes	
35.00	3	7	13	4.6319
35.01	2	4	8	2.7683
35.02	5	12	23	8.0532
35.03	6	15	29	10.5157
35.05	43	109	207	74.0309

Source: Bongiovanni, Borkovec and Sinclair (2006)

Table 8-5 Hidden liquidity estimates

Buys		Sells			Sells	
Size	Price	Price	Size		Price	Size
300	34.99	35.05	500	.	35.00	13
300	34.92	35.07	300	.	35.01	8
	34.90	35.12	500	.	35.02	23
		35.15	600	.	35.03	29
				.	35.05	500
				.	35.05	207
				.	35.07	300
				.	35.12	500
				.	35.15	600

(a) before   (b) after

Figure 8-22 Order book before and after including hidden liquidity estimate

For iceberg orders, an empirical study of CAC 40 stocks on Euronext Paris by D'Hondt, De Winne, and Francois-Heude (2004) found they were focussed around the five best limits of the order book. Figure 8-23 shows their results, plotting the proportion of orders placed against their level of aggressiveness. The categories for order aggressiveness are based on those proposed by Biais, Hillion and Spatt (1995) (see section 8.4) where 1 is the most aggressive and 6 the least.

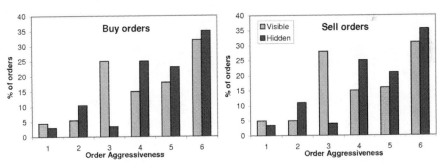

Source: D'Hondt, De Winne, and Francois-Heude (2004)

Figure 8-23 Proportion of orders based on order aggressiveness

As we can see from Figure 8-23, the behaviour of buy and sell orders is similar, with around 25% placed between the best bid and offer (group 4) and over 20% placed at the best price (bid for buys, offer for sells). They are noticeably less aggressive than normal orders with about 35% placed away from the corresponding best bid or offer (group 6).

Another feature of iceberg orders is that the displayed size gives us a baseline for guessing the total order size. For instance, Angelika Esser and Burkart Mönch (2007) observed a strong preference for the chosen display size to be 10% of the overall volume, for the samples in their study of trading on XETRA. Indeed, nearly 40% of all traders followed this trend, with 5% as the next most popular display size. Whilst on Euronext Paris D'Hondt, De Winne and Francois-Heude (2005) found that the median display size for iceberg orders was around 17%. In an earlier study of the French segment of the Euro Nouveau Marché D'Hondt, De Winne, and Francois-Heude (2001) found that more than 70% of the hidden orders displayed less than 30% of their total order size.

Obviously, there is no guarantee that there is hidden liquidity, or how closely it might match these estimates, we shall only find out when we place a buy order (or someone else does). However, these estimates can be some help when trying to choose between venues.

8.6   Estimating execution probability

Execution probability offers another way of looking at order placement. Limit orders sacrifice execution probability for price certainty, whilst market orders do the opposite. As we saw in section 8.4, a wide range of factors such as liquidity, volatility and price trends should be taken into account. By incorporating all these factors into suitable models, we can estimate the probability of execution of any given limit order. Such limit order models allow both traders and algorithms to select limit prices that best match their trading requirements and the current market conditions.

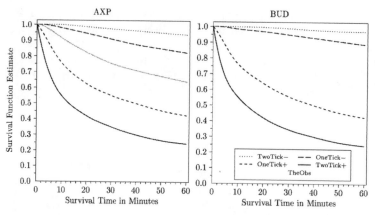

Source: Lo, MacKinlay and Zhang (2002)   Copyright © Elsevier 2002
Reproduced with permission from Elsevier

Figure 8-24 Survival function sensitivity to limit price

Andrew Lo, A. Craig MacKinlay and June Zhang (2002) modelled the dependency of execution times based on the limit price, order size and current market conditions. They used a statistical technique called survival analysis to analyse the lifetimes of limit orders. A survival function is defined and evaluated to determine the probability that a specific limit order is still active after a certain amount of time. This function may then be used to infer the probability of execution, once any cancellations are accounted for. Figure 8-24 shows some examples for two NYSE stocks. Notice how much the probability can vary for different prices. For instance, in this example an order for Budweiser (BUD) has about a 95% probability of surviving 30 minutes when placed one tick below the limit price. Whereas an order placed one tick above has only a 55% chance. Clearly, for a buy order the higher its limit price the lower its survival probability, and so the higher the likelihood of its execution.

The ITG limit order model uses an econometric model of order execution time, also based around survival analysis. ITG (2003) provides a nice example, shown in Figure 8-25. This chart reflects the probability of execution of an order for a range of limit prices over the next half hour. It clearly highlights the non-linear relationships between the probability of execution and both price and time. Note that the shape of each chart will depend on the asset, the order size, the current market conditions and the time of day. For example, the chart shown in Figure 8-25 represents a buy of 500 shares for a liquid NYSE stock. The large rise in probability around the current bid ($23.00) and offer ($23.10) is clearly visible.

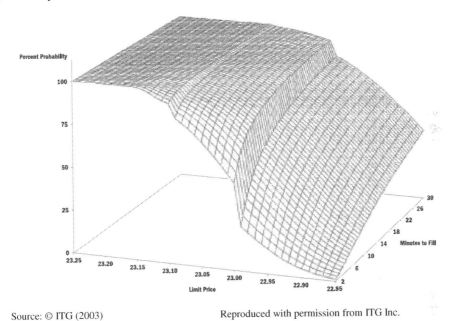

Source: © ITG (2003)   Reproduced with permission from ITG Inc.

Figure 8-25 Execution probability of a limit order

Also, notice that price increments have much more impact in the short term, hence the somewhat skewed surface.

Estimating the likelihood of execution is simply a matter of selecting a limit price from the bottom axis, matching this with the required time horizon and then finding the corresponding probability from the chart's surface. So for this example order, sitting on the bid provides around a 25% probability of execution within the next two minutes, or up to 70% over the next thirty minutes. Raising the limit price increases this, indeed setting the limit at the offer doubles the probability of execution. Therefore, we can use such limit order models to estimate the probability of execution of our orders. Alternatively, by targeting a specific probability of execution and a time horizon we can determine the limit price required to achieve this. For instance, if we require 100% certainty within the first two minutes then Figure 8-25 suggests using a limit price of $23.15.

Clearly, liquidity varies throughout the day and so alters the probability of execution. This can have a considerable effect, particularly for alternate execution venues, such as "dark pool" ATSs, where traders may opt to switch to trading on the main exchange around the close. Figure 8-26 shows a nice example of this, taken from a study for ITG Inc. by Hitesh Mittal and Ronald Taur (2008). For the sample "dark pool" shown in Figure 8-26, we can clearly see a decline in the execution probability (or hit rate) just before the close. The effect is most pronounced for the large-cap stocks. This is probably because substantial volumes will be trading on the main exchanges at the close.

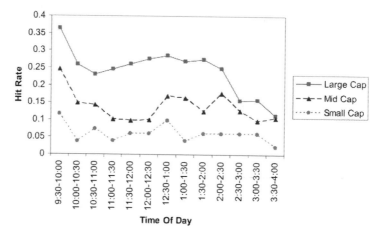

Source: Mittal and Taur (2008)   Reproduced with permission from ITG Inc.

Figure 8-26 Hit Rates for listed stocks in a "dark pool" ATS

So in order to be accurate, limit order models have many different factors that they need to take into account. Though, once created they can be an invaluable aid to the decision making process. As we have seen, we can use them to select appropriate limit prices based on the order size and data for the current market conditions. This should allow us to seek price improvement without sacrificing execution probability.

8.7 Summary

- Price formation is a multi-stage process. The fair value of an asset reflects its actual worth whereas the market price reflects what people are prepared to pay.

- Market microstructure researchers have used a wide range of models to investigate the price formation mechanism. Inventory-based models take the dealer's point of view, whilst information and order book based models assume there are other sources of information, which may in turn affect asset pricing.

- Price discovery / trade execution is generally achieved by bilateral trading (with a market maker) or via auctions (continuous or call-based).

- Continuous auctions typically prioritise orders based on their price. Secondary priority is commonly assigned to time (e.g. equities markets) or pro-rata (size) (e.g. listed derivatives). Though, there is a range of other variants, particularly for pro-rata matching.

- Mid-point matches may be used for venues that do not have their own price discovery mechanism; here the price is sourced externally, often from the primary exchange.

- Order placement decisions require us to choose where we are prepared to trade and how (which order types we will use) as well as how aggressively we will price and size our order/s.

- In today's increasingly fragmented marketplaces, choosing where to place an order can be as important a choice as the price or size.

- Empirical market microstructure research has analysed how order placement decisions and execution probability are affected by market conditions. Order choice and aggressiveness are affected by the:
  - spread
  - order book depth and height
  - volatility
  - other factors such as the time of day

- Hidden orders can be a significant source of additional liquidity, market conditions may also be used to estimate the probability of finding any.

- Limit order models provide estimates for the execution probability of an order. Such models provide a more quantitative basis for order selection.

Chapter 9
Execution tactics

Execution tactics focus on the micro level decisions that need to be made when trading. They are responsible for the actual execution, monitoring the order book and managing order submission.

9.1   Introduction

Execution tactics represent the micro-level choices that must be made during trading. Typically, this means order placement and management. The division of labour between trading algorithms and execution tactics is clearest for the earlier schedule based algorithms. For example, in an all day VWAP algorithm the trading schedule might be based around 15 minute volume "buckets". During the first period, it might aim to trade 3,000, then 2,000 in the next and so on. So for each 15-minute period an execution tactic may be tasked with trading a specific amount. It might simply choose to place a single limit order at the best bid or offer; alternatively, it could slice the amount into a series of smaller orders, as shown in Figure 9-1. In some ways, an execution tactic may be thought of as a mini-algorithm, with a trading horizon of seconds or minutes rather than hours.

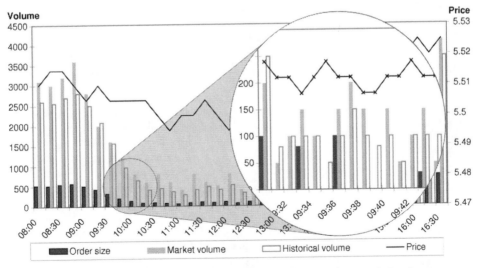

Figure 9-1 Comparing trading algorithm and execution tactic horizons

In order to achieve their objectives, execution tactics often adopt a range of common trading mechanisms. As we saw in Chapter 4, dynamic orders are becoming increasingly sophisticated, so there are often crossovers between common trading tactics and the actual underlying order types. For instance, pegging is obviously related to pegged orders, whilst hiding relies on iceberg and hidden order types. Though, not all venues support these order types, so trading tactics can provide a convenient abstraction. The tactics can then either use the native order types, or adopt an order placement strategy that essentially mimics the required behaviour for venues that do not support them. Alternatively, trading tactics may also employ more complex logic than is currently available via native order types.

As trading algorithms have evolved, many now track market conditions on a tick-by-tick basis. One way of adapting to changing conditions is to use different execution tactics. When market conditions are favourable, an aggressive approach may be employed; then as they become less favourable, it could switch back to using a more passive one.

Note that it is important to realise that there does not have to be a one-to-one relationship between trading algorithms and execution tactics. Some algorithms may use several execution tactics in parallel, leaving passive ones to trade over a longer horizon whilst quicker, more aggressive techniques take advantage of favourable prices.

9.2   Designing execution tactics

The simplest execution tactics are static; so all the logic resides with the trading algorithm. Effectively, these merely consist of splitting child orders to the market with an appropriate price. Passive approaches will adopt limit orders priced at or behind the market whilst aggressive ones use either market or marketable limit orders.

Neutral tactics are more flexible. They may start out passively, seeking price improvement, but if they fail to execute within a certain amount of time they will update or cancel the extant orders, replacing them with more aggressively priced ones. The deadline for execution may just be a fixed period (say five minutes). Alternatively, it could be determined from a limit order model, as we saw in Chapter 8.

Tactics that are more dynamic tend to consider market conditions when making order placement choices. For example, as we saw in Chapter 8, the order book conditions that generally tend to encourage traders to place less aggressively priced orders are:
- wider spreads
- sufficient depth, or prices further apart, on the opposite side of the order book
- insufficient depth, or prices close together, on our side of the order book

Given favourable conditions, a passive price-driven tactic may well price its orders further from the market, seeking price improvement. Alternatively, risk/cost-driven tactics may opt to weigh up the potential costs and decide whether it is better to wait or take an immediate hit. Opportunistic tactics may trade aggressively to take advantage of the current conditions.

So, broadly speaking, execution tactics may be classified based on the goals that drive their usage, just as we categorised trading algorithms in Chapter 5. Some common examples are shown in Table 9-1.

In general, impact-driven tactics seek to further reduce market impact by splitting the order into smaller quantities or by hiding a portion of it. Price/risk-driven approaches strive to dynamically adjust based on the market conditions. Similarly, the opportunistic ones look to take advantage when conditions are favourable.

Impact-driven	Price/Risk-driven	Opportunistic/ Liquidity-driven
Slicing Hiding	Layering Pegging Catching	Seeking Sniping Routing Pairing

Table 9-1 Common trading tactics/mechanisms

Note that a lot of the functionality is applicable amongst the various types so these categorisations are merely guidelines; different approaches may well use them in a "pick 'n mix" fashion. It is important to remember that the trading algorithm is still the main driver of the trading strategy, but by selecting the most appropriate execution tactics, we can further enhance performance.

Impact-driven tactics

Just as impact-driven trading algorithms break down the order into smaller quantities, these tactics apply a similar approach to order placement. Order slicing usually creates tranches that are placed sequentially. Alternatively, the child orders may be hidden, either with the appropriate order types or by sending the order to an opaque ATS.

Slicing

Order slicing is essentially the precursor to the early schedule-driven algorithms. That said, it can still be a useful approach. Reducing the size of an order can lower its market impact and any associated signalling risk, albeit at the cost of execution probability.

Execution tactics usually focus on a much smaller timeframe than a trading algorithm. For example, an over the day VWAP algorithm might need to trade 100,000 of ABC. Though, in a ten-minute period, it may only need the execution tactic to work 3,000. Depending on the market, 3,000 could still be too large to place as a single order, therefore order slicing can be used to reduce this to a series of less noticeable sizes. Randomisation is a way of further reducing signalling risk. This applies to both the quantities to be split and the time between each child order. Otherwise, a very predictable trading pattern emerges, which might be taken advantage of by other market participants. For instance, Figure 9-2 shows two different

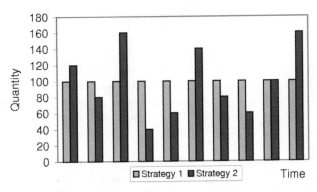

Figure 9-2 Two alternative order splitting tactics

tactics to split an order for 1,000 ABC over the same time period. Clearly, the more random second strategy is harder to second-guess.

Used sequentially, order slicing effectively acts as a hiding mechanism. It may be adopted to create synthetic iceberg orders for venues that do not natively support this order type. Note that there is a key difference between order slicing and native iceberg orders, as we saw in Chapter 4: For native iceberg orders, the hidden portion is still part of the order book, and so may still participate fully in the trade crossing mechanism, albeit with only price priority. Whereas an order slicing mechanism relies on execution confirmations to know when next to send another order slice. Since these are dispatched after the matching process, we will potentially miss out on some crossing opportunities.

For example, consider a requirement to sell 10,000 ABC, from which we have split an initial child order for 1,000 at 101 as S1. Figure 9-3(a-c) shows how an incoming market order to buy 2,200 affects the order book, whilst (d) shows the alternative outcome for a native iceberg.

Buys				Sells					Sells		
Id	Time	Size	Price	Price	Size	Time	Id		Price	Size	Id
	8:25:00	1,000	100	101	1,000	8:20:00	S1		~~101~~	~~1,000~~	~~S1~~
	8:20:25	2,000	99	101	800	8:25:25	S2		~~101~~	~~800~~	~~S2~~
	8:24:20	1,500	98	102	2,500	8:24:09	S3		~~102~~	~~400~~	~~S3~~
									102	**2,100**	S3

(a) before   (b) MO crosses

Buys				Sells					Sells		
Id	Time	Size	Price	Price	Size	Time	Id		Price	Size	Id
	8:25:00	10,000	100	~~101~~	~~1,000~~	~~8:20:00~~	~~S1~~		~~101~~	~~1,000~~	~~S1~~
	8:20:25	50,000	99	~~101~~	~~800~~	~~8:25:25~~	~~S2~~		~~101~~	~~800~~	~~S2~~
	8:24:09	25,500	98	~~102~~	~~400~~	~~8:24:09~~	~~S3~~		~~101~~	~~400~~	~~S6~~
				101	850	8:26:00	S6		101	600	S6
				102	2,100	8:24:09	S3		102	2,500	S3

(c) after for a synthetic iceberg   (d) for a native

Figure 9-3 An order slicing example

The incoming market order will immediately cross 1,000 with our order S1, whilst another 800 will cross with order S2. Since there are no more orders at 101, it will now have to cross the remaining 400 at 102 with order S3. The venue will send out confirmations for these fills. Once the order confirmation is received, we now split another order (S6), this time for 850.

In comparison, for a native iceberg order its price priority would mean the hidden size completed the market order at 101. As we can see in Figure 9-3(d), a new display size would still have been split as order S6, 400 of which completes the incoming market order. The remaining 600 (assuming a display size of 1,000) stays on the order book, and now has price priority. Therefore, an exchange's native iceberg orders can offer both faster execution, and a higher probability of completion.

Clearly, the main disadvantage with order slicing is that we may miss out on crossing opportunities, since our order placement is reliant on the dispatch of execution notifications that take place afterwards. In this example, we only managed to cross 1,000 with the market order, since the crossing mechanism completes the market order by filling with S3 before we are notified that order S1 filled. Note that when selling in an upward trending market missing execution opportunities is less of an issue, but in a downward market this would have resulted in a loss.

The main advantage of order slicing is that we have much more control of the display size, so our second order can be split with a random size, rather than simply splitting 1,000 each time (in this case 850 was used). Order book information and price trend indicators may be used to select the optimal display quantity and even limit price.

Order slicing may also be applied in parallel, allowing simultaneous trading across several execution venues. Similarly, it may also be used to split orders across a range of prices; effectively this is the layering tactic, which we shall discuss shortly. Such versatility means that order slicing can still be a useful tactic, despite its simplicity.

Hiding

Hiding is all about reducing signalling risk. Generally, it is used for orders that would otherwise provide liquidity, namely standing limit orders. This risk reflects the potential losses we can incur from the information that our trading pattern relays to the other market participants. For instance, placing a large buy order gives away our requirements; other traders will then react to this, most likely by raising the price at which they are prepared to sell. They may even cancel their orders to see if we are prepared to go even higher.

Note that in some multi-venue marketplaces hiding can be as straightforward as routing the order to a less obvious venue, where it will face less competition. This applies in particular for U.S. equities since the order protection rule introduced for Regulation NMS means that orders placed at the top of the order book should not be traded through.

Algorithmic orders are implicitly hidden, since most strategies only release a small portion of the order for immediate trading. However, signalling risk is dependent on both the order size and the asset's liquidity. In fact, for illiquid assets even a small order can result in the price shifting away as other traders try to second-guess our requirements. We can further reduce the signalling risk by using hidden order types, as shown in Figure 9-4.

Sells				Sells				Sells		
Price	Size	Id		Price	Size	Id		Price	Size	Id
101	1,000	S1		101	2,000	S1		101	1,000	S1
101	3,000	S2		101	3,000	S2		101	2,000	S2
102	4,000	S3		101	1,000	S3		101	4,000	H1
102	2,000	S4		101	7,000	H1		102	1,000	S4
				102	4,000	S4				
(a)Discretionary				(b) Iceberg				(c) Fully hidden		

Figure 9-4 Hidden order types

Discretionary orders, although fully visible, allow us to hide our actual limit price. For example, in Figure 9-4(a) we have hidden our true intentions by displaying our order S3 with a limit price of 102, even though we are prepared to trade at 101. Admittedly, we could increase the discretionary amount to shift our order deeper into the order book; however, this will place even more orders in front of us in terms of execution priority. The full size is also visible; hence, discretionary orders are generally more suited for smaller orders.

Iceberg orders go further and allow us to display only a portion of the order, whilst the remaining hidden portion retains price priority. For instance, in Figure 9-4(b) we have set the display size to 1,000, again shown as order S3. The remaining 7,000 will remain hidden until order S3 is completed, although it will maintain price priority over order S4. Note that it is important to get the right balance when selecting a display size. Too small a quantity and the order will take longer to complete, since only the visible portion will have both price and time priority. Conversely, selecting too large a display size will allow for faster completion, but at a greater exposure risk. Another factor to consider is the predictability of the display size. In a study of trading on XETRA, Angelika Esser and Burkart Mönch (2007) observed a distinct preference to use a display size of 10% of the parent order. Clearly, this will vary across both assets and markets; however, human nature also plays a part; people will often prefer to use a round number that is easy to calculate. For venues that do not support iceberg orders, we can create synthetic icebergs using randomised order slicing, as we saw in the previous section.

Fully hidden orders can further reduce signalling risk, so in Figure 9-4(c) our entire order H1 is hidden. Some exchanges, such as the Australian Stock Exchange (ASX) used to offer fully hidden orders; however, in an effort to balance the needs of both institutional and retail users many have replaced them with iceberg orders. That said, the introduction of new "dark pools" via alternative trading systems (ATSs) means that fully hidden orders are now making a comeback.

It is important to remember that even the best hiding mechanisms can only really delay the inevitable. Other market participants will undoubtedly be constantly monitoring the order book state and comparing this with the reported trades to try to find hidden liquidity.

Price/Risk-driven tactics

Price-driven tactics may be based on changes in the spread and short-term price trends. For instance, as the gap between best bid and offer narrows we can afford to pay the spread, and so the tactic can issue more marketable limit orders or even market orders. As soon as the spread widens, more passive pricing is used.

Likewise, for price trends, these tactics can react much like the adaptive trading algorithms we saw in Chapter 5. Thus, a passive trading style tends to rely on trends persisting, pricing its orders even further from the market during favourable price trends, to try to maximise price improvement. Conversely, during unfavourable price trends it may price orders closer to the market to try to stem potential losses. Aggressive price-based tactics often rely on price trends mean reverting, and so they behave in the opposite fashion to passive ones, aggressively taking advantage of favourable prices. The price trends may be based on forecasts or inferred from the order book imbalance. For example, a surplus of sell volume on the order book may indicate the price will soon decrease.

Risk-driven tactics may also consider the asset's price volatility and how much time they have left to execute. These may be combined to create a timing factor, which can then be incorporated into the order placement decision. Hence, for a liquid asset at the start of its execution the timing factor is fairly minor; however, it increases as time progresses. For less liquid assets, this factor is more important, and so is more likely to encourage placing more aggressive orders.

In terms of common mechanisms, orders may be layered throughout the order book to try to maximise both execution probability and the potential for price improvement. Alternatively, they may simply be pegged to a market price, or linked with a cost-based latching mechanism to reduce risk.

Layering

The layering tactic simultaneously maintains a range of standing limit orders. The orders are spread throughout the order book, usually with different limit prices. This approach aims to take advantage of favourable price movements. Also for venues where matching is based on price/time priority, the layering tactic helps preserve the time priority for each order. This is because when the market price moves a new order may be split, rather than just updating an existing order to match the new level. This allows the other layered orders to maintain their time priority in the order book queue.

As Michael Aitken *et al.* (2007) point out, time priority is particularly important for liquid stocks that have densely populated order books. The high turnover of orders means that if time priority is lost, the only way to regain it is with a more aggressive price. For example, the order book in Figure 9-5(a) shows our three layered orders S1, S2 and S5 for ABC, ranging in price from 101 to 103. Compared to the single order S3 our combined orders offer more potential for price improvement, should an aggressive order walk up the order book.

Buys		Sells					Sells			
Size	Price	Price	Size	Time	Id		Price	Size	Time	Id
1,000	99	101	1,000	8:25:20	S5		100	500	8:26:20	S7
500	99	101	800	8:25:00	S4		101	1,000	8:25:20	S5
1,800	98	102	2,500	8:24:25	S3		101	800	8:25:00	S4
2,400	98	102	500	8:24:09	S2		102	2,500	8:24:25	S3
900	97	103	1,000	8:23:00	S1		102	500	8:24:09	S2
2,500	97						102	3,000	8:26:05	S6
							103	1,000	8:23:00	S1

(a) before   (b) a new price level is set

Figure 9-5 Layered orders

Admittedly, some execution probability is sacrificed, but the layered orders also allow us more scope to modify orders without losing time priority. For instance, when new orders S6 and S7 arrive, a new price level is set at 100. Assuming we want to participate at this new level, we have several options. If our requirement allows placing an additional order then we can simply split a new order S8 at 100. Though, if we do not want to increase our exposure then we shall need to adjust our existing orders. So we could either:

1.   Update the limit price on order S5 to be 100.
2.   Reduce the quantity of S5 and use this to split a new order S8 at 100.
3.   Reduce the quantities of S1 and S2, then again split a new order S8.
4.   Reduce the quantity just for S1 and split a new order S8.

All these options allow us to participate at 100; in comparison a single order, such as S3, has fewer alternatives in such a situation. Option 1 leaves us with no presence on the order book at 101. If the price reverts slightly we could miss an opportunity to execute. Option 2 addresses this issue, nevertheless, we have still reduced the size of the order that was second most likely to execute. [1] To resolve this problem options 3 and 4 source the required volume using orders further away from the market, reducing the impact on our overall execution probability. Overall, option 4 is probably the best approach [2] since it modifies the order least likely to execute.

So layering orders is useful for highly liquid assets with dense order books where achieving time priority is difficult. Pegging the price of orders to keep up with the market would be an expensive option since it would keep reducing our priority. Whereas by layering orders across the book we can track price moves without significantly affecting our overall

---

[1] Reducing the size would have more effect in a venue using price/pro-rata order matching.
[2] This holds true regardless of whether the venue uses price/time priority or price/pro-rata for its order matching.

execution probability.

Layering is useful for illiquid assets as well, since there is more scope for price improvement, it also improves the visible depth. Deeper books with a lower range of prices tend to promote more aggressive orders from the opposite side. Thus, by filling gaps we can reduce the expected market impact and so try to encourage participants on the other side to place more favourably priced orders. Note that filling gaps means just that, it does not mean filling an empty order book for an illiquid asset with layered orders to give the illusion of depth.

Pegging

Pegged orders are a convenience, they provide dynamically updating limit prices that reduce the risk of mispricing for standing limit orders. Often this tactic is used with passive orders that are trying to benefit from price improvement. Pegging may also be based on the price of another asset, for instance, in pair trading, or versus a market index. Similarly, for options, delta-adjusted orders are effectively pegged based on the price of the underlying asset and the option's delta.

Care must be taken when using pegging since regular trading patterns can lead to considerable signalling risk. Pegging every 30 seconds 0.5 away from the mid is nearly as predicable as the order slicing we saw in Figure 9-2. Hence, randomisation is important to reduce the predictability of pegged trading, both for when updates are made as well as for their size. Two other potential issues with pegging were pointed out by David Brown and Craig Holden (2005): Pegged orders can contribute to momentum since they continually shift liquidity with the prevailing trend. They also generally have a lower execution probability, since in a price/time priority based venue changing the limit price will often place them at the end of the queue (unless a new price level is set).

A more adaptive approach to pegging could incorporate market conditions or short-term price predictions in the decision of whether to peg the order. Note that pegging can just as easily be applied to order sizes. Thus trading based on the available order book depth might peg orders to the best bid or offer size. Note that most venues will allow an order to be reduced in size without losing priority. Increasing the size of an order would clearly disadvantage other similarly priced orders behind it in the order book queue, so to ensure fairness such an update often results in the order losing its priority. Alternatively, it may be better to adopt an order layering tactic.

Catching

This tactic is based on cutting our losses when the price looks to be trending away from us. In some ways, it may be thought of as a visible trailing stop. To start with, we shall adopt a fairly passive latching mechanism, as we can see in Figure 9-6.

Essentially, this is a means of dynamically adjusting our limit price based on the current market price. The main difference from pegging is that it works only in one direction. Generally, price latches are used to try to keep any potential gains from market moves. Consequently, this mechanism is used by both trailing stops and tick-sensitive orders. A positive latch will only move when the price rises (e.g. trailing stop sells and downtick orders); whilst a negative one only tracks price drops (e.g. trailing stop buys and uptick orders).

Figure 9-6 shows a buy order positively latching to the best bid; hence, its limit price only changes when the best bid rises. In addition to the latch, we can assign a trigger limit, much like for a stop order. When the market price reaches this point we will become more aggress-

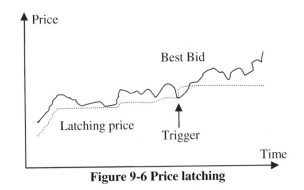

Figure 9-6 Price latching

ive, to try to stem any losses. This is the point labelled trigger in Figure 9-6. So our order will now be priced based on the best offer, paying the spread to prevent any further losses. Alternatively, a market order might even be used, risking further market impact to guarantee execution.

Opportunistic/Liquidity-driven tactics

As with the opportunistic trading algorithms, these tactics tend to strive to maximise the benefits of favourable market conditions, such as liquidity. The seeking tactic aims to source additional liquidity from hidden orders. Tactics may also focus on reducing signalling risk. Clearly, any orders we place will change the available order book depth and so affect the overall order imbalance. For example, if we need to buy but there is already an imbalance skewed towards buy volume then adding another buy order will only increase the probability of a price rise. Sniping tries to take advantage of available liquidity without giving away our own requirements. Finally, routing corresponds to choosing the best destinations to send orders to, based on a variety of criteria.

Seeking

The seeking tactic is all about finding hidden liquidity. Market participants are constantly monitoring the state of the order book and comparing this with the reported trades to try to spot hidden liquidity. Based on this data we can create models to estimate the probability of how much volume is hidden at the various price levels throughout the order book, as we saw in Chapter 8. Note that these are just estimates; the only way we shall really know if there is any hidden liquidity is by issuing an order and, hopefully, being filled with a better price.

Another important concern when searching for liquidity is keeping our own orders hidden; otherwise, we may be exposed to considerable signalling risk. We want to fill our own orders at the best price possible without giving away information about our actual requirements. So a persistent order will not do, instead we will need to use either market orders or marketable limit orders with specific fill instructions. Assuming we want to be able to control our market impact then we can rule out market orders. So the choice is now between the various fill instructions available for limit orders: Of these only immediate-or-cancel and fill-or-kill are suitable, since the others all leave residual orders on the order book. The main difference between the two instructions is that immediate-or-cancel allows partial fills whereas fill-or-kill has a strict 100% execution requirement.

Having identified potential sites in the order book with hidden liquidity, all we need to do now is issue appropriate orders. For instance Figure 9-7(a) shows an example order book for asset ABC. In this example, our estimates suggest that there may be 6,000 hidden to sell at 101 (labelled H1). By sizing our order larger than the visible volume on the order book we are seeking hidden liquidity. If our order is filled then there may well be hidden liquidity at that price point. If sufficient liquidity is not available then our order is immediately cancelled, leaving no trace on the order book. Figure 9-7(b) shows our estimate of what the order book will look like after issuing a limit order to buy 3,000 ABC at 101.

Buys		Sells			
Size	Price	Price	Size	Time	Id
800	100	101	1,000	8:25:00	S1
1,000	99	*101*	*6,000*	*8:20:25*	*H1*
2,500	98	102	2,000	8:21:25	S2
		102	1,500	8:24:09	S3

Sells			
Price	Size	Time	Id
~~101~~	~~1,000~~	~~8:25:00~~	~~S1~~
~~101~~	~~2,000~~	~~8:20:25~~	~~H1~~
101	1,000	8:28:00	S4
101	*3,000*	*8:20:25*	*H1*
102	2,000	8:21:25	S2

(a) before

(b) after

Figure 9-7 An example search for hidden liquidity

In the case of an iceberg order, a new tranche may be issued, such as order S4. Though, neither this, nor a successful execution guarantees that there is any more hidden liquidity. We still need to carefully check the order book state before and after; since potentially we could have crossed with another visible order which hit the order book the same time as ours.

If sufficient hidden liquidity is available then the behaviour of our liquidity seeking order will be the same, regardless of whether we use an immediate-or-cancel or a fill-or-kill instruction. However, let's now assume that the hidden size shown in H1 is only for 1,500. An immediate-or-cancel instruction would mean that our order fills 2,500 ABC at 101, with the best offer becoming order S2 at 102. Having consumed all the hidden liquidity that was available at 101, we can also feedback this size into our hidden order models to help improve future estimates. In comparison, a fill-or-kill order would have failed to cross since there is insufficient hidden liquidity; therefore, the order would be immediately cancelled leaving the order book still looking like Figure 9-7(a). Unfortunately, all this has told us is that there is not sufficient ABC hidden at 101.

Thus, immediate-or-cancel orders offer a way of probing for hidden liquidity that minimises their footprint on the order book and may partially fill, even if our estimate for the amount of hidden liquidity is wrong. Fill-or-kill orders are less forgiving in this last respect due to their 100% completion requirement. Partial fills are important since by the time we resubmit an order someone else may have already found and consumed any hidden liquidity.

Sniping

Sniping is a tactic for capturing liquidity whilst minimising signalling risk. Effectively, it is a way for liquidity demanders to hide their strategy. Alternatively, it is just a version of the seeking tactic for visible liquidity. To reduce the potential for signalling risk we will use marketable limit orders with specific fill instructions. This gives us price control and limits our footprint on the order book.

When liquidity becomes available, an aggressive order is used to cross with it. For instance, Figure 9-8 shows the order book as new order S1 arrives, offering to sell 1,000 ABC at 101.

Buys		Sells			
Size	Price	Price	Size	Time	Id
1,000	100	101	1,000	8:25:00	S1
1,700	99	102	800	8:20:25	S2
2,200	98	104	1,100	8:19:09	S3

(a) before

	Sells			
	Price	Size	Time	Id
.	~~101~~	~~900~~	~~8:25:00~~	~~S1~~
.	101	**100**	8:25:00	S1
.	102	800	8:20:25	S2
.	104	1,100	8:19:09	S3

(b) after

Figure 9-8 An example sniping order

In order to grab this newly available liquidity we issue a fill-or-kill order to buy 900 at 101. By sizing our order just less than the best offer size, we should leave a remainder on the order book, therefore the bid offer spread remains undisturbed at 100-101. This is a reasonable approach since the order book imbalance is currently tilted towards the buys, so if we had taken the whole volume at 101 it is quite possible that the spread would have shifted up to a less favourable 101-102. Note that for sniping either immediate-or-cancel or fill-or-kill instructions can be equally useful, based on whether we want partial fills or not.

Sniping can also adjust to the available liquidity. For example, if order S2 in Figure 9-8 had been priced at 101 we could have executed 1,700 without altering the spread.

Routing

Routing is important for markets that have a range of execution venues. When choosing where to send orders, many different factors should be analysed. Obviously, the price and quantity available are key to the decision, but other important considerations are the probability of hidden liquidity, the likelihood of successful execution, latency and any venue specific costs or fees. Routing mechanisms constantly make these decisions, based on the available data, to try to ensure orders are sent to the optimal destination.

As we saw for liquidity-based trading algorithms, a common way of tackling the difficulty of trading in fragmented markets is to use liquidity aggregation. A virtual order book can be created by collecting data from all the possible execution venues. From this, we can then make more balanced decisions about how much to trade and at what price level. Having decided this we then need to convert our requirements into actual orders. This transformation may be performed by the actual trading algorithm; alternatively, it can be delegated to a routing based execution tactic.

Figure 9-9 shows an extension of the example we saw in Chapter 5 for liquidity based trading algorithms. The virtual order book has been decomposed back into its constituents. These are ordered by price, probability of execution and size. The hidden orders are only estimates, and so are placed after visible orders. Each entry is also flagged with the venue it originated from, whether it is from the primary exchange (Exch-1), an alternative trading system (ATS) or an electronic crossing network (ECN).

We can then use this view to translate order requirements into actual orders. For instance, if price is our key concern then we should clearly try to capture any hidden liquidity at 101 on ECN-2. If we are more concerned about the probability of execution then we should focus on the orders available on Exch-1, ECN-2 and ATS-2. For larger quantities, we shall need to route orders to a wider range of venues.

For example, if we need to immediately sell 10,000 ABC, we could focus on just the visible liquidity, sending the following child orders:

> ATS-2: Sell 700 ABC at 100
> ECN-2: Sell 1,500 ABC at 100

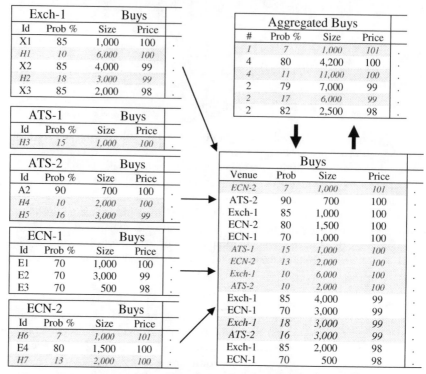

Figure 9-9 An aggregated order book and its breakdown

Exch-1: Sell 5,000 ABC at 99
ECN-1: Sell 2,800 ABC at 99

Alternatively, we could try to consume some of the hidden liquidity by creating orders based on a mix of the probability of execution and the estimated hidden liquidity:

ATS-1: Sell 1,000 ABC at 100
ATS-2: Sell 1,500 ABC at 100
ECN-1: Sell 1,000 ABC at 100
ECN-2: Sell 3,000 ABC at 100
Exch-1: Sell 3,500 ABC at 100

Hence, we are able to easily route orders using various criteria, in an effort to achieve the best execution based on our requirements.

Pairing

As we saw in Chapter 4, some execution venues support a range of contingent order types and conditions; however, the majority of venues do not provide these. Thus, one of the key aspects of the pairing tactic is to emulate this behaviour in order to be able to link orders.

When trading pairs (or baskets) of assets, the trading algorithm focuses on the trigger, i.e. whether the ratio or spread is favourable. Ensuring that each of the assets are successfully bought or sold can be delegated to an execution tactic. Since execution cannot be guaranteed, legging is an important consideration. This is the difference in value in the traded positions for each asset. Certainly, legging often drives the execution for these tactics.

If a reasonable amount of legging is permitted then each order can almost be worked separately. The execution tactic can choose to use standard mechanisms, much like any other static, price or liquidity-based approach. Only when the legging reaches its limit will it need to try to intervene.

For example, let's consider buying 2,000 of asset JKL and selling 2,000 of XYZ. For convenience, we will assume both these assets are priced around $50. Our legging limit is set to $5,000, therefore it equates to around 100 of either JKL or XYZ. So if we have already executed 400 JKL, but only 300 XYZ then we need to address this legging before we can think about buying any more JKL. Similarly, any extant orders for JKL should be cancelled to ensure we do not get even more legged. In order to try to catch up and reduce the legging we can convert any extant orders for XYZ to more aggressive ones, so long as the price of XYZ remains within our limits.

If a negligible amount of legging is allowed then each order will be contingent on the other. Figure 9-10 shows the order books for each asset. Hence, the:

- Buy order for 2,000 JKL (B4) is dependent on being able to sell XYZ at 50.5
- Sell order for 2,000 XYZ (S9) is dependent on being able to buy JKL at 50.8

JKL

Buys			Sells			Buys			Sells		
Id	Size	Price	Price	Size	Id	Id	Size	Price	Price	Size	Id
B1	1,500	50.6	50.8	2,500	S1	B1	1,500	50.6	50.8	2,500	S1
B2	2,000	50.6	50.9	1,000	S2	B2	2,000	50.6	50.9	1,000	S2
B3	800	50.5	50.9	900	S3	B3	800	50.5	50.9	900	S3
B4	2,000	50.5				B4	**1,000**	50.5			

XYZ

Buys			Sells			Buys			Sells		
Id	Size	Price	Price	Size	Id	Id	Size	Price	Price	Size	Id
B6	2,000	50.5	50.6	1,000	S6	~~B6~~	~~2,000~~	~~50.5~~	50.6	1,000	S6
B7	1,000	50.5	50.7	900	S7	B7	1,000	50.5	50.7	900	S7
B8	500	50.4	50.7	1,500	S8	B8	500	50.4	50.7	1,500	S8
			50.8	2,000	S9				50.8	**1,000**	S9

(a) before   (b) after

Figure 9-10 An example of contingent orders

Therefore, when the buy order B6 for XYZ is suddenly cancelled, we can no longer be sure of selling 2,000 XYZ at 50.5, so we need to modify our buy order B4 for JKL, reducing it to be for 1,000, as shown in Figure 9-10(b). Essentially, each order is pegging to what is available on the same side of the order book for the other asset. Note that this can also involve changing the price as well as the size.

In turn, these orders are also linked to the outcome of each other, like the contingent orders that we saw in Chapter 4. This means that we may also need to adjust the size of our sell order S9 for XYZ. Otherwise, we could end up with around $50,000 of legging.

The relative liquidity of each asset is also important: If one asset is significantly less liquid than the other then this becomes a bottleneck. In fact, the orders for the least liquid asset tend to drive the whole process.

9.3   Algorithm selection

In Chapter 5, we saw how various investment objectives could be translated into a range of trading algorithms. In turn, these may then use execution tactics to actually achieve their aims. This division of responsibility helps keep both the algorithms and the execution tactics simpler. Note that it is important to remember that the trading algorithm drives the execution tactics, and not the other way around. For example, a VWAP algorithm that uses price-driven execution tactics is still trying to track the VWAP. The target quantities and hard price limits are still determined by the algorithm. The choice of execution tactic simply makes it slightly more price sensitive in the way it places its orders.

This "divide and conquer" approach also makes it easier to reuse the same logic between different markets or even across asset classes. For instance, we might well be able to "port" a VWAP or implementation shortfall algorithm built to trade U.S. equities to also work in Europe or Asia. Though, as we saw in Chapter 3, the world's financial marketplaces still have some substantial differences. So we shall only get the best performance if we fine-tune the algorithm for each specific region or market. Fundamentally, we are still tackling the same problem so much of the trading algorithm logic can stay the same. However, the actual order execution may need to be quite different. Therefore, we could create execution tactics that are customised for specific regions or markets. These in turn could be reused, potentially allowing us to port other algorithms to new markets much more quickly. This approach could even be extended to port equities-based algorithms to other asset classes, such as futures or FX.

Execution tactics also allow common trading mechanisms to be shared amongst a wide range of algorithms. This is particularly useful given the increasing need for customisation and rapid turnaround of new trading algorithms. For example, modern VWAP and implementation shortfall algorithms may well share some of the same execution tactics, even though at the algorithm level their objectives are very different.

Table 9-2 summarises some of the typical combinations.

Algorithm		Tactics		
		Impact driven	Price/Risk driven	Opportunistic/ Liquidity
Impact	Time Weighted Average Price	●	○	
	Volume Weighted Average Price	●	○	○
	Percentage Of Volume	●	○	○
	Minimal impact	●	○	○
Cost	Implementation Shortfall	●	●	○
	Adaptive Shortfall	●	●	○
	Market On Close	●	●	○
Oppor-tunistic	Price Inline	●	●	○
	Liquidity-driven	○	○	●
	Pairs / Spread trading	○	○	●

● often used   ○ sometimes used

Table 9-2 Execution tactics used by trading algorithms

Note that the relationship between trading algorithms and execution tactics does not have to be strictly one-to-one; in fact, some algorithms may use multiple execution tactics in parallel.

Impact-driven algorithms essentially use order slicing to try to minimise the overall market impact. They may simply be driven by time (TWAP), a historical volume profile (VWAP) or the actual market volume (POV). Thus, the algorithm just needs the execution tactics to work the order as best they can. So we could really use any of these approaches. For instance, a VWAP or POV algorithm using stealth-based or opportunistic tactics might prove to be a good way of reducing market impact.

Cost-driven algorithms have quite a difficult goal to achieve; they need to take account of market impact, timing risk, and even factors such as price trends. So it is important that the execution tactics are attuned to this and do not miss opportunities or incur additional costs. Hence, these algorithms may well adopt multiple tactics. They may switch between approaches, or even run tactics in parallel.

Opportunistic algorithms are focussed on taking advantage whenever the market conditions are favourable; they are less concerned about completing the whole order. So they are much more similar to execution tactics than the other two classes of algorithm. For instance, liquidity-driven algorithms tend to adopt liquidity or stealth-based tactics. Similarly, pair trading implies a pair based, or order contingent approach, although if the legging is sufficient it might also be implemented with a mix of seeking (for illiquid assets) and sniping (for the more liquid ones). Price inline algorithms tend to adopt a wider range, since they are essentially based on an underlying impact-driven algorithm.

Factors affecting the choice of execution tactics

Each trading algorithm bases its trading approach on a wide range of factors, encompassing the investor's goals, the order details and asset-specific information. In Chapter 7 we saw how these factors affect the actual choice of trading algorithm. For execution tactics the main factors affecting their choice are more straightforward. Essentially, this depends on both the current market conditions and how well the algorithm is actually performing.

Market conditions

As trading algorithms have evolved many now track market conditions on a tick-by-tick basis. Internally, they may use this information to alter their target trading patterns. They may also choose to trade more or less aggressively based on whether the market conditions are favourable or not, as we saw for the adaptive shortfall and price inline algorithms.

In terms of their choice of execution tactics, the controlling algorithms may decide to switch between more or less aggressive approaches, based on their perception of the current market conditions. For instance, if the current price trend is favourable the algorithm may adopt a more passive approach, seeking price improvement.

Some algorithms may use multiple execution tactics in parallel. For example, a passive price-based approach might be left running to try to achieve price improvement whilst more aggressive stealth-based tactics might be used to take advantage of any opportunities that arise.

Liquidity is another important factor. Although this is primarily an asset-specific characteristic, we can also characterise this at the market/venue level based on their average spreads and trade sizes.

Average spread

The bid offer spread is one of the most visible indicators of liquidity. Table 9-3 shows the average spreads in basis points for a range of different venues and asset classes.

Asset class		Venue	Average spread / bps
Equity	Stocks	NASDAQ	7
		Euronext Paris	13
		Italy SE	22
		LSE	32
		Hong Kong Ex [3]	47
		Singapore SE [3]	61
Fixed income	U.S Treasury 2yr		~3
	U.S Treasury 10yr		~6
	Corporate bonds	TRACE	25+
FX	Spot	EBS	~1-3
Derivatives	S&P 500 E-mini futs	CME	~2

Source: Equity: EDHEC (2007), FT Mandate (2006), Fixed Income: Edwards, Harris and Piwowar (2007) and author's own estimates

Table 9-3 Average spreads

For markets where a few key assets are highly traded, such as FX or U.S. Treasuries, competition ensures that the spreads are generally much lower. Indeed spreads for these have been as little as 1 or 2 bps or even less. As the liquidity decreases brokers/dealers cover their risk by increasing the spread. For really illiquid assets, spreads may be measured in hundreds of basis points.

Spreads are also closely linked to volatility; since, as we saw in Chapter 2, they represent a premium that market makers apply to protect themselves from the risk of adverse selection. During the 2007-09 financial crisis, spreads increased considerably: Spreads for many stocks doubled, illiquid shares saw even higher rises. Similar increases occurred for other asset classes, pretty much preserving the relative proportions shown in Table 9-3.

There can also be significant geographical differences in the average spread cost. Across Europe, spreads are traditionally somewhat higher than those of the U.S., whilst those in Asia are often even higher. Consequently, aggressive trading tactics can be a lot more expensive in these regions.

When spreads are high it can be worth adopting a more passive trading style to reduce the overall spread cost. Therefore, pegging or layering orders may be used to try to maximise the price improvement. If risk is a significant factor then a catching mechanism might be adopted to reduce the potential losses if the market suddenly moves away.

Average trade size

When we are considering the difficulty of an order it is usual to compare its overall size to the average daily volume (ADV). Thus, an order that is less than 5% of the ADV should be reasonably straightforward to execute. However, it is also worth considering the average trade size. Table 9-4 shows some of the average trade sizes and values for a range of assets and venues.

---

[3] Median figures

Asset class		Venue	Average trade size	Average trade value ($1000s)
Equity	Stocks	NASDAQ	330	9
		NYSE	301	13
		Euronext	956	36
		LSE	6,335	64
		Hong Kong Exch	39,544	18
Fixed income	U.S Treasury 2yr	ICAP BrokerTec	-	8,342
	U.S Treasury 5yr	ICAP BrokerTec	-	2,974
FX	Spot	EBS	-	~3,000
Derivatives	Index futures	CME	3	-
	Interest rate futs	LIFFE	10	-

Source: WFE (2008), Fixed Income: Fleming and Mizrach (2008), FX: Euromoney (2006a)

Table 9-4 Average trade sizes

Electronic trading has helped significantly decrease order sizes, particularly for order-driven venues. Consequently, the lowest average trade sizes/values in Table 9-4 are for the world's stock and listed derivative markets. In comparison, the fixed income and FX markets still have much larger average trade sizes. That said, actual trade sizes might be much lower than these averages. For instance, Galen Burghardt, in a report for the FIA (2006), showed that the most common trade size for E-mini S&P 500 futures was for a single lot.

When dealing with very low average trade sizes, signalling risk can be a major issue. Hence, we should consider splitting orders to ensure they are not significantly larger than those already on the order book. So we will need to use slicing or layering, alternatively we might need to hide them.

Algorithm performance

Internally, most trading algorithms continually track their own performance. This might be versus a target executed quantity or as a comparison of its average executed price versus its benchmark. Therefore the algorithm can easily tell whether it is performing ahead or behind of its own targets.

The algorithm's reaction to under-performance will depend on whether market conditions are favourable and how much time there is left to trade. If conditions are unfavourable, it will probably employ more aggressive trading tactics to try to stem its losses. Conversely, if the conditions are favourable it might hold out for a while longer to see if the extant orders can achieve significant price improvement. Similarly, if there is not much time left to execute the algorithm may revert to using more aggressive execution tactics.

Other factors affecting tactic choice

So far, the focus has been on targeting the specific investment/trading goals. Though, at the micro-level we must also consider market characteristics, such as its fundamental trading mechanism and latency.

Trading mechanism

Clearly, whether a market is quote-driven or order-driven will have a substantial impact on the choice of trading tactic. Indeed, most of the mechanisms we have covered require specialised order types and so need an order-driven or hybrid market. They simply are not viable for request-driven markets. For purely quote-driven markets, we might still use order slicing to spread the order amongst several brokers, but that is about it. Likewise, most of the trading tactics we have covered are primarily intended for continuous trading periods.

The precedence rules that are used for order-driven markets are also significant. If priority is given in terms of price and time then it is important for orders to maintain their position in the queue. Thus, tactics such as layering become more valuable. Conversely, if the secondary priority is assigned on a pro-rata basis, such as for many futures markets, then it is important to have orders with sufficient size at that price level.

Latency

Latency corresponds to the time lag that can occur between sending an order and it reaching its intended destination, and so be able to participate in trading. This lag may be due to delays in the various systems that process the order, as well as the time it takes to actually transmit the information between locations. Latency has the most effect on order routing decisions, but it can also affect dynamic tactics, such as pegging or catching.

A few years ago, latencies were measured in seconds. Although this can still be the case in some emerging markets, the major venues are all now vying to offer platforms with latencies measured in milliseconds or less. Finding an impartial comparison of latencies can be quite difficult, since each venue is keen to stress the speed of their platform. Table 9-5 shows the results of a round-trip test by Exponential-e (2009) for their routing service. This gives an idea of the order transmission times to some key market locations. Latency will be significantly higher for request-driven markets.

From:	*To:*	*Latency ms*
London	Frankfurt	10
	New York	68
	Chicago	85
New York	Toronto	25
	Zurich	90
	Tokyo	246
	Sydney	260

Source: Exponential-e (2009)

Table 9-5 A snapshot latency roundtrip comparison for some key locations

Clearly, sending orders to remote markets can add a considerable amount of latency. Hence, a number of venues now offer co-location services, whereby space is made available for client machines to reduce any transmission delays.

Latency reduces the probability of execution since by the time we have been able to respond another market participant will probably have beaten us to it. Therefore, a tactic like pegging is not suitable for higher latency venues since its reactive nature exacerbates the problem. Instead, it is better to adopt the order layering tactic, so if the market does move orders are already in place at a range of different price levels. The catching tactic may also be used when latency is high, to stem potential losses.

9.4 Summary

- Execution tactics focus on the micro level choices that need to be made for the actual execution, monitoring the order book and managing order submission. They provide common mechanisms to achieve the goals of trading algorithms.

- Tactics are often based around existing order types, for instance, pegging and hiding. For venues that do not natively support these dynamic order types the tactic can adopt an order placement strategy that essentially mimics the required behaviour. They may also employ more complex logic than is currently available via native order types.

- A wide range of common trading mechanisms may be adopted:
  - Slicing is a straightforward means of lowering impact.
  - Hiding takes advantage of hidden order types or using an opaque ATS.
  - Layering places orders throughout the book to maximise execution probability and the potential for price improvement.
  - Pegging provides dynamic adjustments, adjusting the price or even size of orders.
  - Catching uses a price latch to cut losses when the market moves away from us.
  - Seeking actively searches for hidden liquidity.
  - Sniping takes available liquidity without giving away our own requirements.
  - Routing determines the best destination for an order based on a range of criteria.

- The main factors affecting the choice of execution tactic depend on both the current market conditions and how well the algorithm is actually performing.

- Trading algorithms may adapt to changing conditions by switching between execution tactics. Alternatively, they may use several tactics in parallel.

Chapter 10

Enhancing trading strategies

Traders routinely base their decisions on a mix of current market conditions as well as anticipating how these might change in the future. Incorporating such logic into algorithmic trading strategies is a key to enhancing their performance.

10.1 Introduction

Having gone through the basics of both trading algorithms and execution tactics, this chapter aims to highlight some of the ways in which they may be enhanced. These mechanisms are rule-based approaches that respond to market conditions. Though, we can only ever estimate what conditions might be like in the future.

In Chapter 5, we used charts to compare the typical order placement patterns for different trading algorithms. However, during the execution it is important to remember that we just cannot tell what the future holds, as Figure 10-1 tries to show.

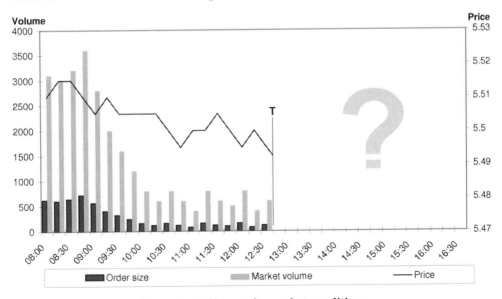

Figure 10-1 Uncertain market conditions

From time T to the close, we do not know exactly what will happen to the market price, volume or liquidity. Hence, trading algorithms and execution tactics are inherently reactive. If a sudden shift occurs in the marketplace, such a reactive approach can be caught out and forced to play catch up, at less favourable prices.

One way of enhancing computerised trading strategies is to incorporate short-term prediction models for key market conditions, such as volume and price. These allow strategies to take a more proactive approach, placing more passively priced orders (provided the forecasts are correct). For instance, a percent of volume (POV) algorithm that only ever trades in response to market volume could incur significant market impact, since it would always be chasing the market. A short-term prediction of trading volume allows the algorithm to layer orders, ensuring it takes part in the market volume rather than simply responding to it. Similarly, for price adaptive trading algorithms, a short-term price prediction will allow them to place appropriate limit orders to take advantage of price trends. If the prediction proves to be inaccurate, the orders may be cancelled.

Estimating potential transaction costs has also become more important, particularly for cost-based algorithms such as implementation shortfall. Many of these cost models are based on a framework by Robert Almgren and Neil Chriss (2000) which uses a random walk model to estimate the current market price in terms of costs.

Another potential enhancement is better handling of specific events, which in turn may be either predictable or not. For example, futures have finite lifetimes, so expiration is a predictable factor for these contracts. Whilst on witching days when major derivatives contracts expire, such as for the S&P 500 index, there will be sizable increases in trading volume, and short-term volatility, on the stock markets. Changes to stock indices are another example, since announcements are made some time before they occur. Given how many investment firms track the major indices, these changes have relatively predictable effects on the short-term trading for the affected stocks, depending on whether they are being added or removed from the index. Unpredictable events are generally triggered by information or news. They may be harder to forecast, but their short-term effects can still be quantified. For instance, trading interruptions, such as halts or volatility auctions, are usually followed by periods of much higher volatility and volumes, although these often dissipate after a few hours. In Chapter 14, we will cover the impact of news in more detail.

10.2 Forecasting market conditions

Traders and investors and have sought to predict prices for as long as markets have existed. Forecasting other market conditions such as volume, liquidity and volatility have also become more important.

Longer-term predictions are more useful for investment decisions. Execution is generally more focussed on short-term price trends. Therefore, the focus of this section is on short-term predictions, typically intraday. Short-term changes in market conditions are closely related to market liquidity. Factors such as order book depth and imbalance can give vital insights for how trade flow will react in the immediate future. In fact, many short-term predictions may be based just on recent market conditions. In Chapter 15, we will see how artificial intelligence can also be used for forecasting.

Predicting asset prices

At the simplest level, an asset's price merely represents what someone else is willing to pay. Imbalances in supply and demand can be a useful indicator for short-term price movements.

An excess of supply (or sells) should lead to a price drop whilst an excess of demand should result in a price hike. Empirical research has considered imbalances in both traded volume and order book depth to test their effectiveness.

A positive correlation between trade imbalances and subsequent price changes was found by Joey Yang (2005) in a study of trades on the Australian Stock Exchange (ASX). He confirmed that the price is more likely to rise if more of the last 30 trades were due to demand on the buy-side, as we might expect. [1]

Imbalances in the best bid and offer sizes were also analysed by Yang (2005) for orders on the ASX. Using an ordered probit model, he established a strong link between future price changes and the logarithms of the best bid and offer sizes. A larger bid size implied price rises were more likely, whilst price drops were more probable when the ask size was larger. Similarly, in an earlier study, Sergei Maslov and Mark Mills (2001) tracked the best quotes on NASDAQ. They focussed on the average price changes around periods when significant imbalances between best bid and offer sizes occurred. [2] Effectively, they were monitoring the short-term market impact of large trades, as shown in Figure 10-2.

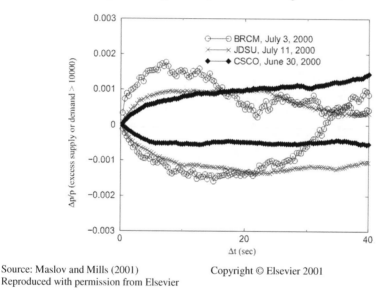

Source: Maslov and Mills (2001)   Copyright © Elsevier 2001
Reproduced with permission from Elsevier

Figure 10-2 The market impact of a large imbalance in best bid and offer size

The positive impacts reflect a surplus of demand for the stock, whilst the negative ones represent an excess supply. Note that the effect is magnified, and more volatile, for the lower volume stocks, Broadcom Corp. (BRCM) and JDS Uniphase Corp. (JDSU), compared to that of Cisco Systems Inc. (CSCO). By normalising their data, they found an approximately linear relationship between the imbalances and short-term average price changes. Given the

---

[1] Note a potential problem with studies based on trade imbalances is the determination of whether the trade was driven by buyers or sellers, as reported by Ekkehart Boehmer and Julie Wu (2006). Most studies adopt the Lee and Ready (1991) algorithm to determine this, although this is not guaranteed to be 100% accurate. For instance, Charles Lee and Balkrishna Radhakrishna (2000) showed that up to 40% of trades observed on the NYSE could not be classified, whilst 7% were incorrectly classified. So caution must be taken when using trade-based imbalances.
[2] Ideally, the limits for this should be based on the average daily volume of each stock; however, for their results they found that a wholesale limit of 10,000 shares gave satisfactory results.

relatively short timescales involved (less than a minute), such trends may be more easy for a computerised system to take advantage of than a busy trader.

Several groups have studied the effect of imbalances for the whole order book. The imbalance I_j for each level j of the order book is just the value of sell orders (supply) minus the value of the corresponding buy orders (demand):

$$I_j = Q_j^s P_j^s - Q_j^d P_j^d$$

where Q_j is the quantity available at a given price P_j and the superscripts s and d correspond to supply and demand. In comparison, the weighted price WP_j is simply the average price based on the available supply and demand at a given level of the order book:

$$WP_j = \frac{Q_j^s P_j^s + Q_j^d P_j^d}{Q_j^s + Q_j^d}$$

The weighted price may also be calculated for specific portions of the order book:

$$WP_{n_1-n_2} = \frac{\sum_{j=n_1}^{n_2} (Q_j^s P_j^s + Q_j^d P_j^d)}{\sum_{j=n_1}^{n_2} (Q_j^d + Q_j^s)}$$

where n_1 is a higher level than n_2, e.g. WP_{1-5} represents the weighted price for the first five levels of the order book. An example order book is shown in Figure 10-3 together with the associated imbalances and weighted prices for each level.

Buys			Sells			Value (thousands)			WP
Id	Size	Price	Price	Size	Id	Buys	Sells	Imbalance	
D1	2,000	100	102	3,000	S1	200	306	106	101.20
D2	6,000	100	103	2,000	S2	594	206	-388	100.00
D3	4,000	99	103	5,000	S3	392	520	128	101.33
D4	3,000	99	104	1,000	S4	291	105	-186	99.00
D5	5,000	98	104	6,000	S5	480	636	156	101.45
					Σ	1,957	1,773	-184	100.81

Figure 10-3 An example order book with its associated imbalances and weighted prices

So for the top of the order book in Figure 10-3 the imbalance and weighted prices are determined as:

$$I_1 = (3,000 \times 102) - (2,000 \times 100) = 106,000$$
$$WP_1 = ((2,000 \times 100) + (3,000 \times 102)) / (2,000 + 3,000) = 101.2$$
$$WP_{1-5} = (1,957,000 + 1,773,000) / (20,000 + 17,000) = 100.81$$

Overall, the imbalance for the first five levels of this order book is $-184,000, so at the moment the demand is outweighing the available supply.

Short-term returns on the ASX were examined by Charles Cao, Oliver Hansch and Xiaoxin Wang (2008). They calculated liquidity measures based on the difference between the weighted price WP_{n1-n2} and the mid-price. They concluded that there is a strong link between these imbalances and future short-term returns. Predominantly, this was for the best bid and offer, but imbalances across the rest of the order book also had an effect.

A similar approach was adopted by Jörgen Hellström and Ola Simonsen (2006) to study returns on the Stockholm Stock Exchange. They modelled the order book shape using weighted price measures (WP_{n1-n2} − mid price) together with a time-adjusted variant. Their results showed that a positive skew in the order book imbalance (a surplus of supply from sell orders) increased the probability of a subsequent decrease in price. Conversely, a surplus of demand from buy orders was linked to subsequent price increases. Though, these relationships were found to be quite short lived, often less than a minute. They also confirmed that, whilst most of this effect could be explained by imbalances at the best bid and offer, taking into account the rest of the order book did have some effect.

The importance of gaps in the order book was highlighted in a study of large price changes on the London Stock Exchange by J. Doyne Farmer et al. (2004). A reasonable assumption for such changes might be large market orders sweeping deep into the order book. Still, their analysis showed that around 85% of the market orders that caused price changes matched the size at the best price. Essentially, they found the price fluctuations caused by market orders to be independent of the volume of orders. Instead, they revealed that the price jumps could be accounted for by liquidity fluctuations caused by gaps in the order book. So an order would take the available volume at the best price, leading to a price shift because the next entry in the order book was at a significantly different level. Interestingly, they found this issue affected even the most liquid stocks, although it was more prevalent for illiquid ones. They went on find that the distribution of gaps in the order book exhibited nontrivial correlations with the position in the book. This highlights the importance of looking past the best bid and offer if we do not want to noticeably affect the current price.

Predicting trading volume

Forecasts for trading volume have generally been based on historical data, or so-called volume profiles. Whilst these can give a reasonable forecast of intraday volume trends, there is still a wide range of factors that can affect daily trading volumes. These range from seasonal factors, such as the summer holidays, to asset specific ones such as news, corporate actions or contract expiration. To improve the relevancy of these forecasts some researchers have decomposed trading volume into both market and asset-specific components.

Volume prediction is important for algorithmic trading, particularly for those algorithms based on statically determined trading schedules such as the original VWAP. If today's trade flow differs considerably from this then the algorithm may well struggle to meet its benchmark. So the performance of a VWAP algorithm often relies on the accuracy of its historical volume profile. Similarly, these are in important input for implementation shortfall models, allowing them to determine the optimal trading horizon for a given order. Short-term trading volume prediction can also be important for purely dynamic algorithms, such as percent of volume (POV). These are driven by market volume and so there is no danger of them following a target trajectory that is out of sync with the market. However, if they only ever issue orders in response to market volume, they could end up chasing the market, and so incur substantial market impact. Short-term volume predictions enable algorithms to effectively place orders in a more proactive fashion, hopefully achieving price improvement.

Volume profiles

A common starting point when predicting trading volume is to create a volume profile based on historical data. As we saw for the VWAP algorithm in Chapter 5, this is just a matter of defining a fixed time interval and then measuring the volume of trading for each period. For example, in Figure 10-4 the daily trading volumes for Mattel Inc. are shown over 30 minute periods in terms of a percentage of the daily total, taken from a study by Dana Hobson (2006). Clearly, there can be considerable variation from day to day.

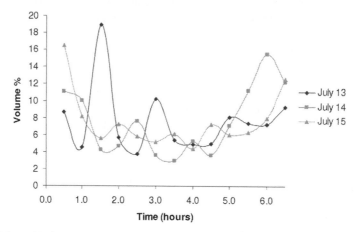

Figure 10-4 Volume profiles for Mattel Inc. in 2005

Though, when these are averaged over longer periods, e.g. a month, the commonality becomes more evident. In this case, as a U.S. stock it exhibits the typical U-shaped curve with higher volumes around the open and close, something like we can see in Figure 10-5.

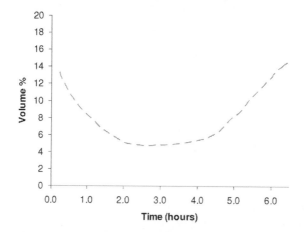

Figure 10-5 An average volume profile based on Figure 10-4

Obviously, the exact shape of the volume profile will differ for each asset and will also depend on the number of days chosen for the average. Over time, these patterns may well change. Therefore, one way of viewing them is a 3-dimensional plot of the historical trading volume. Figure 10-6, shows a plot for a large-cap firm, GlaxoSmithKline, taken from a

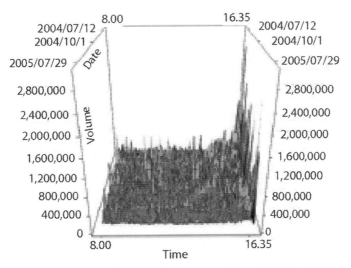

Figure 10-6 Historical volume profiles for GlaxoSmithKline PLC

review by Tracy Black and Owain Self (2005). The trading volumes exhibit a relatively uniform pattern over time, with a clear increase in volume towards the close. Figure 10-7 shows the equivalent plot for the mid-cap technology firm, Logica CMG.

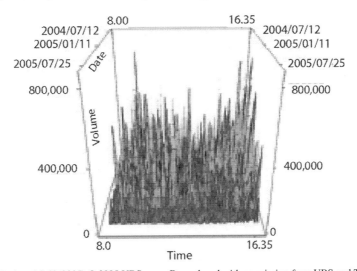

Figure 10-7 Historical volume profiles for Logica CMG PLC

In comparison, for the mid-cap firm, the high levels of variation in daily trading volumes are obvious, so much so that it is difficult to spot a daily volume trend. Also note the difference in volume scales. Overall, more liquid assets tend to have more stable daily volumes, whereas higher growth assets may exhibit much more volatility in their trading volumes. Consequently, historical trading volumes are likely to be more useful as predictors for liquid assets.

Factors affecting trading volume

A wide range of factors can affect daily trading volumes: from general factors which apply across whole regions, or countries, to more localised, market- and asset-specific ones. Examples of general factors are seasonal and calendar-based anomalies, such as summer holidays and the "day of the week" effect. Market holidays and macroeconomic announcements are more market-specific, although they may also have regional and even global effects. Asset-specific factors tend to be based on the asset class, so for stocks this might be news announcements, corporate actions, dividends, mergers and stock splits. Expiration will be a consideration for assets that have fixed maturities such as bonds and futures.

In their aptly titled report, 'Gone Fishin': Seasonality in trading activity and asset prices', Harrison Hong and Jialin Yu (2006) studied the relationship between stock market turnover and vacations for 51 stock markets. They found that trading activity was, on average, 7.9% lower during the summer than during the rest of the year. Note that summer is defined as Q3 (July, August and September) for countries in the Northern Hemisphere and Q1 (January, February and March) for those in the south. The effect was strongest for countries furthest from the equator, where summer vacations are more likely. So, the largest observed falls were 15.6% for Europe and 13.2% for North America. In Asia, they only noted a fall of 3.4%, whilst Australia and New Zealand saw a decline of 6.7% in their Q1 summer. Closer to the equator, the effect was much less, for instance, only a 1.8% drop was observed for Latin American countries.

The "day of the week" effect can also influence turnover. A study of stock market volatility and trading volume for the U.S., Canada and U.K by Halil Kiymaz and Hakan Berument (2003) found average volumes to be consistently lower on Mondays. This also ties in with an earlier study of U.K stocks by Paul Draper and Krishna Paudyal (2002), who observed lower trading volumes on Mondays as well. For currency futures, Pei Hwang Wei and Susan Zee (1998) found volumes to be lower on Mondays and Fridays. Analysis of NYSE stock trading also showed a strong "day of the week" effect, although Tarun Chordia, Richard Roll and Avanidhar Subrahmanyam (2000) noted this more as a decline of liquidity and trading activity on Fridays and an increase on Tuesdays. Many studies have found the middle of the week to have the highest volumes, for instance, Kiymaz and Berument (2003) noted that Wednesdays were the peak for the U.S. whilst it was Thursday for Canada and the U.K.

Specific holidays, such as Christmas, have a noticeable affect as well. Generally, trading volumes drop significantly on the day before the holiday. For example, Figure 10-8 shows a normalised view of trading volume for the Royal Bank of Scotland (RBS) created by Serge Darolles and Gaëlle Le Fol (2003). The proximity of Christmas and the New Year's Day means that the abnormal trading volume can persist for over a week. Note, Figure 10-8 also shows the breakdown of the volume into both stock-specific and common (or market) components, which we shall cover in the next sub-section.

In addition to seasonal effects, asset-specific factors considerably alter trading volumes. Many of these are specific events, which we will cover in more detail in section 10.3. For example, there is generally be an increased turnover on witching days, or when stocks are added to major indices. Similarly, for bonds or futures which are about to expire, there is usually a sudden decline in their trading volumes.

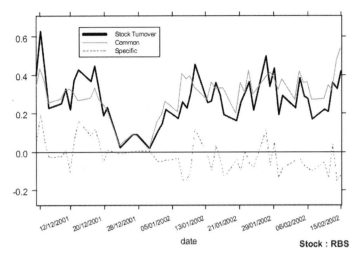

Source: © Darolles and Le Fol (2003)   Reproduced with permission from authors

Figure 10-8 Shift in trading volumes over Christmas holiday

One way of coping with these effects is to determine separate adjustments that compensate for them. These may then be applied to the historical volume profile, and compared with current market conditions to check they are reasonable. Alternatively, custom profiles could be adopted which may more accurately represent the current market trends. Although by using fewer data points, there is more risk in the estimation.

Historical volume profiles are often based on data for the previous weeks or even months. So these factors not only affect current trading, but they also alter the historical averages. For instance, the increased volumes on days when special events occur, such as triple witching, can distort the historical volume profiles for normal days. Hence, they may be excluded from the average volume calculations. Corporate actions, in particular stock splits, also pose a specific problem for the historical volume profile for stocks. Stock splits are usually used to reduce the share price of growth companies, and so encourage more trading. Splitting a $100 share into two $50 shares should lead to significantly higher average daily volumes. Thus, when stock splits occur we need to adjust the historical volumes accordingly, otherwise they will not properly reflect the new levels of trading.

Decomposing trading volume

An alternative method of estimating trading volume is to break it down into its components, namely market volume and asset-specific volume. Essentially, this is the same approach as used for prices in the Capital Asset Pricing Model (CAPM). The CAPM expresses an asset's returns in terms of the expected returns from the market and those of a risk-free asset. Based on this, portfolio risk may be split into both systematic, or market, risk and idiosyncratic risk.

A two-factor model for trading volume was proposed by Andrew Lo and Jiang Wang (2000). Using this approach, turnover models were created by Serge Darolles and Gaëlle Le Fol (2003), and K.J. Cremers and Jianping Mei (2007). Both groups decomposed turnover [3]

---

[3] Note that turnover is used as a more normalised version of trading volume. Turnover is the ratio of the traded volume to the total number of shares outstanding, so it allows for better comparisons between assets than trading volume alone.

into systematic and idiosyncratic components using principal components analysis (PCA). Darolles and Le Fol (2003) applied their model to empirical data for U.K. FTSE stocks, whilst Cremers and Mei (2007) studied NYSE and AMEX stocks.

The market component represents the normal volume that is common across all the traded assets. This should incorporate all the seasonal effects, and so is a non-stationary series (its statistical properties change over time). It may also be viewed as the long-term trading volume of the asset.

The idiosyncratic, or specific, component remains a random, or stochastic, process much like the asset price. It represents the asset-specific unexpected changes in volume.

A later study by Jedrzej Białkowski, Serge Darolles and Gaëlle Le Fol (2007) gives a detailed example of this decomposition for French CAC-40 stocks, one of which is shown in Figure 10-9.

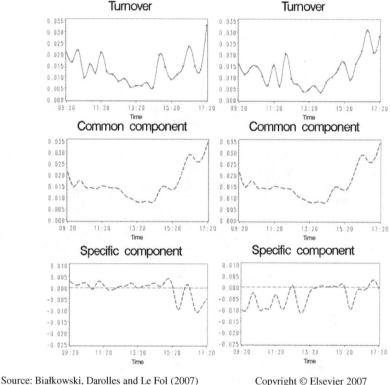

Figure 10-9 Daily volume components for Total on September 9-10 2003

The overall turnover for the energy company Total is displayed in the top charts. This is followed by the common (or market) volume, which was determined as a historical average across all the CAC-40 stocks. Note that this common volume is identical on both days and adopts the common U-shaped pattern. The bottom charts illustrate the stock-specific volumes, which are significantly different between the two days. Thus, the daily differences may clearly be related to the specific component.

Białkowski, Darolles and Le Fol (2007) used two statistical methods for estimating these specific volumes. One was based on autoregressive moving averages (ARMA); the other used a self-extracting threshold autoregressive model (SETAR). Overall, they found that the SETAR model gave the best predictions of daily volume, although both methods were found to be better than a simple historical average. They attributed the performance of the SETAR-based estimations as being due to the ability to discriminate between both turbulent and flat market periods.

Predicting liquidity

In Chapter 8, we saw how limit order models could be used to predict the probability of execution of various limit orders. Short-term predictions of liquidity can allow trading strategies to decide whether they should be more or less aggressive when taking advantage of current market conditions.

Market depth often tends to increase throughout the day. Alexander Kempf and Daniel Mayston (2008) found this for trading on Xetra, as did Catherine D'Hondt, Rudy De Winne and Alain Francois-Heude (2004) for CAC-40 stocks on Euronext Paris. We can also see this trend in Figure 10-10, which is from a study of the Spanish Stock Exchange (SIBE) by David Abad, Sonia Sanabria and José Yagüe (2005).

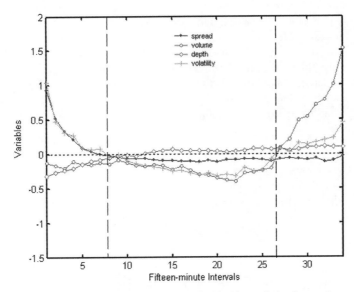

Source: © Abad, Sanabria and Yagüe (2005)   Reproduced with permission from authors

Figure 10-10 Intraday patterns of liquidity, trading activity in the Spanish stock market in 2002

The dashed lines highlight three distinct phases throughout the trading day. Thus, at the start of the day a period of lower liquidity lasts for around two hours, with higher spreads and relatively low quoted depths. This is then followed by an intermediate period where liquidity improves and volatility decreases. The last period is at around 3:30 pm, which coincides with the U.S. open. This leads to a considerable increase in trading volume, although there is only a slight improvement in overall liquidity.

This chart also shows the characteristic U-shaped volume profile. So, just as historical averages are used to predict intraday trading volumes, a similar approach may be taken for liquidity estimates. In periods of lower liquidity, trading strategies can estimate when the depth might improve. They may then evaluate whether the timing risk is sufficiently low to justify waiting; alternatively, they will have to issue more aggressive orders, and risk paying higher market impact costs.

Short-term liquidity predictions are also vital when seeking hidden liquidity, as we saw in Chapter 8. The concealed nature of this liquidity means that all such trading is based on estimates. This is particularly important when trying to choose between execution venues. Again, the availability of hidden liquidity often seems to increase throughout the day. Hendrik Bessembinder, Marios Panayides and Kumar Venkataraman (2008) and D'Hondt, De Winne and Francois-Heude (2004) both found this for hidden orders on Euronext. A similar trend was reported for the Spanish Stock Exchange by Ángel Pardo and Roberto Pascual (2006).

Predicting volatility

Price volatility is an important factor for many trading strategies as it helps determine the execution probability of limit orders. Higher volatility increases the likelihood of execution since it means the observed price range is likely to be wider. However, it also means orders are more likely to become mispriced, and so increases the risk of adverse selection. Higher volatility also makes hidden order usage more likely. Hence, volatility is an important factor for limit order models, used to determine order placement, and the cost models used by shortfall-based algorithms to determine the optimal trading horizon.

As with any market condition, short-term volatility fluctuates intraday, often increasing around the market open and close, as we saw back in Figure 10-10. There are two main ways of estimating volatility, these are based on either historical data or implying it from the prices of options contracts.

Predicting volatility with statistical methods

Historical measurement of volatility may be for a wide range of timescales, from intra-day to monthly, quarterly or even annual values. The volatility σ of an asset's price may be calculated from the standard deviation of its returns, using the following formula:

$$\sigma = \sqrt{\frac{1}{N-1} \sum_{t=1}^{N} (R_t - \overline{R})^2} \qquad (10\text{-}1)$$

where R_t are the returns at time t and $\overline{R}$ is the mean of the returns for N days. The variance is σ^2.

The simplest model for estimating future volatility is just to base it on the previous day's value, often referred to as the random walk model. A slight enhancement of this approach is to determine an estimate based on the average from of a range of historical volatilities. This might simply be the mean of previously calculated volatilities. Alternatively, it might be based on a moving average that just tracks the last 50 days. Exponentially weighted moving averages (EMA) give more weight to the recent values. The EMA method is used by RiskMetrics to model volatility. A detailed summary of all these techniques is provided by Ser-Huang Poon and Clive Granger (2003). They point out that one of the key issues to achieving useful estimates with these two moving average based methods is finding the optimal lag length (e.g. 50 days) or weighting scheme.

Another forecasting method is to create models based on previous values of volatility. The AutoRegressive (AR) model determines the volatility σ_t from the previous value σ_{t-1} using the following formula:

$$\sigma_t = c + \sum_{i=1}^{p} a_i \sigma_{t-i} + \varepsilon_t$$

where c is a constant, each a_i is a parameter of the model and ε_t is an error term. The parameters may be estimated by carrying out least squares regressions on the data series. ARMA (AutoRegressive Moving Average) models are an extension of this approach that include a separate model based on the past volatility errors ε_{t-1}:

$$\sigma_t = \varepsilon_t + \sum_{i=1}^{p} a_i \sigma_{t-i} + \sum_{i=1}^{q} \theta_i \varepsilon_{t-i}$$

where θ_i are the parameters for this error model.

The ARCH (AutoRegressive Conditional Heteroskedasticity) family of models represent a more sophisticated approach. The first ARCH model was proposed by Robert Engle (1982). Instead of using sample standard deviations, the ARCH model uses a common statistical method (maximum likelihood estimation) to determine the best fit for its model, for a given probability distribution. A simple ARCH model determines the conditional variance as a function of past squared returns. The Generalised ARCH (GARCH) model was initially proposed by Tim Bollerslev (1986) and Stephen Taylor (1986). GARCH allows additional dependencies on lagged values; it also assumes a Normal distribution. Poon and Granger note that GARCH is the most popular model for many time series. This has led to a range of extensions such as the exponential, EGARCH, model.

In terms of overall accuracy, the historical volatility based averages tend to give similar results to GARCH models, although some of the later models, such as EGARCH, outperform GARCH. However, Poon and Granger note that the best overall results for volatility forecasts appear to be from implied volatility.

Note this is obviously a very brief introduction to the statistical models for estimating volatility. Indeed, there are even more methods, such as stochastic volatility frameworks and regime-switching models. For further details on these, Poon and Granger (2003) is a good starting point. Also in Chapter 15, we shall see how artificial intelligence is being used to predict volatility.

Using implied volatility

Implied volatility is based on the market prices of options contracts. Option pricing models, such as Black Scholes, allow us to determine what the market price for an option should be, given a certain asset price as well as other factors such as the maturity and interest rates. Therefore, by reversing this process we can use market prices to determine what level of volatility was used to generate them, hence the term implied volatility.

Figure 10-11 highlights the potential differences between a purely historical volatility measurement and an implied one, taken from an example for Instinet's (2006) implementation shortfall algorithm (Wizard).

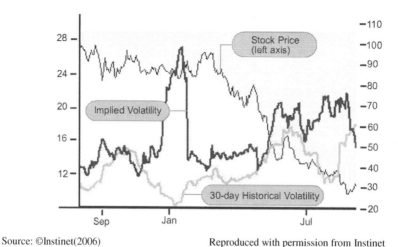

Figure 10-11 Historical and implied volatility, from Instinet (2006)

The chart shows the volatilities and the stock price for CV Therapeutics Inc. (CVTX) in the period 2005-6. Notice how the implied volatility suddenly jumped in early January, coinciding with the company waiting for FDA approval for its new drug. The implied volatility accurately reflects the uncertainty from the options market.

In comparison, the historical volatility based on the stock price is purely backward looking and does not reflect this risk. So investors or traders unaware of the imminent news release might underestimate the potential volatility of the stock if they focus solely on historical volatility. Hence, Instinet uses a weighted average of both historical and implied volatility for its risk estimates.

Implied volatility is not without its own problems, though. As Poon and Granger (2003) point out, the implied volatility reflects the market's expectation of what the volatility will be for the underlying asset over the option's maturity. Thus, options for the same asset, but with differing maturities, will have different implied volatilities. In practice, there are also often significant differences in the implied volatilities for options that have the same maturity but different strike prices. This phenomenon is the characteristic "volatility smile", as shown in Figure 10-12(a). If we then expand this to take account of the different maturities, we get a volatility surface, as shown in Figure 10-12(b).

Poon and Granger (2003) describe two of the main theoretical explanations for this effect, namely the distributional assumption and stochastic volatility; they also outline other potential factors, such as market microstructure and measurement errors.

The distributional assumption refers to the fact that the Black Scholes model assumes the price of the underlying asset has a Log-Normal distribution. But for many risky assets the probability of outliers is higher than expected; the distribution is said to have "fat tails" (or is leptokurtic). So, deeply out-of-the-money options can actually have a probability of exercise which is higher than that expected by the Normal distribution, leading to higher prices than predicted by Black Scholes.

Price/return distributions vary from asset to asset, but the differences are particularly strong across different asset classes. Some nice examples are illustrated in a review by Gunter Meissner and Noriko Kawano (2001). For instance, in the currency and commodities markets, returns often have symmetrical, "fat tailed" distributions. Therefore, deeply out-of-

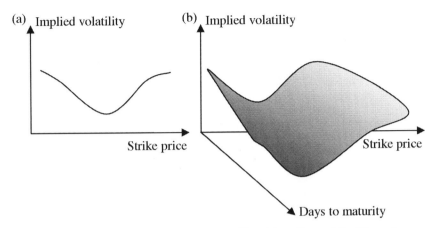

Figure 10-12 An example implied volatility (a) smile and its (b) surface

the-money options have higher volatilities for both high and low strike prices. In comparison, for the stock and bond markets distributions tend to be less symmetrical, with the "fat tails" more predominant on the left hand side of the distribution. This gives rise to a corresponding volatility skew (or grimace) with much lower implied volatilities at high strikes than at low ones.

Using volatility indices

Volatility indices provide a measure of the market expectations for near-term volatility, often based on the prices of stock index options. Potentially, we can also decompose volatility into market and specific components, as we did for trading volume.

The best-known volatility index is the CBOE's VIX, which was started in 1993 and has also been dubbed the "fear index". Originally, the VIX was based on the S&P 100, but in 2003 it was switched to the S&P 500, to be more representative of the U.S. market as a whole. At the same time, a more sophisticated calculation was adopted. The VIX estimation derives the expected volatility for the next 30 days by averaging the weighted prices of a wide range of puts and calls for the index. It is constantly calculated in real-time; in fact, futures and options contracts are now available based solely on the VIX.

Figure 10-13 shows the historical closes for the VIX (based on the new calculation method). The volatility during the 2007-09 financial crisis is easy to see; it is also interesting to compare this to the much smaller spikes from 2001 and 2003. Indeed, October 2008 saw the VIX reach an all time high of 89. Before this, anything over 30 had been considered high. Although it is based on the S&P 500, the VIX has become the de-facto standard for global market volatility. That said, more localised variants are also starting to appear: The VXN caters for the NASDAQ 100, and in Europe there are now indices for the DAX, FTSE 100, CAC 40 and several other major indices. There are even indices for oil, gold and the euro. Over time, the coverage of such indices will probably continue to expand.

Hence, we can also use a volatility index to provide a short-term estimate for future market volatility. This may then be combined with asset-specific estimates to generate a more accurate estimate of an asset's future volatility.

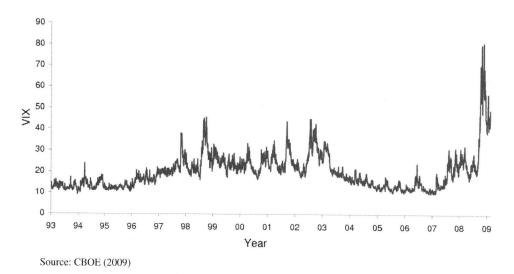

Source: CBOE (2009)

Figure 10-13 VIX closing prices

10.3 Estimating transaction costs

Transaction cost models are essential for providing estimates of potential costs. In his guide to market microstructure for practitioners, Ananth Madhavan (2002) points out three key requirements for successful cost estimation models:

1. Distinguishing between permanent and temporary price impact, since current trades will affect the prices of future ones

2. Incorporating both order specific (size, trading horizon) and asset specific (liquidity, volatility, price level, market) factors

3. Varying estimates with the style of trading, so aggressive tactics which use market orders will incur higher costs than more passive ones

The basis for many of these models is a framework suggested by Robert Almgren and Neil Chriss (2000). This uses a random walk model to estimate the current market price in terms of costs, such as permanent market impact, price trending and volatility. Robert Kissell, Morton Glantz, and Roberto Malamut (2004) express this as:

$$p_n = p_0 + \underbrace{\sum_{j=1}^{n} h(x_j) e^{-(n-j)c}}_{\substack{Temporary \\ market\ impact}} + \underbrace{\sum_{j=1}^{n} g(x_j)}_{\substack{Permanent \\ market\ impact}} + \underbrace{\sum_{j=1}^{n} \Delta p_j}_{\substack{Price \\ appreciation}} + \underbrace{\sum_{j=1}^{n} \varepsilon_j}_{\substack{Price \\ volatility}} \qquad (10\text{-}2)$$

where p_n is the current market price, p_0 is the initial price, p_j is the price and x_j is the trade size for a transaction in period j. The functions $g()$ and $h()$ determine permanent and temporary impact respectively and ε represents random noise. Notice that the temporary impact is dissipated by the function $e^{-(n-j)c}$ where c represents the rate of decay.

Market impact

The price model shown in equation 10-2 is path dependent. As Kissell, Glantz, and Malamut (2004) point out, using it to estimate market impact requires accurate estimations of both the temporary and permanent impacts.

Early models assumed market impact functions were linear. In particular, Albert Kyle's (1985) model derived linear equilibriums from fundamental principles. Similarly, Almgren and Chriss's (2000) first impact models were also based on a linear approach.

The reality is probably something more complex and non-linear. Joel Hasbrouck (1991) reported a good fit for a square root relationship. Fabrizio Lillo, J. Doyne Farmer and Rosario Mantegna (2003) found a significant dependence on the market capitalisation. For low-cap stocks on the NYSE, they found a square root relationship held, whilst for large-cap stocks and for those listed on the LSE they noted that the relationship was more like a power law, with an exponent between 0.2 and 0.3. In the next sub-section, we will review in more detail a model by Almgren *et al.* (2005), which can cater for both linear and non-linear solutions.

Another way of tackling this problem is a more top-down approach. Kissell and Glantz (2003) adopt a cost allocation technique to estimate an average market impact cost based on aggregated trade imbalances. They then allocate this to specific trading periods rather than to individual trades. We shall review this method in more detail later.

A trade level approach

Robert Almgren *et al.* (2005) created a model for market impact estimation using empirical data. This was based on earlier work by Almgren and Chriss (2000) and Almgren (2003). Both the permanent impact function $g()$ and the temporary one $h()$ were modelled as power laws:

$$g(v) = \pm\gamma|v|^{\alpha} \tag{10-3}$$

$$h(v) = \pm\eta|v|^{\beta} \tag{10-4}$$

where v is the trade rate (the order size divided by the available time). The coefficients γ and η and the exponents α and β may be determined from linear or non-linear regressions of empirical data. Thus, one of the aims was to confirm the nature of these functions: whether they were truly linear, or were square roots or had another form.

Their empirical data consisted of a large private dataset of U.S. institutional orders from the Citigroup U.S. equity trading desks. This data also allowed details such as order side and large transactions to be identified. [4] Large orders were excluded, so the dataset was limited to only include orders up to 10% of the ADV. Other simplifications were to assume a constant rate of trading and to ignore co-movement between asset prices.

The model assumes that the price change is actually based on an arithmetic Brownian motion (B). Given an initial market price p_m, the permanent impact function $g()$ determines the price drift (dp) for a given trade rate (v):

---

[4] Many academic studies have used publicly available data, often from the NYSE. Though, there are several issues with using such data. Firstly, buys and sells must be estimated, often using the Lee and Ready (1991) algorithm, since the data does not carry this information. Unfortunately, such estimations (based on comparing the order price with the best bid and offer at that time) are not 100% accurate. Also, public data does not contain any linkages between orders so large transactions may not easily be traced.

$$dp = p_m g(v)d\tau + p_m \sigma \, dB \qquad (10\text{-}5)$$

where σ is the volatility and τ represents "volume time" (the fractional average of the ADV which has executed so far). The temporary impact function $h()$ is used to determine the average execution price ($\bar{p}$):

$$\bar{p}(\tau) = p(\tau) + p_m h\left(\frac{X}{T}\right) \qquad (10\text{-}6)$$

where X is the order size and T is the time.

Impact cost models were derived by integrating equations 10-5 and 10-6. They were then normalised so as to be able to use them across the wide range of assets from their dataset. Hence, the asset specific volatility (σ) was included, and the trading rate (X/T) was adjusted by dividing by the average daily volume (V). The resultant models for permanent and temporary impact (I) are:

$$I_{perm} = \sigma T \, g\left(\frac{X}{VT}\right) + (noise) \qquad (10\text{-}7)$$

$$I_{temp} = I_{real} - \mu I_{perm} = \sigma h\left(\frac{X}{VT}\right) + (noise) \qquad (10\text{-}8)$$

Notice that temporary impact is expressed in terms of the realised and permanent impacts. Almgren et al. (2005) assume that the adjustment factor $\mu = 0.5$. The generic noise factor represents an error expression for each of the estimations.

In addition to normalising the impact functions, they also checked for any asset specific dependencies. They discovered that an additional liquidity factor (L) was required for the permanent impact cost function. [5] This factor is based on the shares outstanding (Θ) and the average daily volume (V) (effectively this is the inverse turnover):

$$L = \left(\frac{\Theta}{V}\right)^{\delta}$$

No such modifications were found to be required for the temporary impact function.

Finally, the power law impact functions, 10-3 and 10-4, were substituted into equations 10-7 and 10-8 to give:

$$\frac{I_{perm}}{\sigma} = \gamma T \, sign(X)\left|\frac{X}{VT}\right|^{\alpha}\left(\frac{\Theta}{V}\right)^{\delta} + (noise) \qquad (10\text{-}9)$$

$$\frac{I_{real} - \mu I_{perm}}{\sigma} = \eta \, sign(X)\left|\frac{X}{VT}\right|^{\beta} + (noise) \qquad (10\text{-}10)$$

To solve the values of the exponents Almgren et al. (2005) used a modified Gauss-Newton optimization algorithm. For their data set, this resulted in the approximate values:

$$\alpha \approx 0.89$$

---

[5] Almgren et al (2005) also considered market capitalisation but only observed a weak dependence on the price effect so they opted to use the simpler shares outstanding measure.

$$\beta \approx 0.60$$
$$\delta \approx 0.27$$

They concluded that a linear function for permanent impact was feasible, since α was so close to one. These results also confirmed the concave nature of the temporary impact function since $\beta < 1$. However, they found in favour of a 3/5ths power law, rather than the square root model. The liquidity factor δ also seems reasonable, suggesting that impact costs are higher for assets with lower average daily volumes.

These exponents were then used to determine the coefficients γ and η. Almgren *et al.* (2005) termed these the "universal coefficients of market impact" since they found them to hold for their entire data set:

$$\gamma \approx 0.314$$
$$\eta \approx 0.142$$

Therefore, by substituting these values into equations 10-9 and 10-10 they were able to accurately estimate market impact costs for any asset from their dataset using the following:

$$I_{perm} = \gamma \sigma \frac{X}{V} \left(\frac{\Theta}{V} \right)^{1/4} + (noise) \qquad (10\text{-}11)$$

$$I_{real} = \mu I_{perm} + sign(X) \, \eta \sigma \left| \frac{X}{VT} \right|^{3/5} + (noise) \qquad (10\text{-}12)$$

It is important to note that their study was for U.S. equities. They concluded that the coefficients, possibly the exponents and maybe even the functional forms might be significantly different across different markets as well as over time. For this reason, such models require careful calibration for each market before use.

Example 10-1: Almgren *et al.* (2005) provide an example estimating the impact costs of buy orders equivalent to 10% of the ADV of IBM and DRI, as shown in Table 10-1. Using their cost model, let's work through these calculations for the potential market impact costs:

In this case, IBM is assumed to have an ADV of 6.561 million, from an outstanding total of 1,728 million shares, and a daily volatility of 1.57%.

Therefore, we can estimate the permanent impact by inputting these values into equation 10-11:

$$I_{perm} = 0.314 * 1.57 * 0.1 * (1{,}728/6.561)^{1/4} = 0.20 = 20 \text{ bps.}$$

Similarly, the realized market impact may then be determined using equation 10-12. If we try to work the trade over half the trading day then $T=0.5$:

$$I_{real} = 0.5 * 0.20 + (sign(0.6561) * 0.142 * 1.57 * |0.1/0.5|^{3/5}) = 0.18 = 18 \text{ bps.}$$

The temporary market impact may then be calculated using equation 10-8:

$$I_{temp} = 0.18 - (0.5 * 0.20) = 0.08 = 8 \text{ bps}$$

Table 10-1 shows the market impact estimates for both IBM and DRI for a range of trade durations, from 0.1 to 0.5 of a day. The costs for DRI are higher than those for IBM; this is mainly due to its higher volatility. If we normalise the market impacts, by dividing them by the relative volatilities, we can see that the order DRI should actually have a lower permanent impact cost. This makes sense, since DRI has a larger turnover so trading 10% of the ADV should have less impact than for IBM. Therefore, DRI has a lower normalised permanent impact (0.096) compared to IBM (0.126). The normalised temporary impacts are the same, since the cost is not dependent on asset specific properties.

		IBM			DRI		
Average daily volume	V	6.561 M			1.929 M		
Shares outstanding	Θ	1728 M			168 M		
Inverse turnover	Θ/V	263			87		
Daily volatility(%)	σ	1.57			2.26		
Normalized trade size	X/V	0.1			0.1		
Norm. perm impact	I_{perm}/σ	0.126			0.096		
Permanent impact bps	I_{perm}	20			22		
Trade duration (days)	T	0.1	0.2	0.5	0.1	0.2	0.5
Normalized temporary	I_{temp}/σ	0.142	0.094	0.054	0.142	0.094	0.054
Temporary impact bps	I_{temp}	22	15	8	32	21	12
Realized impact bps	I_{real}	32	25	18	43	32	23

Source: Almgren *et al.* (2005)

Table 10-1 Cost estimate details for Example 10-1

A cost allocation approach

Kissell and Glantz (2003) take the opposite approach, using a top-down cost allocation model to estimate market impact. This method has proven capable of estimating costs at both the asset and portfolio level. The following provides a brief summary of this model, but for more detailed analysis please see Kissell and Glantz (2003).

The market impact portion of equation 10-2 consists of a permanent impact function $g(x)$ and a temporary impact function $h(x)$:

$$MI(x_j) = \sum_{j=1}^{n} h(x_j)e^{-(n-j)c} + \sum_{j=1}^{n} g(x_j) \qquad (10\text{-}13)$$

The Kissell and Glantz (2003) model relies on the following assumptions:
- Market impact costs are the same for buys and sells. [6]
- Temporary market impact does not persist beyond the current period.
- Only liquidity demanding orders pay temporary market impact.
- All orders have permanent impact.

Based on these assumptions, they then derive average costs for both temporary ($\bar{h}$) and permanent ($\bar{g}$) impact in $/share:

---

[6] Although there is evidence that sells may be more costly, they note that the estimates may be corrected with an adjustment to accommodate this.

$$\bar{h} = \frac{\sum\limits_{j\in side} x_j h}{\sum\limits_{j\in side} x_j} = \frac{b_1 I}{V_{side}} \qquad \bar{g} = \frac{\sum\limits_{j=1}^{n} \sum\limits_{i=1}^{j} x_i g}{\sum\limits_{j=1}^{n} x_j} = \frac{(1-b_1)I}{Q}$$

where I is the total impact cost and Q is the net imbalance between buys and sells. They note that only liquidity demanders pay temporary impact cost, so V_{side} is the traded volume from liquidity demanders (on the same side as the imbalance or $j\in side$). The factor b_1 represents the percentage of temporary impact, so $(1 - b_1)$ equals the percentage of permanent impact.

These averages may then be used to describe the market impact:

$$MI_\$(X) = X \cdot \left(\frac{b_1 I}{V_{side}} + \frac{(1-b_1)I}{Q} \right) \tag{10-14}$$

Kissell and Glantz found that the proportion of temporary impact in any given trading period k was equal to the percentage imbalance at that time (q_k/Q):

$$MI_\$(x_k) = \sum_{k=1}^{n} x_k \left(\frac{q_k}{Q} \cdot \frac{b_1 I}{V_{side}} + \frac{(1-b_1)I}{Q} \right)$$

The market impact may be restated in terms of just order details and expected market volume by using the following assumptions:

- the imbalance is equal to the order size ($Q = X$)
- market volume is distributed evenly between buys and sells

Thus, the liquidity demander volume v_{side} may be restated in terms of the order size x_k and the expected volume for that period v_k[7], i.e. $v_{side} = x_k + 0.5 v_k$. Therefore:

$$MI_\$(x_k) = \sum_{k=1}^{n} x_k \left(\frac{b_1 I x_k}{X \cdot (x_k + 0.5 v_k)} + \frac{(1-b_1)I}{X} \right)$$

Finally, this may be rearranged to show the temporary and permanent components more clearly:

$$MI_\$(x_k) = \sum_{k=1}^{n} \underbrace{\frac{b_1 I x_k^2}{X \cdot (x_k + 0.5 v_k)}}_{Temporary} + \underbrace{(1-b_1)I}_{Permanent} \tag{10-15}$$

Equation 10-15 may be used to determine the market impact solely from the impact I, the order details (total size X and order size x_k for period k) and the expected volume for that period v_k.

In order to actually estimate the model parameters, Kissell and Glantz rearranged the market impact cost for an order (equation 10-14) to be the product of two functions, allowing

---

[7] Kissell and Glantz (2003) also discuss alternatives for situations where market volumes are not evenly distributed between buys and sells.

estimation using non-linear regressions. This is achieved by assuming the order runs over a whole day, with a quantity X equal to the net imbalance Q, and by substituting $\eta^{-1} = Q/V_{side}$. Hence, equation 10-14 may be rearranged to:

$$MI_\$ (X = Q) = \frac{b_1 IQ}{V_{side}} + (1 - b_1)I = I(Q, \sigma) \cdot (b_1 \eta^{-1} + (1 - b_1))$$

Finally, both the cost and imbalance are normalised to allow estimation across a wider range of data. The imbalance is restated as Z, a percentage of the ADV, and the cost (in basis points) may be expressed as the product of both an instantaneous impact function ($I_{bp}^*(Z, \sigma)$) and a dissipation function ($d(\eta)$):

$$MI_{bp} = I_{bp}^*(Z, \sigma) \cdot d(\eta) \qquad (10\text{-}16)$$

Three possible structures for this instantaneous market impact function were investigated by Kissell and Glantz (2003):

$$\begin{aligned}
\textit{Linear}: \quad & I_{bp}^*(Z, \sigma) = a_1 Z + a_2 \sigma + a_3 && = (8Z + 0.30\sigma + 90) \\
\textit{Non linear}: \quad & I_{bp}^*(Z, \sigma) = a_1 Z^{a_2} + a_3 \sigma + a_4 && = (35Z^{0.65} + 0.30\sigma + 15) \qquad (10\text{-}17) \\
\textit{Power function}: \quad & I_{bp}^*(Z, \sigma) = a_1 Z^{a_2} \sigma^{a_3} && = (25Z^{0.38} \sigma^{0.28})
\end{aligned}$$

They used non-linear regression to derive estimates for each of these models, from samples with a range of sizes, volatilities and participation rates. The preferred results for each model are shown on the right hand side. Interestingly, the regression errors were found to be lower for the non-linear and power function based models, implying that the true relationship between impact cost and size is indeed non-linear.

The results proved to be consistent for both size and volatility; but as with any model, we still need to recalibrate it to find the most suitable estimates for specific markets.

Kissell and Glantz (2003) also determined an estimate for the dissipation function as:

$$d(\eta) = (0.95\eta^{-1} + 0.05)$$

The 95% was found in most of their regressions, and appeared to be time invariant and independent of size. Substituting this back into equation 10-16 gives:

$$\hat{I}_\$ = I_\$ \cdot (0.95\eta^{-1} + 0.05) = \underbrace{0.95 I_\$ \cdot \eta^{-1}}_{\textit{Temporary impact}} + \underbrace{0.05 I_\$}_{\textit{Permanent impact}} \qquad (10\text{-}18)$$

So 95% of the total market impact costs are temporary, the cost of demanding liquidity. Therefore, regardless of trading strategy, a 5% permanent impact will result, reflecting the information content of the order.

Let's now put this in practice with an example, loosely based on ones from Kissell and Glantz (2003).

Example 10-2: Consider an order to buy 100,000 EFG, assuming a current price of $50, a daily volatility of 200 bps and an ADV of 1,000,000.

In order to estimate the market impact we will first need a figure for the instantaneous impact cost. Using the estimates shown for equation 10-17, we can substitute Z with 10 (since 100,000 is 10% of the ADV) and σ is 200 bps:

Linear: $I^* = (8*10 + (0.3*200) + 90) * 10^{-4} * 50 * 100,000 = \$115,000$
Non-linear: $I^* = (35*10^{0.65} + (0.3*200) + 15) * 10^{-4} * 50 * 100,000 = \$115,670$
Power: $I^* = (25*10^{0.38} * 200^{0.28}) * 10^{-4} * 50 * 100,000 = \$132,190$
Average $I^* = \$120,953$

Thus, the average instantaneous market impact is approximately $120,000.

We can now feed this instantaneous market impact into equation 10-15 to estimate the overall market impact. Table 10-2 shows an example trading strategy together with the expected market volumes.

Period	1	2	3	4	5	Σ
Shares	20,000	15,000	10,000	25,000	30,000	100,000
E(Mkt volume)	250,000	150,000	100,000	250,000	250,000	1,000,000
Temporary order impact ($)	3,145	2,850	1,900	4,750	6,619	19,264

Table 10-2 Execution details for Example 10-2

Based on this, and using equation 10-15, we can then determine each child order's temporary impact, as shown in the last row. For instance, in the first period the order size x_k is 20,000, whilst the expected volume v_k is 250,000. Therefore, using equation 10-15 the temporary impact for period (1) is defined as:

$$\text{Temporary impact (1)} = 0.95 \times \$120,000 \times (20,000)^2 / 100,000 \times (20,000 + 0.5 \times 250,000)$$
$$= \$ 3,145$$

Note, this assumes we continue to use the same 0.95:0.05 ratio as we saw in equation 10-18, so $b_1 = 0.95$.

As we can see from Table 10-2, the total temporary impact is $ 19,264. Estimating the permanent impact is much easier since it is just a fixed proportion of the instantaneous impact. Therefore:

Temporary impact   = $ 19,264
Permanent impact   = $(1-0.95) * \$ 120,000 = \$ 6,000$
Market impact   = $ 19,264 + $ 6,000 = $ 25,264 = 50 bps.

So with a minimum of required data (price, volatility, ADV) we are able to use the Kissell and Glantz model to provide estimates for both the permanent and temporary market impact.

Timing risk

Timing risk reflects the uncertainty of the transaction cost estimate. Price volatility and liquidity risk are the two main sources of this uncertainty, although other factors such as spread risk may also be considered.

To make the determination of timing risk slightly easier Kissell and Glantz (2003) assume that volume and price movement are independent. This enables them to determine the price volatility and liquidity risk separately:

$$\Re(\phi) = \sqrt{\underbrace{\sigma^2(\mu(x_k))}_{Price\ volatility} + \underbrace{\sigma^2(\kappa(x_k))}_{Liquidity\ risk}} \qquad (10\text{-}19)$$

The price risk for a trading strategy represents the volatility exposure for the remaining position. Hence, for a discrete trading strategy Kissell and Malamut (2005b) define this as:

$$\Re(x_k) = p_0 \sqrt{\sum_{j=1}^{n} r_j^2 \cdot \frac{t\sigma^2}{n}}$$

where r is the residual position and $t\sigma^2/n$ is the per period variance.

The liquidity risk accounts for the variability of liquidity during the trading period. In turn, this affects the market impact estimations. For example, a sudden drop in liquidity will mean orders incur higher market impacts than expected. Kissell and Glantz use the unadjusted temporary impact function from equation 10-15 to determine the liquidity risk. This is beyond the scope of this book, but more details may be found in Kissell and Glantz (2003).

10.4 Handling special events

Computerised trading strategies can react to changing market conditions extremely quickly. We have already seen how short-term predictions can enable them to make more proactive decisions about order placement. Another way of achieving this is to build in rules to recognise and react to specific market events. For instance, a futures contract has a set expiry date; we know from empirical evidence that approaching this date much of the trading volume will switch to the next contract. Therefore, adjustments may be built in to ensure that as it reaches maturity the trading volume estimates are realistic.

These events may be highly predictable, such as contract expiration, or they may be more unexpected, such as a trading interruption due to news. Often they result in sudden rises in volatility and corresponding drops in liquidity. However, once the event has been recognised we can use historical reactions as a guideline, providing short-term predictions for how market conditions will change, and how long this might last. This should help the strategy react more like a real trader might.

Predictable events

Some events happen at set dates or they are pre-announced, so there is a high degree of certainty about them. Thus, it is relatively easy to create custom rules to be applied on these dates. Good examples of this are:

- New bond issues
- Futures contract expiration
- Witching days, when futures and options expire together
- Stock index rebalances

In the following sub-sections, we shall look at empirical examples of these events and examine how they affect market conditions.

New bond issues

For regular issuers of bonds, most typically governments, new issues tend to attract higher levels of liquidity than the contracts that they have effectively replaced. For example, the

U.S. Treasury distributes new issues of 1, 3 and 6-month bills every week, whilst issuance of 2 and 5-year notes is monthly, 10-year notes is quarterly and 30-year bonds is semi-annual. The current issue of any given U.S. Treasury is said to be "on the run". So every week, month or quarter a new batch of Treasury securities become "on the run" and the bills/notes/bonds they have replaced are said to be "off the run".

A study by Michael Barclay, Terrence Hendershott, and Kenneth Kotz (2006) found that once Treasuries become "off the run" their trading volume rapidly drops by 90% within a matter of days. This is illustrated in Figure 10-14, which is based on average trading volumes between January 2001 and November 2002.

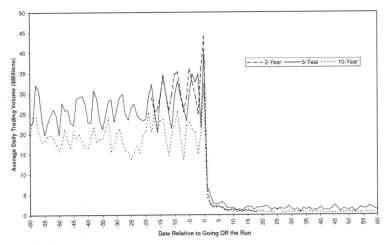

Source: Barclay, Hendershott, and Kotz (2006), Journal of Finance, Wiley-Blackwell
Reproduced with permission from publisher

Figure 10-14 Trading volume for on- and off-the-run U.S. Treasuries

The liquidity of new issues means they can attract a slight premium over their "off the run" equivalents. David Goldreich, Bernd Hanke and Purnendu Nath (2005) found an average premium of 1.5 basis points (bps) for 2-year notes. This dissipates to zero by the time of the next monthly issue. A higher premium of around 12 bps was observed for 30-year bonds by Arvind Krishnamurthy (2002).

Futures contract expiration

Futures have a specific expiration date; just prior to this the exchanges re-designate the lead contract, such as transferring from the June to the September. Changing the lead causes a considerable shift in trading volume as hedgers roll their positions onto the new contract.

Figure 10-15 illustrates this effect for the CME S&P 500 futures contract, taken from a study by Adam Schwartz and Bonnie and Robert Van Ness (2004). On the right hand side we can see that a brand new futures contract starts out with relatively low trading volumes. When the lead (or front-month) future has eight days left to maturity the lead is then switched to the next to expire (next-out) contract. The volume for the former lead contract has a final flurry before suddenly declining, shown at the eight-day marker in Figure 10-15.

For the new lead future, there will be a corresponding surge in trading volume, which we can see at the 98 days to expiry marker. During these crossovers the combined volume of

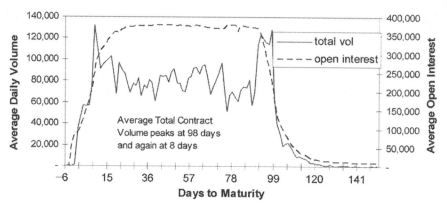

Source: Schwartz, Van Ness and Van Ness (2004), Journal of Futures Markets
Copyright 2004 John Wiley & Sons, Inc.   Reprinted with permission of John Wiley & Sons, Inc.

Figure 10-15, The daily volume and open interest of S&P 500 futures for 1999-2000

both contracts can actually see a net increase of around 30%, as observed for the S&P 500 by Ira Kawaller, Paul Koch and John Peterson (2001). They also found that the volatility of the contracts is closely linked to their trading volume. Hence, the lead contract has consistently lower volatility than the next-out contract.

Figure 10-15 also displays the open interest, which reflects the actual number of outstanding contracts. Again, we can see this suddenly climbs around the 98-day marker, and falls around the eight-day marker. In between these two peaks, the open interest remains relatively static over this period, whilst the trading volume is noticeably lower. This phase represents the secondary trading of contracts.

One way of handling this expiry-related seasonality for trading volume data is provided by Phil Holmes and Jonathan Rougier (2005). They used the change in open interest as an adjustment for the trading volume, so when a contract becomes lead there will be a negative adjustment. This approach was successfully used to interpret the significance of trading volumes for the S&P 500, U.K. long gilts and Brent crude contracts.

Witching days

Witching days occur when several classes of derivatives, for the same underlying asset, all expire on the same date. This is best typified for stock indices where the expiration of index futures and options as well as equity options is known as "triple witching". The introduction of single stock futures has added even more volume, together with the more cumbersome moniker "quadruple witching". The largest witching day is in the U.S., when the quarterly expirations of S&P 500 derivatives converge. A detailed review of this, and its effects on trading at both NYSE and NASDAQ, is provided by Michael Barclay, Terrence Hendershott and Charles Jones (2006). The volumes involved on witching days can be huge, for instance, in terms of S&P 500 futures alone they note that since late 2004 between $50-75 billion are settled on each witching day.

Arbitrageurs account for a sizeable proportion of the volume during witching days. They maintain hedged positions in the cash and derivative markets, since the derivatives usually settle in cash. At expiration, they need to closeout their cash market positions. To make a profit they must target the settlement price of the derivative contracts. Therefore, on witching days the cash markets receive considerable additional order flow from arbitrageurs. For instance, Barclay, Hendershott and Jones (2006) note their activity can increase up to 50 times on witching days, taking normal arbitrage volumes of $0.24 million per stock up to $12.74 million on NYSE, based on data from 2003 to Q3 2005. These shifts can significantly alter the normal balance between supply and demand, potentially causing large, but transient, price changes.

The short-term effects on trading volume for both NYSE and NASDAQ are shown in Figure 10-16. This plots the ratio of witching day volume compared to normal volumes, based on averages for each quarter from 1998 to Q3 2004. Thus, on witching days they found the NYSE opening trade volume was, on average, around seven times larger.

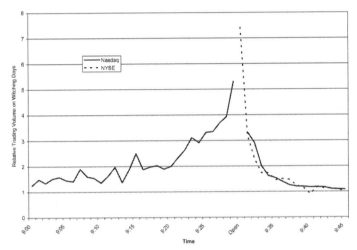

Source: Barclay, Hendershott and Jones (2006)   Reproduced with permission from publisher
Copyright © 2001, School of Business Administration, University Of Washington

Figure 10-16 Relative Witching day trading volume

The 2005 NYSE audit figures actually showed a ten times increase in volumes, with average opening volumes worth $15 million per stock. Similarly, on NASDAQ pre-open volumes reached over five times their usual levels. In both markets, a higher volume persisted after the open. Though, this dissipated rapidly with volumes returning back to their normal levels by around 10am.

A similar effect was observed for short-term volatility, as shown in Figure 10-17. Again, both markets saw a considerable jump in volatility on the morning of the witching. For the NYSE, Barclay, Hendershott and Jones (2006) determined an average increase of nearly 28 bps, whilst an excess of 64 bps was found for NASDAQ. As with volume, both markets also saw a rapid reduction in the excess volatility once the opening auction was completed. Though, by around 10am both markets returned to normal.

The study by Barclay, Hendershott and Jones (2006) is clearly also an interesting comparison between the two major U.S. markets. Some of the differences, particularly in terms of volatility, may be attributed to the variety of companies traded on each exchange.

They also note that the NASDAQ's introduction of an opening call auction in 2004 significantly improved its efficiency at handling witching days. In fact, they suggest that this may have contributed to the 50% jump in open interest in the $&P 500 which occurred in November 2004. This may have also helped triple the witching volume on the NYSE.

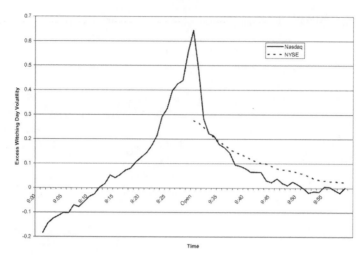

Figure 10-17 Excess Witching day volatility

Index Rebalancing

Stock indices are important benchmarks. In order to accurately reflect the markets they serve periodic rebalances are required. These ensure stocks that now meet the requirements for the index are added, and those that fail to meet them are removed. Hence, by rebalancing indices, such as the FTSE 100 or the S&P 500, manage to keep representing the major stocks for their respective markets.

Since so many investment firms track the major stock indices any such changes are publicised well before they actually happen. This gives the investors sufficient warning to realign their portfolios. To minimize their tracking error, index funds buy stocks added to the index, and sell those that are removed. So being included in a major index can lead to a sudden increase in demand for a company's shares. This can lead to a permanent improvement in its liquidity, in addition to improved coverage by analysts. Numerous studies have found that stocks that are added to an index see an abnormal increase in their returns whilst the stocks that are removed see a decrease.

A lot of research has focussed on the S&P 500, which is hardly surprising given the vast amount of assets that are benchmarked to this index. [8] Since 1989 Standard and Poor's have pre-announced adjustments a week in advance. Honghui Chen, Gregory Noronha and Vijay Singal (2006) analysed the returns for stocks involved in a rebalance, from before the initial announcement to over two months after the index change. Figure 10-18 shows the effect on the prices of these stocks for the period 1989-2002.

On announcement day, abnormal returns were, on average, +5.12% for additions, experienced by over 94% of the sample firms. This increased to +8.37% for the day of the actual rebalance. In contrast, stocks being removed from the index saw, on average, an 8% drop in returns by the day of the announcement, followed by a further decline to -14% on the effective date. Unlike the additions, though, this price effect did not appear to be permanent.

---

[8] Madhavan and Ming (2003) give a conservative estimate of over $830 billion.

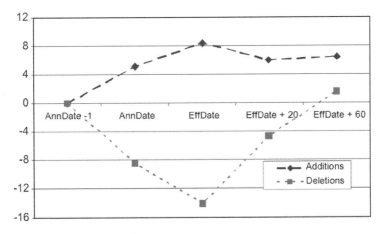

Source: Chen, Noronha and Singal (2006)   Reproduced with permission from JOIM

Figure 10-18 Average price responses to S&P 500 rebalances (1989-2002)

The negative effect disappeared within 60 days of the rebalance.

Similar results for the period between the announcement and the effective date were observed by Ananth Madhavan and Kewei Ming (2003) and Anthony Lynch and Richard Mendenhall (1997). Though, after the effective date Lynch and Mendenhall (1997) only noted a partial reversion in prices. Chen, Noronha and Singal (2006) explain that this difference is most likely due to their study using larger samples, as well as tracking the returns for longer after the event. They also suggested that increased awareness was a potential explanation for the permanent increase in returns for additions. They reason that investors do not suddenly become less aware of stocks which are removed from the index, hence the asymmetry in the returns.

Madhavan and Ming (2003) focussed on the July 19 2002 S&P 500 rebalance when seven non-U.S. companies were replaced. They found that by trading in the period leading up to the actual rebalance investors could dramatically reduce their trading costs without exposing their portfolios to substantial tracking error risk.

Madhavan (2002a) found an equivalent effect for the annual rebalances of the Russell 3000 index. He noted that the subsequent return reversals in July suggested that price pressure might have been an important determinant in generating the abnormal returns. He also concluded that the low liquidity of the stocks being removed might explain some of the asymmetry in the returns between the additions and the deletions.

Comparable short-term abnormal returns were also observed for rebalances of the U.K. FTSE-100 by Bryan Mase (2006). Though, he found no equivalent permanent price effects for additions. Instead, he noted that a reversal occurred for both additions and deletions, within a month their returns were back to normal.

In terms of trading volume, Chen, Noronha and Singal (2006) found turnovers to be over three times higher for affected stocks on the S&P 500 announcement days. They also saw turnovers jump to over 12 times normal levels on the effective dates. After the rebalance, the volumes returned to normal for the newly added stocks, but those removed from the index saw a decline in their volumes. In their study of the S&P 500, Lynch and Mendenhall (1997) reported significantly higher volumes on the day before the effective date. Similarly, Mase (2006) found peaks in trading volume on the day before FTSE-100 rebalances. The peaks applied to both additions and deletions; although post-rebalance there was an appreciable decline in the volumes for the stocks removed from the index.

The impact of index changes have also been analysed for the equity options markets. A study of the S&P 500 by Rong Qi and Libo Sui (2007) tracked the prices and trading volumes for stock options with strikes within 5% of the market price and maturities of 30-117 days. They found that on the day of the announcement call options for the additions saw a considerable price rise whilst the cost of puts fell. For the deletions, the put options saw an even greater price rise, whilst their calls became cheaper. They note that between the announcement and effective dates the highest abnormal return was for put options on the deletions, although the call options on additions also saw a positive return. Again, the price changes seemed to be permanent for the additions, whilst a partial reversal occurred within around 30 days of the effective date for the deletions. Interestingly, they also observed that the option prices started to change up to ten days before the announcement and accelerated at five days before, suggesting that the option market could be a useful leading indicator. Qi and Sui (2007) also reported similar volume spikes. On announcement day, they found up to a 30-times increase for put options on the additions and deletions, up to 50-times for call options on the deletions and around 17-times for call options on the additions. They noted that the open-interest level increased dramatically from announcement to the effective date, then suddenly dropped back to normal levels. Clearly, only so much volume is due to index-funds, they attributed much of the increase to arbitrageurs.

Unpredictable events

Events triggered by information or news are much less predictable. Whilst they may be harder to forecast, their short-term effects can still be quantified. For example, trading interruptions, such as halts or volatility auctions, may be followed by periods of much higher volatility and volumes, although these often dissipate after a few hours.

Trading interruptions

Excessive volatility poses a serious problem for market participants. In an attempt to prevent this, most markets adopt a variety of different methods to try to control things when new information suddenly becomes available, namely:

- Trading halts
- Price limits
- Volatility auctions

Trading halts are imposed by the market authorities; they cease trading for a set period whilst new information is made public. Often these are followed by a call auction to provide a more stable reopening for the affected asset. Price limits act as trading ranges, any trades that would shift the price outside of these are simply not permitted. Alternatively, volatility auctions switch continuous trading to a call auction for a short period. Essentially, they are like micro-halts since they often only last for around five minutes; however, they are generally triggered by set price rules, much like a price limit. This is a key difference between these mechanisms since both volatility auctions and price limits may be maintained automatically by market monitoring systems. Their rule-based nature makes them much easier to predict, In fact, a study by David Abad and Roberto Pascual (2006) even determines the probability of hitting such limits. In comparison, trading halts are more subjective and so harder to predict.

Trading halts are commonly adopted in the U.S. equity markets, whereas price limits are used more in European and Asian stock markets, as well as the U.S. futures markets. Volatility auctions are becoming increasingly popular, especially in Europe. They have also been incorporated into NYSE as Liquidity Replenishment Points (LRPs).

Researchers are still divided over which mechanism is best. Overall, trading halts seem to be preferred over price limits, whilst some studies find volatility auctions more effective than halts. For example, Yong Kim, José Yagüe and J. Jimmy Yang (2008) compared the effect of price limits and halts for trading on the Spanish stock exchange. They concluded that after both interruptions there was increased trading activity. Though, they noted that after trading halts volatility remained the same and the bid-offer spread actually reduced, whereas after price limit hits both the volatility and spread increased.

Note that the main focus of this section is on asset-specific interruptions, since these occur much more frequently than market-wide halts. For instance, in their NYSE study Bidisha Chakrabarty, Shane Corwin and Marios Panayides (2007) analysed 4,020 halts between January 2002 and December 2005, an average of over four a day.

Trading halts

Trading halts may be broken down into two main types, those driven by news and those that arise from order imbalances. Exchange officials instigate news halts when information due to be released is expected to have a significant impact on prices. The halt allows time for this to be disseminated to traders and investors. Order imbalance halts are triggered by a market specialist when the imbalance between buys and sells is too large. During the halt traders may modify, cancel and place new orders, after the halt trading then reopens with a call auction.

NYSE supports both types of halts. In their study, Shane Corwin and Marc Lipson (2000) found the average NYSE halt lasted over 80 minutes. News halts took around 86 minutes whilst order imbalance halts lasted an average of 56 minutes. During this time they noted that order activity increased significantly, both for submissions of new orders and cancellations of existing ones. Hence, by the time the market reopens the order book mainly consists of orders submitted during the halt. Though, due to the uncertainty surrounding halts, they also noted that the depth near the quotes falls to unusually low levels during the halt, even though specialists and floor traders provide additional liquidity. They also observed that order flow could remain at elevated levels for several hours after the halt. Importantly, they found that the market-clearing price after the reopening call auction was a good predictor of future prices. In their sample data, 36% of news halts led to price rises, 43% led to drops and 21% remained unchanged. Whilst for order imbalance halts, 48% led to rises, 41% to drops and 11% were stable. Overall, the average absolute return after a halt was just under 4%.

NASDAQ caters for news-driven halts. William Christie, Shane Corwin, and Jeffrey Harris (2002) found that these led to substantial increases in both volume and volatility. Trading volume and the number of trades were over six times the normal levels for the half hour after the halt, and remained unusually high for up to two hours afterwards. Intraday halts mean market makers cannot start posting prices until five minutes before the resumption of trading. These were found to result in up to nine times the normal levels of volatility, whilst the bid offer spread more than doubled. In comparison, for halts that occur after 4pm there is an extended 90 minute opening the following day. The volatility associated with such openings was significantly lower and the bid offer spread was virtually unaffected. They concluded that there is a clear benefit to allowing more time for price discovery after any halts.

Price limits

Price limits are generally adopted in order-driven markets. They may be static and/or dynamic. Static thresholds are usually applied to a benchmark price, such as the open or the previous close. So a 10% limit from the open restricts the price range between 36 and 44 for an asset that opened at 40. Dynamic thresholds are more versatile and are often based on the last traded price. For example, a 5% limit on an asset whose last traded price was 100 allows a price range of 95.00-105.00. If the next trade is at 104, the allowed price range will shift to 98.8-109.2.

The rules intervene for any trades that would break these ranges and send the market price either above the high limit or below the low. Such trades may then simply not be permitted, in which case the trader must decide whether to alter their price or not trade, forcing them to re-evaluate the market conditions.

Research on the effectiveness of price limits has not been conclusive. Certainly, there are as many studies that find price limits to be inefficient are there are ones finding them beneficial. A good example is an analysis of the Tokyo Stock Exchange by Kenneth Kim and S. Ghon Rhee (1997). They found that price limits could actually lead to higher volatility and volatility spillover on subsequent days. One of the problems with price limits is that the same price rule is often applied to all the assets within a certain market. This can pose issues for illiquid assets, since these can have significantly wider spreads, which can lead to them triggering the limits more often. This is illustrated in a study of the Chinese stock market by Gong-Meng Chen, Kenneth Kim and Oliver Rui (2005), who conclude that wider limits may be appropriate for the less liquid B-shares.

Volatility auctions

Volatility auctions shift continuous trading into a short period call auction, often lasting only about five minutes. This gives traders a brief respite before continuous trading recommences, allowing time for a new price level to be determined. The limits that trigger volatility auctions are usually much less than any daily price limits and so volatility auctions occur more frequently.

These are now in use at NYSE, Euronext and the London Stock Exchange, as well as a variety of other markets. A detailed study of the efficiency of volatility auctions on the Spanish stock exchange is provided by David Abad and Roberto Pascual (2007). They found that volatility started to increase half an hour beforehand, peaking in the ten-minute window around the call auction. In this period volatility levels could shift over six standard deviations away from normal levels. Though, they also noted that volatility rapidly dissipated reaching normal levels again within 90 minutes.

A similar effect was observed for trading volumes, whilst they found that the bid-offer spread was slightly wider for 30 minutes after the auction. However, no marked effect on the displayed order book depth was found. Since the recovery periods were shorter than those observed for NYSE or NASDAQ, they concluded that volatility auctions are an effective means of handling such situations.

Corporate announcements

Corporate announcements can be another relatively unpredictable event. Releases of details, such as company earnings or dividend payments, are often scheduled, but firms are free to change the dates. So, both the information they relay and when they occur can be hard to predict.

A study of dividend announcements for NYSE stocks was carried out by John Graham,

Jennifer Koski, and Uri Loewenstein (2003). Overall, they observed a decrease in liquidity immediately beforehand for notices that were well anticipated. As we might expect, the available depth decreased as traders prepared for the announcement. Afterwards, things returned to normal, although how long this took depended on how well the new information was received. For completely unanticipated announcements, the changes in liquidity were less noticeable beforehand. They observed a considerable and sudden increase in the spread that lasted for up to an hour after the news. The time taken for the available depth to recover also seemed to be longer for such events. Interestingly, they also found that unanticipated events were preceded by abnormal trading volumes. The consistency of this pre-event volume suggested some anticipation by informed traders. Though, their study focused on public news, rather than any other sources of market information or rumours.

Whether the announcement is on time can also give away important information. Firms tend to be keen to announce good news and defer issuing bad news. Mark Bagnoli, William Kross and Susan Watts (2004) analysed this effect for U.S. companies. They found that for each day of delay from the expected date of the announcement there was a fall of one penny/share below the consensus forecasts. In addition to these losses, they also noted that the market reaction on the actual day of the announcement depended on how late it had been. Thus, firms that reported late saw even more adverse reactions to bad results than those with similar results who reported on time. In comparison, they found that the market reaction to be more aggressive for early announcements.

The relatively unstructured format of news can make it very difficult for computer systems to analyse and interpret. In Chapter 14, we will examine methods to overcome these difficulties and analyse the impact of news in much more detail, covering both corporate and macroeconomic news.

10.5 Summary

- Trading algorithms and execution tactics are rule-based approaches responding to market conditions. So generally they are reactive. To enhance their performance we can:
    - Incorporate short-term prediction models for conditions such as price and volume.
    - Improve their spotting and handling of specific events, such as witching or halts.

- Short-term forecasting models for key market conditions enable trading strategies to be slightly more proactive and so take advantage of price improvement by placing more passively priced orders than they might otherwise.
    - Price forecasts may only be for the next few minutes, based on:
        - Imbalances in supply and demand.
        - Gaps in the order book, which trigger price jumps.
    - Volume forecasts tend to be for longer periods, based on:
        - Daily historical trading volume profiles. These may be further adjusted to account for seasonal factors or even specific holidays or events.
        - Volumes may also be decomposed into market and asset-specific components.
    - Liquidity measures, such as the bid offer spread or order book depth may be forecast using intraday averages.
    - Volatility forecasts help determine execution probability for orders, using:

- Statistical estimates, based on methods like EMA, ARMA or GARCH.
- Implied volatility, inferred from the market prices of options.
- Market volatility, estimated using indices such as the VIX.

- Transaction cost estimation helps to gauge the balance between cost and risk. Many of these models are based on a framework by Almgren and Chriss (2000):
  - Market impact models adopt a bottom-up approach.
  - Cost allocation models take a top-down view based on aggregated trade imbalances.

- Identifying specific market events can also enhance performance. For instance:
  - New bond issues lead to lower liquidity for the newly "off the run" assets.
  - Expiration of futures, as liquidity rolls from the current contract to the new one.
  - Witching days often lead to increases in trading volume and short-term volatility.
  - Additions and removals from stock indices lead to increased activity in these stocks.
  - Trading halts and volatility auctions also lead to increases in volatility and volume.

Chapter 11

Infrastructure requirements

Algorithmic trading is just as reliant on its infrastructure as the financial theory upon which its rules are based.

11.1 Introduction

So far, in this book we have focussed on the theory behind trading strategies. However, implementing them also involves a considerable amount of infrastructure. Figure 11-1 shows a high-level overview of the main components that are required for algorithmic trading and DMA.

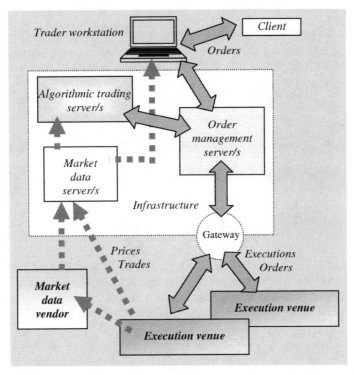

Figure 11-1 A high level view of the infrastructure required for electronic trading

Clearly, order management is a key part of this process, without it nothing much would happen. Before we move on to look at some of the technical considerations for implementing trading algorithms let's first review the mechanics of order management.

11.2 Order management

Order management plays an important role in any trading. Just as orders are the basis of any strategy, so they must be entered and routed to the appropriate destination, as Figure 11-1 shows. Executions (or fills) and updates/confirmations must be propagated back so that we can track the status of any given order. This is all catered for by a wide range of platforms, available from brokers and third-party vendors. There are two main types, namely order management systems (OMSs) and execution management systems (EMSs). Table 11-1 summarises some of the key functions offered by these platforms.

Function		*OMS*	*EMS*
Portfolio management	Modelling and rebalancing, "what-if" analysis	✓	
	Portfolio accounting	✓	
Risk management	Position management and P&L	✓	
	Risk management/exposure analysis	✓	
	Cash management	✓	
	Commission tracking	✓	
Analytics	Pre-trade analysis	✓	✓
	Post-trade analysis	✓	✓
	Real-time execution benchmarks		✓
Execution	Real time market data	✓	✓
	Order book depth		✓
	Connectivity to brokers/routing networks/FIX	✓	✓
	DMA/Trading algorithms/crossing	○	✓
Operations	Trade confirmations/allocations	✓	✓
	Connectivity to back-office systems/STP	✓	✓
	Exception reporting /reconciliations	✓	✓

Table 11-1 Typical OMS/EMS functions

Note that directories of the main OMS and EMS platforms may be found on the Advanced Trading website. [1]

Order management systems were originally developed to help improve workflow. They also encompass post-trade functionality, handling reporting and account allocation ready for clearing and settlement. They may also include portfolio-based functionality.

Execution management systems trace their roots back to the trade blotters and simple order entry screens that traders have relied on for decades. The adoption of DMA and algorithmic trading has led these to become increasingly sophisticated. Similarly, the increasing focus on transaction cost analysis has meant that many such systems now incorporate detailed pre-trade analytics.

At present, the level of convergence between OMSs and EMSs is growing rapidly. Fundamentally, though, whichever platform we use the mechanics of order entry and their subsequent routing are much the same. So let's examine each of these steps more closely.

---

[1] Advanced Trading directories are available at www.advancedtrading.com/directories

Order entry

Clearly, the main points to be captured for any order are:

- the asset (a unique identifier or symbol)
- the direction (whether we are buying or selling)
- the order size
- any price limits (if applicable)
- any additional information detailing the order type and/or conditions

As we saw in Chapter 4, there are a lot more types of order available than just market and limit orders. Similarly, a wide range of conditions may be applied to orders, allowing control over factors such as when and how long they are active, whether they may be partially filled and where they are routed. Therefore, order entry screens need to be able to support whatever order types and conditions are available for any given market.

Traders usually have a lot going on. Order entry needs to be a quick and painless operation. Symbol and account lookups must be fast to help ensure that order entry is as painless as possible. Order entry screens also need to make the appropriate options for order types and conditions easily available to the trader. For instance, Figure 11-2 shows an example order entry screen from the web version of the NASDAQ Workstation. Here we can easily select between different order types, routing destinations or change the time in force (TIF). We may create an iceberg order simply by setting a smaller display quantity. Likewise, there is a checkbox to activate pegging and an associated offset. So from a few drop down menus and check boxes a wide variety of order types is possible.

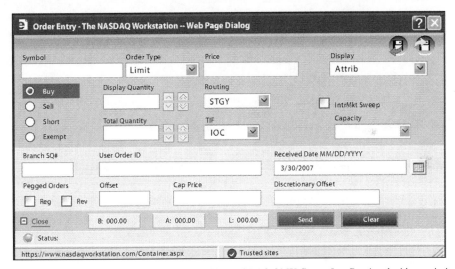

Source: NASDAQ (2008)   © Copyright 2008, The NASDAQ OMX Group, Inc. Reprinted with permission

Figure 11-2 An example order entry screen

Validation is also important, given all the possible permutations of orders and conditions across different venues/markets. Hence, order entry screens should ensure that selected options are all compatible and are valid for the given market. Such validation is particularly important for DMA where the users may not be fully aware of all the intricacies of local market order types/conditions and regulations. It may also make sense to incorporate some "fat finger" logic, such as checking the overall order size or comparing it with the asset's average daily volume (ADV), to try to catch any mistakes.

With trading algorithms, the order entry screens tend to be more customised, since each algorithm has slightly different parameters and requirements. Often vendors also incorporate pre-trade analytics and/or transaction cost estimates to help with algorithm selection. For example, Figure 11-3 shows a sample screen taken from Morgan Stanley's Passport trading application. Since the screens are customised for each algorithm, all the necessary parameters are laid out in an intuitive fashion, allowing easy and accurate order entry.

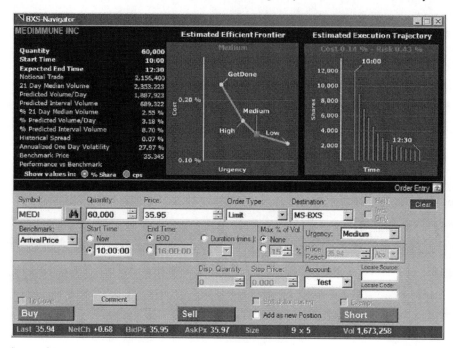

Source: © Morgan Stanley (2007)   Reproduced with permission from Morgan Stanley

Figure 11-3 An example algorithm entry screen

The rapid growth in the popularity of algorithmic trading, and the large number of algorithms involved, poses issues for OMS/EMS vendors. Keeping up with the rapid flow of new algorithms is difficult, particularly for those providing algorithms from a wide range of brokers. The screens for newer algorithms may well be queued up for testing and release by the various vendors. To gain access, clients will often need to upgrade their software. So, there can sometimes be a substantial delay before clients can get access to the latest algorithms.

One potential solution for this has been proposed by the Financial Information Exchange (FIX) group. Their algorithmic trading definition language (FIXatdl) is intended to ease the integration of algorithmic strategies by providing a consistent means of defining them. This XML-based [2] schema provides a standard framework for algorithm parameters, defining:

---

[2] Extensible Markup Language (XML) is a general specification for annotating text, creating custom "languages".

- Core data, such as their type and FIX tag
- Validation rules
- User interface requirements

For example, the following XML snippet shows the configuration details for a "RiskLevel" parameter, based on an example from FIX (2007):

```
<parameter name="RiskLevel" xsi:type="Int_t" fixTag="7078"
use="optional" minValue="1" maxValue="10" mutableOnCxlRpl="true"
controlType="Slider"/>
```

The core data represents the key information about each specific parameter, starting with its name. In this example, RiskLevel is mapped to the FIX tag number 7078. Its type is defined as an integer, although decimals, characters/strings and even enumerations are also supported. The use tag defines this as an optional parameter, whilst the mutableOnCxlRpl tag refers to whether it may be modified in a subsequent update (in this case it can).

Validation rules may just be basic constraints, such as the minimum and maximum values shown in the RiskLevel example. Alternatively, they may be more complex, and based on combinations of parameters. The parameter type will also ensure a basic level of validation, such as between strings or numbers.

The user interface requirements determine how the parameter should appear in an order entry screen. In this case, the RiskLevel parameter will be shown as a slider, allowing the user to pick the most appropriate value between 1 and 10. Other supported widgets are check boxes, radio buttons, drop down list boxes (or combo boxes) and simple input fields for text or dates/times. A separate element, the strategyPanel, allows further control over how various parameters are grouped and displayed. For example, the following XML allows the screen shown in Figure 11-4 to be generated, by grouping together parameters within strategyPanels.

```
<stategyPanel orientation="horizontal">
    <strategyPanel title="Time Parameters" collapsible="false"
            orientation="vertical">
        <parameter name="Start Time" xsi:type="UTCTimeStamp_t"
            fixTag="168" use="optional" controlType="Clock"/>
        <parameter name="End Time" xsi:type="UTCTimeStamp_t"
            fixTag="126" use="optional" controlType="Clock"/>
    </strategyPanel>
    <strategyPanel title="Advanced" collapsible="false"
            orientation="vertical">
        <parameter name="Participation Rate" xsi:type="Percentage_t"
            fixTag="7022" use="optional" controlType="SingleSpinner"/>
        <parameter name="Aggression" xsi:type=" Int_t"
            fixTag="7023" use="optional" controlType="ComboBox">
                <enumPair uiRep="High" wireValue="3"/>
                <enumPair uiRep="Medium" wireValue="2"/>
                <enumPair uiRep="Low" wireValue="1"/>
        </parameter>
    </strategyPanel>
</strategyPanel>
```

For more information on the FIXatdl specification, please see the overview provided by FIX (2008) or their website www.fixprotocol.org.

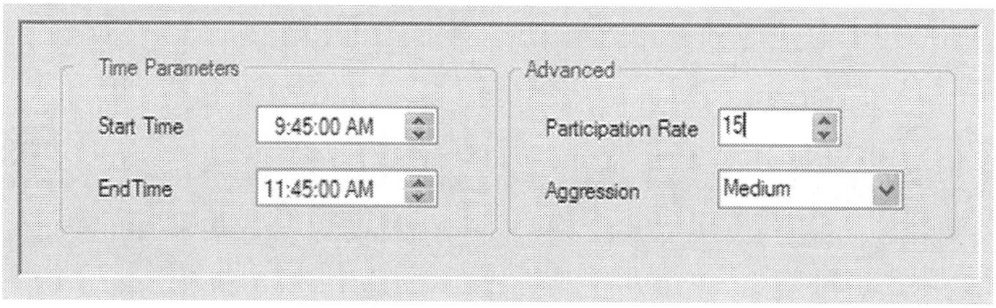

Source: © FIX (2008) www.fixprotocol.org Reproduced with permission from FIX Protocol Ltd.

Figure 11-4 A simple FIXatdl algorithmic parameter screen

Order routing

Once we have successfully entered our order we then need to route it to the required destination. In Figure 11-1 this is simply represented by some arrows going through a gateway process and then magically reaching the appropriate execution venue. In practice, each venue can have its own proprietary protocol for handling orders. Therefore, order routing systems have to convert (or encode) the details of each order into the appropriate format and then transmit them on to the required destination.

Order encoding

Before order routing was handled electronically, order encoding just meant using the right terms with your trader. Similarly, for trading pits, it meant knowing the correct hand signals to communicate the right price, side and size.

As venues have shifted to electronic trading, they have each implemented their own protocols for how orders should be processed. These are often accessed by custom application programming interfaces (APIs). Fortunately, a common messaging scheme, the Financial Information Exchange (FIX) Protocol, has become a de-facto standard for many markets. FIX is intended for the exchange of any information related to securities transactions. Hence, it supports the transmission of orders, market data, security information and settlement details. It exists in two main formats, a strictly machine-readable protocol and one based around an XML schema (FIXML).

The original FIX protocol is based on "Tag=Value" pairings, so an order to buy 1000 shares will contain the string `"54=1^38=1000"`. For the first pair, `54` is the tag number that represents the side whilst the value 1 maps to a buy. Whereas tag `38` maps to the order size.

Each message begins with a standard format; this reflects the version of FIX, the length of the message and the message type (tag `35`). It ends with a checksum that may be used for validation. Thus a message for a new order to buy 5000 shares of IBM looks like this, based on an example from FIX (2008a):

```
8=FIX.4.2^9=251^35=D^49=AFUNDMGR^56=ABROKER^34=2^52=20030615-
01:14:49^11=12345^1=111111^63=0^64=20030621^21=3^110=1000^111=50000
^55=IBM^48=459200101^22=1^54=1^60=2003061501:14:49^38=5000^40=1^44=
15.75^15=USD^59=0^10=127
```

(Note the ^ character is just a representation of the separator between each pair.)

In this example, the message starts by stating the FIX version is 4.2, the message length is 251 bytes and the value of `D` refers to the fact that this message is for a new single order.

Clearly, this approach is fine for sending messages between computer systems, but it is not very amenable for humans to read, for instance, during testing or debugging.

FIXML offers a more readable syntax, and since it is based on XML it allows developers to create custom filters or handlers. So for our example new order a FIXML representation looks something like this:

```
<FIXML>
        <Order   ClOrdID="12345"
                 Side="1"
                 TransactTm="2001-09-11T09:30:47-05:00"
                 OrdTyp="2"
                 Px="93.25"
                 Acct="26522154">
                 <Hdr    Snt="2001-09-11T09:30:47-05:00"
                         PosDup="N"
                         PosRsnd="N"
                         SeqNum="521">
                     <Sndr ID="AFUNDMGR"/>
                     <Tgt ID="ABROKER"/>
                 </Hdr>
                 <Instrmt Sym="IBM" ID="459200101" IDSrc="1"/>
                 <OrdQty Qty="5000"/>
        </Order>
</FIXML>
```

Having replaced the numeric fields with more descriptive tags it is now easier to read the details. The groupings mean that the various parameters are placed with their associated tag, so we can clearly differentiate between the header details and those for the instrument. Though, some translation is still required. For example, the value of 1 for Side means it is a buy order, whilst the value of 2 for OrdTyp means it is a limit order with a limit (Px) of 93.25. The instrument details confirm this is for IBM, both from the symbol and from the ID, which is based on a CUSIP. We can also see that the order is being sent from AFUNDMGR to ABROKER, using account 26522154. Finally, the message itself also has a unique client identifier (ClOrdID), namely 12345.

The main disadvantage with FIXML is the increased size of messages, which can cause capacity and performance issues for the required infrastructure. With earlier variants, the messages could be 3-5 times the size of an equivalent message using the FIX tag=value syntax. In version 4.4, the FIXML schema was updated to incorporate the latest XML enhancements. By streamlining the syntax and using more abbreviations the new FIXML messages are around 70% larger than the tag=value equivalents.

Handling different market types

FIX was originally created to handle the flow of orders. Though, it now also caters for quote-driven markets, supporting both the request for quote (RFQ) and request for stream (RFS) mechanisms that are commonly used in the fixed income and FX markets.

An RFQ based transaction starts with the client sending a Quote Request message to a specific broker. This may optionally specify both the Side and size (OrderQty), but the default is to request a standard market (two-way) quote. The broker must then respond with a corresponding Quote message in which they detail the price/s and size/s they are prepared to trade at. Alternatively, they may send a Quote Request Reject message. The client can then reply to the quote with a Quote Response, in which they can set the QuoteRespType field to "hit or lift" or to negotiate. Finally, if the RFQ results in a transaction the details are sent to the client in an Execution Report.

Streaming prices for RFS are handled via FIX's `Market Data` messages. Again these are triggered by a `Market Data Request`. An initial `Market Data Snapshot` is provided; quotes are then streamed through via subsequent `Incremental Refresh` messages. To trade in response to any given quote simply requires sending a new order based on the quoted price and size.

FIX also supports indications of interest (IOIs). To trade with any given `Indication of Interest` message means replying with an appropriate `Quote Response`, similar to the RFQ mechanism.

Asset specific details

Initially, FIX initially catered solely for equities, but its range of supported asset classes has now expanded to include fixed income, foreign exchange, money market and derivatives. The current version of FIX (5.0) supports:

- Global equities
- US and European government and corporate bonds
- US agency and municipal securities
- Repos
- US and European commercial paper
- FX spot, forwards and swaps
- Listed futures and options

A wide variety of different instrument classification types are also catered for. Hence, fields are provided for data such as the maturity date or strike price. More complex, multi-leg assets, such as swaps, may be defined using the `Security Definition` message. These may then be transmitted between parties, each leg may be handled individually or as part of the whole. A similar approach may be used for futures, or options, spread trading strategies.

Order conditions

Order conditions can offer significant additional functionality (and control of) their associated orders, as we saw in Chapter 4. The most important FIX tag for order conditions is `TimeInForce`; the permitted values are shown in Table 11-2.

Value	Order type
0	Day (or session)
1	Good Till Cancel (GTC)
2	At the Opening (OPG)
3	Immediate Or Cancel (IOC)
4	Fill Or Kill (FOK)
5	Good Till Crossing (GTX)
6	Good Till Date (GTD)
7	At the Close
8	Good Through Crossing
9	At Crossing

Table 11-2 Permitted values for the FIX `TimeInForce` tag

The `TimeInForce` tag may be used to control order lifetimes with values such as Day or Good Till Cancel. For orders that are Good Till Date the deadline is specified with the `ExpiryDate` tag. Alternatively, it may also be used to determine whether the order permits partial fills; hence, there are values for immediate-or-cancel and fill-or-kill. It is also used to specify session requirements, such as at the opening or close.

Order types

FIX supports a wide range of order types, most of which are specified using its `OrdType` tag, as shown in Table 11-3:

Value	Order type
1	Market
2	Limit
3	Stop / Stop Loss
4	Stop Limit
J	Market If Touched
P	Pegged

Table 11-3 Example values for the FIX `OrdType` tag

In addition, each of the order types uses its own custom tags to define additional parameters, such as a trigger price or offset value. Some examples are shown in Table 11-4.

Order type	Specific FIX tags
Stop/StopLimit	`StopPx`
Discretionary	`DiscretionInst` `DiscretionOffsetValue`
Pegged	`PegPriceType` `PegOffsetValue`
Iceberg	`DisplayQty`

Table 11-4 Associated FIX tags for different order types

Stop and stop limit orders used to be specified in FIX by setting both the order type and the `StopPx` price field. In FIX 5.0, this approach has been replaced with a more sophisticated mechanism, based around the `Triggering Instructions` block. This allows for all sorts of triggered behaviours: changing the status, price and even size or type of orders. The `TriggerAction` dictates whether the trigger activates, modifies or cancels the affected order. The `TriggerType` determines what actually acts as the trigger, whether it is a price movement, a new trading session/auction or even partial execution. For price-driven triggers, the `TriggerPrice` is similar to the old `StopPx` tag, whilst the `TriggerPriceType` determines which price is tracked, e.g. the last price or the best bid/offer. A `TriggerPriceTypeScope` field even supports the ability to base this on local market, national or global prices. The `TriggerPriceDirection` field specifies whether the trigger is hit on only rising or falling prices. Triggers may even be based on the prices of other assets, using the `TriggerSymbol` or `TriggerSecurityID` fields. This should permit triggers on futures or options to be based on the price of their underlying asset. In terms of what actually happens when the trigger is activated, the fields `TriggerOrderType`, `TriggerNewPrice` and `TriggerNewQty` allow control over the order's fundamental properties.

Discretionary orders are assigned by setting the `DiscretionInst` tag, relating this to the displayed price. The `DiscretionOffsetValue` defines the size of the price offset.

Pegged orders may be specified in FIX by setting the order type and the `PegPriceType` and `PegOffsetValue` tags. The `PegPriceType` supports pegging versus a wide range of prices, including the last trade, mid, open or even VWAP.

Iceberg, or reserve, orders are created by setting the `DisplayQty` tag. FIX also supports mixing and matching of these various types, so pegged orders may also incorporate discretionary pricing or iceberg behaviour etc., provided this is supported by the destination.

FIX can handle contingent order types as well, such as one-cancels-other. For this, the orders are created as a `New Order - List` and so are linked by their `ListID` tag. The `ContingencyType` tag then determines whether the relationship is one-cancels-other (1) or one-triggers-other (2).

Trading algorithms

FIX handles trading algorithms in a variety of ways. A nice introduction is provided by Roberto Rivero (2005) in FIXGlobal magazine. Clearly, we need to specify both the trading algorithm and its parameters.

There are several ways of setting the algorithm name in FIX messages. Exactly which method is used will depend on the broker/vendor's specific implementation. Table 11-5 shows some of the commoner types, as outlined in a presentation by Scott Atwell (2004) for the FIX Protocol Limited (FPL) Algorithmic Trading and DMA working group.

Type	*FIX fields used*
Text	`TargetSubId(57)` or `Text(58)`
`ExecInst/OrdType`	`ExecInst(18)` or `OrdType(40)`
`TargetStrategy`	`TargetStrategy(847)`
User Defined	FIX custom tags in `5000-9999` range

Table 11-5 Different ways of specifying trading algorithms in FIX

Probably the commonest way is just to pass the algorithm's name ("VWAP", or "ImpShort", "POV") as a text field in one of the instruction tags, or in the user-defined custom fields (in the `5000-9999` range [3]).

For parameters, some existing FIX tags may be used. For instance, the start and end times may be defined by using the respective `EffectiveTime` and `ExpireTime` fields. Though, again it all depends on how the broker/vendor has chosen to implement things. Algorithm specific parameters will often be set using custom user-defined tags.

FIX 5.0 does provide a more generic means of handling algorithm parameters. There is a repeating group (`NoStrategyParameters`), which can contain any number of parameters. For each one a unique name is defined (`StrategyParameterName`) together with its type (`StrategyParameterType`) and value (`StrategyParameterValue`). For example, if an implementation shortfall algorithm needs to be passed a benchmark price and a risk aversion we could set these as follows:

```
NoStrategyParameters(957)      = 2
StrategyParameterName(958)     = BenchmarkPrice
StrategyParameterType(959)     = 8 (Price)
StrategyParameterValue(960)    = 7.4
StrategyParameterName(958)     = RiskAversion
StrategyParameterType(959)     = 1 (Int)
StrategyParameterValue(960)    = 5
```

---

[3] These may be seen at http://www.fixprotocol.org/specifications/fields/5000-9999

As trading algorithms, OMS and EMSs evolve, the level of standardisation should hopefully improve, making it easier for the buy-side to switch between brokers without having to significantly change the format of their FIX messages.

Handling lists/portfolios

The FIX protocol also supports trading lists or portfolios. The `New Order - List` message allows a wave of orders to be sent, based on a unique `ListID`. A `ClOrdLinkID` identifier may also be used to link orders. The constituent orders may still be updated or cancelled. However, FIX also provides an `Order Mass Action Request` that can be used to act on all the orders that match specific criteria. Similarly, there are equivalent requests to cancel orders en-mass or to query their status.

FIX even provides messages to handle the actual mechanics of portfolio trading. In the U.K. and U.S., this is often carried out via a blind auction, in which case the `BidRequest` message can be used to provide a summary model of the portfolio. This describes it in terms of its sectors, countries, indices and liquidity. The participating brokers may then reply with appropriate bids for the trade. The successful bidder will then be sent a `New Order - List` and the details of the actual portfolio. For some countries, such as Japan, the portfolio details may be disclosed for the auction; in which case the portfolio details are provided up-front, although the side may be left undefined. Principal trades are catered for as well, with a `List Strike Price` message, which may be used to detail the agreed strike prices for each constituent. Given that portfolio trades often span many different accounts, FIX messages may also be used to communicate any account allocation details, ready for settlement.

Order transmission

Having considered how to encode the orders, we now need to send them to their required destination. Order transmission brings us to the technical nitty-gritty of actually doing this. For the FIX protocol a lot of this logic is contained within specific FIX engine or gateway servers. These are readily available from a wide range of vendors. They understand the FIX message protocol and provide the necessary logic for establishing connections to other FIX engines/gateways.

Originally, these gateways were just used by clients to establish a direct connection to their brokers, as shown by pathway 1 in Figure 11-5. The broker would in turn have connections to the different execution venues, often these would be implemented using native APIs. Over time, though, an increasing number of execution venues have started to set up their own FIX gateways. Hence, clients now have the possibility of connecting directly to specific venues in addition to routing via their broker, as shown by the various pathways labelled 2 in Figure 11-5.

To ensure the data quality of messages they incorporate both check sums and message lengths, as we saw in the previous section. Thus, the FIX engine can confirm that the received message matches the one that was actually transmitted.

In terms of the actual transmission, clearly we want the connection to the broker/execution venue to be as resilient as possible. Consequently, when the FIX engine makes a connection it establishes a new session. All messages sent during this session are identified by a unique sequence number (`MsgSeqNum`). Messages should be delivered in order so if an engine receives a message whose identifier is out of sequence it can issue a resend request. Likewise, if an engine determines that there may have been a problem with transmitting the

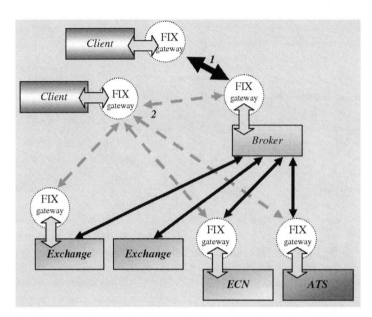

Figure 11-5 Potential transmission routes between clients, brokers and venues

message it may opt to retransmit it, setting the `PossDupFlag` to `"Y"`. It is the responsibility of the receiving engine to then process the message, or discard it if it has already been successfully processed. During periods when no messages are being transmitted, heartbeat messages may also be sent, to confirm that the connection is still okay.

11.3 Algorithmic trading

Algorithmic trading is heavily dependent on both order management and market data services, as we saw back in Figure 11-1. A slightly more detailed infrastructure diagram for a typical algorithmic trading platform is shown in Figure 11-6.

Trading platforms are generally based on client-server technology, so an application on the trader's workstation interacts with a series of back-end servers. The price data for the OMS/EMS client is supplied by market data servers, whilst the actual orders are handled by dedicated order management servers. Algorithmic trading servers make use of both these services as well. They may also use dedicated analytics servers to process historical data or for back-testing. Some proprietary or risk-based algorithms may even use profit and loss (P&L) or risk servers to track their performance and/or exposure.

Most brokers' algorithmic trading platforms have been developed in-house over the last five to ten years. Often these have been built from the ground up. Millions of dollars and years of effort have been invested as each platform seeks to offer "best of breed" algorithms. This is combined with ensuring there is a resilient and scalable trading environment.

Third-party vendors also offer dedicated algorithmic trading platforms, often based on complex event processing (CEP) systems. These provide the basic constructs required for handling market data and processing orders and may even supply trading algorithms that can be extended or used as templates for brand new strategies. So implementing trading algorithms is now a much more viable proposition for the buy-side.

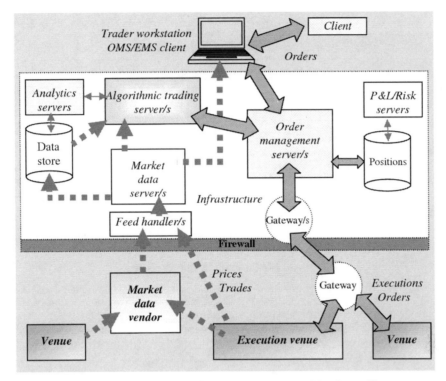

Figure 11-6 A simple infrastructure for algorithmic trading

That said, building an algorithmic trading platform is not a decision to be taken lightly. It takes teams of developers, quants and experienced traders to create effective algorithms.

Infrastructure requirements for algorithmic trading

As the usage of electronic and algorithmic trading continues to increase, the associated infrastructure will play just as key a role as the quality of the actual trading algorithms.

Building a successful platform for algorithmic trading is not just about having the best algorithms. If the infrastructure is not resilient, or sufficiently scalable then its use will be limited. Hence, it is important not to underestimate how much work is involved to create a successful trading platform.

Speed/Latency

Speed has always been important in trading; however, the timescales involved have drastically reduced. People now talk in terms of microseconds (10^{-6}s). To put this in perspective, a blink takes between 100-150 milliseconds (10^{-3}s).

Latency is an often-used term. It represents the inherent delays in transmitting and processing data (for orders or market data prices). Figure 11-7 shows another version of the infrastructure diagram, highlighting the various stages that orders and prices go through.

So to get to the execution venue an order is sent from the client via the various gateways, arriving at the broker, as shown by path A. The algorithmic trading engine then sends out orders (again via gateways) to the execution venue, shown by paths B and C. Finally, the execution venue must receive and process the order (path D).

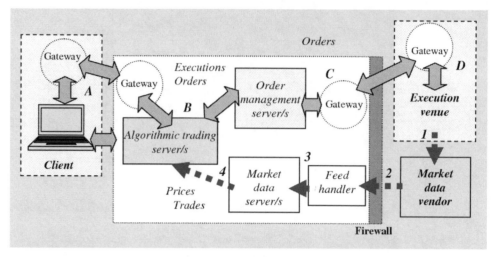

Figure 11-7 Latency in infrastructure

Likewise prices from the execution venue are issued to market data vendors who then distribute them via their own infrastructure. Feed handlers at the broker (or client) receive these and then make them available to any processes that need them, again via their own infrastructure of market data servers. The overall trip times represent the total latency for sending an order or receiving a market data price, as shown by:

Total latency (order) = A + B + C + D
Total latency (price) = 1 + 2 + 3 + 4

So there is no point having a super-fast connection to the external data sources, or execution venues, if internal processes are causing a significant delay. Conversely, there is no benefit in having a fast infrastructure with slow connections to external venues or market data.

Ideally, there should be the minimum number of steps so that data reaches its intended destination as fast as possible. Data messages should be as small as they can. Though, data can only be compressed so much. The time they take to be transmitted also depends on the physical distance they must travel. Table 11-6 shows the results of a round-trip test by Exponential-e (2009) for their routing service, to give an idea of the time it takes to communicate between different locations.

Thus, co-location has become increasingly popular. This allows market participants to host their computerised trading systems in the same machine rooms as the execution venue, thus minimising any transmission-related delays. Otherwise, U.S. based brokers will have considerable latencies when dealing with Asia or Europe, similarly European and Asian firms will be disadvantaged when handling orders for the U.S.

It is important to note that latencies will constantly vary, depending on the overall load. At times when the markets are busiest, or at their most volatile, the latencies will inevitably increase due to the higher workload. Therefore, is important to track latency at peak loads rather than focussing on a minimum figure, which will have been achieved given optimal conditions. In terms of infrastructure, things like careful load balancing can help ensure that processes do not become swamped by their workload, introducing additional delays.

From:	To:	Latency/ms
London	Frankfurt	10
	New York	68
	Chicago	85
New York	Toronto	25
	Zurich	90
	Tokyo	246
	Sydney	260

Source: Exponential-e (2009)

Table 11-6 A snapshot latency roundtrip comparison for some key locations

Capacity

Over the last few years, electronic and algorithmic trading have led to smaller trade sizes and more frequent order updates. Consequently, the number of market data messages has massively increased, as we can see in Figure 11-8.

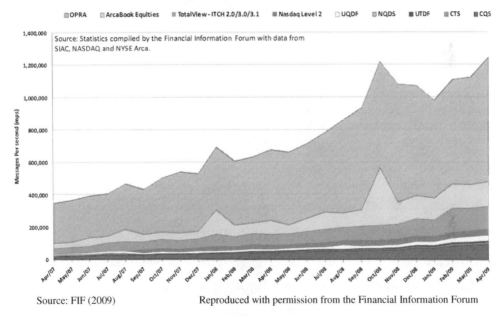

Source: FIF (2009)   Reproduced with permission from the Financial Information Forum

Figure 11-8 OPRA and consolidated equities 5 second peak rates

This shows the historical 5-second peak rates from the main market data feeds for U.S. equities and listed options. The increase is most notable for U.S. options. In fact messages from OPRA (Options Price Reporting Authority) now exceed 1.2 million messages per second, having nearly tripled in just two years.

In comparison, the equity feeds have lower update rates; indeed, all but the depth of book feeds (for NYSE ArcaBook, NASDAQ TotalView ITCH and NASDAQ Level 2) are at the very bottom of Figure 11-8, with peak update rates below 200,000 messages per second.

These include the Consolidated Quotation System (CQS) and Consolidated Tape System (CTS) which carry the quote and trade updates for the NYSE (Tape A), Regional (Tape B) and the UTP Quotation Data Feed (UQDF) and UTP Trade Data Feed (UTDF) for NASDAQ (Tape C) stocks. They may be much lower, but the trend is the same, these have all seen considerable increases in update rates over the last few years.

Clearly, the numbers in Figure 11-8 are huge; however, they cover all the traded assets whose prices/trades are broadcast on each of the respective feeds. So the number of market data updates per second for a specific asset will obviously be a lot lower. No one algorithm will be exposed to hundreds of thousands of updates per second. Still, at any one time an algorithmic trading platform may be trading hundreds or thousands of different assets. Hence, these massive update rates become relevant, and the infrastructure will need to be able to cope with them.

Other factors

Speed and capacity are obviously important. However, reliability is also vital. A fast car is great, unless it breaks down every other day. So the infrastructure also needs to cope with every-day usage, as well as handling the loads at peak times. In modern markets, this may mean the infrastructure being available 24x7 (or as close as possible). Therefore, all of the server-side processes we saw back in Figure 11-6 also need to be:

- Resilient
- Manageable
- Scalable

Hardware (or software) issues should not result in catastrophic failure. Therefore, if a machine or process fails there should be another machine/process ready to immediately take over in its place. This might be achieved by running machines/processes in fault-tolerant pairs, or using "server farms" to handle processes. Failures should also not be allowed to propagate, so a problem with analytics should not disable the algorithmic trading server.

Problems will always occur, so the infrastructure needs to be manageable. Failures should be simple to spot and correct. Monitoring should highlight the servers/processes that are under heavier load, since these may be more likely to fail in the future. Load balancing may also be adopted to try to ensure that the work is distributed evenly amongst the various processes/machines.

Scalability is another key issue. Obviously, for the long-term it is desirable to be able to easily extend capacity. There can also be short-term peaks in demand, so a flexible infrastructure where new servers can easily be added can be extremely useful.

Designing an environment for algorithmic trading

Having considered some of the infrastructure surrounding electronic trading let's now take a closer look at how actual trading platforms might be designed and implemented. In Chapter 5, we saw a wide range of different trading algorithms. Still, they all share quite a lot of common functionality. Fundamentally, it all starts with an order, which details the trading requirements as well as the specifics for the algorithm. An instance of the algorithm will then be created with all these details. The trading algorithm's order placement decisions are fundamentally based on market data. Thus, it needs access to see the available prices and probably the liquidity. It also needs to be able to create, send and update orders to specific destinations, which will be one (or several) execution venues. Figure 11-9 shows a simple outline of these relationships.

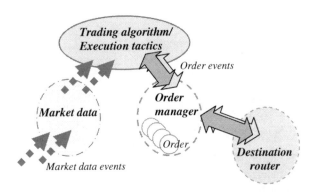

Figure 11-9 A simplified algorithmic trading environment

In terms of object-oriented programming (OOP), the above ellipses may be viewed as objects. Each of these is an instance of a specific class, which we will go through in the following sub-sections. They all "encapsulate" the required logic and data they need to work. In turn, they can be made up of other objects. For example, the order manager maintains a list of child orders which it is able to send on to the required destination.

Essentially, this also represents a minimal design for an algorithmic trading platform. In practice, it is slightly more complex than this, but by designing the environment based around suitable classes a lot of the complexity may be hidden.

Trading algorithm

The trading algorithm is effectively created from a parent order, which encapsulates the basic requirements such as the asset details, target size and direction (buy/sell) together with any price limit or specific conditions. The parent order also needs to maintain client details to ensure they can be provided with order status updates.

Based on the specified trading algorithm type and any associated parameters, the appropriate algorithm may then be launched. The trading algorithm contains all the various information needed for its execution. So it maintains market data subscriptions to get access to the prices etc. The algorithm also manages a list of all the child orders it has spawned, so if it is cancelled it can easily cycle through and cancel any extant orders. It also retains details such as the current position and maybe even its performance relative to any benchmarks. This information may then be used to determine whether it is ahead or behind of its targets, and so decide how aggressively future orders should be priced/sized. Obviously, there are also the actual trading rules; we will consider these in more detail in the next section.

Market data

Market data is generally provided for a specific asset at a set venue, although some vendors also provide consolidated feeds. Therefore, a subscription to the market data for an asset provides us with streaming updates for each time the price or size changes, or for when trade reports are issued.

Throughout this book, we have used order books to visualise the available liquidity, as shown in Figure 11-10. Because of the additional information value held within the order book, many exchanges and market data venues have variable charges for the different depths. Level 1 usually corresponds to the best bid and offer quotes, whilst Level 2 provides

Market data:	Buys				Sells			
	Id	Time	Size	Price	Price	Size	Time	Id
Level 1	B1	8:24:00	1,000	100	101	1,000	8:25:00	S1
Level 2/3	B2	8:21:25	5,000	99	102	1,500	8:20:25	S2
	B3	8:23:25	2,500	98	104	2,000	8:19:09	S3
	B4	8:24:09	1,000	97	106	3,000	8:15:00	S4

Figure 11-10 An example order book

a fuller view of the order book, although sometimes this aggregates orders. Sometimes there is even a Level 3, which gives a full view of the order book, except for hidden orders, of course. This data might be sourced from a single subscription, but often several different market data subscriptions will be required.

A dedicated order book class may be used to merge all this data together to provide a coherent image. Obviously, this translation needs to be fast so as not to introduce any significant additional latency. The order book class will also need to define its own custom events to correspond to any changes in the order book. In turn, classes for our trading rules may then subscribe to these events so as to be notified when the order book changes. This should allow our trading algorithms or execution tactics to react to any changes in liquidity.

Market data is also important for tracking reported trades. Algorithms such as POV need to track the market traded volume. Note that there can sometimes be substantial delays in trade reporting data; in fact, some might even be for previous days. So when reacting to trade ticks it is important to also check that the trade time and any conditions flags are appropriate.

Examining the reported trades is also important for tracking hidden liquidity, as we saw in Chapter 8. A custom order book class could be created which incorporates estimates for hidden liquidity. Though, again it is important to ensure that any calculations are performed as fast as possible, otherwise new data updates may render it meaningless.

Orders

Each child order that is spawned by the trading algorithm needs to contain its specific requirements. Namely, the asset details, target size and direction (buy/sell), together with any limit price or other conditions. It also needs some sort of identifier so that it may be linked back to the parent order/algorithm.

Orders lend themselves well to being implemented in a class. For instance, to send an IOC order with a limit price of 7.9 to a specific destination we could simply use code like:

```
Order myOrd = new LimitOrder( 7.9 );
myOrd.setCondition( ImmediateOrCancel );
myOrd.send( destination );
```

The send() method will handle the necessary encoding and transmission details. Hence, all the implementation details we saw in the previous sections remain hidden, keeping things a lot simpler.

One key consideration when handling orders is their state. Just because we have sent an order does not mean it has yet reached its intended destination. The transmission might fail or the destination may reject the order. So we should treat it as a pending order until we receive a successful acknowledgement. The same applies for any order updates or cancellations. This may mean certain actions are prevented, for example, a pending cancel might fail if the destination issues an update that the order has just been filled.

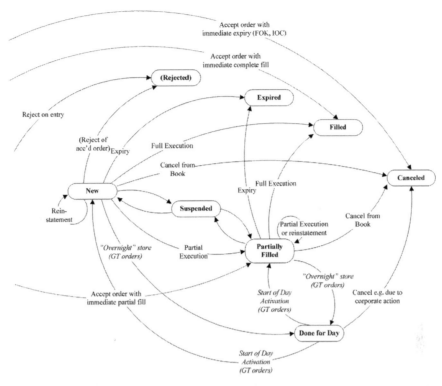

Source: © FIX (2008b) www.fixprotocol.org   Reproduced with permission from FIX Protocol Ltd.

Figure 11-11 FIX order states

A nice representation of the different states for a FIX order is provided in the documentation from FIX (2008b), as shown in Figure 11-11.

Destination

Orders clearly need to be sent somewhere. Therefore, another key object that needs to be implemented is some sort of destination. This may simply be a wrapper for a connection to a FIX engine. The destination object might also incorporate additional logic, such as average latency information and details of any extra fees. This could then be used by any strategies that need to decide between execution venues.

Other classes

Trading algorithms may also use a wide range of additional classes. For instance, VWAP algorithms need access to historical volume profiles. Cost-driven algorithms will need access to market impact and risk models. Liquidity-driven algorithms may use a diverse range of liquidity metrics. The logic associated with all of these analytics may be encapsulated in dedicated classes, which can then be shared between different trading algorithms.

Implementing trading rules

So far, the trading algorithm class has just been a container. In order to recreate the algorithms we saw in Chapter 5 we need to add some actual trading logic to this. Typically, this means creating trading rules that respond to specific events or situations, as shown in Figure 11-12.

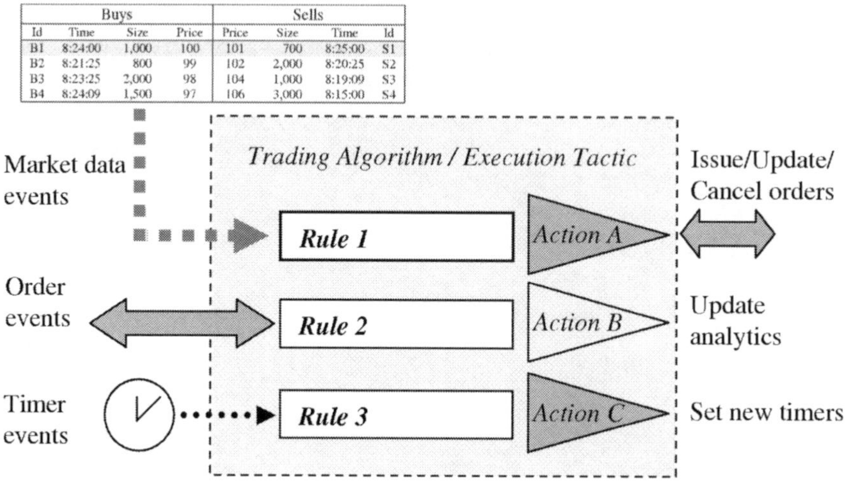

	Buys				Sells		
Id	Time	Size	Price	Price	Size	Time	Id
B1	8:24:00	1,000	100	101	700	8:25:00	S1
B2	8:21:25	800	99	102	2,000	8:20:25	S2
B3	8:23:25	2,000	98	104	1,000	8:19:09	S3
B4	8:24:09	1,500	97	106	3,000	8:15:00	S4

Figure 11-12 A rules-based trading algorithm

This event-based approach is common to most algorithmic trading platforms. Obviously, the key events are those related to market data, for prices and liquidity, and to orders, for fills and changes in status. Each rule will react to an event in a specific way, often by performing a set action. For example, a POV algorithm will need to take account of any new market volume; it might then update its target quantity or simply issue a new child order. Similarly, adaptive algorithms will react to changes in the market price or liquidity.

Coding trading rules

Most algorithmic trading platforms are event-driven, built using an object-oriented language such as Java or C++; so trading rules are often written directly in code.

In event-driven programming, each event represents a message that may be transmitted between objects. The objects are said to be either producers (publishers) or consumers (subscribers) for a specific event. So all the interested objects can register to ensure they are notified when an event occurs. These registrations may be handled by a separate intermediary, which allows the components to be "loosely coupled". Hence, the producers and consumers do not actually need to know any specifics about each other; all they require is access to the intermediary. This allows us to dynamically add new consumers or even change to use a different producer object. Such an approach provides a lot of flexibility.

The actual triggers are called event handlers. These respond every time a specific event happens. For instance, each time an order receives a fill an OrderFillEvent may be triggered. By registering a dedicated event handler for these we can be notified by this event each time the order gets a fill. We can then update our overall position based on the new fill size, as shown in the following sample event handler:

```
public void onOrderUpdate( OrderFillEvent oe ){
    if ( notYetProcessed( oe.getFillID() ) ) {
        position = position + oe.getFillSize();
        flagAsProcessed( oe.getFillID() );
```

```
            adjustTarget();
        }
    }
```

In addition to updating the position we might also use this event to adjust our targets, as shown by the `adjustTarget()` placeholder. Note that the `notYetProcessed()` function simply protects us from situations when we might receive multiple confirmations for the same fill.

Market data provides two main types of information, firstly basic order book data such as the best bid and offer and their sizes. For example, let's consider recreating a simple pegging order. On each market data update (or tick) we check if the best bid or offer has changed:

```
public void onMarketDataUpdate( MarketDataEvent mde ){
    if ( mde.hasBestBidOrOfferChanged()
            && priceChangeSufficient() ){
                doPeg();
    }
}
```

If the price change is sufficient, we need to change the price of our extant order, this decision is handled by the placeholder function `priceChangeSufficient()`. The `doPeg()` method contains all the necessary logic for the actual pegging. All the trading rule really does is act as a link to trigger this, based on the market data changing.

Market data events may also deliver information from trade reports. For example, a simple reactive Percent of Volume (POV) algorithm will need to respond to market data trade reports, setting its new target based on the additional volume:

```
public void onMarketDataUpdate( MarketDataEvent mde ){
    if ( mde.isTradeTick() && isValidTrade( mde ) ) {
        adjustTarget( mde.getTradeSize() );
        if ( targetChanged() )
            sendOrder();
    }
}
```

The `isValidTrade()` function allows us to check the trade report flags and date to ensure this is volume the algorithm should be tracking. If the trade is valid a new target is then set. For a truly reactive POV approach, we can then issue an order, provided that the target size has changed sufficiently. Note that this is just a simple example, as we saw in Chapter 5 such a reactive approach is not the best way of implementing a POV algorithm.

Obviously, event handlers can be much more complex than these basic examples. For orders we also need to deal with rejections, cancellations etc., similarly for market data we need to handle order book information as well. We also need to deal with infrastructure issues, for instance, possible failures in the connections for our orders or our data feeds.

However, the key point is that complex behaviours can be built up from a large number of relatively simple rules. If they are designed well, the rules can often be used across a wide range of different strategies, and so helping to speed up development time for new strategies.

Scripting trading rules

Some vendor's platforms provide applications that allow trading rules to be scripted. A good example of this is the Apama Event Modeler as shown in Figure 11-13.

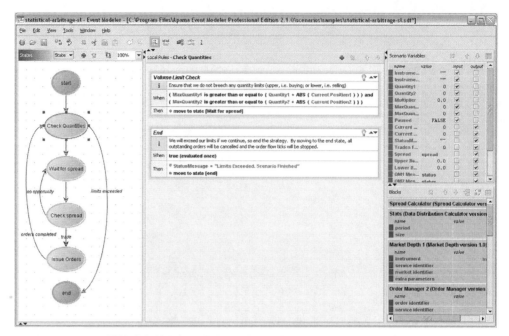

Source: Apama (2008) © 2008 Progress Software Corporation. Used with permission

Figure 11-13 A screenshot of the Apama Event Modeler

The Event Modeler provides a state-driven approach; the various potential states may be seen on the left hand side of Figure 11-13. The example scenario displayed is driven by the spread between the prices of two assets. The arrows show the progression from one state to another: So after starting and checking the quantities, the scenario effectively loops between the "wait for spread" and "check spread" states. Only when the spread is favourable will it shift to "issue orders". In the middle of Figure 11-13, we can also see the rules for the "check quantities" state. If it passes the 'volume limit check' rule then it will move to the "wait for spread" state. Otherwise, it will terminate with a status message noting that the limits have been exceeded.

This approach allows traders to create strategies by scripting appropriate rules within a custom application. Obviously, significant testing is still required, but it can offer a rapid means of prototyping new strategies.

Testing

Testing is clearly a vital part of the process. The basic mechanism of each trading strategy and rule must be verified, so a dedicated test environment is usually required. This enables us to test each separate component for a wide range of market conditions. Back-testing may then be used to analyse the overall performance, based on historical data.

Note that whilst test environments are important there is no substitute for the real thing. Therefore, once they have passed all the various tests and performance analyses trading algorithms will often undergo a period of small-scale live testing. Only after careful real-world performance monitoring and analysis will the algorithms be ready for more widespread use.

Test environment

A test environment needs to be able to realistically recreate the actual infrastructure, so it will look similar to the layout we saw in Figure 11-1. Market data is important, similarly we need be able to dispatch orders and see their effect. Clearly, all these processes need to operate separately from the live production instances so that there is no confusion (or any accidents).

Testing against live market prices is certainly useful; however, historical (or "canned") data is often used as well. Live market prices are inherently uncertain, whereas using historical data allows us to control exactly what the market conditions are. This enables us to replay specific scenarios and so test the performance of a range of trading strategies, or rules, based on exactly the same conditions. A number of vendors already provide solutions which can store and replay historical data.

Validating the encoding and transmission of orders is also important, although admittedly these will change much less frequently than the trading rules. Often this will require a mix of visual inspection by the developers and routing orders through to test exchanges.

Another factor worth considering is latency. As strategies increasingly search for liquidity amongst different execution venues, they need to be able to take account of latency. Unfortunately, test environments often perform very differently to the real world, so simulators can play an important role in reproducing the effect of latency.

Validating trading rules

As we have already seen, trading algorithms may be broken down into sets of trading rules. Each of these must be individually verified. So a developer may create specific tests to ensure that given the required market conditions each rule will react as expected. Thus, replaying historical market data is invaluable, since it allows fine-grained control of the market conditions. In comparison with live data, we simply cannot predict exactly how the market will move throughout the day, so there is no guarantee that a test condition will be triggered.

It is also important to test for extreme market conditions, such as during the 2007-09 financial crisis. Consequently, testing may also be carried out using historical datasets for periods in which there was a strong price trend, volatility, trading halts or even sudden liquidity crises.

We also need to confirm how trading rules perform "en-masse" as part of an algorithm. For example, a perfectly reasonable stop-loss rule might actually play havoc with performance when incorporated into a liquidity-seeking algorithm. Careful post trade analysis can highlight the child orders that contributed most to the overall transaction costs. Then it is a matter of drilling down to understand why they were placed and to confirm whether this was the best approach.

Back-testing

Back-testing is an important method for verifying the potential performance and profitability of trading strategies. For instance, let's consider a trading strategy that relies on price forecasts based on historical moving average (MA) prices, as shown in Figure 11-14.

If the 10-day moving average rises above the 30-day moving average then we will treat this as a signal to buy the asset. Conversely, when it falls below the 30-day average we shall look to sell the asset. For this one example the rule seems to work quite well. Still, that does not guarantee its future success. A common way of validating its potential is to check how it does over time. By back-testing for the last few months we can determine whether the rule

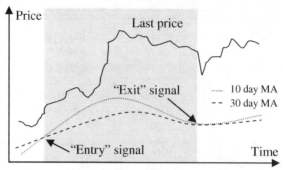

Figure 11-14 A simple trading strategy

holds true or whether it breaks down over time. Usually, this is gauged by determining the overall profit and loss (P&L) of a simulated strategy. Based on this figure we can then compare the performance of different trading strategies.

Note it is vital to remember that just because a rule holds for a certain period of historical data does not mean it will necessarily continue to do so in the future. As its name implies all back-testing does is highlight the performance based on data from the past. Factors such as transaction costs also play a key role: Just because a strategy seems profitable based on close prices does not mean it will actually be viable.

Trading algorithms can be back-tested, although the focus will usually be on performance rather than the overall P&L, since the decision to buy or sell remains a separate choice. Obviously, this requires a lot more data than simple close prices, simulations will need to incorporate data for each price "tick" and all the trades, as a bare minimum. They will also usually recreate the order book, so as to be able to replicate the exact market conditions.

Historical market data is invaluable for testing the fundamental behaviour of trading algorithms and rules. It is also important to remember that our trading strategies actually change market conditions. Each of our orders adds to the overall buying or selling pressure and so has an effect on both the market price and overall trading volume. Consequently, there is always some uncertainty about how the market will actually react to our orders.

Market impact and signalling risk are important factors, so for performance testing we need to try to simulate these effects. Though, as we saw in Chapter 10, accurately estimating market impact is non-trivial. Hence, simulators are often used to try to provide a realistic market for testing purposes. Any simulation must take into account competition from other participants and provide a realistic reaction to any test orders, whilst applying the same trade matching rules as the execution venue. Many of these will have been developed in-house, although increasingly vendors are offering exchange simulators that provide this.

The overall quality achieved using back-testing owes a lot to the accuracy of the market simulation. In Chapter 15, we will see how artificial intelligence is being used to try to make these simulations more accurate.

11.4 Other requirements

This chapter has mainly focussed on the technical requirements for implementing trading strategies. In order to successfully implement such strategies there are also some other important considerations: Generating thousands of electronic orders is all very well, but it could easily swamp the clearing and settlement department. Thus, it is vital to ensure that their infrastructure is able to cope with the potential load. In addition, trading platforms must adhere to the rules set out by the different execution venues that they use. So it is also important to audit them for regulatory compliance.

Clearing and settlement

The ultimate goal of any trading platform is to execute trades quickly and efficiently. Although getting an execution back from an exchange is only half the story, since settlement still needs to take place.

Electronic trading has led to markedly increased trading volumes, which could have swamped the clearing and settlement departments. Fortunately, the shift away from manual trading has helped streamline the process, since most (if not all) of the trade-related information may now be processed electronically. This has increased the accuracy and allowed clearing and settlement to become more highly automated.

Just as the FIX Protocol has proved invaluable as a means of linking trading platforms, it also offers solutions for post-trade reporting and settlement. Once an order has been completed, an `Execution Report` message may be sent, detailing how much was filled and the average price. The client may then send an `Allocation` message to specify the actual accounts that should be used for settlement. Alternatively, they can even include this pre-trade in their `New Order` message. Finally, the broker may issue `Confirmation` messages that confirm each trade allocation, as well as the fees, account/s and other settlement details. More details can be found on the FIX website (www.fixprotocol.org).

As with any other piece of infrastructure, for a trading platform to be successful it is important that all its components are well integrated. Hence, the appeal of common protocols, such as FIX, which provide a uniform messaging structure allowing straight-through processing (STP) from pre-trade right through to settlement.

Regulations compliance

Trading must abide by market regulations, whether it is carried out manually or electronically. There is also scope to prevent potential problems by ensuring that systems perform basic "sanity checks" to ensure that orders are reasonable. These may be enforced by management or by dedicated compliance departments.

One of the advantages of electronic (and algorithmic) trading is that it is much easier to implement a full audit trail, tracking any order placements, changes and resultant executions, than it is for manual execution. This makes it easier to find the cause of any issues, should they occur.

Sanity checks

Over the last few years, there have been several major instances of so-called "fat finger" trades. These are when someone accidentally enters an order with a ridiculous price or quantity, usually sending the asset's price spiralling downwards and resulting in the suspension of trading. It is important to ensure that there are systems and procedures in place to prevent such trades. This can be achieved by ensuring there are certain sanity checks to control orders':

- Price
- Size
- Value

If any of these are significantly different from the norm then they probably warrant checking. These validations might be placed within the order entry screen, the order management system or both.

Clearly, the limit price is an important benchmark. If it bears no relation to the current market price this may be due to an input error. Alternatively, it might reflect a problem with currency conversion, or even issues with the market data source. For stocks, there might also have been a stock split or dividend, so it might be based on an old price.

Order sizes may be compared to the average daily volume (ADV). An order size that is more than 50% of the ADV might be a typo, or at least should be discussed carefully with the broker/dealer since it will need special handling.

By determining the overall value of the order we can add an extra level of validation. For example, both the price and size might be reasonable; however, if a client generally sends orders no larger than $2 million then suddenly an order worth $20 million arrives it may be an error.

Note that all of these checks are based on market data, so for them to be meaningful it is vital that the prices are valid and up to date. Thus, it is important for the order management system to have monitoring in place to ensure that market data is reliable and there is no significant latency in updates. Similarly, an algorithmic trading platform is blind without data, so such monitoring is even more important for these.

Trading algorithms also often make use of historical data and analytics, so it is important to ensure that there are mechanisms in place to check the validity of these as well. Again, a good example is coping with the historical adjustments required for stock splits.

Market regulations

Traders must pass exams in order to trade on most organised exchanges. This ensures that they have a thorough knowledge of the rules and regulations associated with trading and settlement. For instance, they will need to be aware of the:

- Trading sessions, both continuous and auction, and opening and closing times
- Order types and conditions, and permitted combinations during each session
- Trading halts/suspensions and market-wide halts
- Reporting requirements
- Code of conduct

Clearly, these regulations must be followed whether the trader is on the floor of the exchange, sending orders from a screen or using a trading algorithm. Therefore, order management systems must also be aware of these rules. Ideally, they should be able to prevent any incorrect orders from being sent to the execution venue. Order entry screens should also be aware of these and try to make life easier for the trader by only offering the appropriate options and/or combinations.

Algorithmic trading platforms must also incorporate the appropriate rules and regulations within their logic. For example, they should certainly be aware of the different trading sessions, such as continuous trading or a call auction, and adjust accordingly. They must also be aware of any market halts, or delays in opening or closing the market. Again, should this happen they need to be able to adjust their strategy accordingly, or as a minimum they ought to flag that there has been an issue and they require attention or manual intervention. Some venues even stipulate that electronic and algorithmic trading platforms have to be able to be turned off during periods of market instability. There should also be processes in place to handle any technical problems, such as failure of a market data server or the link to the exchange.

It is also important to review the logic behind trading algorithms, in order to try to prevent any accidental breaches of market regulations. As an example, let's consider an algorithm which is some way behind its targets. In trying to be filled, it might place an aggressive order. Though, if the market has already moved substantially throughout the day this might be enough to tip the balance and trigger a price-based halt. Ideally, there ought to be price checks in place to prevent this. Again, it is essential to test how algorithms respond to such events.

Clearly, a full system audit is a time consuming process; however, it is important to check that systems are compliant. In general, market regulations do not usually change that frequently. Thus, compliance checks are mainly needed when trading platforms and algorithms expand to cater for new markets. That said, this can all change when the markets become volatile. A good example of this is the rapid change of regulations for short-sales during the 2007-09 financial crisis. Indeed, given the resultant market turmoil regulation is likely to increase. For instance, there is the possible reintroduction of some form of uptick [4] rule for U.S. equities. Therefore, testing and auditing is a process that must continually evolve in order to keep pace with changes in the world's markets.

11.5 Summary

- Order management plays an important role in any trading strategy, it comprises of:
  - Order entry, allowing specification of any necessary trade conditions or parameters
  - Order encoding, to convert the details into a format the target venue can use
  - Transmission of order-related information to and from the venue

- Order management (OMS) and execution management (EMS) systems provide an important front-end for managing orders, as well as offering functions like pre- and post-trade analytics. They also connect to back-end servers, which handle the order encoding and routing.

- The Financial Information Exchange (FIX) protocol offers a common messaging scheme for the exchange of any information related to securities transactions. It handles the transmission of orders, market data, security information and settlement details. FIX (5.0) supports equities, bonds, repos, FX spot, forwards, swaps and listed futures and options.

- Algorithmic trading and DMA are reliant on their implementation, they need easily accessible platforms that are stable and can deal with heavy loads. They should also be easily extendable to increase capacity and allow new functionality.

- Trading rules may be coded or scripted to respond to specific events, typically these are:
  - Market data, for prices and liquidity
  - Order notifications, for fills and changes in status

- Testing is a vital part of this process. Individual trading rules must be verified, but it is

---

[4] Until its removal in 2007 this meant that short sales could only be carried out after the price had moved upwards.

also important to see how they perform en-masse, as part of an algorithm. Replaying specific scenarios allows the performance of a range of different rules to be compared based on exactly the same conditions. Though, it is also always important to test against live market data. Hence, brokers generally use algorithms internally for a while before making them available to their clients.

- Clearing and settlement must also be considered; it is important to ensure they can cope with the trading volume from electronic and algorithmic trading.

- Trading platforms must also adhere to the rules set out by the different execution venues that they connect to, so it is essential to audit them for compliance.

Part IV

Advanced trading strategies

This final part of the book focuses on some of the more advanced techniques that are still at the cutting edge of algorithmic trading.

- Chapter 12 considers how algorithms may be used for trading portfolios. It also looks at the potential for portfolio-optimised algorithms that take account of portfolio risk and diversification.

- Chapter 13 introduces multi-asset trading and reviews many of the common cross-asset trading strategies. It highlights the additional factors that must be considered when creating algorithms for these.

- Chapter 14 examines the potential for incorporating news. This covers the various sources of information and the analytics used to create meaningful indicators. There is also a review of market reactions to news events.

- Chapter 15 shifts the focus to data mining and artificial intelligence (AI). This shows how they may be applied to enhance trading performance by mining for relationships and providing short-term predictions.

Hopefully, by the end of these four chapters you should have a good idea of some of the techniques that may be more commonly adopted in the not too distant future.

Chapter 12
Portfolios

Portfolio trading is not just about multi-tasking. Significant risk reductions can be achieved by tracking and managing portfolio risk.

12.1 Introduction

Portfolio trading provides investors with a cost-effective means of trading whole baskets of assets. This may be used to convert new cash flows, liquidate existing positions, or a combination of the two for portfolio rebalances. It may even be used to assist the transition of entire investment portfolios, also known as transition management.

Just as with single asset trading, portfolios are traded on either an agency or principal basis. Agency trades may simply be worked on "best efforts", or target benchmarks such as the VWAP or daily close. Principal trades are agreed for a specific strike time, at which point a snapshot of all the asset prices is taken. Quotes may be obtained from a number of brokers, although information leakage is obviously a key concern. Hence, trading may also be performed blind, in which case the broker is just given a description of the portfolio. This offers only an approximate value, number of assets, and factors such as weightings for the countries, indices and/or sectors. Clearly, with such blind trades the broker/s will tend to quote more conservatively to protect themselves from the additional uncertainty.

There are some hybrid trading types as well, namely incentive agency and guaranteed benchmark trades. An incentive agency trade means the broker's commission depends on the performance relative to the benchmark, whilst a guaranteed benchmark trade enforces a strict target that the broker must meet.

Portfolio trading is also an important tool for risk control and efficiency. Most brokers provide comprehensive pre-trade and real-time trading analytics, which allow investors to more precisely assess the impact of trading. This information may also be useful for their hedging strategies. Detailed post-trade analytics allow accurate performance measurement. The high level of automation associated with portfolio trading also enables the streamlining of post-trade allocation and settlement.

One of the key considerations when trading baskets of assets is portfolio risk. So we will start this chapter by reviewing this in more detail. Then after seeing how transaction cost analytics may be applied, we shall focus on optimal portfolio trading strategies. This includes techniques such as hedging and determining the optimal portfolio makeup. Finally, we will consider a how best to apply trading algorithms for executing portfolio trades.

12.2 Portfolio risk

A portfolio's return is the weighted sum of the returns for its constituent assets. So the associated portfolio's volatility is the standard deviation of these returns. Portfolio risk is somewhat harder to define. For the purposes of this book, we shall assume that this may be defined in terms of the portfolio volatility (σ_p) and an error term (ε):

$$Portfolio\ risk = \sigma_p + \varepsilon \qquad\qquad (12\text{-}1)$$

The error term reflects the uncertainty associated with any risk estimates. Given that portfolio volatility forms the basis for this risk, the two terms are often used interchangeably.

Another important concept closely linked to portfolio risk is diversification. This is a significant risk reduction that occurs when the individual risks in the portfolio offset one another. Diversification helps to reduce the overall volatility of a portfolio's value, and so ensure a more consistent performance. Often this may be achieved simply by increasing the number of assets in the portfolio. For example, Figure 12-1 shows a plot of risk for portfolios of various sizes.

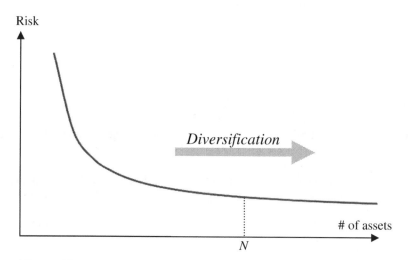

Figure 12-1 A comparison of risk between various sizes of portfolio

A study of stock portfolios by Burton Malkiel (2004) confirmed this effect. Although he found that the risk reduction soon became negligible once portfolios were larger than 15 stocks (equivalent to the point N in Figure 12-1). The key to achieving diversification is to group together assets that are uncorrelated. This means that price rises/drops will not affect all the assets in the portfolio uniformly. Thus, Malkiel (2004) found that portfolios containing international stocks had much lower risk than those concentrated on U.S. stocks.

Portfolio volatility

The relationship between portfolio volatility and that of its constituent assets is actually non-linear. So unlike the returns we cannot just determine it from the weighted sum of each asset's volatility. This was first pointed out by Harry Markowitz (1952) in his landmark paper "Portfolio Selection". He noted that each constituent's contribution to the overall portfolio risk depends on three key factors:

- its proportion/weight in the portfolio
- the variance of its returns
- the covariance of its returns with all other assets in the portfolio

Covariance is a measure of how much two variables vary together. [1]
Therefore, the portfolio volatility (σ_p) may be defined as:

$$\sigma_p = \sqrt{\sum_{i=1}^{n} \omega_i^2 Var(r_i) + \sum_{i \neq j} \omega_i \omega_j Cov(r_i, r_j)} \qquad (12\text{-}2)$$

where r_i is the return for constituent asset i and $Var(r_i)$ is its variance, ω_i and ω_j represent the weights of specific assets i and j and $Cov(r_i, r_j)$ is the covariance between their returns. Note that the covariance of a variable with itself equals its variance. We can further simplify equation 12-2 to:

$$\sigma_p = \sqrt{\sum_{j=1}^{n} \sum_{i=1}^{n} \omega_i \omega_j Cov(r_i, r_j)} \qquad (12\text{-}3)$$

The overall volatility (σ_p) of a simple portfolio with two equally weighted assets, which have corresponding volatilities σ_1 and σ_2, may be determined as:

$$\sigma_p = \sqrt{(0.5 * \sigma_1)^2 + (0.5 * \sigma_2)^2 + 2 \cdot (0.5 * 0.5) * Cov(1,2)} \qquad (12\text{-}4)$$

Example 12-1: Let's examine the risk for a range of portfolios based on different compositions of two sample assets. Asset EFG has a volatility of 40% whilst HIJ has one of 25%. The covariance between these assets is 0.05.

So a portfolio that is 100% EFG will have 40% volatility, whilst one based solely on HIJ will have 25%.

Based on equation 12-4 a portfolio with 50% of each stock has a volatility of:

$$\sigma_p = \sqrt{(0.5 * 0.40)^2 + (0.5 * 0.25)^2 + 2 * (0.5 * 0.5) * 0.05} = 28\%$$

In comparison, the weighted sum of asset volatilities is 32.5%.

This lower volatility is due to the low covariance between the two assets. In other words, the overall risk is reduced because they are not perfectly correlated. If we plot the actual portfolio risk for all the potential mixes, we get the curve shown in Figure 12-2. Based on this, the lowest portfolio volatility of 24.74% may be achieved for a basket comprising of about 10% EFG and 90% HIJ.

---

[1] A positive covariance between two variables means they behave similarly, so if one is higher than expected then it is likely the other one will be as well. Conversely, a negative covariance means that they behave in opposite fashions, so a high value for one implies a lower expected value for the other. A covariance of zero shows that the items are completely independent, so no inference may be made from either value. For more details on calculating covariance see Addendum A at the end of this chapter.

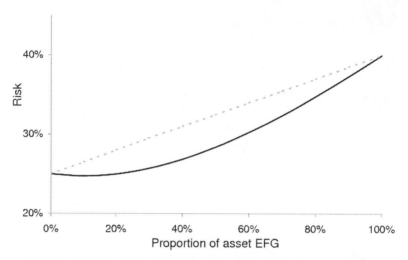

Figure 12-2 Portfolio risk for a range of portfolio compositions

The dotted line shown in Figure 12-2 marks the weighted averages for each portfolio composition. It corresponds to the risk that would be achieved if the two were 100% correlated.

The strength of the relationship between these two assets' returns may be quantified using a correlation coefficient (ρ). Essentially, this is their covariance divided by the product of their standard deviations, as outlined in Addendum A at the end of this chapter.

Using equation 12-9, we can determine the actual correlation (ρ) between these assets:

$$\rho_{i,j} = \frac{Cov(I,J)}{\sigma_i \sigma_j} = \frac{0.05}{0.40*0.25} = 50\%$$

Example 12-1 highlights the fact that the overall portfolio risk may be less than or equal to the weighted sum of the individual asset risks, and that this is largely due to the correlation between them. For instance, if the correlation between EFG and HIJ was zero the portfolio risk could be further reduced to around 20%.

Clearly, portfolios usually have more than just two constituents. Since they can in fact be quite large, matrices are often used to simplify the calculation of portfolio volatility. Thus an alternative notation for equation 12-3 is:

$$\sigma_p = \sqrt{w^T \Omega w} \qquad (12\text{-}5)$$

where Ω is the covariance matrix, w is the vector of asset weights and w^T is its transpose. The covariance matrix represents all the possible permuations across the portfolio, and for the purposes of this calculation is often expressed in terms of $/share. Note, for more details on how to construct a covariance matrix see Addendum A at the end of this chapter.

Example 12-2: Consider a simple portfolio with three assets. The portfolio is long 120 of asset ABC (volatility=0.245) and short 80 DEF (volatility=0.161) and 40 HIJ (volatility=0.387). The vector of asset weights (w) and the covariance matrix (Ω) are:

$$
w = \begin{pmatrix} 120 \\ -80 \\ -40 \end{pmatrix} \quad \Omega = \begin{pmatrix} 0.060 & 0.033 & 0.021 \\ 0.033 & 0.026 & 0.002 \\ 0.021 & 0.002 & 0.150 \end{pmatrix}
$$

Substituting these into equation 12-5, the expected portfolio volatility (in dollars) is:

$$
\sigma_p = \sqrt{\begin{pmatrix} 120 & -80 & -40 \end{pmatrix} \begin{pmatrix} 0.060 & 0.033 & 0.021 \\ 0.033 & 0.026 & 0.002 \\ 0.021 & 0.002 & 0.150 \end{pmatrix} \begin{pmatrix} 120 \\ -80 \\ -40 \end{pmatrix}} = \$21.17
$$

Consequently, our simple portfolio has an expected volatility of $21.17.

Note that it is important to remember that all of these are simply estimates. They rely on forecasts for the individual volatilities and correlations, which will usually be based on historical data. Their accuracy depends on how well these forecasts match reality. Hence the importance of the error term (ε) in equation 12-1.

Diversification

Diversification can result in a significant decrease in the overall portfolio risk, as we saw back in Figure 12-1. Indeed, its effect is probably best summed up by Burton Malkiel (2004) as the closest thing there is to a free lunch in finance.

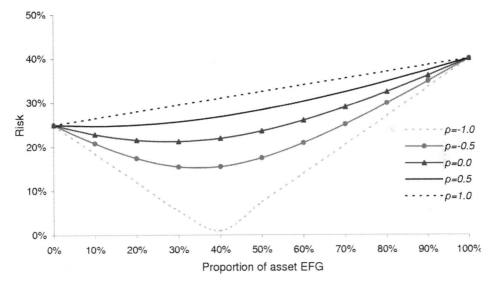

Figure 12-3 Portfolio risk for a range of different correlations

If we go back to our two-asset portfolio from Example 12-1, we can see how a lower correlation between the assets leads to a lower portfolio risk, as shown in Figure 12-3. This makes sense because with a correlation of -1.00 the price rise of one asset will be offset by an equivalent drop in the price of the other. In comparison, a correlation of 1.00 means that both prices will rise, so there is no implicit hedging.

Successful diversification relies on grouping together assets that are uncorrelated, so their covariance is zero. Therefore, price rises/drops will not affect all the assets in the portfolio uniformly, reducing the overall volatility of the portfolio and ensuring a more consistent performance. For example, correlation should be lower for stocks across different sectors, industries or countries.

Another way of visualizing the relationship between correlation and risk is shown in Table 12-1 which directly maps the correlation to the proportion of diversifiable risk which may be eliminated:

Intra-portfolio correlation	Percent of diversifiable risk eliminated
1.00	0.00
0.75	12.50
0.50	25.00
0.25	37.50
0.00	50.00
-0.25	62.50
-0.50	75.00
-0.75	87.50
-1.00	100.00

Source: Wikipedia (2006)

Table 12-1 The relationship between intra-portfolio correlation and the amount of diversifiable risk

This risk reduction may be harnessed to determine the optimal composition of portfolios, as Markowitz suggested. For each group of assets, the optimal composition may be discovered by altering the weightings of the constituents to find the solution with the lowest risk. This is effectively what we did in Example 12-1.

However, it is also important to take into account the returns for each asset; hence, we can plot a chart of risk versus returns for the various portfolio combinations. An example of this is shown in Figure 12-4, based on the assumption that the returns for assets EFG and HIJ are 10% and 5% respectively.

This type of portfolio risk curve is sometimes called a Markowitz efficient frontier. The shape of each curve is dependent on the correlation between the two assets: When the assets are perfectly correlated, the frontier forms a straight line. The curvature of this frontier increases as the assets become less correlated. Few assets exhibit perfect correlation, consequently diversification is possible. Note, few assets are perfectly negatively correlated either.

Decomposing portfolio risk

Portfolio risk may also be decomposed into simpler components, just as we did for transaction costs in Chapter 6. A common approach used for returns is the single factor model. This expresses returns in terms of an expected out-performance compared to a specific factor. In this case, the factor represents the performance of a key benchmark (or the market). Hence, the returns (r) may be expressed as:

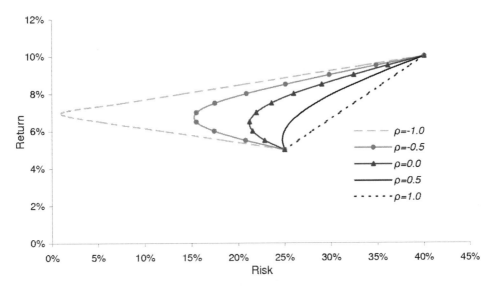

Figure 12-4 Example Markowitz efficient frontiers

$$r = \alpha + \beta\, r_B + \varepsilon$$

where α represents the out-performance, r_B is the benchmark (or market) return and ε is an independent error factor. The beta (β) factor determines how much impact the benchmark has on the overall returns. In comparison, the out-performance (α) and the error factor represent returns that are uncorrelated with the benchmark (or market).

A similar approach may be used to model the variance of these returns, or portfolio risk. Nadine Gottschalk (2003) shows that the variance may be represented as:

$$\sigma_i^2 = \beta_i^2 \sigma_B^2 + Var(\varepsilon) \tag{12-6}$$

where σ_B is the variance of the benchmark (or market) returns and $Var(\varepsilon)$ represents an independent error factor. So the portfolio risk may be broken down into two main components:

- a systematic benchmark (or market) risk
- a non-systematic or asset specific risk

The systematic (or market) risk represents the risk of a market move. Again, the beta factor determines how much impact this actually has on the overall portfolio, with higher betas implying more risk. Note that this also represents the baseline level of risk that may not be reduced by diversification. Although separate hedging strategies may still be used, for instance, trading futures to counteract the market risk.

The non-systematic (or specific) risk is actually the independent error factor in equation 12-6. It represents the risk that may be reduced by diversification.

Specific risk factors

Specific risk may in turn be broken down into a range of other common risk factors together with an asset specific residual risk. The common factors represent risks that may not be felt market-wide, but do exert an effect on specific groups of assets.

A common means of decomposing risk is to replace the single factor model with more complex multi-factor models. The study by Eugene Fama and Kenneth French (1993) is a well-known example of this. They analysed the returns for a mix of U.S. stocks and bonds (government and corporate). Overall, they found three common risks for stocks, namely the market and factors related to the firm size and book-to-market equity (which relates the firm's balance sheet value to its actual market value). For bonds, they noted common factors based on their maturity and default risk. Other common factors may correspond to the asset's country of issuance or currency; or for firms the industries or sectors with which they are most aligned. Hence, one way of viewing this breakdown of portfolio risk is shown in Figure 12-5.

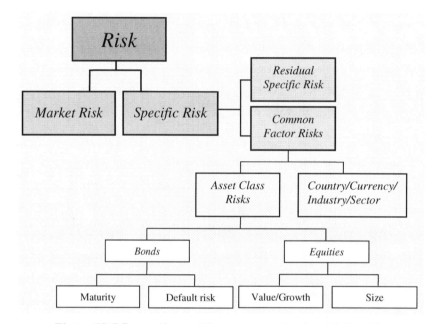

Figure 12-5 Separating out the components of portfolio risk

A nice illustration of the impact of some of these factors is provided by Ananth Madhavan and Jian Yang (2003). They analysed data from the annual reconstitution of the Russell indices, the results are shown in Figure 12-6. Overall, they note that in 2002 the active risk was more than 2% between the pre and post-reconstitution of the indices, based on market capitalisation. Whilst much of this risk was systematic or market risk, it is interesting to see how much was attributed other common factors. In particular, for both indices the style-based Value/Growth factor was extremely important. Similarly, it is worth noting just how small the asset specific residual risk can be: For the Russell 1000, we can see it was merely equal to the combined industry and sector risk.

Clearly, such risk breakdowns will be different for each portfolio, but as Figure 12-6 shows, the common risk factors can play a significant role and so should be considered rather than focussing solely on asset specific risk.

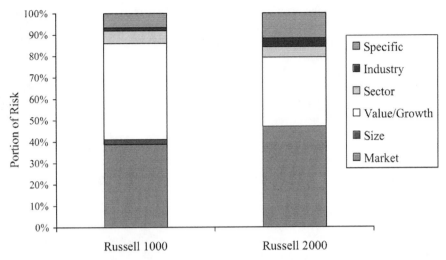

Figure 12-6 A breakdown of portfolio risk factors

Portfolio risk measures

Quantifying and tracking portfolio risk are vital in order to minimise it. A variety of risk measures are used in both pre and post-trade analytics. Some are even used during execution to track the ongoing performance. Based on the previous decomposition of risk, we can fairly easily divide portfolio risk into systematic (or market) and non-systematic (or specific) components.

Market risk may be tracked using the portfolio's overall beta coefficient, as we saw in equation 12-6. This allows us to quantify the level of non-diversifiable risk that we may need to hedge.

Tracking error provides a measure of how closely a portfolio follows a specific benchmark. If the benchmark corresponds to the market then the tracking error reflects the specific risk component. Thus, a high tracking error implies a considerable proportion of specific risk.

An alternative approach to risk measurement is offered by the marginal contribution to risk (MCR). This is measured for each constituent of a portfolio. It reflects how the overall portfolio risk might change if the position of a specific asset is increased. Therefore, the key to risk reduction is to target the constituents which have a high MCR.

Beta

The beta coefficient relates to the volatility of an asset's or portfolio's returns in comparison with the rest of the market. Essentially, it acts as a measure of the non-diversifiable market (or systematic) risk. A higher beta suggests greater volatility and so more risk.

The beta for an asset is based on the covariance of its returns with the market:

$$\beta_i = \frac{Cov(r_a, r_m)}{Var(r_m)} \qquad (12\text{-}7)$$

where r_a corresponds to the asset's returns and r_m represents those of the market. Hence, it is the ratio of the covariance of the two sets of returns divided by the variance of the market's returns. Note the market will often be represented by a key benchmark price, such as that of a major stock index.

For example, an asset (or portfolio) whose returns change in line with the market has a beta of 1. Thus, a 10% increase in the market will also mean a 10% increase for the asset, whilst a 10% decrease will lead to a similar drop. A beta of 2 means that the price swings are twice as rapid for the asset as the market, so a 10% rise in the market now leads to a 20% rise in the asset. Conversely, a beta of 0.5 means the sensitivity is halved, so a market fall of 10% only results in a drop by 5% for the asset. Assets with a negative beta actually move in the opposite direction to the market. For instance, during market crises the prices for precious metals often increase, so firms whose income is dependent on this can exhibit negative betas. A beta of zero is harder to find, this means there is absolutely no correlation between the two sets of returns.

Equation 12-7 may also be used to determine the beta of a portfolio, based on the covariance of the portfolio's returns with those of the market. Alternatively, we can determine the portfolio beta from the weighted average of the betas of its constituent assets. For each constituent the beta is determined from its covariance with the other portfolio members. Using the matrix based notation we can express this as:

$$\beta_i = \frac{\sum_{j=1}^{n} \Omega_{i,j} w_j}{\sigma_p^2}$$

where $\Omega_{i,j}$ is the covariance matrix, w_j is the weight of each asset (j) and σ_p^2 is the variance of the entire portfolio.

In theory, if we could construct a portfolio of assets with a beta of zero it would have no non-diversifiable risk. Consequently, we could use diversification to reduce the overall risk to a negligible amount. Realistically, though, most assets have some degree of correlation with each other.

Tracking error

Many portfolios are managed to a benchmark, such as an index. Passive funds will often aim to match the returns of a specific benchmark index, whilst active funds will try to outperform them. Tracking error provides a measurement of how closely a given portfolio follows the benchmark. Therefore, managers of passive index tracking portfolios will seek to minimise their tracking error. In general, tracking error is calculated from the standard deviation of the difference between the portfolio and index returns:

$$TE = \sqrt{\frac{\sum_{i=1}^{n} (R_P - R_B)^2}{N-1}}$$

where R_P represents the portfolio returns and R_B are those of the benchmark for N time periods. A high tracking error reflects a significant deviation from the benchmark. Essentially, it also reflects the active risk of a portfolio, which is a measurement more commonly adopted by active fund managers.

Marginal contribution to risk

The marginal contribution to risk (MCR) may be used by investors to determine the portfolio's risk sensitivity to a specific asset. It reflects the actual change in overall portfolio risk, so diversification is taken into account. Therefore, a comparatively risky asset may have a lower MCR than expected.

For any given portfolio the vector of marginal contributions to risk may be defined as:

$$MCR_i \equiv \frac{\partial \sigma_p}{\partial w_i} = \frac{(\Omega w)_i}{\sigma_p} = \frac{Cov(r_i, r_p)}{\sigma_p} \tag{12-8}$$

where Ω is the covariance matrix, w is the vector of asset weights, σ_p is the standard deviation of the entire portfolio and r_i and r_p are the returns of the asset (i) and the portfolio respectively.

Note that generally the MCR is measured by determining the effect of varying the existing position of the given asset by 1%. Thus, the standardized change in portfolio risk may simply be determined by dividing equation 12-8 by 100.

Based on the similarity with equation 12-7 we can also express the MCR in terms of the asset's beta:

$$\frac{\partial \sigma_p}{\partial w_i} = \beta_i \cdot \sigma_p$$

So, the MCR is equivalent to a beta adjusted portfolio risk. Traders cannot vary the contents of a trade list; however, they can use the MCR as a guideline for how trading will affect the residual risk, as Robert Kissell and Morton Glantz (2003) point out. If a particular asset has a high MCR then trading it more quickly will help reduce the overall risk. Conversely, assets with negative MCRs actually act as natural hedges; therefore, it makes sense to trade these more slowly to prolong this benefit.

12.3 Transaction cost analysis for portfolios

Portfolio risk and diversification mean that transaction cost analysis is slightly more complicated when dealing with portfolios. In the following sections, we will briefly consider how the cost estimates we saw in Chapter 10 may be extended to deal with this.

Market impact

Market impact costs are additive, therefore the market impact calculation for a portfolio is just a case of summing all the constituent impacts. Using the Kissell and Glantz (2003) market impact model, we can express the market impact cost for a portfolio of m stocks as:

$$MI = \sum_{i=1}^{m} \sum_{j=1}^{n} \frac{0.95 x_{ij}^2 I_i}{X_i * (x_{ij} + 0.5 v_{ij})} + \sum_{i=1}^{m} \sum_{j=1}^{n} \frac{0.05 x_{ij} I_i}{X_i}$$

where I_i is the instantaneous impact cost, X_i is the total order size for each asset and for each period j the order size is represented by x_{ij} whilst v_{ij} is the expected volume. Though easy to compute, the additive nature also means that market impact costs are not reduced by portfolio diversification. So impact costs are an important consideration for portfolios.

Timing Risk

Just as in Chapter 6, timing risk for portfolios may still be split into separate price and liquidity risks. The price risk is based on the portfolio risk of the remaining positions. From equation 12-5 Robert Kissell and Roberto Malamut (2005b) define the price risk for a portfolio as:

$$\sigma(x_j) = \sqrt{\sum_j r_j^T C r_j}$$

where r_j is the vector of residual portfolio positions that are left to be traded for each period j, and C is the covariance matrix in $/share.

Liquidity risk represents the risk that our market impact estimations will be inaccurate due to unexpected market volumes. By assuming that any liquidity surprises are uncorrelated, Kissell and Glantz (2003) are able to base liquidity risk on the variance of their temporary market impact function. So, for any given asset the liquidity risk may be defined as $\sigma(h(x))$:

$$\sigma(h(x)) = \sqrt{\sigma^2 \left(\frac{I}{X} \sum_j \frac{x_j^2}{(x_j + 0.5v_j)} \right)}$$

where I is the instantaneous market impact, X is the total order size and for each period j the order size is represented by x_j whilst v_j is the expected volume.

Across an entire portfolio, the liquidity risk may be represented as the sum of these individual risks:

$$\sigma(x_j) = \sqrt{\sum_i \sigma^2(h(x_j))}$$

So as a whole, the portfolio timing risk may be expressed as:

$$\Re(x_j) = \sqrt{\sum_j r_j^T C r_j + \sum_i \sigma^2(h(x_j))}$$

Thus, the main difference to the portfolio volatility examples we saw in section 12.2 is the addition of liquidity risk. This is covered in some more detail in Kissell and Glantz (2003).

12.4 Optimal portfolio trading

In Chapter 7, we noted that achieving an optimal trading strategy requires us to meet the investor's specified trading objectives, which may be to:
- Minimize the expected cost for a given level of risk
- Achieve price improvement over a given level of cost
- Balance the trade-off between expected cost and risk

The same principles apply for portfolio trading with the added complication of trying to maximise diversification, and so minimise the portfolio risk. Again, the set of optimal trading strategies is represented by the efficient trading frontier. This may be found by solving the following optimisation for the expected cost ($E(x)$):

$$\min_{x}(E(x)+\lambda V(x))$$

where $V(x)$ corresponds to the expected risk and λ is represents the level of risk aversion. To find the optimal solutions, mean-variance optimization techniques can help minimise the expected impact cost, whilst covariance or multi-factor risk models may be used to provide the expected portfolio risk.

That said, when trying to minimise the expected cost for a given level of risk, the optimal solutions are a constantly moving target. This is because the portfolio risk is based on the residual trading positions, and so it must be re-evaluated each time the portfolio changes. Hence, each change requires the creation of a new efficient trading frontier, from which the minimum cost may then be targeted. Consequently, the minimum impact costs will vary over time. So to maintain the same level of risk we may have to alter the pattern of our trading, as shown by the sample path in Figure 12-7.

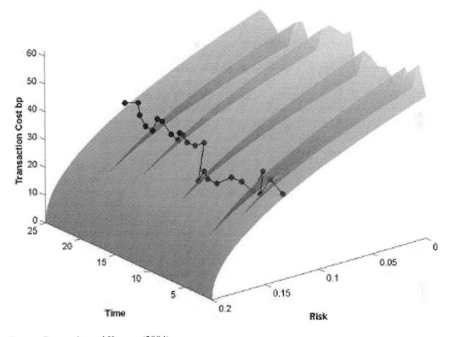

Source: Domowitz and Krowas (2004)
Reproduced with permission from ITG Inc. and Institutional Investor

Figure 12-7 Tracking portfolio risk and cost over time

Likewise, achieving price improvement over a given level of cost faces the same problem. Effectively, both these goals now have to dynamically balance the trade-off between expected cost and portfolio risk. For example, from a cost perspective it may make sense to aggressively trade one of the assets. However, if this was acting as a natural hedge for the residual portfolio (a negative MCR) then the reduced diversification may lead to a significant increase in portfolio risk. Therefore, we need to determine which effect is more important and act accordingly.

Thus, finding the optimal trading strategy for a portfolio requires both cost-based execution models and techniques from portfolio optimisation. Increasingly, these are converging to provide dedicated portfolio execution models.

Additional goals for portfolio trading

Portfolio risk may be decomposed into a range of different factors, as we saw in Figure 12-5. Thus, portfolio managers may also track risk in terms of its market or asset specific components. So they may consider issues such as country, currency or sector risk. Alternatively, they might focus on minimising the tracking error for their fund. Therefore, investors often adopt a range of additional strategies to try to minimise risk for their portfolios, such as:

- Cash balancing
- Beta/Market neutrality
- Sector/Country neutrality
- Minimising index tracking error

The easiest of these approaches is cash balancing, which just balances the value of the long and short positions, making the portfolio cash neutral. Still, this can leave exposure to market risk. Therefore, market neutral hedging tries to ensure that the net beta of the portfolio is zero. Similarly, even market neutral portfolios may still be exposed to considerable risk from other common risk factors; hence, sector/country neutrality may be targeted. Each of these approaches requires careful balancing of the various groups. This also applies for tracking error, where a portfolio may be divided into the assets that help or hinder the index tracking. Clearly, if multiple goals are required this balancing act can become even more complicated; hence, it may be useful to prioritise them.

The portfolio manager needs to control the risk for the entire investment portfolio. This also includes the basket of assets that have been sent for trading. Brokers/traders may also need to be able to support these additional goals when trading portfolios. Otherwise, during the trading/transition process the investment portfolio could be exposed to unnecessary risk, particularly if trading spans days or even weeks. These goals may also enhance the overall performance. So, not only do portfolio trading strategies need to balance impact costs with portfolio risk, they may also need to take account of any such additional requirements.

Hedging

Incorporating hedging requirements into a portfolio trading strategy can pose some difficulties. We need to strike the right balance between enforcing the hedging and allowing the constituent orders to trade optimally.

Essentially, this is similar to what we saw for the pair trading strategy, except that it can involve multiple groups. For instance, if the executed value for one group starts to lag behind then we may need to either:

- Trade more aggressively for that group
- Slow down trading for the other group(s)

As a simple example, let's consider the following cash balanced trade list shown in Table 12-2, essentially we can view this as a three-asset portfolio. As long as we manage to trade each asset in line with each other, we should maintain this natural hedging. Thus, for the first period (t_1) we can issue 10% of each target position as a limit order.

Let's assume that by the end of this period only the orders for ABC and XYZ have completed, so the limit order for 50 HJK is still unfilled (or extant).

Side	Asset	Price	Target	Position at t_1	
				Sent	*Filled*
Buy	ABC	31	500	50	50
	HJK	31	500	50	0
Sell	XYZ	31	1,000	100	100
			Net	0	-50

Table 12-2 A simple two-sided trading portfolio

So by the end of the first period our rudimentary hedging has already broken down. To remedy this we could:

1.   Wait for the buy order for HJK to complete before placing more orders.
2.   Convert the remaining buy to a more aggressive limit or market order.

Option 1 could prove to be expensive if the more liquid assets ABC and XYZ have unfavourable price trends. Effectively, we have stalled trading until the illiquid asset catches up, exposing ourselves to timing risk for the other constituents. Likewise, option 2 could also prove to be expensive, since we may simply not be able to buy any HJK within acceptable price limits. The cost of catching up, to become cash neutral again, could actually outweigh the benefits of hedging.

In this case, because we are only striving to be cash neutral, a possible short-term solution to this problem is to make up the balance by additionally buying another 50 of the more liquid ABC. Though, for more complex hedging requirements such an approach may not always be possible.

A common solution is to incorporate a legging value, much as we saw for pair trading. This allows one of the groups (in this case one side of the portfolio) to lag the other/s by a specific amount. This gives the trading strategy some breathing space before any remedial action is taken to enforce the hedging requirements. Otherwise, we could potentially miss out on good trading opportunities for some assets just because an order for a less liquid asset is struggling.

Note that if there is a significant mismatch in the liquidity of the portfolio constituents then cost effective hedging may be difficult to achieve. In some cases, it may well be worth handling the more illiquid assets separately. This highlights the importance of pre-trade analysis, to spot any such potential issues and determine how much of a problem they might pose before trading commences.

Cash balancing

Cash balancing obviously only applies for two-sided portfolios. The aim is to stay "dollar neutral" so that the two sides offset one another. Essentially, the proceeds from selling cover the costs of the purchases.

We have already seen a simple example of cash balancing, back in Table 12-2. Another example of a cash balanced trade list is shown in Table 12-3. The buy and sell sides are already balanced so we can split off child orders for the first period based on a percentage of their value. For the buy side, we have simply assigned the target for the first period as 10% of the position, as shown in the column labelled target (*Tgt*). Whilst for the sell side, the target quantities have been assigned slightly more randomly. This allows us to take into account factors such as short-term liquidity or favourable prices. Though, in terms of remaining cash neutral, the sum of our target sell side positions still meets our target.

Buys

Asset	Prc	Pos	Tgt	Value
ABC	30	1,200	120	3,600
DEF	40	500	50	2,000
GHI	60	800	80	4,800
JKL	50	600	60	3,000
MNO	80	200	20	1,600
Σ				15,000

Sells

Asset	Prc	Pos	Tgt	Value
PQR	20	1,300	104	2,080
STU	30	700	84	2,520
VWX	70	600	66	4,620
YZA	40	400	32	1,280
BCD	90	500	50	4,500
Σ				15,000

Table 12-3 Example trading targets to maintain a cash balanced portfolio

Market prices change constantly, so it is unlikely to achieve perfect cash balancing simply by trading percentages. Adjustments will need to be made based on real time price changes. Though, it is impractical to constantly change the size of extant orders; particularly for venues where this would result in a loss of priority on the order book, or those that charge for order updates. Hence, strategies may incorporate minimum limits to ensure that the price change is large enough to warrant changing the orders.

This approach may also be used for portfolios that are not actually cash balanced. For instance, we could modify the trading strategy to bias the trading rates for the buy and sell sides to try to improve the balance. If the portfolio was net long, we could trade the buy side more aggressively until it balanced with the sell side. However, for very unbalanced portfolios Anna Bystrik and Richard Johnson (2005) suggest that it may be worth trading each side separately, since risk management techniques tend to be more effective for balanced portfolios.

Market-neutrality

A portfolio is typically said to be market-neutral if its net beta is zero. In other words, the portfolio returns must be uncorrelated with the market. This approach is popular with fund managers since it means general market risk is minimised, leaving them only exposed to the specific risks that they are focussed on.

Therefore, when trying to maintain a market-neutral approach the assets with a higher beta will often be traded faster than those with a lower one. For example, let's consider the trade list shown in Table 12-4.

Buys

Asset	Prc	β	Position	β-wgt	Target	Residual Position	Residual Mkt Val	Residual β-wgt
ABC	30	2.0	1,200	0.480	480	720	21,600	0.384
DEF	40	1.0	500	0.133	100	400	16,000	0.142
GHI	60	1.5	800	0.480	240	560	33,600	0.448
JKL	50	0.5	600	0.100	60	540	27,000	0.120
MNO	80	0.5	200	0.053	20	180	14,400	0.064
Σ				1.247			112,600	1.157

Table 12-4 Example buy trading targets to maintain a market neutral portfolio

Assets ABC and GHI have the highest betas, combined with their relative positions this means they contribute most to the overall net beta, as can be seen in the beta weight (β-wgt) column.

As a baseline, we can trade 20% of each of the assets in the next period. Though, this will do nothing to alleviate the relative beta imbalance. A simple way of changing this is to adjust this proportion by each asset's beta, so we actually trade 40% of ABC and only 10% of JKL. If these fully execute this leaves residual positions with a significantly lower net beta, as shown in Table 12-4. So it should reduce by around 8% from 1.247 to 1.157.

Although this simple beta adjustment works for single-sided trade lists (or portfolios), we need to be more careful with two-sided ones. For example, let's now assume that the sells shown in Table 12-5 represent the other half of our list.

Sells						Residual		
Asset	Prc	β	Position	β-wgt	Target	Position	Mkt Val	β-wgt
PQR	20	1.5	1,300	0.260	390	910	18,200	0.243
STU	30	0.8	700	0.112	112	588	17,640	0.126
VWX	70	1.3	600	0.364	156	444	31,080	0.360
YZA	40	1.5	400	0.160	120	280	11,200	0.150
BCD	90	1.2	500	0.360	120	380	34,200	0.365
Σ				1.256			112,320	1.243

Table 12-5 Example sell trading targets to maintain a market neutral portfolio

Using the same beta adjusted approach we can reduce the net beta for this side to 1.243. The reduction is less marked because unlike the buys the betas are more evenly balanced.

This simple approach results in a buy side with a net beta of 1.157 and a sell side with 1.243. The market values are virtually the same; though, our residual list is still more exposed to market risk on the sell side. So it is important to also consider the net beta when handling two-sided lists/portfolios.

A different approach might be to trade 20% of the buy side, maintaining its net beta as 1.247. Whilst on the sell side the beta-adjusted approach may be used, reducing it to 1.243. Alternatively, we could also use a scaling factor to trade more of the higher beta assets on the sell side, to try to address the imbalance.

Categorised neutrality

Portfolios may also have substantial exposure to common factors, such as country, currency or sector risk. To reduce this we can try to trade the portfolio in such a way as to neutralise these risk factors.

For instance, Table 12-6 shows the country assignments for our example trade list, using the ISO Country codes for France (FR), Germany (DE) and the U.K. (GB). The net balances are shown in Table 12-7. Notice that the buys and sells are reasonably balanced, although there is more net exposure to U.K. assets than the other countries. Again, we shall aim to trade 10% of this list in the next period. To try to reduce the country risk we can bias trading towards the side that is largest for each country. So for the U.K., the focus will be on reducing the $42,000 worth of assets to sell, whilst for France and Germany the focus will be on reducing the buys. Similarly, since the U.K. has the largest net imbalance we should also target these assets more than the others.

Buys

Asset	Prc	Ctry	Position	Mkt Val	Target	Residual Position	Residual Mkt Val
ABC	30	FR	1,200	36,000	90	1,110	33,300
DEF	40	GB	500	20,000	54	446	17,840
GHI	60	DE	800	48,000	88	712	42,720
JKL	50	FR	600	30,000	52	548	27,400
MNO	80	GB	200	16,000	28	172	13,760
Σ				150,000			135,020

Sells

Asset	Prc	Ctry	Position	Mkt Val	Target	Residual Position	Residual Mkt Val
PQR	20	FR	1,300	26,000	38	1,262	25,240
STU	30	FR	700	21,000	26	674	20,220
VWX	70	GB	600	42,000	150	450	31,500
YZA	40	FR	400	16,000	18	382	15,280
BCD	90	DE	500	45,000	25	475	42,750
Σ				150,000			134,990

Table 12-6 Example trading targets to aim for a category neutral portfolio

One way of assigning the target trades is to base them purely on the imbalances. Given a sum total of $30,000 for both buys and sells, we can assign half of this to redress the balance for U.K. assets, whilst the remainder is split evenly between France and Germany.

The net imbalances may then be used as a starting point, assigning this to the side that has the greatest value. The residual may then be split evenly between buys and sells. Hence, for the U.K. $6,000 will target sells, leaving $9,000 to split between them. So our target values are $4500 for U.K. buys and $10,500 for sell orders. The remaining target values are shown in Table 12-7.

Ctry	Market Value Buys	Sells	Net	Target Value Buys	Sells	Residual Value Buys	Sells	Net
DE	48,000	45,000	3,000	5,250	2,250	43,200	43,200	0
FR	66,000	63,000	3,000	5,250	2,250	59,400	59,250	150
GB	36,000	42,000	-6,000	4,500	10,500	32,400	32,550	-150

Table 12-7 Net balances for a category neutral portfolio

Since the list is cash balanced, we will also try to preserve this, as there is no point introducing additional risks. In this example, the target buys and sells still add up to $15,000 so there is no need to make any more changes.

Finally, we now need to convert the target balances into target shares for each of the assets. For simplicity, we shall evenly assign them for each country, although factors such as liquidity or price trends could also be taken into account. Adjustments could also be made to ensure quantities are rounded to meet their lot sizes. Sample target quantities are shown in Table 12-6.

Provided we manage to trade these targets, we can see from Table 12-7 that the net values for the residual list will be almost zero. Though, the need to balance other requirements means that the category imbalances will often be reduced more gradually than this. Also, note that exactly the same principles may be used for other common factors such as currency or sector risk.

Minimising tracking error

Tracking error relates the portfolio returns to those of a specific benchmark. An alternative way of viewing this is to say that a portfolio with a minimal tracking error should have a net beta of 1.0. In other words, the performance of the portfolio exactly matches its benchmark, so changes in value are inline with each other.

We have also seen how adjustments could be made to try to achieve a net beta of 0.0 for market neutral portfolios. A similar approach may be used to minimise tracking error, except the target net beta is now 1.0. So again, we target the constituents with the highest beta weights, as we saw in Table 12-4.

Minimising the overall portfolio risk

We can also seek to minimise the overall portfolio risk based on the matrix formation we saw in equation 12-5. By using the first derivative of this equation, we can try to find a possible minimum:

$$\frac{\partial(Risk)}{\partial w} = \frac{w^T \Omega}{\sqrt{w^T \Omega w}} = 0 \;\; \Rightarrow w^T \Omega = 0$$

where Ω is the covariance matrix, w is the vector of asset weights and w^T is its transpose. Kissell and Glantz (2003) find that solving this for w yields:

$$w_{optimal} = A * B * w$$

where A and B are the following matrix operations:

$$A = \text{-}inverse(diagonal(\Omega))$$
and
$$B = \Omega + inverse(A)$$

They stress the fact that this solution is only valid for the execution of a single asset. The resultant position change will affect the whole portfolio's risk, so for each subsequent trade a fresh solution must be recalculated.

As an example, let's reuse the portfolio and covariance matrix from Example 12-2:

$$w = \begin{pmatrix} 120 \\ -80 \\ -40 \end{pmatrix} \quad \Omega = \begin{pmatrix} 0.060 & 0.033 & 0.021 \\ 0.033 & 0.026 & 0.002 \\ 0.021 & 0.002 & 0.150 \end{pmatrix}$$

We can then use the appropriate matrix operations to determine the product:

$$A * B * w = \begin{pmatrix} 0.000 & -0.550 & -0.350 \\ -1.269 & 0.000 & -0.077 \\ -0.140 & -0.013 & 0.000 \end{pmatrix} \begin{pmatrix} 120 \\ -80 \\ -40 \end{pmatrix} = \begin{pmatrix} 58 \\ -149 \\ -16 \end{pmatrix} \Rightarrow v = \begin{pmatrix} 62 \\ 69 \\ -24 \end{pmatrix}$$

This implies that the optimal weightings are 58 of asset ABC, -149 of DEF and -16 of HIJ. Given our current positions, this implies the vector v, which represents the possible transitions to reach this optimal state. Note that we cannot trade any DEF since the optimal position of -149 lies outside our permitted range. Thus, we may sell 62 of ABC or buy 24 HIJ.

Using equation 12-5, we can now apply each of these potential positions to confirm which gives the lowest risk. For example, inputting the values for ABC gives:

$$\sigma_p = \sqrt{(58 \quad -80 \quad -40)\begin{pmatrix} 0.060 & 0.033 & 0.021 \\ 0.033 & 0.026 & 0.002 \\ 0.021 & 0.002 & 0.150 \end{pmatrix}\begin{pmatrix} 58 \\ -80 \\ -40 \end{pmatrix}} = \$14.74$$

Trading ABC reduces the portfolio risk to $14.74 whereas trading HIJ only reduces it to $18.97. Therefore, the optimal trade is to sell 62 shares of ABC.

As we saw back in Figure 12-7, the optimal solution when trying to minimise the expected cost for a given level of risk is a constantly moving target. Each trade changes the overall portfolio composition and so the overall risk. Therefore, to find the next optimal trades we must simply keep repeating this process until the execution is complete.

12.5 Portfolio trading with algorithms

Conventional trading algorithms may easily be used for trading portfolios, although clearly there are complications when trading lists that span multiple markets, currencies and/or time zones.

Another important consideration is how the chosen trading strategies affect portfolio risk, or achieve any of the other specific goals covered in the previous section. Standard single asset algorithms have no inbuilt mechanisms to accommodate this. Therefore, we will also look at some methods for tailoring algorithms to cope with these requirements.

Portfolio trading with standard trading algorithms

In general, any of the single asset trading algorithms we saw in Chapter 5 may be used for portfolio trading. A trading list might comprise of tens, or even hundreds of assets, which might be buys, sells or a mixture of the two. These may all be traded with a single algorithm, targeting a benchmark such as VWAP or their arrival price. Alternatively, they might be for a range of different algorithms, depending on the relative difficulty of each order. The trading algorithms might be specified by the investor, or determined by the broker/dealer.

Can "one size fit all"?

When choosing trading algorithms for portfolios we should first consider whether a single algorithm is appropriate for all the constituents of the trading list. An interesting example is given by Ian Domowitz and Henry Yegerman (2005a) from ITG. This is based on a large portfolio transition that was benchmarked using the daily VWAP for each asset. The strategy resulted in transaction costs that were approximately double the estimate from pre-trade analysis. By analysing the volatility and order sizes of the constituents, they concluded that costs might have been reduced by adopting differing trading strategies, rather than a "one size fits all" approach. This is illustrated in Figure 12-8.

To find a better alternative they classified the orders into three main groups, based on each asset's volatility and the relative size of the order compared to the average daily volume (ADV). At the two extremes, they found small orders for volatile assets and large orders for assets with a much lower volatility.

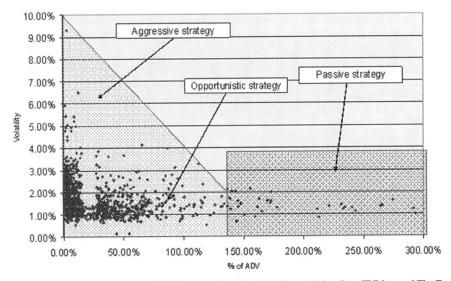

Source: Domowitz and Yegerman (2005a)   Reproduced with permission from ITG Inc. and The Trade

Figure 12-8 Volatility versus percentage of ADV

As we saw in Chapter 7, volatile assets suit a more aggressive trading style, countering the associated timing risk. This is also helped by the small order size, which means lower market impact costs. Hence, Domowitz and Yegerman proposed an aggressive strategy for such orders. For example, we might use an implementation shortfall algorithm.

Conversely, for the larger orders a more passive approach makes sense, to try to reduce the overall market impact. Similarly, since the volatility of these assets is lower, the price risk will not be as significant. So a VWAP over the whole day may be an appropriate choice. That said, timing risk comprises of both price risk and liquidity risk, so liquidity can also be a considerable factor for large orders, as Domowitz and Yegerman point out. Thus, opportunistic trading may also be appropriate, depending on the uncertainty of the transaction cost estimates. Those orders, which are more than 40% of the ADV trading, may span multiple days. In such cases, a more aggressive strategy may be suitable for the first day, followed by more passive trading on any subsequent days.

Between these two extremes are orders that may be suitable for more opportunistic trading. In terms of trading algorithms, this might range from a VWAP with a short horizon, a percent of volume or a price inline. Alternatively, an implementation shortfall or even a liquidity-based algorithm might be used. The choice also depends on other factors such as investor risk aversion, liquidity and price momentum.

Standard trading algorithms and portfolio risk

Clearly, trading algorithms designed for executing single assets have no consideration of portfolio risk. They are solely focussed on optimising the execution of their individual orders. So the trader handling the list will have to do this manually. They may decide to split it into waves (or slices), each weighted to try to maintain the diversification. Alternatively, the riskier assets might be handled first; so trading algorithms may also be selected based on whether they are optimal for the portfolio as a whole, rather than for a specific order.

Only the simplest schedule-driven approaches, such as TWAP, provide a consistency of trading across the whole portfolio. For instance, if all the orders are traded using TWAP, we know that halfway through trading we should have 50% of the desired positions for each and every constituent.

In comparison, using more dynamic algorithms will often lead to a shift in the portfolio composition as they are traded. For example, Figure 12-9 shows how different the resultant trading schedules can be for a range of orders using an implementation shortfall (IS) algorithm (in this case Instinet's Wizard algorithm).

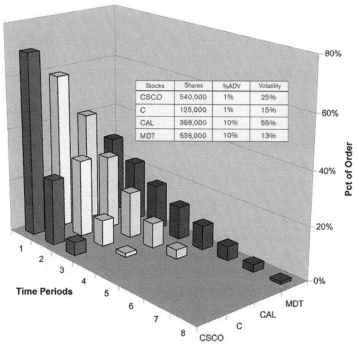

Figure 12-9 Example implementation shortfall schedules

Since the implementation shortfall algorithm is trying to adopt the optimal trading strategy for each order, the resultant trading patterns are clearly very different. The larger orders (in terms of percentage of ADV) are allowed longer to trade to reduce the market impact, whilst a more aggressive approach is taken for the volatile assets to reduce timing risk. So, for this example, the relatively small orders for Cisco (CSCO) and Citigroup (C) should complete first, with the more volatile Cisco traded fastest. Next to complete should be the order for Continental Airlines (CAL), whose high volatility means that aggressive trading is required. Finally, the order for Medtronic (MDT) takes the longest, since its relatively low volatility allows the order to be traded more passively.

Taken in turn, each of these schedules may well be the optimal trading strategy for the corresponding order. Still, this does not necessarily mean it is the best trading strategy for the portfolio as a whole. Diversification is heavily dependent on portfolio makeup. So a significant change in the relative portfolio positions could lead to a considerable shift in the portfolio risk. For instance, let's compare the example portfolio in Figure 12-9 between time periods 1 and 3. Initially, the largest outstanding position is for Cisco, followed by Medtronic, Continental Airlines and finally Citigroup. By following the target schedules, at the start of period 3 the position for Cisco has fallen to be only the third largest position, just above Citigroup. So the residual portfolio is now dominated by Medtronic and Continental Airlines. Hence, the overall portfolio risk may be very different between these two periods.

Unsurprisingly, this problem is not unique to shortfall-based algorithms. Other trading algorithms will also face this issue, since trading is unlikely to be evenly balanced across the portfolio. In particular, this concerns dynamic algorithms that are driven by market conditions. It also affects schedule-driven algorithms like VWAP, since there is no guarantee that the volume profiles for the various assets will be similar enough to preserve the portfolio mix. Illiquid assets will also lag behind more actively traded ones. Again, this could reduce the overall diversification. Thus, a more aggressive trading strategy may be necessary to compensate for this.

Note that this issue is not just restricted to algorithm choice. A similar problem arises for portfolios that span multiple countries. Although marketplaces such as Europe are becoming more uniform, there can still be slight differences in market open and close times. Thus, some orders might begin trading before others, causing an imbalance. Explicit start and end times may be set to prevent this, although this obviously reduces the potential trading horizon. Things become even more complex for truly global portfolios where the time-zone differences make simultaneous trading difficult (if not impossible). For instance, during the European morning just after the Asian markets have closed and before the U.S. have opened.

However, maintaining a consistently weighted portfolio is not necessarily the best way to minimise portfolio risk. In fact, all it does is ensure that the portfolio risk stays consistent. Instead, we need to evaluate each order to determine how much it contributes to the overall risk. To minimise this overall risk we therefore need to focus on reducing the positions of those assets that contribute the most. Also, note that the largest risk contributors will not necessarily be the orders for the riskiest assets, since natural hedging will occur between the assets in the portfolio. So instead of selecting the optimal algorithm based on the specific order requirements we should try to determine the best approach for the entire portfolio.

Tailoring algorithms for portfolio trading

Customising trading algorithms to incorporate portfolio risk makes a lot of sense. Although hedging requirements can prove quite complex, the potential risk reduction and related cost savings can be substantial.

Extending existing trading algorithms to incorporate portfolio models has been a typical (and logical) solution. As demand grows, some vendors are also creating sophisticated new algorithms, designed from the ground up to cater for portfolio trading.

An alternative approach is offered by Robert Kissell, Andrew Freyre-Sanders and Carl Carrie (2005). They describe an "algorithm of algorithms" which manages the portfolio trading requirements whilst individual algorithms may still be used for each constituent order. The macro/micro-level split is similar to the division of labour we adopted between trading algorithms and execution tactics in Chapter 5. This offers the prospect of reusing existing single asset trading algorithms to provide a wide variety of trading styles.

In the following sections, we shall outline these two main approaches in some more detail. As the market for algorithmic portfolio trading grows, it will be interesting to see what other variants appear in the future.

Algorithms incorporating portfolio risk models

We can incorporate portfolio risk models into trading algorithms by extending existing algorithms or by creating new portfolio specific algorithms from scratch. Either way, shortfall-based algorithms, with their inbuilt cost models, provide a good starting point.

The core of any such approach is a centralised portfolio risk model. One way of achieving this is to have the algorithm for each constituent asset tracking a combination of its own market impact model together with this shared portfolio risk model. Thus, each algorithm is able to make decisions that take into account all the other current portfolio positions. Correlations between the assets may also be used to find natural hedges, and so maximise diversification. Adjustments may be made to try to preserve these relationships, minimising the overall portfolio risk. Since the portfolio risk must be re-evaluated as positions change, this also allows traders to take advantage of other opportunities, such as blocks from crossing networks.

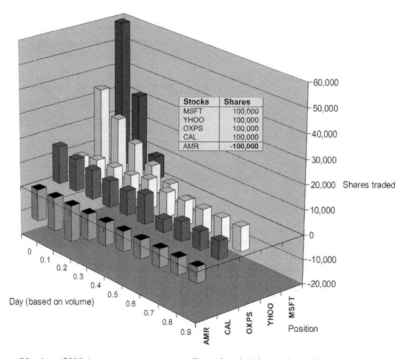

Source: ©Instinet (2006a)   Reproduced with permission from Instinet

Figure 12-10 Example portfolio optimised implementation shortfall schedules

For instance, Figure 12-10 shows an example two-sided portfolio, each order is traded in parallel using a portfolio optimised implementation shortfall algorithm (in this case Instinet's Wizard PRO [2] which incorporates Northfield Information Services' short-term factor risk model). Each algorithm adjusts its own optimal strategy based on correlations with the other constituents in order to help minimise the overall portfolio risk.

---

[2] Note Instinet's Wizard PRO has since been replaced with their Portfolio IS algorithm.

In this example, the two airline stocks, Continental Airlines (CAL) and the AMR Corporation (AMR), are highly correlated. Hence, these orders actually act as effective hedges for each other since both CAL and AMR have similar prices and we are buying and selling equivalent amounts. The risk reduction achieved from this hedging allows us to trade them more passively, despite them being reasonably volatile stocks. As we can see in Figure 12-10, the trading for both orders is spread throughout the day, helping to reduce their market impact.

A similar level of correlation exists between Microsoft (MSFT) and Yahoo (YHOO). Though, since these are both buy orders the resultant sector concentration could actually increase the potential portfolio risk. Thus, both of these orders are executed reasonably quickly, more like a typical implementation shortfall algorithm. The illiquid Options Xpress (OXPS) has no natural hedges in the portfolio, so it left to trade throughout the day, primarily to minimise impact costs.

Clearly, if we compare this with a purely implementation shortfall based approach, which we saw back in Figure 12-9, one of the most noticeable differences is the fact that many of the orders are now traded throughout the day. This is because of the risk reduction afforded by diversification. It allows for more passive trading, to try to reduce the market impact costs.

Another way of viewing the effectiveness of portfolio-optimised algorithms is to compare their performance in terms of risk. For instance, Figure 12-11 shows an example from Olivier Thiriet (2006) at Credit Suisse. This charts the tracking error for a portfolio of 214 Japanese stocks, with 104 buys, worth $20 million, and 110 sells, worth $22 million. Their customised PHD (Portfolio Hedging Device) algorithm achieves a lower tracking error than using standard single asset market inline (effectively POV) algorithms, and much less than the ubiquitous VWAP.

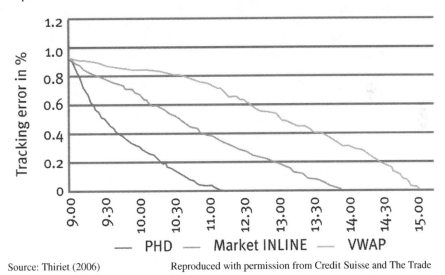

Source: Thiriet (2006)   Reproduced with permission from Credit Suisse and The Trade

Figure 12-11 Comparing portfolio risk for a range of different algorithm types

An "algorithm of algorithms"

The "algorithm of algorithms" is a portfolio-focussed approach outlined by Kissell, Freyre-

Sanders and Carrie (2005). It is responsible for managing the portfolio trading requirements whilst individual algorithms are still used for each constituent order. Therefore, a portfolio algorithm can track the overall risk, issuing adjustments to alter the trading patterns of the algorithms for the portfolio constituents.

This innovative approach should allow single asset trading algorithms to be used for optimal portfolio trading with the minimum of changes. The primary requirement is that they support dynamic updates of their parameters, allowing the portfolio algorithm to dynamically control them. Therefore, instead of adopting a "one size fits all" approach we can use the algorithm that is most appropriate for each constituent order, given factors such as the asset's volatility and the order's size. Thus, a portfolio might employ of a range of POV, VWAP, implementation shortfall or liquidity-based algorithms. The standalone portfolio algorithm tracks the progress of each of these orders, adjusting them when it becomes necessary in order to maintain the minimum overall risk.

Obviously, some algorithms are more suited to this approach than others. The target participation rate of POV algorithms makes them extremely easy to control, since the portfolio algorithm can alter the trading pattern simply by increasing or decreasing this target. A similar approach may be taken with algorithms with support a tilt factor, such as some TWAP or VWAP variants. For shortfall-based algorithms, the risk aversion parameter could be updated to trigger more or less aggressive trading. Alternatively, the portfolio algorithm could also slow algorithms down by setting, or modifying, price limits.

Over time, as the portfolio risk profile changes, the most appropriate algorithm for a constituent order might also change. So the portfolio algorithm might need to cancel the order for the original algorithm and replace it with a new order for the residual position. Thus, portfolio constituents might be swapped from a VWAP algorithm to a shortfall or liquidity based one.

In terms of the actual portfolio algorithm, clearly this needs to carefully track the portfolio risk of the residual positions, as well as determining the optimal trading strategy for each constituent order. In addition, it needs to ensure that the projected savings achieved from diversification outweigh any incurred by altering each individual order's optimal trading strategy.

An approach that lends itself well to this is based on the marginal contribution to risk (MCR) measure, as described by Bystrik and Johnson (2005). By determining the MCR for each constituent, we can quantify their effect on the portfolio risk. Hence, positions that have a large positive MCR should ideally be reduced sooner, whilst those with a negative MCR should be preserved since they are actually helping offset the overall risk. These adjustments may then be applied to the constituent trading algorithm.

For example, Figure 12-12 illustrates how the target participation rate might be varied over time for a range of different risks. Initially, the target participation rates are raised for the constituents that have a positive MCR, whilst they are lowered for those with a negative one. As trading progresses, the urgency to trade those with a positive MCR decreases, whilst it becomes more important for the others to catch up.

Also, notice that no adjustments are needed for the constituents that have a negligible contribution to risk. Alternatively, where two constituents with different liquidities both have a similar positive MCR, it may be more cost effective to trade the liquid one faster, since aggressive trading of the illiquid one could lead to prohibitive costs.

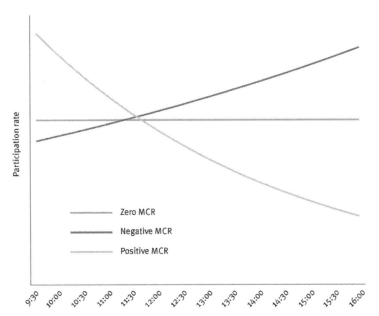

Source: Bystrik and Johnson (2005)   Reproduced with permission from Miletus Trading and The Trade

Figure 12-12 Participation rates based on marginal contribution to risk

12.6 Summary

- Portfolio trading provides a cost-effective means of trading whole baskets of assets. Significant risk reductions can be achieved by tracking and managing portfolio risk.

- Portfolio volatility is simply the standard deviation of the portfolio's returns. However, the relationship between overall risk and each portfolio constituent is non-linear. Each constituent's contribution to the overall risk depends on its proportion/weight in the portfolio, the variance of its returns and the covariance of its returns with all other assets in the portfolio.

- Diversification reduces portfolio risk, it occurs because the individual risks can offset one another. Simply increasing the number of assets can reduce the overall risk.

- Portfolio risk may also be decomposed into:
  - Systematic benchmark (or market) risk
  - Non-systematic (or asset specific) risk, which may be reduced by diversification

- Portfolio managers may have additional trading goals, since they might also track risk in terms of other components, such as market, sector or country risk:
  - Cash balancing
  - Beta/Market neutrality

- Sector/Country neutrality
- Minimising index tracking error

▪ Optimal portfolio trading lowers portfolio risk by reducing the positions of those assets that contribute the most. Note that the largest risk contributors will not necessarily be the orders for the riskiest assets, due to natural hedging.

▪ Conventional trading algorithms may easily be used for trading portfolios. Though, dynamic algorithms will often lead to a shift in the portfolio composition since portfolio risk is not considered.

▪ Portfolio optimised algorithms need to track risk for the whole portfolio. There are two main ways of doing this:
   - Extending existing algorithms to incorporate portfolio models
   - Adopting an "algorithm of algorithms" to manage the portfolio trading requirements whilst individual algorithms are still used for each constituent order

Addendum A: Covariance

Covariance is just a measure of how much two variables I and J vary together:

$$Cov\ (I, J) = E((I - \mu)(J - v))$$

where the function $E()$ represents the expected value (or mean), and variables μ and v are the respective mean values for variables I and J. A positive covariance means that the two items vary together, so if the value of I is more than its average then it is likely that J will also have a higher than normal value. Conversely, a negative covariance means that they behave in opposite fashions, so a high value for one implies a lower expected value for the other. A covariance of zero shows that the items are completely independent, so no inference may be made from either value.

Sometimes the relationship between variables is compared using the correlation coefficient (ρ). Essentially, this is their covariance divided by the product of their standard deviations:

$$\rho_{i,j} = \frac{Cov(I, J)}{\sigma_i \sigma_j} = \frac{E((I - \mu_i)(J - \mu_j))}{\sigma_i \sigma_j} \tag{12-9}$$

where μ_i, μ_j and σ_i, σ_j are the means and standard deviations of variables I and J respectively.

Example 12-3: Let's determine the covariance between the four assets whose sample prices are shown in Table 12-8.

Asset	Price series										μ	σ^2
	1	2	3	4	5	6	7	8	9	10		
A	3.50	3.50	3.28	3.34	3.69	3.86	3.58	3.69	3.12	3.17	3.47	0.06
B	4.41	4.42	4.28	4.34	4.69	4.86	4.58	5.00	4.22	4.03	4.48	0.09
C	5.42	5.54	5.58	5.68	5.44	5.03	5.82	5.93	5.61	5.94	5.60	0.07
D	6.42	6.54	6.58	6.34	6.69	6.86	6.58	6.93	6.30	6.94	6.62	0.05

Table 12-8 Sample time series for covariance calculation

Table 12-9 shows the intermediate calculations for determining the covariance between the prices of assets A and B. Δ_A corresponds to the series of differences to the mean (μ).

	Series									
	1	2	3	4	5	6	7	8	9	10
Δ_A	0.02	0.03	-0.19	-0.13	0.22	0.39	0.11	0.22	-0.35	-0.30
Δ_B	-0.07	-0.07	-0.20	-0.14	0.21	0.38	0.10	0.52	-0.26	-0.46
$\Delta_A\Delta_B$	0.00	0.00	0.04	0.02	0.05	0.15	0.01	0.11	0.09	0.14

Table 12-9 Sample intermediate calculations for covariance

The sample covariance for assets A and B is equal to the sum $\Sigma(\Delta_A\ \Delta_B)$ adjusted by dividing by $(n-1)$ where n is the sample size:

$Cov(A,B) = \Sigma(\Delta_A \Delta_B)/(n-1)$
$= (0+0+0.04+0.02+0.05+0.15+0.01+0.11+0.09+0.14)/9$
$= 0.07$

This process is then repeated for all the other possible combinations.

Note that $Cov(A, B) = Cov(B, A)$, similarly $Cov(A, A) = Variance(A)$ or σ^2 as shown in Table 12-8. Hence, the covariance matrix (Ω) for this example set may be defined as:

$$\Omega = \begin{pmatrix} 0.06 & 0.07 & -0.03 & 0.02 \\ 0.07 & 0.09 & -0.02 & 0.03 \\ -0.03 & -0.02 & 0.07 & 0.01 \\ 0.02 & 0.03 & 0.01 & 0.05 \end{pmatrix}$$

Chapter 13
Multi-asset trading

Multi-asset trading is nothing new; however, trading between different asset classes poses a whole new set of issues for trading algorithms.

13.1 Introduction

Multi-asset trading is starting to attract nearly as much hype as algorithmic trading. In its simplest form, it means single systems that allow investors and traders to manage trading across multiple asset classes. Though, in terms of algorithmic trading the most interesting prospect is cross-asset trading. This offers the potential of simultaneously trading a wide variety of different asset types using a single trading strategy.

Historically, the world markets have been highly segmented, both regionally and across asset classes. Electronic trading has helped open up markets, allowing a much broader range of access. Trading any asset globally is rapidly becoming a straightforward technical issue. Increasing numbers of order (OMS) and execution management systems (EMS) now provide unified platforms that enable trading across a range of asset classes. Similarly, communications protocols such as FIX have expanded to cater for equities, bonds, FX and an array of derivatives.

Hedge funds are arguably the principal driver behind the current trend towards multi-asset trading. Their strategies are becoming increasingly complex as they constantly seek new sources of profit, or alpha. Risk management has also become progressively more sophisticated in its use of derivatives for hedging. Consequently, the overall buy-side use of derivatives has spiralled over the last few years, leading to increased demand for multi-asset support.

The sell-side has had to evolve to cope with a new era of lower margins and higher volumes. Many firms have started reorganizing themselves; the old asset class silos are disappearing. Equities and derivatives businesses are merging, in some cases even fixed income and equities desks are integrating. Sales desks are becoming more customer-focussed, able to cater for trading a wide range of assets. The aim is to try to achieve greater efficiencies of scale and so reduce the overall costs. Cross-asset trading strategies also offer them a significant means of differentiation, as well as the benefits associated with being first-to-market.

Competition amongst execution venues is also helping. As we saw in Chapter 3, the competition is now truly global and has even started to span across asset classes. Exchanges are increasingly catering for equities, derivatives and even fixed income trading. For example, both NYSE and NASDAQ have expanded to offer trading in ETFs, futures and options. The NYSE has even relaunched its bond-trading platform. Many of the European and stock exchanges also handle bonds, whilst some of the Nordic exchanges also cater for derivatives. In Asia, Australia, Korea and Singapore have all seen mergers between their stock and derivatives exchanges. Likewise, the major derivatives exchanges have started branching out into other asset classes as well. For instance, Eurex also caters for bond trading whilst the ISE has created its own stock market. Competition is also increasing between the "dark pool" ATSs. Indeed, if some of the newer ATS entrants in FX and options prove successful, we may see mergers and takeovers in this arena as well.

Regulations will also play an important part in the expansion of multi-asset trading. In Europe, MiFID means that regulations now span across a broad section of asset classes, which should help clear the way for cross-asset trading. Though, in the U.S. the disparate regulatory bodies mean that it may be more complicated, as evidenced with difficulties over newer assets such as ETFs and single stock futures.

Another factor that will be crucial to the growth of multi-asset trading is the provision of unified mechanisms for clearing and settlement. Prime brokerage services will need to expand across the various asset classes. Netting agreements for collateralization and margin requirements will also have to encompass a much wider range of assets.

Although the divisions between the world's markets are becoming increasingly blurred, the exact outcome of all this change is still uncertain. At present, very few execution venues actually provide cross-asset trading. Some of the reasons for this are highlighted in an article by Ivy Schmerken (2006): Many exchanges still run separate platforms and matching engines for each asset class, some may have half a dozen different systems. Whilst there may be interest, the demand has still not been sufficient to justify the expense of merging these systems. That said, as exchanges migrate to new platforms support for multiple asset classes is becoming a key consideration. Another important factor is that whilst linked orders may be convenient, such "one-stop shopping" runs counter to broker's best-execution obligations. In the short-term, many of the cross-asset trading solutions are likely to be from brokers and other third-parties. Complex orders can easily be split into multiple legs and routed to different venues. Reduced latencies have also helped to reduce the legging risk for such strategies. Hence, it is likely that for the foreseeable future much of the innovation in cross-asset trading will be provided by specialised algorithms/platforms as brokers seek to continue to differentiate themselves with new value-added services.

13.2 Multi-asset trading strategies

Despite all the hype, cross-asset trading is nothing new. Cash positions in stock, bonds and commodities have been hedged with futures and options ever since the creation of derivative contracts. The ability to protect against a broad spectrum of risks has made derivatives a virtually indispensable tool. Cross-asset arbitrage is nothing new, either. In particular, index arbitrage and basis trading have been around for decades. Though, the high cost of entry has meant that historically such arbitrage has been monopolised by market makers, dealers and proprietary traders. More recently, electronic trading has helped lower the cost of entry. Easier access and decreasing transaction costs have made cross-asset trading viable for a much wider range of investors and traders. On the downside, it has also substantially reduced the timescales; many opportunities might now only last minutes, seconds or even less.

Ten years ago, the precursors of modern trading algorithms were efficiency tools, helping traders cope with the ever-increasing order flow. Finally, they were packaged up into discrete strategies and made available to clients as trading algorithms. Dealers' hedging and arbitrage systems arguably contain a lot more proprietary techniques. However, there is no real reason why the more established ones could not undergo a similar transformation. In fact, several broker dealers have already started releasing algorithms that provide hedging and other types of cross-asset trading. Similarly, hedge funds and other investment institutions have begun creating their own dedicated algorithms, to protect their own proprietary techniques. Vendors have already started to provide platforms geared up for this, for example, Flextrade, Progress Apama and AlgoTrader's OptimEx.

Unlike for existing trading algorithms, it is slightly more difficult to predict exactly what future multi-asset algorithms might look like. Broadly speaking, we can use some of the existing types of trading as a basis, as outlined in Table 13-1:

Strategy type	*Examples*	*Assets involved*	
Utility	FX cash trades	Stock	FX
	Covering short sales	Stock	Stock Lend/Rev repo
Structured	Principal protected notes	Bond	Option
Hedging	Hedging market risk	Stock/s	Future/s
	Hedging interest rates	Bond/s	Future/s
	Hedging the "Greeks"	Option/s	Stock/s
Arbitrage	ADR arbitrage	DR	Stock
	Basis trading	Future/s	Bond/s
	Index arbitrage	Future/s	Stocks
	Option arbitrage	Options	Stocks/Bonds
	Futures and options arbitrage	Options	Future/s
	Dividend arbitrage	Stock	Option/s

Table 13-1 Some examples of cross-asset trading types

The utility strategies are relatively straightforward additions, such as incorporating FX cash trades with stock trading in order to facilitate cross currency trading or covering short sales using stock lending or reverse repos.

Structured products are combinations of cash and derivative assets designed to meet specific investment objectives, such as enhancing returns or reducing risk. The more straightforward products, such as principal protected notes, may well form the basis for some multi-asset trading strategies.

Likewise, hedging provides a mechanism for offsetting risk, generally via derivatives. Although this is often simply applied to existing positions, hedging may also be used in tandem with normal trading, such as for portfolio transitions. Hedging also forms the backbone of many of the arbitrage techniques that seek to extract risk-free profits when price imbalances occur.

Note that a reasonable grasp of derivatives is important for many of these trading strategies. So if you are new to these instruments, it may be worth rereading the corresponding parts of Chapter 3 and Appendix E. Alternatively, for a more detailed review 'Understanding Futures Markets' by Robert Kolb and James Overdahl (2006) or 'Options, Futures, and Other Derivatives' by John Hull (2003) are both good starting points.

In the following sections, we shall look at each of these various strategy types before reviewing some of the key considerations for multi-asset trading algorithms.

13.3 Utility strategies

These are simple extensions of procedures, which are routinely carried out manually. For example, when trading assets denominated in foreign currencies we could automate the FX cash trades. Automatic handling could also cover short sales, by finding lending or reverse repos to borrow the required asset. As volumes continue to increase and traders get busier the market for such conveniences may well expand.

FX cash trades

When trading pairs or portfolios of assets with multiple currencies the exchange rates are an important consideration. Admittedly, settlement currencies may often be specified; however, any changes in the exchange rate could mean settling at a disadvantageous rate. Therefore, when trading assets denominated in a different currency it may be appropriate to also perform an FX cash trade, to ensure there is a sufficient amount of local currency for settlement.

Trading systems may be extended to issue FX cash trades to match the value traded. Depending on the value and the volatility of the currency, this could be carried out automatically upon completion of the order. Alternatively, the currency could be traded in parallel with the order. Existing trading algorithms could be extended to incorporate currency handling, or it could be done manually using DMA. The client may also want to perform this across multiple assets, so a net currency position could be traded. This might be handled by the broker or, if execution information is sent back to the client in real-time, they could take charge of this for themselves.

For example, let's consider a pairs trade between the pharmaceutical firms Genentech (U.S.) and GlaxoSmithKline (U.K.) for $10 million. The ratio algorithm will steadily build positions in the two companies. To ensure our U.K. sterling cash account is sufficient for settlement the algorithm could also incrementally issue FX cash orders for sterling based on the current size of our GlaxoSmithKline position. This might simply mean issuing limit orders; alternatively, a separate algorithm could be used to handle the FX trading.

Covering short sales

To sell short most cash assets we will usually need to cover the position by borrowing the asset, either via stock lending or reverse repos. As the markets for stock lending and repos become increasingly electronic this also opens up the possibility of automating short covering. Hence, an algorithm could scan the lending and/or repo markets to source the required asset. Since it may be more difficult to borrow the asset, the short sale could even be made dependent on the success of this transaction. It could even take account of the cost of borrowing when placing the short sell orders to ensure the fees are covered.

13.4 Structured strategies

Structured products are synthetic assets created to meet specific investment requirements, such as enhancing the yield, increasing tax efficiency or reducing risk for a given asset. Financial engineering is used to determine the required combinations of cash and derivative assets to meet these objectives.

Structured products have primarily been targeted at retail investors, although usage by institutional investors is also growing. Over $100 billion of new issues were made in 2007 according to estimates from the Structured Products Association (SPA) (2008). [1] Indeed, their increasing popularity means they are starting to emerge as a separate asset class. Note that they are principally designed to be kept to maturity, so this is an OTC only marketplace with little or no secondary trading.

Although structured products may be highly complex and tailored to the needs of a specific investor, there are also some increasingly common variants such as structured notes, as Chris Biscoe (2005) points out. Trading algorithms may well evolve which approximate to some of the more common or straightforward products.

Principal protected notes

Principal protected notes offer a guarantee to return a set percentage (usually 100%) of the amount invested at maturity. As well as this, they also offer the potential of additional returns, derived from the performance of other asset/s. Note that a participation rate may be set on the enhanced returns, so the investor might receive 70 or 80% of them.

Equity linked notes are effectively debt instruments combined with an option on a specific stock or index. They do not usually have any coupon payments; instead the returns at maturity are based on the gains of the underlying equity. The investment amount is protected to maturity, although it is still exposed to issuer default risk.

Interest rate linked notes are based on the moves for market benchmark rates, such as Fed Funds or LIBOR. Range accrual notes only accrue interest on days when the reference rate is within a set range.

Currency (or FX) linked notes augment their returns from the performance of a currency, or basket of currencies. There are also range accrual notes where interest is accrued only on days when the currency is within set bounds.

Hybrid linked notes even allow the performance to depend on multiple asset classes.

Many of these structured notes have a maturity of between 1-3 years. The basic principle behind them is to invest in risk-free bonds which provide the protection. For instance, zero coupon bonds may be bought at a discount to achieve this. The remaining funds may be used to purchase derivatives to enhance the returns. This might be purchasing long-term call options for the required stock, currency or commodity. Alternatively, some structures may incorporate more exotic derivatives, such as barrier options.

As an example we might construct a $1 million two year principal protected note by purchasing two year zero coupon Treasury notes with a notional of $1 million. These are priced at 90, leaving $100,000 to purchase two-year call options to provide the enhanced returns. A customised trading algorithm could be used to link these two orders together.

13.5 Hedging strategies

Hedging is simply a mechanism for offsetting risk. Since positions may be constantly exposed to market risk, hedging is effectively a continual cycle comprising of the following three stages:

- analysing the various risks for existing positions
- determining what is required to counteract them
- issuing orders to achieve the target hedge positions

For cash assets, such as stocks or bonds, hedging often uses derivatives. Whilst for

---

[1] Based on data from MTN-I, Prospect News and StructuredRetailProducts.com.

derivative positions the hedging may be based on the underlying assets, other derivatives or a combination of the two.

Transaction costs mean that it is not necessarily cost effective to constantly adjust the hedging positions. As always, it is a careful balancing act between risk and cost. That said, electronic trading has made it much more viable to perform hedging in real-time.

For existing positions, investment firms already maintain their own hedging, which may then be traded manually or via trading algorithms or DMA. For portfolio trades the brokers could also incorporate any required hedging, as we saw for FX cash trades. In Chapter 12, we saw that dedicated portfolio trading algorithms that incorporate portfolio risk are already available. Extending these to also handle hedging with derivatives is not that great a leap.

For example, consider an investment fund worth $1 billion hedged with S&P 500 futures. A portfolio trade to increase the fund by 10% would need a corresponding increase in the futures cover. So in addition to the portfolio of stocks the broker could also trade the additional futures for the hedging. Alternatively, if the broker is supplying frequent status updates, the buy-side traders could manage the futures hedging themselves, although they may be disadvantaged by any delays.

In the following sub-sections, we shall outline some of the commoner types of hedging which might be incorporated into custom algorithms.

Hedging market risk

Futures can provide a cost-efficient means of hedging market risk, particularly for portfolios. For stock portfolios, an index future allows us to offset market risk. The number of futures contracts required can be determined based on the overall beta of the portfolio (β_P), using the following equation:

$$Number\ of\ Contracts = -\beta_P \frac{V_P}{V_F} = -\beta_P \frac{V_P}{P_F \cdot m} \tag{13-1}$$

where V_P and V_F are the corresponding market values of the portfolio and of a futures contract. The futures value may also be expressed in terms of its price P_F and its contract multiplier m.

Remember that the actual beta of a portfolio for a specific index may be determined by comparing its returns with those of the index, as we saw in Chapter 12. The portfolio beta (β_P) may in turn be derived from its covariance:

$$\beta_p = \frac{Cov(r_p, r_m)}{Var(r_m)}$$

where r_p and r_m are the respective returns for the portfolio and the index.

Example 13-1: Let's assume we need to add $5 million of S&P 500 stocks to our portfolio. To protect against a falling market we can sell an equivalent number of September futures contracts. For convenience, we will base this on their closing value (1,559.7) with a multiplier of $250/point. Since this is a basket of S&P stocks, we shall assume the beta is 1.0.

Using equation 13-1, we get:

Number of contracts = - $5,000,000 / ($250 * 1,559.7) = -12.82 ≈ -13

Therefore, selling 13 futures contracts should provide sufficient hedging for our portfolio. A month later, the S&P 500 fell from 1549.37 to 1445.94, whilst the futures price fell to 1449.9. Hence, the stock position sees a loss of nearly 7%, or $333,780. Conversely, the value of the short futures hedge actually increased, due to the 109.8 drop in price. This equates to $250 x 13 x (1559.7-1449.9) = $356,850.

Table 13-2 summarises the market values at each date. Overall, the hedge worked: If we needed to liquidate the portfolio in August, the losses realised from the stock sales would be more than compensated for by the gain from our futures.

Date	Position	Market Value/$	Net Value/$
16 Jul	Stock portfolio	5,000,000	
	S&P 500 SEP futures	-5,069,025	-69,025
17 Aug	Stock portfolio	4,666,219	
	S&P 500 SEP futures	-4,712,175	-45,956

Table 13-2 An example of short futures hedging

Example 13-2: Let's now consider shorting a $5 million basket of stocks. Compared to the S&P 500 the basket has a beta of 1.5. To protect against a rising market we will need to buy more futures than before:

Number of contracts = - 1.5 * $-5,000,000 / ($250 * 1,559.7) = 19.23 ≈ 19

So in this case we need to buy 19 futures to hedge our short basket. The beta also means that the falling market will probably have even more effect on this portfolio. Indeed, by the 17th August it is only worth $4,475,000. So if we were to buy back the stocks we could realise a profit of $525,000. However, these potential profits will be reduced by losses from the futures hedge. The market values and the β-adjusted equivalents are shown in Table 13-3:

Date	Position	Market Value/$	β-adjusted Market Value/$	Net Value/$
16 Jul	Stock portfolio	-5,000,000	-7,500,000	
	S&P 500 SEP futures	7,408,575	7,408,575	2,408,575
17 Aug	Stock portfolio	-4,475,000	-6,712,500	
	S&P 500 SEP futures	6,887,025	6,887,025	2,412,025

Table 13-3 An example of long futures hedging

The long futures position decreases in value by 250 x 19 x (1559.7-1449.9) = $521,550. Thus, the hedging prevented us from realising any significant directional profits. More importantly, though, it protected us from any losses due to a rising market.

For instance, let's consider if the S&P had actually risen to 1600, and the SEP future to 1605. Our short stock position would instead be worth $5,250,000, effectively a loss of $250,000. This is offset by a gain of $215,175 in the value of the futures position, as shown in Table 13-4. Although not perfect, this hedge has still provided an important insurance mechanism against market moves.

Date	Position	Market Value/$	β-adjusted Market Value/$	Net Value/$
16 Jul	Stock portfolio	-5,000,000	-7,500,000	
	S&P 500 SEP futures	7,408,575	7,408,575	2,408,575
17 Aug	Stock portfolio	-5,250,000	-7,875,000	
	S&P 500 SEP futures	7,623,750	7,623,750	2,373,750

Table 13-4 An alternative scenario for long futures hedging

Hedging interest rate risk

Fixed income assets are obviously affected by changes in interest rates. When market interest rates increase bond prices decrease, and vice versa. This is because the cash flows are fixed, so a higher interest rate reduces their present value.

For a standard bond we may represent its current value (V) as the sum of all its future cash flows (C_i) each discounted to their present value ($P(i)$) based on the rate (r):

$$V = \sum_i P(i) = \sum_i C_i e^{-r\Delta T_i}$$

where T_i is the time left to maturity for each payment (in years). Note the rate (r) is effectively the yield to maturity (YTM) of the bond. It represents the overall interest rate that would be earned by buying it at the current market price and holding to maturity.

Example 13-3: Let's consider a 2-year bond with an annual coupon of 5% for a notional value of $100,000. It is priced such that its yield to maturity (YTM) is also 5%.

So at the end of the first year we receive a coupon of $5,000, which has a current value of $(5,000 * e^{-0.05*1}) = \$4,756$.

At the end of the second year, we receive both the final coupon payment and the full notional amount. This gives a total current value of $99,764, shown in Table 13-5.

Time (years)	Cash flow	YTM=5.00%				YTM=5.01%	YTM=4.99%
		Present value	Weight	Weighted time		Present value	Present value
1	5,000	4,756	0.05	0.05		4,756	4,757
2	105,000	95,008	0.95	1.90		94,989	95,027
Total		99,764	1	1.95		99,745	99,784

Table 13-5 Calculating value of a bond

Now let's consider the situation if interest rates increase by one basis point (bps). The bond's yield to market will also increase to 5.01%. The present value of the second year payment is now $(105,000 * e^{-0.0501*2}) = \$94,989$, so the overall value of the bond decreases by $19. Conversely, if rates decrease by one basis point the value increases to $99,784, or $20.

Thus, the average change in value for a 1 bps change in interest rates = $(19+20/20) = \$19.5$. This risk measure is sometimes referred to as the PVBP (price value of a basis point), whilst if measured in dollars it is called the *DV01* (dollar value of a basis point change).

Alternatively, we can use duration to represent the sensitivity of a bond to interest rate movements. This is inversely related to the coupon rate, so higher rate bonds have shorter durations, whilst for zero coupon bonds the duration is equal to their maturity. The duration (D) may be expressed as the sum of the weighted maturities for the associated cash flows:

$$D = \sum_{i=1}^{n} \frac{P(i) \ T_i}{V}$$

For Example 13-3, the weight column in Table 13-5 is simply each present value divided by the total. Hence, the duration for the bond is 1.95 years when the yield to market is 5%.

These risk metrics may also be applied to portfolios of bonds, as a weighted sum based on the size of each bond's position. Hull (2003) shows that the number of interest rate futures (N) required to hedge this risk may be determined using the following equation:

$$N = -\frac{D_S \cdot S}{D_F \cdot F}$$

where D_S is the duration of the portfolio (or bond) and D_F is the duration of the underlying (cheapest to deliver) bond for the future. The value of the portfolio is S and the value of a future is F. Alternatively we can express this based on $DV01$:

$$N = -\frac{DV01_{bond}}{DV01_{future}} \times \frac{S}{F} \tag{13-2}$$

There are several ways to determine the $DV01$ for a future, the easiest is to make an approximation based on the $DV01$ of the most economical underlying asset, the "cheapest to deliver" (CTD). So the $DV01_{future}$ is in turn based on the $DV01$ of this CTD bond and a conversion factor (CF).

$$DV01_{future} = -\frac{DV01_{CTD}}{CF}$$

Example 13-4: A bond portfolio worth $10 million has a $DV01$ of $195. The current futures contract for a ten-year bond is priced at 94.20, with a notional of $100,000.

Each futures contract is worth (94.2/100) x $100,000 = $94,200.
At the future's maturity, the cheapest to deliver bond has a $DV01$ of $250.
For simplicity, let's assume the conversion factor is 1, so the $DV01$ of our future is $250.

Using equation 13-2:

$$\# contracts = -\frac{195}{250} \times \frac{\$10,000,000}{\$94,200} = -82.8$$

Therefore, by selling 83 futures contracts we should have hedged our bond portfolio. If interest rates increase, both the bond portfolio and the futures contracts will be worth less. The loss in value from the bond portfolio should be offset by profit from the short futures position. Conversely, a drop in interest rates will make the bond portfolio worth more, whilst the futures position will realise a loss.

There are some other important assumptions with this approach: Firstly, it relies on the cheapest to deliver bond not changing. Neither does it account for basis risk, the possibility that the spot price of the asset and the futures price do not converge, towards the expiration date. Basis trading is covered in more detail in section 13.6.

It is also important to remember that *DV01* applies to small changes in interest rates. Still, this is not a linear relationship. With large changes in rates more significant price changes may occur. This is due to a property called convexity: Bonds or portfolios with higher convexity will see higher increases in value as rates decline than those with lower convexity. To compensate for this it is possible to adjust the hedge calculation to also incorporate convexity.

Finally, there is no guarantee that interest rate changes will apply uniformly across the yield curve. If this does not happen, the portfolio will be exposed to different risks depending on the maturity. This may be handled by identifying these "gaps" and adding extra hedging for them. More details about all these considerations may be found in Hull (2003).

Hedging derivative risk factors (the "Greeks")

Hedging derivatives requires us to fully understand their sensitivities to the price of the underlying asset as well as factors such as interest rates. There are many different pricing models for derivatives; however, the Black Scholes (1973) is easily the best known:

A call option's price *(C)* may be defined as a function of the price of its underlying asset *(S)* and the time left to expiry *(T)*:

$$C(S,T) = S\Phi(d_1) - Ke^{-rT}\Phi(d_2) \qquad (13\text{-}3)$$

where K is the option's strike price, r is the interest rate and Φ is the standard normal cumulative distribution function. The first component $(S\,\Phi(d_1))$ corresponds to a probability weighted estimate of the asset price at expiration, whilst the second $(Ke^{-rT}\,\Phi(d_2))$ represents a discounted exercise price. In turn, the factors d_1 and d_2 are defined by:

$$d_1 = \frac{\ln(S/K) + (r + \sigma^2/2)T}{\sigma\sqrt{T}} \qquad d_2 = d_1 - \sigma\sqrt{T} \qquad (13\text{-}4)$$

where σ is the asset's price volatility. The option price is sensitive to all of these key parameters, each of which has been assigned its name based on the name for their mathematical symbol. Since most of these are Greek, they became known as the "Greeks".

Delta represents the rate of change in value with respect to the underlying price. Rho measures the sensitivity to changes in the interest rate. Vega reflects the impact of changes in volatility and theta corresponds to the effect of time on the derivative's value. Gamma is a secondary risk factor, rather than directly mapping to one of the parameters in equations 13-3 or 13-4 it measures the rate of change in delta based on changes in the underlying price.

Since the focus of this chapter is cross-asset trading, we will concentrate on the hedges targeting risk from changes the underlying price, namely delta and gamma.

Delta Hedging

Delta hedging balances some of the risk from an option position by buying or selling a set amount of the underlying asset. This protects against price moves in the underlying.

The value of delta ranges between -1.0 and 1.0. A delta of 1.0 means that for every rise (fall) of $1 in the underlying asset the derivative's price will also rise (fall) by $1.

Conversely, a negative delta means that the derivative's price moves in the opposite direction. So a delta equal to -0.5 means that a price increase of $1 for the underlying asset will result in a price drop of $0.5 for the derivative.

Using the Black Scholes model, equation 13-3, the delta for a call option is actually equal to the weighting $\Phi(d_1)$, so these have deltas ranging from 0 to 1.0. Conversely, for put options the delta is $(\Phi(d_1) - 1)$, so these vary from 0 to -1.0.

The size of the delta reflects how likely the option is to be exercised. An option is said to be at-the-money when its strike price is equal to the market price of its underlying. A call (put) option is in-the-money when the underlying market price is higher (lower) than its strike price, whilst if the opposite holds true it is said to be out-of-the-money. At-the-money options tend to have deltas around ±0.5, as they become deeper in-the-money this becomes closer to ±1.0, whilst deeply out-of-the-money options have deltas approaching 0.0. Nearer to expiration, deltas tend to become closer to ±1.0. Deltas also vary based on changes in the underlying asset price, volatility and interest rate, as we can see from equation 13-4.

When calculating the delta risk for positions we must also incorporate whether they are long or short. This is done by negating the deltas of short positions. Thus a long call position and a short put position are both actually delta positive, due to the double negatives for the short put. Similarly, short call and long put positions are both delta negative.

For instance, a long position of 50 call options with a delta of 0.5 has a delta-adjusted position of 50 x 0.5 = 25. To delta hedge this position we can sell 25 shares of the underlying asset. Alternatively, we might buy 100 out-of-the-money puts each with a delta of -0.25 (although hedging with another option can introduce additional risk factors). Either way we achieve our goal of achieving a delta neutral position.

Example 13-5(a): We have sold 100 OCT 50 call options for EFG at $4. EFG is currently trading at $45 and its volatility is 20%.

Since we have sold a call option we are delta negative, therefore we can hedge this by buying shares of EFG. Given that the call option delta is initially 0.15, this means buying 15 shares. The hedge will be updated on a daily basis for the lifetime of the option. Table 13-6 shows how this progresses over time.

Date	Asset price	Option delta	Delta shares	Hedging P/L $
13 Aug 07	45.30	0.15	15	
14 Aug 07	46.90	0.19	19	30.4
15 Aug 07	47.80	0.33	33	29.7
16 Aug 07	48.60	0.44	44	35.7
..	..	..	..	..
17 Sep 07	53.80	0.75	75	
18 Sep 07	55.60	0.89	89	160.2
19 Sep 07	56.25	0.92	92	59.8
20 Sep 07	57.50	0.95	95	118.8

Table 13-6 An example of delta hedging

As the call options become deeper in-the-money, their delta approaches 1.00, so by the end of September we effectively have a fully covered call position. It is likely that the option will be assigned, causing us to realise a loss. Though, the delta hedging means that much of this loss will be covered by gains from our long hedge.

With any hedging strategy, it is vital to strike the right balance between cost effectiveness and risk. This is particularly true for delta hedging since the delta is affected by so many factors. Changes in the underlying asset price, its volatility, the interest rate and the time left to expiry may trigger a change in the delta. In theory, we should constantly adjust the hedge position to ensure we remain delta neutral. Unfortunately, due to transaction costs this is impractical.

Re-hedging may be carried out in an ad-hoc fashion based on (1) time, (2) delta or (3) the underlying price, as Euan Sinclair (2008) points out in his book 'Volatility Trading'. Thus position adjustments may be made at discrete time intervals, when the delta reaches a specific level or when the underlying asset reaches a set price level, such as for every \$1 or 1% move. Alternatively, Sinclair (2008) outlines some more systematic approaches based on utility theory, which take into account the risk aversion of the trader. These use delta banding, with hedging only undertaken when the delta moves outside its allowed range. Short positions are hedged more defensively whilst long positions are handled more loosely (the deltas are allowed "to run"). The width of the delta band corresponds to the trader's risk aversion.

The type of volatility being used for these calculations can also play an important role. As we saw in Chapter 10, implied volatility is based on the market prices of options contracts, whilst realised volatility is determined from the underlying asset price changes. Both of these may be used to try to forecast what future volatility may be. For delta hedging, Sinclair (2008) notes that using implied volatility lowers the variance of the profit and loss (P&L) over time, although the final P&L is less certain when compared to using realised volatility.

Delta hedging is an important tool; hence, venues have already started offering linked orders between a stock and its options. For example, the International Securities Exchange (ISE) introduced "buy-write" orders in 2004. The stock leg is sent to NYFIX for execution, upon completion the option leg then becomes active on the ISE's order book. Initially, only a 1:1 ratio was supported, although this has since been extended to support any ratio.

Gamma Hedging

Gamma hedging is an extension of delta hedging which also aims to keep the gamma close to zero. Delta hedging works well for small moves in the price of the underlying. However, the delta can change rapidly when the option is almost at-the-money. By controlling the gamma, we can slow this rate of change and so improve the effectiveness of delta hedging.

As we have already seen, gamma is a second derivative risk measure which represents how much the delta will change when the underlying asset's price moves by one unit, such as \$1. For instance, let's consider a call option priced at \$6 with a delta 0.5 and a gamma of 0.25. When the underlying asset price increases by \$1, the delta means the call option will increase to \$6.5, whilst its delta will increase to 0.75 because of the gamma.

Based on the Black Scholes model, equation 13-3, we can actually define gamma as:

$$\frac{\varphi(d_1)}{S\sigma\sqrt{T}}$$

where φ is the standard normal probability density function, S is the underlying asset's price, σ is its volatility, T is the time to expiry and d_1 is as defined in equation 13-4.

Unfortunately, the gamma of the underlying asset or any futures/forwards is zero. Thus, gamma hedging relies primarily on options, or any other derivatives that have a non-linear relationship with the underlying asset's price.

Example 13-5(b): Let's add a gamma hedge to our position from Example 13-5(a).

Initially, the call option delta is 0.15 and the gamma is 0.1.

Our net delta is -100 x 0.15 = -15. This is offset to 0.0 by buying 15 EFG.
Our net gamma is currently -100 x 0.1 = -10.

We can offset this gamma with a long option position in a cheap out-of-the-money call. For this example, let's assume the call's delta is 0.088 and its gamma is 0.08. Buying 125 of these options offsets the gamma by 125 x 0.08 = 10, making us gamma neutral. Though, it also alters our net delta:

Net delta = (-100 x 0.15) + 15 + (125 x 0.088) = 11.

So to remain delta neutral we need to reduce our long position in EFG from 15 to 4.

Note that care must be taken when gamma hedging, since the new option positions can also introduce other risks. For instance, being delta and gamma neutral may well lead to volatility (vega) risk. Hedging against vega also relies on options. So to become vega neutral we may well need to take on a new option position and rebalance the portfolio in order to achieve the desired risk characteristics. Time (theta) and interest rate (rho) based risks may also be introduced. These are beyond the scope of this book, but Hull (2003) is a good starting point.

13.6 Arbitrage strategies

Simple arbitrage, such as assets listing with different prices on multiple venues, is easy to understand and take advantage of. Essentially, "we buy low and sell high". Though, all trading has associated risks: For example, having bought the asset at the first venue, what if the market price at the second venue has adjusted? Suddenly, our profit margin may have disappeared, plus we must also take account of transaction costs. Hence, to try to guarantee profits any successful arbitrage must minimise risk by incorporating hedging techniques.

As well as simple price arbitrage, each asset class can also have its own particular arbitrage opportunities. For instance, yield curve arbitrage takes advantage of discrepancies in the pricing between short, medium or long-term bonds. Similarly, cash-flow arbitrage decomposes bonds into their effective constituents. If there are cheaper alternatives to create the same cash-flow, arbitrageurs may take advantage of the discrepancy. An example of this is stripping the coupons from bonds, such as U.S. Treasuries, and trading the zero-coupon bonds and their coupon strips separately.

However, the focus of this chapter is multi-asset trading: Arbitrage opportunities trading across different countries may involve multiple currencies, hence an FX cash trade may also be necessary to minimise the currency risk. For example, there can still be price discrepancies between dual listed companies, or stocks and their depositary receipts.

Derivatives are the main source of multi-asset arbitrage. In fact, one of the oldest types of arbitrage is basis trading. This is typically used to take advantage of mispricing between futures and their underlying commodities or bonds, although the principle may just as well be applied for options. Since both futures and options can be based on the same underlying cash assets, there is actually the potential for a three-way set of arbitrages between them. This is demonstrated for stock indices by pathways (a), (b) and (c) in Figure 13-1, which is based on a diagram from Sheri Markose and Hakan Er (2000).

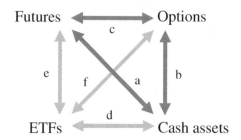

Figure 13-1 Cross-asset index arbitrage opportunities

Index arbitrage focuses on mispricing between index futures and the underlying cash index, as shown by pathway (a) in Figure 13-1. Like basis trading, it is based on the concept of the future's fair value. For options, arbitrage is often based on the principle of Put-Call parity, shown by pathway (b). Pathway (c) shows the potential arbitrage between futures and options; this is driven by the Put-Call-Futures parity relationship.

The introduction of ETFs has provided additional opportunities for arbitrage. Thus, Figure 13-1 also shows pathways (d), (e) and (f) for cash indices. The daily creation and redemption mechanism (d) for ETFs provides a natural arbitrage with the underlying assets, whilst ETFs may act as substitutes for the cash assets in index arbitrage (e) and potentially even Put-Call option arbitrage (f). The creation of single stock futures based on ETFs should add even more permutations.

Note that many of the pathways shown in Figure 13-1 may also be applied for other types of underlier. There are also other derivative-based arbitrages, such as dividend arbitrage.

Clearly, speed plays a key role in successful arbitrage. Hence, electronic trading has had a huge effect. The simplest arbitrages have almost disappeared, since even for fragmented markets it is now relatively easy to spot and take advantage of any such opportunities within milliseconds. Even the more complex multi-market or multi-asset opportunities are likely to be monitored closely. Often, the timescales involved, and the associated margins, for such opportunities have been drastically reduced. So it is vital to get the hedging right.

It is also important to note that just because an arbitrage opportunity exists, that does not necessarily mean it is profitable. The cost of hedging must be considered, plus the associated transaction costs. So cost minimisation is another key focus. Taking advantage of any facilities such as netting trades via a CCP or cross-margining (to reduce margin payments for any futures positions) can also make a significant difference.

Given the progression of electronic and algorithmic trading, it is likely that in the future arbitrage opportunities will become even more complex, possibly involving exotic derivatives. As the saying goes, *"There is no such thing as a free lunch"*; arbitrage opportunities may well be out there, but making a profit from them is often non-trivial.

Multiple listing/depositary receipt arbitrage

Some companies are dual-listed or listed on multiple exchanges. However, the most widespread arbitrage opportunity comes from trading between depositary receipts and their underlying local stocks.

Figure 13-2 shows some examples of the price differences between ADRs and other cross-listed shares in the U.S., taken from an extensive study by Louis Gagnon and G. Andrew

Karolyi (2003). Each chart plots both the U.S. dollar price of the ADR and the local price of the stock converted into dollars. Mispricing opportunities arise from both the difference in currency and local information. Different time zones and languages can mean that information flows to the markets at differing rates. For large cap stocks from developed countries, such as British Petroleum (BP) and Toyota Motor Corp., this should pose less of a problem. Indeed, we can see very few price discrepancies for these. Though, for smaller cap stocks or those from developing countries there can be quite substantial inconsistencies. For example, Figure 13-2 shows clear differences for Taiwan Semiconductor Manufacturing and Infosys Technologies. They also found that cross-listed stocks tended to follow U.S. market indices more closely than other domestic stocks.

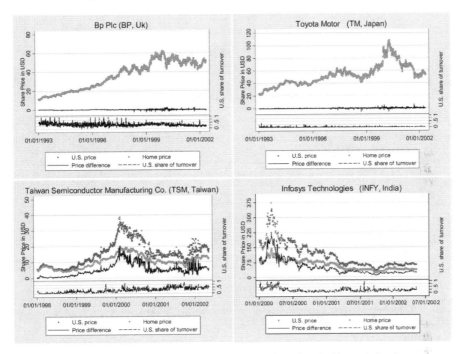

Source: © Gagnon and Karolyi (2003)   Reproduced with permission from authors

Figure 13-2 ADR prices versus their local shares

Another factor to consider for depositary receipts is the administration fee that is charged for their conversion. When this is taken into account, it can significantly reduce the number of arbitrage opportunities.

In order to implement this arbitrage we need a model that compares both prices, accounting for any currency differences and any additional fees. The orders for the ADR and the stock must also be dependent, much like for pair trading. As with any cross currency arbitrage, in order to take full advantage of price imbalances it is important to minimise the currency risk. So, as we saw for cross currency trades, a separate FX cash trade may be used. In fact, brokers are already starting to provide automated conversion services, notably ADR Direct from BNY ConvergEx. This allows clients to convert to and from ADRs as well as providing an automatic currency conversion.

Basis trading

In general, basis trading refers to an arbitrage between a futures contract and its underlying cash product. Though, in theory it could also be applied to the arbitrage between other derivatives and their corresponding underlying assets. The name is derived from the concept of the future's basis (B), which is the difference between the current cash market price (S) and the futures contract's price (F):

$$B = S - F \quad \equiv \quad F = S - B \tag{13-5}$$

This is also sometimes referred to as the total basis or the gross basis. Note that when the gross basis is positive the futures price is below the cash price, which is referred to as normal backwardation. Alternatively, a negative basis means the futures price is higher than the cash price, sometimes described as contango.

The basis changes over time, although generally it is less volatile than either the cash or the futures prices. However, towards expiration of the future the two prices will start to converge, since at expiry there is no real difference between a futures contract and the cash asset, barring transaction costs. This convergence means that the basis must also decrease, and should reach zero when the futures contract expires, as shown in Figure 13-3.

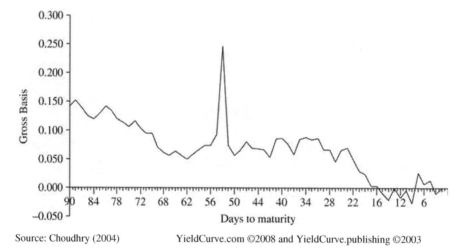

Source: Choudhry (2004)   YieldCurve.com ©2008 and YieldCurve.publishing ©2003

Figure 13-3 Convergence of basis towards zero

Another way of expressing the relationship between the cash and futures prices is the cost of carry model:

$$F = S + C \tag{13-6}$$

where the cost of carry (C) represents the net costs associated with the cash position:

Cost of carry = Funding cost + Storage cost – Income earned

In turn, this cost may be represented as:

$$C = (S \cdot r^{T/365}) + A - I \tag{13-7}$$

where r is funding interest rate, T is number of days until the futures contract expires, A represents the storage costs and I corresponds to the income earned.

The funding cost is the interest that would have to be paid to fund a cash position for the period of the futures contract, often this is based on the repo rate. The storage costs and income earned will differ depending on what the underlying asset is. For instance, with investment assets, such as bonds or stocks, the storage costs will be negligible whilst the income earned may be considerable (Bonds may earn accrued interest whilst equities may receive dividends.). Alternatively, for commodities the storage costs may be sizeable whilst no income will be generated.

When the net cost of carry is positive the futures position is more attractive since we will not need to make any payments until the future reaches expiry, apart from margin calls. Whereas if the cost of carry is negative it actually pays to take on the cash position instead.

The net basis, also termed the value basis, adjusts the gross basis for the cost of carry:

$$Net\ basis = Gross\ basis + Cost\ of\ carry$$

Hence, the net basis represents the difference between the fair value of the future and its actual market price. A positive value shows it is underpriced, whilst a negative one means it is overpriced.

Buying the basis means issuing a buy order for the cash asset whilst simultaneously selling the corresponding futures contract. This is also called cash-and-carry trading. When we are long the basis, we benefit from any increases in the basis; in other words, from price rises for the cash asset or price drops for the future. Effectively, being long the basis allows us to earn the cost of carry.

Selling the basis is the opposite process, so the cash asset is sold and the future is bought. This is also known as reverse cash-and-carry trading. A short basis position will benefit from a decreasing basis; effectively it pays the cost of carry.

These strategies may effectively be implemented by using an appropriate pricing model and linking the orders for the future and the underlying asset/s.

Index arbitrage

Index arbitrage focuses on the profit opportunities that arise between index futures and their underlying constituents. Typically, most index arbitrage is carried out for stock indices, although it could also be applied to bond indices or even CDS indices. Effectively, it is another example of basis trading, except that the cash position corresponds to a basket of assets.

Based on equation 13-6, we can use the cash price and the net cost of carry to determine the fair value of the futures contract. Opportunities for arbitrage arise when the market price for the index future deviates significantly from this fair value. If the futures price exceeds the fair value then a cash-and-carry trade can profit by buying the constituents of the index whilst selling the overpriced futures contract. Conversely, when the futures price is less than its fair value we can use a reverse cash-and-carry trade to buy the futures and sell the index. Generally, these positions will be closed out once the price discrepancy has disappeared, rather than when the futures contract expires.

As we noted for the cost of carry, the income earned is dependent on the underlying asset. Thus, accurately estimating the dividend cash flows is key to successful stock index arbitrage. The issuance of dividends is reasonably seasonal; however, even for short periods they may be delayed or even brought forward. Similarly, whilst analysts can offer reasonable estimates for the normal dividend amounts, special dividends can be much harder to predict. Unfortunately, special dividends often make a substantial proportion of the overall dividend cash flow, as James Cummings and Alex Frino (2007) note. Clearly, the risk of inaccuracy is greater for larger indices, such as the Russell 2000, and for longer periods.

Example 13-6: Let's determine the cost of carry and fair value for the S&P 500 SEP 2007 future using the following data for the 26th of June 2007, from www.IndexArb.com (2007).

- The SEP 07 contract has 87 days to expiry
- The short-term interest rate is around 5.52%.
- The cash index value is 1492.89

Before we can substitute these values into equation 13-7, we need to estimate a figure for the income earned from dividends *(I)*. The estimate from www.indexArb.com (2007) for this is $57,411, which we may convert into index points by using an appropriate divisor. In this case, the divisor is 8,883.46 giving an adjusted dividend of 6.46 index points. Note we shall assume the storage cost is zero. Thus, the cost of carry may be determined as:

$$C = (1492.89 * 1.0552^{\,87/365}) - 6.46 = 12.78$$

Using equation 13-6 the fair value of the future is (1492.89 + 12.78) = 1505.67.

Example 13-6(a): Let's now assume the current S&P 500 SEP 07 futures price is 1510.00.

Compared to our fair value of 1505.67 the futures contract seems overpriced, with a basis of -17.11. Therefore, it may be worth considering a cash and carry trade, selling the September future and buying the equivalent basket of stocks. Table 13-7 shows the resultant cash flows for such a strategy.

Date	Action	Underlying cash flow/$	Futures cash flow/$
26 June	Buy stocks for $250 x 1492.89 Borrow cash at 5.52% Sell SEP future at 1510.00	-373222.50	
21 Sept	Sell stocks for $250 x 1533.38 Receive dividends, $250 x 6.46 Interest payments for 87 days loan Future expires, $250 x (1510.00-1533.38)	383,345.00 1,615.00 -4,810.58	 -5845.00
	Gross amounts	6,926.92	-5845.00
	Total		1,081.92

Table 13-7 Example cash flows for cash and carry index arbitrage

Note that the S&P 500 is a market capitalization based index, so each constituent has a weighting based on their company's size. To make things slightly easier we will assume we can create a basket of stocks equivalent to the value of the futures contract. The value of this basket is equal to the futures multiplier ($250) times the index closing price. [2] The S&P 500 futures contract expires on the third Friday of the delivery month, in this case September 21st; at which point we must sell back our stocks (with market on open orders) whilst the future is settled for cash.

---

[2] Alternatively, we could use the E-Mini contract that has a multiplier of $50.

Also, note that throughout the lifetime of this trade there will be various other cash flows, such as the daily futures margin payments and loan interest payments. Stock dividends will also be paid out intermittently over the period, and may be reinvested until expiry to further reduce costs. For simplicity, all these cash flows are merely presented in Table 13-7 as accumulated sums to be paid at expiry.

Overall, we can see that in this example the profit is derived solely from the cash leg, which had a gross profit of nearly $7,000. Much of this was due to the overall increase of the stock index, although the dividend payments actually ensured that the strategy did more than break even. Offsetting this were the interest payments and the loss of nearly $6,000 on the futures position. The futures leg did provide a successful hedge, since if the index had fallen we would have been in the opposite position. If this had happened, the profit from the futures contract would have compensated for the loss on the stocks.

Example 13-6(b): In actual fact the S&P 500 SEP 2007 futures price closed at 1497.80 on the 26th of June.

Compared to our fair value of 1505.67 the futures contract now seems underpriced, with a basis of -4.91. Therefore a reverse cash and carry trade is actually more appropriate. So we should consider buying the September future and selling the equivalent basket of stocks. The resultant cash flows for this approach are shown in Table 13-8.

Date	Action	Underlying cash flow/$	Futures cash flow/$
26 June	Sell stocks for $250 x 1492.89 Lend cash at 5.52% Buy SEP future at 1497.80	373222.50	
21 Sept	Buy stocks for $250 x 1533.38 Interest from 87 days loan Future expires, $250 x (1533.38-1497.80)	-383,345.00 4,810.58	8,895.00
	Gross amounts	-5,311.92	8,895.00
	Total		3,583.08

Table 13-8 Example cash flows for reverse cash and carry index arbitrage

This time, our long futures position actually benefits from the increase in the index level, leading to a gross profit of $8,895. In comparison, our short cash position realised losses of $10,122, which were offset by the $4810 income from interest. Though, since we were short stock, there was no additional income from dividends.

Note that for both of these examples the final value of the stock basket is actually based on the futures settlement price (1533.38), rather than the opening price of the S&P 500 on the 21st (1520.11). This is because the index's opening price is based on when the NYSE opened rather than when all the morning's opening auctions had completed, which could actually be some time after the official open. Therefore, the official index open is actually based on some stocks' close prices from the 20th. So at expiry the CME instead provides a special opening quotation (SOQ), which is not finalised until all of the index constituent's official opening prices are set. This ensures that arbitrageurs can liquidate their trades at coordinated levels. Though, it does mean that there can sometimes be a sizable difference between these two prices. The SOQ was introduced in June 1987 to try to minimise the volatility, prior to this settlement was based on the closing price. For more information, please see the CME (2005) documentation.

There are some further complications, which were omitted from Example 13-6 (a) and (b) for clarity. Real-world arbitrage strategies must cope with the risk that the cost of carry is uncertain. Over the length of the trade short-term interest rates could shift, similarly the dividend cash flow may differ from its estimate. Arbitrageurs must also account for factors such as transaction costs, interest rates and market regulations.

Transaction costs obviously have a direct impact on arbitrage opportunities; high costs can make even significant mispricings unprofitable. Consequently, arbitrage models should also factor in the bid offer spread for the stocks and futures, as well as any fees or commissions. For larger waves, market impact could be an important factor as well. Also, when shorting stocks the cost of borrowing them must also be considered. This means that index futures are more often underpriced than overpriced, as Catherine Shalen (2002) points out.

Funding rates can also have an effect. The same funding rate was used throughout Example 13-6 (a) and (b). Though, the interest rates to borrow will be slightly higher than this market rate, whilst those for lending will be lower.

Market regulations can also have a noticeable impact on arbitrage. Short selling restrictions, such as the up-tick rule, make it more difficult to keep the cash and futures legs synchronized. Market collars also pose a considerable problem. For example, the NYSE Rule 80A enforces a collar based on the DJIA index; when triggered it requires index-arbitrage orders for the S&P 500 stocks to be stabilizing. So if the index falls 190 points (from the prior close) arbitrage orders can only be sold on an up-tick; conversely, if it rises by this amount buy orders must be on a down-tick.

To counter some of these issues, arbitrageurs often close out of their positions before the futures contract expires. Indeed a study of the NYSE by George Sofianos (1990) found this to be true for over 70% of positions, with liquidation occurring upon reversal of the original mispricing or within a few days. Arbitrageurs may also sometimes trade only a portion of the actual index, instead creating a subset that acts as a proxy. Although this offers reduced transaction costs, it does create the potential risk of tracking error between the proxy and the actual index.

Clearly, successful index arbitrage is non-trivial. Whilst there is still plenty of money to be made from this, it is not without some risk or difficulty. To automate this process we require detailed price models that need to take account of all of these factors. Similarly, to perform the trading we shall need to use approaches for handling baskets of orders, as we saw in Chapter 12. This will also need to be linked to the futures trading.

ETF Index Arbitrage

The daily creation and redemption mechanism for ETFs ensures that there is a natural arbitrage between these funds and their underlying assets. Therefore, when the ETF trades at a premium (discount) to its net asset value (NAV) dealers can simply sell (buy) the ETF and buy (sell) the underlying assets. This ensures that any mispricing for the ETF is kept to a minimum.

The rapid growth of the ETF marketplace has given rise to new arbitrage opportunities. In particular, for index arbitrage they can replace the cash leg. ETFs are attractive to arbitrageurs because they are:

- based on the actual index
- easy to short

- not subject to any up-tick rules
- potentially much cheaper to trade than a basket of stocks

Since ETFs represent a pro-rata share in a fund modelled on the index they should have a negligible tracking error. Their inherent daily creation mechanism means that short sales pose no issues. As Gary Gastineau (2003) notes, this also means short squeezes are not possible. The lack of an up-tick rule also makes them much more flexible when selling. Thus ETFs circumvent many of the issues we saw in the previous section. They offer a low risk and cost efficient alternative for index arbitrageurs, provided they have sufficient liquidity.

There is one key difference between using a basket of stocks or an ETF for the cash leg of an index arbitrage, as Andrew Economopoulos (2005) highlights: For ETFs, dividends are accumulated in the fund and distributed 45 days after the ex-dividend date. The value of these accumulated dividends will actually be discounted, so the market price of an ETF will be slightly lower than its net asset value (NAV). This also means the ETF may actually trade at a slight premium to the index, which will also be reflected in any futures fair value based on the ETF price.

Arguably, the main appeal of ETFs is their potential to substantially reduce transaction costs. For instance, Economopoulos (2005) gives an example of the S&P 500, where ten SPDR shares are equivalent to the index. For a portfolio worth $25 million he estimated a total cost of $170,362 for trading the cash index. In comparison using the SPDR ETF cost $45,357 whilst the futures only cost $2,777. Table 13-9 helps to explain these differences.

	Shares purchased	Average spread ($)	Cost (bps)
Cash index	714,185	0.219	68
ETF	266,810	0.15	18

Source: Economopoulos (2005)

Table 13-9 Round trip cost comparison between cash and ETFs

The main cause is the sheer number of stocks which have to be traded. Combined with a higher spread this leads to a total cash index cost of 68 bps, whereas the ETF costs some 50 bps less. Even accounting for the fund management costs of 4.6 bps the ETF offers a considerable saving over trading cash equities.

Note that realizing these savings requires the ETF to have enough liquidity. So the liquidity premium must be sufficiently low; otherwise it will cancel out any savings. For instance, Economopoulos (2005) points out that prior to 1996, even though the SPDR ETF offered a cost advantage, its liquidity was insufficient to attract traders as a cash substitute. He also notes that the mispricing relationship declined after November, 1997, suggesting increased arbitrage. This seems to be linked to the CME halving the denomination of the S&P 500 futures contract, and their earlier introduction of the E-mini contract. Likewise, an earlier study by Lorne Switzer, Paula Varson and Samia Zghidi (2000) found that the introduction of the SPDR ETF had improved the pricing efficiency in the futures market, observing that mispricing was negatively related to SPDR volume.

Another benefit of arbitrage using ETFs is that we no longer need to trade baskets of assets. Thus a more straightforward pair trading approach may be used, although we will still clearly need a sophisticated pricing model.

Option arbitrage

Put-call parity is a key principle in option pricing, most notably demonstrated by Hans Stoll (1969). He highlighted the relationship between the fair values for a pair of identical European call and put options and their underlying asset, as shown in equation 13-8:

$$C_t + Xe^{-rt} = P_t + I_t \qquad\qquad (13\text{-}8)$$

where C is the price of the call option, P is the price of the put, I is the price of the underlying, X is their strike price, r is the interest rate and t is the time left to expiry. Note that this depends on the put and the call having the same strike price and expiration.

Stoll showed that by using this principle the payoff of any one of the trio may be recreated by an appropriate combination of the other two. Hence, the whole concept of synthetic option positions was spawned. For example, a synthetic long call is just a long position in the underlying combined with purchasing an at-the-money (ATM) put. Alternatively, a synthetic long put corresponds to a short position in the underlying together with the purchase of an ATM call option.

Using put-call parity we should always be able to infer the fair price for a call or a put option based on the prices of the other two assets. So, any mispricing may be easily spotted and taken advantage of by arbitrageurs. If the call option is relatively overpriced then a conversion strategy may be used. This means selling the call and hedging by creating a synthetic long call position. Alternatively, if the put option is overpriced we may adopt a reversal, or reverse conversion strategy, which consists of selling the overpriced put and hedging with a synthetic long put.

A conversion strategy comprises of selling ATM call options, and buying the underlying and ATM puts. Alternatively, we can view this as going long the underlying and creating a synthetic short position. Figure 13-4 shows the payouts for this strategy.

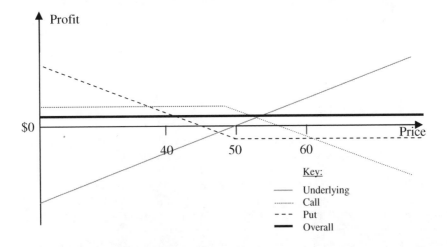

Figure 13-4 Payouts for the conversion strategy

Any gains in the underlying will be offset by losses from the calls; similarly, any losses will be compensated for by gains in the puts. Hence, the position is completely hedged.

Example 13-7(a): Asset HJK is currently trading at $50. The OCT 50 call is priced at $3 whilst the OCT 50 put is $2. The interest rate is 5.52%.

Based on equation 13-8, we should first determine the discount factor, assuming that both options will expire in a month, so $e^{-rt} = e^{-1/12 \times 0.0552} = 0.995$.

We can now substitute these values into the put-call parity equation (13-8):

$$3 + (50 \times 0.995) = 2 + 50 \Rightarrow 52.75 \neq 52$$

Clearly, either the call option is overpriced or the put is underpriced. Assuming that the call option price is fair then the put option should actually be $2.75.

Either way, we can take advantage of this with a conversion strategy:

	Income		Outgoings
• Buy underlying			$50 x 100 = $5,000
• Sell ATM calls	$3 x 100 = $300		
• Buy ATM puts			$2 x 100 = $200
Total = $ -4,900 =	$300	-	$5,200

Setting up the conversion trade has cost $4,900, so it is $100 cheaper than simply buying the underlying. This saving is due to the difference in pricing between the ATM calls and puts. This profit is immediately locked in, as Figure 13-4 shows.

In October, if the asset price rises to $60 the call options will be in-the-money and so will be exercised. The long underlying position may be used for delivery. The put options will become worthless. Overall, we shall receive $5,000, giving a gross profit of $100.

Conversely, if the price fell to $40 the puts will be in-the-money whilst the call options will be worthless. So we can exercise the put options to sell our underlying position for $5,000, again leaving a gross profit of $100.

Alternatively, if the price does not change we can sell the underlying for $5,000, with a gross profit of $100.

Regardless of the outcome, a gross profit of $100 should be achieved. All that remains is to subtract any interest payments and transaction costs.

For a reversal strategy, we sell ATM put options, and sell the underlying and buy ATM calls. We can also view this as shorting the underlying and creating a synthetic long position. Figure 13-5 plots the potential payouts for this approach.

Example 13-7(b): Asset HJK is still trading at $50, but now the OCT 50 call has fallen to $2 whilst the OCT 50 put has risen to $3.

Let's assume the call price is fair, in which case, based on the discount we calculated in Example 13-7(a), the put should be priced at $1.77. This time the put is overpriced relative to the call, in which case we can adopt a reversal:

	Income		Outgoings
• Sell underlying	$50 x 100 = $5,000		
• Buy ATM calls			$2 x 100 = $200
• Sell ATM puts	$3 x 100 = $300		
Total = $ 5,100 =	$5,300	-	$200

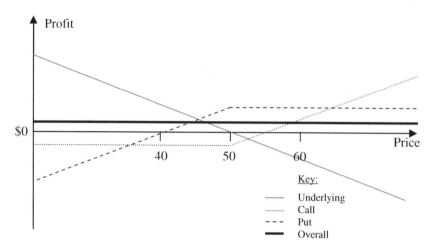

Figure 13-5 Payouts for the reversal strategy

Again, setting up the reversal trade has proven more profitable than simply shorting the underlying. Once more, the profit is derived from the difference in pricing between the ATM calls and puts, and is instantly locked in. As we can see from Figure 13-5, any losses on the underlying are offset by gains from the calls, whilst any gains are neutralised by the puts.

In October, if the asset price rises to $60 the call options will be in-the-money and so will be exercised, allowing us to flatten our underlying short for $5,000. The puts will expire worthless. Hence, the overall gross profit remains $100.

If the price falls to $40 then our call options will expire worthless. Though, the put options we sold will expire in-the-money, so the purchaser will want to sell us 100 HJK for $5,000. This flattens our short position, leaving us with $100 profit again.

If the price does not change, we can flatten our short position, at a cost of $5,000.

The net profit for this strategy will also incorporate any interest earned for the $5,000 over the month, which will help offset any borrowing costs associated with shorting the underlying.

Futures and options arbitrage

The put-call parity relationship we saw in equation 13-8 relates the prices of options with the price of the underlying asset. Similarly, we can relate these to futures positions, as Alan Tucker (1991) showed with the Put-Call-Futures (P-C-F) parity relationship.

The price of a stock index future may be related to the underlying index price *(S)* by its forward value:

$$F_t = S_t e^{(r-q)\tau}$$

where q is a constant rate representing income from dividends, r is the risk-free rate and τ is the time to expiry. Sheri Markose and Hakan Er (2000) rearrange this to show that discounting the futures price gives the underlying stock index price adjusted for dividends:

$$F_t e^{-r\tau} = S_t e^{-q\tau}$$

We can substitute this into the right hand side of the put-call parity equation (13-8) to express it in terms of the futures price, and so define the P-C-F parity:

$$C_t + X e^{-r\tau} = P_t + F_t e^{-r\tau}$$

If the futures contract is underpriced relative to the options we can take advantage using a conversion strategy. Essentially, this is the same as we saw in Example 13-7(a), except we go long the futures contract rather than the underlying. To counter this position, a synthetic short future is created by selling ATM calls and buying the equivalent puts. The synthetic future is completed by lending an additional cash amount, based on the discounted difference between the strike price and the futures price i.e. $(X - F_t) e^{-r\tau}$.

Whereas if the futures contract is overpriced compared to the options then we can adopt a reversal strategy, as we saw in Example 13-7(b). Again, rather than shorting the underlying we sell the futures contract. This is then hedged with a synthetic long futures position, from buying ATM calls and selling the puts and borrowing $(X - F_t) e^{-r\tau}$.

Trading a futures contract is a much cheaper alternative to trading a basket of stocks. So trading based solely on index futures and options can prove a cost-effective and efficient means of index arbitrage.

In their study of FTSE-100 P-C-F arbitrage, Markose and Er (2000) note that when the index future is at its fair value the put-call and put-call-futures parity conditions are identical. They concluded that some of the most profitable P-C-F arbitrage opportunities were for futures contracts further from maturity, such as 20-50 and 50-80 days. They also noted that the so-called Black effect could have a substantial impact on the opportunities for arbitrage. This is due to market makers for index options often using the Fisher Black (1976) pricing method, a modification of the Black Scholes formula that is based on the futures price rather than the index. The effect can mean that overpriced index futures lead to overpriced calls and underpriced puts, and vice-versa. Markose and Er (2000) found that the Black effect limited the efficiency of P-C-F arbitrage and in some circumstances noted that arbitrage could even exacerbate the futures underlying mispricing.

Dividend arbitrage

Company dividend payments can be an important source of earnings. Dividend arbitrage combines a position in the stock with deep in-the-money options in order to lock in profits.

When a dividend is formally announced, the company will specify when the payment will actually be made, termed the due date. They also stipulate the record date that determines the actual entitlement, since only the shareholders of record at this time will receive payments. However, since it takes time for trades to be cleared and settled, the exchange will usually set a separate deadline. This is the ex-dividend (or ex-div) date, which is often two days before the record date. Anyone purchasing the stock before the ex-dividend date will receive the dividend, even if they subsequently sell the stock. Thus, the market price usually reflects this fact with a price drop equal to the dividend, as shown in Figure 13-6.

If we buy the stock just before the ex-div date we are effectively paying a premium based on the dividend value. The price drop at the ex-div date will realise an immediate loss for long positions. Only at the subsequent due date will the dividend actually be paid. So a quick sale will often return a loss, or at best a negligible profit. To lock in any profits from the dividend there are two main types of arbitrage based on either buying put options or selling call options.

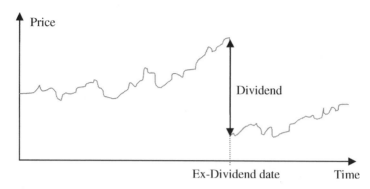

Figure 13-6 The price effect of stock dividend payments

By purchasing an in-the-money put option at the same time as buying the stocks, we have locked in an exit price. Although, there will be a significant premium to be paid for such options. In order for this strategy to be profitable, this premium must be less than the exercise profit and the dividend payment.

Example 13-8: Stock EFG is trading at $50; it goes ex-div on the 20th September paying $2/share. A SEP 55 put costs $6.

To lock in dividend profits we can buy 100 EFG and 100 SEP 55 puts. The resultant cash flows are shown in Table 13-10:

Date	Action	Cash flow/$
18 Sept	Buy stocks for $50 x 100	-5,000
	Buy SEP 55 put for $6 x 100	-600
20 Sept	Exercise put for $55 x 100	5,500
	Dividend payment $2 x 100	200
	Total	100

Table 13-10 Dividend arbitrage using puts

The exercise cost is $100 whilst $200 is made from the dividend; therefore, the SEP 55 puts are sufficiently cheap to result in a net profit of $100. This trade is risk free since we have flattened our long position by exercising the puts, so we are unaffected by price changes on the ex-div date.

The alternative approach is to sell an in-the-money call option. Though, this relies on the fact that assignment does not occur before the ex-div date (that is the purchaser does not exercise them). At which point, the price drop will affect both the stock and its options. We should be able to buy back the call option more cheaply, which will offset the losses from our stock position, leaving the dividend payment as profit.

Example 13-9: Stock HJK is trading at $60; it goes ex-div on the 16th October paying $2/share. An OCT 50 call costs $10.

We can lock in the dividend profits by going long 100 HJK and selling 100 calls. Assuming that the call options were not assigned, the cash flows for the stocks and options balance out leaving $200 profit from the dividend, as shown in Table 13-11.

Date	Action	Cash flow/$
15 Oct	Buy stocks for $60 x 100	-6,000
	Sell OCT 50 call for $10 x 100	1,000
16 Oct	Sell stocks for $58 x 100	5,800
	Buy call for $8 x 100	-800
	Dividend payment, $2 x 100	200
	Total	200

Table 13-11 Dividend arbitrage using covered calls

Thus, the main risk with this strategy is the likelihood of the call option being assigned before the ex-div date, which would lead to a loss of the dividend profits. Further examples may be found at TheOptionsGuide.com (2007).

13.7 Adapting algorithms for multi-asset trading

In many ways, multi-asset trading algorithms are similar to the two-sided portfolio trading algorithms we saw in Chapter 12. Though, since they involve a more diverse range of markets they are more likely to suffer from marked differences in liquidity. This could pose real problems for achieving best execution. Therefore, risk models need to start expanding to cope with this.

Factors to consider for multi-asset trading algorithms

Obviously, the main starting point for any multi-asset trading is to already have successful algorithms in place for trading each of the target asset classes. This ensures that any asset class specific issues have already been identified and appropriate adjustments have been made.

Multi-asset trading adds an extra level of complexity since it will invariably mean trading across different trading platforms, currencies and time-zones. Hence, it is vital that any trading algorithms can cope with differences in:

- Liquidity
- Latency
- Transparency
- Consistency
- Dependency

Otherwise, there may be a considerable additional risk exposure.

Liquidity

As we saw in Chapter 3, liquidity varies considerably between the various markets and asset classes, just as it does between specific assets. Multi-asset trading algorithms need to balance their trading based on the liquidity of the target assets. Simplistically, this means focussing on the lowest common denominator, so the most illiquid asset drives the rate of trading.

For instance, when trading a corporate bond against its stock, orders might only be placed for the stock leg once an execution has been confirmed for the less liquid bond. Alternatively, we could use legging to provide some more flexibility over execution, just as we saw for pairs trades. Though, for very illiquid assets this could expose us to significant risk. Whilst such approaches will work, they could miss opportunities for the more liquid assets.

Latency

Latency can be just as important as liquidity. It makes it harder to rely on the prices we can see, since by the time our order is handled the price may have shifted.

Each asset class may well be traded over different platforms, across different execution venues and possibly even spanning time-zones. Exchanges are now focussed on reaching turnaround times less than 10 ms. However, there are still plenty of venues where this figure is more like 100 ms or more. So there are bound to be differences in latency between the venues.

The actual trading mechanism is another key factor for latency, since it is quite possible that trading might need to span both order books and request-for-quote (RFQ) or request-for-stream (RFS) based platforms. In such cases, the difference in latencies might range from milliseconds to seconds.

For example, let's consider executing a simple pairs trade, both assets have the same liquidity except one trades at a venue with a latency of 50ms whilst for the other it is 500ms. If we place a matching buy and sell order for each asset there is at least 450ms of uncertainty. A busy trader might not notice this lag; after all, it is equivalent to a few blinks. However, it can still have an appreciable effect. In order to compensate for this, the trading algorithm will have to bias trading towards the venue with higher latency.

Transparency

Transparency can also vary considerably between markets. Within a single market, differing levels of transparency have proved fairly successful. Highly transparent primary venues allow for easy price discovery, whilst more opaque venues enable volume discovery. Indeed, the "dark pool" ATSs have proven so successful for equities because although being opaque their price discovery tends to be based on the primary exchanges.

Across asset classes, differences in transparency can pose more of a problem, since there are no equivalent links. For instance, the entire order book might be visible when trading stocks, but for other assets we might only be able to see the best bid and offer. Although we might have confidence of best execution for our stock trading, it is much harder to have this for the other assets.

Consistency

Consistency is another major factor for ensuring successful multi-asset trading, particularly for transaction costs. As we saw in section 13.6, there is a wide range of arbitrage opportunities between asset classes. For these to be profitable it is vital that any additional costs are considered when looking at relative prices. This might be as obvious as incorporating the different bid offer spreads, commissions or routing/handling fees. However, it must also include asset specific factors such as storage/delivery fees, accrued interest or dividend payments.

Dependency

Over the years, microstructure studies have analysed the price relationships across many of the different asset classes. For example, studies have focussed on whether the futures markets lead or lag the markets for their underlying assets. Such inter-market relationships are an important source of information for short-term predictions of prices and other market conditions, as we will see in Chapter 15. Taking advantage of these could be the difference between a profitable trading strategy and a loss-making one.

Minimising risk

Lower transaction costs may be achieved for portfolios by maximising the natural hedging, or diversification, for as long as possible. Therefore, it is quite likely that risk-based models, similar to those we saw for portfolio trading, will be at the heart of next generation multi-asset algorithms. Clearly, constructing multi-asset risk models is more complex than the existing single asset ones. However, these should hopefully provide the flexibility required to achieve best execution for all the assets in a mixed portfolio.

For example, let's consider the dummy trade list shown in Table 13-12.

Asset	Size/$mm	Side	Liquidity	Risk
Euro mid-cap stock	10	Buy	Medium	High
Euro equity put options	2	Buy	Low	Medium
Euro FX	10	Buy	High	Medium
U.S. equity put options	2	Buy	Medium	Low
U.S. large-cap stock	10	Buy	High	Low

Table 13-12 Potential prioritisation for a sample portfolio

In this particular case, the European mid-cap stock and its put options have the lowest liquidity. Note that the put options are intended for hedging and so may be made dependent on the underlying stock position. The out-of-the-money puts for the U.S. large-cap stock are assigned a lower overall risk than the FX trade, since the required size is less. Hence, for this basket the mid-cap stock position poses the most risk, so we can target this more aggressively. This is clearly a simplistic example, but it highlights the fact that liquidity should not be the sole determinant when evaluating trading strategies.

A more quantitative approach would be to determine the marginal contribution to risk (MCR) for each order in the trade list and then adjust their execution accordingly, as we saw in Chapter 12. We should also try to incorporate factors such as latency into the estimates for timing risk.

Trading algorithm choice

The simplest multi-asset orders could be handled by slight extensions to existing algorithms. For example, we could extend the pairs/spread trading mechanism that we saw in Chapter 5. An additional leg could incorporate handling FX cash trades with relative ease.

Alternatively, for strategies where there is a clear dependency between the orders, a conditional algorithm could be created; essentially, this would just use conditional orders. This could be used to try to cover short sales with orders for lending/repos. It might also provide the mechanism for simple structured notes, or even some hedging.

For more complex strategies, the "algorithm of algorithms" approach that we saw in Chapter 12 seems a reasonable starting point. Again, the portfolio algorithm would need to contain the required control logic, whilst the individual orders could continue to use standard single asset algorithms. So stock, bond, currency, future and option positions could each be handled by their own algorithms, which the portfolio algorithm continually checks and adjusts. If the links between the investor and the broker are sufficiently fast and reliable, there is no real reason why the portfolio algorithm could not reside on the buy-side, with updates sent to the individual algorithms being worked on the sell-side.

Similarly, since hedging and arbitrage rely on position information and potentially proprietary analytics these are good candidates for in-house development by the buy-side.

13.8 Summary

- Multi-asset trading strategies are now more widely accessible due to electronic trading:
    - Utility strategies incorporate FX cash trades or cover short sales.
    - Some structured products may be recreated using algorithms.
    - Hedging strategies offset risk, whether this is for duration, beta, delta or gamma.
    - Arbitrage strategies take advantage of mispricing between assets, even between asset classes. Hedging is also vital to lock these profits in by staying risk-free.

- To cope with trading across different asset classes it is vital that strategies take account of differences in:
    - Liquidity
    - Latency
    - Transparency

- For best execution, strategies must also ensure that prices are compared consistently, by including any relevant asset specific costs or factors.

- Strategies may also use established inter-market price relationships to gain an edge from short-term price forecasts.

- Multi-asset trading may require extensions to existing trading algorithms to deal with:
    - Adding conditional orders
    - Adopting a pairs/spread trading approach
    - Handling the different legs as a portfolio, possibly adopting an "algorithm of algorithms" to minimise risk

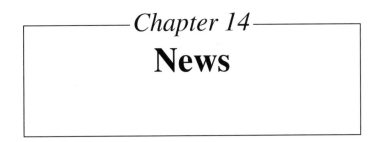

Information is everything. Automated news handling and interpretation can be complex, but these techniques offer the potential to further enhance trading strategy performance.

14.1 Introduction

The world's markets are driven by information, much of which is reported in news headlines and stories. Adapting to breaking news events can give traders a significant edge over the rest of the market. Over the last few years, the incorporation of news into algorithmic trading systems has attracted more and more attention.

Clearly, the relentless increase in both the speed and capacity of computers offers a massive potential for news-based analysis. Nevertheless, people are still much more adept at interpreting news and events than machines. Computer-based news analysis is a non-trivial task. Part of the difficulty is simply the fact that news is often based on unstructured text so it is difficult for rule-based systems to process it, and even harder for them to reliably interpret it. The increasing digitisation of news to computer-readable formats is helping to bridge this gap. Complex artificial intelligence and natural language processing techniques are also being employed. As we shall see in the following sections, progress is being made on computer-based analysis, but there is still quite a long way to go.

14.2 Types of news

News items can represent a wide variety of information. Broadly speaking, we can categorise most news items into three main classes: global/regional, macroeconomic and corporate.

Event	*Examples*
Global/regional	Political events, wars and terrorism, natural disasters
Macroeconomic	Interest rate, US non-farm payroll, Gross Domestic Product (GDP) announcements
Corporate	Mergers and acquisitions, bankruptcies, board/executive changes, product releases, quarterly/annual reports, dividend announcements

Table 14-1 Key news types

Table 14-1 shows some examples. Note that all three types of news can have distinct effects on the volume and volatility of both markets and specific assets. Though, the full effects of global/regional news can be quite difficult to interpret. Hence, this chapter focuses on the impact of both macroeconomic and corporate news.

Macroeconomic news

Most macroeconomic news comes in the form of regular announcements that provide information on key economic indicators. There is a wide range of different indicators; some of the main ones for the U.S. economy are shown in Table 14-2.

Class	Announcement Type	Freq	Time
GDP	Gross Domestic Product (GDP)	Q	8:30
Consumption	Personal Consumption Expenditures	M	8:30
Investment	Business Inventories	M	8:30
	Durable Goods Orders	M	8:30
	Factory Orders	M	10:00
	Construction Spending	M	10:00
	New Home Sales	M	10:00
Net Exports	Trade Balance	M	8:30
Government Expenditure	Government Budget	M	14:00
FOMC	Target Federal Funds Rate	6W	14:15
Money supply	M2	W	16:30
Real Activity	Non-Farm Payrolls/Employment	M	8:30
	Initial Unemployment Claims	W	8:30
	Industrial Production Capacity Utilization	M	9:15
	Retail Sales	M	8:30
	Personal Income	M	8:30
	Consumer Credit	M	15:00
Prices	Producer Price Index (PPI)	M	8:30
	Consumer Price Index (CPI)	M	8:30
Forward-Looking	Index of Leading Indicators	M	8:30
	ISM/NAPM Index	M	10:00
	Consumer Confidence Index	M	10:00
	Housing Starts	M	8:30

Table 14-2 Some of the key U.S. macroeconomic announcements

The classification scheme is based on those commonly adopted in economic literature. In the U.S., most of the announcements are made monthly (M), although some are issued quarterly (Q) or weekly (W). Indicators may also be referred to as procyclical or countercyclical; this just shows whether they move in the same direction as the economy or not. For instance, GDP and Non-Farm payrolls are procyclical indicators, whilst unemployment claims is a countercyclical one.

The *Gross Domestic Product* (GDP) is probably the best-known indicator of an economy. It represents the total value of goods and services produced by a country, usually over a year. Another way of expressing GDP is:

GDP = Consumption + Investment + Net Exports – Government Expenditure

GDP announcements are generally made quarterly and often in several stages, beginning with an advance figure, followed by preliminary and then final figures. The Real GDP is a GDP based indicator that includes adjustments for price changes and inflation.

Consumption represents private consumption; in other words, household expenditures on food, clothing and bills for utilities, health, education and insurance.

Investment corresponds to the investment in capital, which in turn is broken down into several sub-categories: *Business Inventories* reflects the three stages of production, namely manufacturing, wholesaling and retail. Effectively, it acts as a leading indicator for consumer demand. *Durable Goods Orders* measures the number of orders placed with manufacturers, similarly *Factory Orders* monitors the total order placements. These give an indication of the health of the factory/manufacturing sectors. The remaining investment indicators highlight the state of the building/housing markets. *Construction Spending* provides an estimate of the total domestic expenditure on all types of construction, whilst *New Home Sales* focuses on family dwellings. These may be used to estimate the future demand for mortgages. Housing market indicators also often act as a leading indicator for the general health of the economy.

Net Exports are reflected by the balance of trade. Essentially, this is the difference between the value of an economy's imports and exports.

Government Expenditure is represented by the overall budget, which incorporates the cost of government services and projects as well as the wage bill for government sector employees.

Another important economic indicator is the *Target Federal Funds rate*, which reflects U.S. monetary policy. For the money markets, the *M2* indicator measures the total U.S currency held in reserves, checking, savings or current accounts.

The *Real Activity* indicators provide a view on key economic activities such as employment, retail sales, credit and personal income. *Non-Farm Payrolls*, or the *Employment* report, provides a count of the number of paid full and part-time employees. Whilst the *Initial Unemployment Claims* shows the number of people newly out of work. *Industrial Production* gives a measure of the output of domestic industries. *Retail Sales* values the total sales from retail stores, and so reflects consumer spending. *Personal Income* measures the total income before and after taxes, whilst *Consumer Credit* measures the level of personal debt.

The *Price Indices* provide measures of the average costs for manufacturers (PPI) or for consumers (CPI). Therefore, they act as indicators for inflation, whether it is for commodity prices or domestic.

Most of the indicators so far mentioned provide a lagged measure of economic performance. The *Index of Leading Indicators* tries to provide a forecast for the economy in the next six to nine months. The *Institute for Supply Management* (ISM) *Survey*, formerly the National Association of Purchasing Management (NAPM), gives an indication of whether the manufacturing sector is expanding or contracting. Similarly, the *Consumer Confidence* survey measures the level of optimism held by consumers.

Macroeconomic indicators may differ slightly for other countries, but essentially they all offer the same kind of information.

Corporate news

For corporations, news arrives in two main forms: Company reports provide regular indications on the economic strength of a firm. Other corporate news is just a catch-all for any important event that might happen for a firm.

Company reports provide results, showing their historical performance, and estimates for future earnings and growth. Often these are made yearly, although for some countries, such as the U.S., they are filed quarterly. Unlike macroeconomic indicators, these are not tied to specific dates, firms may freely choose to bring forward or delay their reports. The same applies for any dividend announcements.

In terms of other corporate news, a wide range of specific events may occur. This can include anything from:

- New issues or repurchases, of shares or debt
- New or lost orders/sales
- New product releases
- Joint ventures/mergers/takeovers
- Management changes
- Lawsuits
- Bankruptcy
- Analyst upgrades/downgrades

Obviously, such news tends to be less predictable, both in terms of when it is released and how the market reacts to it.

14.3 The changing face of news

News has been steadily changing over the last few years, from how it is delivered to where it is being sourced.

Increasingly, news items are being fully digitised into machine-readable formats. This is making it much easier for computer programs to filter and even analyse the information from news stories.

The internet has also had a significant impact, making alternative sources of information, such as message boards and blogs, easily accessible. In fact, these are even starting to compete with the mainstream news services to deliver scoops, although credibility and reliability are still issues.

Digitisation of news

News has been available digitally, in one form or other, for decades. Though, only over the last few years have we seen more efforts to make it easier for computers to actually process and interpret it.

When news screens first became accessible digitally, they were simply copies of the original terminal screens. An example is simulated in Figure 14-1.

```
09:06 NEWS Futures slip as fears persist on subprime
09:05 NEWS DEF Corp Q2 results $0.25 EPS
09:04 NEWS AN Other Corp raise offer for Target One to $5.50/sh
09:03 VEND Target One shareholders getting impatient over bidding
09:01 NEWS BANK-2 writes down $7 bn on subprime, sector falls
09:00 NEWS AN Other says merger makes sense
08:55 HOT1 More doom and gloom, poll expects turmoil to continue
08:51 ALER Commodities rally as oil reaches new high
08:49 NEWS AFG Inc expands into Asia with $500 mn new plant
```

Figure 14-1 An example news terminal screen

The only real way to handle news in this format is to extract the raw text, also known as "screen scraping". Just like web page scraping, this has been used as a means of merging headlines from a range of sources or adding rudimentary filtering. Although such an approach is useful for delivering headlines for traders to read, it is less suitable for computerised news analysis and interpretation.

In the early '90s, vendors introduced news feeds that could deliver separate headlines and stories. For example, Reuters journalists tagged each headline and story with specific categories. The categories covered markets, countries, languages, industries and companies. This was a more versatile delivery mechanism, making storage and retrieval of news much easier. The category codes could be easily used to filter news items. However, the news was still in a single body of text, which had to be parsed for interpretation and analysis.

```
Headline: 09:05 NEWS DEF Corp Q2 results $0.25 EPS
                                         |Symbol|DEF.Q|Type|Research
Story:
|Time|09:05            |Source|VEN1
|Symbol|DEF.Q           |Type|Research         |Country|US
|Title|DEF Corp Q2 results $0.25 EPS
|Story|  * Second quarter earnings per share $0.25
         * Second quarter revenue rose 15 percent to $100 million
         * Estimates second quarter earnings per share $0.20
           revenue view $85 million
```

Figure 14-2 An example categorised news headline and story

A simulated example is shown in Figure 14-2 based on the headline we saw in Figure 14-1 for DEF Corp. The data is delivered in a fully digital format, so for readability it is shown as plain text with the different fields separated (using | characters). The natural progression from this has been for vendors to start digitising the actual news content.

```
<News>
    <Headline>DEF Corp Q2 results $0.25 EPS</Headline>
    <Time>09:05 EST</Time>                    <Source>RTRS</Source>
    <Category>CorpEarnings</Category>         <Country>US</Country>
    <Sector>Tech</Sector>        <Identifiier>DEF.Q</Identifier>
    <Results>
        <Type>EPS</Type>
        <Value>25</Value>
        <Units>CPS</Units>
    </Results>
    <Estimate>
        <Type>EPS</Type>
        <Value>20</Value>
        <Units>CPS</Units>
    </Estimate>
  <Story>
      * Second quarter earnings per share $0.25
      . . .
  </Story>
</News>
```

Figure 14-3 An example elementized news story in XML

Indeed, they have started converting their news feeds for delivery in various formats, often based on the Extensible Markup Language (XML). So our example story might now look something like Figure 14-3 (again reformatted for readability). Clearly, this allows more fields to be added to the data and makes the information easier to access. For this example, both the actual earnings per share (EPS) and the estimate figures are now readily accessible for computerised systems, without the need for any text parsing. This allows programs to read in these values in much the same way as they might use bid and offer prices from market data feeds. Hence, they are much more easily incorporated into rules for trading strategies and algorithms. This technology is already available; for example, the Dow Jones Elementized News Feed publishes key corporate and economic data elements such as earnings numbers while simultaneously publishing the news stories about the earnings.

Digitisation of corporate reports/research

Digitisation is also starting to be established for corporate reporting and research. The eXtensible Business Reporting Language (XBRL) provides a framework for corporations to create machine-readable reports. Instead of just being treated as blocks of text and tabular data, XBRL reports ensure that each item has its own unique tag. Thus, every item on the balance sheet or expenses is tagged, and may even be assigned to groups or linked to other items. A taxonomy acts as the classification scheme that enables the data and tags to be correctly interpreted. This allows the same set of information to be viewed and processed in a variety of different ways whilst maintaining consistency. Being machine-readable, this should allow automated systems to perform most of the routine data processing and validation steps. The hope is that this will free up analysts, allowing them to focus on more value-added aspects, whether they are sell-side researchers, buy-side investors, auditing accountants or regulators.

For the companies themselves, XBRL will clearly require a lot of work. Hopefully, it will help streamline the process of corporate data collection and reporting, allowing finance divisions to more quickly and reliably generate management reports and financial statements. Still, the uptake of XBRL is most likely to be determined by regulation, rather than long-term efficiency gains.

Clearly, the migration to something like XBRL is a much bigger task than elementized news feeds. Instead of a handful of major news vendors there are hundreds of thousands of companies across dozens of countries with a wide range of accounting and reporting practices.

The main driving force behind the adoption of XBRL will be the U.S. The SEC has already paved the way for filing in XBRL by U.S. companies and is looking to transform its company information database (EDGAR). To date, this has been a voluntary filing programme, although it should be mandatory for the largest companies from 2009 and for all public companies by 2011. Other countries have also started adopting XBRL. For instance, in Europe the Spanish Stock Exchange now uses it to receive and distribute reports from over 3,000 listed companies. The National Bank of Belgium has plans to migrate the filing of accounts for commercial and industrial companies to XBRL. Similarly, the UK government plans to make XBRL mandatory for the filing of company accounts. The shift to IFRS (International Financial Reporting Standards), a unified set of accounting standards, should also help ease Europe's transition to XBRL. In Asia, the task is more complex, since every country has its own set of accounting standards, each of which will need to be handled by their own XBRL taxonomies. That said, in 2005 more than 800 Chinese companies filed their half-year reports with the Shanghai Stock Exchange using XBRL. The Tokyo Stock

Exchange has also launched a pilot scheme.

Closely linked with XBRL is the Research Information eXchange Mark-up Language (RIXML). This framework is intended for the distribution of investment and financial research. Taken together, these projects mean that most corporate-related reports will be available in completely machine-readable formats. Whilst this is most applicable for quantitative investment systems, trading algorithms may also benefit from the ability to quickly interpret the key information, such as earnings figures/estimates, in real-time updates. More information on XBRL may be found at www.xbrl.org, whilst the homepage for RIXML is www.rixml.org.

Changing sources of news

The internet is steadily transforming the news, in terms of how information is supplied and how quickly, as well as from where it may be sourced. The major news wires and press services have been electronic for a long time. However, conventional media is starting to face fresh competition from social media, which covers the raft of technologies now used to share information and opinions, such as blogs, message boards, wikis and podcasts. Social media sites can offer glimpses of information well before it reaches the mainstream media as official press releases and news wires. Figure 14-4 gives a nice illustration of this shift:

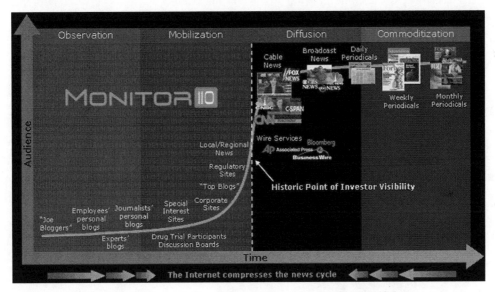

Source: ©Monitor110 (2007)   Reproduced with permission from Monitor110, Inc.

Figure 14-4 The new information dissemination cycle

Companies, such as Collective Intellect, trawl through thousands of web sites and message boards to glean useful information. Official press releases and other information may be extracted from a range of government, regulatory and corporate web sites, whilst opinions and rumours may be sourced from blogs and discussion boards.

Services that aggregate both conventional and alternative media sources are also being established. These provide a uniform means of accessing data from a huge range of feeds. For instance, Relegence's First Track product scans over 18,000 different business-centric sources, ranging from the news wires and business media, to domestic and foreign newspapers, as well as government and corporate web sites and blogs. Their Mail Track product can even incorporate email and its attachments. This is particularly useful given how much information is communicated over email, from internal memos to newsletters and research notes. The major news agencies are also starting to offer similar facilities, for example, news and information from Dow Jones is available through their own current awareness solution (Dow Jones Factiva).

Thus, a new breed of alternative and complementary news services has been created. Will these be the equivalent of ECNs for news?

Potential benefits

Sourcing information from alternative sources can give a significant head start over more conventional news feeds. For instance, over a fortnight before Google's Q4 2005 earnings announcement a blog created by a Yahoo technologist predicted that they would miss their Q4 estimates. Admittedly, this could be seen as misinformation from the competition, in fact CNN Money picked up the story on January 31st with a report titled "Rival trashes Google's growth prospects". However, the prediction proved to be accurate with the stock falling by up to 10% shortly after the earnings announcement, as shown in Figure 14-5(a). Clearly, it is much easier to judge such information with hindsight. Although an alternative point of view from a domain expert is still useful, even if it had proven to be incorrect.

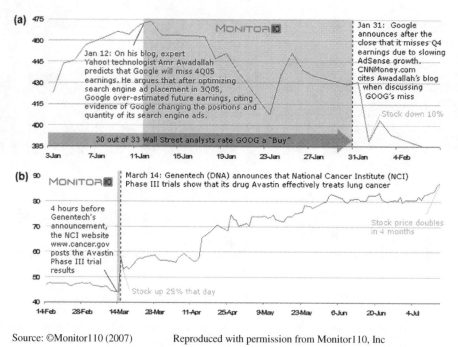

Source: ©Monitor110 (2007)   Reproduced with permission from Monitor110, Inc

Figure 14-5 Two examples of information available before the news wires

Blogs and forums are not the only source of news leads; regulatory bodies can also give an insight into upcoming announcements. This is particularly appropriate in the field of medicine. For example, Figure 14-5(b) highlights an example for Genentech: Avastin is their trade name for Bevacizumab, an anti-angiogenic drug that has been approved for use against colorectal cancer since 2004. On March 14th 2005, the National Cancer Institute (NCI) posted the results of Phase III trials using Bevacizumab combined with chemotherapy for patients with advanced lung cancer. Around four hours later, Genentech released this news to the press, resulting in a 25% hike in its stock price. Anyone who made the connection between Bevacizumab and Genentech could have had a significant market lead.

A note of caution

Credibility is vital for news. The news wires and press services have carefully built their reputations over the last century. Still, human or technical errors may mean incorrect news or old stories can sometimes be picked up: Chief executives have been given premature obituaries and company reports from years before have appeared as if just issued.

Clearly, when using information taken from alternative sources, such as internet blogs or news forums, more caution must be taken. Fake news announcements are not uncommon for micro-cap or penny stocks, with fraudsters adopting "pump and dump" tactics. Though, as David Leinweber and Ananth Madhavan (2001) point out, large-cap stocks are not immune to such fraud either: They use the example of Lucent Technologies, which in March 2000 saw its market cap drop $7 billion in a day, triggered by a series of fake postings. The scam was successful because at the start of the year internet bulletin boards and chat rooms were full of negative rumours about the company, which were confirmed when Lucent issued an earnings warning on January 6th. So on March 22nd, when a series of postings suggested that Lucent would not meet their Q1 earnings projections these carried more weight than might have been expected. Indeed, Lucent's stock price started to fall rapidly. Then in the same evening, a new posting was made titled "LUCENT RELEASES EARNINGS WARNING! DAMN!" together with comments from a disappointed investor and what appeared to be a press release from Lucent, similar to the one from January. This was forwarded to over 20 different message boards. The next day, Lucent's price continued to fall before the company was finally able to convince the market that the news was fraudulent. A subsequent SEC investigation found that a single fraudster had used a trio of aliases to post the fake news item together with a barrage of replies and comments to lend credibility to it. The names used were specifically chosen to be similar to those of established posters, although with user names like "hot_1ike_wasabe" it is clearly hard to tell friend from foe. How did they find the fraudster? Well, unsurprisingly, he made a huge profit from buying Lucent on the 22nd and 23rd of March.

Hence, vendors sourcing data from social media sites are incorporating filters and ranking mechanisms to ensure that only the most reliable sources are used. Analysts are sometimes involved to ensure additional data quality. Some vendors even use voting systems to incorporate end-user feedback on the quality/relevancy of particular articles and sources. Gaining a solid reputation takes both time and results, so for the moment experience gives the established media the edge.

14.4 Computerised news handling techniques

Computerised news handling was originally based on simple categorisation and filtering techniques. In an effort to analyse and interpret this information these have evolved into even more complex mechanisms.

News filtering

Given the amount of information available, news filtering is vital to ensure traders and investors notice the stories that are important to them, rather than being distracted by the general flow of news.

Back in the days of terminals, the news services directly controlled the filtering, providing specific pages for key news topics. Whilst "screen scraping" techniques could be used, it was difficult to achieve 100% accuracy, particularly for companies since a wide range of names and abbreviations may be used. Filtering became much easier when vendors started tagging news with additional data, such as the Reuters News 2000 category codes. Adding this meta-data allowed users to configure custom filters for themselves, based on any combination of category codes. Similarly, elementized news feeds offer the prospect of even finer grained filtering. Instead of having to rely on the categorisations assigned by news editors and/or journalists, we can now create filters which match on the actual contents of the news.

Outside of the mainstream news services, information on web sites, blogs and forums is much more unstructured. Again, these were initially handled with simple "screen scraping" programs. This has since progressed to more advanced techniques based on textual and statistical analysis, or even natural language processing. Commercial software to do this data processing is becoming available, similarly alternative news feed services have started attaching additional meta-data to the raw information, which may then be used for more standardised filtering.

Clustering is closely aligned with filtering, ensuring that we do not see a handful of headlines, from various sources, all for the same event. This can be as simple as removing duplicate headlines. Alternatively, more sophisticated approaches cluster based on their interpretation of the actual information, coping with the fact that each source may use slightly different headlines for the same story. This is offered by systems like Relegance's First Track and Infonic's Burst>.

News association

News stories all differ in their effects. However, implicit relationships mean that beyond the immediate impact, secondary and tertiary effects can also propagate throughout the markets. For instance, macroeconomic factors will often have more immediate impact on the fixed income and foreign exchange markets; ultimately, though, they can also affect stock prices. Likewise, bad news for a company may cause its price to drop, but it may also affect the price of its main competition or even the whole sector.

Ideally, we would like to see any associated news that might affect us. For example, we could simply reduce the level of filtering, e.g. by shifting the focus from company-level to sector-level. Still, we do not want to be so inundated with news that we miss key items. The goal is to strike the best balance between these two extremes. One way of tackling this is to incorporate a dependency model that reflects all the key relationships. For instance, consider a supply chain. It is highly likely that a problem with a component supplier may also affect other companies, both upstream and downstream. In the U.S., firms must disclose financial information for any customer representing more than 10% of the total sales, or any industry segment that comprised more than 10% of consolidated yearly sales, assets or profits. This data may be used to infer the main dependencies.

There are several ways to construct dependency models. For example, services like TextMap create them based on analysis of distinct entities from historical news archives. Figure 14-6 shows an association map for news stories about Google.

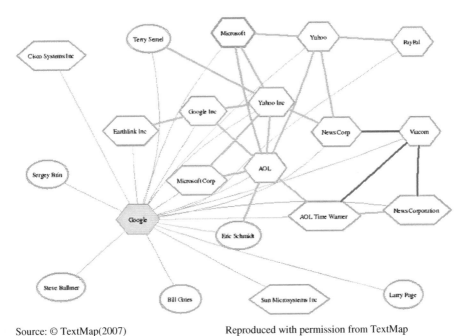

Figure 14-6 An association map for Google

We could also weight the importance of each relationship based the number of news matches. Though, we should probably also try to incorporate how these correlate with actual asset prices. Therefore, for the time being the most accurate dependency models are still created manually, and generally based on fundamental analysis. Hence, Relegence's Connect service incorporates proprietary mappings of corporate relationships and supply chains from the broker Credit Suisse.

A nice example of just how useful such relationships can be is given by Lauren Cohen and Andrea Frazzini (2008). In 2001, the Callaway Golf Corp. was the major customer for Coastcast Corp.'s golf club heads, accounting for 50% of their production. On the 7th of June 2001, Callaway was downgraded by one of the analysts covering it; the following day it lowered its Q2 revenue projections by $50 million. Effectively, this meant nearly a 50% reduction in its expected earnings per share (EPS), falling from 70 down to 35-38 cents per share. This resulted in a 30% drop in its market price to close at $15.03 on the 8th of June. However, such negative news about its largest customer did not seem to affect Coastcast's share price at all. Cohen and Frazzini searched the archives for the newswires and financial publications but could find no mention of Coastcast in the two months after Callaway's slump. It was not until July 5th that the price of Coastcast began to steadily decline, announcing an EPS of -4 cents on July 19th.

Figure 14-7 shows the price changes over this period (normalised relative to 1st May 2001 levels). Anyone closely tracking both companies would have had nearly a month before the price of Coastcast Corp. dropped in a similar fashion to Callaway Golf Corp. To prove their point Cohen and Frazzini tested a strategy of buying firms whose customers had the most positive returns in the previous month and shorting those with the worst. They found

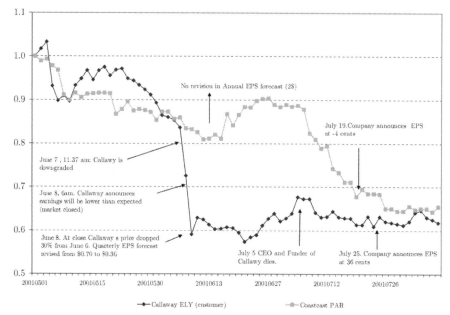

Source: Cohen and Frazzini (2007), Journal of Finance, Wiley-Blackwell
Reproduced with permission from publisher

**Figure 14-7 Delayed reaction of Coastcast Corp.'s price to the slump in its leading
customer Callaway Golf Corp.**

potential annualized returns of 18.6%. Unsurprisingly, association based analysis is proving
to be increasingly popular.

News analysis

At present, the most common form of news analysis is interpreting its sentiment. Once we
can reliably determine whether a specific news item is good or bad we can then start to
estimate its impact on the market.

The simplest way of trying to determine sentiment is to look for, and count, specific
words, such as "exceeds" or "profits". Clearly, this has its limits, since the text may contain
words that by themselves may be construed as positive, e.g. "rising", but in context are
actually negative, e.g. "debt is rising". The next logical progression is to extend the counting
to phrases. A study by Young-Woo Seo, Joseph Giampapa and Katia Sycara (2002) used
bigrams (two linked keywords) to infer sentiment. Their technique extracts the key phrases
by first removing any unnecessary words or identities, so "Shares of ABC Company rose"
becomes the bigram "Shares rose" for ABC. These bigrams are then translated into a
sentiment based on a range of five different classifications, as shown in Table 14-3.

News stories also differ in terms of whether they are reporting facts after the event or
reflecting predictions for the future. So news that is certain uses phrases like "revenue rose"
or "shares fell", whereas uncertain news includes words like expect, forecast, anticipate or
warning. Overall, this technique can achieve reasonable results, in particular for simpler text
such as news headlines. However, everything that does not contain a good or bad bigram is
classified as neutral, so useful information may be ignored. Therefore, they concluded that its

Class	Examples
GOOD	... Shares of ABC Company rose ½ or 2 percent on the Nasdaq to $24-15/16. ... *Bigrams*: "revenue rose", "exceeds expectations", "share rose", "rose profit"
GOOD, UNCERTAIN	... ABC Company predicts fourth-quarter earnings will be high. ... *Bigrams*: "expect earnings", "forecasts earnings", "anticipate earnings"
NEUTRAL	... ABC and XYZ Inc. announced plans to develop an industry initiative. ... *Bigrams*: "alliance company", "alliance corp", "announces product"
BAD, UNCERTAIN	... ABC (Nasdaq: ABC) warned on Tuesday that Fourth-quarter results could fall short of expectations. ... *Bigrams*: "warning profits", "short expectation", "warning earnings"
BAD	... Shares of ABC (ABC: down $0.54 to $49.37) fell in early New York trading. ... Bigrams: "share off", "share down", "profit decrease", "fall percent", "sales decrease"

Source: Seo, Giampapa and Sycara (2002)

Table 14-3 Example sentiment classifications

inability to cope with complex grammar prevented it from exceeding 75% accuracy.

A further complication is the fact that news articles frequently contain information on a range of items or companies. Therefore, to ensure an accurate sentiment analysis we really need to be able to extract the exact context of any key words or phrases. This lead Seo, Giampapa and Sycara (2002) to consider future approaches based on more sophisticated natural language processing (NLP) techniques and semantic analysis. These techniques are more appropriate, since they can cope with more complex grammar. For example, they break down sentences into grammatical units, so phrases such as "profits falling" can be attributed to a specific entity.

Commercial systems capable of large-scale sentiment analysis are now becoming available. For instance, Infonic's Sentiment> offers a potential capacity of 10 articles/second at high levels of accuracy. It adopts a hybrid approach: the first phase performs linguistic analysis to extract the key features from each document. The second phase of processing performs the actual classification, based on machine learning. Numeric sentiments are then assigned for each story, together with a confidence level. It can also assign separate scores if the story concerns multiple companies. The major news services are starting to offer sentiment analysis as well. Indeed, Reuters has used the Infonic software to make available sentiment analysis for their own news feeds via their NewsScope Sentiment Engine.

News interpretation

The logical progression from sentiment analysis is for systems to be able to perform a full interpretation of the news. Rather than simply deciding whether a given story is good or bad, they start to estimate how much the information should change the asset's price. So interpretation systems will need to identify and extract all the key information from the news story. Again, this may use NLP based approaches. Alternatively, with the increasing availability of machine-readable news and corporate reports this may just be a matter of extracting data using the required tags.

However the information is sourced, it must then be used to determine its effect on the asset's price. Asset pricing is non-trivial, so in order to interpret the potential impact on prices the new information will need to be incorporated into dedicated asset pricing models. Obviously, this is easier to do for some stories than others. For example, an announcement of a new contract can mean adjustments to figures for expected sales and costs, whilst the resignation of a senior executive is more difficult to quantify. More advanced news interpretation techniques may even try to "read between the lines". For example, a study by Antonina Kloptchenko *et al.* (2004) found that the tone used in company reports often better reflects future performance than the reported results.

The new target prices generated by this analysis may then be used to make investment decisions. Still, in terms of execution its use is debatable. The changes may not be reflected soon enough in the markets for execution systems to benefit from this information in real-time.

News mining

News mining combines the analysis of historical data with information from news archives. At present, much of the research focuses on interpreting the text from news headlines/stories and using this to explain price changes. Pattern recognition techniques are used to infer the market impact of news. Artificial intelligence (AI) techniques, such as neural networks or support vector machines, are then trained on this historical data in order to learn how to predict future changes.

As we saw in the previous sub-sections, accurately interpreting the meaning of news is a complex task. Many studies struggle to achieve better than 50% accuracy. Though, given time, it is likely that semantic analysis will improve sufficiently to make such techniques a worthwhile addition (in the not too distant future). In the meantime, data is also becoming available in machine-readable formats such as XML.

Analysing the short-term impact of news is an easier goal than estimating its mid and long-term effects. By comparing the news data, such as EPS figures, with market expectations we can determine how much of a surprise the news actually is. If the news meets expectations then the market will most likely already have incorporated this information into the asset's price, so a significant price change is unlikely. Whereas if the news is a huge surprise then a period of volatility will be likely, whilst the market adjusts to this new information. Section 14.5 provides a review of empirical market studies detailing these short-term effects.

Note that when trying to assess the impact of a particular news story or headline, rather than treating it as a discrete event we can look back over previous news items to confirm how much new information it actually contains. By chaining together news stories, we can determine the relative amount of new information each one contains. Thus, we can start to analyse whether news has a substantial momentum effect. This could also enable us to study how effectively new information is assimilated by the market, and whether it under or over-reacts to news.

An interesting example is given in a study by Gur Huberman and Tomer Regev (2001). EntreMed Inc. (ENMD) is a pharmaceutical company focussed on releasing drugs for the treatment of cancer and inflammatory diseases. On May 3rd 1998, the Sunday edition of the New York Times (1998) had an article on its front page titled "HOPE IN THE LAB: A special report; A Cautious Awe Greets Drugs That Eradicate Tumors in Mice". This outlined the potential of endostatin, an anti-angiogenic protein. Endostatin was found to inhibit the growth of cancer tumours, and in studies on mice had demonstrated no onset of drug resistance. In fact, after repeated cycles it was even found to remove the tumours in mice altogether, effectively curing the cancer. The article also mentioned EntreMed, since they had the licence for producing the drugs based on this research. On the following Monday, EntreMed's price opened at 85 falling to close at around 52, up from 12.063 on the previous Friday, a 330% increase. This is shown in Figure 14-8.

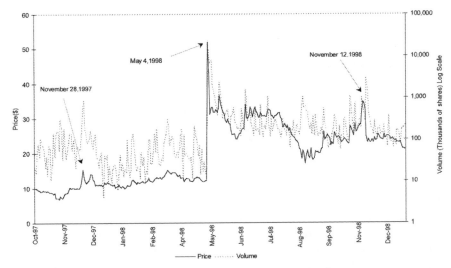

Source: Huberman and Regev (2001)   , Journal of Finance, Wiley-Blackwell
Reproduced with permission from publisher

Figure 14-8 EntreMed trading price and volume around news of its new drug

Still, as Huberman and Regev note the news story did not actually bring any significant new information to the market. In fact, it was just a fuller version of an earlier article printed in the New York Times (1997) the previous November 27th, titled "Tests on Mice Block a Defense by Cancer". This covered the publishing of the same research results in the journal Nature. There was also coverage on CNN's MoneyLine and CNBC's Street Signs on November 27th. Although this earlier news was released around Thanksgiving, it still saw a sizeable market reaction with a 28.4% price increase. They concluded that the key difference would seem to be due to being placed on the front page of the New York Times versus page 28, generating corresponding increases of 330% versus 28%. Certainly, there was an over-reaction to the news in May. The persistent price increase in EntreMed may reflect an under-reaction by professional investors in November; alternatively, it may also reflect the massive additional publicity that the company received. So when tracking the impact of news we should also consider how much attention the information might receive.

News mining may also be used to infer relationships that are more complex. For instance, the spillover effects and correlations that can occur between assets, typically across stock industries and sectors. In the case of EntreMed, Huberman and Regev (2001) note that on May 4th the seven firms of the NASDAQ Biotechnology Combined Index (excluding ENMD) saw a daily average return of 4.89% whilst the spotlight was on this sector.

It is also important to consider other sources of information when carrying out news mining. Asset pricing is complex, so key factors, such as market conditions or fundamental data, are necessary to explain the asset's price changes. For example, consider the substantial price lag, which we saw for the supplier-customer relationship between Coastcast Corp. and Callaway Golf Corp. Data mining could be used to check whether any other market variables might explain such a lag, other than investor under-reaction.

As with any forecasting method, caution must be taken to ensure that data is not over-fitted, as we will see in Chapter 15. A common method is to exclude a set period of the historical data and news archives, often the most recent. Any relationships based on the main dataset may then be retested on the excluded period to check their suitability. Any rules that survive this test may then be exposed to further testing with real-time news and prices.

14.5 Market reactions to news

News announcements represent a flow of information to the markets. Since most asset prices are based on such information it is hardly surprising that news can have a marked effect.

A large number of empirical studies have analysed the impact of news for most of the major markets. In this section, we will review these to see the effects of both macroeconomic and corporate news on prices, trading volumes, liquidity and volatility. We shall also consider how other factors, such as the business cycle, affect the market response to news.

Reactions to macroeconomic news

Macroeconomic news gives a regular indication of the performance of an economy. The announcements may be used to predict future economic growth, so they can have a marked effect on the trading of most asset classes. For instance, if key indicators show signs of a recession then governments may be prompted to change interest rates or alter their fiscal policy. Companies may well have to adjust their expected earnings in the light of these new conditions. Likewise, investors may choose to alter their portfolios, shifting to safer larger cap stocks or increasing the proportion of bonds.

The impact of news on asset prices varies somewhat for different asset classes. For example, news of an interest rate drop will help increase the price of existing bonds, whilst it weakens the currency. For corporations, the picture is slightly more complex, since they may benefit from lower interest rate but may also suffer from the weaker currency. Though, in terms of trading volume, liquidity and volatility, the reaction is generally a significant short-term increase for all asset classes.

Price

In their study of U.S. Treasuries, Pierluigi Balduzzi, Edwin Elton and T. Clifton Green (1997) found that the Non-Farm Payroll announcement had the most impact on prices. The impact was persistent and almost immediate; it also behaved roughly symmetrically between positive and negative surprises. In addition to Non-Farm Payrolls, they found that announcements for PPI, CPI, Consumer Confidence, ISM/NAPM survey, New Home Sales, Durable Goods Orders, Housing Starts and Initial Jobless Claims all had a noticeable impact on the market price. For example, Figure 14-9 shows the reaction to the Consumer Price Index for the 10-year note.

A comparable effect was observed for the 5-year Treasury note in analysis by Michael Fleming and Eli Remolona (1997). The key announcements were broadly similar, with Non-Farm Payrolls dominating, whilst PPI, CPI, Consumer Confidence, ISM/NAPM survey and

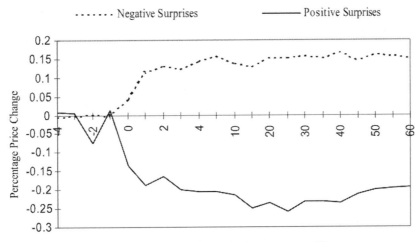

Figure 14-9 Price responses of the active 10-year Treasury note to surprises in CPI

New Home Sales were also found to be significant. Though, they found Durable Goods Orders and Housing Starts had much less effect. Instead, they observed that Retail Sales and the Federal Funds Target rate were more important, as we can see from their relative rankings in Table 14-4.

Unfortunately, the complexity of the relationship between macroeconomic indicators and bond prices means that each study seems to find slightly different relationships. Some of this may be related to the investment timescales associated with different assets. Balduzzi, Elton and Green (1997) analysed the effect on 3-month bills, 2-year notes and 30-year bonds. They observed that the size of the reaction tended to increase with the maturity of the Treasury, highlighting the increased volatility of longer-term bond prices. A later study by Fleming and Remolona (1999) also focussed on this trend. They found this effect to occur for most announcements with the exception of the price indices (CPI and PPI) where the reaction seemed to remain constant for maturities over four years.

The number of announcements that affect different securities also seems to vary based on the maturity date. Balduzzi, Elton and Green (2001) reported that nine announcements significantly affected the price of the 3-month bill, whilst there were 13 for the 2-year note, 16 for the 10-year note, then falling back to 10 for the 30-year bond. This could be due to differences in the applicability of each announcement to both short and long-term expectations.

For exchange rates, Alain Chaboud *et al.* (2004) analysed the impact of announcements using data from EBS. They found sudden increases in price occurred almost instantly, but only lasted for about 5-10 minutes and generally stabilised in less than an hour. Surprises for GDP and Non-Farm Payrolls generally had the most effect. Overall, they found that news that indicated stronger than expected activity for the U.S. was systematically followed by dollar appreciation. A similar trend was reported in an earlier study by Torben Andersen *et al.* (2003). They observed the largest price changes for Non-Farm Payrolls and Trade Balance surprises, followed by Durable Goods Orders, Retail Sales and the Federal Funds

Announcement [1]	Effect on: [2]		Ranking by:	
	Price	Volume	Price	Volume
Employment (Non-Farm Payrolls)	-23.1	60.52	1	2
Producer Price Index	-8.59	27.87	2	8
Retail Sales	-6.51	39.03	5	4
Consumer Price Index	-6.48	24.56	6	12
New Single-Family Home Sales	-5.08	23.97	7	13
Federal Funds Target Rate	-4.61	60.8	8	1
Consumer Confidence	-4.42	9.62	9	16
NAPM Survey	-4.17	35.83	11	5
Industrial Production	-3.87	17.81	12	14
Housing Starts	-3.42	12.05	13	15
Gross Domestic Product	-3.2	29.04	14	7
Trade Balance	-2.5	4.94	15	21
Construction Spending	-1.79	-5.35	16	19
Consumer Credit	-1.7	2.24	17	23
Factory Inventories	1.61	27.55	18	9
Durable Goods Orders	-1.41	-5.1	19	20
Leading Indicators	-0.46	2.28	22	22
Federal Budget	-0.29	-1.86	23	24
Personal Income	0.19	-1.66	24	25
Business Inventories	0.05	24.88	25	11

Source: Fleming and Remolona (1997)

Table 14-4 Impact of macroeconomic announcement surprises on the 5-year U.S. Treasury note

Target Rate. Though, there were slight differences for the various exchange rates, for instance, the Trade Balance had the most impact for the yen/dollar, whilst GDP advance notices were important for both the euro and the Swiss franc versus the dollar.

For equities, a study by Rui Albuquerque and Clara Vega (2007) analysed the response of the stocks in the Dow Jones Industrial Average (DJIA) and Portugal's PSI-20 indices to macroeconomic news. They grouped the announcements into classes, such as consumption and investment, but also analysed the impact of individual announcements. In general, for the DJIA, U.S. macroeconomic announcements led to an immediate response that stabilised within the first hour. Though, for the price indices (CPI and PPI) and Initial Unemployment Claims they found the impact was only appreciable for around the first ten minutes. Overall, the most positive responses were for good news in Personal Consumption Expenditures, Capacity Utilization, Personal Income, the Index of Leading Indicators and the Trade Balance. The most negative responses were for news on the GDP Advance, ISM/NAPM survey, Housing Starts, New Home Sales and the Federal Funds Target Rate. For instance, they found that a one standard deviation unexpected surprise in the Federal Funds Target

---

[1] Note that Fleming and Remolona (1997) also included the results of Treasury auctions in their study. These have been excluded for ease of comparison with other studies. For reference the auction results for the 10-year note had the 3rd most significant effect on prices and the 6th most effect on volumes. The 30-year bond auction was 4th in terms of prices and 3rd for volumes.

[2] The effect column shows the actual coefficients from regressing the price and volume with the surprise factor which is based on the difference between the actual announcement and the expected forecast figures.

Rate could lead to a 0.5% decrease in the DJIA. Similar studies that focussed on the impact of FOMC announcements found around a 1% response for Federal Funds surprises. Michael Ehrmann and Marcel Fratzscher (2004) analysed the impact on the S&P 500 and Ben Bernanke and Kenneth Kuttner (2005) studied the CRSP value weighted index. Albuquerque and Vega (2007) reason that the difference in results is due to their sample being based on the DJIA which is a small sample of large firms, which are often less affected by monetary policy surprises.

A useful comparison of the effects for a range of futures contracts is provided in a study by Andrew Clare and Roger Courtenay (2001), shown in Figure 14-10. Using data for 1994-99, they investigated the impact of U.K. macroeconomic and interest rate announcements, which are generally released at 9:30am and 12:00pm. The aim of their study was to determine the effect of operational independence being granted to the Bank of England in 1997 allowing the Monetary Policy Committee to set interest rates.

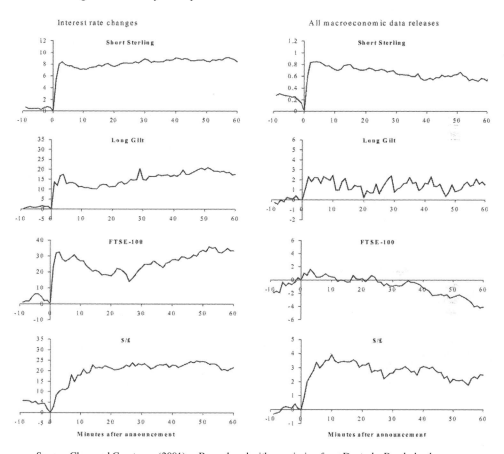

Source: Clare and Courtenay (2001)   Reproduced with permission from Deutsche Bundesbank

Figure 14-10 Impact of macroeconomic news on the prices of futures and currencies

They tracked the price reaction of currencies and LIFFE futures contracts for short-term (Short Sterling) and long-term (Long Gilts) debt and the FTSE-100 stock index. The average hourly responses are shown in Figure 14-10. From these charts, it is clear that the interest rate changes have much more considerable effect on both the futures and the currency than other macroeconomic data. Interestingly, the largest overall impact for interest rates was for the FTSE-100 futures, although these had much less response to more general U.K. macroeconomic announcements. In comparison, the currency and Long Gilts appeared to be the most affected by general macroeconomic news. The Long Gilts also seemed to be more volatile than the Short Sterling, which is similar to what we have seen for U.S. Treasuries.

Volume

The fixed scheduling of many U.S. macroeconomic announcements makes their effect on trading activity and volumes easy to spot. For instance, the sudden peak in inter-dealer trading activity for Treasury notes at 8:30am is clear to see in Figure 14-11, taken from a study by Fleming and Remolona (1997). There is also a noticeable peak for the 10:00am news. Fleming and Remolona (1998) observed an almost identical trend for traded volume.

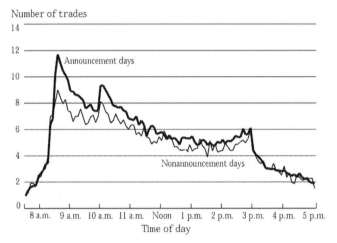

Source: Fleming and Remolona (1997) Reproduced with permission from Federal Reserve Bank of New York

Figure 14-11 Intraday activity on announcement days for five year U.S Treasury notes

Therefore, key macroeconomic announcements can lead to large, but short-term, increases in trading volume. This has been reported by a wide range of studies. For example, Fleming and Remolona (1998) observed elevated volumes in the 5-year note for over 90 minutes after Employment and CPI/PPI price index announcements. Similarly, a study of the effect of FOMC announcements by Michael Fleming and Monika Piazzesi (2005) analysed the impact for 3 and 6-month bills and 2, 5 and 10-year notes. They found a significant volume increase that lasted for around 45 minutes after the announcements, whilst volumes remained higher than normal for 1½ to 2½ hours.

In the previous section, we saw how each type of announcement had a markedly different effect on the market price. Fleming and Remolona (1997) also analysed the impact of each announcement on the trading volume. The results are displayed back in Table 14-4. The largest influence was held by the Federal Funds Target Rate and the Non-Farm Payrolls, which had virtually identical coefficients from the regression analysis. In terms of importance, these were then followed by Retail Sales, the ISM/NAPM survey, GDP, and PPI announcements. In total, around a dozen of the announcements had a notable impact on trading volume. Balduzzi, Elton and Green (2001) found a similar number of key announcements.

The volume effects tend to be comparable across the range of Treasury securities, although the relative sizes differ. Fleming and Piazzesi (2005) found the largest percentage increases for the 3 and 6-month bills, with peaks of around 400%. In comparison, the increases for five and ten year notes reached about 150%. Likewise, a study by Balduzzi, Elton and Green (2001) found volume for the 10-year note peaked at around 170-200% of normal levels within the first fifteen minutes after the announcement. Though, for the 3-month bill they found the volume effects to be much weaker.

Another trend Fleming and Piazzesi (2005) reported was a slight decrease in volumes around an hour before the announcements. They attribute this as being "the calm before the storm" when traders wait to see what news the announcement brings. Fleming and Remolona (1998) noted a slight lag of up to two minutes after the announcement when volumes remain at normal levels. This might be attributed to a delay whilst the market reacts to the news.

For exchange rates, Chaboud et al. (2004) focussed on a subset of indicators in their study of the impact of macroeconomic announcements. The reactions shown in Figure 14-12 are for Employment (Non-Farm Payrolls), since this had the largest impact. Note this is essentially a percentage change, since 100 represents the average one-minute volume. For comparison, the average volumes for non-announcement days are shown as dotted lines.

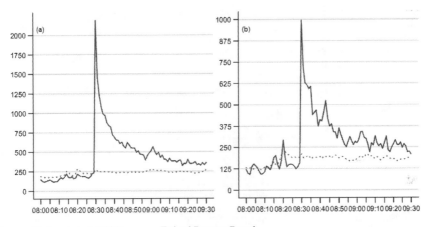

Source: Chaboud et al. (2004)   Federal Reserve Board

Figure 14-12 Average one-minute volume on announcement days for (a) Euro/Dollar, (b) Dollar/Yen

GDP has nearly as much effect, followed by Retail Sales, Trade Balance and the Producer Price Index. The FOMC results had less immediate impact; however, their overall effect seemed to last longer. In addition, as we can see from the relative scales in Figure 14-12, the Dollar/Yen was much less affected than the Euro/Dollar; this trend was consistent across the other macro indicators.

Liquidity

An appreciable increase in the bid offer spread often accompanies macroeconomic announcements. For instance, Fleming and Remolona (1998) observed sharp increases in the spread for five year U.S. Treasury notes around 8:30 and 10:00am on announcement days. Empirical studies also find a consistent trend for the effect on the bid offer spreads: Just before the announcement, they start to widen, peaking around the time of the news. The spreads remain at higher than normal levels for between half an hour to two hours afterwards. Fleming and Piazzesi (2005) found the 10-year note recovered fastest, in around 30 minutes. The 3 and 6-month bills and the 2-year note took much longer to recover. A similar effect was noted by Fleming and Remolona (1997a) and Balduzzi, Elton and Green (2001). The latter study also notes that the Employment report caused the most effect, both in terms of the size of the spread increase and its duration.

Volatility

The effect of news on short-term volatility can be extremely important, often more so than its effect on trading volumes. Some of the volatility is due to the market adjusting to the new information delivered in the news announcement, whilst some of it is also due to the sudden changes in trading volume and liquidity.

For U.S. Treasuries, the distinctive spikes in response to macroeconomic news at 8:30am and 10:00am are again evident in Figure 14-13 (as a standard deviation of log price changes), taken from Fleming and Remolona (1997).

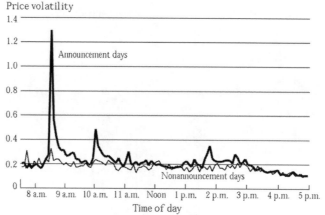

Source: Fleming and Remolona (1997) Reproduced with permission from Federal Reserve Bank of New York

Figure 14-13 Intraday volatility on announcement days for 5 year U.S Treasury notes

Studies by Fleming and Piazzesi (2005), Fleming and Remolona (1997a) and Balduzzi, Elton and Green (1997) all found that volatility increased immediately after the announcement, remaining at higher than normal levels for over an hour. For instance, Balduzzi, Elton and Green (1997) found that the volatility for the ten-year note stayed at more than twice its normal levels for 30-45 minutes afterwards. Fleming and Piazzesi (2005) found that the largest changes in volatility were for the 3-6 month bills and the 2-year notes.

In terms of the actual announcement types, Balduzzi, Elton and Green (2001) found that the largest increases in volatility were for the employment and PPI announcements, both for 3-month bills and 10-year notes.

For exchange rates, there is a similar spike in volatility around the announcement, as shown by the average absolute one-minute returns in Figure 14-14, taken from a study by Chaboud et al. (2004).

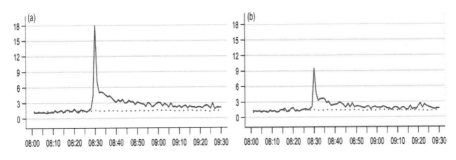

Source: Chaboud *et al.* (2004)   Federal Reserve Board

Figure 14-14 Intraday volatility (in bps) on announcement days for (a) Euro/Dollar, (b) Dollar/Yen

They found that volatility also follows the same trends that we saw for FX trading volumes. Hence, announcements for employment, GDP and target federal funds rate had the most impact, followed by retail sales, trade balance and the PPI.

Reactions to corporate news/announcements

Corporate news is obviously much more closely linked to specific assets than macroeconomic news. That said, the information may also have a considerable effect on other firms in the same industry/sector, or the supply chain.

Earnings announcements are the corporate equivalent of macroeconomic indicators, so there is a lot of activity around these. Indeed, analysis of S&P 500 companies by Paul Tetlock, Maytal Saar-Tsechansky and Sofus Macskassy (2008) found that company news tended to cluster around earnings announcements.

Price

In a study of French stocks, Angelo Ranaldo (2008) confirmed that news events, and particularly earnings announcements, triggered significant short-term price changes. The effect on prices was much larger and lasted for up to an hour for earnings announcements, reflecting the additional information that they convey. He also noted that for intraday announcements the shift in prices actually started around ten minutes before a corresponding news item in his data. Potentially, these premature market movements are due to the fact that there are many sources of information available to traders, whilst his study focussed on Reuters headlines.

An interesting analysis of the effect of overnight earnings announcements was carried out by Louhichi Wael (2008), again for French stocks. Overall, he found that prices could increase by 1.7% for stocks where the announcement was good news, whilst bad news led to a fall of around 1%. These abnormal returns persisted for well over an hour for both types of news. Since his study focussed on overnight announcements most of these changes were achieved in the opening auction, yielding an increase of 0.96% for good news and -1.28% for bad news. He also observed a slight reversal around half an hour after announcements of bad news, suggesting a possible initial overreaction.

For stocks, the effects of news can last days, weeks or even longer. Wael's (2008) study also analysed the performance for six days before and after each announcement. He found the abnormal results were mainly centred on the announcement day, although there were some minor reversals over the following days, particularly for bad news. The mid-term effect of news items on U.S. stock returns was also analysed by Paul Tetlock, Maytal Saar-Tsechansky and Sofus Macskassy (2008). They tracked around 350,000 news articles for S&P 500 companies. The news was taken from both the Dow Jones News Service (DJNS) and the Wall Street Journal (WSJ) from 1980 through to 2004. Stories were classified as positive or negative using lexicon-based sentiment analysis. Overall, they found effects persisted for over ten days after the announcement. Figure 14-15 shows a plot of the abnormal event returns covering ten days before and after a news story.

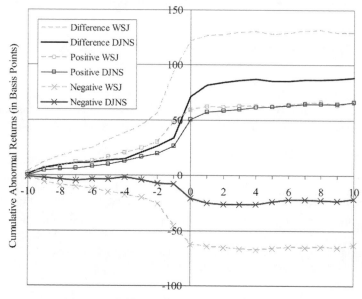

Source: Tetlock, Saar-Tsechansky and Macskassy (2007), Journal of Finance, Wiley-Blackwell
Reproduced with permission from publisher

Figure 14-15 Firms' valuations around news stories

As we can see in Figure 14-15, positive news led to similar improvements in returns, although the reaction to news from the Dow Jones news wire seemed to lag behind that for the Wall Street Journal. Whereas for negative news, there was a marked difference in the losses, with more effect seen from news published in the Wall Street Journal. They also noted that the market anticipated the news over the preceding days. In fact, the returns the day before the announcement could be nearly as important as those on the actual day the story broke. There was also a noticeable delay in seeing the full effect of the news, suggesting that it takes the market a while to fully react to it. This drift can actually last several days. The slight reversal that is visible for the reaction to bad news from Dow Jones also suggests that there may be a slight overreaction for bad news.

An earlier study of U.S. stocks by Wesley Chan (2002) found broadly similar results. He noted that stocks experiencing negative returns associated with news stories continued to under-perform their peers. In comparison, stocks with similar negative returns but no public news tended to see a price reversal in the following month. Much less price drift was evident with positive returns. He also found the drift to be more pronounced for smaller and less liquid companies.

One of the factors that make corporate announcements different from macroeconomic news is that the exact dates of these notices can vary considerably. Estimates for these used to be from calendar-based calculations, although it is becoming more common for firms to provide the expected dates for their next announcement. Products such as Thomson Financial's First Call Corporation now provide centralised sources for these dates. Other than providing a warning for upcoming announcements, the estimated dates may actually be used to help predict whether the news will be good or bad. This is because firms tend to be keen to announce good news and defer issuing bad news. A more quantitative analysis of this effect was performed by Mark Bagnoli, William Kross and Susan Watts (2004). They analysed the returns for U.S. stocks based on the lag between the estimated dates and the actual corporate announcements, for around 26,000 examples between 1995-8. They found that, on average, late announcements contained bad news 44.5% of the time, whilst this was only 36.1% for early or on-time announcements. The proportion increased so that after seven days late more than 50% of notices had bad news. For reporting losses they found that this was more than 90% more likely with late announcements than on-time ones. They found no such obvious trends for firms that made early reports.

Overall, Bagnoli, Kross and Watts (2004) discovered an average fall of one penny/share below the consensus forecasts for each day of delay from the expected date of the announcement. In terms of market prices, they observed similar declines for stocks that were late in making announcements. For instance, a delay of four days led to a cumulative loss of around 1% of returns. In addition to these losses, they also noted that the market reaction on the actual day of the announcement depended on how late it had been. Firms that reported late saw even more adverse reactions to bad results than those with similar results who reported on time. In comparison, they found the market reaction to be more aggressive for early announcements.

Volume

Unsurprisingly, corporate news also leads to noticeable short-term volume increases. Ranaldo (2008) observed this in terms of both volume and number of trades in his study of French stocks. Wael (2008) also found that for both good and bad news trading volumes increased slightly up to thirty minutes before the news breaks. Though, the most significant shift was still centred in the ten minutes around the actual announcement. He also noted that the heightened trading volumes persisted for around two days when the news was bad, and for five days after good news. Similar volume effects were found for the Spanish stock exchange by David Abad, Sonia Sanabria and José Yagüe (2005). They noted that both trading volume and frequency were unusually high up to three hours before the announcement, together with a sizeable increase when the news was released. These effects then persisted at abnormal levels for the rest of the trading day.

As we have already seen with prices, the effect of news on trading volumes can often be more prolonged for stocks; indeed, the volume increase can drift over days and weeks. For example, a study of U.S. stocks by Joon Chae (2005) found announcements had a considerable effect on volumes for more than 15 days afterwards. He also noted that the volume preceding scheduled earnings announcements actually decreased slightly in anticipation of the results. Although for unscheduled announcements, such as changes in Moody's ratings, takeovers or acquisitions, he found that the volume increased noticeably in the days beforehand.

Liquidity

The effect of corporate news on liquidity is less clear-cut, since the results of empirical research are mixed. Some studies find marked decreases in liquidity around announcements whilst some report increases and others find the changes to be negligible.

A decrease in liquidity around corporate announcements has been noted for studies of the NYSE by Kenneth Kavajecz (1999), Itzhak Krinsky and Jason Lee (1996) and Charles Lee, Belinda Mucklow and Mark Ready (1993). These showed how the quoted spreads increased whilst the available depth, from both specialists and the order book, decreased. Similarly, Jean-François Gajewski (1999) found that spreads widened after corporate announcements for French stocks.

A noticeable increase in liquidity was found to occur after the announcement in a study of the Spanish stock exchange by Abad, Sanabria and Yagüe (2005). They used a wide range of measures to analyse the available liquidity. In the time before the announcement, they found no notable changes in the bid offer spread or order book depth. Though, for around 90 minutes after the announcement, they observed a marked narrowing of the spread and an increase in the available depth. After this period, these returned to more normal levels. Wael (2008) found a similar decrease in spreads for French stocks, but also noted that spread levels were noticeably higher in the days preceding the news. Alternatively, Kazuhisa Otagawa (2003) found a consistent decrease in spreads both before and after quarterly earnings announcements for Japanese stocks. On the announcement day, market depth was found to improve slightly as well.

Not all research has found a noteworthy change in liquidity around corporate news events. For example, in a study of German stocks Peter Gomber, Uwe Schweickert and Erik Theissen (2004) tracked changes using the Xetra Liquidity Measure (XLM). Overall, they found no significant changes in the available liquidity at the time of the actual news item. Though, they did observe a slight decrease in liquidity in the fifteen minutes before the news release, which they attribute to traders having access to multiple information sources. The effect was most noticeable for the less liquid non-DAX stocks. Fifteen minutes after a news item, their XLM cost had increased by around 3% hence giving a slight reduction in their overall liquidity. In comparison, DAX stocks actually saw around a 3% reduction in their XLM cost after a news item, suggesting a slight improvement.

Some of these differences may be attributable to the markets being studied. For instance, markets where liquidity is provided by market makers or specialists may well exhibit increased spreads around announcements, as dealers try to minimise the cost of trading with more informed traders. Though, as Ranaldo (2008) points out, this effect may be reduced by competition between liquidity providers. In some markets, the liquidity may shift to hidden orders or on to "dark pool" ATSs. For instance, a study of the INET ECN (now part of NASDAQ) by Bidisha Chakrabarty and Ken Shaw (2006) showed that both the number and average size of hidden orders increased around earnings announcements, lasting up to seven days afterwards.

The information content of the news is another potential factor. An increase in liquidity after an announcement may suggest a decline in information asymmetry between traders. A study of French stocks by Faten Lakhal (2008) found that the uncertainty around earnings forecasts triggered an increase in spreads, leading to a decrease in the available liquidity. In comparison, the certainty of quarterly announcements was found to lead to an increase in liquidity. Wael (2008) also noted that the immediate impact on liquidity after an announcement was very much dependent on what information was imparted.

Announcements that met expectations (no news) saw an immediate decrease in their spreads, which then gradually reverted to normal levels over the next 90 minutes. Unexpected news took longer to react: For good news, spreads returned to normal about half an hour after the announcement, whilst for bad news they took nearly an hour. Similarly, unexpected news seemed to lead to much higher spreads in the half hour before each announcement, again this effect was most pronounced for bad news.

The level of information may also be reflected in differences between quarterly and annual reports. A study of earnings announcements by Theresa Libby, Robert Mathieu and Sean Robb (2002) found that the changes in liquidity were greater for quarterly announcements than annual ones.

Dispersion in market expectations may be another factor accounting for these differences. For instance, a study of NASDAQ by John Affleck-Graves, Carolyn Callahan and Niranjan Chipalkatti (2002) found that firms with less predictable earnings had consistently higher spreads, particularly in the days around announcements.

One last potential factor is the timing of the announcements. A study of the Spanish stock exchange by Abad, Sanabria and Yagüe (2005) found that overnight announcements led to an immediate improvement of liquidity at the following open. They reasoned this was because investors and traders had the time to properly evaluate the information. For intraday announcements, they found that it took around 90 minutes after the news before a notable improvement in liquidity was observed. They also noted a tendency for Spanish firms to prefer intraday releases when earnings were lower than expected.

Volatility

Volatility is usually higher immediately after a corporate announcement. Ranaldo (2008) found higher levels to persist for 10 minutes after firm-specific news and for over 40 minutes after earnings announcements. Likewise, Abad, Sanabria and Yagüe (2005) noted significantly raised levels of volatility for around 45 minutes after earnings announcements.

The volatility may also be affected by whether the news is good or bad. Unsurprisingly, after bad news Tetlock, Saar-Tsechansky and Macskassy (2008) found there to be higher levels of volatility. Wael (2008) also noted that it takes longer for the market to adjust to bad news than good. Thus, higher volatility persisted for nearly an hour after bad news, compared to around half an hour for good news.

Other factors which affect the impact of news

The effect that news has obviously depends on the information that it brings to the market. News provides information that either confirms or confounds the market consensus. So the degree of surprise indicates how the market will react. The timeliness of news also dictates whether it is new information or simply a confirmation of existing data.

Market conditions and the business cycle are another important consideration, since these reflect investor sentiment. In a declining market, even good news can fail to buck the trend. Therefore, the reaction to news is also dependent on the prevalent conditions.

Reactions to surprises

In order to gauge the degree of surprise, we need a common source of expectations. For macroeconomic indicators this means data from consensus forecasts. These are provided in publications such as the Wall Street Journal and Barron's. Another source, widely used in research studies, is the consensus forecasts from Money Market Services International (MMS). These surveys of money market managers provide estimates for what they expect the upcoming economic announcements to be. Based on these expected values, we can then determine how much of a surprise the actual announcements really are.

In their analysis of U.S. Treasuries, Balduzzi, Elton and Green (1997) confirmed that the size of the surprise affected the price change. They highlighted the potential impacts by expressing the price changes caused by a one standard deviation surprise, as a percentage of the daily volatility, shown in Table 14-5.

Macroeconomic announcement	Price change as % of daily volatility
Non-Farm Payrolls	89
PPI	39
CPI, Durable Goods Orders, Retail Sales, NAPM Index, Consumer Confidence	25-30
Initial Jobless Claims, Capacity Utilization, Industrial Production, New Home Sales	12-19
Factory Orders, M2 Medians	4-9

Source: Balduzzi, Elton and Green (1997)

Table 14-5 Effect of macroeconomic surprises on U.S. 10-year Treasury notes

For example, a one standard deviation surprise in Non-Farm Payrolls was around 110,000. An unexpected announcement with a corresponding increase could lead to a price change equivalent to nearly 90% of the daily volatility. Given a daily volatility of 0.47% for the 10-year note, this equates to a price change of 0.418% due to the surprise. They also confirmed that procyclical indicators, such as Non-Farm Payrolls, had a negative effect on bond prices, whilst counter-cyclical ones, such as Initial jobless claims, had a positive effect.

In terms of trading volume, Balduzzi, Elton and Green (1997) found little evidence for it being affected by the size of surprises. They reasoned that the trading volume is more closely related to the dispersion of views across the market.

Timeliness

The timeliness of an announcement particularly applies to the regular macroeconomic announcements. It helps quantify their information content by relating them to the data they are based on. Fleming and Remolona (1997) used the timeliness of an announcement to help explain its impact on U.S. Treasury prices. Likewise, David Veredas (2006) used it to explain the behaviour of Treasury futures.

For example, Figure 14-16 shows some of the major U.S. macroeconomic announcements ordered in terms of the data they are based on, taken from an article by Fleming and Remolona (1997). Consequently, the forward-looking Consumer Confidence measure is on the far left hand side. The majority of announcements are in the middle since they report on results for the previous month. On the right hand side, the Trade Balance reports two month old data, so as an announcement it imparts less new information to the market when compared to other indicators. Less timely reports are likely to have less impact on prices and volumes, which is indeed what Fleming and Remolona (1997) observed for the U.S. Treasury markets. Hence, the timeliest reports, such as Employment, PPI, CPI and Retail Sales tend to have the strongest effects.

In comparison, the forward-looking indicators, namely Consumer Confidence and the ISM/NAPM survey have slightly less impact. This is probably because they are forecasts

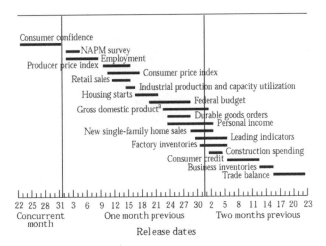

Source: Fleming and Remolona (1997) Reproduced with permission from Federal Reserve Bank of New York

Figure 14-16 U.S. macroeconomic announcement release dates

rather than actual reports, so the bond markets attribute more weight to the real data.

Veredas (2006) took a similar approach in his study of the 10-year U.S. Treasury note future. He used timeliness to rate the impact of different announcements, as shown in Figure 14-17. The forward looking consumer confidence (CC) and ISM/NAPM surveys were given more weight by the futures market, whilst employment remained the most significant report. As with the underlying bonds, important announcements such as GDP and the trade balance actually had only a limited effect, since they relay very little new information.

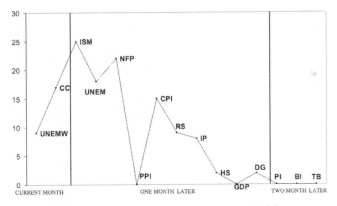

Source: Veredas (2006), Journal Empirical Economics, Physica-Verlag Heidelberg,
Reproduced with permission from publisher

Figure 14-17 The impact of timeliness for the U.S. 10-year Treasury note future

Another point to consider is that market reactions are not always for the latest figures. Revisions to key macroeconomic indicators can have a considerable effect as well. Indeed, Veredas (2006) notes that the repeated revisions for GDP help to reduce market interest in it as an indicator.

Market conditions

In their study of the response of U.S. Treasuries to news, Fleming and Remolona (1997) also considered the potential effects caused by market conditions. They demonstrated that the price reaction for a given surprise was often greater during conditions of increased uncertainty. As indicators for market uncertainty, they used the implied volatility of Treasury futures options together with the expected change in the Federal Funds Target Rate. For the price impact on the 5-year note, they found that the uncertainty from implied volatility helped explain the market reaction to announcements for Durable Goods Orders, Housing Starts and GDP surprises. The expected change in the Federal Funds Target Rate helped explain the reaction of Employment and Durable Goods Orders surprises.

In terms of trading volume, they noted that both indicators still had an effect, although the links were somewhat weaker than for prices. Both indicators of uncertainty helped explain the increases for CPI, PPI and Trade Balance surprises. As with prices, the expected Federal Funds Target Rate also helped to account for the increases for Employment and Durable Goods Orders surprises.

Business cycle

The business cycle is closely related to market conditions. We can break down the cycle into four main stages which reflect when the market is at its top or bottom, and when it is either expanding or contracting. News surprises may well have considerably different impacts depending on what stage of the business cycle the market is at. Intuitively, we might expect the most impact to be in the expansion and contraction parts of the cycle, since these phases are more likely to have higher uncertainty/volatility.

One measure of the business cycle is an index from the Institute for Supply Management (ISM). Unlike factors like the GDP, it is a forward-looking measure, based on a survey of market expectations from the manufacturing industry. More details about the ISM may be found in Niemira and Zukowski (1998).

David Veredas (2006) used the ISM to confirm whether business cycles do indeed alter the impact of macroeconomic news on the price of U.S. 10-year Treasury note futures. He found a strong inverse correlation (-0.71) between the futures price and the ISM, which is shown in Figure 14-18. For each peak in the ISM, the price of the Treasury future was generally at a low, and vice versa: Based on historical data, Veredas (2006) concluded that when the ISM was above 55 the business cycle was at a top, whilst below 50 it was at a bottom. In between this range, a rising value was treated as the expansion part of the cycle, whilst a falling one indicated a contraction.

Veredas also analysed the impact of surprises on the price of the futures contract during specific cycles. Overall, he found that news tended to have more effect in down cycles than in up cycles. He noted that bad news had more impact in good times than bad, whilst good news had less effect when the cycle was already depressed. As an illustration of this Figure 14-19 shows corresponding plots of the impact of surprises in the figures for Consumer Confidence. Note that the solid lines show the average response whilst the dotted lines are only negative surprises and the dashed lines only positive ones. The time axis represents ten-minute intervals.

When the business cycle is down or contracting (shown on the right hand side of Figure 14-19) we can see that any type of news has a negative impact on prices. Interestingly, in these depressed phases positive surprises seem to cause the most impact.

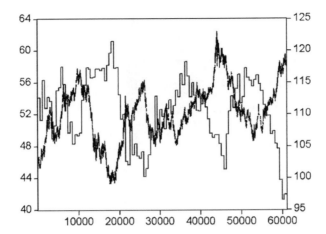

Source: Veredas (2006), Journal Empirical Economics, Physica-Verlag Heidelberg,
Reproduced with permission from publisher

Figure 14-18 ISM versus the U.S. 10-year Treasury note price (continuous, right axis)

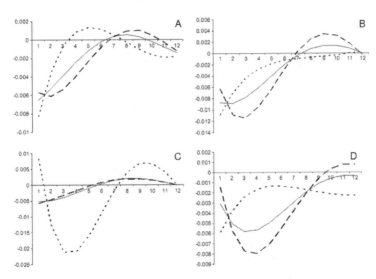

Source: Veredas (2006), Journal Empirical Economics, Physica-Verlag Heidelberg,
Reproduced with permission from publisher

**Figure 14-19 Impulse responses of U.S. 10-year Treasury note price to shocks in
Consumer Confidence when economy is in the (a) top, (b) bottom, (c) expansion, (d)
contraction part of the cycle**

When the cycle is at a top or in expansion (shown on the left hand side of Figure 14-19),
we can see that negative surprises led to the largest price drops. Overall, for Consumer
Confidence the most significant price drop seems to be caused by negative surprises in an
expansion cycle. Veredas notes that whenever the indicator was against the trend it seemed

to have more impact, probably due to more publicity. It is also worth noting that in most of these cases the initial impact dissipated reasonably quickly, with the prices returning to normal within one or two hours of the news.

14.6 Incorporating news into trading strategies

Precognition, or "second sight", would clearly be a very useful add-on for most investment and trading strategies. However, the focus of this book is on execution, not investment. Though we may not be able to reliably predict exactly what information news will bring, we can still estimate how the market might react, as we saw in the previous section. These short-term predictions of market conditions may enable our trading strategies to take advantage of the market response, rather than simply reacting to the rapidly changing conditions.

Even though we are using news to augment trading strategies, rather than to generate investment ideas, certain precautions are still necessary. Correct interpretation is vital otherwise, the estimates for the market response will be wrong. The accuracy and validity of information is also important.

An easy way of incorporating news into trading strategies is to use indicators. They provide a simple means for algorithms to interpret whether news is good or bad, and so respond accordingly. These may then be added to adaptive trading algorithms alongside the price trend and short-term liquidity indicators that many already use. In the future, we might also start to see more opportunistic news-driven algorithms.

Precautions for automated news handling

We have become used to trading algorithms and execution tactics routinely making automatic decisions about the location, price and size of orders. These decisions are often based on a mix of historical and real-time market data, and the responses are driven by rules specified by expert traders and subjected to rigorous testing. Increasingly, though, algorithms are becoming even more adaptive, responding dynamically to changing market conditions, such as liquidity. Therefore, reacting to news may just be viewed as another real-time adaptation. Just as with anything else, the standard computer maxim of "Garbage in, garbage out" applies. Bad data or poor interpretations could lead to expensive mistakes.

Market conditions, such as prices, spreads or depths, correspond to actual quantifiable factors. News is always an interpretation, even if this is done by a vendor rather than in-house systems. Thus, accuracy and authenticity are obviously key concerns when leaving a system to automatically react to news headlines/stories. Though, in the short-term, whether it is inaccurate or even false is less significant, since the whole market reacts to the same news.

Given that bad news data of one sort or another is almost certain to creep through at some point, it is important to apply some additional controls/sanity checks. If the market reacts as expected then we may assume the news is being treated as valid by other market participants. If not, then it may be safer to trigger an alert allowing a trader to monitor the situation and either intervene or resume the trading algorithm. These checks may need to be performed repeatedly after any news announcements. So an immediate aggressive response to a news item may not be the best approach, although neither is waiting until the market reaction has subsided. We need to strike some sort of balance, trying to safely capitalise on advantageous conditions without taking excessive risks, much like the behaviour of an adaptive shortfall or a liquidity-based algorithm.

On the other hand, we may not even be alerted about a news story. The news filtering may not identify the story as being relevant for our order. News handling systems may fail to correctly identify the key entities affected by the story. Alternatively, the news vendor might accidentally miss an important tag, or fail to consistently tag all stories in the same way. Whatever happens, though, the news will still spread and the market will still react. Hence, in such cases we are reliant on the trading algorithm simply adapting to the changing market conditions, just as it would if there were no news component.

Potential news-based indicators

Converting textual information from news into a numeric indicator makes it much easier for computer-based systems to react to it. Obviously, this is easier to do for some news, such as macroeconomic or earnings announcements, than others. As we saw in section 14.3, the increasing digitization of news and corporate reports means that soon much of this key information will be readily available digitally.

News indicators can range from a simple count of the number of stories to more complex sentiment-based analysis. They can also be used to quantify the difference between consensus estimates and actual announcements.

News flow

Following the old adage *"There is no smoke without fire"*, news flow is itself an important trading signal. The sheer volume of news items can be just as much an indicator as the actual information they convey. Clearly, we cannot reliably use the number of headlines to predict future prices; for that we need to know whether the news was good or bad. Though, a sudden rush of headlines does suggest that volatility may increase, since uncertainty breeds volatility. Therefore, by tracking the amount of news generally associated with a given topic or asset we can determine historical averages.

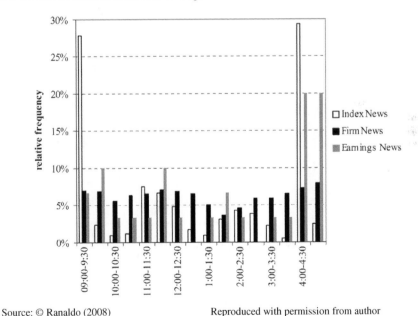

Source: © Ranaldo (2008)   Reproduced with permission from author

Figure 14-20 Intraday news patterns

Time of day effects may need to be taken into account as well, since news events can cluster around the open and close, as we can see in Figure 14-20. This shows the results from a study of news patterns for French stocks by Ranaldo (2008). In particular, he found the peaks for news were most pronounced for the CAC 40 index compared to firm specific news.

Thus, when news levels rise significantly above the historical average we have an immediate indicator that something unusual is happening. This gives us a very quick and easy way of tracking potential issues, since we do not even need to read or interpret the actual news stories. For example, Relegence calculates a news heat index, based on the number of stories for a specific company, converting this to a scale ranging from -4 to +4.

For traders, a news flow indicator acts as a simple alert, allowing them to study the situation more carefully. Whilst for trading algorithms, it can be used as an indicator that short-term volatility is likely to increase. So, risk and cost-based algorithms can then adjust their trading strategies accordingly.

News sentiment

In section 14.4, we saw how news items could be analysed to extract whether they represented good, bad or neutral information. By assigning these sentiments numeric scores we can calculate averages, so we can determine the prevalent market sentiment hour by hour or day by day. We can also track sentiment over time just as if it were price or return data. For instance, Figure 14-21 shows charts of the stock prices and sentiment for two companies, from a study by Sanjiv Das (2005). The sentiments were determined from statistical analysis of bulletin board messages; each point on the charts represents the arrival of a new message.

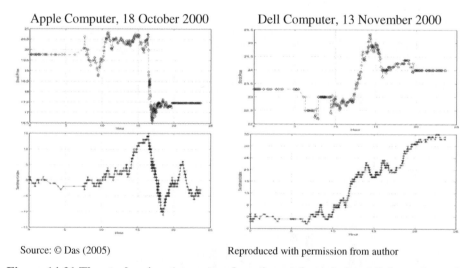

Source: © Das (2005)   Reproduced with permission from author

Figure 14-21 The stock prices (upper) and sentiment (lower) charted throughout the trading day

Obviously, substantial changes in price can have a marked impact on the associated sentiment, as we can see in Figure 14-21. Though, inferring future changes in price based on the sentiment is more complex. For example, the continued shift in sentiment for Dell Computer seen in Figure 14-21 is not immediately reflected in the market price. So, at the level of individual companies, the complex relationship between sentiment and price can make it difficult to reliably take advantage of this information.

Sentiment scores may also be aggregated across sectors or indices to create broader indicators, as shown in Figure 14-22. Sanjiv Das and Mike Chen (2007) found a significantly stronger correlation between sentiment and returns for indices than for individual stocks. In their study, they aggregated the sentiment for the 25 stocks in the Morgan Stanley High Tech Index (MSH), based on nearly 150,000 bulletin board messages. The correlation between the two series shown in Figure 14-22 was relatively low, only 0.48. Though, using regression analysis Das and Chen found that the MSH 35 index was strongly related to its value from the previous day and was also significantly related to the sentiment index value from the prior day. In comparison, the sentiment index was found to have no such dependency on the stock index, so they concluded that the causality flowed from the sentiment to the stock index. Thus, sentiment offered some explanatory power for the level of the MSH 35.

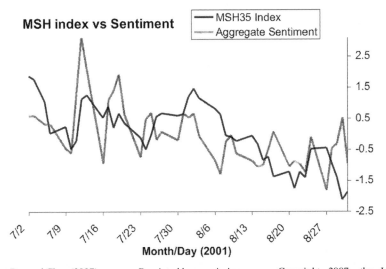

Figure 14-22 Comparing the MSH Index with aggregated sentiments

They also found that higher trading volume was significantly correlated with positive sentiment, but could find no relationship between volume and the previous day's sentiment.

News surprises

As we have already seen, the size of the surprise information contained in a news story can often have a substantial effect on market conditions, particularly prices. Some news obviously lends itself to this approach more than others. Macroeconomic or corporate announcements deliver new numbers to the market, whether they represent Non-Farm Payrolls figures or a firm's quarterly earnings. These may quickly be compared with expected figures to determine how much of a surprise they represent. A nice example of this is given in a study by Linda Goldberg and Deborah Leonard (2003). Figure 14-23, reproduced from this study, shows the monthly changes in Non-Farm Payroll data together with the market expectations from MMS surveys between January 2000 and June 2002.

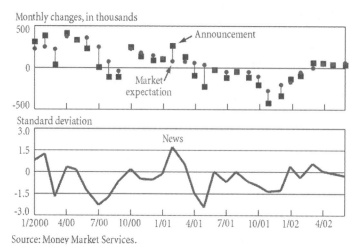

Source: Money Market Services.

Source: Goldberg and Leonard (2003)
Reproduced with permission from Federal Reserve Bank of New York

Figure 14-23 U.S. Non-Farm payrolls: Announcements, expectations and news

To quantify the size of any surprises they normalised the difference between actual and expected figures by dividing by the standard deviation of Non-Farm Payrolls relative to expectations for the period. For real-time analysis, we could adopt a similar approach using a standard deviation based on historical data. The normalisation confirms that events such as the ones at 7/00 and 2/01 are statistically significant. Based on the empirical results we have already seen, we might expect the surprise factor of such events to have a noticeable effect on the market. Since this news is easy to interpret, it is also likely that the impact will be relatively short-lived, as the market can rapidly incorporate the information into its prices.

Other types of news may require much more analysis in order to interpret their information. Quantitative models or fundamental analysis may be required to recalculate new fair values for assets. Some news may be extremely difficult to quantify, such as the resignation of a senior executive or losing a key contract. Hence, such news tends to take longer for the market to react to. There may also be a wider range of interpretations, so this dispersal of views could lead to an increase in volatility. There might even be a decline in liquidity while the market analyses the potential effects. So even for more complex news items without fully interpreting them we may be able to make some simple estimates of their short-term effect on the market's liquidity and volatility.

News-based algorithms

News-based algorithms have already attracted the moniker "news flow" algorithms. Note that our focus remains on execution, rather than automated trading. Consequently, news is simply treated as information that affects our execution decisions. Unlike price, volume, liquidity or volatility, news is not a core market variable - it arrives sporadically. The arrival of news is a factor that has a clear short-term impact on these market variables, as we saw in section 14.5. Focussing solely on news cannot guarantee to meet specific investment objectives such as minimising market impact or transaction costs. For this reason, news-based algorithms are clearly more opportunistic in nature.

Incorporating news handling into existing algorithms

Just as price and liquidity-adaptive behaviour is being incorporated into existing algorithms, the same can be done for news. Adding a news handling capability may well improve their performance when news events do occur. For example, VWAP algorithms could modify their target volume profiles to account for the news release, whilst shortfall-based algorithms could alter their short-term volatility estimates. Similarly, temporary adjustments could be made to limit order models used by cost-based algorithms or execution tactics to determine the optimal approach for order placement. Thus, news just becomes another factor, like price and liquidity, upon which algorithms and execution tactics base their order placement decisions.

News-adaptive algorithms

These are the news-based equivalents of price-adaptive algorithms. In which case a news-adaptive algorithm might trade a sell order less aggressively when good news arrives, whilst for a buy order it might be more aggressive. Clearly, this approach is closely related to price-adaptive algorithms. However, since news is the trigger the decisions are effectively making short-term estimates of how they think the price will react to the news. So long as the market reaction behaves as expected, the news adaptation should give slightly better results than the more reactive price-based approach. Again, this highlights the importance of inbuilt monitoring to ensure that the market does react as our interpretation of the news suggests.

News-driven algorithms

Market prices and trades vary continuously throughout the day, hence algorithms such as percent of volume or price inline can constantly track this data and adjust their trading patterns accordingly. In comparison, the arrival of news is a much more discrete event. Each day there might only be a handful of news stories that might affect an order, and often there may be none. Even for a worst case scenario there is likely to only be a few pieces of significant news arriving in a day. There may well be 30 or 40 different stories, but many of these will simply be the same information from different sources, possible revisions, or daily summaries outlining the effect the news has had on the market. Thus, if an order is to be driven solely by news it will tend to behave more like a conditional order, only being activated if good (or bad) news appears. For some investment firms news-conditional orders may act as a useful placeholder to reduce (or increase) their position if a certain event occurs. Essentially, though, it is much like a stop order, but based on information rather than price. In fact, a stop order (or trailing stop) might be used just as well, given a reasonably accurate estimate for the potential impact of the news.

In the future news-driven algorithms may well become more complex, but at the moment it is hard to tell what form these might take.

14.7 Summary

- Adapting to breaking news events can give traders a significant edge, although people are still more adept at interpreting news and events than machines.

- Major news wires and press services have been electronic for a long time. Conventional media is now facing competition from social media, such as message boards and blogs.

- Computer-based news analysis is a non-trivial task Complex artificial intelligence and natural language processing techniques are being employed to analyse unstructured text:
  - News filtering searches for keys to narrow the amount of information.
  - News association uses relationships to spot secondary/tertiary effects.
  - News analysis is primarily sentiment analysis at the moment.
  - News interpretation combines information with asset pricing models for forecasts.
  - News mining combines the analysis of historical data with information from news archives, helping to find causal relationships between the news and market prices.

- Market reactions to news depend on the information relayed and market conditions.
  - With macroeconomic news, the reaction varies for different assets. For instance, news of an interest rate drop will help increase the price of existing bonds, but weakens the currency. Corporations may benefit from lower interest rate, but may also suffer from the weaker currency.
  - For corporate news, the reaction is more closely linked to specific assets, although it may also have an effect on other firms in the same industry/sector.

- News-based indicators may easily be added to existing trading algorithms:
  - News flow can help to forecast future volatility.
  - Sentiment can be tracked over time just as if it were price or return data.
  - Surprise relates to the difference between consensus estimates and actual figures.

- News is not a core market variable like price. Each day there might only be a handful of news stories that affect an asset. So:
  - News-adaptive algorithms use appropriate indicators for short-term estimations of how the market may react to the news.
  - News-driven algorithms are likely to be more like conditional orders, triggered by a set outcome or information.

Chapter 15

Data mining and artificial intelligence

Trading is a complex process; markets keep getting faster and the volumes of data keep escalating. Data mining and artificial intelligence offer the potential to give traders an edge by spotting or predicting trends.

15.1 Introduction

Trading algorithms and execution tactics are inherently reactive, responding to market conditions based on predefined rules. In Chapter 10, we saw how they may be enhanced by using short-term prediction models for key market conditions, such as volume and price. These allow a more proactive approach, placing more passively priced orders.

However, in volatile markets, such as those during the 2007-09 financial crisis, sudden unexpected shifts can occur. These are hard to predict and can wrong-foot forecasts based on statistical analysis of historical data. Techniques such as data mining and artificial intelligence offer the potential to improve short-term predictions for key market variables, even during volatile markets. This is because they can incorporate a much wider range of factors in their forecast models. They may also be able to cope better with today's more complex marketplaces, where trading is fragmented between multiple venues.

Data mining is all about finding and confirming trends and/or relationships, some of which may be obvious whilst others may be much more subtle. Many of these techniques are purely statistical in nature. Certainly, much of the market microstructure analysis we have already seen in Chapters 8 and 10 may be viewed as a form of data mining. Likewise, textual analysis can be incorporated. So associations may also be inferred from information in news stories or company reports, as we saw in Chapter 14.

Artificial Intelligence (AI) systems are designed to adapt and learn, and so they can effectively think for themselves. There are two main types, namely conventional AI and computational intelligence. Conventional AI is a top-down approach, which applies logic and rules to make decisions. Essentially, trading algorithms are an example of conventional AI. Computational intelligence takes a bottom-up approach, and is inspired by biological mechanisms. For instance, neural networks try to reproduce the action of our brain's neurons, whilst genetic computation simulates evolution.

In terms of trading and finance, there are three main applications for these techniques: [1]

- Prediction
- Finding associations/relationships

---

[1] As suggested in a review by Stephen Smith (1998).

• Generating trading strategies

All of these are quite closely related. Prediction and association mining often use similar methods to find relationships in the data. These may form the basis of new trading rules or strategies. Artificial intelligence systems are able to test a huge number of variations in parallel, seeking the optimal solution. Hence, they can also help in the creation, testing and fine-tuning of rules for trading strategies/algorithms and their associated parameters.

In the following sections, we will review these techniques and survey some of the reports on their effectiveness, particularly for short-term forecasts. We will also consider how they might be incorporated to enhance execution.

15.2 Data mining

As its name suggests, data mining is all about data. By applying analytical techniques, trends and/or relationships may be found within data, or between different datasets.

Data mining techniques

Dongsong Zhang and Lina Zhou (2004) provide a nice overview of data mining for the financial markets. There are several main types, namely:

• Classification and clustering analysis
• Time-series mining
• Association rule mining

These employ a range of different statistical analysis/inference methods. They may also incorporate AI-based mechanisms such as neural networks and genetic algorithms.

Classification and clustering analysis

Classification and clustering analysis both seek to identify common features in the data. Any commonalities may then be used for predictions, since if the results are known for one entity (or may be accurately estimated) they are likely to be comparable for those with similar properties. Note that often such predictions will focus on the direction rather than the potential value. For example, specific conditions might be used to determine whether a stock index or exchange rate will increase or decrease in a certain time span. These analyses may also be used for risk management or for spotting potential investments.

Classification may be strictly hierarchical, in which case properties such as country, currency, industry and sector are useful. Other factors such as the financial ratios (e.g. price to book) may also be used. Cluster analysis may also be applied to create intermediate hierarchies, based on results such as price returns or volatility.

Alternatively, a more geometric approach may be taken. This is often achieved using AI-based techniques, which we shall cover in section 15.3. For instance, the k-nearest neighbour algorithm classifies based on a majority vote from its neighbours. Likewise, probabilistic neural networks employ a weighted vote for each category based on the distance from test cases. Support vector machines may also be used to seek the plane/s which optimally separate/s any categories or clusters.

Time-series mining

In finance, time series analysis is often used for forecasting. As we saw in Chapter 10, regression-based models, such as ARMA, are used to make short-term predictions for prices or volatility. Historical volume profiles are another example, using average-based models to estimate future trading volumes.

Time series analysis can also use factor models to try to identify any regular features, such as cyclical or seasonal effects. Thus, data is often de-trended and normalised. Curve fitting techniques may be applied as well, using lagged data, simple moving averages or even Fourier transforms or wavelets to try to model the data. Transformations may also be used: shifting, scaling or warping the data to try to highlight any patterns. Due to the non-linear nature of many of these patterns, AI techniques, such as neural networks and support vector machines, have proved to be effective forecasting tools. We will cover this more fully in section 15.3.

In addition to purely quantitative forecasting, these techniques may also be used more qualitatively. For example, a common application is identifying turning points in the time series, to determine when a sudden change in direction is likely.

Association rule mining

Association rules are probably best known for their shopping basket examples. Supermarkets can use their huge databases to determine relationships, such as what type of milk customers will buy based on their choice of breakfast cereal.

In statistics, an association represents any relationship between two variables that makes them dependent. In terms of probability, this means the occurrence of one event makes it more likely that the other will occur. Correlation is often used to measure statistical associations. As we saw in Chapter 12, the correlation coefficient can be found by dividing the covariance of the two variables by the product of their standard deviations.

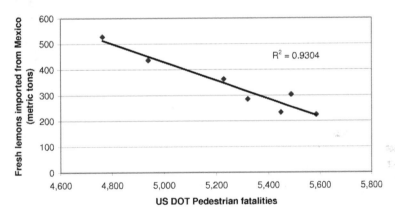

Source: US DOT (2009), US DOA (2009)

Figure 15-1 Association and causality

Note, it is important to differentiate between association and causality. A statistical association between two types of data is simply that; it does not imply anything more. Stephen Johnson (2008) illustrates this with two clearly unrelated datasets, namely the U.S. imports of fresh lemons from Mexico and the U.S. Highway fatality rate. Figure 15-1 shows a similar plot of lemon imports versus pedestrian fatalities for the period 1994-2000. For this sample, the correlation coefficient (ρ) is -0.965. As we can see from the negative slope in Figure 15-1, there seems to be a significant negative association between the two, with fatalities decreasing as lemon imports increase.

When looking at associations, it is also important to consider the measure of confidence we can have in them. R^2 is a statistical measure of the "goodness of fit" between different data sets. In the case of statistical models, it shows how likely future outcomes are to be predicted by the model. An R^2 of 1.0 (or 100%) represents a perfect match, so the R^2 of 0.93 means we can be confident that this association holds for this sample data.

However, can we really infer any link between lemon imports and traffic accidents? Even when we find a statistically significant association, it is difficult to prove a causal link. Probability models may quantify the likelihood of each occurrence, whilst Bayes' theorem helps to relate the conditional probabilities between two such events. Prediction models can also be used, to see if an event may be linked to subsequent events or specific reactions. Though, it is important to remember that we are still dealing in probability, not certainty.

Finding patterns/associations

In Chapter 10, we saw how statistical analysis of historical data could be used to provide forecasting models for key market variables, such as price, volatility and liquidity. Much of this focussed on data for a specific asset. However, useful information may also be inferred from relationships between assets, both in the same market and across different markets or even asset classes. Data mining can help to find these associations, allowing us to create forecasting models that are based on a wider range of data.

Some of these associations are already well known, such as the beta of a stock versus its index. Others require some more work to find. For instance, lead/lag relationships may be found between some key sectors and the market as a whole, or in the supply chain. They can also exist between countries and between the cash and derivative markets. Therefore, automated data mining techniques provide a way of searching for useful or promising relationships. The results may then be examined more closely to see how viable they are as predictive indicators. They may also be related to other sources of information, such as news and macroeconomic indicators, as we saw in Chapter 14.

Relationships between assets and markets are also heavily dependent on market conditions. At the most basic level, many of the world's markets are driven by a mixture of fear and greed, which is why volatile conditions can so easily spread between markets. For example, the Mexican Peso crisis, the Asian currency crisis, Russia's devaluation, the collapse of LTCM, and the 2007/8 sub-prime debacle all led to substantial downturns, which spread across the world's markets. In such volatile times, tracking other key markets, such as the U.S., can be another useful predictive indicator. The "flight to quality" is a well-established phenomenon, with investors shifting to safer, or more liquid, assets during troubled times. Therefore, it can also be useful to look across asset classes, for instance during volatile markets investors may well shift to hold more bonds than equities.

Intra-market relationships

Many of the studies examining intra-market relationships have focussed on corporations, due to their ease of classification via industries and sectors.

A detailed study of the co-movements for U.S. industry sectors was carried out by Jarl Kallberg and Paolo Pasquariello (2008). They created a model for returns based on four fundamental factors. Three of these were the systematic risks identified by Eugene Fama and Kenneth French (1993): market, book-to-market and small-firm risk. The fourth factor was sector risk. They found a significant amount of excess co-movement, based on the co-variation between asset prices. For some sectors, such as utilities and non-cyclical services, the excess was much higher than average. Whilst for others, such as general industrials, non-cyclical consumer goods, financials and cyclical services, the excess was slightly below average. This is summarised in Table 15-1, which is ordered based on their findings.

	Sector	*Examples*
Higher	Utilities	Electricity, gas distribution, water providers
	Non-Cyclical Services	Food/drug retailers, telecom providers
	Resources	Mining, oil and gas
	Information Technology	Hardware, software and computer services
	Cyclical Consumer Goods	Automobiles, household goods and textiles
	Basic Industries	Chemicals, construction /building materials, forestry and paper, steel and other metals
	General Industrials	Aerospace and defence, diversified industrials, engineering and machinery
	Non-Cyclical Consumer Goods	Beverages, food producers, health, pharmaceuticals, tobacco
	Financials	Banks, insurance, investment companies
Lower	Cyclical Services	General retailers, leisure, media, transport

Table 15-1 Excess co-movement for specific sectors

Their fundamental model was only able to explain 27% of the excess co-movement for the market as a whole. Whilst for some sectors, such as resources and utilities, it was much more effective. Thus, a sizeable proportion of the co-movement was attributable to non-fundamental factors. However, there was also a considerable amount, which was not. Kallberg and Pasquariello went on to investigate some additional factors that might explain the remainder of the excess co-movement. They found that it was negatively related to market volatility and the level of short-term interest rates.

Co-movement also appeared to be negatively related to U.S. monetary and real output developments. Conversely, it was positively related to the dispersion and the number of analysts' earnings forecasts, which acts as a proxy for information flow. Momentum, contemporaneous and lagged returns were found to have negligible explanatory effects. Overall, these other factors were able to explain another 23% of the excess co-movement.

An additional factor that might help explain excess co-movement is firm size. Kewei Hou (2002) observed a significant lead/lag effect for stocks in the U.S., with the returns of large firms leading those of smaller companies. Lior Menzly and Oguzhan Ozbas (2004) found that for small and medium-sized firms cross-industry momentum could be significant, whilst it was negligible for larger firms (above the NYSE median market capitalisation cut-off).

The supply chain is another potential factor for relating the price moves between different sectors. A lead/lag relationship seems reasonable since problems with upstream suppliers could well affect the future returns of firms that are dependent on their goods. For instance, Y.L. Hsieh, Don-Lin Yang and Jungpin Wu (2006) used genetic algorithms to analyse the price relationships between firms in Taiwan's technology industry. Rules were created based on the daily returns. Using these, they found they could predict future price changes with 60-70% accuracy. In the U.S., Menzly and Ozbas (2004) used the input-output survey from the Bureau of Economic Analysis to quantify the supply chain. They found a significant momentum from upstream and downstream industries. The effect from upstream industries was about double the size of the cross-industry momentum, whilst for downstream industries it was less, but still around 50% larger.

Certain industries can also act as an important indicator for the market as a whole. Harrison Hong, Walter Torous and Rossen Valkanov (2007) analysed the relationship between industry and market returns in a range of countries. For the U.S., they found that the returns from stocks in over a dozen industries showed a significant lead, of around a month, versus the market as a whole. In terms of economic significance, the banking sector led, followed by real estate, print, apparel and services. They also found a negative relationship for some of the resource-based industries, such as petroleum and metals. Overall, they concluded that the industries that led the market also acted as indicators of economic activity. A similar effect was found for other countries, including the U.K., Canada, Germany, and Japan, although there was more variation in the number of key industries.

Inter-market relationships

The intraday dynamics between international equity markets have been analysed by Kari Harju and Syed Hussain (2006a). Once the returns were deseasonalized, they found a correlation of 0.54 between the returns for the U.K. FTSE and the German DAX. Interestingly, this increased to 0.7 at around 15:30 Central European Time (CET), which coincides with the U.S. open. The significance of the U.S. open is also highlighted in a similar study by Harju and Hussain (2006), where they compared the average intraday returns for major European indices between days when the U.S. markets were open or closed. They found a clear shift in the returns at around 15:30 CET on the days when the U.S. markets were open.

Harju and Hussain (2006a) also used a vector autoregressive exponential GARCH model to analyse the volatility. They found that significant price spillovers from Germany and the U.S. rapidly spread to the U.K. The German market also affected U.S. returns, but they could find no evidence of the U.K. significantly affecting either the U.S. or Germany.

A similar analysis was carried out by Kate Phylaktis and Lichuan Xia (2008). They analysed the returns of stocks across Europe, Asia and Latin America. Overall, they found the Asian stocks to be more responsive to the US market than to the regional markets, whilst European and Latin American stocks showed more reaction to regional markets than the U.S. That said, a notable exception is information technology, which was found to be globally responsive for firms from every region.

Robin Brooks and Marco Del Negro (2003) broke down returns into global, country and industry specific components for stocks from 20 countries. They confirmed that the level of risk for a stock was dependent on its international exposure. A 10% increase in international sales was found to increase the stock's exposure to global shocks by 2%, whilst reducing its country specific risk by 1.5%.

Cross asset class relationships

A lot of research has focussed on the lead/lag relationships that can exist between asset classes, particularly between cash and derivatives. The potential for arbitrage means that the price differences between markets should generally not be any larger that the costs of executing the arbitrage.

Jeff Fleming, Barbara Ostdiek and Robert Whaley (1996) analysed the relationships between stock indices and their futures or options markets. They found that the lead/lag return relations amongst these markets were consistent with their relative trading costs. The cost-efficient index derivatives appeared to lead prices in the stock market, in turn the prices of index futures tended to lead those of index options. Similar results were found in an analysis of the Korean KOSPI 200 index by Jangkoo Kang, Soonhee Lee and Changjoo Lee

(2004). They noted that both the futures and the options markets led the cash index prices by up to ten minutes, even when accounting for transaction costs. They also analysed the relationship for volatility and found the cash market again lagged the others, this time by around five minutes.

The lead/lag relationship for S&P 500 index options was analysed by Phelim Boyle, Soku Byoun and Hun Park (2002). They also found that the contracts led the cash index. In another study, Fleming, Ostdiek and Whaley (1996) noted that, in terms of the lead/lag relationship, the prices of index calls and index puts moved together. Though, analysis of short-term at-the-money (ATM) CAC 40 index options by Alexis Cellier (2003) noted a marked difference between calls and puts. The call options led the cash index by up to five minutes, although a significant effect was found to last for up to fifteen minutes. The puts were found to be more contemporaneous with the index.

For single stock options, Richard Holowczak, Yusif Simaan and Liuren Wu (2006), and Sugato Chakravarty, Huseyin Gulen and Stewart Mayhew (2004) analysed the price discovery with U.S. stocks. Both groups found stocks tended to lead options prices. Though, they also noted that during periods of substantial options trading the options market became more informative. In their study, Chakravarty, Gulen and Mayhew (2004) estimated that the option market's contribution to price discovery was around a fifth, so there was a meaningful two-way flow between the two markets. In earlier work, Matthew O'Connor (1999) also found that the stock market led the options market. He observed that the lead was related to the options' trading costs. Whilst Holowczak, Simaan and Wu (2006) noted that the increasing use of automated quoting algorithms by options market makers was helping increase the reliance on the stock market for prices.

The relationships between the corporate bond, credit default swaps (CDS) and stock markets were analysed by Lars Norden and Martin Weber (2005), for a sample of 90 firms from Europe, the U.S. and Asia. Stock returns were seen to lead changes in the spreads for both bonds and CDSs. They also found that CDS spread changes were likely to have more influence on bond spreads than vice versa. The stock market lead may be ascribed to its higher liquidity and trading volumes, as well as the relative ease of shorting stocks. Similar results were found in an earlier U.S. based study by Francis Longstaff, Sanjay Mithal and Eric Neis (2003). They noted that both the stock and CDS markets led the corporate bond market. In their study, Norden and Weber (2005) found that CDSs were more sensitive to moves in the stock market than bonds, and this effect increased for firms with lower credit ratings. This additional sensitivity was explained by the fact that CDSs represent pure issuer credit risk, whilst bonds are a bundle of both credit risk and market risk.

For currencies, Tiffany Hutcheson (2003) analysed the differences between the intraday returns based on CME FX futures contracts and Reuters spot prices for the euro and the U.S. dollar. She found that the spot market led the futures market, within a 5-minute period.

The relationships for commodity prices were studied by Frank Asche and Atle Guttormsen (2001). They analysed the relationship between spot and futures prices for gas (or heating) oil on the International Petroleum Exchange (IPE). They saw that the futures price did indeed lead the spot prices. They also reported that the prices of futures contracts with a longer time to expiration led those that were closer to expiry.

Crises and contagion

The relationships that exist within and between markets can change considerably during extreme periods. In terms of intra-market relationships, research has shown that correlation tends to increase for downward moves, so this can be an important issue for forecasts.

Param Silvapulle and Clive Granger (2001) analysed the daily returns for the Dow Jones Industrial stocks between 1991-9. They confirmed that the correlation between them increased for large negative market movements, whilst there was no notable difference for large positive movements. They concluded that this reaction reduced the benefits of diversification, so in downturns portfolios can be exposed to more risk than expected. A similar increase in correlation during market falls was reported by Andrew Ang and Joseph Chen (2002). In their analysis of the correlations between U.S. stocks and the market as a whole, they noted the effect was strongest for the most extreme drops. They also found that the largest changes in correlation were for firms that were smaller, had seen low returns recently or could be categorised as "growth" stocks. A significant change was also observed for the traditionally defensive sectors, such as petroleum and utilities. Interestingly, stocks with lower betas were affected most; higher risk stocks were less affected.

Across markets, Donald Lien, Y.K. Tse and X.B. Zhang (2002) analysed the relationship between stock and futures markets for the Nikkei 225 index between 1995 and 1999. They found three clusters of structural changes. The first of these originated in the futures market, as we might expect; however, the other two were led by the stock market. They also found another structural shift in the stock market, although this did not seem to be large enough to affect the futures. Hence, the traditional lead/lag relationships that we saw in the previous sub-section do not always hold during crises.

A global increase in correlation has also been observed during crises. François Longin and Bruno Solnik (2001) used "extreme value theory" to derive the distribution of extreme correlations between the U.S., European and Asian stock markets. They established that the change in correlation was related to the market trend rather than the market volatility. Thus, correlation was seen to increase in bear markets but was less affected in bull markets. There was a notable shift in correlation for a drop of 10% whereas a rise of 10% behaved as expected. They concluded that the probability of having large losses simultaneously on two markets is larger than might be expected. Simón Sosvilla-Rivero and Pedro Rodríguez (2004) also studied the relationship between the S&P 500, FTSE 100 and the Nikkei 225 stock indices. They found that the S&P 500 seemed to lead the other two markets in terms of extreme positive or negative returns.

Research has also focused on how these crises spread across markets. For instance, a nice summary of the Asian currency crisis is provided by Jarl Kallberg, Crocker Liu and Paolo Pasquariello (2005). They examined both returns and volatility for currencies and stocks and tracked how the information shocks moved from country to country in the 1992-1998 time period. For volatility, they found that the first breaks actually clustered around the 1994-5 Mexican Peso crisis for Malaysia, Taiwan and Thailand. Volatility breaks were found for the other Asian countries towards the end of 1997. The equity markets were then affected by the currency volatility. Return shocks were found to affect Malaysia and South Korea in early 1998, these then spread across the rest of Asia. Phylaktis and Xia (2008) also examined both the Mexican and Asian crises in their sectoral analysis. They found that nearly half the sectors in Europe, Asia and Latin America were affected by the Mexican crisis. Yet, in the Asian currency crisis, they found no additional contagion in Europe or Latin America.

The effects of contagion have also been studied for the debt markets. Amar Gande and David Parsley (2005) analysed the publicly traded U.S. dollar denominated sovereign debt for 34 countries across Europe, Asia and the Americas. They found that, on average, a one-notch downgrade, such as from AA+ to AA, for a country's credit rating led to an increase in the spreads of sovereign bonds for the other countries. Assuming a 6% yield, they estimated this could lead to a change of 12 bps in the spread. They also found evidence for competitive spillovers occurring, so a downgrade for a country with highly negatively correlated trade or capital flows to the U.S. actually led to a decrease in the spreads for similar countries.

During crises, there is often a "flight to quality". George Theocharides (2006) found evidence of this for U.S. bonds; resulting in wider spreads for corporate bonds and a drop in the yields for U.S. Treasuries. He also noted a tendency for older bonds to be traded during these periods. But for U.S. corporate bonds, he found that company specific shocks had negligible effects on the bonds from firms in the same industry.

Research is still divided about exactly how and why contagion occurs. Data mining has been applied to try to identify the causes of contagion. For example, it has been linked to the dynamics of economic fundamentals, such as interest rates. In fact, Robert Shiller (1989) found that a marked proportion of the excess covariance between U.S. and U.K. stocks could be explained by positively correlated interest rates. A nice summary of research into contagion is provided by Kallberg and Pasquariello (2008): Studies by Kathy Yuan (2005), Albert Kyle and Wei Xiong (2001) and Guillermo Calvo (2002) have focussed on liquidity shocks due to the trading activity of financially constrained investors. Other researchers such as Paolo Pasquariello (2007) and Jeff Fleming, Chris Kirby and Barbara Ostdiek (1998) have concentrated on investors' portfolio rebalancing activity. Both are probably contributory factors, although further research will be needed to fully quantify their relative importance.

Important precautions for data mining

Statistical analysis is an important tool, but it can also be a dangerous one. Indeed, there are lies, damned lies, and statistics, as popularised by Mark Twain (1907). As with any analysis, due care must be taken to check any potential relationships which may be discovered. It is essential to apply economic sanity checks and a wide range of testing before too much is read into any relationship.

Stefan Zemke (2002) provides a nice review of some of the potential pitfalls that should be considered when handling financial data. In particular, he emphasises the importance of the data pre-processing. To start with, we must be sure that the data quality is good enough. The old maxim "garbage in, garbage out" holds just as true for statistical analysis as for computer programs. Therefore, it is important to have checks in place to inspect and, if necessary, clean the data. Apparent outliers may in fact be genuine; they may be due to events such as stock splits or dividends. Similarly, missing data may need to be back-filled, or simply excluded.

Inferring relationships from data must also be done with some caution. Again, it is important to remember that any associations often simply reflect a probability, rather than a truly causal relationship: Just because one event has happened, it does not necessarily guarantee anything – although it may make related events more likely to occur. A commonly cited example is the "Texas sharpshooter" fallacy: If we just look at a target with several shots in the dead centre, we might assume that the shooter had a good aim. However, without having seen the shots we do not know how far they were taken from, or even whether the target was painted on afterwards! In other words, it is always important to check whether the discovered relationships make economic sense. This may also mean taking into account factors such as transaction costs.

For relationships to be meaningful, they must be based on a reasonably sized dataset. Two points can always be joined by a straight line (with an R^2 of 1.0 or 100%). For instance, back in Figure 15-1 we saw that the data for U.S. lemon imports and pedestrian fatalities were very closely related, with an R^2 of 0.93. However, this is only for annual results from 1994-2000; in fact, this range was chosen solely because it happened to give a high correlation and

R^2. If we expand the period up to 2008 the correlation drops to -0.554, with an R^2 of only 0.31.

Another risk when data mining is the potential for over-fitting data. Essentially, this means that the discovered relationship works perfectly for the test data; but as soon as it is exposed to real data it gives completely useless results. For example, let's consider if there might be any link between the Dow Jones Industrial Average (DJIA) and U.S. traffic accidents from 1995-2007, as shown in Figure 15-2.

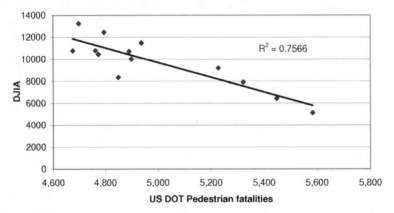

Source: US DOT (2009)

Figure 15-2 The dangers of over-fitting data

Again, the correlation of -0.87 and an R^2 of 0.75 shows a reasonably close fit between these datasets. Maybe if we added some other datasets, a meaningful relationship might be found. David Leinweber (2000) carries out a brilliant example of this: he starts with the returns for the S&P 500, finding a reasonable fit with the level of butter production in Bangladesh, achieving an R^2 of 0.75. Determined to improve the model he then found that incorporating U.S. cheese production and the sheep population of both countries raised the R^2 to 0.99 for the test period. Equally high R^2 were achieved for models using fitted polynomials based on the year's digits. So associations can be found between almost anything if you look hard enough.

Obviously, these are purposefully outlandish examples. Unsurprisingly, the relationships are non-existent outside the test period. However, Leinweber makes the key point that just because regression charts for interest rates or GDP seem plausible, the statistics can sometimes be just as meaningless. So when examining data, it is important to hold back a portion to allow for "out-of-sample" testing. Leinweber also suggests that this should be done on both a temporal and a cross-sectional basis.

15.3 Artificial Intelligence

The term Artificial Intelligence (AI) was first coined by John McCarthy in 1956 during a workshop on computers and intelligence at Dartmouth. AI systems are designed to adapt and learn, and so effectively think for themselves.

The progress of AI has certainly had its fair share of "ups and downs". Buoyed by early success in the 1960s AI seemed unstoppable. A brief slowdown in the 1970s was followed by a surge in the 1980s as the sudden availability of personal computers helped it become more commercial. In fact, by 1985 the market for AI systems had reached a billion dollars, according to Daniel Crevier (1993). In the mid 1980s, AI systems spread to finance and more specifically trading, heralding the dawn of AI-driven automated trading. Although the harsh realities of dealing on the world's markets meant that many such systems became write-offs within a few years. Overall, a lack of results meant the honeymoon ended and much of the corporate and government funding for AI research disappeared.

The 1990s saw a resurgence of AI techniques, particularly in the technology industry. It again became headline news in 1997, when IBM's Deep Blue computer managed to beat the Grand Master Gary Kasparov at chess, nearly fifty years after the first AI researchers had begun. Unsurprisingly, financial applications for AI are once again being found.

Types of artificial intelligence

AI can actually be split into two main approaches:
- Conventional AI
- Computational intelligence

Conventional AI is a top-down approach that uses logic and rules to make decisions. This generally relies on data that has been translated into known symbols, employing custom-made knowledge bases or statistical analysis. Examples of conventional AI include expert and case-based reasoning systems, as well as Bayesian networks.

On the other hand, computational intelligence is a bottom-up approach that takes its inspiration from biological mechanisms. For instance, neural networks try to reproduce the action of our brain's neurons, whilst evolutionary computation simulates populations. Other examples are hybrid intelligent systems, which are a combination of neural and evolutionary mechanisms, whilst fuzzy logic offers probability based solutions.

Conventional AI

Conventional AI is generally based on logic. Experts define rules for how to identify specific situations and what actions to take in response to them. These may be broken down into simple logical statements: IF <this happens> THEN <do this> ELSE <do this instead>. Rules also need to be placed in context; hence, structures like decision trees may be used to ensure they are followed in a sensible order. Once enough of these are defined, a system has all the basics of how to cope. Obviously, though, there are some subtle nuances - there will always be situations that simply do not follow the rules.

All of this sounds rather familiar, since a trading algorithm is essentially a complex collection of rules each designed to respond to various events. The rules themselves have generally been determined by experienced traders or quants. So, in essence, a trading algorithm is just an instance of an AI expert system.

Conventional AI may be also used to make forecasts; however, the reliance on explicit rules means it is less adaptable than techniques involving computational intelligence.

Computational intelligence

Computational intelligence, or soft computing, applies an array of different techniques, using elements of learning, optimisation and adaptation/evolution.

Machine learning is used by computer systems to recognize complex patterns in data, and make intelligent decisions based on this. There are three main categories:
- Supervised learning

- Unsupervised learning
- Reinforcement learning

Supervised learning is adopted by many soft computing techniques, from the k-nearest neighbour algorithm to neural networks and support vector machines. During training, the ideal outputs are provided for test inputs. Hence, the learning mechanism will try to validate its own outputs against these target values. Repeated cycles should mean it optimises itself to produce output much closer to the ideal. With unsupervised learning, no test outputs are provided, so the mechanism must find another way to validate itself. Reinforcement learning takes a different approach: instead of using a dedicated training period, it relies on constant feedback from its environment. Some neural networks use unsupervised or reinforcement learning.

Optimisation is also important. For many problems, there is an optimal solution, which may be found by searching through the possible solutions. Computational intelligence may be employed to search the solution space more efficiently.

Likewise, adaptation is another key consideration. One of the downfalls of conventional AI is the fact that situations can arise for which none of the pre-determined rules fit. By being able to adapt, or evolve, computational intelligence has a better chance of dealing with such situations.

In the following sub-sections, we shall examine some of these methods in more detail, starting with the simplest k-nearest neighbour algorithm then progressing on to neural networks and support vector machines and finally genetic algorithms and programming.

k-nearest neighbour algorithm

The k-nearest neighbour (k-NN) algorithm classifies objects based on a majority vote from its closest k neighbours, where k is a small number. To start with, we need to seed the mechanism with some sample assignments. For instance, Figure 15-3 shows an example where objects have already been classified as type 1 or type 2.

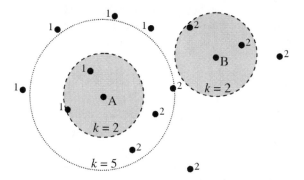

Figure 15-3 An example of k-NN classification

When classifying sample objects, if $k = 2$ then A will be classed as type 1 since its closest two neighbours are both type 1, whilst B will be classed as type 2, as shown by the shaded circles. If we now use $k = 5$, for sample A three of the five closest neighbours are now type 2, so A would be reclassified as type 2. Although this is a simple 2D example, the concept may also be extended for multiple dimensions.

The k-NN mechanism may be used for regression as well, so the ideal value for our sample object is based on the average values for its k nearest neighbours, each weighted by their distance from the sample. Note, there is very little training for the k-NN algorithm; it simply consists of storing the details for the seeded training samples. The rest is done in the classification phase.

Neural networks

Artificial neural networks (ANNs), also known as neural nets, take their biological inspiration from the mechanism of neurons. The brain is a complicated network of interconnected neurons where information is passed by electrical stimulation. Signals are received by a neuron's dendrites, or branches, which in turn connect to many other neurons. If sufficient electrical signals are received, the neuron may become activated; in which case it will transmit a signal to other neurons via its axon. The human brain has around a hundred billion (10^{11}) neurons whilst there may be 100-500 trillion (10^{12}) connections (or synapses), based on estimates from David Drachman (2005).

Each node in a neural network mimics the biological structure fairly closely, as Figure 15-4 tries to show. A node takes inputs $I_{1,2,3}$ which are then processed and the resultant output O_n is transmitted. The actual processing may be split into two, firstly summing the input data then determining what kind of output signal is appropriate (if at all).

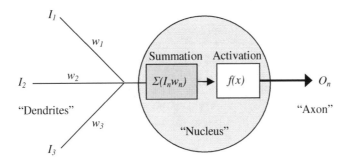

Figure 15-4 A neural network node

Note that the summation function applies distinct weights $w_{1,2,3}$ to the corresponding inputs, so the signals from some connections may be given more importance than others. The activation function determines the appropriate output for the node, based on this input information. Often the activation function is a reasonably simple method that normalises the summed inputs to become a value in the ranges [-1, 1] or [0, 1]. This might be achieved with a threshold function (which will only output a set value if the inputs are more than a specific limit) or with continuous Gaussian, trigonometric or sigmoid functions.

The node shown in Figure 15-4 is effectively an example of a perceptron, which was invented by Frank Rosenblatt in 1957. By itself, this is of limited use; however, when multiple nodes are connected together the resultant networks can be much more powerful and versatile. Figure 15-5 shows some example networks where each circle represents an individual node. In turn, each of these nodes may be classed as being input, output or hidden. Generally, there is one input node for each variable being investigated. The number of output nodes will depend on the information that the network must generate. In between these, there may be any number of hidden nodes, acting as the intermediate steps in the transition from input to output data. They are often arranged in layers, although grids may be used as well.

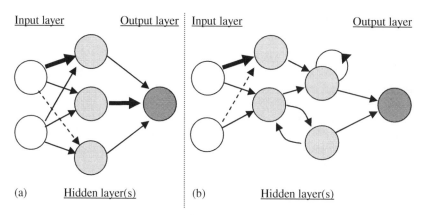

Figure 15-5 Example (a) feed-forward and (b) recurrent neural networks

The overall size of a network is an important consideration. Too few nodes and it may fail to fit the data well enough, too many and it becomes a significant computational burden. There is also the risk of over-fitting data, which can lead the network to start modelling random noise. Unfortunately, there is no real consensus on exactly how best to size a network. As a rough rule of thumb, Lou Mendelsohn (1993) suggests using between half and double the number of input variables as hidden nodes.

That said, the architecture of a neural network is much more than just how many nodes it employs. It also specifies how the nodes are interconnected and how signals flow through the network. In terms of how signals flow through networks Figure 15-5 shows the two main types, namely feed-forward and recurrent. Feed-forward networks process signals in a linear fashion. So they are organised much like the internals of each node. Recurrent networks allow signals to flow in both directions. Nodes may connect to themselves or even nodes in earlier layers, as we can see in Figure 15-5(b). These feedback loops mean that recurrent networks can retain additional state information, allowing them to better adapt to input signals that change over time.

There is also a range of other architectures catering for specific applications, such as probabilistic and general regression neural networks. For more details of these approaches, a nice overview is provided on the DTReg (2008) website and by Joarder Kamruzzaman, Rezaul Begg and Ruhul Sarker (2006).

The training of the network is also an important consideration. Back propagation is a commonly adopted method for supervised learning. The error value is the difference between the output value and the desired figure. In back propagation, this error value is passed backwards through the network, so that each hidden node can then compare this with its own inputs to see how strongly these relate to the required output. The hidden nodes then modify the weights for these to reduce the overall error. After a series of cycles, the weightings should be optimised.

One of the disadvantages of neural networks is their "black box" nature. After training, a model may provide useful results, but to determine how this has been achieved means decoding the various weightings to discover the relationships. That said, interpreters can be created to handle this; indeed, researchers have been using other AI techniques, such as genetic algorithms or programming, to do this automatically.

Support vector machines

A support vector machine (SVM) classifies objects by seeking the plane that optimally separates them. For example, Figure 15-6(a) shows the classification problem we considered back in Figure 15-3. The solid line marks a plane between the two types.

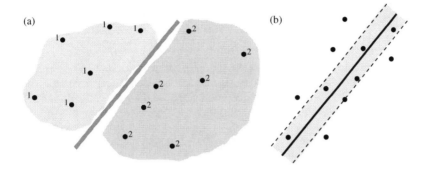

Figure 15-6 Examples of SVM (a) classification and (b) regression

SVMs may also be applied to regression, as shown in Figure 15-6(b), by using Vladimir Vapnik's (1995) error-insensitive loss function. The bold line represents the best plane for the data values, from which we can actually interpolate the ideal values. The dotted lines show additional boundaries that incorporate a maximum permitted error. Any data outside this boundary is effectively ignored.

The examples shown in Figure 15-6 have straightforward linear solutions; however, SVMs are also able to deal with problems spanning multiple dimensions. For a more detailed review of SVMs Kristin Bennett and Colin Campbell's (2000) report is a good starting point.

In many ways, SVM models are actually quite similar to neural networks, although their training is very different: Essentially, it is like solving a quadratic programming problem with linear constraints. So for optimisation problems this means that a unique and globally optimal solution will be found. There is no risk of solutions reaching local minima, which can happen with techniques like back propagation.

Evolutionary computation

Evolutionary algorithms are based on the theory of natural selection, first proposed by Charles Darwin (1859). Traits or properties that are successful become increasingly common over successive generations of a population. This is due to the increased likelihood of survival of individuals with those traits. Evolution relies on the transmission of these traits by genetic inheritance, as well as the innovation provided by mutation.

Computer simulations of evolution started in the 1950s, but one of the most well known models is still John Conway's (1970) Game of Life, a deceptively simple grid-based cellular automaton.

Genetic algorithms

Genetic algorithms (GAs) became popular in the 1970s, most notably based on work by John Holland (1975). For GAs, the population of individuals represent potential solutions to a given problem. A fitness function is used to gauge the quality of each individual. Evolutionary cycles are then repeated, with selection biased to ensure that the next generation is based on those with the highest scores. A nice summary of this cycle is provided by Jin Li and Edward Tsang (1999):

1. Create an initial population.
2. (a) Assess the fitness of each individual.
   (b) Select the set of parents for the next generation.
   (c) Create a new generation of individuals.
3. Repeat step 2 until the required cycles are completed or the time is up.

The aim is that once these iterations are finished the population should be dominated by the highest scoring individuals, and so hopefully the best potential solutions for the problem. Though, this does not guarantee that the global optimum will be reached.

Each individual in the population may be defined as a sequence of genes, which in turn correspond to a set of specific settings or parameters for the required solution. Often these are encoded in a binary fashion, as shown in Figure 15-7:

Figure 15-7 Binary representation for an individual GA solution

This is because the bitwise format is very easy to manipulate when simulating reproduction and mutation. The reproduction is based on a genetic crossover, as shown in Figure 15-8(a): The genes of each parent are cut in two at some random point (marked by the dotted line) and then spliced with the corresponding remainder from their partner. This generates siblings that share parts of each parent's characteristics.

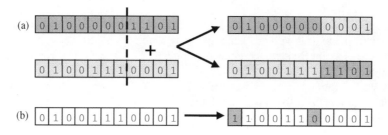

Figure 15-8 Examples of GA (a) reproduction and (b) mutation

The fitness function is obviously central to finding good solutions. Often determining the fitness of a potential solution will entail running a separate simulation. For instance, the individual's settings might correspond to settings for a set of trading rules. These will then need to be back tested to determine their effectiveness. Only then may the overall fitness be rated.

Since there is the danger that the population might simply revolve around a single good solution, it is also important to incorporate mutation, which adds the potential for completely new variants. As we can see in Figure 15-8(b), with a bitwise implementation this is extremely simple, since all we need to do is toggle the value at random points. Mutation helps increase the potential for the population to span a wider range of possible solutions, and so scan more of the search space for the optimal solution. An alternative to mutation is to use immigration, in which case completely new individuals are randomly generated and introduced into each cycle, as suggested by Jurgen Branke (1999).

Genetic programming

Genetic programming (GP) is a natural progression of the work done by genetic algorithms. Instead of relying on simple bit-strings, the individuals are based on more complex data structures, such as trees. This allows even more sophisticated modelling. The early work in this field was led by John Koza (1992). Initially, much of the focus was on evolving actual computer programs; however, this has since expanded to encompass fields as diverse as quantum computing and electronic design.

Tree-based structures are ideally suited for mathematical expressions, for example, Figure 15-9(a) shows a tree for the equation (8 * ((3 + 2) / 4)). Similarly, they may be also be used to encode trading rules. For example, Figure 15-9(b) shows a trading rule that requires the Bid price to be less than 10 and the corresponding size to be more than 500.

(a)   (b)

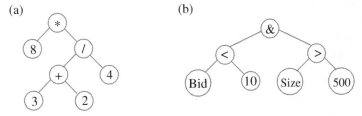

Figure 15-9 Example trees for (a) mathematical and (b) trading rules

Processing for genetic programming is just as with genetic algorithms. Crossover and mutation are essentially the same, except that it is based around nodes of the tree rather than bits in the bit-string. Potential issues with this approach are that over a reasonable number of cycles the trees can become quite complex. In addition, some crossovers or mutations may lead to defunct expressions such as 1 = 1. Note that it is important to leave the trees alone during testing. This is because further crossovers and mutations can easily change defunct expressions to become useful ones, as Jean-Yves Potvin, Patrick Soriano and Maxime Vallée (2004) point out.

Predicting data and trends

In terms of applications, AI has often been used as a forecasting tool. This expands on the forecasting techniques we saw in Chapter 10. Again, the goal is to enhance execution rather than find investment opportunities, since when an order is received the decision to buy or sell the asset has already been made. Hence, we will focus on short-term predictions of market conditions. The results of these predictions may be used within cost or risk models as a factor in determining order choice and placement. These should help the algorithms/tactics decide on an appropriate level of aggressiveness. Note that for such decisions directional trends can be just as useful as actual numbers.

Predicting asset prices

Understandably, much of the research has focussed on forecasting asset prices. In terms of AI-based models, neural networks are the commonest approach, although support vector machines are increasingly being adopted.

Price prediction with neural networks

Neural networks were first applied to stock price prediction in a study by Halbert White (1988). He employed a feed-forward network to analyse the daily stock returns of IBM in order to test the Efficient Markets Hypothesis (EMH), which asserts that asset prices follow a random walk. Although no predictive rules were found, his research highlighted the potential for such analysis. Indeed, a later study of six other U.S. stocks by George Tsibouris and Matthew Zeidenberg (1995) found some predictive ability from historical prices. Further prediction studies of stock returns, such as those by Apostolos-Paul Refenes, Achileas Zapranis and Gavin Francis (1995) and Manfred Steiner and Hans-Georg Wittkemper (1995), found that neural networks outperformed comparable statistical techniques, such as regression models. Some studies have even incorporated aspects of technical analysis, for instance, K. Kamijo and T. Tanigawa (1990) used an Elman recurrent network to predict stock prices for Japanese stocks. Their method sought to find triangle patterns to determine whether price rises might be permanent, based on historical highs, lows and closes.

Predicting stock indices has been a particularly popular area of research. Amol Kulkarni (1996) performed a study of the S&P 500, with weekly data covering both the crash of October 1986 and the bull run of 1994. His network was a straightforward feed-forward net, with 19 input neurons and a single hidden layer of 7 neurons. The model incorporated both short- and long-term interest rates together with historical prices. It was trained with 275 weeks of data. He found that for out-of-sample testing the network gave reasonable predictions one week ahead of the actual index, as shown in Figure 15-10.

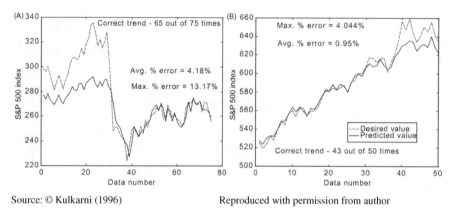

Source: © Kulkarni (1996)   Reproduced with permission from author

Figure 15-10 Predicted values for the S&P 500 (a) during the 1986 crash and (b) the 1994 bull run

It also correctly predicted the overall price trend 65 out of 75 times for the period of the 1986 crash, and 43 out of 50 times for the 1994 bull-run. In particular, he ascribed its success over the period of the 1986 crash to having incorporated the effect of rising long-term interest rates, since there was no hint of this from the index price trends.

In their study of the S&P 500 index, Tim Chenoweth, Zoran Obradović and Sauchi Lee (1995) also used interest rate data, namely the US Treasury rate, lagged by two and three months. They employed two separate neural networks, which were trained with either upward or downward trending index data. The quality of the prediction was found to be sufficient to yield an annual rate of return close to 15%.

Another study which looked at both "bull" and "bear" markets was carried out for the Madrid stock market's General Index by Fernández-Rodríguez, González-Martel and Simón Sosvilla-Rivero (2000). They used a feed-forward network with nine inputs for the previous close prices and a single hidden layer with four neurons. Their results proved superior to a simple buy-and-hold strategy; although incorporating transaction costs showed the ANN underperformed buy and hold during bull markets.

Other factors have also been incorporated into models, such as FX and the prices of other major indices. Thomas Ankenbrand and Marco Tomassini (1995) carried out a study of the Swiss Performance Index. Their model incorporated interest rates, relative performance to the S&P 500 and the DEM/USD exchange rate, due to the importance of exports for Swiss companies. Overall, the prediction accuracy was around 70% out-of-sample.

Technical indicators such as moving averages and RSI were also used as input together with the historical prices for the main indices on the Kuala Lumpur stock exchange by Jingtao Yao, Chew Lim Tan and Hean-Lee Poh (1999) and Yao and Poh (1995). They tested feed-forward networks with back propagation for a range of different network configurations. Networks with two hidden layers seemed to give the best results, both in terms of accuracy and from paper-trading profits. Overall, they estimated that annual returns of up to 26% could be achieved from these predictions for the 1990 data, taking into account 1% transaction costs.

Using neural networks for predicting prices is not solely limited to equities; they have been applied to most of the major asset classes, such as bonds, FX, futures and options.

Forecasts of U.S, U.K and German 10-year government bond yields were made by Christian Dunis and Vincent Morrison (2004). The inputs for their ANN-based models incorporated a range of daily close prices for 2001-3, including currencies, leading stock indices and commodities like oil. They actually found the ARMA model to give consistently more accurate predictions; however, the ANN-based models proved to be the best at predicting the directional trends. Hence, their trading simulation actually saw the most profit from the ANN-based models.

A study of the U.S. dollar/euro exchange rate, using daily data from 1994-2001, by Christian Dunis and Mark Williams (2003), noted that ANN-based models outperformed statistical techniques such as ARMA. The exchange rates for six different currencies versus the U.S. dollar were modelled by Yao and Tan (2000), using weekly moving averages from 1984-95 as inputs. They found that for most of the currencies the neural network outperformed ARIMA based models, reaching accuracies of over 70% with relatively low deviations. Similar results were found by Joarder Kamruzzaman and Ruhul Sarker (2003), in their study based on a range of currencies versus the Australian dollar. Weekly data was used with training over 500 weeks. Two of the out-of-sample forecasts (spanning 65-weeks) are shown in Figure 15-11. Another feature of their research was the comparison of a range of learning mechanisms. They reported that scaled conjugate gradient-based learning gave significantly better results than back propagation.

The short-term dynamics of daily prices for S&P 500, Libor and Deutsche Mark futures were analysed using Elman recurrent networks by Ludmila Dmitrieva, Yuri Kuperin and Irina Soroka (2002). The best predictions were achieved for the S&P 500. Similarly, ANNs were used to predict NYMEX crude oil future prices by Saeed Moshiri and Faezeh Foroutan (2004). Their ANN-based predictions outperformed both ARMA and GARCH models.

Neural networks have also been applied for predicting the prices of options. Gunter Meissner and Noriko Kawano (2001) forecasted the daily prices of options on ten U.S. high-tech stocks from 1999-2000. They compared standard feed-forward networks with those based on radial basis functions (RBF) and probabilistic and generalised regression networks. The inputs were based on those for the Black Scholes model, so they used the ratio of the spot to the strike price, the maturity, the risk-free rate and a GARCH estimate of the volatil-

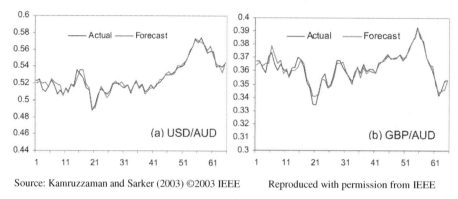

Figure 15-11 ANN based 65 week currency forecasts

ity. The standard feed-forward networks performed best, outperforming all the other types including the standard Black Scholes model. Subrata Mitra (2006) also saw improved performance when using an ANN to modify the Black-Scholes based pricing model for call options on India's Nifty stock index. Whilst Alex Faseruk and Lev Blynski (2006) used a simple back-propagation ANN to forecast the price of the OEX S&P 100 index option from the CBOE, using data from 1986-93. They also noted that the ANN model outperformed the conventional Black-Scholes pricing model when both were based on historical volatility. Switching both models to use implied volatility gave improved results; although the ANN's relative outperformance was less.

Most of the examples, so far, have been based on feed-forward or recurrent networks, but other types have also been successful. For example, a probabilistic neural network was used to predict the Singapore Stock Price Index by Steven Kim and Se Hak Chun (1998). Whilst Sung-Suk Kim (1998) used a time delay recurrent network to forecast the Korean Stock Market Index.

Price prediction with SVMs

Support vector machines (SVMs) have also been applied to forecast prices. A study of the Nikkei 225 stock index, using weekly data from 1990-2002, was performed by Wei Huang, Yoshiteru Nakamori and Shou-Yang Wang (2004). They compared the SVM's predictions with an Elman recurrent neural network and found that the highest accuracy was achieved by the SVM (73%), followed closely by the neural net (69%). A similar analysis was performed for six major Asian stock market indices by Wun-Hua Chen, Jen-Ying Shih and Soushan Wu (2006). They used SVMs to predict the returns for the Nikkei 225, Australia's All Ordinaries, Hong Kong's Hang Seng, the Singapore Straits Times, Taiwan's weighted index and Korea's KOSPI indices. Daily close prices were used with test data from 1984-2001. For comparison, they also tested auto regressive (AR1) models and back propagation (BP) neural nets. Overall, they found mixed results for the performance of both SVMs and neural nets. In terms of accuracy, the SVM models performed better for the indices in Hong Kong, Taiwan and Korea, whilst for Japan and Singapore the neural nets were better. In out-of-sample testing there was no appreciable difference between the two models for Australia, as shown in Figure 15-12. Both SVMs and neural nets performed better than autoregressive models, except for predicting the direction of returns.

Tony Van Gestel et al. (2001) used least squares SVM regressions to predict the time series and related volatility for U.S. short-term interest rates, as well as the German DAX

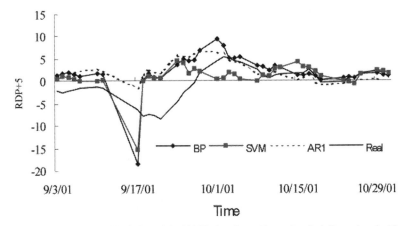

Figure 15-12 A comparison of the relative differences in percentage of price (RDP) for the All Ordinaries index

stock index. The accuracy of prediction for the sign of future returns was over 5% higher for the SVM models compared to both autoregressive (AR) and GARCH methods.

SVMs have also been used to predict the prices of futures, Francis Tay and Lijuan Cao (2001) studied five contracts, covering both stock indices (S&P 500 and CAC 40) and major government bonds (U.S. 10 and 30 year, and German 10 year bunds). Daily close prices were used with a training period of over 900 days. A neural network was used for additional comparison. Overall, the forecasts from the SVMs were better than from the neural net. The deviations from the actual were smaller and the predictions of the directional trend were more accurate.

For option prices, Michael Pires, Tshilidzi Marwala (2007) found that SVM's offered the most effective price forecasts for American options, with significantly less deviations when compared to ANN-based models.

Predicting volatility

R. G. Donaldson and Mark Kamstra (1997) created a non-linear GARCH model, based on a neural net, to study the return volatility of stocks from the U.S., Canada, U.K. and Japan. They found that the neural network captured volatility effects overlooked by traditional GARCH and EGARCH methods.

For stock indices, Fernando Gonzalez Miranda and Neil Burgess (1997) used neural networks to predict the intraday volatilities from Spain's IBEX 35 index options. Again, the networks were found to outperform more traditional linear methods. Apostolos-Paul Refenes and Will Holt (2001) also found that neural networks generally outperformed other statistical methods for volatility prediction. Likewise, a study by Peter Tiňo, Christian Schittenkopf and Georg Dorffner (2000) found neural networks effective in predicting the volatility of the U.K. FTSE and Germany's DAX stock index options. Though, they noted that on average simple binary Markov models outperformed both GARCH and neural network based techniques in simulated trading tests.

Valeriy Gavrishchaka and Supriya Banerjee (2006) used a support vector machine to forecast the volatility of the S&P 500 index. They found that it was comparable to be best

GARCH model across different volatility regimes, and even outperformed GARCH in some.

Currency volatility was modelled by Christian Dunis and Xuehuan Huang (2002). They used both feed-forward and recurrent neural networks to predict the volatility of the British pound and the Japanese yen versus the U.S. dollar, using daily data from 1993-99. Again, both the ANNs performed well compared to GARCH models, giving the best simulated trading results. The recurrent networks marginally outperformed the feed-forward ones in terms of directional accuracy. Overall, though, the highest accuracy was achieved by a combination model that incorporated both the neural and GARCH estimates.

Even the volatility for options on index futures has been analysed. Shaikh Hamid and Zahid Iqbal (2004) used ANNs to study the S&P 500, using daily prices from 1984-94. They found that the volatilities from the neural network outperformed implied volatility forecasts, and were not significantly different from realized volatility.

More exotic neural models have also been used to predict volatility. For instance, Dirk Ormoneit and Ralph Neuneier (1996) used a conditional density estimating neural network to predict volatility of the DAX. They found that this outperformed a standard feed-forward network. Similarly, a mixture-density network was applied to the DAX index by Christian Schittenkopf, Georg Dorffner and Engelbert Dockner (2000). This is essentially a set of neural networks used to estimate the parameters for a mixture density model. They found that their predictions had a higher correlation with the implied volatilities than those of the GARCH model. In an earlier work Schittenkopf, Dorffner and Dockner (1998) also studied the volatility of the Austrian stock market.

Genetic programming (GP) has been used to forecast volatility as well. In a study of the S&P100 index, using intraday data from 1987-2003, Irwin Ma, Tony Wong and Thiagas Sankar (2007) found they could achieve 75-80% accuracy within a hundred generations. Wo-Chiang Lee (2006) used both ANN and GP models to forecast the volatility of Taiwan's TAIEX index. He found that empirically both types performed reasonably well in forecasting out-of-sample volatility compared to other methods, such as GARCH.

Predicting volume

A study forecasting the total daily trading volume on the NYSE was carried out by Blake LeBaron and Andreas Weigend (1994). They applied a bootstrapping, or resampling, technique, to simple feed-forward networks. The inputs were the aggregate turnover and the level of the DJIA. The turnover was detrended by dividing by its 100-day moving average. (Note logarithms were used to ensure the distributions of the input series were less skewed.) Contrary to their expectations, they found that the neural network did not give a marked improvement over standard linear models, although they reasoned that better results might be achieved by using additional forecast variables.

More promising results were found in a subsequent study of trading volume for six futures contracts on the on the Winnipeg Commodity Exchange by Iebeling Kaastra and Milton Boyd (1995). They again used feed-forward networks, but with an expanded set of input parameters. These were individually selected as predictors for futures trading volume. So the models were based on lagged trading volume, the futures price volatility, open interest and the average cash price as well as a proxy for the overall hedging demand. The neural network outperformed both naïve and ARIMA models, providing forecasts for up to nine months into the future.

15.4 Incorporating in trading strategies

Trading algorithms and execution tactics can adapt to market conditions. Limit order models may be used to determine the execution probability of orders, whilst cost-models help estimate the potential market impact and risk associated with a trading strategy. Hence, it is not a great leap to consider adding short-term forecast models. These may also be used to augment models for execution probability and/or cost estimates.

Algorithms may be broken down into specific trading rules. Generally, these are defined by experienced traders, or quants, based on experience of what works best for a specific market. Often this requires a substantial amount of testing and fine-tuning. Artificial intelligence systems offer a way of enhancing this process, since they can dynamically test a huge number of variations in parallel. Evolutionary algorithms may be used to fine tune trading rules and/or their parameters. Alternatively, whole rule-sets or algorithms could be evolved. Closely linked with this, is the ability to back-test the rules or strategies to determine their performance. By successfully automating both of these processes, we should be able to harness the power modern computers provide to literally test thousands of combinations.

Applying short-term forecast models

In Chapter 5, we used charts to compare the typical order placement patterns for a range of trading algorithms. However, during the execution it is important to remember that we do not know exactly what the future holds. So from time T in Figure 15-13 all we really have is uncertainty.

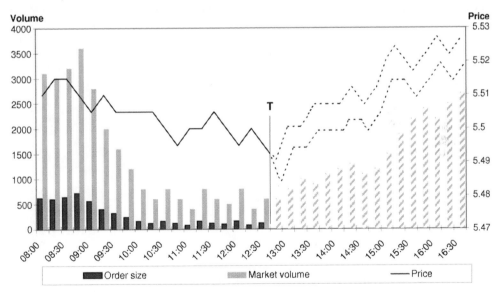

Figure 15-13 Using short-term estimates for future market conditions

Modern trading algorithms are used to making dynamic adjustments to cope with changing market conditions. Though, if a sudden shift occurs such a reactive approach can be caught out and forced to play catch up at less favourable prices, leading to sub-optimal performance.

Data mining and artificial intelligence offer the potential to improve our short-term predictions for key market variables, such as price, volume and liquidity. This may be direct, using specific forecasting techniques, or indirect, based on changes in other assets or markets where data mining has shown a clear association.

Volume prediction is important for many trading algorithms. If future trade flow differs markedly from the historical volume profile then VWAP algorithms will probably struggle to meet their benchmarks. Even implementation shortfall algorithms need an accurate idea of the daily trading volume in order to determine the optimal trading horizon. A sudden spike or lull in volume will affect its performance. Likewise, a sudden shift could lead a dynamic percent of volume (POV) algorithm to chase the market, incurring considerable market impact. Using a short-term forecast would enable POV algorithms to place more passively priced orders in anticipation of future trading volume.

As we saw in Chapter 10, historical volume profiles go some of the way towards this, particularly when seasonal or even asset specific factors are incorporated. AI-based models can also offer useful short-term volume predictions, which may perform better in volatile markets. They might also be able to cope better with today's complex marketplaces, where volume is fragmented between multiple venues. However, so far there seems to have been little AI-based research into this.

Similarly, the market price may exhibit a consistent price trend, or there may be a reversion as in Figure 15-13. In Chapter 5, we saw how price adaptive algorithms can easily adapt to this. A passive in-the-money (PIM) strategy assumes any trends will persist and so prices orders more passively when market conditions are favourable, seeking to maximise the potential price improvement. Conversely, an aggressive in-the-money (AIM) tactic takes the opposite approach, assuming that trends will soon mean revert and so aggressively takes advantage of favourable prices. For instance, let's assume we are selling asset ABC, three potential short-term price forecasts are shown in Figure 15-14.

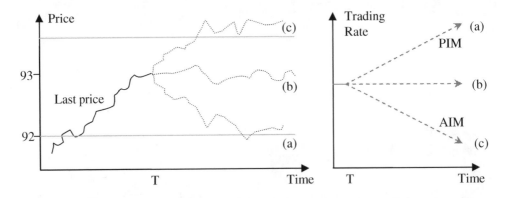

Figure 15-14 Linking expected trading rate to future conditions

So at time T, a PIM strategy might expect the favourable trend to persist (pathway c) and so will continue to passively price its orders. If the trend slows down (pathway b) or even reverts (pathway a) it will need to trade more aggressively, trying to stem the now less favourable price trend. In comparison, an AIM strategy would expect reversion, so if the trend actually persists it will under perform.

Reacting to the changes as they happen will mean seeking immediate fills and so paying half the spread as well as any market impact costs. Whereas if at time T we could accurately forecast such a reversion, our trading algorithm could alter its approach. Less passively priced orders could be placed, reducing our potential spread and impact costs.

In terms of their choice of execution tactics, the controlling algorithms may decide to switch between more or less aggressive approaches, based on their perception of the current market conditions. For instance, if the current price trend is expected to stay favourable the algorithm may adopt a more passive tactic, such as layering orders, to try to maximise the price improvement.

Price volatility is another important factor for many trading strategies. Historical volatility is certainly useful, but in highly volatile markets, it can still underestimate the actual volatility. AI-based methods have proven to give more accurate forecasts than estimations based on implied volatility and statistical analysis.

This approach may also be adopted for other market conditions, such as liquidity or spreads. Provided the short-term forecasts are accurate, we should be able to benefit from more proactive order placement. If they are not then the orders may be cancelled, and more aggressively priced orders may be used to catch up.

Incorporating forecast models

In Chapter 11, we looked at how a simplified algorithmic trading environment might be set up. Figure 15-15 illustrates how this could be extended in order to incorporate short-term estimation models.

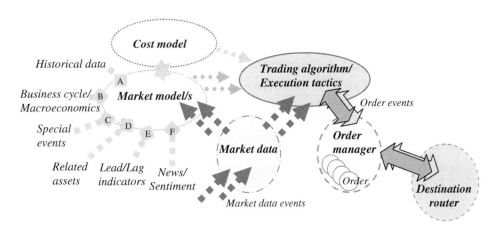

Figure 15-15 Extending an algorithmic trading environment

Keeping the models separate from the actual algorithm allows them to be reused more easily. Each trading algorithm, or even execution tactic, may then use these short-term market estimates as part of their decision making process, choosing how much weight to give this information.

In fact, several models may be used, weighting the results from each and adjusting for optimal performance, as we saw for the neural network node back in Figure 15-4. This is similar to a technique called ensemble learning, which may be used to improve the accuracy of forecasting. Multiple models are employed for the forecast; each one is given a weighted vote (labelled A-E in Figure 15-4), based on its accuracy from prior testing. Even if models are not that accurate to start with, by combining them in this way the probability of a correct forecast increases. Hence, a variant of this technique is called boosting.

The models themselves may be purely statistical, as we saw in Chapter 10, or use AI or relationships learned from data mining. For example, short-term price estimation might be achieved by looking to the futures or options markets, or other major market indices, based on historical lead/lag relations. Another model might track prices across stock industries or sectors based on historical correlations. For example, in Chapter 14 we saw how news in one company led to a spillover effect across the whole sector (in this case biotechnology). A further model might simply give an indication of whether the price is likely to increase or decrease, based on analysis (statistical or AI-based) of previous prices.

Clearly, each model will need access to a range of data, from:

- Market data for the specific asset
- Market data for other related assets and/or indices/indicators
- News/sentiment data
- Business cycle/Macroeconomic data
- Historical data for any/all of the above

There should also be monitoring to ensure that the forecast models are improving the overall performance of the trading algorithms. A control might even use market data to check the accuracy of the model/s, and make adjustments based on whether the market reaction is more or less than expected. Factors such as performance and reliability play a part as well, as we saw in Chapter 11. Any analytics must also be calculated fast enough to be useful for execution and/or order placement decisions.

Generating trading strategies/rules/parameters

Trading algorithms and execution tactics are sets of trading rules that are chosen to meet specific objectives. These rules are generally defined by traders, but there will also have been a significant amount of testing and fine-tuning to ensure they perform sufficiently.

Tree-based expressions, supported by genetic programming techniques, provide a very flexible means of generating or evolving trading rules, as we saw back in Figure 15-9. Evolutionary algorithms are potentially well suited to such fine-tuning; since they have the ability to test a huge number of variations in parallel. The changes being tested might be as simple as different parameters, alternatively whole sets of rules may be evolved.

Much of the research into trading rule generation has concentrated on investment decisions. Technical trading rules for the S&P 500 index were created by Franklin Allen and Risto Karjalainen (1999), using daily price data. The rules were specified in expression trees that incorporated variables, such as market prices, and functions, such as moving averages. A similar approach was adopted by James Butler (1997) and Edward Tsang et al. (2000) to create the EDDIE (Evolutionary Dynamic Data Investment Evaluator) system. They also incorporated fundamental data, such as the price-earnings ratio, together with market prices in the rules. EDDIE was used by Butler (1997) and Li and Tsang (1999, 1999a) to predict whether a specific rate of return (or more) could be achieved within a given timeframe (1-3 months) for the S&P 500 and DJIA stock indices. In each case, they found that it was indeed possible to generate rules that could outperform random tests and common technical rules. A variant was even created by Tsang, Markose and Er (2005) to investigate the futures call-put parity arbitrage for the FTSE-100 index, which outperformed naïve arbitrage rules.

However, generated trading rules may be just as easily be used for execution tactics, such as order placement decisions. Figure 15-16 shows what the rule-tree might look like for a sample execution tactic. This models the decision for choosing between market order and a limit order placement.

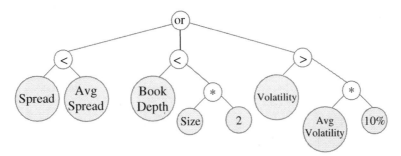

Figure 15-16 An example order placement rule

The rules are based on order book conditions and asset specific variables, as we saw in Chapter 8. Thus, less aggressively priced limit orders are placed when:

- the spread is less than its historical intraday average, or
- the book depth (on the same side) is less than double our order size, or
- the short-term volatility is 10% greater than normal.

This approach could also be applied to choose between execution venues in fragmented markets, or to try to minimise legging risk for contingent/pairs and portfolio trades.

Back-testing

Back-testing is an important means of verifying the potential performance and profitability of any trading strategy. It allows us to see how the strategy might have performed under market conditions. Testing can also show how the strategy copes with specific situations, such as news events or market crashes.

A nice overview of the key considerations for back-testing is provided by Steve Oppenheimer and Thomas Parry (2007) in eForex magazine. As they point out, it is important to be able to simulate how the market might have reacted to our orders. To do this accurately we need to consider the available liquidity, as well as taking into account factors such as latency. Another important consideration is how deterministic the simulation is. For example, when testing trading rules or parameters we want to be able to see the impact of just these changes. If the simulation is deterministic then each time the results will be the same, making it easier to isolate the effect of any rules changes. In comparison, random (or stochastic) simulations will give completely different results each time. Ideally, it would be useful for the simulation to be able to toggle between these two types, giving us the most flexibility.

So far in this book, we have concentrated on empirical studies; however, there has also been a lot of research based on artificial markets. These offer one potential solution for back-testing. In particular, artificial markets allow us to test a wide variety of conditions such as trending or volatile markets or even sudden liquidity crises. An alternative approach is to base the simulation on real market data. In which case the simulator somehow needs to merge the test orders with this data and try to emulate the appropriate reactions.

Testing with artificial markets

Artificial intelligence is being used to create simulated marketplaces that are populated with electronic agents, although some also allow human participants. Unlike real markets, these simulations may be controlled and configured, allowing active experimentation. Research is primarily focussed on market microstructure analysis and testing the performance of specific trading strategies. The data from these simulations may then be compared with theoretical predictions and empirical evidence from real markets.

Artificial agents

The artificial agents used to simulate trading can range from simple random order generators to rule-based agents or even ones based on sophisticated AI techniques. A nice summary of the various types is given by Blake LeBaron (2000).

Purely random agents are easily implemented, but they can often lead to high volatility. In comparison, experiments involving human traders generally achieve quite a rapid price convergence. LeBaron (2000) notes that market efficiency tests assign random agents at between 50-100%, whilst human traders are much closer to 100%.

One step up from purely random order generators is the zero-intelligence agent, as outlined by Dhananjay Gode and Shyam Sunder (1993). These still place random orders to buy or sell, but they also adhere to strict budget constraints. LeBaron (2000) notes that such budget constrained agents allocate assets at over 97% efficiency, which is close to the performance of humans in similar tests.

Dave Cliff's (1997) zero-intelligence plus (ZIP) traders further extend this model to include a variable profit (or utility) margin. Each ZIP agent has an inbuilt price limit. In addition to this, there are three main parameters, namely its profit margin, learning rate and a momentum term. Using these, each agent can determine a target price, based on its price limit and the desired profit margin together with a random factor. The learning rate parameter controls the rate of convergence between the agent's order prices and their target price. The momentum term dictates how much history the agent takes into account when re-evaluating its margin. Essentially, this adjustment is based on how successful the agent has been at getting its orders filled, as well as the dynamics of the market price. A genetic algorithm may be used to optimise these parameter settings.

Similarly, Steven Gjerstad and John Dickhaut (1998) created agents that maintain an order and trade history. From this, they form a subjective "belief" function that represents their estimated probability of the fair price.

Other studies have used agents that are even more sophisticated. For instance, Marco Raberto *et al.* (2003) created them based on particular investment styles. Momentum and contrarian agents used simple technical trading rules to make decisions, whilst fundamental agents traded based on a firm view of the asset's value. Gilles Daniel (2006) created self-referential agents, which acted as informed and rational arbitrageurs. Agents have also been designed to adopt the role of market makers. For example, Sanmay Das (2005a), Yi Feng, Ronggang Yu, and Peter Stone (2003) and Alexander Sherstov and Peter Stone (2004) all report on market making agents.

The performance of both human and electronic agents in a continuous double auction was analysed by Rajarshi Das *et al.* (2001). Several different agents were used, including ZIP traders. To their surprise, they found that the electronic traders consistently outperformed their human counterparts by around 20%.

Artificial markets

Research into trading strategies and market microstructure has yielded a range of different market simulators. A nice overview of these is provided by Julien Derveeuw *et al.* (2007), Gilles Daniel (2006) and LeBaron (2001).

The Santa Fe artificial stock market was one of the earliest simulated markets to be created. Trading evolves around two assets, a risk-free bond and a risky stock. In the first version, outlined by Richard Palmer *et al.* (1994), the market was driven solely by the decision of the agent traders to buy or sell. In later versions, described by Blake LeBaron (2001a), agents could predict the value of the stock based on estimates for its future dividend.

The Genoa artificial stock market, outlined by Marco Raberto *et al.* (2001), supports the same two assets as the Santa Fe simulator, but agents may issue limit orders. Using this model, they were able to see some of the key features of price dynamics, namely volatility clustering and fat-tailed distributions.

The NatLab market simulator provides a fully asynchronous event driven platform. The design is based around a central order book and supports both market and limit orders. By using a mixture of different agent trader types the simulator has been able to reflect phenomena such as financial bubbles, crashes and recoveries, as detailed by Lev Muchnik, Yoram Louzoun and Sorin Solomon (2006).

Another notable platform is the U-Mart simulator, reported by Yoshihiro Nakajima *et al.* (2004), which provides an artificial futures market for both human and machine agents.

Simulating real markets

Artificial agents and markets can be useful for testing. However, basing the simulation on real market data gives an immediate head start in terms of realism. The simulator needs to be able to recreate the order book and apply the same trade matching rules as the venue it is simulating. Though, simply giving an immediate fill for every test order with a matching price does not provide sufficient realism. The simulator also needs to take into account competition from other participants. Otherwise, the strategy/algorithm being tested may perform poorly when transferred to the real world. Therefore, it is also vital that the simulator provides a realistic reaction to the test orders. Figure 15-17 shows an example of what this might look like.

As we saw with market impact, it is difficult to predict the long-term effect of placing additional orders. Though, based on the short-term responses we saw from the empirical studies in Chapter 8, simulators can make slight adjustments to the historical data in response to the test orders. For instance, subsequent orders might be priced more passively if the test orders increase the available depth on the order book. The simulator might also take into account other market conditions, such as volatility or price trends.

Some research groups have already created their own simulations based on real data. Most notably the Penn-Lehman Automated Trading Project (PLAT), as described by Michael Kearns and Luis Ortiz (2003). This order book based platform integrates data from the former Island ECN. The Penn Exchange Simulator augments the order book data from the ECN with its own simulated orders. Additional realism is provided by competition from multiple agents. Thus, agents' orders may end up executing with simulated ones from the ECN or with orders from a competitor. Based on this approach Sheri Markose, Azeem Malik, Wing-Lon Ng (2007) also report on a simulator for London's SETS limit order book.

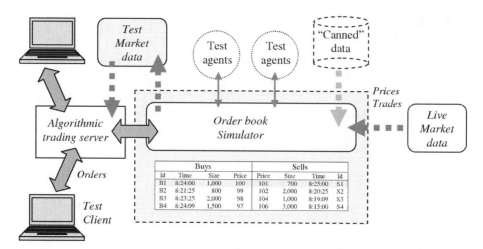

Figure 15-17 An example test environment

Commercial simulators are available as well. These are focussed on catering for the testing needs of algorithmic trading systems. For instance, Allied Testing's Exchange Simulator (SIM) [2] provides both live and playback modes, much like PLAT. The order book is recreated using exchange data feeds. It can also be reconstructed using the order book depth and by inferring the order flow based on trade details from level two market data. Instead of using competing agents, the simulator responds to user orders based on the available liquidity. It adjusts the historical data in response to the user's trading activity and even simulates new orders to mimic the typical market reactions. These reactions also take account of stock-specific behaviour, so orders tend to queue for assets with large spreads whilst for more liquid assets simulated orders compete by using more aggressive pricing and filling any gaps in the order book. Hence, the simulator is able to provide behaviour tailored to the typical dynamics and microstructure properties of each asset.

Both PLAT and SIM support real-time and replay modes, so simulations may be performed live or back-tested by replaying historical data. This provides a very flexible framework for testing and training. Note that single agent testing is likely to be more deterministic, and so more suited to reproducibly testing changes for trading rules and parameters. Further testing may then be performed in a multi agent environment.

15.5 The future

Artificial intelligence often evokes images of the "black box" supercomputers used to play chess. However, chess is a game with defined board and a very strict set of rules, so despite the billions of permutations a computer can potentially learn every move, as James Finnegan points out in CFA Magazine (2006).

Financial markets are a lot more complex than chess; for starters, there are a lot more participants, and the rules are less well defined and constantly evolving. Relying on a computer's processing power and brute force is not going to solve the problem of best execution. Artificial intelligence may well offer a solution, although it still appears to be

---

[2] A free online trial version of Allied Testing's simulator is available at http://exchangesimulator.alliedtesting.com

some way in the future.

Autonomous vehicles may offer a closer approximation to the required complexity than chess. These also highlight the rapid progress that is being made in AI. In 2004, the objective of the DARPA (Defense Advanced Research Projects Agency) Grand Challenge was for autonomous vehicles to navigate a 142-mile long course through the Mojave Desert. The vehicles relied on a combination of satellite navigation, radar, laser range finding, and video cameras. The AI systems somehow needed to take all these disparate inputs and use them to keep control of the vehicle and navigate safely to the destination. On this first run within a few hours all of the fifteen competitors had failed, been disqualified or withdrawn. However, the 2005 rerun was much more successful with five teams finishing. Stanford University's robot-car "Stanley" completed the course in less than seven hours. In fact, all but one of the 2005 entrants surpassed the 7.36 mile limit, which had been achieved in 2004.

On the back of this rapid progress, DARPA significantly raised the goals for their 2007 Urban Challenge. This time, the vehicles had to negotiate 60 miles through a mock city avoiding obstacles. The AI systems also had to contend with other vehicles, and more complex driving patterns such as overtaking and parking. The entry from Carnegie Mellon won, but all the cars showed considerable improvements over the previous models. This is a closer approximation to the financial markets, since they had to contend with other drivers and other AI-based systems.

The techniques we have covered in this chapter may seem somewhat esoteric. Still, if AI systems can be used to drive a car 60 miles through town and park it without crashing, then there is certainly some scope for them to be applied to the financial markets. It is important to remember that we are not talking about recreating human intelligence. Best execution seems like a fuzzy goal, but it is still less complicated than life. AI systems for trading are not conscious and they cannot communicate. In terms of raw intelligence, the goal is probably more like that of an insect, which (in theory) should be a lot more achievable.

That said, the financial markets have thousands of traders, each with their own opinions and strategies. Collectively their behaviour shapes the markets, and so affects the prices of assets. Advances are certainly being made in collective intelligence, using massive multi-agent simulations. But this an incredibly complex phenomenon, so the science of forecasting market reactions is still evolving.

Admittedly, some of the studies we have seen in this chapter have failed to show AI techniques performing substantially better than statistical models. Nevertheless, computers continue to get more and more powerful. Over the next few years, they will be able to support increasingly complex data mining and artificial intelligence techniques. Therefore, their accuracy and speed are likely to increase. Hardware innovations, such as memristors, may even make building dedicated artificial intelligence hardware viable. As for whether this latest progress in AI will be successfully applied to trading - only time will tell.

15.6 Summary

- Artificial intelligence (AI) and data mining offer the potential to give traders an edge by spotting or predicting trends; they may even be used to generate trading strategies.

- Data mining is a mix of statistical analysis and inference techniques:

- Classification and clustering analysis seek to identify common features in the data.
- Time-series mining is generally used for forecasting or spotting trends.
- Association rule mining searches for correlation patterns.

- Relationship based data mining has analysed:
  - Intra-market relationships, such as co-movements between industries and sectors.
  - Inter-market relationships, highlighting the correlation between major markets.
  - Crises and contagion, highlighting that relationships can change significantly during extreme periods. For instance, correlation tends to increase with downward moves.

- AI can actually be split into two main approaches
  - Conventional AI is a top-down approach using logic and rules to make decisions. This often relies on data from statistical analysis or custom-made knowledge bases.
  - Computational intelligence is a flexible bottom-up approach, inspired by biological mechanisms. Neural networks try to reproduce the action of our brain's neurons, whilst evolutionary computation simulates populations.

- Trading algorithms are already an example of conventional AI since they encapsulate trading logic within a rules-based framework.

- Short-term predictions of conditions, such as prices and volatility have been shown as effective, using neural networks, support vector machines and statistical analysis.

- Evolutionary algorithms and genetic programming can test a huge number of variations in parallel, making them suitable for checking trading strategies and their parameters.

- Back-testing is an important means of verifying the potential performance and profitability of any trading strategy. AI can help create simulated marketplaces for this.

Epilogue

It is hard to say what the trading environment will look like in five or ten years time, but algorithmic trading and DMA are here to stay.

The preface of this book started by noting that today's trading environment bears very little resemblance to that of the 1980s, or even the early 1990s. Certainly, trading has experienced some major changes over the last 20 years. At the moment, it is hard to see what might cause a similar impact in the 2010s. Therefore, over the next few years we are more likely to see evolutionary changes rather than major paradigm shifts.

Algorithmic trading is still work in progress, doubtless in ten year's time some of the earlier algorithms will seem positively naïve. The following points try to highlight some of the key "take-homes" from this book.

Algorithmic trading has already proven itself

The 2007-09 financial crisis certainly shook things up for the world's markets. Trading volumes, liquidity and volatility saw huge shifts. However, algorithmic trading platforms proved their mettle. The financial press was not inundated with stories of trading algorithms "blowing up", bringing down exchanges (or even banks). Market share for algorithmic trading has continued to steadily increase, despite the challenging market conditions.

Algorithmic trading will continue to spread

The world's markets have predominantly shifted towards electronic trading. Algorithmic trading is the next logical progression.

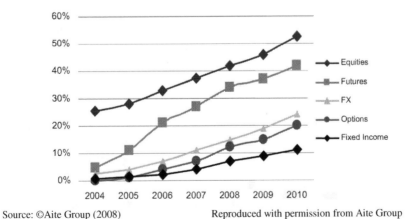

Source: ©Aite Group (2008)   Reproduced with permission from Aite Group

Figure Ep-1 Estimates for the adoption of algorithmic trading

Rates of adoption of are continuing to increase across all the major asset classes, as Figure Ep-1 shows.

Trading algorithms will continue to evolve

So far, there have been three main generations in the evolution of trading algorithms:

- The first algorithms were natural evolutions of simple order slicing, focussing on specific benchmarks, such as TWAP or VWAP. Initially, these were schedule driven, and often based on historical data; variants then evolved which were more dynamic.
- The second generation of trading algorithms were created in response to the application of transaction cost analysis; such as implementation shortfall algorithms striving to minimise cost by balancing both market impact and risk.
- The third generation of algorithms have tended to be more adaptive and opportunistic focussing on liquidity, due to the fragmentation of major markets and the arrival of "dark pool" ATSs.

Brokers have already started to consolidate their algorithms to make the selection process easier. Those that remain are now more highly configurable, allowing much more client-specific customisation.

As algorithmic trading continues to spread across asset classes, new types of algorithm will doubtless be created, such as the volatility-driven and multi-leg algorithms we considered in Chapter 5.

Algorithms will become even more adaptive

Adaptive shortfall and liquidity-driven algorithms have already become commonplace.

The market volatility during the 2007-09 financial crisis showed how important it can be for algorithms to cope with (and take advantage of) such changeable conditions.

Algorithms will increasingly try to take advantage of short-term predictions of market conditions and even news/sentiment-based indicators.

Portfolio-based and cross-asset algorithmic trading will increase

As portfolio-optimised algorithms continue to improve, many of the hurdles to cross-asset trading will also be reduced. In other words, algorithms will be better able to cope with significant differences in liquidity and latency across one and two-sided trading lists.

Many of the major OMS and EMS platforms now support multiple asset classes, so multi-asset trading is already a reality. Algorithms will make cross-asset trading easier, but may also reduce the opportunities for arbitrage.

The demand for some structured products may even decline, with trading algorithms offering similar functionality.

World markets will continue with waves of consolidation and fragmentation

As the Greek philosopher Heraclitus put it: *'The only thing constant is change'* ....

Appendices

The following appendices provide an overview of each of the major asset classes and their main markets. The focus is on their adoption of electronic trading and the provision of algorithmic trading and DMA. They also examine the regional differences between the Americas, Europe and Asia.

Invariably, any review of the world markets will date rapidly given how quickly the markets are changing. Nevertheless, the main sources of information remain the same, namely the:

- World Federation of Exchanges (WFE) (www.world-exchanges.org)
- Bank for International Settlements (BIS) (www.bis.org)
- Securities Industry and Financial Markets Association (SIFMA) (www.sifma.org)

Each of these organisations publishes annual (and sometimes monthly) statistics for the world's major markets.

For analysis that is even more comprehensive, the reports by consultancies, such as the Aite Group, Celent, Greenwich Associates and the TABB Group, are invaluable.

Note that no particular reading order is required for these appendices. You may prefer to jump straight to the markets that are most relevant to you. Still, it is worth coming back to review the other material since there is a lot to gain from seeing how things are done in the other markets.

Appendix A

Equity markets

The world's equity capital markets account for a quarter of the global financial market value, as we saw back in Chapter 3. Historically, stock markets have developed around strong inter-dealer networks, usually centred on major exchanges. In part, this is due to the highly standardised nature of stocks. Trading on these exchanges is still mainly carried out by brokers. They act as intermediaries, acting as an agency through which to trade orders on the exchanges; broker/dealers may also be prepared to deal in principal with OTC trades. The equity markets have proven to be ideally suited for implementing electronic and algorithmic trading. Hence, the levels of adoption of these techniques are still significantly higher for the equities markets than any other asset class.

Asset specific

The equity in a corporation represents the value of the remaining assets once all the liabilities have been deducted. A share in a company (also known as stock) represents a portion of this total equity. A finite number of shares are issued by public corporations. Though, they may periodically choose to issue new shares or buy back some of the outstanding ones. If the company performs well its value (and so its share price) should increase. However, if it fails and falls into bankruptcy, shareholders rights are subordinate to those of creditors, so they are typically left with little or nothing. Therefore, shares are forward looking investments; investors expect the value of their shares to increase in order to compensate them for the risk of default. Alternatively, periodic dividend payments may also be made by the company to reimburse investors.

Growing companies tend to need cash so they will often rely on share price rises to appease investors. Whereas more established companies may prefer to issue larger dividends. This flexibility explains part of the appeal of issuing shares for companies.

The kind of equity issued by a company may differ in terms of voting rights and in the distribution of dividends and assets, in case of bankruptcy. The two main types are common stock and preferred stock. Common stock allows the holder to vote in certain corporate decisions, such as the election of directors, issuance of new shares and approving takeovers. Preferred stock has priority over common stock when dividends are issued and in liquidation; however, they tend to have less voting rights.

The total value of the outstanding shares is referred to as the corporation's market capitalisation, or market cap. In U.S. terms, a large-cap, or blue-chip, stock has a value of greater than $10 billion. Mid-caps have values between $1 and $10 billion, small-caps are below $1 billion and micro-caps have values less than $100 million. The values for these categories will vary for other countries, but the relative sizes will be similar.

Pricing and trading

Determining the fair value for equities is non-trivial. Present value theory states that the value of an asset is the discounted sum of its future payments. For stocks, these correspond to their future dividend payments, which in turn depend on future earnings. Though, dividend payments can be difficult to predict. Firms may also choose to reinvest some of their income rather than increasing dividend payouts. A range of estimation models try to take such factors into account. Alternatively, cross-sectional regression analysis may be used to infer prices by comparing key ratios such as Price/Earnings (P/E) with similar firms, or across whole sectors/industries.

Investors also have varying information about each company and so their valuations will be dissimilar. Thus, market prices reflect the average of all these valuations combined with the effects of supply and demand. Consequently, the market capitalisation will often be different to the fundamental value of a corporation's (its assets minus its liabilities).

In terms of trading, stocks are readily transferable in a domestic context, so markets like the U.S. have seen a huge amount of local competition, between both exchanges and other execution venues. Electronic access and remote memberships, for foreign investors/traders, are helping to increase access to venues. There is also a buoyant depositary receipt market for trading foreign stocks. Essentially, these are just proxies allowing foreign stocks to be traded locally (they are covered in more detail in Appendix F). Together, all these factors mean that stocks are starting to become truly global assets that may be traded 24 hours a day. For instance, Mark Howarth (2004) uses Sony as an example to demonstrate how such trading is now possible for many major firms. Table A-1 shows some of the potential trading venues for this throughout the day.

Time (Japan Standard Time)	Trading venue
08:00 – 09:00	Tokyo pre-trade
09:00 – 15:00	Tokyo
15:00 – 24:00	London, GDR IOB
18:00 – 24:00	Tokyo after-hours markets
22:30 – 05:00	U.S. ADR
05:00 – 08:00	U.S. after-hours markets

Table A-1 Potential trading venues for a Japanese stock

Once the Tokyo stock exchange has closed, trading may continue either on its after-hours platform (ToSTNeT) or on other local after-hours markets, such as SBI JapanNext. Trading can also shift to London stock exchange's International Order Book (IOB). Similarly, before London closes the U.S. opens, allowing depositary receipts to be traded here and on after market venues until Tokyo opens again.

World equity markets

The world's equity markets continue to be centred on stock exchanges. However, an increasing array of new execution venues such as Electronic Communications Networks (ECNs) and Alternative Trading Systems (ATSs) have brought both competition and fragmentation. That said, the high level of electronic trading and access via DMA and algorithmic trading mean that the world's equity markets have arguably the highest level of client-side accessibility.

Table A-2 shows the world's top fifteen stock exchanges in terms of their domestic market capitalisation and total value of share trading for 2007 and 2008, based on data from the World Federation of Exchanges (WFE) (2009). Clearly, the U.S. dominates the world's equity trading with both the NYSE and the NASDAQ exchanges. The Tokyo, Euronext and London stock exchanges also have significant market shares and turnovers.

Exchange	Domestic market cap in $ billions		Total value of share trading in $ billions	
	2008	2007	2008	2007
NYSE Euronext U.S.	9,209	15,651	33,639	29,114
Tokyo Stock Exchange	3,116	4,331	5,607	6,413
NASDAQ OMX (U.S.)	2,396	4,014	36,447	28,116
NYSE Euronext Europe	2,102	4,223	4,411	5,640
London Stock Exchange	1,868	3,852	6,272	10,334
Shanghai Stock Exchange	1,425	3,694	2,600	4,029
Hong Kong Exchanges	1,329	2,654	1,630	2,134
Deutsche Börse	1,111	2,105	4,679	4,325
TSX Group	1,033	2,187	1,716	1,635
BME Spanish Exchanges	948	1,781	2,411	2,970
SIX Swiss Exchange	857	1,271	1,500	1,883
Australian Stock Exchange	684	1,298	1,213	1,372
Bombay Stock Exchange	647	1,819	302	344
National Stock Exchange India	600	1,660	725	751
BM&FBOVESPA	592	1,370	724	598

Source: WFE (2009)

Table A-2 Major world stock markets

Although some global execution is possible, stock markets are generally focussed on domestic trading. In part, this is due to the much higher level of regulation for the stock markets. Still, over the last few years exchanges have started to become truly global entities. The mergers between NYSE and Euronext, NASDAQ and OMX are a good example of this. Hence, global competition is likely to increase significantly in the coming years.

Electronic trading has become ubiquitous for the world's stock markets, particularly for the sell-side. Buy-side levels of adoption of DMA and algorithmic trading are also high, especially in the U.S. Figure A-1 shows both the current levels of adoption of algorithmic trading and projections for 2010, based on estimates from the Aite Group (2007a) consultancy. Clearly, it will still take some time before the levels of adoption for algorithmic trading in Europe and Asia reach those of the U.S.

American equity markets

North America obviously dominates the region with some of the world's largest exchanges, as shown in Table A-2. The markets in Canada and Latin American are much smaller.

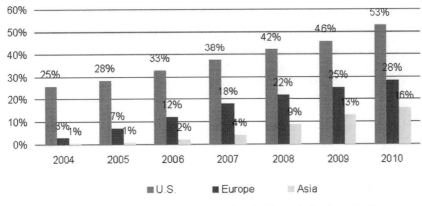

Figure A-1 Regional adoption of equity algorithmic trading

U.S. equity market

The U.S. equity market is led by two of the largest stock markets in the world, the New York Stock Exchange (NYSE) and the NASDAQ (originally an acronym for the National Association of Securities Dealers Automated Quotations). Figure A-2 shows an estimate for the breakdown of the market-share in December 2008.

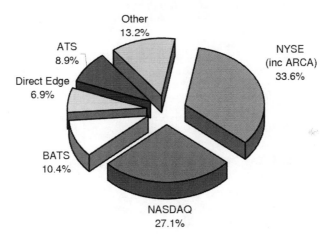

Source: FIF (2009), [1] Direct Edge (2009) and Rosenblatt Securities (2009)

Figure A-2 U.S. equity market share in 2008 (December)

Although they still lead the U.S. marketplace, both NYSE and NASDAQ have had to constantly evolve in order to maintain their position. They have also kept an eye on the global marketplace: As evidenced by NYSE's merger with Euronext and NASDAQ's acquisition of OMX. The rest of the U.S. market is split between BATS and Direct Edge, the regional exchanges, brokers, and around 40 distinct electronic communication networks

---

[1] Statistics compiled by Financial Information Forum with data from BATS Trading.

(ECNs) and alternative trading systems (ATSs). The intense competition has made the U.S. a very fluid marketplace. In fact, the two leading competitors, BATS and Direct Edge, have evolved from ECNs into full exchanges (or are in the process of doing so). Hence, the market-share breakdown for 2009/10 may be noticeably different from Figure A-2.

The U.S. equities market leads the world for the level of adoption of DMA and algorithmic trading. Uptake has been greatest on the sell-side where traders have relied on remote electronic access for many years. Trading algorithms are often used by traders as an efficiency tool, although buy-side usage has also increased. In their 2007 U.S. Equity Investors Study, Greenwich Associates (2007) found that three-quarters of investment managers and mutual funds used algorithmic trading strategies, whilst for hedge funds the figure was more than 85%.

A TABB Group (2008) survey of U.S. institutional trading found that 55% of U.S. equity trades were executed via DMA (9%), algorithms (24%), crossing networks (11%) or program trading (11%) in 2008. Note that in 2007 this total was actually 63%. The 2007-09 financial crisis and ensuing market volatility led to increased levels of high touch trading. However, the proportion of algorithmic trading has continued to grow, up from 22% in 2007. Other surveys put the level of DMA even higher. For example, the Celent (2008b) consultancy estimates that DMA accounts for around 15-18% of the share volume, predicting this to increase to 20% by 2010. Similarly, an earlier report by the Aite Group (2007a) consultancy put the level of DMA at around 19%, whilst they estimated that algorithmic trading had reached 18%.

Regulation has played a significant part in shaping the U.S. equity marketplace; it has generally been used to try to increase competitiveness, or correct practices that are perceived as being anti-competitive. Table A-3 outlines some of the key regulatory milestones and their effects.

Year	Regulation	Direct effects
1963	Restructuring OTC trading	NASDAQ created
1975	National Market System (NMS)	ITS created
1997	NASDAQ order handling rules	ECNs
2001	Decimalisation	Reduced spreads
2007	Regulation NMS	More competition

Table A-3 Milestones in U.S. equity market regulation

Starting in 1963, the Securities and Exchange Commission (SEC) recommended restructuring over the counter (OTC) trading, leading to the creation of NASDAQ. Whilst the National Market System (NMS) was introduced to consolidate price and trade information amongst the various exchanges, as well as provide an inter-market system (ITS) to route orders between them. Then in 1997, NASDAQ order handling rules were introduced to offer investors more protection for their limit orders, and to ensure that dealers always displayed their best quotes. The ruling to display client limit orders (when priced better than the dealer's quote) helped push NASDAQ away from being a purely quote-driven market to incorporating behaviour more like a limit order book. Notably, though, it was the quote ruling which had the most impact. Previously, dealers had been able to use private inter-dealer systems to trade at better prices; the new ruling meant that these prices should also be available to the public. In effect, this opened a window on NASDAQ for external execution venues, and suddenly many new ECNs were created, all competing for market share.

Decimalisation was introduced in 2001, leading to lower bid offer spreads. The resultant 0.1 cent tick size also encouraged the practice of "pennying" (jumping ahead of an existing order simply by upping the price by a penny). Decimalisation has helped continue the trend of smaller order sizes and so has encouraged traders with large orders to use alternative venues, in particular the newer ATSs or so-called "dark pools". Last, but not least, Regulation NMS was implemented in 2007, providing rules for:

- Fair access
- Order protection
- Abolishing sub-penny pricing
- Market data revenue allocation

In part, these rekindle the earlier 1975 regulations, although they meant scrapping the ITS. Instead, the fair access rule mandates that private links must be established to allow venues to route orders between each other. In addition, venues capturing a significant proportion of the ADV must provide a market quote. The order protection (or "trade-through") rule requires that trades must be executed at the best displayed price accessible in under a second. So an order placed on the NYSE will actually be routed and executed wherever the best quoted price is, be it NASDAQ or an ECN. In comparison, the ITS allowed a 30 second time window for an order to be acted on, whilst this may have seemed reasonable 30 years ago, in a market where trading is now often measured in milliseconds this delay is a lifetime. In fact, this huge delay put the ITS order creator at a considerable disadvantage to the market, as Larry Tabb points out in an article for the TABB Group (2003). Regulation NMS should help increase market competition, but its long-term impact remains to be seen.

The 2007-09 financial crisis also triggered a fresh look at many aspects of the U.S. marketplace by regulators. Initially, the focus was on short selling, but has since expanded to look at the "dark pool" ATSs and the use of IOIs, as well as "flash" orders and high-frequency trading. Only time will tell what new regulations result and how they affect the markets.

The U.S. equity marketplace has arguably seen more changes than any of the world's markets. As we saw in Figure A-2, the major exchanges still lead the market share; however, they are facing stiff competition. Since stocks are so fungible, trading in them can happen at virtually any of these venues, regardless of where they are actually listed.

Venue	% of Tape A (NYSE)	% of Tape B (Regional)	% of Tape C (NASDAQ)	% of Total
NYSE (inc Arca)	42.77	28.08 [2]	15.64	33.55
NASDAQ	19.90	32.37	40.79	27.09
BATS	8.57	15.10	10.41	10.36
Direct Edge	7.10	5.55	7.83	6.93
ATSs (dark pools)	n/a	n/a	n/a	8.90
Other	21.66	18.90	25.33	13.17

Source: FIF (2009), [3] Direct Edge (2009) and Rosenblatt Securities (2009)

Table A-4 U.S. equity matched market share breakdown in 2008 (December)

Table A-4 quantifies this by showing the market share breakdown for NYSE and

---

[2] Includes Amex.
[3] Statistics compiled by Financial Information Forum with data from BATS Trading.

NASDAQ listed stocks across each of the major venues for December 2008. Figure A-3 tries to illustrate this in a slightly different way, with the major exchanges at the centre and all the alternative venues above and below them, free to trade in any of their stocks.

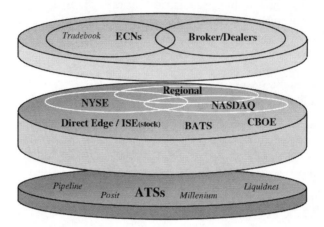

Figure A-3 An alternate view of the U.S. equity market

The NYSE is by far the world's largest stock exchange. Historically, trading has been based around specialists, [4] who are responsible for maintaining a "fair and orderly" market for each stock. Early on, the NYSE was one of the first exchanges to offer electronic order routing; namely via the 1976 Designated Order Turnaround (DOT) system. This was followed by SuperDOT in 1984, which went on to handle more than 75% of the order flow, even though such routing meant the specialist was still required to manually match orders (which could be up to 100,000 in size). Though, the NYSE has been slower than some exchanges in the shift to fully electronic trading, in part due to the success of its trading floor and specialists. Fully automated execution was first offered in 2000 for small orders (up to 1,099 shares) by NYSE Direct+. The next major step forward was the introduction of the NYSE Hybrid market in 2005. This offers the automated execution of Direct+, but for orders of up to a million shares; it also removes the time restrictions and is fully integrated with OpenBook to allow off-market participants a much more detailed view of the available market depth. By Q2 2007, electronic trading accounted for over 90% of NYSE trading with over 80% of the total share volume, as noted on NYSE Exchanges (2007). NYSE Hybrid has significantly reduced average execution times. A review in Trading Talk by Rosenblatt Securities (2007) notes that it also helped to reduce quoted spreads, although volatility was found to increase slightly. Structural changes have also been made. In 2008, the NYSE changed the role of specialist to become designated market makers (DMMs). DMMs are able to trade at parity, rather than having to give priority to client orders, encouraging them to provide additional liquidity, as outlined by Ivy Schmerken (2008). In addition, supplemental liquidity providers (SLP) are also able to make markets in NYSE stocks. Such innovation, both in terms of market structure and technology, is vital for NYSE to maintain its position.

---

[4] Peter Bennett (2005) retells the accidental story of how specialists first came about. Legend has it that a leading broker, James Boyd, broke his leg in 1875. Unable to walk between trading posts, he did all his business from a chair at the Western Union post. Other brokers then started to have him work their Western Union orders for commission, leaving them free to run between the other trading posts.

Increased competition has meant that over time NYSE's market share has noticeably decreased. In 2005, it was over 80%; however, since then it has dipped below 50%, the estimate for December 2008 is shown in Table A-4. Incorporating the Arca exchange in 2006 helped in consolidating its position. The market structure and trading platform changes also seem to have helped.

NASDAQ was originally created in 1971 as a bulletin board, allowing OTC trading of stocks, but it soon became a multi-dealer quote-driven market. Like the NYSE, the systems behind NASDAQ have been extensively updated over the last few years. Fully electronic trading was first provided in 1984 by the Small Order Execution System (SOES). Then in 1988 the release of SelectNet allowed dealers to negotiate electronically. These were later merged to form SuperSOES. The next major step was the release of Super Montage in 2002, which displayed market depth (the three best buy and sell orders), fully supported limit orders and allowed anonymous trading by using the SIZE moniker. Continuing its transformation, electronic call auctions were introduced for both the opening and closing in 2004. In terms of market share, NASDAQ has also faced a lot of competition, indeed in 2005 ECNs had a combined market share greater than 60%, leaving NASDAQ with less than a third of the market. Though, NASDAQ has managed to regain its position, notably by buying two of its largest competitors, namely Brut in 2004 and INET in 2005. These additional order books were fully integrated with SuperMontage in Single-Book in 2007. NASDAQ has also managed to capture an increasing proportion of trading in NYSE listed stocks, whilst its new listing segment (Global Select Markets) should help bolster its own listings.

BATS Trading started life as an ECN in 2006, although in 2008 it became an exchange in its own right. Initially, NASDAQ market share was targeted with aggressive pricing schemes. For instance, in January 2007 more was awarded in rebates than fees, growing its NASDAQ share to 14%, although this dropped slightly afterwards. BATS has also managed to significantly increase its proportion of NYSE volume. By August 2008, average daily volumes were around 750 million shares; about half of what traded on NYSE Arca, making it the third most important venue in the U.S. Volume has steadily continued to increase since then.

Direct Edge is another venue that started out as an ECN. The International Securities Exchange (ISE) stock exchange is now a wholly owned subsidiary. Direct Edge is continuing plans to become an exchange in its own right. Interestingly, it provides two execution platforms, EDGA and EDGX. EDGA charges the same fee for adding or removing liquidity, it is intended for more pro-active traders. EDGX follows a maker/taker fee schedule, so liquidity providers receive a rebate.

The regional exchanges, namely the American (AMEX), Boston, Chicago (Midwest) and National (Cincinnati) stock exchanges have managed to maintain some presence in both NYSE and NASDAQ stocks, as well as smaller listed companies. Many of them have also embraced the options markets. However, market consolidation and competition has had a massive effect on them. The Pacific exchange was taken over by Archipelago before being incorporated into the NYSE. Likewise, AMEX has also been bought and is now called NYSE Alternext; its focus is on listing smaller firms and options. The Boston Equities exchange closed its doors back in 2007; it has since become NASDAQ OMX BX. This has pricing designed to attract liquidity takers, giving NASDAQ a dual structure like Direct Edge. Clearly, such consolidation makes the outlook for the remaining regional exchanges less certain. Despite their relatively small market share, they can still be attractive propositions as independent entities since they offer the chance to recoup revenue from market data and exchange fees, as noted by Joshua Galper (2006).

As we have already seen, ECNs have had a huge impact on the exchanges, particularly NASDAQ. By the millennium there were over a dozen ECNs, all vying for market share; although the market was dominated by Island, Instinet and Archipelago. Since then, the competition has increased, but there has been a large amount of consolidation. In fact, of the original four ECNs founded after the 1997 SEC order handling rules, only Bloomberg Tradebook remains. The Arca ECN merged with REDIBook in 2002, forming the Archipelago Exchange; it then went on to merge with the Pacific Exchange before being bought by NYSE in 2006. Similarly, Island merged with Instinet in 2002 to form the INET ECN, which was bought by NASDAQ in 2006, two years after its purchase of the Brut ECN. Meanwhile BATS has now become an exchange and Direct Edge is in the process of becoming one. Soon, independent ECNs may be something of a rarity.

In the last few years, ATSs (or the so-called "dark pools" or "dark books") have become more prominent. Their number is growing just as rapidly; currently there are around 40 venues, double that of early 2006. This is understandable when average execution sizes of up to 40-50,000 shares may be accomplished on some of them, in comparison to less than 500 on NYSE or NASDAQ. Rosenblatt Securities provide a regular report detailing the volume traded on "dark pool" venues. Table A-5 shows their adjusted average daily crossing volumes (for April 2009) for some of the key venues, together with the corresponding market share. The adjustments try to take account of the double counting which can occur when orders are matched across multiple venues.

Venue	Average trade size	Adj. ADV April 2009 (in millions of shares)	Adj market share %
BIDS	324	9.7	0.09
BNY ConvergEx Vortex	437	6.9	0.06
Citi Match	386	35.5	0.32
Credit Suisse CrossFinder	319	133.9	1.19
Direct Edge	283	99.4	0.89
GETCO Execution Services	344	140.5	1.25
Goldman Sachs SigmaX	570	150	1.34
Instinet CBX	306	29	0.26
ISE Midpoint Match	231	9.6	0.09
ITG POSIT	~6,000	~21.1	0.19
Knight Link	357	116	1.03
LeveL	341	57	0.51
Liquidnet	52,428	~35.7	0.32
Millennium	288	17.3	0.15
Morgan Stanley MS Pool	277	46	0.41
Pipeline	~47,105	~10.4	0.09
UBS PIN Cross	n/a	~41.9	0.37

Source: Rosenblatt Securities (2009)

Table A-5 Non-displayed U.S. liquidity pool volumes

A detailed review of many of the main ATS venues is provided in an article from Rosenblatt Securities (2007a). To categorise them we will use the same types as in Chapter

2, so the crossings are scheduled or continuous, and are negotiated, advertised, blind or internal.

Scheduled crossings have been provided since 1987 by ITG's POSIT. Currently, this offers a dozen separate intraday crosses together with two after the close. Effectively, each cross is an anonymous call auction, priced at the midpoint of the national best bid and offer (NBBO). Instinet offer a similar service, with 7 intraday crosses (IDX) and an after the close (LDX); in addition there are two morning crosses which use a VWAP price (VWAPX).

Continuous crossing systems have grabbed a significant proportion of the market share. A notable example is Liquidnet, a buy-side oriented system launched in 2001 that offers a negotiation-based crossing mechanism. Liquidnet constantly tries to find matches between its clients' buy and sell order requirements, when it finds them notifications are sent to each party. They are then free to enter into anonymous bilateral negotiations for both the size and price. Although the negotiation is anonymous, Liquidnet employs a scorecard (like eBay's ratings) to reflect each user's history of successful crossings. This approach has proven extremely popular with the buy-side, in part because of the added sense of security that no sell-side or proprietary traders have access.

Continuous blind crossing systems have also become increasingly popular. In 2001, the Millennium ATS [5] was launched by NYFIX, offering "pass through" orders. ITG released POSIT Now in 2002, providing a continuous version of their popular crossing mechanism. LeveL is another noteworthy venue, which has seen rapid growth since its launch in 2006 by a consortium of Boston Stock Exchange (BSE) investors. For many of these blind crossing networks, "pass through" orders have become a notable source of liquidity. As their name suggests, these orders first try to match with the liquidity available within the ATS, before then being routed on to their intended destination, whether that is a primary/regional exchange, ECN or possibly even another ATS. Similar approaches are offered by Instinet's Continuous Block Crossing (CBX) and Liquidnet's H_2O network. Liquidnet H_2O allows smart order routers to send sell-side flow to Liquidnet to cross with buy side orders. The fact that the interaction is only at the smart order router level, ensuring no human intervention, minimises information leakage for the buy side.

Advertised crossing is another important mechanism, for which Pipeline is probably the best-known example. It maintains a block-board of stocks, which are highlighted in orange when liquidity is present. Block price ranges are available as a guideline, although no sizes are displayed. Users may then place firm orders to execute with the available liquidity. Pipeline enforces strict minimum share thresholds to prevent predatory trading. The Millennium ATS also provides its clients with an optional Plus order type, which sends liquidity alerts to a group of passive liquidity partners (PLPs) once the order reaches Millennium. These PLPs are other dark pools or internal crossing engines that allow for automated responses without any human intervention. Again, this ensures that the alerts are not visible to traders whilst maximising their chance to be filled. In 2005, ITG released POSIT Alert, [6] based on indications it alerts users when liquidity is available, leaving them to decide whether to execute. Buy-side firms may also choose to only notify other buy-side users.

Constant market evolution means hybrids of the above crossing types are also being developed. For instance, in 2006 a consortium of broker/dealers announced the Block Interest Discovery Service (BIDS) for both the buy and sell side. This uses firm and

---

[5] BNY ConvergEx announced they have agreed to acquire Millennium in 2009.
[6] POSIT Alert was previously known as BlockAlert (when it was a joint venture with Merrill Lynch).

conditional orders to support both continuous blind crossing as well as negotiated crossing using scorecards. BNY ConvergEx's VortEx combines "actionable" Indications of Interest (IOIs) from a large network of external liquidity providers with its continuous blind crossing platform to securely provide additional liquidity. Other innovations are Instinet's CBX, which allows users to fully configure what information (price, size) they may wish to share with other participants. The LeveL ATS can even incorporate client preferences for specific counterparties in its matching logic.

Brokers' own crossing networks have rapidly become a major force in terms of "dark pool" liquidity, as shown by their respective market shares in Table A-5. Originally, these were just internal crossing networks that allowed them to save the fees from executing on exchanges or other venues. Still, over the last few years these have progressively opened up for direct client access, effectively transforming them into ATSs in their own right. The volumes passing through the brokers mean that these are now major competitors in this space. Prominent amongst these are Credit Suisse's CrossFinder, Goldman Sachs' Sigma X and UBS's Price Improvement Network (PIN). In 2008, Goldman Sachs, UBS and Morgan Stanley also made agreements that will allow their clients access to liquidity from each other's networks.

"Dark pools" linked to market making operations have become another important source of liquidity. For example, GETCO Execution Services is an ATS that provides execution via IOC orders, with liquidity sourced from the GETCO market makers.

Unsurprisingly, exchanges and ECNs have also been keen to enter this arena, as they attempt to retain and attract liquidity from the ATSs. In 2006, the International Securities Exchange (ISE) created MidPoint Match, a blind crossing venue that supports pass-through flow to its electronic market. It also allows orders to advertise via firm Solicitations of Interest (SOIs). The Direct Edge ECN allows orders to be routed to a range of ATSs including Liquidnet H$_2$O. Similarly, in 2007 NASDAQ launched its own crossing network with an aggressive pricing scheme, whilst 2008 saw NYSE launch Matchpoint, its own anonymous crossing service. In 2009, the New York Block Exchange (NYBX) was launched; this is a joint venture between NYSE Euronext and BIDS Holdings. Unlike many of the other ATSs, NYBX has full access to the NYSE order book, including its non-displayed liquidity. Other financial institutions are also creating their own internal crossing systems, such as Fidelity's CrossStream.

Despite all these changes and the acute competition, it is still widely expected that further cycles of fragmentation and consolidation will occur. As usual, liquidity and order flow will be the keys to survival.

Canadian equity market

The Canadian market is still dominated by the primary exchange, the six main banks, and their brokerage arms. A nice overview of the market is provided by Alison Crosthwait (2009) from ITG Canada Corp. In 2006, new regulations were passed to ensure best execution, as well as allowing the establishment of alternative trading systems. Effectively kick-starting the same processes we have seen in the U.S. Prior to this, around a third of all trading was still carried out off-exchange in the upstairs market. In fact, Crosthwait (2009) estimates this had fallen to around 16% in 2008.

Historically, much of the competition for trading Canadian stocks has been from the U.S. In fact, around 200 of the 1,500 Canadian companies are cross-listed on U.S. exchanges. For these, the U.S. accounts for a considerable amount of trading, although the majority still takes place on the primary exchange. ITG Inc. even offers a Best Market Server smart router that adjusts for FX and so can trade such stocks by automatically routing orders between the U.S. and Canada.

Local competition arrived in 2003, in the form of the Canadian National Stock Exchange (CNSX) (formerly the Canadian Trading and Quotation System, Inc.) which offers an alternate site for listing emerging companies. This is a fully electronic trading platform, now based on the X-stream trading engine from NASDAQ OMX.

ECN-like venues have also been established, such as Pure Trading. This was launched in early 2008 with maker/taker based pricing. Like the CNSX, it is also based on the X-stream engine. The Alpha ATS is another new electronic order book based venue; launched in November 2008 by nine major Canadian brokers, based on Cinnober's TRADExpress ATS platform. Alternatively, a fully anonymous order book is provided by the Omega ATS, which was launched in 2007.

The major players from the U.S. have also started tailoring their platforms for Canada. For example, Instinet has launched a Canadian version of Chi-X, based on the same software as used in its European crossing market. Bloomberg Tradebook has also established itself.

Several "dark pool" execution venues have already been established in Canada. Liquidnet offers their continuous negotiation driven crossing platform. Likewise, ITG's Match Now ATS provides a virtually continuous blind auction (every 30s) which also incorporates streaming liquidity to other venues. Perimeter Financial's BlockBook also offered a dark pool ATS, but it has been reported that it is shutting down due to lack of business.

Other American equity markets

The Latin American markets are much smaller than those in the U.S. Although its largest market Brazil is one of the top twenty in the world, in terms of capitalisation and trading volume. For comparison, Table A-6 shows most of the American exchanges.

Exchange	Market cap ($ billions)		2008 ADV ($ millions)	2008 Avg value ($ thousands)
	2008	2007		
NYSE Euronext U.S.	9,209	15,651	132,960	8.3
NASDAQ OMX (U.S.)	2,396	4,014	144,057	9.6
TSX Group	1,033	2,187	6,837	9.2
BM&FBOVESPA	592	1,370	2,908	14.8
Mexican SE (BMV)	234	398	438	24.2
NYSE Amex	132	258	2,219	n/a
Santiago SE	132	213	144	41.6
Colombia SE	88	102	82	34.7
Buenos Aires SE	40	57	26	7.0
Lima SE	38	69	25	17.7

Source: WFE (2009)

Table A-6 Other American stock markets

The Bolsa de Valores de São Paulo (BOVESPA) is both Brazil's and the region's largest stock exchange. It is a completely electronic market; the trading floor was closed in 2005. In 2008, it merged with the Brazilian derivatives exchange (Bolsa de Mercadorias & Futuros). BOVESPA's trading platform MegaBolsa provides a fully transparent order book, based on the Nouveau Système de Cotation (NSC) platform. Market makers provide additional liquidity for stocks. Brokers offer DMA and have also started providing algorithmic trading.

Mexico's Bolsa Mexicana de Valores (BMV) is the region's second largest exchange. This has been fully electronic since 1999, based on its BMV-SENTRA Captiales central limit order book. Brokers also offer DMA and algorithmic trading is becoming available.

However, around as much volume for Brazil and Mexican companies is traded via depositary receipts as is traded on exchange. These are proxies, allowing stocks to be traded as if they were domestic shares in the U.S. or Europe. For instance, in 2008, $750 billion traded on BM&FBOVESPA and $112 billion traded on the BMV, based on data from the WFE (2009). In comparison, $899 worth of Brazilian and $191 billion worth of Mexican depositary receipts were traded, according to the Bank of New York Mellon (BNYM) (2008). Therefore, the key competitor for the Latin American stocks is actually the depositary receipt market, which we shall cover in more detail in Appendix F.

EMEA equity markets

Europe is clearly the largest market in the Europe, Middle East and Africa (EMEA) region. The European equity market is second in size only to the U.S. Indeed, four of the top ten stock exchanges (by 2008 market cap) are European. The European Union has helped unify the marketplace, particularly with the creation of the single currency in 1999. There has also been some consolidation amongst the exchanges, notably the creation of Euronext. Still, Europe consists of thirty states so there is a diverse range of currencies, regulations and trading mechanisms.

Just as in the U.S., regulation is likely to be a major factor in shaping the future of the European marketplace. In November 2007, the Markets in Financial Instruments Directive (MiFID) took effect. This aims to encourage competition between trading venues, improve pre and post-trade transparency and enforce "best execution" requirements. Previously, concentration rules in countries such as France, Spain and Italy prevented significant off-exchange trading. For broker/dealers the compulsory post-trade reporting means their OTC trades must be reported. Firms that provide off exchange trading venues may be classified as Systematic Internalisers (SIs) and so become subject to regulations much like the exchanges. For example, SIs must publish firm quotes during market hours, report all trades and may not offer price improvement on orders below a specific market size. Alternatively, rather than managing this by themselves there is always the option to join one of the Multilateral Trading Facilities (MTFs), such as Turquoise. In the short to medium term, MiFID has resulted in a spate of new execution venues competing for liquidity from the exchanges, but also sourcing new liquidity that previously may have been hidden. A report by the Aite Group (2009) consultancy notes that MTFs should reach 20% market share of European trading in 2009, and could achieve 50% by 2013. Hence, Europe is entering a cycle of fragmentation, which may well be followed by a consolidation phase.

Electronic trading is pretty much universal on the sell-side, with levels of algorithmic trading growing rapidly. Though, buy-side uptake has tended to lag the U.S. A report by the TABB Group (2007b) consultancy notes that in 2007 electronic order routing was used by over 50% of firms, and should grow to 65% by 2009, most of this routing over FIX. In terms of volume, the Celent (2008b) consultancy estimates that DMA accounts for 8% of the flow, projecting this to grow to 15% by 2011. The buy-side adoption of algorithms is also growing; the TABB Group (2007b) reported it at 41%, expecting it to reach 58% by 2009.

Most of the region's venues are based on electronic central limit order books, often using call auctions for the open and close. Many also incorporate dedicated market makers or liquidity providers. The widespread adoption of electronic order books can be traced back to the competition that London's International Order Book spawned in 1986. Each country's primary exchange generally still has a monopoly over its listed stocks. Though, since the implementation of MiFID they are now starting to face stiff competition from a wide range of MTFs. Table A-7 shows the breakdown of market capitalisation and trading volumes for the region's main exchanges.

Exchange	Domestic market cap ($ billions)		2008 ADV ($millions)	2008 Avg value ($thousands)
	2008	2007		
NYSE Euronext Europe	2,102	4,223	17,231	23.0
London SE	1,868	3,852	24,691	31.1
Deutsche Börse	1,111	2,105	18,420	33.0
BME Spanish Exchanges	948	1,781	9,491	64.5
SIX Swiss Exchange	857	1,271	5,977	35.7
NASDAQ OMX Nordic Exchange	563	1,243	5,268	24.1
Borsa Italiana	522	1,073	5,926	21.6
Johannesburg SE	483	828	1,574	22.7
Oslo Børs	146	353	1,756	26.1

Source: WFE (2009)

Table A-7 European equity markets

Euronext was created in 2000 by the merger of the Paris, Brussels and Amsterdam stock exchanges. These were joined in 2002 by Portugal; it has also established membership/ access agreements with the Helsinki and Warsaw stock exchanges. Though, clearly the most notable merger was completed in 2007 with the NYSE. Euronext is based on an electronic order book that allows access for dedicated liquidity providers. Originally, this was the Nouveau Système de Cotation (NSC); however, early in 2009 equity trading migrated to the new Universal Trading Platform (UTP) which offers even greater capacity and lower latency.

On the London Stock Exchange (LSE), the electronic central limit order book for FTSE 100 companies is provided by its Stock Exchange Electronic Trading Service (SETS), which dates back to 1997. Although in 2007, the platform was upgraded with a new transaction engine (TradElect). Around 800 mid and small cap stocks are also catered for by SETS with registered market makers providing liquidity to the order book via displayed quotes. (Note these were formerly handled by the SETSmm hybrid market, whose quote functionality was rolled into SETS as part of the preparations for MiFID.) Less liquid main market stocks are currently handled by SETSqx, which combines a quote based market with four intraday crosses to improve overall liquidity and to help member firms to meet MiFID requirements. The Borsa Italiana has also migrated to the LSE's TradElect platform, as has the Johannesburg Stock Exchange. Norway's Oslo Børs is also planning to adopt TradElect; currently their trading is based on the NASDAQ OMX's SAXESS platform.

The Deutsche Börse operates the Frankfurt Stock Exchange. Xetra, its electronic platform, offers a hybrid marketplace, based on an electronic order book that allows designated market makers to provide additional liquidity. They have introduced discounts to encourage algorithmic trading. It is estimated that around 40% of their volume now originates from such systems. Xetra is also used by the Vienna, Irish and Budapest stock exchanges.

The Spanish Bolsas y Mercados Españoles are linked through an electronic system (SIBE), and have seen considerable volume growth over the last few years.

The Stockholm, Copenhagen and Helsinki stock exchanges are part of the NASDAQ OMX Group, as are the Baltic exchanges for Riga, Vilnius and Tallinn. Trading is based on their INET platform (previously the SAXESS platform was used).

For smaller companies, there is a range of dedicated exchanges, most notably London's Alternative Investments Market (AIM). This is operated by the LSE, and is now the world's leading market for small-cap stocks. By 2008, AIM had over 1600 quoted companies including 300 international ones and a combined market cap of over $170 billion. It uses SETS for its fifty most traded stocks, whilst the quote driven SEAQ is used for the less traded, although ultimately this will probably migrate to SETSqx. Euronext's Alternext market, Spain's Nuevo Mercado and the NASDAQ OMX First North also offer alternative marketplaces, although these are much smaller than AIM. Germany's Neuer Markt has been incorporated back into the main market. In the U.K., the PLUS Markets Group has established some local competition; its exchange has over 180 listings and a total market cap of nearly $4 billion. It provides trading for around 7,500 U.K. and European small and mid-cap stocks.

Pan-European execution venues have also been established. In the past, their success has been somewhat mixed; venues such as Chi-X have flourished whilst others such as EASDAQ [7] and Jiway [8] floundered. In part, this has been due to national concentration regulations that favoured many of the primary exchanges. In addition, the rapid adoption of electronic order books by the European exchanges meant that ECNs initially had much less impact in Europe than the U.S. Though, the introduction of MiFID meant that regulations now actively encourage such competition. Hence, MTFs from Turquoise, NASDAQ OMX Europe and BATS were launched in 2008. NYSE Euronext launched its own MTF in 2009, as did Equiduct and Burgundy, other venues are also due.

Instinet's Chi-X MTF has proven that liquidity can be shifted away from the major exchanges. Launched in 2007 it currently offers trading in stocks for most of the major European indices and has managed to attract large sell-side firms to provide liquidity. In terms of market share, it estimated to have captured around 17% of trading for the U.K.'s FTSE 100 stocks, around 13% of France's CAC 40 firms and Amsterdam's AEX stocks and around 9% of Germany's DAX 30, based on the companies own data in November 2008. For its top stocks, it is capturing anything from 30-50% of the daily volume, reporting average price improvements of 4 bps. This rapid success may be attributed to a mix of its pricing structure and its speed. Interestingly, it also offers trading to 3 decimal places for all stocks, and so allows trading between the spreads quoted on the major exchanges. This is something that Regulation NMS removed from ECNs in the U.S. (the Sub-Penny rule).

The Turquoise MTF has been driven primarily by a group of broker/dealers and was launched in September 2008. It provides an electronic order book for most of the major European indices, together with support for fully hidden orders. The platform is based on Cinnober's TRADExpress, which also powers the London Metals Exchange. An article in

---

[7] EASDAQ was founded in 1996 to try and emulate the success of NASDAQ, who in turn bought it and created NASDAQ Europe in 2001. However, with only 60 listings it proved vulnerable to the post-millennium tech downturn, closing in 2003.

[8] Jiway was launched in 2000 as a joint venture between the OMX Group and Morgan Stanley, but it failed to source enough liquidity from retail flow and so closed two years later.

The Trade News (2008) notes that in early November it had captured around 7% of trading for stocks in France's CAC and Switzerland's SMI indices, 5% or more for the Dutch AEX, German DAX and UK's FTSE, as well as a smaller portion of trading in Italy's MIB and Sweden's OMX indices. The London Stock Exchange has announced plans to purchase a majority share in Turquoise, so it will be interesting to see what effect this has.

The NASDAQ OMX Europe MTF went live in September 2008. It caters for over 1,200 stocks, covering the major indices for markets in the U.K., Germany, France, Netherlands, Italy, Switzerland, Austria, Belgium, Denmark, Finland, Ireland, Norway, Sweden and Spain. Based on NASDAQ OMX's INET platform it also supports pan-European order routing to the region's other main exchanges and MTFs.

BATS also launched its own MTF in October 2008, aiming to recreate the success of its U.S. operation for European stocks. Trading encompasses stocks from all the major European indices.

Meanwhile, March 2009 saw the introduction of NYSE Arca Europe. Based on their UTP platform, it supports trading for the blue-chip European stocks, which are not already handled by its Euronext markets.

Equiduct's MTF also went live in March 2009, supporting trading for the most liquid stocks from the LSE, Euronext and Deutsche Börse. Its HybridBook platform is an electronic order book that also supports trading at proprietary benchmarks, namely the Europe-wide Best Bid and Offer (EBBO), which is based on consolidated prices from the major markets. A Volume weighted Best Bid and Offer (VBBO) is offered as well, although there is a premium for these benchmark trades.

The Burgundy MTF launched in May 2009, backed by major Nordic brokers. This focuses on trading mid-cap and small-cap Nordic stocks and also offers hidden (or "dark") order types. It is based on Cinnober's TRADExpress trading system.

In response to such competition, the European exchanges are already making changes to try to retain their liquidity post MiFID. They are altering their fee structures, adopting a maker/taker approach and offering reductions for trading in volume. London, Xetra and Euronext have all either released, or are in the process of updating their trading systems to support greater volumes and lower their latencies to below 10ms, to compete with the likes of Chi-X. NYSE Euronext has also started reducing the tick sizes of many of its stocks, introducing support for pricing to three decimal places, like Chi-X. The Deutsche Börse has also launched a pan-European trading segment, the Xetra International Market (XIM), to further compete with the MTFs.

In terms of order internalisation, the Deutsche Börse was one of the first exchanges to recognise the importance this, introducing Xetra-BEST in 2002. This allows brokers to internalise their retail orders, gaining MiFID compliance and saving on settlement fees, whilst retail clients benefit from a mandatory price improvement. They have also reduced their fees and cut the mandatory price improvement to €0.001 to encourage more brokers to adopt BEST. Likewise, in early 2007, Euronext announced that it was developing a new trading mechanism to ensure best execution, allowing members to be MiFID complaint without having to become Systematic Internalisers.

The ramp-up in "dark pools" of liquidity has also been slower in Europe, although given that significant amounts trade off-exchange, particularly in the U.K. and Germany, there is plenty of opportunity. A report by the Celent (2007c) consultancy predicts that ATSs will capture around a 5% market share by 2011. In part, this is because the major European exchanges have offered hidden and/or iceberg orders for some time, helping to accommodate block trading. The Deutsche Börse supports intraday blind crossings, every 15 minutes (except during auctions on the main market) via their XETRA-XXL platform. The LSE also offers a crossing service via SEAQ Crosses, although it is intended primarily for less liquid stocks. Undoubtedly, the other exchanges will also consider providing crossing systems to try to retain their liquidity.

In terms of continuous "dark pools", Xetra MidPoint offers a closed order book with continuous midpoint trading. Likewise, SWX has launched "Swiss Block" in partnership with NYFIX. In 2009, NYSE Euronext launched SmartPool, as a joint project with several major international banks. SmartPool provides continuous mid-point crossing together with four daily periodic crosses; it also offers routing to the NYSE Euronext central order book. Also in 2009, NASDAQ OMX launched its continuous dark pool, NEURO Dark. Based on INET it offers mid-point crossing from the primary market and caters for over a thousand European stocks (it supports internalised orders as well). In the same year, Chi-X's Chi-Delta and the BATS Europe Dark Pool were launched, providing continuous mid-point crossing. The LSE will also provide a dark pool for the region.

Unsurprisingly, the major U.S. ATSs, namely ITG and Liquidnet, have already established themselves in Europe. For scheduled crossing systems POSIT is arguably the leader, being established here since 1998. It covers over 9,000 stocks across 15 countries with eight matching sessions each day (biased towards the open). ITG acquired its main direct European competition (E-Crossnet) in 2005. Other types of crossing are also available in Europe, the negotiated crossing system Liquidnet went live in Europe in 2002, and offers trading in 22 markets, allowing institutional users to trade liquid stocks in much larger average sizes than those available on the exchanges. It is also considering expanding into the Middle East. ITG has introduced a European version of its POSIT Alert platform as well, complementing its continuous blind crossing system, POSIT Now, which was released in 2007. Likewise, Euro Millennium was launched by NYFIX in 2008; this is a European version of its continuous blind crossing platform, although it is now owned by NYSE Euronext.

Many of the major brokers have also established European internal crossing networks, for example, Credit Suisse's CrossFinder.

In order to cope with all these new venues and to try to reduce the impact of fragmentation, pre- and post-trade information need to be aggregated. Presently, this is handled by the main market data providers. Markit's Boat (formerly "Project Boat") also provides a single interface for pan-European trade reporting. The UK's Financial Services Authority has proposed the creation of dedicated Trade Data Monitors to meet this requirement.

Another area that may see further consolidation across Europe is its settlement systems. For instance, Table A-8 shows some of the potential settlement options for the company Royal Dutch (Shell).

Execution venue	Central Securities Depository
Euronext Amsterdam	Euroclear Amsterdam
London Stock Exchange	
Instinet Chi-X	
Virt-x	Euroclear Bank
Deutsche Börse	Clearstream Banking Frankfurt

Source: Instinet (2007)

Table A-8 Potential settlement destinations for a European stock

Life would be a lot simpler, and more efficient, if there were a single depository like the U.S. Depository Trust & Clearing Corp. (DTCC). The choice of depository can also affect the trade cost since each may have different settlement costs. Therefore, liquidity aggregation is only really appropriate for prices from venues that share the same depository, as noted in a white paper on market data consolidation from Instinet (2007). Otherwise, additional costs may be incurred which are not reflected in the price. Cross-border settlement has traditionally been expensive in Europe.

A report by the Deutsche Börse Group (DBG/Clearstream) (2002) noted that wholesale trades could be 30% more expensive, whilst retail ones were up to 150% more. Thus, until there is further consolidation amongst Europe's depositories, smart order routing systems and trading algorithms will need to take these additional costs into account. Fortunately, there are some signs that this situation should improve. A subsidiary of the U.S. DTCC has launched EuroCCP, which provides a unified clearing and settlement facility that is used by Turquoise.

Asian equity markets

The Asian equity marketplace has seen huge increases in trading volume in the last few years, as well as significant returns. However, this is much more fragmented than either Europe or the U.S. There is no common currency, or legal framework, so sovereignty is still a major factor for each country's exchanges. Despite these issues, many exchanges have started to form agreements and alliances with each other. There has also been a lot of consolidation within each country, particularly between the stock and derivative markets, e.g. Korea and Singapore.

Most of the region's execution venues support electronic trading; although, in terms of adoption, Asia is still some way behind both Europe and the U.S., particularly for the buy-side. DMA and algorithmic trading have also been quite slow to take off. Though, this is changing as buy-side attention starts to focus more on execution costs. A survey by Greenwich Associates (2009) found that in 2008 electronic trading accounted for 15% of equity trading in Asia, up from 11% in 2007. This breaks down into 9% for DMA, 5% via algorithms and 1% in "dark pools" and crossing networks. They also estimate this figure could rise to 28% in three years. The Aite Group consultancy estimates that the region's algorithmic trading could increase to around 16% by 2010 from 4%, as noted by Cristina McEachern (2007). Levels of adoption are slightly higher in Japan, although uptake has been faster with foreign investors. A survey of Japanese equity trading by Greenwich Associates (2008) found that in 2008 electronic trading accounted for 17% of institutional volume. DMA increased to 9%, from 8% in 2007, whilst algorithmic trading rose from 5% in 2007 to 7% in 2008. By 2012, they project electronic trading to reach 35%, with DMA at 16% and algorithmic trading at 15% of the volume.

The Asian marketplace is dominated by exchanges and broker/dealers. Table A-9 gives a breakdown of the largest exchanges in terms of market cap. The exchanges have been quick to move to electronic trading, but for many capacity and latency still pose issues. That said, over the last few years, the pace of upgrading exchanges has increased significantly.

Japan is still the largest market in Asia. The Tokyo Stock Exchange (TSE) is the second largest in the world (by 2008 domestic market cap). The TSE closed its trading floor and became fully electronic in 1999. Trading is purely order driven with two daily sessions of continuous trading (referred to as the Zaraba method) are augmented by call auctions (Itayose) at the open and close of each. Its trading system is known as "arrowhead", which

Exchange	Domestic market cap ($ billions)		2008 ADV ($millions)	2008 Avg value ($thousands)
	2008	2007		
Tokyo SE	3,116	4,331	22,887	n/a
Shanghai SE	1,425	3,694	10,656	2.0
Hong Kong Exchanges	1,329	2,654	6,652	14.6
Australian SE	684	1,298	4,776	11.4
Bombay SE	647	1,819	1,226	0.5
National Stock Exchange India	600	1,660	2,948	0.5
Korea Exchange	471	1,123	5,776	2.2
Taiwan SE Corp.	357	664	3,333	4.1
Shenzhen SE	353	785	5,076	1.9
Singapore Exchange	265	539	1,031	n/a
Bursa Malaysia	189	325	382	6.9

Source: WFE (2009)

Table A-9 Asian equity markets

went live in 2010 replacing the former CORES platform. This brings a much-anticipated boost in performance and capacity. Japan's second largest exchange, the Osaka Securities Exchange (OSE), is the leading Japanese derivatives exchange, but it also lists over 1,000 companies, and is used to trade TSE listed stocks as well. The OSE has also announced plans to migrate to a new trading platform, from the NASDAQ OMX Group. Further competition is offered by the JASDAQ, a Japanese version of the NASDAQ, with a market cap now similar to the OSE. For small-cap stocks, the TSE incorporates a dedicated segment called the Mothers market, which lists around 130 stocks, with a market cap of around $40 billion.

The Hong Kong exchange (HKEx) provides a gateway for access to mainland China. Trading is provided via an electronic order book, based on its third generation Automatic Order Matching and Execution System (AMS/3). Algorithmic trading is already established, analyst estimates put algorithmic flow at around 3-4%, as reported in Securities Industry News (SIN) (2007). In mainland China, the most important venues are the Shanghai and Shenzhen stock exchanges. Both are again based on limit order books, the Shanghai's trading system is adapted from the Deutsche Börse's Xetra. The Shanghai and Shenzhen exchanges saw massive annual turnover increases in 2007 (500-600%), with a corresponding increase in their overall market cap of 300-400%, based on data from the WFE (2007, 2008). If their growth continues, they will soon be serious competitors for domination of the regional marketplace. Smaller companies are catered for by Hong Kong's Growth Enterprise Market (GEM), which lists around 200 stocks.

The Australian Securities Exchange (ASX) is a product of the 2006 merger between the Australian Stock Exchange and the Sydney Futures Exchange. It operates a fully electronic order book using its Integrated Trading System (ITS), which is based on NASDAQ OMX's CLICK-XT. In 2006, it altered its pricing structure from per-trade to a value based approach, mainly to encourage DMA and algorithmic trading, which now accounts for around a fifth of its order flow.

The Korea Exchange (KRX) was formed in 2005, from a merger between the Korean

Stock, Futures and KOSDAQ exchanges. This merger also incorporated the region's first ECN, founded in 2001 by Korea ECN Securities. The KRX provides an order driven trading system, with call auctions for the open and close, via its Automated Trading System (KATS). It also allows market makers to provide liquidity for less traded stocks and newer issues. For smaller companies, the KOSDAQ arm of the KSX caters for around 900 stocks, with a combined market cap of around $50 billion, making it globally just behind AIM in terms of size. Algorithmic trading is starting to take hold in Korea: In 2007, its first commercial algorithmic platform was created by a joint venture between Koscom (a subsidiary of the KRX) and Progress Apama.

The Bombay Stock Exchange (BSE) is India's largest, by market cap, and has around 4,800 listed companies. Though, it faces stiff competition from the National Stock Exchange (NSE), which was created in 1994 to encourage market reform. Originally, the BSE was based on open outcry, its Bombay On-line Trading (BOLT) system was introduced in 1995 in response to the fully automated NSE. BOLT provides a hybrid electronic market, which incorporates two-way quotes from "jobbers", or market makers. In comparison, the NSE runs an anonymous pure limit order book, based on its National Exchange Automated Trading (NEAT) system. Brokers are also starting to offer DMA for these exchanges, a report from the Celent (2008) consultancy estimates this could reach 11% of trading by 2010. The ever-expanding trend of exchange globalisation has also seen NYSE-Euronext purchase 5% of the NSE whilst the Singapore exchange and the Deutsche Börse have each taken 5% of the BSE.

The Taiwan Stock Exchange operates a continuous limit order book together with periodic call actions for the lunch break and close. This is based on its Fully Automated Securities Trading system, which was introduced in 1993.

The Singapore Exchange (SGX) was formed in 1999 by the merger of the Stock Exchange of Singapore and the derivative Singapore International Monetary Exchange; both are based on central limit order books. SGX stock trading is carried out on its Quest-ST platform, which is based on the NASDAQ OMX's CLICK-XT exchange software. It is also planning to reduce the average bid offer spread to improve its competitiveness. Between 10 and 15% of trading is currently estimated to be traded algorithmically, as noted in an article on TradingMarkets (2007). For smaller companies, listing and trading is handled by the SESDAQ.

The Bursa Malaysia has updated its trading platform, migrating to Bursa Trade, which is based on the NSC platform from Euronext and the Atos Origin Consultancy. This provides much lower latencies (down from 5s for the old platform to milliseconds) and enables DMA. It has been handling Malaysian derivatives trading since 2006.

Alternative trading venues have yet to capture a sizeable proportion of the Asian marketplace. A report by Greenwich Associates (2007a) notes that crossing networks are expected to capture about 1% of the total market share, although this could reach up to 3% in Japan. In part, this is due to the prevalence of electronic central limit order books amongst the exchanges, as in Europe. Local regulations can also pose problems, as noted by Maria Trombly (2007). For instance, China has severe restrictions for foreign investors whilst India does not allow off-exchange crossing. Other market peculiarities can also pose problems, such as Taiwan's requirement that trades be pre-funded with cash. None of these are insurmountable, indeed alternative venues have already started to appear in Asia.

ECNs have spread to Japan, aided by their 1998 legislation for Proprietary Trading Systems (PTS). This allows the creation of private markets intended to augment the existing exchanges. Instinet's CBX ASIA was launched in 2001, providing a central limit order book for Japanese and Hong Kong equities. Likewise, in 2003 Japan Securities Agents was granted status as a PTS, providing dealers an off-exchange mechanism. SBI Holdings launched its JapanNext in 2007, catering for after-hours stock trading. Australia should see its first ECN in the form of AXE in 2009/10. Interestingly, this venture is partially owned by the New Zealand stock exchange. Instinet has also announced plans to establish Chi-X in the Asia Pacific region.

Crossing networks and "dark pool" ATSs are also spreading across the region. 2001 saw the establishment of Instinet's JapanCrossing. This PTS offers a pre-market VWAP cross as well as a morning close and an afternoon close. Though initially slow to take off, by Q1 2006 it had captured around 4% of the TSE's daily turnover, this growth has continued. CLSA has launched its BlocSec ATS, providing crossings for Singapore, Hong Kong, Japan, and Australia. Liquidnet brought its continuous negotiated crossing mechanism to Japan, Hong Kong, Singapore and South Korea in 2007 and to Australia in 2008. ITG also has a presence in Asia; POSIT Match offers intraday crossings for Japan, Australia and Hong Kong. ITG Australia has also launched its continuous crossing system, POSIT Now, together with its POSIT Alert continuous indications system. Instinet has also released its continuous blind crossing system CBX in Japan. Other broker's liquidity pools have started appearing as well, for example, Credit Suisse's CrossFinder is live in Japan, Australia, Hong Kong, Singapore and South Korea. Instinet has also established an agreement with Credit Suisse to allow mutual access to each other's liquidity pools. Combined this forms one of the largest "dark pools" of liquidity currently available in Asia.

Summary

- Electronic trading is now ubiquitous for the world's stock markets.

- Buy-side levels of adoption of DMA and algorithmic trading are high, particularly in the U.S.

- It will still take some time before the levels of adoption for algorithmic trading in Europe and Asia reach those of the U.S., but the pace of change is increasing.

Appendix B
Fixed income markets

The fixed income marketplace accounts for a third of the global financial market, in terms of value, as we saw back in Chapter 3. Fixed income trading has developed around the OTC mechanism, mainly because the assets are much less standardised than stocks. However, strong inter-dealer markets have become established for some fixed income securities, which are sufficiently uniform, such as government bonds. These securities have tended to be the ones that have most successfully migrated to electronic trading, although the overall level of adoption still lags many of the other asset classes.

Asset specific

A fixed-income asset represents a debt for a specific amount (the principal), whereby the issuer is obliged to repay the holder at some future date (the maturity date). Debt can be issued by governments, other agencies and by companies. A variety of names are used for these, for example, the U.S. Treasury terms them based on their maturity, namely bills (<1 year), notes (2-10 years) and bonds (>10 years). For simplicity, in this book all such debt will generally be referred to as bonds. Debt may also be issued based on pools of loans, which is the essence of asset-backed securities. Similarly, mortgage-backed securities are the equivalent for real estate debt.

The return for an investment in bonds is usually more predictable than for stocks, and is bounded by their principal value. Investors are typically looking for safer returns than the potential growth offered by equities. Therefore, some of the largest investors are pension funds and insurance companies. Since these firms often adopt buy-and-hold strategies, the liquidity of bonds traded in the secondary markets can be much less than for stocks.

The issuer of a bond will usually pay interest (the coupon) to the holder at a given frequency for the lifetime of the loan, e.g. every 6 months. Alternatively, zero coupon bonds make no such payments; instead, their price is discounted by an equivalent amount. Either way, at maturity the bond should redeem its principal amount, or face value. Hence, the main risk with bonds is that the issuer defaults on the debt. This risk is generally reflected by the bond's interest rate, so riskier debt pays higher coupons to compensate investors. The bond's price will also reflect this, so higher risk bonds usually trade at a much deeper discount than others.

The effective interest rate that a bond issuer must pay depends on the maturity date of the contract, as well as their credit rating and the current market rates. Bonds will sometimes have additional collateralization or credit protection to reduce the credit risk, allowing issuers to use slightly lower rates. For secured bonds, specific assets (collateral) have been pledged which may be sold to ensure the debt holders are paid in case of bankruptcy. Debts may also be differentiated in terms of their seniority when it comes to bankruptcy hearings, with senior debt taking priority over subordinated debt. All these specifics should be detailed in the bond's indenture, which formally specifies the rights of bondholders. It also contains details of any covenants that may relate to the finances of the issuer, e.g. pledging to maintain specific capital requirements, or even restricting the levels of dividends. Often such covenants are intended to protect the income stream for bondholders, so again they can affect the coupon rate.

Bonds may also have a range of conditions associated with their maturity date. Extendable bonds allow the issuer to extend the maturity date, for instance, when the market rates become unfavourable. Callable bonds allow the issuer to redeem the bond before it matures. Thus, to compensate the bondholders for such provisions the issuer must pay a premium. On the other hand, some bonds incorporate an option that allows the bondholder to force redemption on specific dates, for which they must in turn pay a premium.

Pricing and trading

In general, bonds are more straightforward to price than equities. Essentially, the fair price of a bond is the present value of all its future interest and principal payments. The present value incorporates a discount for the market rate of return, which in turn depends on the bond's characteristics. So for a government bond issued in the local currency with negligible default risk the market rate should approximate to the risk-free rate. For higher risk issuers, the rate will need to be higher. Macroeconomic factors, such as inflation expectations, will also have a considerable impact on the price of bonds.

The main risk with bonds is that the issuer defaults on the debt. This is reflected in both their interest rate and price, so riskier bonds usually trade at a deeper discount than others.

Bonds are priced in terms of a percentage of their par value, where 100 represents 100% of the face value. They can also trade at a premium where the price will be above 100, for instance, when the bond's coupon is more attractive than the prevailing market rates. Bonds are still quoted in fractions for many markets, so 95:05, 95-05 or 95'05 are not the same as 95.05. Some bonds quote in eighths, whilst U.S. treasuries are quoted in $1/32^{nd}$s, so 95-05 is actually 95 5/32 = 95.15625, whilst 95-05+ adds another 1/64 so it is 95.171875. Hopefully, decimalisation will continue to spread.

Another factor that can affect bond prices is related to the interest that has been accrued since the last coupon payment, which must also be transferred when the bond is traded. Some markets include this interest in the bond's current price, also referred to as a "dirty price", whilst others exclude it - instead adopting a "clean price".

A bond's yield to maturity (YTM) represents the annualised rate of return it would give if held to maturity. This is inversely related to the bond price, so the higher the price the lower the YTM and vice versa. So, when market interest rates rise, bond prices should fall. In fact, bonds are often referred to by their yield, rather than their price.

Unlike stocks, a single issuer can have a huge range of bonds, each differing in terms of when they were issued and their maturity, their interest rate and payment structure, any collateralization/credit-protection as well as the specifics of the indenture. Indeed, the number of different bonds is phenomenal. For example, in the U.S alone there are more than three million bonds, that is two hundred times more than the number of equities available globally. This diversity can pose serious liquidity problems, since for many assets it will be difficult to find sufficient depth in a given bond for a continuous market. Only the markets for reasonably standardised debt, such as U.S. Treasuries, tend to have sufficient volume to be viable for continuous trading. One factor that helps is the fact that many bond investors trade based on specifications, such as credit rating and maturity, rather than seeking a specific bond. This provides more liquidity to a market that would otherwise be much sparser.

Liquidity for bonds can often differ significantly over their lifetime. For instance, most of the activity is focussed on the current issue of a bond (when it is "on the run"). As soon as the next issue is released, the trading volume of the previous (now "off the run") asset plummets. In fact, a study by Michael Barclay, Terrence Hendershott, and Kenneth Kotz (2006) found that "off the run" U.S. treasuries fall to around 10% of their former volume. The prevalence of "buy and hold" strategies, particularly for corporate bonds, means that shortly after issuance, many bonds are simply not available for trading.

Bonds tend to trade in much larger size than stocks, but often with much lower frequencies. For example, a report by the U.K. Financial Services Authority (FSA) (2005) notes that the average trade size for gilts was £5 million compared with only £43,000 for U.K. equities, in 2004. Whilst even the most heavily traded issue in the gilt market only saw around 200 trades in a day, whereas for stocks this figure is at least an order of magnitude more.

Corporate debt is even less heavily traded. A study of U.S. corporate bonds by Amy Edwards, Lawrence Harris and Michael Piwowar (2007) found that, on average, bonds traded less than 1.9 times a day, with more than 60% of the trades worth less than $100,000. Similarly, a European study by Bruno Biais et al. (2006) found an average of 3.07 trades per day for euro denominated corporate bonds and only 2.23 for U.K. sterling ones, with a maximum number of trades no more than 50 a day. Bonds with lower associated credit ratings tend to trade less regularly, although the trends for maturity date were less conclusive with Biais et al. (2006) noting that short and long-term debt seemed to be the most heavily traded.

World fixed income markets

Globally there is over $85 trillion of outstanding fixed income debt. This is based on data for the total outstanding domestic and international debt in H1 2008, from the Bank for International Settlements (BIS) (2008). Government debt accounts for around $30.7 trillion (36%) of this. A further $45.5 trillion is owed by financial agencies (53%) whilst the remaining $9 trillion is from corporate debt. Much of this debt is actually concentrated in a handful of countries, as Figure B-1 shows. Overall, the Americas account for 42%, followed by 40% for the EMEA region and 18% for Asia.

Bond markets differ based on the type of debt. Government bond markets tend to issue more standardised contracts, whereas corporate debt is often more customised. Hence, the government debt markets tend to be larger and more liquid. The governments also have much more control over how these markets are structured and run.

The secondary markets for most of the world's bonds are dealer-based and much of the trading is still done over-the-counter (OTC). The markets are segmented between inter-dealer and dealer-to-client trading. The lack of centralised markets, or exchanges, means that for clients most trading is principal.

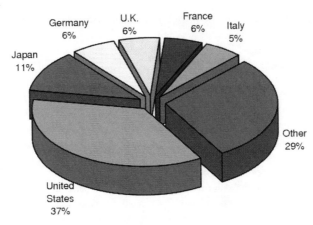

Source: Authors own calculations based on data from BIS (2008)

Figure B-1 Global market share of fixed income market

American fixed income markets

The U.S. dominates the world's fixed income marketplace, as is clear from Figure B-1. Though, Canada and Latin America also have significant debt markets.

U.S. fixed income market

The U.S. fixed income market is huge; it caters for a debt of around $25 trillion, together with a daily trading volume of more than a trillion dollars. Over half of this daily volume consists of government debt trading. Though, as Table B-1 shows, much of the U.S. outstanding debt is actually issued by other agencies, municipalities and corporations.

Type	Outstanding debt H1 2008 ($ billions)	Daily trading volume H1 2008 ($ billions)	% of daily volume
U.S. Treasury securities	4,700	615.1	54
Federal agencies	3,100	116.5	10
Municipal securities	2,700	23.1	2
Mortgage-backed securities	7,600	365.1	32
Corporate securities	6,200	18.8	2

Source: SIFMA (2008, 2008a) [9]

Table B-1 U.S. fixed income market [10]

U.S. treasuries are the most liquid fixed income assets, accounting for nearly two thirds of the daily volume, which is not that surprising given the demand for treasury debt and the amount available. This liquidity is, in part, due to the essentially risk-free nature of the issuer. It is also helped by the relative standardisation, in terms of the characteristics of each bond issue. The benchmark asset for U.S. Treasury debt is the 10-year note. In fact, these are often used as an indicator for long-term interest rates. Although in 2006 the Treasury also

---

[9] Data from the Federal Reserve Bank of New York, Municipal Securities Rulemaking Board, NASD TRACE.
[10] Money market and asset-backed debt is worth around $7 billion, based on estimates from SIFMA (2008a).

reintroduced quarterly issues of its 30-year bond. About 70% of the trading volume is solely attributable to the currently on-the-run assets. So most trading activity is concentrated on this small subset, as Frank Fabozzi and Michael Fleming (2004) note, despite the wide range of bonds that are available.

In comparison, agency and municipal debt is much less heavily traded. To compensate for the slightly greater credit risk they offer tax benefits, so they are generally held by single investors, insurance companies or trusts (hence their low daily turnover).

Likewise, the turnover for U.S. corporate debt is negligible, considering the size of the outstanding debt. As we can see in Table B-1 it accounts for around 2% of the average daily volume. In fact, the corporate debt market turns over only about once a year. [11] In comparison, treasuries turn over thirty times a year, as Harrell Smith (2005) points out. This lack of liquidity is partly due to the fact that much corporate debt is held to maturity.

Although there have been no massive structural changes in the U.S. fixed income marketplace, at the height of the dot.com bubble there were over a hundred vendors offering electronic trading platforms. Intense competition and rationalisation has whittled this down to a more realistic marketplace. A report by the Celent (2008a) consultancy estimates that electronic trading accounts for 57% of the U.S. fixed income market's average daily volume. They predict that this should reach 62% by 2010. The highly liquid U.S. Treasuries lead the way with nearly 80% of the volume traded electronically. They found much lower levels for the other classes. For instance, only 32% of mortgage-based security trading was electronic.

The inter-dealer broker market for U.S. Treasuries is dominated by a few brokers. These have effectively taken the place of bond exchanges, as Larry Tabb (2004) notes. Electronic trading accounts most of the trading in on-the-run treasuries; even the off-the-run market has around 50% electronic trading. The market share is split between ICAP's BrokerTec (58%) and BGC's eSpeed (41%) platforms, given estimates from ICAP (2007). Both systems allow anonymous order matching, so the market place for 2, 5 or 10-year treasury notes is much like the equity markets. BrokerTec also supports "workups", allowing dealers to negotiate the trade quantity. In terms of volume, ICAP (2009) reported average daily trading figures of $141 billion for U.S. Treasuries in 2008 (note this also includes T-bills). ICAP also has a major presence in the electronic inter-dealer market for mortgage-backed securities. BrokerTec supports agency and corporate debt trading as well. For municipals, the MuniCenter provides a similar inter-dealer platform, which also competes for agency and corporate debt.

In the dealer-to-client marketplace there is a lot less liquidity. Tradeweb is the market leader in offering electronic access, via a request-for-quote mechanism, with average daily volumes of around $300 billion in 2008, based on figures from the company. It caters for trading government, agency, mortgage-backed and corporate debt, as well as money market, credit and derivatives. Bloomberg's BondTrader provides a similar service. In terms of corporate debt, MarketAxess leads the market for electronic trading, with its multi-dealer RFQ based platform. Further competition in the dealer-to-client market should have arrived in the form of LiquidityHub, which was to provide clients with a request-for-stream based trading mechanism for government bonds, aggregating the liquidity from a consortium of over a dozen banks. Unfortunately, the 2007-09 financial crisis helped put an end to this venture.

The U.S. is seeing a gradual shift in market structure. Investment firms/hedge funds have started to become an important part of the inter-dealer market. A paper by the European

---

[11] This is when the cumulative traded volume equals the level of outstanding debt.

Primary Dealers Association (EPDA) (2007) notes that these were reported to account for five of the top ten participants on BrokerTec and three of the top ten on eSpeed. A thriving arbitrage business has developed between the two systems and the futures market, as reported in an article by Daniel Safarik (2005). In this article, the CEO of electronic brokerage at ICAP, David Rutter, explains that much of this is due to a small number of quantitative trading firms laying off risk against bond-based futures contracts from the CBOT. Interestingly, he also highlighted that algorithmic trading was their fastest growing customer segment, with more than half of the bids and offers from computerised systems. The advent of such trading has also helped to reduce price discrepancies and become an important source of liquidity.

Exchange based trading was rekindled in 2007 with NYSE re-launching its bonds trading platform. This is based on the electronic order book from its Arca platform; trading is anonymous and both limit and reserve/iceberg style orders are supported. In addition to the main trading segment, there is also an early trading session from 4am, and a late session lasting until 8pm. It currently caters for over 3,000 bonds, although ultimately this figure should double. It will be interesting to see how much market share this captures, and how it affects the overall market in the long term.

"Dark pools" have not quite spread to the U.S. fixed income market. That said, State Street Global Markets FICross is a pretty close approximation. A nice summary of FICross is provided by Cristina McEachern (2008). Effectively, it offers a bulletin board where users can post anonymous orders or indications of interest. Matching is still done manually with State Street acting as the intermediary, although they are also planning to offer an automated process. At present, the coverage is for cash bonds with most of the activity in corporate and asset-backed instruments.

Post-trade transparency has also been improved for the corporate debt market by the Trade Reporting and Compliance Engine (TRACE) initiative, first approved by the SEC in 2001. This mandated reporting of trade prices for all dealers and brokers, and does seem to have helped reduce overall costs. A study by Michael Goldstein, Edith Hotchkiss and Eric Sirri (2007) found that the increased transparency had a neutral or positive effect on market liquidity, based on measurements of trading volume and effective spreads. Though, some market participants still feel that overall liquidity has declined since the introduction of TRACE.

Other American fixed income markets

Canada is the second largest debt market in the Americas, although as Table B-2 shows it is closely followed by Brazil.

Country	Outstanding domestic debt H1 2008 in $billions			Outstanding international debt H1 2008 in $billions		
	Total	Govern.	Corporate	Total	Govern.	Corporate
Canada	1126.0	727.8	135.5	506.9	92.3	128
Brazil	1162.6	789.4	8.7	126.2	54.0	13.5
Mexico	428.3	214.4	32.3	95.1	41.8	20.3
Argentina	77.6	65.8	7.5	63.5	56.7	3.6

Source: BIS (2008)

Table B-2 Outstanding debt for other American debt markets

The Canadian debt market has started to attract more interest, particularly from U.S. investors. Though, trading levels are still relatively low compared to the U.S. Overall, the Investment Industry Association of Canada (IIAC) (2008) reported that $7 trillion was traded in 2007. The turnover ratio for government debt is around 6.8, versus over 30 for the U.S. The Canadian corporate debt market is also tiny compared to the U.S., with only around $250 billion in outstanding debt. In terms of electronic trading, a consolidated view of the market is provided by CanPX, which has merged quotes from inter-dealer brokers since 1999. In the dealer-to-client space, CanDeal and Bloomberg's Bondtrader were launched in 2002; both provide RFQ trading for institutional clients. There is also an alternative execution venue run by Collective Bid (CBID) Markets Inc. CBID offers an anonymous electronic order book for both dealers and clients, although it also provides an RFQ mechanism for less liquid bonds.

Brazil has a substantial debt market, most of which is for government debt, since its corporate market is relatively undeveloped. However, the trading volumes are relatively low; in 2005, the annual turnover for government bonds was $433 billion, based on a BIS (2006) report. In fact, based on the turnover ratio it appears to be even less liquid than the U.S. corporate debt market. It will be interesting to see how much impact the setup of MTS Brazil has, which is due to create a dedicated electronic platform for Brazilian sovereign debt.

Mexico is the next largest source of debt in Latin America, although it is around half the size of the Brazilian market. Government securities are quite heavily traded, the BIS (2006) report found that annual turnover was more than five times the outstanding notional value in 2005.

EMEA fixed income markets

The introduction of the Euro currency in 1999 helped create the second largest debt market in the world. The main Euro-zone countries are Austria, Belgium, Finland, France, Germany, Greece, Ireland, Italy, Netherlands, Portugal and Spain. Their combined outstanding domestic debt is worth over $14 trillion, based on figures from BIS (2008). Another $1.4 trillion comes from the U.K., together with $1.4 trillion for Denmark, Norway, Sweden and Switzerland combined.

Despite this sizeable debt, the trading volumes are much lower than the U.S. The average daily volume for the Euro-zone secondary government debt market is around $90 billion (€65 billion), according to BearingPoint (2007), as compared to around $500 billion for U.S. treasury. In part, this is due to the fact that the Euro-zone represents a diverse range of issuers, so the market is much more fragmented. Most of the trading, around 70%, is concentrated on German, French and Italian government debt. The largest of these is the German bond market with around €20 billion traded daily.

The inter-dealer market accounts for around half of the Euro-zone government bond trading volume. Of this, BearingPoint (2007) estimate that around 50% is handled by electronic platforms whilst the remainder is voice brokered. An earlier study by Peter Dunne, Michael Moore and Richard Portes (2006) puts this at closer to two thirds for electronic trading. The electronic trading marketplace is dominated by the MTS platform, which has around an 80% market share. The remainder is split mainly between Greece's HDAT (15%), Eurex Bonds (4%) and Spain's SENAF (1%), based on the BearingPoint (2007) survey.

Originally, the MTS (Mercato Telematico dei Titoli di Stato) was created in 1988 to improve the secondary market for Italian government bonds. Since the late '90s it has expanded across the Euro-zone with separate national markets. EuroMTS was launched in

1999 to cater for benchmark government bonds and other high quality debt from Euro-zone countries. MTS aggregates market maker's firm two-way prices and provides anonymous trading. By 2004, it had reached an average daily volume of around €25 billion, according to a report from the Bond Market Association (TBMA) (2005).

In terms of the other platforms, Greece's HDAT quote-driven trading system is based on the same technology as List Group's FastTrack-ATS. SENAF and Eurex Bonds both provide anonymous electronic order books. All of these systems predominantly cater for local debt, although Eurex Bonds has started to move beyond Germany to cover Euro-zone benchmark government and corporate debt as well. The UK Gilt market adopts a hybrid trading environment that incorporates anonymous quote-driven trading, although it is somewhat less liquid than the Euro-zone. Unlike in the U.S., ICAP's BrokerTec and BGC's eSpeed have found it harder to gain a sizeable market share in Europe. As Avinash Persaud (2006) explains, primary dealerships have often been awarded based on trading on local platforms, usually MTS, so there has been less incentive for dealers to use alternatives such as BrokerTec or eSpeed. That said, things have started to improve, for example, Austrian, Belgian and Dutch state treasury agencies have now formally recognised BGC's European Government Platform.

For the dealer-to-client marketplace, BearingPoint (2007) estimate that around 40% is handled electronically. They also report that Tradeweb is the market leader with 52% market share, followed by MTS's BondVision (25%) and Bloomberg's BondTrader (21%) multi-dealer system. Other systems, such as Reuters RTFI trading system only account for around 2%. These proportions have not changed significantly since the 2004 report from TBMA (2005) when Tradeweb had an average daily volume of €8 billion, compared to €3 billion for both BondVision and BondTrader. MarketAxess also offers its multi-dealer platform for European corporate debt. Again, all of these systems are generally based on request-for-quote trading mechanisms.

Europe is also starting to see some changes in the overall market structure. The MTS Group is considering providing access for hedge funds. Eurex Bonds has also been looking to incorporate a wider range of investment firms and hedge funds.

Asian fixed income markets

The financial crisis that spread throughout Asia in 1997-98 highlighted the need for a well-developed domestic bond market. Before this, banks and corporations had relied on foreign currency based funding, taking advantage of low overseas interest rates. When market perceptions changed in 1997, this loan market dried up and so intensified the crisis, as Atsushi Takeuchi (2005) points out. Some ten years later, the Asian bond market has now grown to nearly the same size as Europe, in terms of outstanding domestic debt. Japan still accounts for the majority (66%) of this, followed by China (14%), South Korea (7%) and Australia (5%), based on data from BIS (2008).

Japan has the largest outstanding government debt in the world, at around $7.8 trillion, based on H1 2008 data from BIS (2008). In comparison, its corporate debt is unusually low, at less than $0.7 trillion, or around 7% of the government debt. Average daily volumes are lower than in the U.S. Figures from Asian Bonds Online (2007) put the ADV for Japanese government bonds at around $150 billion, whilst corporate debt trades less than $2 billion.

Despite its size, the market for Japanese government debt, or JGBs, has been slow to embrace electronic trading. The inter-dealer market for JGBs is led by Japan Bond Trading; the brokerages ICAP Totan Securities and BGC Securities also have a considerable presence.

Some trading is also carried out on the Tokyo, Osaka, and Nagoya stock exchanges. Electronic trading is steadily increasing, based on Celent's (2006a) figures it should increase to nearly 60% by 2009 from around 35% in 2005. Japan Bond Trading has around a 60% market share, based on data from an article in the International Herald Tribune (IHT) (2006). It provides both a FIX interface as well as BB Super Trade, an order-driven platform initially created for trading short-term government bills (TB and FB), outlined in more detail by the Bank of Japan (BOJ) (2001) Market Review. It has also formed an alliance with Instinet. Electronic trading is also catered for by ICAP's ETC and BGC's eSpeed platforms. Though, MTS-Japan closed in 2003 after struggling to cope with an initially dormant market, which then became extremely volatile. Unlike in Europe the market makers did not have the benefit of being primary dealers, as noted by Tomohiko Taniguchi (2003), so the cost of providing liquidity in such a market was simply too high. For the dealer-to-client (D2C) market, trading is still generally handled by phone. The small electronic market, barely 2% in 2005, consists of multi-dealer platforms, such as Yensai.com, JBond and Bloomberg's Tradebook, and single broker systems. The Celent (2006a) consultancy estimates that electronic D2C trading may increase to nearly 13% by 2009.

China has the next largest government debt to Japan, with $0.9 trillion outstanding, based on data from the Asia development bank's Asia Bond Monitor (ABM) (2007). Government debt markets in Hong Kong and China have an average daily volume of over $4 billion each. Corporate debt in China accounts for nearly $0.5 trillion. This is a significant increase due to growing numbers of Chinese corporations being allowed to directly issue their own bonds. Average daily volumes for corporate debt are around $1.3 billion. Secondary trading for all types of bonds takes place mainly on the quote-driven inter-bank bond market and the order books of the Shanghai and Shenzhen stock exchanges. The MTS group have also signed a letter of intent with the China Foreign Exchange Trade System to cooperate with the development of an MTS-like market for government debt.

South Korea has less than $0.5 trillion each of outstanding government and corporate debt. The government debt market is more liquid with daily market volume of nearly $5 billion versus only $1 billion for corporate debt. Around 95% of the total bond trading in on the OTC market, again based on figures from Asian Bonds Online (2007a). The remainder is traded on the Korean Exchange's dedicated bond platform, which will also form the basis for Malaysia's new platform.

Summary

- Electronic trading is becoming more widespread for fixed income assets, particularly for the more liquid government bonds in the U.S. and Europe.

- The most scope for algorithmic trading is currently in the inter-dealer markets, which are often based on hybrid electronic order books. Though, it is also possible using the RFQ and RFS platforms commonly provided in the dealer-to-client markets.

- It will take some time before the adoption of electronic and algorithmic trading reaches that of equities, but the size of this market means it is a significant opportunity.

Appendix C
Foreign exchange markets

The foreign exchange (FX) market enables the transfer of money across different currencies. This ranges from spot transactions, which lock-in exchange rate for cash settlement, to forwards, and swaps that arrange transfers for months or even years in the future. This is a huge market, accounting for daily trading volumes of over $3 trillion. Historically, the FX markets have developed around inter-dealer networks (but not exchanges). Electronic trading has been common for some time in the FX marketplace; direct access trading via DMA and algorithms is also becoming more widespread.

Asset specific

Foreign exchange represents the trading of currencies, essentially by the transfer of ownership of deposits. Therefore, a U.S. dollar / Japanese yen trade consists of one counterparty selling U.S. dollars to another in exchange for a specific amount of yen. For this deal, the exchange rate might be 118.50, which means a single dollar buys 118.5 yen. [12] Generally, exchange rates are expressed in terms of dollars, it is said to be the base currency whilst the other currency is referred to as the quoting or counter currency. Note that British pounds and Australian dollars are an exception to this rule, these also act as base currencies and so the exchange rate is expressed in terms of them.

What we first think of as foreign exchange is spot trading. This corresponds to a cash trade at the current exchange rate, which will usually be settled within two days. FX forwards, or outrights, offer a means of locking-in an exchange rate that will then be used for an exchange at a specified date in the future. Rather than being straight cash transactions, forwards are based on binding contracts. The forward rate will try to reflect the expected future exchange rate, and so it incorporates the volatility of the two currencies. The availability of forwards allows both counterparties to hedge against shifts in the exchange rate; conversely, speculators will try to predict and benefit from them. An FX option is similar, although it gives the purchaser the right to buy or sell, rather than an obligation.

Foreign exchange swaps consist of two legs, a standard spot FX transaction linked with a simultaneous FX forward trade. Initially, the two currencies are exchanged, and when the outright matures, they are swapped back again, at the pre-agreed rate. A currency swap is slightly different since it represents an exchange of interest payments for underlying fixed income assets in two distinct currencies. At maturity, it may also involve exchanging the

---

[12] Note that in FX the tick (or smallest quote increment) is termed a pip, for $/yen a pip=0.01; however, for most other currency pairs a pip=0.0001.

notional amount of the underlying fixed income assets. This provides a means for foreign companies to borrow at the more favourable interest rates that are available to domestic companies. Both of these swaps are often used for much longer-term exchanges than FX forwards (years rather than months).

Pricing and trading

FX trading is largely concentrated on a small subset of currencies. In fact, around two thirds of all trading involves just four major currencies. The 2007 triennial survey by the Bank for International Settlements (BIS) (2007b) reports that 86.3% of all transactions involve the U.S. dollar, 37.0% the European euro, 16.5% the Japanese yen and 15.0% the British pound sterling (Bearing in mind that each trade involves two currencies, so the total sums to 200%). In terms of actual currency pairs, they reported that, for the overall turnover in April 2007, 27% was for the U.S. dollar / Euro, followed by 13% for U.S. dollar / Japanese yen and 12% for the U.S. dollar / British pound (known as cable). Emerging market currencies accounted for around 20% of trading.

Pricing foreign exchange rates can be quite difficult, since they are affected by a wide range of economic factors. Traditional exchange rate determination models based solely on macroeconomic factors have failed to explain and forecast fluctuations in exchange rates. This has been clearly noted in studies by Yin-Wong Cheung, Menzie Chinn, and Antonio Garcia-Pascual, (2005) and Richard Meese and Kenneth Rogoff (1983). An alternative method of pricing is to adopt a market microstructure-based approach. This has been pioneered by Martin Evans and Richard Lyons (2002), and Lyons (2001). In these models, macroeconomic information affects exchange rates directly, but also indirectly via order flow, or net buying pressure. Subsequent studies have shown that order flow can both explain and forecast changes in exchange rates. For more information, see the work by Dagfinn Rime, Lucio Sarno and Elvira Sojli (2008) and Evans and Lyons (2005).

Both exchange rates and order flows react to macroeconomic factors such as changes in economic growth, inflation, interest rates or budget/trade balances. Any such information, which might reflect future order flows, can have an important, and often immediate, effect on exchange rates. This can make the trading volumes quite volatile. Indeed, the spot market can vary by up to 30% day to day, as noted by Naureen Malik from the Wall Street Journal (WSJ) (2004). Whilst the actual news is publicly broadcast, global order flow is still relatively opaque. Clearly, the major banks have an advantage here since the more clients they have then the more order flow information they possess.

Another factor, which can have a considerable effect on foreign exchange, is the possibility of central bank interventions. Although these may be able to smooth short-term fluctuations, it is just no longer feasible to prop up a currency for any length of time. For instance, the infamous Black Wednesday (16th September 1992) when the U.K. finally announced it was withdrawing from the European exchange rate mechanism. This netted over a billion dollars profit for speculators, who had shorted up to $10 billion in pounds sterling in the previous two weeks, anticipating of the pound's fall from grace. Central bank intervention is also an interesting signal for investors, since it can indicate future changes in monetary policy.

Global FX markets

The FX market is enormous; the BIS (2007b) triennial survey reported a total average daily turnover of $3.2 trillion in 2007 for both spot and "traditional" FX derivative trading (forwards and FX swaps). This figure increases to around $3.5 trillion when currency swaps and FX options are included in the total. To put this in perspective, that is well over ten times the daily volume of all the world's stock exchanges. The rapid growth of the FX market is such that the 2007 turnover is nearly double the recorded volume for 2004, and nearly three times the figure for 2001. Estimates for 2009/10 predict this to grow to between $4-5 trillion. Table C-1 shows a breakdown of this volume by instrument type.

Foreign Exchange	Global average daily volume ($ billions)		U.K. average daily volume ($ billions)		
	Apr 2007	Apr 2004	Oct 2008	Apr 2007	Apr 2004
Spot	1,005	631	605	335	222
Outright forwards	362	209	210	124	103
Foreign exchange swaps	1,714	954	719	899	428
Currency swaps	32	21	18	18	16
FX options	212	117	108	106	64
Other	129	108	0	0	0
NYSE stocks	80	45			

Source: BIS (2007b), FX JSC (2007, 2008) and NYSE (2009)

Table C-1 Average daily FX trading volumes

The spot market alone now trades over a trillion dollars every day. FX swaps have higher daily volumes than even OTC interest rate derivatives, making them the world's most heavily traded asset. That said, the 2007-09 financial crisis has certainly had an effect on FX, volumes decreased in the latter part of 2008, but they have started to recover.

In terms of location, London is still the biggest centre of FX trading (34.1%) followed by the U.S. (16.6%), Switzerland (6.1%), Japan (6.0%) and Singapore (5.8%). London and Switzerland have seen the most gains in market share since 2004, based on figures from BIS (2007b).

The proportion of electronic trading within the FX marketplace is increasing rapidly. In fact, a report from the Aite Group (2007) consultancy notes that it increased from only 22% in 2001 to over 56% by the end of 2006. They predict that this could reach up to 75% by 2010. Likewise, the TABB Group (2007e) consultancy estimates electronic trading reached around 62% by the end of 2006, and should reach 80% by 2010. The adoption of electronic trading is highest in the inter-dealer market. Globally, the Aite Group (2007) found electronic trading levels of around 66% for the inter-dealer market. Data from the U.K. foreign exchange Joint Standing Committee (FX JSC) (2008) shows that 61% of inter-dealer volume was electronic in October 2008. In comparison, the proportion is still lower in the dealer-to-client marketplace. However, buy-side adoption of electronic trading is still increasing. For instance, the annual buy-side FX survey by Greenwich Associates (2007a) found that over 53% reported using e-trading systems for FX. The Aite Group (2007) found 45% electronic trading in the dealer-to-client marketplace. The FX JSC (2008) data shows that 20% of client volume was traded on single broker systems and another 7% on multi-broker platforms. [13]

---

[13] Although actual levels may be higher since some electronic trading volume may not have been reported as such.

Algorithmic trading is also starting to take hold in FX. Estimates for the total proportion of algorithmic trading are around 7%, with this predicted to rise to up to 15% by 2010, from an Aite Group (2008a) report. The Celent (2007b) consultancy estimates that on some venues algorithmic trading may already account for over 20% of the volume.

The FX marketplace is still segmented with strong inter-dealer networks and separate dealer-to-client markets. Though, inter-dealer trading is declining in importance as the proportion of client-driven trading increases, particularly from hedge funds. The BIS (2007b) survey shows 43% of FX trading was due to inter-dealer activity, down from 59% in 2001. In comparison, trading between dealers and financial institutions increased to 40%, whilst retail FX trading reached 17%.

Over the last few years, the FX marketplace has seen many new entrants. Table C-2 shows estimates of market share for the key participants in both the inter-dealer and dealer-to-client markets, based on data from the TABB Group (2007) consultancy:

2007 market share estimates	*Inter-dealer* *(Sell-side) %*	*Dealer-to-client* *(Buy-side) %*
Bank platforms	23	46
EBS/Reuters/Bloomberg	27	15
FXAll/State Street/Currenex/Hotspot	27	31
Lava	14	8
CME	9	0

Source: TABB Group (2007)

Table C-2 FX global market share

The inter-dealer market has been dominated by Reuters and EBS (the Electronic Brokers Service) for some time. Whilst this has provided competition, a segregation of the traded currency pairs has occurred. EBS leads for the Euro-Dollar, Dollar-Yen and a range of other Euro based crosses whilst Reuters leads for Sterling-Dollar and for the Euro-Sterling.

Reuters pioneered electronic trading for FX by introducing their monitor dealing service in 1981, based on a "conversational" approach. Effectively, this negotiation is much like the request-for-quote (RFQ) model. Then in 1992, they incorporated a matching service for FX spot orders into the Dealing 2000 platform, and so providing a hybrid order book based execution model. Subsequently, this has been extended to support both forwards and options. They have also introduced an interface designed to cater for algorithmic trading.

EBS was launched in 1993 by a consortium of banks, primarily to compete in the spot marketplace, although it has since been acquired by the inter-dealer broker ICAP. It also provides a hybrid order book marketplace that includes quotes from multiple dealers. EBS is now a major venue for spot FX, trading reached an average of $217 billion a day in 2008, based on figures from ICAP (2009). Their Spot-API provides an interface specifically catering for algorithmic trading.

In the dealer-to-client space, the large multi-national banks still prevail. Though, competition has meant that the dealer market has continued to consolidate. In fact, the 2008 Euromoney FX poll shows that the five most active banks accounted for just over 60% of the trading, as detailed in Euromoney (2008). These were Deutsche Bank (21.7%), UBS (15.8%), Barclays Capital (9.12%), Citi (7.49%) and RBS (7.3%). The banks offer clients a mix of phone-based trading, dedicated platforms or trading via white label offerings (as services that may then be repackaged by other companies). To compete, Reuters have introduced their Trading for FX platform, and EBS is now available via Bloomberg terminals.

The major banks also participate in the multi-broker dealer-to-client platforms such as FXAll and State Street's FX Connect and Currenex. Generally, these systems all either provide an RFQ market or stream prices direct to clients (RFS). Currenex adopts a hybrid mechanism that also supports limit orders, although there is no visible order book. In terms of trading volume, FXAll achieved average daily volumes of more than $60 billion in 2008, based on the companies own figures. Estimates from the Celent (2007b) consultancy give FX Connect and Currenex average daily trading volumes in the $40-50 billion range.

Many of the dealer-to-client platforms do not support anonymous trading, since the client identity is important for credit checking. However, anonymous trading is becoming available to clients, based on prime brokerage style arrangements to address the issue of credit risk. For example, FXAll have extended their streaming prices to support anonymity via their QuickFill mechanism. EBS has also created EBS Prime, which enables financial institutions to trade on their platform. In fact, in 2006 it accounted for over 14% of the average daily volume, according to the Celent (2007b) report.

ECNs have also become established for the FX marketplace, the first was Hotspot FXi. Based around visible, but anonymous, central limit order books these systems are targeting hedge funds, a rapidly growing portion of the marketplace. Hotspot was joined by Lava Trading's LavaFX in 2006, whilst Bloomberg offers Tradebook FX. Similarly, FXAll released its own ECN called Accelor in 2007. FXAll has also signed an agreement to purchase LavaFX, so the FX market is also starting to see some consolidation.

The natural progression of such order book based venues might be to create a dedicated exchange. Indeed, a joint venture between Reuters and the Chicago Mercantile Exchange resulted in the creation of FXMarketSpace in 2007. This was the first dedicated FX exchange, catering for both inter-dealer and institutional trading. It was based on a fully electronic order book providing straight-through processing, centralised clearing and settlement (much like the central counterparties for some stock exchanges) and credit checking. Initially, it focussed on spot FX in the six major currencies and six cross-currency pairs, with plans to extend the product to swaps and forward outrights. Unfortunately, the venture failed to meet its targets and so closed down in October 2008.

"Dark pool" ATS and crossing networks have also become available for FX. Instinet's FX Cross, a joint venture with Citigroup, was established in 2002, providing three anonymous crossing sessions a day in 17 currencies. Flextrade's MilanFX, announced in 2007, is the first continuous block trading venue for FX, providing fully hidden crossing for large orders.

Summary

- Electronic trading is now commonplace for foreign exchange.

- Levels of adoption of algorithmic trading are increasing.

- The increasing competition and the huge size of this market means it is a significant opportunity.

Appendix D
Money markets

The money markets are key to the provision of short-term financing for banks, institutions and corporations. Often this is for short periods of time, from overnight to around a month, although it can be for as much as a year.

In the following sub-sections, we will review the markets for unsecured short-term debt, repurchase agreements and stock lending. In Appendix E, we shall also touch on some of the key money market derivatives, such as overnight interest rate swaps. Note that a more detailed overview of the U.S. money markets is provided in Chapter 4 of the New York Fed's (1998) book 'U.S. Monetary Policy and Financial Markets'.

Short-term debt

Short-term debts encompass a variety of assets, from traditional fixed income contracts to tradable loans/deposits and commercial paper. There is a considerable market for such debt, although it is often handled as part of the fixed income or FX markets.

Asset specific

Generally, the lifetime for short-term debt is less than a year, and is often anything from overnight to a month. Hence, the risk of default is lower than their longer-term counterparts.

Government bonds provide a comparatively risk-free investment, particularly over the short-term. Usually, short-term issues are traded at a discount, rather than paying coupons. The best-known example is U.S. Treasury bills. Their European counterparts are Germany's Bubills, France's BTF bills, Italy's BOT bills and the Dutch DTC bills. Short-term government agency and municipal debt is also available, such as federal agency discount notes. Other than their shorter lifespan, none of these instruments is that different from the fixed income assets that we saw in Appendix B.

Inter-bank lending is an important source of short-term liquidity for banks, particularly overnight, for banks. Both U.S. federal funds and Eurodollars are sources of immediately available funds for banks, and through them large financial institutions. U.S. federal funds refer to depository accounts held with the Federal Reserve. Banks that have excess liquidity can loan it out to those that may need additional overnight cover. The rate at which these deals occur is based on the federal funds rate. Eurodollar deposits represent dollar accounts held in banks outside of the U.S. The London Interbank Offer Rates (LIBOR) are the rates at which highly rated banks may borrow Eurodollar deposits, from overnight to three or six months.

Deposits usually pay slightly higher interest than government bills, since there is more credit risk. Their rate is also obviously linked to the set term period. A time (or term) deposit represents money that may not be withdrawn from an account for a set amount of time. Negotiable deposits may be traded in the secondary markets, whilst non-negotiable ones are held to maturity. Large time deposits are classified in the U.S. as those with a value greater than $100,000. A certificate of deposit (CD) is just a type of time deposit, where all the details used to be printed on a certificate.

A banker's acceptance is a money draft to pay a set amount on a certain date. Once accepted by a bank they become liable for the amount, in turn they may then choose to trade it on the secondary markets.

Commercial paper (CP) provides an alternative to bank loans for corporations. Effectively, these are unsecured promissory notes, often issued at a discount. Due to the credit risk, these obviously pay higher rates than government bills. Still, these are often lower than the corporation could achieve funding via a bank; hence their appeal to both firms and investors. In the U.S., commercial paper generally has a maturity date of less than 270 days since this is the limit before registration with the SEC is required.

Unlike the previous instruments, asset-backed commercial paper (ABCP) represents a secured loan. Generally, these are issued against a special purpose vehicle (SPV) company, which was setup specifically to provide these secured loans.

Global short-term debt markets

The world's money markets are sizeable. For the U.S. alone, they account for around $5.5 trillion of outstanding notional value, as shown in Table D-1.

Type	*Outstanding amount Q3 2008 in $billions*
Treasury bills	1,484.3
Commercial paper	1,555.3
Large time deposits	2,413.3
Bankers acceptances	0.0

Source: SIFMA (2008b, 2008c) [14]

Table D-1 U.S. money market

Short-term government debt is an important and highly liquid segment of the money market. In the U.S., Treasury Bills are issued weekly for periods of 4, 13 and 26 weeks. Although off-the-run bills suffer a significant fall in trading volume, the weekly issuance ensures this is still a highly liquid market. For 2008, the U.S. primary dealers association reported average daily trading volumes of around $77 billion, according to the New York Fed (2009). The U.S. electronic inter-dealer market mainly consists of ICAP's BrokerTec and BGC's eSpeed platforms. In Europe, Germany's Bubills are important benchmarks for short-term government debt. There are inter-dealer markets for these on both MTS and Eurex Bonds. Other important European government bills are France's BTFs and Italy's BOTs, which are also tradable on Euro MTS. ICAP caters for trading of these key European benchmark bills as well.

Overnight unsecured lending for banks in the U.S. is provided by the Fed funds market.

---

[14] Based on data from the U.S. Treasury, Federal Reserve System

ICAP's i-Feds platform provides a multi-dealer venue where live prices are posted for the overnight Fed funds market. They estimate that over 40% of the total market is represented by the providers using i-Feds, with over a thousand registered lenders and over 130 active sellers. In Europe, e-MID has offered electronic trading for inter-bank deposits since 1990, starting with the Lira then moving on to cater for the Euro, U.K. sterling and U.S. dollar. In 2007, e-MID saw average daily volumes of over €30 billion, but the 2007-09 financial crisis led to a considerable decline in turnover for deposits, so by Q2 2008 this had fallen to around €15 billion, based on data from the ECB (2009) review. Across Europe, the ECB estimate that 17% of such unsecured trading is electronic.

Corporate short-term debt, in the form of commercial paper, was also significantly affected by fallout from the financial crisis. This hit the U.S. asset backed commercial paper (ABCP) segment particularly hard. In fact, from its high of nearly $1.2 trillion outstanding in 2007, U.S. ABCP has since fallen to $758 billion in H1 2008, based on figures from SIFMA (2008a). Unsecured commercial paper accounts for nearly another trillion dollars, with $817 billion from financial institutions and $165 billion from non-financial firms. The European market for ABCP has seen a similar decline to around €70 billion outstanding (from €175 billion) based on data from the ECB (2009) review. In terms of electronic trading, there is some but commercial paper is still predominantly traded OTC via the phone.

The dealer-to-client marketplace for money market assets is catered for by a range of offerings, including those from the major fixed income and foreign exchange markets as well as dedicated platforms.

For instance, Tradeweb not only caters for short-term government debt, but also provides trading for U.S. agency notes, CDs and both U.S. and European commercial paper. Bloomberg offers similar trading via its BondTrader and Money Markets platforms. These both offer firm dealer quotes as well as a request-for-quote (RFQ) mechanism. In Canada, CanDeal provides a multi-dealer to client RFQ platform for trading Canadian Treasury bills and money market assets. Whilst in Europe, MTS's BondVision provides trading for short-term government debt.

Many of the foreign exchange platforms have also expanded to incorporate money market trading. FXAll provides trading of cash loans and deposits via its multi-dealer quote-driven mechanism, which also allows electronic negotiation. Similarly, Currenex have extended their multi-dealer platform to enable trading of loans and deposits. Whilst the 360t platform not only caters for deposits but also allows trading of commercial paper and forward rate agreements (FRAs), which are effectively money market derivatives.

There are dedicated offerings as well, such as the SunGard Transaction Network (STN) Money Markets service. This helps connect institutional investors and corporate treasurers, allowing them to trade CDs and commercial paper directly with the issuers. Brokers have also extended their single dealer-to-client platforms to cater for the money markets. Noteworthy examples are Deutsche Bank's Autobahn and Barclays' BARX platforms, which support both request-for-streaming (RFS) prices and RFQ trading.

Repos

Repos reflect both the money markets and the bond markets. Their short terms place them in the category of money market assets, but since the underlying collateral is often a bond they are also affected by the same factors which influence bonds.

Asset specific

A repo is the common name for a sale and repurchase agreement, essentially this is a secured loan. The seller provides securities in return for cash, but they also commit to repurchase them back at a specified date for a set price together with an interest payment. The interest paid is based on a pre-negotiated repo rate, which will often be offset from a benchmark, such as the Fed funds rate. A reverse-repo transaction is simply the opposite of a repo. A sell/buy back is similar to a repo, although the sale and repurchase are simultaneous. This is because the repurchase is achieved with a forward transaction. The repo rate is implied in this forward price. A more detailed introduction to repos is provided by Moorad Choudhry (2006).

Specific repos are for a certain security. In the U.S., these are often termed special collateral repos or "specials". In comparison, general collateral (GC) repos allow the security to be fungible so any acceptable security that meets the set requirements may be used. The difference between the general collateral repo rate and the specials rate reflects the demand to borrow the specific security. Although repos have traditionally been used for bonds, the market for equity repos is steadily growing.

During the term of the repo, the legal title to the securities is transferred. Though, the repo seller remains exposed to the risk of owning them, since they have committed to repurchasing them at a set price. Therefore, if the market value of the collateral securities drops they will suffer a loss. In comparison, the repo buyer remains unaffected.

Repos have become extremely important for central banks as a means of implementing their monetary policies. They trade repos with the primary dealers to inject reserve balances into the banking system, whilst reverse-repos allow them to reduce the available balances. Thus, they enable them to control the overall liquidity. They also allow both dealers and investment firms to finance their positions at lower interest costs.

The standardisation of repos, using the International Capital Market Association's (ICMA) Global Master Repurchase Agreement, makes them well suited for electronic trading. Triparty repos are also becoming increasingly popular. These involve a third party clearing bank with which both parties must have cash and collateral accounts. Essentially, this acts like a central counterparty (CCP) allowing for anonymous trading, as opposed to the more bilateral delivery versus payment settlement.

Global repo markets

The global repo market accounts for a daily notional outstanding value over $16 trillion, most of which is split between the U.S. and Europe. Over $6.5 trillion of this involves U.S. government financing with the primary dealers, based on Q3 2008 figures from the Federal Reserve (2009). The European repo market accounts for around another $8.1 trillion, or €6.4 trillion, based on a market review by Celent (2007). The European market has more than trebled in size since 2001, although in the last few years its size has stabilised. In Asia, repo levels are lower; for instance, Japan's market is worth around $1 trillion, according to a report from the Nomura Research Institute (NRI) (2007).

Adoption of electronic trading is growing. In Europe, the ECB (2009) survey found that 48% of trading was carried out electronically. A similar value was reported in the Celent (2007) analysis. The Bearing Point (2007a) consultancy predicts that by 2012 over 75% of trades should be electronic, accounting for a third of the total volume. Automation is also starting to be applied to OTC repo trading via trade matching and confirmation systems, such as ETCMS and Trax II.

The wholesale inter-dealer repo market in the U.S. focuses on overnight repos. ICAP supports trading over their electronic BrokerTec platform, as well as via voice. They allow trading for any institutions that are netting members of the Fixed Income Clearing Corporation (FICC). BrokerTec automates the process for general collateral deals, allowing traders to easily change the assigned security. In 2008, they achieved average daily volumes of around $195 billion, based on data from ICAP (2009). Tullett Prebon's TradeBlade, also offers anonymous matching for bids and offers from any netting member of FICC. BGC's eSpeed platform is available for repos as well, for the 18 U.S. primary dealers who trade with the Federal Reserve BNY. Longer-term repos tend to be handled more by voice brokers.

The European inter-dealer market is also led by ICAP followed by Eurex Repo and MTS. ICAP Europe trades repos for European government securities, UK Gilts, Euro Supra National Agencies and Sovereigns, as well as covered bonds, corporate bonds and U.S. treasuries. In terms of volume, ICAP (2009) reported average daily figures of $259 billion for European repos in 2008. Eurex Repos caters for repos on European and German government securities as well as other bonds. It has also introduced GC Pooling, allowing a much wider range of European Central Bank (ECB)-eligible collateral. MTS's Money Market Facility is a dedicated MTS segment for repos and buy/sell backs, which was established in 1997. MTS focuses on repos for European government securities, Italian bonds and German covered bonds. There is also an important local market for repos on Spanish bonds traded via SENAF. Note that a further complication for European repo trading is the multitude of clearing and settlement venues, whereas the U.S. has a central clearing counterparty.

In Japan, repo trading has been mainly voice based. Though, Japan Bond Trading Co. has announced that it will introduce an electronic marketplace for repos.

In the dealer-to-client markets, voice trading is still the norm, although there are some electronic alternatives. Tradeweb provides an electronic trading platform for triparty repo with average daily volumes in excess of $175 billion, based on their own figures (Tradeweb (2008)). Bloomberg has a repo offering as well; there are also single broker solutions, such as Morgan Stanley's RepoLink. The European dealer-to-client market is much smaller.

Securities lending

Securities (or stock) lending is like a repo without the loan; the securities are simply lent for a fee. Over the last few years, the securities lending business has seen a considerable level of growth as hedge funds have increasingly needed to borrow securities to support their short positions. However, the 2007-09 financial crisis had a considerable effect, particularly with governments introducing regulations to restrict short selling for certain sectors.

As with repos, the type of lending may be classified into general and specific. General lending is equivalent to a repo with general collateral so the security just needs to match a set of criteria. Again, the fees for lending depend on the scarcity of the security, so general lending costs significantly less.

Global securities lending markets

The global securities lending market is sizable and steadily growing. A report by the Celent (2007a) consultancy notes that around $3.6 trillion worth of assets are involved in lending, from an available total of about $16 trillion. The U.S. accounts for around $2.7 trillion, whilst Europe is around $900 billion. By 2009, Celent estimate that the U.S. market may reach $2.9 trillion, and Europe $1 trillion.

At present, securities lending is still very much a relationship driven marketplace, with most of the trading being phone based. However, Celent (2007a) note that 10-15% of deals were traded over electronic platforms. They expect this to increase to around 20% in 2009.

The earliest electronic trading platforms for lending offered either bilateral order routing or auction-based trading mechanisms. As its name suggests, SunGard's Loanet Centralized Order Routing system provides a network dedicated to handling equity lending. It was launched in 1999 and by 2006 was processing over 100,000 borrow requests a day. Indeed, SunGard (2006) reported handling 22 million requests in 2005, worth $6 trillion. Another notable platform is EquiLend; launched in 2002 by a consortium of ten large financial institutions it offers several types of trading services. Their AutoBorrow mechanism allows borrowers to review the available securities. Borrowers may direct orders to their lending counterparty, any successful executions are then returned to proprietary settlement systems. This bilateral mechanism also supports electronic negotiation through a service called Trade$_2$O, which allows lenders and borrowers to upload specific positions or whole portfolios. It is targeted at the non-GC market in global equity and fixed income securities. EquiLend also allows lenders to run their own open or blind auctions via AuctionPort, to which the lender may invite specific bidders. In 2007, annual transaction volumes reached $2.9 trillion for equity lending and $277 billion for fixed income securities, based on data from EquiLend (2008). As of October 2008, they were executing up to 20,000 trades a day. Other noteworthy platforms offering a purely auction driven approach are eSecLending and BNY Mellon's I-Bid.

Centralised order-driven markets are also starting to appear for securities lending, notably SecFinex, Eurex's SecLend and ICAP's I-Sec. SecFinex was established in 2000, and now is part of NYSE Euronext. It caters for lending in U.S., European and Japanese equities; providing an order driven market that supports pre-trade anonymity and credit checking, whilst a separate service allows entire portfolios to be auctioned. SecFinex also offers a private market, based on a bilateral trading mechanism that supports negotiation. The private market provides a search mechanism allowing borrowers to check for the availability of a particular stock across their entire lender base. They were also the first system to make available executed trade information, helping to improve the post-trade transparency for this market. Eurex's SecLend has been around since 2005, enabling electronic lending for fixed income or equities. Around $150 billion worth of assets are available for lending in SecLend. In 2007, ICAP's I-Sec was launched, based on their BrokerTec platform. It supports an anonymous order driven market for equity lending in similar markets to SecFinex, also providing an anonymous bilateral negotiation mechanism.

Summary

- Electronic trading is increasingly available for the money markets, often based on platforms also used for fixed income or foreign exchange.

- Short-term debt seems the most likely candidate for algorithmic trading, although cross-asset trading strategies may well start to incorporate repos and securities lending as well.

Appendix E
Derivatives markets

The derivatives markets are by far the largest financial markets in the world. Figures for H1 2008, from BIS (2008), show that the total notional amount outstanding reached $766 trillion, up 25% from 2007. A breakdown of these notional amounts is given in Table E-1.

Derivative type		*Notional $billions*		*%*
		Jun-08	*Jun-07*	*change*
Equity	Forwards and swaps	2,657	2,470	8
	Options	7,520	6,119	23
	ET index futures	1,584	1,315	20
	ET index options	7,088	8,897	-20
Interest rate	FRAs	39,370	22,809	73
	Swaps	356,772	272,216	31
	Options	62,162	52,288	19
	ET futures	26,874	30,165	-11
	ET options	46,905	55,986	-16
FX	Outright fwds/forex swaps	31,966	24,530	30
	Currency swaps	16,307	12,312	32
	Options	14,710	11,804	25
	ET ccy futures/options	367	303	21
Commodity-based [15]		13,229	7,567	75
Credit default swaps		57,325	42,580	35
Other		81,708	61,713	32

Source: BIS (2008, 2007a)

Table E-1 Outstanding notional amounts for derivative contracts

Note that forwards and forward rate agreements (FRAs) are effectively the OTC equivalent of exchange traded (ET) futures.

Unfortunately, the BIS figures do not incorporate notional amounts for exchange traded (ET) single stock or commodity derivatives. Despite these omissions, the majority of the outstanding notional is clearly for interest rate swaps, which are still generally traded OTC. In fact, around $684 trillion of the outstanding notional is for derivatives traded OTC, 53% of which is just for interest rate swaps (IRSs).

---

[15] The figures for commodity-based derivatives do not include exchange traded contracts.

Most OTC derivatives are still traded manually. Therefore, in the following sub-sections we will primarily focus on the exchange traded futures and options. We shall also cover swaps and CDSs since there are now electronic platforms that cater for these as well.

Futures and options markets

The futures and options markets primarily represent the exchange-traded segment of the derivatives marketplace. As we saw in back in Table E-1, their outstanding notional value is easily overshadowed by OTC derivatives. Though, in terms of trading volume, the positions are reversed. For instance, in 2007 over $6 trillion worth of interest rate futures and options contracts were traded daily on the world's exchanges, compared to just over $4 trillion traded OTC, based on data from the 2007 triennial survey by the Bank for International Settlements BIS (2007b).

	Futures		*Options*	
Underlying asset	*Number of contracts (millions)*	*% of total*	*Number of contracts (millions)*	*% of total*
Equity index	2,286.0	29.4	4,077.1	44.0
Single stock	1,058.9	13.6	4,367.9	47.2
Interest rate	2,565.1	33.0	609.6	6.6
Currency	331.7	4.3	49.9	0.5
Commodities	1,541.9	19.8	153.7	1.7
Total	7,783.5	100.0	9,258.2	100.0

Source: Based on data from WFE (2009)

Table E-2 Global exchange traded futures and options market for 2008

Futures and options may be based on a wide range of underlying assets. As Table E-2 shows, there is a marked difference in trading volumes between futures and options. (Note the market volumes for futures and options are commonly compared in terms of numbers of contracts rather than their corresponding value.) Clearly, trading in futures is led by interest rate products, much like their OTC counterparts. In comparison, trading for options contracts seem to be much more concentrated on equities. Though, the high value of interest rate contracts means that these still account for over 80% of the total market turnover for both futures and options, despite their lower levels of volume, based on BIS (2007b) data.

Asset specific

Futures and options represent agreements to buy or sell a set quantity of a certain asset, whether this is a stock, a bond or even a commodity such as oil. Where they differ is that a futures contract is binding, whilst an option contract gives the owner the right, but not the obligation to trade.

Futures

A forward contract is an agreement to buy (or sell) a fixed quantity of a given asset at a certain price on a specific date in the future, e.g. a contract to buy 5,000 bushels of grain in July for $3. When the maturity date is reached, the contract expires and the transaction must then be settled. A futures contract is simply a forward with standardised terms (e.g. amounts, prices, dates) which is traded on an exchange. The standardisation makes futures more readily tradable than forwards. Historically, these contracts were focussed on commodities, since they allow both producers and consumers to hedge their risks. Much of the market liquidity is actually provided by intermediaries and/or speculators. Without them, producers and consumers would still struggle to find sufficient market liquidity, although too much speculation makes the markets volatile.

Having bought (or sold) a contract we have locked in a set price. Futures contracts are not generally held to expiry, but are instead traded out of. For example, we may have taken up a futures position just to capitalise on our view of where the market price should move to. If this still has not been reached just prior to the contract's expiry we can roll our position over to the next contract. This is achieved by selling (buying) our current position and buying (selling) the next maturing contract. So we might sell our July contract and buy an equivalent September future. Effectively, this has given us a synthetic position in the underlying asset. At expiry, if we are still holding a contract and the market price is higher then we have made money; however, if the price has fallen then we have lost the difference.

Futures contracts may be physically settled. This means that at expiry a buyer must pay the notional amount to the exchange in return for the underlying asset, whilst a seller must deliver the asset to the exchange. Alternatively, cash settlement was introduced in the early 1980s. This allowed futures to expand beyond commodities and incorporate a diverse range of financial assets, since settlement is based on a cash amount determined from the settlement price.

Pricing and trading

The price of a futures contract reflects the expected future value of its underlying asset, discounted to give a present value. Some other factors also need to be considered, such as any additional costs (for storage etc.) or incomes (e.g. dividends). A more detailed review of pricing futures contracts is given by Robert Kolb and James Overdahl (2006).

Clearly, the price of a futures contract is affected by the underlying asset, as well as the market's expectations of how that price will change over time. Hence, the factors that affect it are asset dependent. Single stock futures will be affected by stock specific or sector related news. Interest rate or currency futures will react to economic news and events. Agricultural futures will be affected by forecasts for crop yields and weather predictions.

In terms of risk, these contracts could have considerable exposure, since they represent trades that will take place in the future (e.g. 3, 6 or 12 months). Futures contracts remove counterparty risk since the exchange acts as a central counterparty, so the trade is effectively split into separate trades between each counterparty and the exchange. The other risks are reduced by ensuring that an initial margin is deposited with the exchange as collateral. This is then adjusted daily by marking-to-market the contract, so any resultant profits (or losses) are settled each day.

Options

Option contracts are similar to forwards and futures in that they allow a price to be struck to trade a set quantity of a given asset at a specific future date. The settlement price is called the strike price of the option. The premium represents the actual price paid for the option. An option contract to buy is called a call, whilst a contract to sell is a put.

The main difference with forwards and futures is that the owner of an option is not obliged to trade. If the market price is more favourable they may choose not to exercise their option contract (hence its name). Though, the creator (writer) of the option contract is obliged to trade, should the purchaser wish to do so.

Options may also be classified as European or American style. This refers to when they can actually be exercised. American style options may be exercised at any time prior to the expiry date, whereas European style options may only be exercised at maturity. This flexibility means American style options usually trade at a premium to corresponding European ones.

Pricing and trading

Options may be traded OTC or on exchanges. Like futures, exchange traded options are standardised contracts. Whilst there is generally a single future for a given maturity date, there are a wide range of options, both calls and puts for an array of strike prices. For instance, major corporations may have hundreds of exchange tradable options (if not more). Clearly, such diversity affects the available liquidity, so options tend to be less liquid than futures.

One of the main differences with options is the ability to buy and sell call and put options. For futures contracts, and their underlying cash assets, things are much simpler; we are either a natural buyer or a seller at a given price. In comparison, with options we are trading rights. The risk characteristics of these are very different: buying a put or call gives us the right to execute at the strike price, so the most we can lose is the option premium. However, writing an option obliges us to trade at the strike price if the owner wishes to exercise the contract, so our losses could potentially be infinite. Therefore, whilst there may be plenty of investors who want to buy calls or puts, much fewer may be prepared to sell them. Thus, specialised broker/dealers often play a vital role as liquidity providers and market makers.

Though pricing options can be quite complex, there are many standard models out there, such as the ubiquitous Black Scholes equation created by Fisher Black and Merton Scholes (1973). These can compute the fair value of an option based on factors such as the contract's strike price, the underlying asset's market price and its volatility, the time left to expiry and the risk-free interest rate. Other factors that may need to be considered are whether it is a European or an American option, also asset-specific factors such as dividend payments. What this means is that there are a lot more factors exerting pressure on the option price than just the market price of its underlying asset. Thus noticeable price shifts may occur even when there does not appear to be important new information, or changes in the levels of liquidity, supply and demand.

World futures and options markets

Exchanges are still the focal point of trading for listed futures and options contracts. They provide the main inter-dealer marketplace, since membership is usually held by brokers. Client access is still reasonably segregated with brokers acting as agents for investor's orders, or dealers negotiating principal trades. Still, the increasing adoption of electronic trading has meant that clients may now access markets more directly via DMA and even algorithmic trading.

Listed derivatives may be standardised products, but they are still not as readily transferable (or fungible) as cash or equities. A futures contract or option bought from one exchange will generally not be tradable elsewhere. Consequently, the exchanges that were first to market have had the most advantage. Thus, liquidity tends to concentrate around the major exchanges. Table E-3 shows the worlds top ten exchanges in terms of traded contracts, based on data from the WFE (2009).

Exchange	Number of contracts traded in 2008 (millions)		
	Total	Futures	Options
CME Group	3,277.2	2,776.7	500.5
Korea Exchange	2,867.3	100.8	2,766.5
Eurex	2,164.8	1,231.4	933.4
Chicago Board Options Exchange	1,167.3	0.0	1,167.3
Liffe	1,049.7	610.0	439.7
International Securities Exchange	1,007.7	0.0	1,007.7
BM&FBOVESPA	681.9	278.1	403.8
National Stock Exchange India	601.6	439.6	162.0
NASDAQ OMX PHLX	543.3	0.0	543.3
Johannesburg Securities Exchange	478.1	446.2	31.8

Source: Based on data from WFE (2009)

Table E-3 Global exchange traded futures and options

Competition in the marketplace has become increasingly global as exchanges try to launch equivalent products. A combination of technological innovation and reduced costs has allowed exchanges to grab market share, proven by the success of Eurex and the International Securities Exchange (ISE). This has also helped transform the marketplace, shifting from floor-based open-outcry auctions to side-by-side and fully electronic trading. In fact, most of the world's listed futures and options are now either traded electronically, or side-by-side with open-outcry.

Computerisation has also helped turn this into virtually a 24-hour marketplace. For instance, CME's Globex platform allows trading up to 23 hours each day, five days a week, starting in Asia-Pacific and following the morning through to Europe and the U.S.

American futures and options markets

The Americas are clearly still a major force in the listed derivatives marketplace. Half of the top ten exchanges shown in Table E-3 come from this region. Based on data from the Futures Industry Association (FIA) (2008) around 40% of both the exchange traded futures and options volume was for North American based assets.

U.S. futures and options markets

The U.S. is clearly one of the main markets for exchange-listed derivatives. In fact, it dominated the global futures and options marketplace until the late '90s, when competition arrived from venues such as Eurex and Liffe. Table E-4 shows the breakdown of the 2008 figures for futures and options trading on the major U.S. exchanges.

The last few years have seen a considerable shift with the major U.S. exchanges increasingly moving from floor-based to electronic trading. Nowadays, at least 75-85% of the most liquid contracts are traded electronically. Many brokers/vendors provide DMA access to the major exchanges. Some brokers have even started expanding their algorithmic trading offerings to incorporate futures and options trading. Though, the adoption of these low-touch strategies still lags behind the equities market. A review of equity derivative trading by the TABB Group (2007d) consultancy estimates that around 47% of futures traders used DMA whilst 53% still used the phone. They also found that only 27% of options traders adopted DMA, with the remainder again using the phone. By 2009, they predict that DMA uptake may have risen to 58% and 40% respectively for futures and options trading. Overall, they noted that 68% of buy-side derivatives orders were handled by high-touch trading with only 32% adopting low-touch strategies. Again, by 2009 they expect the adoption of low-touch strategies, such as DMA and algorithmic trading, to increase to 40%. Interestingly, they also found that smaller firms seemed to be adopting these new techniques more rapidly than larger ones.

Exchange	Number of contracts traded in 2008 (millions)		
	Total	Futures	Options
CME Group	3,277.2	2,776.7	500.5
Chicago Board Options Exchange	1,167.3	0.0	1,167.3
International Securities Exchange	1,007.7	0.0	1,007.7
NASDAQ OMX PHLX	543.3	0.0	543.3
NYSE Arca Options	416.9	0.0	416.9
NYSE Amex	207.3	0.0	207.3
Boston Options Exchange	177.6	0.0	177.6
ICE Futures U.S.	81.0	63.4	17.5

Source: WFE (2009)

Table E-4 U.S. exchange traded futures and options

The U.S.'s two largest derivatives exchanges, namely the Chicago Mercantile Exchange (CME) and Chicago Board of Trade (CBOT) merged in 2007. Whilst this has created a huge local monopoly, it is more understandable from a global point of view, since the combined entity has a similar daily volume to Eurex, which has merged with the International Securities Exchange (ISE).

The Chicago Mercantile Exchange (CME) originated from the Chicago Butter and Egg Board; however, it has since moved away from agricultural contracts and is now one of the world's leading financial exchanges. This shift may be traced back to 1972 when it created the world's first financial futures. These were currency futures for British pounds, Canadian dollars, Deutsche marks, French francs, Japanese yen, Mexican pesos and Swiss francs. Nowadays, currency trading only accounts for around 10% of CME's volume. The majority of its trading is from interest rate products. The most important of which is the Eurodollar, a short-term debt contract that it introduced back in 1981. The Eurodollar was the world's first cash settled future; it is now the most traded futures contract and a key benchmark for U.S. short-term debt. Together with Eurodollar options, they account for around half of the volume traded on the CME. Equity index contracts account for another third of the CME's volume. The Standard & Poor's (S&P) 500 index future was first introduced in 1982, whilst the NASDAQ-100 contract was created in 1996. Though, CME index trading volumes are now dominated by their E-mini counterparts. E-mini futures were first introduced in 1997; they are a fifth of the size and traded electronically. They have proven to be extremely popular, particularly with portfolio hedgers and retail investors. The most important of which is the E-mini S&P 500 index future, the 2nd most traded listed derivative in the world, based on the 2008 review by the FIA (2009). Other indices such as the NASDAQ, Russell 1000 and 2000 and the S&P MidCap 400 are also catered for. Globally, the CME continues to face stiff competition, which has helped spur the migration of volume from the floor to Globex, its trading system. Globex provides an electronic order book, as well as supporting lead market makers. This second-generation system was introduced in 2002, based around the NSC trading engine. In fact, the majority of trading is now carried out on Globex.

The Chicago Board of Trade (CBOT) has also become predominantly a financial exchange. Although nearly a fifth of its daily volume is still attributable to agricultural, metal and energy based contracts. The most important contracts are based on long-term interest rate futures; namely the 10 year Treasury Note, followed by the 5 year note and 30 year bond futures. The CBOT has faced competition from the bond market, where lower spreads made it cheaper to trade treasuries, whilst in 2004 Eurex also started listing Treasury note and bond futures. In response, it has shifted more trading away from open-outcry auction to be electronic. Originally, its electronic order book was based on Liffe's Connect platform; however, this has now been completely migrated to Globex in line with its merger with the CME. Electronic trading now accounts for the majority of trading. Settlement is straightforward since CBOT already used the CME to clear its trades.

The New York Mercantile Exchange (NYMEX) is another venue that has had to rapidly embrace electronic trading in the face of new global competition, in particular from the IntercontinentalExchange (ICE). Primarily, NYMEX is an exchange for energy-based derivatives although it also handles contracts for metals. Its electronic trading platform is provided by the CME's Globex, which has helped it realise a sizeable increase in trading volumes. In 2008, it became part of the CME Group.

The remaining exchanges shown in Table E-4 are mainly involved in the trading of U.S. equity options, which we will review more fully in the next sub-section.

There are also some other U.S. exchanges which cater for derivatives trading, such as OneChicago and the U.S. Futures Exchange. OneChicago is a joint venture between the CME Group, CBOE, and the IB Exchange Corp. It provides a fully electronic exchange, primarily for single stock futures but also futures on ETFs. Lead Market Makers ensure liquidity and the platform is based on the CBOEdirect match engine, although it also caters for Globex users. The U.S. Futures Exchange (USFE), formerly Eurex U.S., is another Chicago-based electronic futures exchange. It offers futures on a variety of fixed income, equity and commodity based funds/indices, as well as new derivative products. For example, it offered a binary event future based on the outcome of a CME-CBOT merger.

Further local competition is also arriving. NYSE Liffe U.S. was launched in 2008, based on the precious metals business it bought from the CME Group. It will also have transatlantic links to Europe's Liffe exchange. The NASDAQ OMX Futures Exchange (NFX), formerly the Philadelphia Boards of Trade (PBOT), offers trading of futures for interest rates swaps, currency and sector indices. Also the Electronic Liquidity Exchange (ELX) was launched in 2009, backed by a consortium of major brokers, institutions and technology firms. Its electronic exchange is based on the eSpeed platform. Initially, it is targeting trading for treasury futures, although it also plans to cover other key assets in the future.

ATSs are starting to appear for derivatives as well. LiquidityPort has announced plans to offer an electronic block-trading platform for both futures and options contracts.

U.S equity options market

The U.S. equity option marketplace has seen some of the highest levels of growth of any of the world's listed derivatives markets. Having noted that most futures and options are not fungible, this marketplace is an interesting exception since a common clearing mechanism ensures that the options are readily transferable. Therefore, U.S. stock options may be traded on any one of seven exchanges, making this the most competitive listed option marketplace in the world. Figure E-1 highlights the difference in growth between the U.S. equity option marketplace and the rest of the world.

Source: BIS (2008)

Figure E-1 Global Exchange Traded Equity Option growth

Figure E-1 also shows the disparity in growth between option trading for equities and indices. Admittedly, this is not all attributable to market competition, but also due to changing investment and hedging styles. Nevertheless, it does help emphasise just how important competition can be.

There has been a phenomenal growth in the trading of U.S. equity options. This the largest market of its kind in the world, accounting for nearly two thirds of the globally traded volume. As a marketplace, it has become a microcosm of its cousin, the stock market. Trading is now dispersed amongst seven main venues. Table E-5 shows a breakdown of their trading volumes. Unlike many other markets there now a split in how venues actually match orders, with the newer venues such as NYSE Arca, Boston and NASDAQ all offering a price/time based order book, rather than the pro-rata matching traditionally offered by the other derivatives exchanges.

Much of the current market structure is due to changes in regulation. This dates back to 1999 when the Justice Department and the SEC won settlements agreeing that competition had been blocked by selective trading practices. Suddenly, by the end of the year stock options were no longer concentrated at specific venues, but instead could be traded at any of the options exchanges. The resultant competition helped reduce spreads and led to a significant increase in overall trading volumes. Decimalisation has also helped, so in 2007 the SEC instigated a pilot program to further reduce the tick size from $0.05 to $0.01. Early indications are that this "penny pilot" program is working. However, it also appears to have encouraged even lower trade sizes and higher overall volumes, mimicking the effect seen in the equities market. New portfolio margining regulations that allow positions to be netted may well cause a further increase in volumes, since they help lower the cost of entry.

Algorithmic trading is starting to take hold as well. A report by the TABB Group (2009) consultancy found that 23% of the hedge funds and 9% of the long-only funds they surveyed were already using trading algorithms.

The International Securities Exchange (ISE) has rapidly become the leading exchange for U.S. equity options, since its creation in 2000, with repeated year on year growth of over 30%. Its trading system is based on NASDAQ OMX's CLICK platform. Trading is via a hybrid mechanism, based on a fully electronic order book with both primary and secondary

Exchange	Order Matching	# of contracts traded (in millions)	
		2008	2007
International Securities Exchange	Pro-rata	988.1	787.9
Chicago Board Options Exchange	Pro-rata	933.8	713.9
NASDAQ OMX PHLX	Pro-rata	537.9	399.1
NYSE Arca	Price/Time	416.9	335.8
NYSE Amex	Pro-rata	199.8	226.5
Boston Options Exchange	Price/Time	177.6	129.7
NASDAQ Options Market	Price/Time	n/a	n/a

Source: WFE (2009)

Table E-5 U.S. Equity Option Marketplace

market makers. The ISE also allows order preferencing (for specific market makers) as well as directed orders, which initiate a price improvement mechanism (effectively a one-second bilateral auction). Block crossing is catered for as well; a separate mechanism advertises the order to members who may then respond with the prices and sizes at which they are willing to trade. It has led the way in terms of transparency, ensuring that the top three price levels of the order book are visible. The ISE has also announced plans to develop a new global trading system that will replace its current system in early 2011. The new system is a joint development project between the technology teams at the ISE and the Deutsche Börse Group.

The Chicago Board Options Exchange (CBOE) was the world's first equity options exchange, founded in 1973. In response to the increasingly competitive marketplace, it has created a hybrid trading system. This blends its floor-based technology with CBOE Direct, its dedicated electronic trading platform. Designated primary market makers are responsible for overseeing the market for each stock's options. Additional liquidity is provided by "in-crowd" and remote market makers.

The NASDAQ OMX PHLX (formerly the Philadelphia Stock Exchange) provides another hybrid electronic market. This was formerly based on the PHLX XL system, but has since been migrated to the INET platform. There are still specialists, and other market makers may participate as well. Order flow may also be directed to specific dealers. NASDAQ OMX has another separate venue, the NASDAQ Options Market, which went live in 2008. This is based on INET as well, but it adopts a price/time priority.

NYSE Arca's involvement with options dates back to the Pacific Exchange, which merged with Archipelago to form Arca, before merging with the NYSE. This electronic market uses Lead Market Makers to provide liquidity, particularly for the more thinly traded options, in return they are guaranteed 40% of the incoming order flow (so long as they are quoting at the NBBO). The NYSE has also bolstered its offering by incorporating the Amex (formerly the American Stock Exchange), which has moved its trading floor to the NYSE and has migrated to the Arca platform.

Between the options exchanges there is an inter-market linkage program, which aims to ensure that market orders execute with the NBBO. This is due to be replaced with a decentralised order routing approach, similar to the U.S. equity markets. Liquidity aggregation is also starting to be offered by some vendors. For example, Orc Software has launched a U.S. Options Montage, which consolidates quotes across all the exchanges and allows smart order routing to achieve best execution.

Current regulation means that ECNs/ATSs are not yet possible since trades must be handled by an exchange, as pointed out in an article by Emily Fraser (2007). However, new platforms to allow block crossing are still being created For instance, 2008 saw the launch of Ballista. This provides a hybrid approach, combining auctions with electronic negotiations. Each order is placed in an electronic auction, which is open to other members for up to five minutes; the user can also specify how much information the order reveals (size or direction). A successful counter bid from another member then triggers an exclusive negotiation between the two. Ballista also allows members to place orders for complex strategies, comprising of up to three option legs and/or their underlying stock. Meanwhile Pipeline's Archangel takes a different approach. It adopts a blind auction, similar to those used for portfolio trading. Therefore, participants only have access to the key characteristics of the available orders. So decisions are based on risk factors such as the "Greeks" (delta, gamma, theta etc), order size indications and other static information such as the industry sector. Once a match is agreed, the orders are then routed to the corresponding venues, such as the CBOE or ISE. In addition to protecting the details of orders, this model-driven approach should also improve the number of matches. Given the size of the option universe, finding an exact match for a specific contract would otherwise be difficult. If (or once) the trading regulations change we may well see other entrants look to expand into the block crossing space.

Other American Futures and Options Markets

Though dwarfed by their U.S. counterparts Latin America still has some of the world's largest derivatives exchanges, as shown in Table E-6.

Exchange	Number of contracts traded in 2008 (millions)		
	Total	Futures	Options
BM&FBOVESPA	681.9	278.1	403.8
Mexican Derivatives Exchange	70.1	69.5	0.6
Montreal Exchange	38.1	22.0	16.0
Buenos Aires SE	25.2	0.0	25.2

Source: WFE (2009)

Table E-6 Other American futures and options exchanges

Brazil has the region's two largest exchanges. The São Paulo Stock Exchange (BOVESPA) caters for equity options, whilst the Bolsa de Mercadorias & Futuros (BM&F) covers fixed income, currency and commodity based contracts. These merged in 2008 to become BM&FBOVESPA. Their main contract is a one-day inter-bank deposit future; in fact, in 2007 this was the 9th most traded listed derivative, according to the FIA (2008). Their trading systems are based on the order-driven NSC platform. Although there is still some open-outcry trading, much of the volume has become electronic. They have been keen to encourage DMA access as well. In 2009, they established a link to route orders to the CME; this is also used to allow CME users to trade BM&F contracts.

The Mexican Derivatives Exchange was founded in 1998. Its most successful contract is a future based on a short-term interest rate, the TIIE 28 day inter-bank rate, which was the 11th most actively traded derivative in 2007, based on the FIA (2008) report. It also offers a range of other fixed income, equity and FX contracts. The exchange provides a fully automated and anonymous marketplace, as well as supporting FIX.

EMEA futures and options markets

Over the last ten years, the major European derivative exchanges have consolidated their position as leading venues in the global marketplace. Certainly, the merger between the CME and CBOT owes much to their competition. Table E-7 outlines the breakdown in terms of traded contracts in 2008 for the region's top exchanges.

Exchange	Number of contracts traded in 2008 (millions)		
	Total	Futures	Options
Eurex	2,164.8	1,231.4	933.4
Liffe	1,049.7	610.0	439.7
Johannesburg Securities Exchange	478.1	446.2	31.8
ICE Futures Europe	153.0	152.3	0.6
NASDAQ OMX Nordic Exchange	143.4	80.4	63.1

Source: WFE (2009)

Table E-7 Top European futures and options exchanges

Eurex originated in 1998 from a merger of the Deutsche Terminbörse (DTB) and the SWG's SOFFEX derivative markets. It offers a fully electronic order book with provision for market makers to supply liquidity. By 1999, it had become the world's largest futures and options exchange. Eurex's success led the way for trading electronically, causing the open-outcry based venues to re-examine the benefits of electronic access. Its most heavily traded contracts are fixed income benchmark futures, namely the Euro-Bund (10y), Euro-Bobl (5y) and the Euro-Schatz (2y), together with futures and options for the Dow-Jones Euro Stoxx 50 stock index. Eurex is the leading marketplace for European stock options and has also expanded into single stock futures, becoming the world's third largest exchange for these. In 2007 Eurex merged with the International Securities Exchange (ISE), adding considerably to its market share of the option and U.S. markets, and creating a truly global exchange.

The London International Financial Futures Exchange (Liffe), founded in 1982, was initially modelled on the CBOT and CME open-outcry markets. Mergers with other London derivative markets led it to become Europe's leading derivatives exchange by 1996. Still, it faced increasing competition from the DTB and subsequently Eurex, causing it to shift to a fully automated marketplace by 2000. In 2002 Liffe was acquired by Euronext, which already incorporated the derivatives markets for Amsterdam, Brussels and Paris, most notably the MATIF. Liffe has remained an important competitor in the global derivatives marketplace. Trading on Liffe is based on an order book, running on the Connect system. Liffe's main contracts are its short-term interest rate futures, namely the Euribor (3m) and Sterling (3m) futures. Trading volumes are lower for equity and index based contracts; but an article by Joe Morgan (2007) notes that these have seen a steady increase in automated trading, with levels reaching up to 50% for the more liquid contracts. This is encouraged by their liquidity provider system, which gives market makers a mass quoting facility, enabling them to rapidly submit updates, which is particularly useful for options.

The South African Futures Exchange (SAFEX) merged with the Johannesburg Securities Exchange (JSE) in 2001. Offering fully automated trading it has since become the world's most active exchange for single stock futures.

The NASDAQ OMX derivatives market is dominated by equity derivative trading, with futures and options for both single stocks and indices. Trading for these is fully electronic, based on the CLICK trading platform. For fixed income derivatives, SAXESS is used by designated market makers to provide indicative quotes. Note that the actual trading for these takes place off-exchange, and is separately reported to the NASDAQ OMX for clearing.

The IntercontinentalExchange was created in 2000, with the intention of creating a fully electronic around-the-clock energy exchange. A year later, it incorporated the International Petroleum Exchange (IPE) to become ICE Futures. ICE offers a hybrid marketplace; market makers provide firm quotes, whilst centralised credit management allows anonymous order matching. ICE's Brent crude oil futures are the fourth most highly traded futures contract globally. It has become competition for NYMEX, particularly with its new West Texas Intermediate (WTI) crude oil contract. ICE has continued to expand, buying the New York Board of Trade (NYBOT) in 2007; it also sought a merger with CBOT.

Further competition is also starting to appear in Europe. A group of broker/dealers has announced Project Rainbow, a derivatives equivalent of Turquoise. This plans to compete with the established exchanges, initially for short term interest rate contracts.

Asian futures and options markets

Asia lags both the U.S. and Europe in terms of the number of futures and options contracts traded on exchanges, except for the behemoth that is the Korean options market. Table E-8 shows the top exchanges based on the number of contracts traded in 2008.

Exchange	Number of contracts traded in 2008 (millions)		
	Total	Futures	Options
Korea Exchange	2,867.3	100.8	2,766.5
National Stock Exchange India	601.6	439.6	162.0
Dalian Commodity Ex (China)	313.2	313.2	0.0
Zhengzhou Commodity Ex (China)	222.6	222.6	0.0
Australian SE	175.2	153.2	22.0
Osaka SE	163.7	131.0	32.7
Shanghai Futures Exchange	140.3	140.3	0.0
Taiwan Futures Exchange	136.7	37.7	99.0
Hong Kong Exchanges	105.0	44.7	60.3

Source: WFE (2009)

Table E-8 Top Asian futures and options exchanges

The KOSPI 200 options, traded on the Korea Exchange, lead the global exchange traded derivatives volume. Alone they account for 45% of the total volume traded by the top ten contracts in 2008, based on the FIA (2009) report, and around 15% of the global volume. Trading by institutions and foreign investors makes up around 60% of the volume, although historically retail trading was more dominant. Since much of the retail trading was speculative, this trend has meant the volatility of the KOSPI has declined. As the market matures, the rapid growth in trading for these contracts has also declined slightly. Trading is based on an electronic order book provided by the KOSPI futures-trading-system, which has proven able to cope with these huge trading volumes.

The National Stock Exchange of India is currently the world's second most active market for single stock futures. The rest of its volume is mainly from index futures trading for the

S&P CNX Nifty, the leading 50 stocks on the NSE.

China's largest derivatives exchange is the Dalian Commodity Exchange, which specialises in agricultural commodity futures. Electronic trading is available, based on its own dedicated platform. Most of its trading volume is in contracts for corn and soy meal, for which it is the world's largest market. Other agricultural contracts, such as sugar, cotton and wheat are tradable on the Zhengzhou Commodity Exchange. Metal, rubber and fuel contracts are traded on the electronic Shanghai Futures Exchange (SHFE). Exchange trading of purely financial derivatives has not yet taken off. That said, 2006 saw the foundation of the China Financial Futures Exchange (CFFEX), its first exchange dedicated to purely financial derivatives. The first traded contract will be a future on the CSI-300 (China Securities Index). Note that futures contracts will provide a way to synthetically short stocks, which is not currently possible on the cash market. Once the CSI-300 has gone live, contracts for bonds and currency are also expected. Commodity options are also likely to be introduced. Another dedicated commodities exchange should be launched in 2009/10, the Hong Kong Mercantile Exchange. Initially, its focus will be on oil contracts, the platform will be based on Cinnober's TRADExpress system. The U.S. has also been eager to capitalise on China's rapid growth, for instance, the CME has launched a mini-futures contract linked to an index for China's top 25 equities (by market cap).

The Australian Securities Exchange was formed in 2006 by a merger between the Sydney Futures Exchange (SFE) and the Australian Stock Exchange. Listed derivative trading has been electronic since 1999 when the SFE closed its trading floor. Its SYCOM trading system provides 24 hours access and includes a FIX gateway. The most heavily traded contract is the future for the 3 year Treasury bond; there is also significant trading for the S&P/ASX 200 stock index as well as other fixed income futures, ranging from 90-day bank bills to 10-year treasury bonds.

The Taiwan Futures Exchange (TAIFEX) is fully electronic, based on its in-house Electronic Trading System. Around 85% of its trading volume is accounted for by TAIEX index options, whilst nearly another 10% is for the TAIEX future. It has started supporting DMA and is looking to provide spread order functionality. The exchange has also begun listing dollar-based contracts and is looking to expand the range of futures, which may be traded by foreign investors.

In Japan, financial derivatives are traded on separate exchanges. Equity index contracts are traded on the corresponding stock exchanges. The Nikkei 225 is catered for by the Osaka SE; currently the most successful contract is the Nikkei 225 mini future, which was introduced in 2006. The TSE handles derivatives for the TOPIX; it also provides sector index futures. In 2009, it released its new options trading platform Tdex+, based on Liffe Connect. In terms of fixed income contracts, the Tokyo Financial Exchange (TFX, formerly TIFFE) trades contracts for the 3 month Euro-Yen; its platform is also based on Liffe Connect. Futures and options on JGB bonds are actually traded on the TSE. For commodity derivatives, the Tokyo Commodity Exchange (TOCOM) is the largest venue, with a market share of nearly 70%. Primarily, it trades contracts for gold and other metals, rubber, gasoline and other energy products. It has offered electronic trading since 1991 with a continuous market as well as call auctions. In 2009, it saw a major upgrade with a trading engine from NASDAQ OMX. Note there are three other commodity exchanges, the Central Japan Commodity Exchange (C-COM), the Tokyo Grain Exchange (TGE) and the Kansai Commodity Exchange (KEX). Although this is down from 16 in 1989, it is quite likely that further consolidation will occur for Japan's derivatives exchanges.

Swaps markets

Swaps are one of the most important types of derivative, accounting for around half the global outstanding notional value in the first half of 2008, as we saw back in Table E-1. Essentially, a swap is an agreement between two counterparties to exchange cash streams. These streams may be linked to fixed/floating interest rates, currencies, or even dividend payments. Thus, they offer a flexible means of controlling cash flows, which goes some of the way to explaining their popularity.

Swaps are still essentially viewed as an OTC derivative. Though, the sheer volume of interest rate swaps means there can be considerable liquidity for the more standardised contracts. Hence, electronic trading is becoming more important.

Asset specific

A swap contract is a bilateral agreement to exchange cash streams for a principal amount over a set time period. Generally, the associated cash streams are based on interest rates or currencies (or both), although they can also incorporate flows from equities or commodities. For example, a cash stream might correspond to the income or interest payments from a specific bond, the interest rate of a specific fixing (such as LIBOR) or the gains/losses from marking to market a stock position. As with bonds, swaps may be classified by the maturity date: short-term range from a week to less than 1-2 years, medium term range from 1-10 years whilst long term may last up to 50 years. Swaps give organisations an extremely flexible means of controlling their cash streams, although their individuality also means they have primarily been traded OTC.

The commonest type is an Interest Rate Swap (IRS). Note that the principal (or notional) amount is not actually exchanged; only the associated interest payments are swapped. A vanilla interest rate swap consists of one leg based on a floating rate of interest whilst the other is based on a fixed rate. For the floating leg, the actual payments are determined by the fixing schedules for the interest rate, e.g. quarterly for the three-month London Interbank Overnight Rate (LIBOR), whilst the fixed leg is usually paid semi-annually. Alternatively, a basis swap is one where both legs are based on floating rates, albeit with different fixing sources or schedules.

As its name suggests, a currency swap adds exchange rates into the mix. However, it also requires exchange of the notional amount at maturity and optionally at the start of the contract. This allows companies to borrow in the currency where they can obtain the best interest rate then convert it to the currency they actually need. The most common type of currency swap involves a floating U.S. dollar rate (often based on LIBOR) with a fixed rate in another foreign currency. Note that a currency swap should not be confused with a forex swap, which just represents an exchange of currencies. A forex swap is the combination of a spot FX transaction together with a forward contract to reverse this initial exchange and so close out the deal; interest payments are not involved. Effectively, a forex swap represents a spread trade between the spot FX rate and the forward rate.

An overnight indexed swap (OIS) is similar to a vanilla IRS, with a leg linked to an overnight fixing. At maturity, the difference between the accrued interest for the fixed rate and the average of the floating rates is exchanged. These are usually short-term swaps with maturities ranging from a week to two years.

A total return swap exchanges periodic interest payments for the total return of an asset or basket of assets. This allows investors access to capital gains, without having to actually hold the asset/s, since the ownership is not transferred. Effectively, they provide the purchaser with a synthetic position in the given asset. If a large price drop or even a default occurs then the purchaser will actually have to compensate the seller. So they are exposed to both the asset's market and credit risk. An equity swap is basically a total return swap based on an underlying stock, portfolio or stock index.

Asset swaps are the combination of an interest rate swap with a fixed rate bond, where the interest from the bond should be sufficient to pay for the swap rate (the IRS fixed rate). Therefore, the swap effectively cancels out the interest rate risk of the bond, leaving the holder exposed to a mix of bond credit risk and counterparty risk for the swap.

Other, more exotic types of swaps are also available, including features such as being callable or incorporating price ratcheting, but these are beyond the scope of this book.

Global swaps markets

The global market for swaps is huge; its notional value has increased nearly eight-fold since 1998 to over $370 trillion in the first half of 2008. Of this, interest rate swaps account for over 95%, whilst less than 5% is due to currency swaps.

In terms of trading volume, interest rate swaps had an average daily turnover of $1.21 trillion in 2007, based on data from BIS (2007b). That is about double the volume recorded in their 2004 triennial survey, which in turn was double the value for 2001. Clearly, the growth in turnover is considerable. In comparison, currency swaps had a daily turnover of around $80 billion in 2007, although this is actually four times its 2004 level.

Swaps are generally for the Euro and U.S. dollar. In fact, over 44% of interest rate swaps are based on the Euro and 27% on the dollar. In comparison, only 10% are for U.K. sterling, 9% for Japanese Yen and the remaining 10% covers all other currencies. Likewise, three quarters of all currency swaps involve the dollar. The sizeable volumes of Euro denominated swaps may seem surprising. However, for the Eurozone swaps have proven invaluable as a means of generating pan-European interest rates, as Joseph Mariathasan and Mark Bannister (2007) point out. This is also reflected by the fact that around 42.5% of the trading is based in London, whilst the U.S. only accounts for around 23.8%.

The maturities of swaps are spread relatively evenly, with around 38% of interest rate swaps lasting up to a year, 36% between one to five years and around 26% for even longer periods, based on the BIS (2007c) report. Whilst for currency swaps the BIS data shows that around three quarters of them are arranged for less than a year.

The swap marketplace is still strongly segmented with separate inter-dealer and dealer-to-client markets. In terms of electronic trading, progress has actually been faster in the dealer-to-client segment, although the inter-dealer space is catching up. A report from the Celent (2006) consultancy estimates that by 2009 electronic dealer-to-client trading should account for around 42% of the market, up from 9% in 2006, whilst inter-dealer trading may reach around 22%. In Europe, a study by the ECB (2009) found that interest rate swaps had reached around 16% electronic trading by 2008, whilst for overnight indexed swaps it was only 8%.

Competition is growing in the inter-dealer market. The first dedicated electronic marketplace for these was e-MIDER, created in 2000 by a consortium of banks, based on a request for quote mechanism. Although, at present, the two main inter-dealer systems providing the widest range of electronic swap trading are i-Swap and the Swapstream, both introduced in 2003. The ICAP brokerage's i-Swap caters for overnight, short and medium-term interest rate swaps. Although initially the focus has been on the euro, it also supports trading in pounds, dollars and yen. Orders may be entered electronically and are also transcribed from phone-dealing into a visible order book. This hybrid marketplace is actually based on the NASDAQ OMX's X-stream platform. i-Swap also supports implied orders, allowing additional liquidity from trading strategies such as spreads. The CME bought Swapstream in 2006; it offers trading for U.S. dollar and euro swaps versus Libor or Euribor with maturities from 6 months to 30 years as well as short-term overnight indexed swaps. EuroMTS has also launched a dedicated swap market for trading overnight indexed swaps.

The dealer-to-client segment consists of a mix of single and multi-dealer platforms. Barclay's were quick to capitalise on the opportunity offered by electronic trading, displaying live prices via Bloomberg and setting up a dedicated trading system in 2003. Since then, other brokers have gone on to release their own trading platforms. Other vendors have also been keen to create swap trading platforms; Reuters introduced its Matching for Interest Rates in 2004 followed by Bloomberg's SwapTrader and Tradeweb in 2005. These cater for short, medium and long-term euro and dollar swaps, generally using an RFQ mechanism to allow prices to be compared between several dealers before trading. Tradeweb also supports streaming (RFS) prices for Euro and GBP interest rate swaps. The banks and exchanges have noticed the success of these systems, and are working on their own competing platforms. The CME has also introduced sPro, a dealer-to-client version of Swapstream, which offers a hybrid market with streaming prices. LiquidityHub was proposed as a gateway for brokers to provide streaming prices for euro and dollar swaps, although the 2007-09 financial crisis helped put an end to this project.

Centralised clearing is starting to be offered for swaps trading as well, which may help further increase the adoption of electronic trading platforms. In particular, the CME has introduced Clearing360, which provides a mechanism for substituting interest rate forwards and swaps. Indeed, one of the main advantages of swaps traded on Swapstream is that they are centrally cleared through CME Clearing 360. Hence, this platform offers full straight-through-processing (STP) for electronic swaps trading.

Credit derivative markets

Credit derivatives were first created in 1990s as banks sought custom guarantees to hedge and diversify the credit risk associated with their loans. They have rapidly become a major asset class, enabling investors to trade credit risk without having to actually manage or fund loans. As Nishul Saperia and Jean Gross (2008) point out, increasing standardisation and a ready supply has allowed traders to track a single credit spread curve for any given entity, as opposed to following a large range of bonds. This led the credit derivative market to become a primary indicator of creditworthiness. In fact, they note that the volume of trading in credit derivatives outstripped the volume of bonds outstanding some time ago.

Although still primarily traded OTC, noteworthy steps have been made in the electronic trading of credit derivatives.

Asset specific

Credit derivatives act as financial guarantees that may be used to provide protection against a variety of credit events, but most typically default or bankruptcy. They include single entity credit default swaps, basket swaps, index-based credit swaps and synthetic collateralised debt obligations as well as some other credit based products.

A credit default swap (CDS) is a contract in which the credit risk for a notional amount of debt issued from one (or more) entities is transferred. The purchaser gains protection from this credit risk, whilst the seller is paid regular premiums for the lifetime of the contract. If a credit event occurs then the seller must compensate the purchaser and the contract expires. The key features, which differentiate each CDS, are the:

- Coverage, in terms of entities and notional amount of debt
- Premium payments
- Types of credit event allowed
- Settlement procedures

CDSs provide credit protection for debt issued from a variety of entities, ranging from companies to governments or their agencies. Note that when multiple entities are involved the swap is sometimes referred to as a basket CDS. The notional amounts vary depending on the entity's credit rating. Generally, investment grade CDSs have a notional value of around $10-20 million whilst riskier, higher yield contracts are often between $2-5 million. The allowed credit events may range from failure to pay, defaulting or bankruptcy, to debt restructuring or credit rating changes.

The required premium, or spread, is based on the credit rating of the entities and the notional amount of debt to be covered. The typical maturity for a CDS contract is five years. Generally, the premium is quoted in terms of basis points per annum, and paid quarterly. Note that for constant maturity swaps the credit spread is periodically reset based on the current market level.

Like futures, CDSs may be settled either physically or via a cash settlement. When triggered by a credit event physical settlement means the purchaser must deliver the corresponding debt in exchange for the cash notional amount from the seller. Though, cash settlement is becoming increasingly popular. This requires the seller to pay the difference between the notional amount and the current market value. Often, post-default the current market value will be determined by an auction of the defaulted debt, such as the Credit Event Auctions administered by Creditex and Markit, more details of this are given in Saperia and Gross (2008).

A credit-linked note is effectively a funded CDS that provides securitisation to protect the purchaser against counterparty risk. In case of default, this acts as a guarantee to ensure that the buyer is compensated. Often this is achieved through an intermediary special purpose company.

CDS indices represent a natural evolution from single entity or basket CDSs. These standardised credit swaps often cover more than a hundred separate companies. Usually, these are equally weighted so each company is covered by an equal share of the notional amount. They have proven to be incredibly popular, since they allow investors to make much broader macro trades for credit risk. In addition, it is possible to buy or sell tranches of CDS indices, allowing investors to define limits for the protection coverage. For instance, a 3-7% tranche for the CDX index means that protection is provided for losses of between 3 and 7% of the notional amount, but not above or below these levels. Leading exchanges have even started to offer futures and options based on underlying CDS indices.

Another use for CDSs has been for structured products that involve credit risk. Collateralized debt obligations (CDO) are asset-backed securities based on an underlying portfolio of bonds or loans. A synthetic CDO replaces these underlying assets with credit default swaps, the income from which is invested in low risk bonds. Effectively, a synthetic CDO is a portfolio of CDSs combined with low risk assets.

Pricing credit derivatives is non-trivial. Unlike an interest rate swap, we must also incorporate the probability of default together with the recovery price for the asset. A variety of methods are used to price credit derivatives, but these are beyond the scope of this book.

A brief review is provided by Brian Eales (2007) and David Mengle (2007). These sources also provide a more detailed review of credit derivatives in general.

Global credit derivative markets

Credit derivatives have experienced phenomenal growth over the last ten years. In 1997, the global notional outstanding volume was just $180 billion. For 2008 the International Swaps and Derivatives Association Inc. (2009) reported a total notional outstanding of $38.6 trillion. Admittedly, the credit crunch has dampened the growth of the credit markets; in fact, the 2008 figure was down 38% from the 2007 year-end. The 200% increase in outstanding notional between 2005 and 2007 now seems a distant memory. Still, it is important to remember that credit derivatives are well established as a major asset class.

Trading is focussed in London and New York, each with around a 40% market share, whilst the rest of Europe accounts for around 10%. In terms of asset types, much of the trading is concentrated on CDSs and CDS indices, each accounting for over 30% of the market whilst CDOs account for around 16%, based on the 2006 Credit Derivatives Report from the British Bankers' Association (BBA) (2006). In terms of maturity, BIS (2007c) note that around 60% of the CDSs range between one to five years whilst another third are for periods longer than this.

Standardisation has played an important role in the level of growth which credit derivative trading has achieved. Standards have helped make the contracts and transactions more uniform. But the most noticeable impact has been from the introduction of CDS indices. These have experienced an extraordinary surge in usage since 2004, when they had less than 10% market share, based on the BBA (2006). In Europe, much of this is due to the enhanced liquidity that arose from the 2004 merger of the iBoxx and Trac-X indices into the iTraxx Europe, which consists of 125 investment grade companies. The Dow Jones CDX is the main U.S. index, covering investment grade debt from 125 North American corporations. There are also a wide range of other indices covering Asia, emerging markets as well as high yield and specific industry sectors.

Credit derivatives are still generally traded OTC with brokers. Though, electronic trading is making noteworthy progress, particularly for the more standardised products such as CDS indices. A report by the Celent (2004) consultancy noted that around 25% of index based trading was electronic, predicting it would increase to around 50% by 2007. These predictions seem to have been met in Europe, where a Euromoney (2008a) report notes that around 45% of inter-dealer transactions were electronic. Adoption in North America and Asia is still at an early stage. The rate of progress for less standardised products, such as single entity CDSs, is also likely to be slower.

The inter-broker market has a range of electronic platforms which cater for CDSs, most notably Creditex's RealTime platform, GFI's CreditMatch and ICAP's BrokerTec. The Euromoney (2008a) report notes that these three accounted for 90% of the European inter-dealer market. The focus has primarily been on the liquid CDS indices, although systems are increasingly catering for single entity CDSs and other less liquid products. In addition, to cater for correlation trading, vendors are also starting to provide for trading large portfolios of single entity CDSs. These orders can be huge, with aggregate notional amounts of more than a billion dollars and encompassing over 100 CDSs. In particular, in 2007 Creditex launched a platform dedicated to handling such trades (called Q-WIXX), providing live prices from up to four different dealers.

In the dealer-to-client market, electronic trading has seen less significant uptake. Initially, single vendor systems were the norm, such as those from BNP Paribas and Barclays Capital. Multi-dealer platforms have also started to appear, in the form of MarketAxess and Tradeweb. Again, the initial focus has been on the highly liquid CDS indices, based around an RFQ trading mechanism. Both platforms have integrated real-time prices to provide users with indicative quotes. It is also likely that vendors will soon cater for clients who require CDS portfolio trading.

The leading exchanges have proven keen to enter the credit market as well, starting with the Eurex's launch of futures based on the iTraxx indices. In the U.S., the CBOT announced an index future based on the CDR Liquid 50 index. The CME has also announced a joint venture with the Citadel Investment Group LLC for a CDS trading platform called CDMX. This will provide an RFQ mechanism for trading both single entity and CDS indices, coupled with a central counterparty clearing facility. Whilst the CBOE also has plans for CDS based options. At the moment, it is still too early to gauge how successful these ventures will prove to be, but given the size of this market, even a small percentage would be important.

The 2007-09 financial crisis also focussed attention on the clearing and settlement procedures for credit derivatives. The counterparty risk associated with CDS contracts made it hard to trade out of them, particularly with the collapse of several major banks. Hence, regulators are seeking to mandate centralised clearinghouses to try to reduce this risk. In the U.S, centralised clearing proposals from NYSE Euronext Liffe and the CME have already been approved. Likewise in Europe there is growing support for central counterparties, with a number of banks already committed to using them. Centralised clearing should also make it easier to implement fully electronic trading platforms in the future, as Ivy Schmerken (2009) points out.

Streamlining the settlement process is also important to allow for continued market growth. In fact, the 2006 BBA report highlights that trade confirmations were more than two months late for almost 10% of trades. Tales of huge back-office backlogs for settlement are not unheard of. That said, steps are being made to improve the provision of straight-through processing. For instance, vendors such as T-Zero now offer dedicated platforms to streamline the confirmation and assignment processes.

Summary

- Electronic trading is now commonplace for listed derivatives (futures and options); it is even available for swaps and credit derivatives, which traditionally are traded OTC.

- Algorithmic trading is becoming established for listed derivatives, particularly futures. The rapid growth and fragmentation of the U.S. equity options marketplace means this is likely to be a focal point for algorithm development as well.

- Other derivatives may also be electronically traded as part of cross-asset trading strategies.

Appendix F

Other markets

A few types of financial asset do not quite fit in the main categories. Most notably, depositary receipts and exchange traded funds. Both asset classes have seen considerable growth over the last few years.

Depositary receipts (DRs) are securities that represent the shares of a foreign company. They provide an important means of accessing the major financial markets for foreign companies, as well as offering a cheaper alternative to cross-border trading. In a sense, DRs may be viewed as derivatives, since they have an underlying asset. However, there is no contract based on some future value of the underlier, as in futures and options. So really, they are more a proxy than a derivative.

Exchange traded funds (ETF), as their name suggests, represent tradable investment funds. Like depositary receipts, they have helped provide an easier and cheaper means for investors to access assets from other markets. Since they represent baskets of assets, they are an extremely efficient means for investors to gain much broader exposure to sectors or markets, much like futures.

Depositary receipts

Depositary receipts allow trading in shares of foreign companies without having to carry out any cross-border transactions. Note that these are for single companies and bear no relation to the similarly named Standard & Poor's Depositary Receipt (SPDR), which is an exchange-traded fund (ETF).

Asset specific

Depositary receipts (DRs) essentially act as proxies for foreign shares that may be traded locally either at exchanges, other execution venues or OTC. They are issued by a domestic bank or brokerage against their own inventory of the foreign stock. Note that the ratio of shares does not have to be 1:1, so a single depositary receipt might translate to 0.5, 5, 10 or even 100 foreign shares, depending on the share price. A sponsored DR means that the depositary bank is also involved with the foreign company, for instance, organising proxy votes for the DR holders. An un-sponsored DR is issued without such involvement, so holders may not receive the same shareholder benefits or voting rights. Any dividends are generally paid in the local currency, and for a fee the depositary bank will convert the receipts back into the underlying stock. So in many respects they behave much like domestic stocks.

DRs are attractive to companies since they allow them to raise capital from abroad, without having to undertake many of the onerous reporting and accounting requirements, which would otherwise be necessary for dual listing.

An American Depositary Receipt (ADR) for a foreign company is priced in dollars and may be traded OTC or on the major U.S. exchanges. The first ADR was in fact issued by JP Morgan in 1927 for the London department store Selfridges & Co. There are several levels of ADR available to issuers. These dictate how and where they may be traded, and are based on how much U.S. reporting the company is prepared to do. The easiest starting point for firms is to issue them as restricted stock, under SEC Rule 144(a), although this restricts trading to only be for large institutional investors (or qualified institutional buyers). Alternatively, Regulation S allows trading, but only for offshore non-U.S. residents. Neither of these options enforces any specific reporting requirements on the company. A Level I ADR has minimal reporting requirements, but still only permits OTC trading of the company's ADRs. Quarterly and annual reporting to the SEC is not mandatory, similarly there is no requirement to follow the U.S. generally accepted accounting principles (GAAP) standards. For Level II ADRs, the company must file a GAAP compliant annual report with the SEC. This allows them to be traded on a U.S. exchange, provided they meet the appropriate listing requirements. Finally, a Level III ADR has the highest level of reporting requirements since it means the company is actually issuing new shares in the U.S.

Depositary receipts are also used outside the U.S., European depositary receipts allow trading and settlement on Europe's stock exchanges. Likewise, global depositary receipts (GDRs) are effectively global equivalents of ADRs. They allow trading in more than one country, often this means both Europe and the U.S.

A similar approach is used for the large number of Canadian companies that are cross-listed on U.S. exchanges. These so-called Canadian ordinaries do not require a depositary bank as an intermediary, so there are no restrictions on trading and no conversion fees. Though, as Louis Gagnon and G. Andrew Karolyi (2003) point out, they are not 100% fungible, since those traded on U.S. exchanges must be held in U.S. dollar accounts and their dividends are also made in U.S. dollars.

Global registered shares (GRS), or global ordinaries, adopt a similar approach to Canadian ordinaries. These may be traded internationally, such as on the NYSE, as well as on their domestic exchange. Again, there are no conversion fees, although the process does need to be coordinated between agents. The GRS was first created in 1998 for DaimlerChrysler AG, currently only a handful of companies use this structure.

Pricing and trading

A depositary receipt is based on an underlying asset, namely a foreign stock. Its value is dependent on the current market price of this underlying asset, rather than some future value. Therefore, the price of a DR should be similar to the price of the foreign stock, adjusted by the current market exchange rates. Note that the conversion ratio is usually chosen by the depositary agent to best reflect the value of the foreign shares. Hence, the price of most ADRs is between $10 and $100. So for cheaper stocks each ADR share might equate to hundreds of actual shares in the company.

There are some complications, though: A true price comparison should also factor in the fees associated with converting a DR into the actual stock. The savings in management and settlement costs which the DR offers may also be reflected in the price of the DR. Also there is the transaction cost associated with any FX trades to consider. So differences in the prices of the two assets do not necessarily represent arbitrage opportunities.

When trading DRs, it is vital to remember that they are based on foreign stocks. Consequently, they are much more likely to be impacted by shifts in the exchange rate. Whilst for DRs based on emerging market companies there may also be the risk of inflation to consider. Time-zones can also have a considerable effect since the market for the underlying stock may well be closed whilst its DRs are being traded, or vice versa.

Research into the relationship between prices for ADRs and their underlying stocks confirms that the most information is held by the underlying stock. Though, analysis by Gagnon and Karolyi (2003) also found that cross-listed stocks tend to have higher systematic price co-movements with the U.S. and lower co-movements with local indices than other stocks. We review such relationships in more detail in Chapter 13.

Global DR markets

Worldwide, there were 2,130 depositary receipts at the end of 2008. An increase of 30% on the year before, based on figures from the annual review by the Bank of New York Mellon (BNYM) (2008). [16] They encompass companies from 77 countries. The BRIC [17] countries dominate the market in terms of numbers, accounting for a third of the issued depositary receipts. In fact, India has the highest number of depositary receipts for any country (276) followed by Russia (176), whilst Brazil has 128 and China 110. Developed countries also play a major role, for instance, the U.K. has 141 depositary receipts and Australia has 125.

The majority of these are actually GDRs (1,013) followed by U.S. Level I ADRs (716) and U.S. listed Level II and III ADRs (403). The popularity of GDRs is, in part, due to the stricter regulatory requirements in the U.S. Though, a change in rulings by the SEC has simplified the process for un-sponsored DR programs which are to be traded OTC. So the balance may change; indeed, 2008 saw 605 new un-sponsored depositary receipts created.

In terms of investment value, by the end of 2008 over $1.2 trillion was invested in depositary receipts, a decrease of about 25% since 2007. U.S. listed ADRs accounted for $773 billion, European listed DRs were only worth $214 billion, whilst the remaining OTC and other receipts were worth around $163 billion. In terms of issuance, the largest proportion was for western European companies ($452 billion), whilst the remainder was split fairly evenly between firms from Emerging Europe and Africa ($249 billion), Latin America ($237 billion), and Asia Pacific ($212 billion).

For 2008, the global value of depositary receipt trading was around $4.4 trillion, a third higher than the year before. In comparison, 2007's volumes were 72% higher than those of 2006, so the financial crisis slowed the massive growth that the DR markets were seeing. DRs for firms from the BRIC countries accounted for the majority of this trading with around 54% of it. Specifically, Brazil led with $899 billion worth of trading, from China's $792 billion and Russia's $579 billion. Most of the trading is executed at stock exchanges, in fact only 2% was traded OTC. Table F-1 shows a more detailed breakdown of the trading volumes at major venues.

The U.S. is clearly the largest market for DRs. Given that around $70 trillion traded on the two major U.S. exchanges in 2008, DRs accounted for around 5% of this total. Though, the trading is quite concentrated. In fact, the top five ADRs accounted for 27% of the total U.S. exchange turnover. This was led by China's Baidu Inc. ($331bn) and Brazil's Petrobras ($244bn) and Vale ($204bn). The top ten also included Finland's Nokia, Mexico's America Movil, the UK's BP and Australia's BHP Billiton.

---

[16] Note that unless otherwise stated all the figures for this section come from this report.
[17] The BRIC countries represent the fast-growing developing economies of Brazil, Russia, India and China.

Venue	Number of sponsored DRs	Trading volume in $billions		% volume change
		2008	2007	
NYSE	291	3,000	2,288	31
NASDAQ	109	698	620	31
London/IOB Luxembourg	388	523	387	35
OTC		99	76	30
Other	15	45	40	13

Source: BNYM (2008)

Table F-1 Global traded volumes of Depositary Receipts

The NYSE is still the world's largest market for DRs, with more than two thirds of the global market share. The BNYM (2008) report points out that 44 DR programs had a trading value greater than $25 billion in 2007, 40 of these were listed on the NYSE. Trading DRs is supported electronically via NYSE Hybrid, just like any normal stock. Similarly, the NASDAQ supports ADR trading just as if they were stocks. There are no figures for levels of trading on ECNs and ATSs, although venues such as ITG POSIT and Pipeline also allow them to be traded.

The London Stock Exchange's International Order Book (IOB) is still the leading competitor for the U.S exchanges. It handles much of the European DR trading. Most of the IOB turnover is actually for Russian companies, which were eight of its top ten most actively traded DRs in 2008. In fact, Gazprom was the 4th most heavily traded DR in 2008, with total volumes of $177 billion. The LSE provides continuous electronic trading on an order book similar to SETS, although it additionally permits member firms to display their identity via named orders. For less liquid DRs, there is an auction-only model, which comprises of three daily auctions, each providing a two-hour call period before the final matching takes place. They offer an International Bulletin Board as well, which allows dedicated market makers to provide liquidity for the electronic trading of certain DRs. The IOB also supplies the trading platform for Luxembourg Stock Exchange listed DRs.

Electronic venues for OTC DR trading have been established as well. In 2007, Pink Sheets LLC (now Pink OTC Markets Inc.) launched the International OTCQX Market, which provides an electronic platform for OTC trading of Level I ADRs. The market comprises of two segments, PremierQX for those companies that meet the U.S. national exchange listing requirements, and PrimeQX for smaller firms. The NASDAQ PORTAL market trading system was also launched in 2007. This provides electronic trading for Rule 144(a) securities, including ADRs. The BNYM (2008) report estimates that around $141 billion traded on Pink OTC Markets in 2008. They also predict that these levels are likely to rise higher due to the SEC easing of OTC DR listing regulations.

Another interesting innovation in the DR market is ADR Direct from the BNY ConvergEx Group. This platform enables institutional investors to trade stocks overseas and then automatically convert them into ADRs. This handles the FX transaction, and sources liquidity to try to achieve the best price for the ADR. Services such as this should help smooth out any price discrepancies between ADRs and the underlying shares.

Exchange Traded Funds

Investment funds are collective investment schemes. However, they can also be traded as assets. Funds may be categorised as either open-ended or closed-ended. This relates to their size; open-ended funds can continuously expand or reduce, whereas closed-ended funds maintain a fixed size.

Perhaps one of the best-known types of open-ended fund is the U.S. mutual fund. For new investors the fund manager must issue additional shares, whilst for departing investors they must redeem them for cash or securities. Historically, open-ended funds were bought or sold based on the day's close prices.

Closed-ended funds (CEFs) behave more like stocks. There is an initial distribution of a fixed number of shares in the fund, much like an IPO. Subsequently, investors wanting to join or leave the fund will generally need to trade the shares on the secondary markets.

The exchange-traded fund (ETF) was first introduced in the early 1990s. Initially, these were simply open-ended funds which were tradable intraday on the secondary market, just like closed-ended funds. Exchange traded funds are becoming an increasingly popular way for fund managers to gain an overall market exposure, or to provide hedges for risk management. In fact, they have proven to be so successful that a range of closed-ended funds now also class themselves as ETFs.

Asset specific

ETFs are generally classified as either being index or optimised funds. Index funds passively track or replicate a specific benchmark, whilst optimised funds try to beat market benchmarks and so adopt similar techniques to active investors.

Initially, most open-ended ETFs concentrated on major stock indices as their benchmarks. Nowadays, sector specific ETFs are becoming commonplace, as are ETFs containing foreign assets. They are not just restricted to equities; ETFs may also be created based on portfolios of bonds or even commodity futures. Fixed income ETFs are useful because the fund manager is responsible for maintaining the portfolio, so bonds are rolled before they mature and coupon payments are reinvested. Likewise, for commodity ETFs the manager handles the margin requirements and again rolls any contracts before expiry.

Optimised ETFs often track custom benchmarks, which are created by applying strict rules and quantitative techniques. This allows them to preserve their transparency. ETFs have even been created to cater for specific investment styles. For instance, the Claymore MacroShares Oil Down fund comprises of assets that will benefit from a drop in oil prices, whilst their Insider ETF invests in 100 stocks in which insiders have recently been buying.

ETFs offer several advantages to other types of investment funds:

- Transparency
- Lower fees / overall cost
- Tax efficiency

In general, ETFs employ fixed compositions, often published daily, so they are more transparent than other types of funds. In comparison, for some actively managed mutual funds or closed-ended funds the publicly available compositions may be months old, in part to protect their investments. ETFs also tend to have lower fees, particularly for the more straightforward index trackers. For instance, the SPDR ETF, which covers the S&P 500 index, has an expense ratio of 9.45 bps, whilst many mutual funds quote an equivalent cost around double this. Meanwhile active funds may charge anywhere from 100-150 bps or more. Similarly, for bonds, Rebecca Knight (2007) points out that many of the newer ETFs have expense ratios around 20 bps, in comparison to the average annual ratio of 109 bps for typical bond funds. Tax efficiency may also be achieved for stock ETFs, since investors can exit the fund with equivalent positions in the underlying, and so avoid incurring capital gains tax.

Pricing and trading

The net asset value (NAV) of a fund is simply the total value of all the assets in the fund divided by the number of shares issued. For an open-ended fund the NAV represents the price investors must pay (have redeemed) when they join (or leave), in addition to any fees.

Arbitrage ensures that the market value of the ETF keeps in line with the NAV, since if the ETF trades at a premium (discount) the dealers will just sell (buy) the ETF and buy (sell) the underlying assets. In comparison, closed-end funds may trade at a considerable premium or discount to their NAV, based on analysts/traders estimates for the actual value of their composition. Likewise, ETFs for funds holding foreign assets will tend to trade with a more noticeable difference between their market price and the NAV. This is similar to what we saw for depositary receipts. Variations may be caused by changes in the exchange rate, information flow or simply due to time-zones. For example, some funds will be priced based on stale data, since the native market is closed. Price discrepancies can also be highlight new and forward-looking information. For instance, in a study of Asian ETFs traded in the U.S., Timothy Jares and Angeline Lavin (2002) found that discounts for the ETF were a significant negative predictor for the subsequent daily return in Japan/Hong Kong.

ETFs may be freely bought and sold on the secondary markets throughout the trading day. Unlike mutual funds, they are not subject to any minimum holding periods. They may also be lent, and so allow short sales. All these factors mean that ETFs tend to be much more liquid than any other type of investment fund.

Although ETFs may be traded much like equities, it is still important to remember they are different. Most notably open-ended funds are not subject to a fixed fund size. Instead, an in-kind creation and redemption process allows specialised dealers, sometimes known as authorized participants, to react to the demands of the secondary market by trading large blocks of ETFs with the fund sponsor. Therefore, supply and demand have less impact on price than for equities: If demand is outstripping supply the dealers will just create more ETFs, alternatively they can redeem them to reduce the supply. Hence, trading volume is somewhat less important as an indicator for ETFs.

Global ETF markets

ETFs may be traced back to the TIPS-35 a fund launched in 1990 which tracked the stocks in Canada's TSE 35 index. Some three years later saw the introduction of the now ubiquitous Standard & Poor's Depositary Receipts (SPDRs), which track the S&P 500 index of U.S. firms. By 2001, ETFs were well established in North America and Asia and were being introduced across Europe.

A detailed review of the worldwide market is provided by Barclays Global Investors (BGI) (2009): Globally, there are around 1600 ETFs, 472 of these were launched in 2008 with plans to launch another 600 in the near future. Overall, these cover around $710 billion worth of assets under management. The majority of these investments are equity-based, with over 1300 ETFs, for a total value $596 billion. Though, fixed income ETFs have steadily grown in popularity, with more than 160 funds and $104 billion now invested in them. Nearly 50 commodity-based funds have also been established; although investment in them is still much lower, at around $10 billion. There are also some funds for currencies and mixed investments.

Despite the economic downturn, investment in ETFs is still growing. The BGI (2009) report estimates that the total value invested in them could reach $2,000 billion by 2011; a similar value was predicted by Morgan Stanley in the FT (2007). This is a comparable rate of growth to that seen for U.S. mutual funds in the 1980s and '90s.

In terms of the investment firms issuing ETFs, the global marketplace is led by Barclays Global Investors (BGI) whose iShares funds account for about 50% of the U.S. and nearly 40% of the European markets, again based on data from the BGI (2009) review. In the U.S., State Street and Vanguard also stand out as major players, although there are 18 fund managers in total. In Europe, there is nearly double the number of providers, but again 80% of the market is catered for by just three, namely BGI, Lyxor Asset Management and Deutsche Bank.

The average daily traded volume for ETFs has also grown significantly, with a global average of $80.4 billion in 2008, a third higher than the year before, based on BGI (2009). Trading is mainly concentrated at the major stock exchanges, often sharing the same systems as stocks. So the potential for electronic and algorithmic trading is good. Globally, $10 trillion worth of ETFs were traded on exchanges in 2008, based on figures from the WFE (2009). Table F-2 outlines the top exchanges in terms of volume traded.

Exchange	Value traded in $ billions		% change	Number of ETFs listed in 2008
	2008	2007		
NYSE Euronext U.S.	6,821	2,710	152	1048
NASDAQ OMX	1,906	n/a	n/a	46
NYSE Amex [18]	283	270	5	356
Deutsche Börse	205	173	19	408
NYSE Euronext Europe	143	119	20	396
TSX Group	141	73	92	96
London SE	101	n/a	n/a	305
Borsa Italiana	70	49	40	326
Hong Kong Exchanges	56	20	175	24
Shanghai SE	39	15	150	3
Mexican Exchange	35	23	54	159

Source: WFE (2009)

Table F-2 Top exchanges by value of ETFs traded

The U.S. leads the world ETF marketplace, followed by Europe then Asia. Emerging markets, such as Mexico, are also seeing considerable levels of trading. The U.S. market has continued to grow rapidly, with 144 new ETFs issued in 2008 alone, resulting in $497 billion in assets invested in over 698 funds and an average daily trading volume of $77 billion, based on data from BGI (2009). ETF trading volumes now account for a sizeable proportion of trading in the U.S. In fact, in 2008 they reached around a third of the total equity trading

---

[18] Excludes data for December 2008.

volume. During some of the worst market moves in November, ETFs accounted for nearly 40%. Given such volumes, it is hardly surprising that competition for this trade flow is increasing. ETFs are now regularly the most traded assets at many U.S. venues. Note that the bulk of ETF trading in the U.S. is concentrated on a few key funds, as shown in Table F-3. Stock index tracking funds dominate the market, with the ubiquitous "Spiders" for the S&P 500, "Qubes" for the NASDAQ-100, iShares Russell 2000 and the DJIA based "Diamonds".

ETF	ADV Q4 2008 $ millions	Assets Dec 2008 $ millions
SPDR S&P 500 ETF (SPY)	43,278	93,922
PowerShares QQQ (QQQQ)	7,466	12,537
iShares Russell 2000 (IWM)	5,436	11,018
ProShares Ultra Short S&P 500 (SDS)	4,902	2,251
DIAMONDS Trust (DIA)	3,550	8,966
iShares MSCI Emerging Markets (EEM)	3,472	19,210

Source: Author's own estimates based on NSX (2009)

Table F-3 Most traded U.S. ETFs for Q4 2008

ETFs were initially championed in the U.S. by the American Stock Exchange (Amex). However, competition soon arrived from the NYSE when unlisted trading privileges meant that venues could trade the same funds without them having to be dual listed. This combined with the NYSE's purchase of Arca has helped make the NYSE the largest venue for ETF trading in the world. NYSE Euronext also took over the Amex in 2008. NYSE ETF trading now uses the ARCA platform where dedicated liquidity providers ensure there is sufficient liquidity. In 2007 NASDAQ launched its own dedicated ETF market; again using designated liquidity providers. Unsurprisingly, other venues such as BATS and the National Stock Exchange (NSX) are also competing for ETF market share.

Europe was slower to embrace ETFs, due to regulatory issues, although since 2000 their uptake has been rapid. In fact, the EDHEC (2006) European ETF survey points out that in 2005 nearly two-thirds of the global market growth was from this region. In 2008, over 630 ETFs were offered in Europe, accounting for more than $140 billion of assets and an average daily trading volume of $2 billion, based on data from BGI (2009).

As we can see from Table F-2, two European exchanges make the top five venues globally. Based on their own figures for Q1 2008, the Deutsche Börse (DBG) (2008) leads with around 37% of the region's market share, followed by Euronext's ETF segment with 34%. Whilst the Borsa Italiana has nearly 13% and the London Stock Exchange has over 6%. Chi-X also supports ETF trading. The Deutsche Börse XTF platform is essentially based on Xetra with liquidity provided by Designated Sponsors. A similar approach is adopted for Euronext's ETF segment; both venues also continuously publish indicative NAVs. London's ETF segment is based on their SETS platform. In terms of actual funds, the DAX EX is the most heavily traded, followed by the Dow Jones and iShares Euro STOXX 50 funds. Though, volumes are much lower than those of the giant U.S. funds, for example, the DAX EX has an ADV of about $375 million. Pan-European and local stock indices are still in the majority, although international and fixed income ETFs are also gaining importance. Commodity funds are increasing as well; in fact, the London Stock Exchange has a dedicated exchange traded commodity (ETC) segment.

The Asian ETF market is noticeably smaller than Europe. BGI (2009) reports a total of 200 ETFs with over $50 billion invested. More than half of this value is invested in the 61 Japanese ETFs. Japan also leads the way in terms of trading volumes, at both the Tokyo and Osaka stock exchanges. This has also been helped by cross-listing agreements with the U.S. That said, volumes are increasing across the region, in particular at the Hong Kong and Shanghai exchanges.

Summary

- Electronic trading is commonplace for many depositary receipts and exchange traded funds, since they are generally traded on the world's stock markets.

- Buy-side levels of adoption of DMA and algorithmic trading for these assets are likely to increase. They may also be incorporated in cross-asset trading strategies.

Abbreviations & Acronyms

e.g.	exempli gratia (for example)
et al.	et ali(i/ae/a) (and others)
i.e.	id est (that is)
ABCP	Asset Backed Corporate Paper
ADR	American Depositary Receipt
ADV	Average Daily Volume
AI	Artificial Intelligence
AIM	Aggressive in the money
ANN	Artificial Neural Network
AON	All or None
API	Application Programming Interface
AR	Autoregressive
ARCH	Autoregressive Conditional Heteroskedasticity
ARMA	Autoregressive Moving Average
AS	Adaptive shortfall
ASX	Australian Securities Exchange
ATM	At the money
ATS	Alternative Trading System
BIS	Bank for International Settlements
BNY	The Bank of New York
BNYM	The Bank of New York Mellon
BP	Basis Point
BRIC	Brazil, Russia, India and China
CBOE	Chicago Board Options Exchange
CBOT	Chicago Board of Trade
CCP	Central Counterparty
CDA	Continuous Double Auction
CDS	Credit Default Swap

CFA	Chartered Financial Analyst
CME	Chicago Mercantile Exchange
CPI	Consumer Price Index
CTD	Cheapest to deliver
DBG	Deutsche Börse Group
DJIA	Dow Jones Industrial Average
DMA	Direct Market Access
DMM	Designated Market Maker
DOT	Designated Order Turnaround
DR	Depositary Receipt
DTCC	Depository Trust & Clearing Corporation
DV	Dollar value
ECB	European Central Bank
ECN	Electronic Communications Network
EGARCH	Exponential Generalized Autoregressive Conditional Heteroskedasticity
EMA	Exponential Moving Average
EMEA	Europe, Middle-East and Africa
EMS	Execution Management System
EPS	Earnings Per Share
ET	Exchange Traded
ETF	Exchange Traded Fund
FIA	Futures Industry Association
FIX	Financial information exchange protocol
FIXML	FIX Markup Language
FOK	Fill or Kill
FOMC	Federal Open Market Committee
FPL	FIX Protocol Limited
FRA	Forward Rate Agreement

FT	Financial Times	**NAV**	Net Asset Value
FX	Foreign exchange	**NBBO**	National Best Bid and Offer
GA	Genetic Algorithm	**NMS**	Normal Market Size
GARCH	Generalized Autoregressive Conditional Heteroskedasticity	**NN**	Neural Network
		NYSE	New York Stock Exchange
GC	General Collateral	**OHLC**	Open High Low Close
GDP	Gross Domestic Product	**OMS**	Order Management System
GDRs	Global Depositary Receipt	**OTC**	Over The Counter
GP	Genetic Programming	**PIM**	Passive in the money
GWAP	Gamma Weighted Average Price	**POV**	Percent of Volume
ICE	IntercontinentalExchange	**PPI**	Producer Price Index
IDB	Inter Dealer Broker	**RFQ**	Request For Quote
IOB	International Order Book	**RFS**	Request For Stream
IOC	Immediate or Cancel	**RPM**	Relative Performance Measure
IOI	Indication of Interest	**SE**	Stock Exchange
IS	Implementation Shortfall	**SEC**	Securities and Exchange Commission
ISE	International Securities Exchange	**SI**	Systematic Internaliser
ISM	Institute for Supply Management	**SIFMA**	Securities Industry and Financial Markets Association
ITS	Intermarket Trading System	**SIN**	Securities Industry News
LIBOR	London Interbank Borrow Rate	**SPDR**	Standard & Poor's Depositary Receipt
LP	Liquidity Provider		
LSE	London Stock Exchange	**STP**	Straight Through Processing
MA	Moving Average	**SVM**	Support Vector Machine
MBF	Must be Filled	**TCA**	Transaction Cost Analysis
MC	Market Close	**TWAP**	Time Weighted Average Price
MCR	Marginal Contribution to Risk	**VIX**	Chicago Board Options Exchange Volatility Index
MI	Market Impact		
MiFID	Markets in Financial Instruments Directive	**VWAP**	Volume Weighted Average Price
MO	Market Order	**WFE**	World Federation of Exchanges
MTF	Multilateral Trading Facility	**WSJ**	The Wall Street Journal
NAPM	National Association of Purchasing Management	**XBRL**	Extensible business reporting language
NASDAQ	National Association of Securities and Dealers Automated Quotation	**XML**	Extensible markup language
		YTM	Yield to maturity

References

Abad and Pascual (2006) Abad D. and Pascual R., 'On the Magnet Effect of Price Limits', *European Financial Management,* vol:13 (5), p 833-852, doi:10.1111/j.1468-036X.2007.00399.x

Abad and Pascual (2007) Abad D. and Pascual R., 'Switching to a Temporary Call Auction in Times of High Uncertainty', *EFA 2006 Zurich Meetings*

Abad, Sanabria and Yagüe (2005) Abad D., Sanabria S. and Yagüe J., 'Liquidity and information around annual earnings announcements: an intraday analysis of the Spanish stock market', *Instituto Valenciano de Investigaciones Económicas, S.A., Working Papers. Serie EC*

ABM (2007) 'Asia Bond Monitor', *Asian Development Bank (asianbondsonline.adb.org)*

Advanced Trading (2008) 'Algorithmic Trading Directory', *Advanced Trading (www.advancedtrading.com)*

Affleck-Graves, Callahan and Chipalkatti (2002) Affleck-Graves J., Callahan C. and Chipalkatti N., 'Earnings Predictability, Information Asymmetry, and Market Liquidity', *Journal of Accounting Research,* vol:40 (3), p 561-583, doi:10.1111/1475-679X.00062

Ahn, Bae and Chan (2001) Ahn H.J., Bae K.H., Chan K., 'Limit Orders, Depth, and Volatility: Evidence from the Stock Exchange of Hong Kong', *Journal of Finance,* vol:56 (2), p 767–788, doi:10.1111/0022-1082.00345

Aite Group (2007) 'Electronic FX: Welcome to the Banks' Neverland', *Aite Group (www.aitegroup.com)*

Aite Group (2007a) 'Algorithmic Trading: Top 10 Keys to Success in 2007', *Aite Group (www.aitegroup.com)*

Aite Group (2008), 'Order Execution Management: Convergence and Multi-Asset Capabilities', *2008 FPL (FIX Protocol Ltd.) Canadian Electronic Trading Conference*

Aite Group (2008a) 'Algorithmic Trading in FX: Fad or Reality?', *Aite Group (www.aitegroup.com),* September 2008

Aite Group (2009) 'European Multilateral Trading Facilities: The Post-MiFID Exchange Landscape', *Aite Group (www.aitegroup.com)*

Aitken *et al.* (2007) Aitken M., Almeida N., Harris F.H. and McInish T.H. 'Liquidity Supply in Electronic Markets', *Journal of Financial Markets,* vol:10 (2), p 144-168

Aitken, Berkman and Mak (2001) Aitken M.J., Berkman H. and Mak D., 'The use of undisclosed limit orders on the Australian Stock Exchange', *Journal of Banking and Finance,* vol:25 (8), p 1589-1603

Albuquerque and Vega (2007) Albuquerque R. and Vega C., 'Economic News and International Stock Market Co-movement.', *EFA 2006 Zurich Meetings*

Allen and Karjalainen (1999) Allen F. and Karjalainen R., 'Using genetic algorithms to find technical trading rules', *Journal of Financial Economics,* vol:51 (2), p 245-271

Almgren (2003) Almgren R., 'Optimal execution with nonlinear impact functions and trading-enhanced risk.', *Applied Mathematical Finance,* vol:10, p 1–18

Almgren and Chriss (2000) Almgren R. and Chriss N., 'Optimal Execution of Portfolio Transactions', *Journal of Risk,* vol:3, p 5-39

Almgren *et al.* (2005) Almgren R., Thum C., Hauptmann E. and Li H., 'Direct Estimation of Equity Market Impact', *Risk magazine (www.risk.net),* July 2005, p 57-62

Anand and Weaver (2004) Anand A. and Weaver D., 'Can order exposure be mandated?', *Journal of Financial Markets,* vol:7 (4), p 405-426, doi:10.1016/j.finmar.2004.04.001

Andersen *et al.* (2003) Andersen T.G., Bollerslev T., Diebold F.X. and Vega C., 'Micro Effects of Macro Announcements: Real-Time Price Discovery in Foreign Exchange', *American Economic Review,* vol:93 (1), p 38-62

Ang and Chen (2002) Ang A. and Chen J., 'Asymmetric correlations of equity portfolios', *Journal of Financial Economics,* vol:63 (3), p 443-494, doi:10.1016/S0304-405X(02)00068-5

Ankenbrand and Tomassini (1995) Ankenbrand T. and Tomassini M., 'Multivariate Time Series Modelling of Financial Markets with Artificial Neural Networks', *Proceedings of the International Conference on Artificial Neural Networks and Genetic Algorithms ICANNGA'95 (Alès, France, April 18-21, 1995) D. W. Pearson, N. C. Steele and R. F. Albrecht (Eds.),* p 257-260

Apama (2008) 'Screenshot: Apama Event Modeler', *Progress Software Corporation (www.progress.com/apama)*

Asche and Guttormsen (2001) Asche F. and Guttormsen A., 'Lead lag relationships between futures and spot prices', *Institute for Research in Economics and Business Administration (SNF) Working paper*

Asian Bonds Online (2007) 'Market Liquidity: Trading Volume', *Asian Bonds Online (asianbondsonline.adb.org)*

Asian Bonds Online (2007a) 'Asian Bonds Korea Market Infrastructure Exchanges and Trading Platforms', *Asian Bonds Online (asianbondsonline.adb.org)*

Atwell (2004) Atwell S., 'FPL Algorithmic Trading and DMA Working Group Update', *FPL (FIX Protocol Ltd.) Americas Conference 2004*

A-Team Group (2009) 'Algorithmic Trading Directory - 2009 edition', *A-Team Group (www.a-teamgroup.com)*

Bae, Jang and Park (2003) Bae K.H., Jang H. and Park K.S., 'Traders' choice between limit and market orders: evidence from NYSE stocks', *Journal of Financial Markets,* vol:6 (4), p 517-538, doi:10.1016/S1386-4181(02)00047-2

Bagnoli, Kross and Watts (2004) Bagnoli M., Kross W., Watts S.G., 'The Information in Management's Expected Earnings Report Date: A Day Late, a Penny Short', *Journal of Accounting Research,* vol:40 (5), p 1275-1296, doi:10.1111/1475-679X.t01-1-00054

Balduzzi, Elton and Green (1997) Balduzzi P., Elton E.J. and Green T.C., 'Economic News and the Yield Curve: Evidence from the U.S. Treasury Market', *Journal of Financial and Quantitative Analysis,* vol:36 (4), p 523–543

Balduzzi, Elton and Green (2001) Balduzzi P., Elton E.J. and Green T.C., 'Economic News and Bond Prices: Evidence from the U.S. Treasury Market', *Journal of Financial and Quantitative Analysis,* vol:36 (4), p 523-543

Barclay, Hendershott and Jones (2006) Barclay M., Hendershott T. and Jones C., 'Order Consolidation, Price Efficiency, and Extreme Liquidity Shocks', *forthcoming Journal of Financial and Quantitative Analysis*

Barclay, Hendershott and Kotz (2006) Barclay M.J., Hendershott T. and Kotz K., 'Automation versus Intermediation: Evidence from Treasuries Going Off the Run', *Journal of Finance,* vol:61 (5), p 2395-2414, doi:10.1111/j.1540-6261.2006.01061.x

BATS (2008) Website, *BATS (www.batstrading.com)*

BBA (2006) Barrett R. and Ewan J., 'BBA Credit Derivatives Report 2006', *British Bankers' Association (www.bba.org.uk)*

BearingPoint (2007) 'Electronic Bond Market 2007 survey', *BearingPoint (www.bearingpoint.com)*

BearingPoint (2007a) Gast F., 'Electronic Trading Platforms – European Repo and Bond Markets, ACI Germany Conference', *BearingPoint (www.bearingpoint.com)*

Beber and Caglio (2005) Beber A. and Caglio C., 'Order Submission Strategies and Information: Empirical Evidence from the NYSE', *EFA 2003 Annual Conference Paper No. 875; FAME Research Paper No. 146*

Bennett (2005) Bennett P., 'End of the road or new beginning for NYSE Specialists?', *Exchange Handbook (www.exchange-handbook.co.uk),* 2005 edition

Bennett and Campbell (2000) Bennett K.P. and Campbell C., 'Support Vector Machines: Hype or Hallelujah?', *ACM SIGKDD Explorations Newsletter archive,* vol:2 (2), p 1-13, doi:http://doi.acm.org/10.1145/380995.380999

Bernanke and Kuttner (2005) Bernanke B.S., Kuttner K.N., 'What Explains the Stock Market's Reaction to Federal Reserve Policy?', *Journal of Finance,* vol:60 (3), p 1221-1257, doi:10.1111/j.1540-6261.2005.00760.x

Bessembinder, Panayides and Venkataraman (2008) Bessembinder H., Panayides M. and Venkataraman K., 'Hidden Liquidity: An Analysis of Order Exposure Strategies in Electronic Stock Markets', *Working paper*

BGI (2009) 'ETF Industry Preview Year End 2008', *Barclays Global Investors (barclaysglobal.com)*

Biais *et al.* (2006) Biais B., Declerck F., Dow J., Portes R. and von Thadden E.L., 'European Corporate Bond Markets: transparency, liquidity, efficiency', *Centre for Economic Policy Research,* May 2006

Biais, Glosten and Spatt (2005) Biais B., Glosten L. and Spatt C., 'Market microstructure: A survey of microfoundations, empirical results, and policy implications', *Journal of Financial Markets,* vol:8 (2), p 217-264, doi:10.1016/j.finmar.2004.11.001

Biais, Hillion and Spatt (1995) Biais B., Hillion P. and Spatt C., 'An Empirical Analysis of the Limit Order Book and the Order Flow in the Paris Bourse', *Journal of Finance,* vol:50 (5), p 1655-1689

Białkowski, Darolles and Le Fol (2007) Bialkowski J., Darolles S. and Le Fol G., 'Improving VWAP strategies : A dynamical volume approach old - Decomposing Volume for VWAP Strategies', *Journal of Banking & Finance,* vol:32 (9), p 1709-1722, doi:10.1016/j.jbankfin.2007.09.023

BIS (2006) Jeanneau S. and Tovar C.E., 'Domestic bond markets in Latin America: achievements and challenges', *Bank for International Settlements (www.bis.org) Quarterly Review,* June 2006, p 51-64

BIS (2007a) 'Quarterly Review Statistical Annex - September 2007', *Bank for International Settlements (www.bis.org),* September 2007

BIS (2007b) Heath A., Upper C., Gallardo P., Mallo C. and Mesny P., 'Triennial Central Bank Survey December 2007 Foreign exchange and derivatives market activity in 2007', *Bank for International Settlements (www.bis.org),* December 2007

BIS (2007c) Upper C., Gallardo P. and Mallo C., 'Triennial and semiannual surveys on positions in global over-the-counter (OTC) derivatives markets at end-June 2007', *Bank for International Settlements (www.bis.org),* November 2007

BIS (2008) 'BIS Quarterly Review, December 2008 Statistical Annex', *Bank for International Settlements (www.bis.org),* March 2008

Biscoe (2005) Biscoe C., 'Multi-asset class trading', *FIX Global (www.fixglobal.com),* Vol 1 Issue 8 Q4 2005

Black (1971) Black F., 'Towards a fully automated exchange, part I', *Financial Analysts Journal,* vol:27, p 29-34

Black (1976) Black F., 'The Pricing of Commodity Contracts', *Journal of Financial Economics,* vol:3, p 167-79

Black and Scholes (1973) Black F. and Scholes M., 'The Pricing of Options and Corporate Liabilities', *Journal of Political Economy,* vol:81 (3), doi: 10.1086/260062

Black and Self (2005) Black T. and Self O., 'Choosing the right algorithm for your trading strategy', *'Algorithmic Trading, A Buy-Side Handbook', 1st edition (2005), publisher The Trade (www.thetradenews.com),* p 41-50

Blank (2007) Blank J.J., 'Implied Trading in Energy Futures', *Journal of Trading,* Summer 2007

BNYM (2007) 'The Depositary Receipt Markets 2007 Year End Review', *Bank of New York Mellon*

BNYM (2008) 'The Depositary Receipt Markets 2008 Year End Review', *Bank of New York Mellon*

Boehmer and Wu (2006) Boehmer E. and Wu J., 'Order flow and prices', *AFA 2007 Chicago Meetings Paper*

BOJ (2001) 'Increasing Use of Electronic Trading Systems and Its Implications on Japanese Financial Markets', *Bank of Japan Financial Markets Department*

Bollerslev (1986) Bollerslev T., 'Generalized autoregressive conditional heteroskedasticity', *Journal of Econometrics,* vol:31 (3), p 307-327, doi:10.1016/0304-4076(86)90063-1

Bongiovanni, Borkovec and Sinclair (2006) Bongiovanni S., Borkovec M. and Sinclair R.D., 'Let's Play Hide-and-Seek: The Location and Size of Undisclosed Limit Order Volume', *Journal of Trading,* Summer 2006

Boni and Leach (2004) Boni L. and Leach C., 'Expandable limit order markets', *Journal of Financial Markets,* vol:7 (2), p 145-185, doi:10.1016/j.finmar.2003.10.001

Boyle, Byoun and Park (2002) Boyle P., Byoun S. and Park H., 'The lead-lag relation between spot and option markets and implied volatility in option prices', *Research in Finance,* vol:19, p 269-284, doi:10.1016/S0196-3821(02)19012-5

Brandes *et al.* (2007) Brandes Y., Domowitz I., Jiu B. and Yegerman H., 'Algorithms, Trading Costs, and Order Size', *'Algorithmic Trading, A Buy-Side Handbook', 2nd edition (2007), publisher The Trade (www.thetradenews.com)*

Branke (1999) Branke J., 'Evolutionary Approaches to Dynamic Optimization Problems - A Survey', *GECCO Workshop on Evolutionary Algorithms for Dynamic Optimization Problems*

Brooks and Del Negro (2003) Brooks R. and Del Negro M., 'Firm-Level Evidence on International Stock Market Comovement', *Review of Finance,* vol:10 (1), p 69-98, doi:10.1007/s10679-006-6979-1

Brown and Holden (2005) Brown D.P. and Holden C.W., 'Pegged limit orders', *Working paper*

Burr (2005) Burr D., 'Vision: In the Blink of an Eye', *Current Biology,* vol:15 (14), p 554-556

Butler (1997) Butler J., 'EDDIE Beats the Market, Data Mining and Decision Support Through Genetic Programming', *Reuters: Developments,* vol:1

Butler (2007) Butler G., 'Liquidity Aggregation: What Institutional Investors Need to Know', *Journal of Trading,* Spring 2007

Bystrik and Johnson (2005) Bystrik A. and Johnson R., 'Basket algorithms The next generation', *'Algorithmic Trading, A Buy-Side Handbook', 1st edition (2005), publisher The Trade (www.thetradenews.com)*

Calvo (1999) Calvo G., 'Contagion in emerging markets: when Wall Street is a carrier', *proceedings from the International Economic Association Congress, vol. 3, Buenos Aires, Argentina 2002. Also in G. Calvo 'Emerging Capital Markets in Turmoil: Bad Luck or Bad Policy?', Cambridge, MA: MIT Press 2005.*

Cao, Hansch and Wang (2008) Cao C., Hansch O. and Wang X., 'The Informational Content of an Open Limit Order Book', *Journal of Futures Markets,* forthcoming

Cao, Hansch and Wang (2008a) Cao C., Hansch O. and Wang X., 'Order Placement Strategies in a Pure Limit Order Book Market', *Journal of Financial Research,* vol:31 (20), p 113-140, doi: 10.1111/j.1475-6803.2008.00234.x 10.1086/260062

CBOE (2009) VIX historical data, *Chicago Board Options Exchange* (www.cboe.com/VIX)

Celent (2004), 'E-Credit Trading: A Screen-Based Future?', *Celent (www.celent.com)*

Celent (2006) 'Interest Rate Swaps 2006: New Participants, New Challenges', *Celent (www.celent.com)*

Celent (2006a) 'eJGBs: e-Trading in The Japanese Government Bond Market', *Celent (www.celent.com)*

Celent (2007) 'The European Repo Market', *Celent (www.celent.com)*

Celent (2007a) 'Securities Lending: Topic, Technology, and Trends', *Celent (www.celent.com)*

Celent (2007b) 'Electronic Platforms in Foreign Exchange Trading', *Celent (www.celent.com)*

Celent (2007c) 'Alternative Trading Systems in European Equities', *Celent (www.celent.com)*

Celent (2008) 'Impact of Direct Market Access in India', *Celent (www.celent.com)*

Celent (2008a) 'Electronic Bond Trading: Reaching the Tipping Point', *Celent (www.celent.com)*

Celent (2008b) 'The Evolution of Direct Market Access (DMA) Trading Services in the US and Europe', *Celent (www.celent.com)*

Cellier (2003) Cellier A., 'Lead Lag Relationships between Short Term Options and the French Stock Index CAC 40: The Impact of Time Measurement', *Brussells Economic Review / Cahier Economique de Bruxelles,* vol:46 (2), p 65-82

CFA Magazine (2006) Opiela N., 'Hype and Algorithms Is algorithmic trading the way of the future or "just okay"?', *CFA Magazine, March-April 2006*

Chaboud et al. (2004) Chaboud A., Chernenko S., Howorka E., Krishnasami Iyer R., Liu D. and Wright J., 'The High-Frequency Effects of U.S. Macroeconomic Data Releases on Prices and Trading Activity in the Global Interdealer Foreign Exchange Market', *Federal Reserve (www.federalreserve.gov)*

Chae (2005) Chae J., 'Trading Volume, Information Asymmetry, and Timing Information', *Journal of Finance,* vol:60 (1), p 413-442, doi:10.1111/j.1540-6261.2005.00734.x

Chakrabarty and Shaw (2006) Chakrabarty B. and Shaw K., 'Hidden Liquidity', *Journal of Business, Finance and Accounting,* forthcoming

Chakrabarty, Corwin and Panayides (2007) Chakrabarty B., Corwin S.A. and Panayides M.A., 'The Informativeness of Off-NYSE Trading during NYSE Market Closures', *2007 FMA Conf. (Orlando)*

Chakravarty, Gulen and Mayhew (2004) Chakravarty S., Gulen H., Mayhew S., 'Informed Trading in Stock and Option Markets', *Journal of Finance,* vol:59 (3), p 1235-1258, doi:10.1111/j.1540-6261.2004.00661.x

Chan (2002) Chan W.S., 'Stock price reaction to news and no-news: drift and reversal after headlines', *Journal of Financial Economics,* vol:70 (2), p 223-260, doi:10.1016/S0304-405X(03)00146-6

Chan (2005) Chan Y.C., 'Price Movement Effects on the State of the Electronic Limit-Order Book', *Financial Review,* vol:40 (2), p 195-221, doi:10.1111/j.1540-6288.2005.00100.x

Chen, Shih and Wu (2006) Chen W.H., Shih J.Y. and Wu S., 'Comparison of support-vector machines and back propagation neural networks in forecasting the six major Asian stock markets', *International Journal of Electronic Finance,* vol:1 (1), p 49-67

Chen, Kim and Rui (2005) Chen G.M., Kim K.A. and Rui O.M., 'A note on price limit performance: The case of illiquid stocks', *Pacific-Basin Finance Journal,* vol:13 (1), p 81-92, doi:10.1016/j.pacfin.2004.05.002

Chen, Noronha and Singal (2006) Chen H., Noronha, G. and Singal V., 'S&P 500 Index Changes and Investor Awareness', *Journal of Investment Management,* vol:4 (2), p 23

Chenoweth, Obradovic and Lee (1995) Chenoweth T., Obradovic Z. and Lee S., 'Technical trading rules as a prior knowledge to a neural networks prediction system for the S&P 500 index', *Northcon 95. IEEE Technical Applications Conference and Workshops,* p 111, doi:10.1109/NORTHC.1995.485023

Cheung, Chinn and Garcia-Pascual (2005) Cheung Y.W., Chinn M.D. and Garcia Pascual A., 'Empirical exchange rate models of the nineties: Are any fit to survive?', *Journal of International Money and Finance,* vol:24 (7), p 1150-1175, doi:10.1016/j.jimonfin.2005.08.002

Chi-X (2008) Website, *Chi-X (www.chi-x.com)*

Chordia, Roll and Subrahmanyam (2000) Chordia T., Roll R. and Subrahmanyam A., 'Market Liquidity and Trading Activity', *Journal of Finance,* vol:56 (2), p 501-530, doi:10.1111/0022-1082.00335

Choudhry (2004) Choudhry M., 'The Government Bond Basis', *YieldCurve.publishing (www.yieldcurve.com)*

Choudhry (2006) Choudhry M., 'Financial market liquidity and the Repo instrument', *YieldCurve.publishing (www.yieldcurve.com)*

Christie, Corwin and Harris (2002) Christie W.G., Corwin S.A., Harris J.H., 'Nasdaq Trading Halts: The Impact of Market Mechanisms on Prices, Trading Activity, and Execution Costs', *Journal of Finance,* vol:57 (3), p 1443-1478, doi:10.1111/1540-6261.00466

Clare and Courtenay (2001) Clare A. and Courtenay R., 'What can we learn about monetary policy transparency from financial market data?', *Deutsche Bundesbank, Research Centre Discussion Paper Series 1: Economic Studies*

Cliff (1997) Cliff D., 'Minimal-intelligence agents for bargaining behaviours in market environments', *Institution Technical Report HPL-97-91, HP Labs, 1997*

CME (2005) Labuszewski J., 'Understanding the Special Opening Quotation (SOQ)', *Chicago Mercantile Exchange (www.cme.com)*

CME (2006) 'Developer's Guide for CME iLink 2.X', *Chicago Mercantile Exchange (www.cme.com)*

CME (2006a) 'CME Eurodollar Futures', *Chicago Mercantile Exchange (www.cme.com)*

Cohen and Frazzini (2008) Cohen L. and Frazzini A., 'Economic Links and Predictable Returns', *Journal of Finance,* vol:63 (4), p 1977-2011, doi: 10.1111/j.1540-6261.2008.01379.x

Comerton-Forde and Rydge (2004) Comerton-Forde C. and Rydge J., 'A Review of Stock Market Microstructure', *SIRCA working paper*

Conway (1970) Conway J., 'Mathematical games: The fantastic combinations of John Conway's new solitaire game "life"', *Scientific American October 1970,* vol:223, p 120-123

Copeland and Galai (1983) Copeland T.E. and Galai D., 'Information Effects on the Bid-Ask Spread', *Journal of Finance,* vol:38 (5), p 1457-1469

Corwin and Lipson (2000) Corwin S.A. and Lipson M.L., 'Order Flow and Liquidity around NYSE Trading Halts', *Journal of Finance,* vol:55 (4), p 1771-1805, doi:10.1111/0022-1082.00267

Cremers and Mei (2007) Cremers K.J.M. and Mei J., 'Turning Over Turnover', *Review of Financial Studies,* vol:20 (6), p 1749-1782, doi:10.1093/rfs/hhm038

Crevier (1993) Crevier D., 'AI: The Tumultuous Search for Artificial Intelligence', *publisher Basic Books, NY*

Crosthwait (2009) Crosthwait A., 'Is Chaos Good? Canadian Equity Market Evolution: What Institutional Investors Need To Know', *ITG Inc. (www.itg.com)*

Cummings and Frino (2007) Cummings J.R. and Frino A., 'Time-dependent risk measurement for stock index arbitrage', *SIRCA (Securities Industry Research Centre of Asia-Pacific) Limited*

Cushing and Madhavan (2001) Cushing D. and Madhavan, A., 'The Hidden Cost of Trading at the Close', *'Transaction Costs', Institutional Investor Investment Guide,* p 12-19

D'Hondt, De Winne and Francois-Heude (2001) D'Hondt C., De Winne R. and Francois-Heude A., 'Hidden Orders : an Empirical Study on the French Segment of Euro.NM', *Working paper*

D'Hondt, De Winne and Francois-Heude (2004) D'Hondt C., De Winne R. and Francois-Heude A., 'Hidden Orders on Euronext:Nothing is quite as it seems', *Working paper*

D'Hondt, De Winne and Francois-Heude (2005) D'Hondt C., De Winne R. and Francois-Heude A., 'To Hide or Not to Hide?', *Working paper*

Daniel (2006) Daniel G., 'Asynchronous simulations of a limit order book', *University of Manchester PhD Thesis Dec 2006*

Daníelsson and Payne (2002) Daníelsson J. and Payne R., 'Liquidity determination in an order driven market', *LSE Working paper*

Darolles and Le Fol (2003) Darolles S. and Le Fol G., 'Trading volume and Arbitrage', *Working paper*

Darwin (1859) Darwin C., 'The Origin of Species'

Das (2005) Das S., 'Information Structure and Investor Sentiment Extraction using the Internet', *Working paper*

Das (2005a) Das S., 'A learning market-maker in the Glosten-Milgrom model', *Quantitative Finance*, vol:5 (2), p 169-180

Das and Chen (2007) Das S.R., Chen M.Y., 'Yahoo! for Amazon: Sentiment Extraction from Small Talk on the Web', *Management Science*, vol:53 (9), p 1375-1388, doi: 10.1287/mnsc.1070.0704

Das et al. (2001) Das R., Hanson J.E., Kephart, J.O. and Tesauro G., 'Agent-human interactions in the continuous double auction', *Proceedings of the International Joint Conference on Artificial Intelligence*, vol:2, p 1169-1176

DBG (2008) 'Deutsche Börse Europe's Market Leader in ETF Trading', *Deutsche Börse (deutsche-boerse.com)*, April 2008

DBG/Clearstream (2002) 'Cross-Border Equity Trading, Clearing & Settlement in Europe', *Deutsche Börse Group and Clearstream International*, April 2002

De La Vega (1688) de la Vega J., 'Confusion de Confusiones'

De Winne and D'Hondt (2005) De Winne R. and D'Hondt C., 'Hidden Liquidity in a Pure Order-Driven Market', *Finance Letters*, forthcoming

Degryse et al. (2005) Degryse H., de Jong F., van Ravenswaaij M. and Wuyts G., 'Aggressive Orders and the Resiliency of a Limit Order Market', *Review of Finance*, vol:9 (2), p 201-242, doi:10.1007/s10679-005-7590-6

Demsetz (1968) Demsetz H., 'The cost of transacting', *Quarterly Journal of Economics*, vol:82 (1), p 33-53

Derveeuw et al. (2007) Derveeuw J., Beaufils B., Mathieu, P. and Brandouy, O., 'Testing double auction as a component within a generic market model architecture', *Lecture notes in Economics and Mathematical Systems*

D'Hondt (2008) D'Hondt C., 'Which Execution Improvement for Orders on Euronext?', *Banque & Marchés*, vol:95, p 15-26

Direct Edge (2009) 'Direct Edge Monthly Volume for December 2008', *Press Release*

Dmitrieva, Kuperin and Soroka (2002) Dmitrieva L., Kuperin Y. and Soroka I., 'Neural Network Prediction of Short-Term Dynamics of Futures on Deutsche Mark, Libor and S&P500', *Lecture Notes in Computer Science*, vol:2331/2008), p 1201-1208, doi:10.1007/3-540-47789-6

Domowitz and Krowas (2004) Domowitz I. and Krowas, J., 'Where Risk Control Meets Cost Control in Analytics Development', *Journal of Investing*, vol:13, p 82-87

Domowitz and Yegerman (2005a) Domowitz I. and Yegerman H., 'Measuring and Interpreting the Performance of Broker Algorithms', *'Algorithmic Trading, A Buy-Side Handbook', 1st edition (2005), publisher The Trade (www.thetradenews.com)*

Domowitz, Finkelshteyn and Yegerman (2008) Domowitz I., Finkelshteyn I. and Yegerman H., 'Cul de Sacs and Highways An Optical Tour of Dark Pool Trading Performance', *ITG Inc. (www.itg.com)*, August 2008

Donaldson and Kamstra (1997) Donaldson R.G. and Kamstra M., 'An artificial neural network-GARCH model for international stock return volatility', *Journal of Empirical Finance*, vol:4 (1), p 17-46, doi:10.1016/S0927-5398(96)00011-4

Drachman (2005) Drachman D.A., 'Do we have brain to spare?', *Neurology*, vol:64, p 2004-2005

Draper and Paudyal (2002) Draper P. and Paudyal K., 'Explaining Monday Returns', *Journal of Financial Research*, vol:25 (4), p 507-520, doi:10.1111/1475-6803.00034

DTReg (2008) Website, *DTReg (www.dtreg.com)*

DuCharme (2007) DuCharme M., 'First Steps in Foreign Exchange Transaction Cost Analysis', *Journal of Performance Measurement,* vol:11 (3), p 19

Dunis and Huang (2002) Dunis C.L. and Huang X., 'Forecasting and trading currency volatility: an application of recurrent neural regression and model combination', *Journal of Forecasting,* vol:21 (5), p 317-354, doi:UK 10.1002/for.833 US: http://dx.doi.org/10.1002/for.833

Dunis and Morrison (2004) Dunis C.L. and Morrison V., 'The Economic Value of Advanced Time Series Methods for Modelling and Trading 10-year Government Bonds', *European Journal of Finance,* vol:13 (4), p 333-352, doi: 10.1080/13518470600880010

Dunis and Williams (2003) Dunis C.L. and Williams M., 'Applications of Advanced Regression Analysis for Trading and Investment', *'Applied Quantitative Methods for Trading and Investment', eds Dunis C., Laws J., Naïm P., publisher John Wiley & Sons Ltd.,* doi:10.1002/0470013265.ch1

Dunne, Moore and Portes (2006) Dunne P., Moore M. and Portes R., 'European Government Bond Markets: transparency, liquidity, efficiency', *Centre for Economic Policy Research,* May 2006

Eales (2007) Eales B., 'The Case for Exchange-Based Credit Futures Contracts', *Eurex publication,* May 2007

Easley and O'Hara (1987) Easley D. and O'Hara M., 'Price, Trade Size, and Information in Securities Markets', *Journal of Financial Economics,* vol:19 (1), p 69-90

ECB (2009) 'Euro Money Market Study 2008', *European Central Bank. ECB publications are freely available at http://www.ecb.int*

Economopoulos (2005) Economopoulos A.J., 'The Impact of S&P Depository Receipts on the S&P Cash & Futures Market', *Investment Management & Financial Innovations,* vol:2 (2), p 72-82

EDHEC (2006) Amenc N., Giraud J.R., Le Sourd V., Goltz F., Martellini L. and Ma X., 'EDHEC European ETF survey 2006', *EDHEC (www.edhec-risk.com)*

EDHEC (2007) Giraud J.R. and D'Hondt C., 'Transaction Cost Analysis in Europe: Current and Best Practices European Survey', *EDHEC (www.edhec-risk.com),* January 2007

Edwards, Harris and Piwowar (2007) Edwards A.K., Harris L.E. and Piwowar M.S., 'Corporate Bond Market Transaction Costs and Transparency', *Journal of Finance,* vol:62 (3), p 1421-1451

Ehrmann and Fratzscher (2004) Ehrmann M. and Fratzscher M., 'Taking Stock: Monetary Policy Transmission to Equity Markets', *Journal of Money, Credit, and Banking,* vol:36 (4)

Elkins McSherry (2008) 'Newsletter', *Elkins McSherry LLC (www.elkinsmcsherry.com),* May 2008

Elkins McSherry (2008a) 'Newsletter', *Elkins McSherry LLC,* August 2008

Ellul *et al.* (2003) Ellul A., Holden C.W., Jain P. and Jennings R., 'Determinants of Order Choice on the New York Stock Exchange', *Working paper*

Engle (1982) Engle R.F., 'Autoregressive Conditional Heteroscedasticity with Estimates of the Variance of United Kingdom Inflation', *Econometrica,* vol:50 (4), p 987-1007

EPDA (2007) 'EPDA Third Party Access Discussion Paper', *European Primary Dealers Association*

Equilend (2008) Website, *Equilend (www.equilend.com)*

Esser and Mönch (2007) Esser A. and Mönch B., 'The navigation of an iceberg: The optimal use of hidden orders', *Finance Research Letters,* vol:4 (2), p 68-81, doi:10.1016/j.frl.2006.12.003

Euromoney (2006a) 'The growing pains of foreign exchange', *Euromoney (www.euromoney.com),* March 2006

Euromoney (2008) '2008 Euromoney FX Poll', *Euromoney (www.euromoney.com),* April 2008

Euromoney (2008a) 'Crunch wakes US to CDS e-trading', *Euromoney (www.euromoney.com),* February 2008

Evans and Lyons (2002) Evans M.D. and Lyons R.K., 'Order Flow and Exchange Rate Dynamics', *Journal of Political Economy,* vol:110 (1), doi: 10.1086/324391

Evans and Lyons (2005) Evans M.D. and Lyons R.K., 'Meese-rogoff redux: Micro-based exchange-rate forecasting', *American Economic Review,* vol:95 (2), p 405-414, doi: 10.1257/000282805774669934

Exponential-e (2009) Website, Exponential-e (www.finance.exponential-e.com)

Fabozzi and Fleming (2004) Fabozzi F. and Fleming M., 'US Treasury and Agency Securities', *'The Handbook of Fixed Income Securities',* 6th edition, publisher McGraw Hill, New York, NY

Fama and French (1993) Fama E. and French K., 'Common risk factors in the returns of stocks and bonds.', *Journal of Financial Economics,* vol:33, p 3–56

Farmer *et al.* (2004) Farmer J.D., Gillemot L., Lillo F., Mike S. and Sen A., 'What really causes large price changes?', *Quantitative Finance,* vol:4 (4), p 383-397, doi:10.1080/14697680400008627

Faseruk and Blynski (2006) Faseruk A. and Blynski L., 'Comparison of the Effectiveness of Option Price Forecasting: Black-Scholes vs. Simple and Hybrid Neural Networks', *Journal of Financial Management and Analysis,* vol:19 (2)

Federal Reserve (2009) 'Financing by U.S. Government Securities Primary Dealers', *SIFMA*

Feng, Yu, and Stone (2003) Feng Y., Yu R. and Stone P., 'Two Stock-Trading Agents: Market Making and Technical Analysis', *Lecture Notes in Computer Science Agent-Mediated Electronic Commerce,* vol:3048/2004, p 18-36, doi:10.1007/b99040

Fernández-Rodríguez, González-Martel, Sosvilla-Rivero (2000) Fernández-Rodríguez F., González-Martel C. and Sosvilla-Rivero S., 'On the profitability of technical trading rules based on artificial neural networks: Evidence from the Madrid stock market', *Economics Letters,* vol:69 (1), p 89-94, doi:10.1016/S0165-1765(00)00270-6

FIA (2006) Burghardt G., 'Annual Volume Survey - 9,899,780,283 Contracts Traded', *Futures Industry Magazine (www.futuresindustry.org),* March/April 2006

FIA (2008) Burghardt G., 'Volume Surges Again: Global Futures and Options Trading Rises 28% in 2007', *Futures Industry Magazine (www.futuresindustry.org),* March/April 2008

FIA (2009) Burghardt G. and Acworth W., '2008: A Wild Ride Global Futures and Options Volume Rises 13.7%, But Credit Crisis Damages Liquidity in the Core Markets', *Futures Industry Magazine (www.futuresindustry.org),* March/April 2009

FIF (2009) Website, Financial Information Forum (www.fif.com)

FIX (2007) 'FIX Algorithmic Trading Definition Language', *FPL Press Briefing July 25th, 2007*

FIX (2008) 'Algorithmic Trading Definition Language: Introduction and Tutorial', *FIX Protocol Ltd. (FPL) (www.fixprotocol.org)*

FIX (2008a) 'Financial Information Exchange Protocol (FIX) Version 5.0 Service Pack 1 Vol 1', *FIX Protocol Ltd. (FPL) (www.fixprotocol.org)*

FIX (2008b) 'Financial Information Exchange Protocol (FIX) Version 5.0 Service Pack 1 Vol 7', *FIX Protocol Ltd. (FPL) (www.fixprotocol.org)*

Fleming and Mizrach (2008) Fleming M.J. and Mizrach B., 'The Microstructure of a U.S. Treasury ECN: The BrokerTec Platform', *Working paper*

Fleming and Piazzesi (2005) Fleming M. and Piazzesi M., 'Monetary Policy Tick-by-Tick', *Working paper*

Fleming and Remolona (1997) Fleming M.J. and Remolona E., 'What Moves the Bond Market?', *Federal Reserve Bank of New York Economic Policy Review,* vol:3 (4)

Fleming and Remolona (1997a) Fleming M.J. and Remolona E., 'Price formation and liquidity in the U.S. Treasury Market: Evidence from intraday patterns around announcements', *New York Fed (www.newyorkfed.org)*

Fleming and Remolona (1998) Fleming M.J. and Remolona E., 'Price Formation and Liquidity in the U.S. Treasury Market: The Response to Public Information', *Journal of Finance,* vol:54 (5), p 1901-1915, doi:10.1111/0022-1082.00172

Fleming and Remolona (1999) Fleming M.J. and Remolona E., 'The Term Structure of Announcement Effects', *EFA 2001 Barcelona Meetings; BIS Working Paper No. 71; FRB of New York No. 76.*

Fleming, Kirby and Ostdiek (1998) Fleming J., Kirby C. and Ostdiek B., 'Information and volatility linkages in the stock, bond, and money markets', *Journal of Financial Economics,* vol:49 (1), p 111-137, doi:10.1016/S0304-405X(98)00019-1

Fleming, Ostdiek and Whaley (1996) Fleming J., Ostdiek B. and Whaley R.E., 'Trading Costs and the Relative Rates of Price Discovery in Stock, Futures, and Options Markets', *Journal of Futures Markets,* vol:16(4), p 353-387

Foucault (1999) Foucault T., 'Order flow composition and trading costs in a dynamic limit order market', *Journal of Financial Markets,* vol:2 (2), p 99-134, doi:10.1016/S1386-4181(98)00012-3

Fraser (2007) Fraser E., 'Options in the Dark', *Waters magazine (www.watersonline.com),* November 2007

FSA (2005) 'Trading transparency in the UK secondary bond markets', *Financial Services Authority*

FT (2007) 'Surge in volume of exchange traded funds', *Financial Times website (ft.com),* May 31 2007

FT Mandate (2006) 'Getting Asia to adopt algorithmic trading', *Financial Times Mandate (www.ftmandate.com),* June 2006

FX JSC (2007) 'BIS triennial survey of foreign exchange and over-the-counter derivatives markets in April 2007 – UK data - results summary', *www.bankofengland.co.uk/markets/forex/fxjsc*

FX JSC (2008) 'Results of the Semi-Annual FX Turnover Survey in October 2008', *www.bankofengland.co.uk/markets/forex/fxjsc*

Gagnon and Karolyi (2003) Gagnon L. and Karolyi G.A., 'Multi-Market Trading and Arbitrage', *Dice Center No. 2004-9*

Gajewski (1999) Gajewski J.F., 'Earnings Announcements, Asymmetric Information, Trades and Quotes', *European Financial Management,* vol: 5 (3), p 411-424, doi:10.1111/1468-036X.00102

Galper (2006) Galper J., 'Against the Duopoly: The New Economics for U.S. Regional Stock Exchanges and Equity ECNs', *Journal of Trading,* Spring 2006

Gande and Parsley (2005) Gande A. and Parsley D.C., 'News spillovers in the sovereign debt market', *Journal of Financial Economics,* vol:75 (3), p 691-734, doi:10.1016/j.jfineco.2003.11.003

GAO (2005) 'Securities Markets: Decimal pricing has contributed to lower trading costs and a more challenging trading environment', *United States Government Accountability Office report to congressional requesters,* May 2005

Garman (1976) Garman M., 'Market Microstructure', *Journal of Financial Economics,* vol:3 (3), p 257-75

Gastineau (2003) Gastineau G.L., 'Is Selling ETFs Short a Financial "Extreme Sport?"', *'Short selling: strategies, risks, and rewards', Fabozzi F., published 2004 by John Wiley & Sons, Inc., NJ*

Gavrishchaka and Banerjee (2006) Gavrishchaka V. and Banerjee S., 'Support Vector Machine as an Efficient Framework for Stock Market Volatility Forecasting', *Computational Management Science,* vol:3 (2), p 147-160, doi:10.1007/s10287-005-0005-5

Gjerstad and Dickhaut (1998) Gjerstad S. and Dickhaut J., 'Price Formation in Double Auctions', *Games and Economic Behavior,* vol:22 (1), p 1-29, doi:10.1006/game.1997.0576

Gode and Sunder (1993) Gode D.K. and Sunder S., 'Allocative Efficiency of Markets with Zero-Intelligence Traders: Market as a Partial Substitute for Individual Rationality', *Journal of Political Economy,* vol:101 (1), doi: 10.1086/261868

Goldberg and Leonard (2003) Goldberg L. and Leonard D., 'What Moves Sovereign Bond Markets? The Effects of Economic News on US and German Yields', *Federal Reserve Bank of New York Current Issues in Economics and Finance,* vol: 9 (9)

Goldreich, Hanke and Nath (2005) Goldreich D., Hanke B. and Nath P., 'The Price of Future Liquidity: Time-Varying Liquidity in the U.S. Treasury Market', *Review of Finance*, vol:9 (1), p 1-32, doi: 10.1007/s10679-005-2986-x

Goldstein, Hotchkiss and Sirri (2007) Goldstein M.A., Hotchkiss E.S. and Sirri E.R., 'Transparency and Liquidity: A Controlled Experiment on Corporate Bonds', *Review of Financial Studies*, vol:20 (2), p 235-273, doi:10.1093/rfs/hhl020.

Gomber, Budimir and Schweickert (2006) Gomber P., Budimir M. and Schweickert U., 'Volume Discovery: Leveraging Liquidity in the Depth of an Order Driven Market', *Electronic Markets*, vol:16 (2), p 101-111, doi: 10.1080/10196780600643688

Gomber, Schweickert and Theissen (2004) Gomber P., Schweickert U. and Theissen E., 'Zooming in on Liquidity', *EFA 2004 Maastricht Meetings Paper No. 1805*

Gonzalez Miranda and Burgess (1997) Gonzalez Miranda F. and Burgess N., 'Modelling Market Volatilities: The Neural Network Perspective', *European Journal of Finance*, vol:3(2), p 137-157, doi:10.1080/135184797337499

Gordon (1962) Gordon M.J., 'The investment, financing, and valuation of the corporation', *publisher RDIrwin, Homewood, Ill.*

Gottschalk (2003) Gottschalk N., 'Portfolio Theory Covariance and the Optimal Portfolio', *Master Thesis in "Mathematical Finance", Oxford (2003)*

Graham, Koski and Loewenstein (2003) Graham J.R., Koski J.L. and Loewenstein U., 'Information Flow and Liquidity around Anticipated and Unanticipated Dividend Announcements', *Journal of Business*, vol:79 (5), doi:10.1086/505236

Grammig, Heinen and Rengifo (2004) Grammig J., Heinen A. and Rengifo E., 'Trading activity and liquidity supply in a pure limit order book market', *EFA 2005 Moscow Meetings Paper*

Greenwich Associates (2007) 'U.S. Equities Balancing Act: Cheaper Trades Versus Sell-Side Service', *Greenwich Associates (www.greenwich.com)*

Greenwich Associates (2007a) 'Electronic Trading Systems Capture One Half of Global FX Volume', *Greenwich Associates (www.greenwich.com)*

Greenwich Associates (2008) '2008 Japanese Equity Investors Study', *Greenwich Associates (www.greenwich.com)*

Greenwich Associates (2009) 'Asian Equity Investors – Asian Equities for 2008', *Greenwich Associates (www.greenwich.com)*

Griffiths et al. (2000) Griffiths M.D., Smith B.F., Turnbull D.A.S and White R.W., 'The Costs and the Determinants of Order Aggressiveness', *Journal of Financial Economics*, vol:56, p 65-88

Hall and Hautsch (2006) Hall A. and Hautsch N., 'Order aggressiveness and order book dynamics', *Journal Empirical Economics*, vol:30 (4), p 973-1005, doi:10.1007/s00181-005-0008-7

Hamid and Iqbal (2004) Hamid S.A. and Iqbal Z., 'Using neural networks for forecasting volatility of S&P 500 Index futures prices', *Journal of Business Research*, vol:57 (10), p 1116-1125, doi:10.1016/S0148-2963(03)00043-2

Handa and Schwartz (1996) Handa P. and Schwartz R., 'Limit Order Trading', *Journal of Finance*, vol:51 (5), p 1835-1861

Handa, Schwartz and Tiwari (2003) Handa P., Schwartz R. and Tiwari A., 'Quote Setting and Price Formation in an Order Driven Market', *Journal of Financial Markets*, vol:6 (4), p 461-489, doi:10.1016/S1386-4181(02)00041-1

Harju and Hussain (2006) Harju K. and Hussain M., 'Intraday Seasonalities and Macroeconomic news announcements', *Working paper*

Harju and Hussain (2006a) Harju K. and Hussain M., 'Intraday Linkages across International Equity Markets 2006', *Working paper*

Harris (1991) Harris L., 'Stock price clustering and discreteness', *Review of Financial Studies*, vol:4, p 389-415

Harris (1996) Harris L., 'Does a large minimum price variation encourage order exposure', *Working paper*

Harris (1999) Harris L., 'Trading and Exchanges: Market Microstructure for Practitioners', *publisher Oxford University Press, USA*

Hasbrouck (1991) Hasbrouck J., 'Measuring the Information Content of Stock Trades', *Journal of Finance,* vol:46 (1), p 179-207

Hasbrouck and Saar (2002) Hasbrouck J. and Saar G., 'Limit Orders and Volatility in a Hybrid Market: The Island ECN', *Stern School of Business Dept. of Finance Working Paper FIN-01-025*

Hellström and Simonsen (2006) Hellström J. and Simonsen O., 'Does the Open Limit Order Book Reveal Information About Short-run Stock Price Movements?', *Umeå Economic Studies*

Hobson (2006) Hobson D., 'VWAP and Volume Profiles', *Journal of Trading,* Spring 2006

Holland (1975) Holland J.H., 'Adaption in Natural and Artificial Systems: An Introductory Analysis with Applications to Biology, Control and Artificial Systems', *publisher University Press of Michigan*

Hollifield, Miller and Sandas (2004) Hollifield B., Miller R.A. and Sandås P., 'Empirical Analysis of Limit Order Markets', *Review of Economic Studies,* vol:71 (4), p 1027-1063, doi: 10.1111/0034-6527.00313

Holmes and Rougier (2005) Holmes P. and Rougier J., 'Trading Volume and contract rollover in futures contracts', *Journal of Empirical Finance,* vol:12, p 317-338, doi:10.1016/j.jempfin.2004.01.003

Holowczak, Simaan and Wu (2006) Holowczak R., Simaan Y.E. and Wu L., 'Price discovery in the U.S. stock and stock options markets: A portfolio approach', *Journal Review of Derivatives Research,* vol:9 (1), p 37-65, doi: 10.1007/s11147-006-9004-0

Hong and Wang (2000) Hong H. and Wang J., 'Trading and Returns under Periodic Market Closures', *Journal of Finance,* vol: 55 (1), p 297-354, doi: 10.1111/0022-1082.00207

Hong and Yu (2006) Hong H. and Yu J., 'Gone Fishin': Seasonality in Trading Activity and Asset Prices', *Working paper*

Hong, Torous and Valkanov (2007) Hong H., Torous W. and Valkanov R., 'Do industries lead stock markets?', *Journal of Financial Economics,* vol:83 (2), p 367-396, doi:10.1016/j.jfineco.2005.09.010

Hou (2002) Hou K., 'Industry Information Diffusion and the Lead-lag Effect in Stock Returns', *Review of Financial Studies,* vol:20, p 1113-1138, doi:10.1093/revfin/hhm003.

Howarth (2004) Howarth M., 'Best execution across multiple pools of liquidity via FIX', *FIX Global (www.fixglobal.com),* Vol 1 Issue 1 Q1 2004

Hsieh, Yang and Wu (2006) Yang D.L., Hsieh Y.L. and Wu J., 'Using Data Mining to Study Upstream and Downstream Causal Relationship in Stock Market', *Advances in Intelligent Systems Research JCIS-2006 Proceedings,* doi:10.2991/jcis.2006.191

Huang, Nakamori and Wang (2004) Huang W., Nakamori Y. and Wang S.Y., 'Forecasting stock market movement direction with support vector machine', *Computers & Operations Research Applications of Neural Networks,* vol:32 (10), p 2513-2522, doi:10.1016/j.cor.2004.03.016

Huberman and Regev (2001) Huberman G. and Regev T., 'Contagious Speculation and a Cure for Cancer: A Nonevent that Made Stock Prices Soar', *Journal of Finance,* vol: 56 (1), p 387-396, doi:10.1111/0022-1082.00330

Hull (2003) Hull J., 'Options, Futures, and Other Derivatives', *5th edn, publisher Prentice Hall, New Jersey, USA*

Hutcheson (2003) Hutcheson T., 'Lead-lag Relationship in Currency Markets', *SIRCA working paper*

ICAP (2007) 'Preliminary Results Presentation', *ICAP (www.icap.com),* May 2007

ICAP (2009) Monthly volume data, *ICAP (www.icap.com)*

IHT (2006) Ujikane K. and Morita I., 'Computer hitch shuts down Japan bond trading', *International Herald Tribune,* 30 June 2006

II (2006) Paulden P., 'Keep the change', *Institutional Investor Magazine,* December 2006

IIAC (2008) 'An Issue of Debt: Inside Canada's Debt Markets', *Investment Industry Association of Canada*, Q1 2008

Inoue (1999) Inoue H., 'The Stylised Facts of Price Discovery Processes in Government Securities Markets: A Comparative Study', *publisher BIS Committee Publications*

Instinet (2005) 'Algorithmic trading: An overview', *Instinet (source: www.northinfo.com)*

Instinet (2006) 'Instinet Algorithms: Wizard', *Instinet (www.instinet.com)*

Instinet (2006a) 'Instinet Algorithms: Wizard PRO', *Instinet (www.instinet.com)*

Instinet (2007) Misra H., 'European Market Data Consolidation in a fragmented landscape', *Instinet (www.instinet.com)*

International Swaps and Derivatives Association (2009) 'News release: ISDA Publishes Year-End 2008 Market Survey Results', *www.isda.org*

ITG (2003) 'ITG Connect', *ITG Inc. (www.itg.com),* Spring 2003

ITG (2008) 'ITG Global Trading Cost Review', *ITG Inc. (www.itg.com),* February 2008

ITG (2009) 'ITG Global Trading Cost Review', *ITG Inc. (www.itg.com),* May 2009

Jain (2005) Jain P.K., 'Financial Market Design and the Equity Premium: Electronic versus Floor Trading', *Journal of Finance,* vol: 60 (6), p 2955-2985, doi: 10.1111/j.1540-6261.2005.00822.x

Jares and Lavin (2002) Jares T.E. and Lavin A.M., 'Japan and Hong Kong Exchange-Traded Funds (ETFs): Discounts, Returns, and Trading Strategies', *Journal of Financial Services Research,* vol:25 (1), p 57-69, doi:10.1023/B:FINA.0000008665.55707.ab

Johnson (2008) Johnson S., 'The Trouble with QSAR (or How I Learned To Stop Worrying and Embrace Fallacy)', *Journal of Chemical Information and Modeling,* vol:48 (1), p 25-26, doi: 10.1021/ci700332k

Kaastra and Boyd (1995) Kaastra I. and Boyd M.S., 'Forecasting Futures Trading Volume Using Neural Networks', *Journal of Futures Markets,* vol:15(8), p 953-970, doi:10.1002/fut.3990150806

Kallberg and Pasquariello (2008) Kallberg J. and Pasquariello P., 'Time-series and cross-sectional excess comovement in stock indexes', *Journal of Empirical Finance,* vol:15 (3), p 481-502

Kallberg, Liu and Pasquariello (2005) Kallberg J., Liu C.H. and Pasquariello P., 'An Examination of the Asian Crisis: Regime Shifts in Currency and Equity Markets', *Journal of Business,* vol:78 (1), doi: 10.1086/426523

Kamijo and Tanigawa (1990) Kamijo K. and Tanigawa T., 'Stock price pattern recognition-a recurrent neural network approach', *Neural Networks, 1990., 1990 IJCNN International Joint Conference on,* vol:1, p 215-221, doi: 10.1109/IJCNN.1990.137572

Kamruzzaman and Sarker (2003) Kamruzzaman J. and Sarker R.A., 'Forecasting of currency exchange rates using ANN: a case study', *Neural Networks and Signal Processing, 2003. Proceedings of the 2003 International Conference on,* p 793-797, doi: 10.1109/ICNNSP.2003.1279395

Kamruzzaman, Begg and Sarker (2006) Kamruzzaman J., Begg R.K. and Sarker R.A., 'Artificial Neural Networks in Finance and Manufacturing', *publisher Idea Group Publishing Hershey, PA, USA*

Kang, Lee and Lee (2004) Kang J., Lee S. and Lee C., 'An Empirical Investigation of the Lead-Lag Relations of Returns and Volatilities among the KOSPI200 Spot, Futures and Options Markets and their Explanations', *Journal of Emerging Market Finance,* vol:5 (3), p 235-261, doi:10.1177/097265270600500303

Kavajecz (1999) Kavajecz K.A., 'A Specialist's Quoted Depth and the Limit Order Book', *Journal of Finance,* vol:54 (2), p 747-771, doi: 10.1111/0022-1082.00124

Kawaller, Koch and Peterson (2001) Kawaller I.G., Koch P.D. and Peterson J.E., 'Volume and Volatility Surrounding Quarterly Redesignation of the Lead S&P 500 Futures Contract', *Journal of Futures Markets,* vol:21 (12), p 1119-1149

Kazakov (2003) Kazakov V., 'Optimal VWAP trading on the ASX', *PhD Thesis*

Kearns and Ortiz (2003) Kearns M. and Ortiz L., 'The Penn-Lehman automated trading project', *Intelligent Systems, IEEE,* vol:18 (6), p 22-31, doi: 10.1109/MIS.2003.1249166

Kempf and Mayston (2008) Kempf A. and Mayston D., 'Liquidity commonality beyond best prices', *Journal of Financial Research,* vol:31 (1), p 25-40, doi: 10.1111/j.1475-6803.2008.00230.x

Kim (1998) Kim S., 'Time-delay recurrent neural network for temporal correlations and prediction', *Neurocomputing,* vol:20 (1-3), p 253-263, doi:10.1016/S0925-2312(98)00018-6

Kim and Chun (1998) Kim S.H. and Chun S.H., 'Graded forecasting using an array of bipolar predictions: application of probabilistic neural networks to a stock market index', *International Journal of Forecasting,* vol:14 (3), p 323-337, doi:10.1016/S0169-2070(98)00003-X

Kim and Rhee (1997) Kim K.A. and Rhee S.G., 'Price Limit Performance: Evidence from the Tokyo Stock Exchange', *Journal of Finance,* vol:52 (2), p 885-901

Kim, Yagüe and Yang (2008) Kim Y., Yagüe J. and Yang J.J., 'Relative performance of trading halts and price limits: evidence from the Spanish Stock Exchange', *International Review of Economics and Finance,* vol:17 (2), p 197-215, doi:10.1016/j.iref.2007.06.003

King and Yaroshevsky (2005) King J. and Yaroshevsky Y., 'The Ticker', *Abel/Noser (www.abelnoser.com),* Fall 2005

Kissell (2006) Kissell R., 'The Expanded Implementation Shortfall: Understanding Transaction Cost Components', *Journal of Trading,* Summer 2006

Kissell and Glantz (2003) Kissell R., Glantz M. and Malamut R., 'Optimal Trading Strategies: Quantitative approaches for managing market impact and trading risk', *publisher American Management Association*

Kissell and Malamut (2005) Kissell R. and Malamut R., 'Understanding the Profit and Loss Distribution of Trading Algorithms', *'Guide to Algorithmic Trading', publisher Institutional Investor Inc.,* Spring 2005

Kissell and Malamut (2005b) Kissell R. and Malamut R., 'Algorithmic Decision-Making Framework', *Journal of Trading,* Winter 2006

Kissell, Freyre-Sanders and Carrie (2005) Kissell R., Freyre-Sanders A. and Carrie C., 'The future of algorithmic trading', *'Algorithmic Trading, A Buy-Side Handbook', 1st edition (2005), publisher The Trade (www.thetradenews.com)*

Kissell, Glantz and Malamut (2004) Kissell R., Glantz M. and Malamut R., 'A practical framework for estimating transaction costs and developing optimal trading strategies to achieve best execution', *Finance Research Letters,* vol:1 (1), p 35-46, doi:10.1016/S1544-6123(03)00004-7

Kiymaz and Berument (2003) Kiymaz H. and Berument H., 'The day of the week effect on stock market volatility and Volume: International Evidence', *Review of Financial Economics,* vol:12 (4), p 363-380, doi: 10.1016/S1058-3300(03)00038-7

Kloptchenko et al. (2004) Kloptchenko A., Eklund T., Back B., Karlsson J., Vanharanta H. and Visa A., 'Combining data and text mining techniques for analyzing financial reports', *International Journal of Intelligent Systems in Accounting, Finance, and Management,* vol:12 (1), p 29-44, doi: 10.1002/isaf.239

Knight (2007) Knight R., 'Fixed-income ETFs in market to stay', *Financial Times website (ft.com),* 4 June 2007

Kolb and Overdahl (2006) Kolb R.W. and Overdahl, J.A., 'Understanding Futures Markets', *publisher Blackwell Publishing*

Koza (1992) Koza J.R., 'Genetic Programming: On the Programming of Computers by Means of Natural Selection', *publisher MIT Press*

Krinsky and Lee (1996) Krinsky I. and Lee J., 'Earnings Announcements and the Components of the Bid-Ask Spread', *Journal of Finance,* vol:51 (4), p 1523-1535

Krishnamurthy (2002) Krishnamurthy A., 'The bond/old-bond spread', *Journal of Financial Economics,* vol:66 (2-3), p 463-506, doi:10.1016/S0304-405X(02)00207-6

Kulkarni (1996) Kulkarni A., 'Application of Neural Networks to Stock Market Prediction', *Report*

Kyle (1985) Kyle A.S., 'Continuous Auctions and Insider Trading', *Econometrica,* vol:53(6), p 1315-1335

Kyle and Xiong (2001) Kyle A.S. and Xiong W., 'Contagion as a Wealth Effect', *Journal of Finance,* vol:56 (4), p 1401-1440, doi: 10.1111/0022-1082.00373

Lakhal (2008) Lakhal F., 'Stock market liquidity and information asymmetry around Voluntary earnings announcements: New evidence from France', *International Journal of Managerial Finance,* vol:4 (1), p 60-75, doi: 10.1108/17439130810837384

Larison (2008) Larison S., 'Transaction Cost Analysis and Liquidity Discovery with Equity Options', *Journal of Trading,* Winter 2008

LeBaron (2000) LeBaron B., 'Agent-based computational finance: Suggested readings and early research', *Journal of Economic Dynamics and Control,* vol:24 (5 -7), p 679-702, doi:10.1016/S0165-1889(99)00022-6

LeBaron (2001) LeBaron B., 'A builder's guide to agent-based financial markets', *Quantitative Finance,* vol:1 (2), p 254-261

LeBaron (2001a) LeBaron B., 'Empirical regularities from interacting long and short memory investors in an agent-based financial market', *IEEE Transactions on Evolutionary Computation,* vol:5, p 442-455

LeBaron and Weigend (1994) LeBaron B. and Weigend A.S., 'Evaluating neural network predictors by bootstrapping', *Proceedings of International Conference on Neural Information Processing (ICONIP'94),* p 1207-12

Lee (2006) Lee W.C., 'Forecasting high-frequency financial data volatility via nonparametric algorithms: evidence from Taiwan's financial markets', *New Mathematics and Natural Computation (NMNC),* vol:2 (3), p 345-359, doi: 10.1142/S1793005706000543

Lee and Radhakrishna (2000) Lee C.M.C. and Radhakrishna B., 'Inferring investor behavior: Evidence from TORQ data', *Journal of Financial Markets,* vol:3 (2), p 83-111, doi:10.1016/S1386-4181(00)00002-1

Lee and Ready (1991) Lee C.M.C. and Ready M.J., 'Inferring Trade Direction from Intraday Data', *Journal of Finance,* vol:46 (2), p 733-746

Lee, Mucklow and Ready (1993) Lee C.M.C., Mucklow B. and Ready M.J., 'Spreads, depths, and the impact of earnings information: an intraday analysis', *Review of Financial Studies,* vol:6, p 345-374

Leinweber (2000) Leinweber D.J., 'Stupid Data Miner Tricks: Overfitting the S&P 500', *Journal of Investing,* Spring 2007

Leinweber (2002) Leinweber D., 'Using information from trading in trading and portfolio management: ten years later', *Working paper*

Leinweber and Madhavan (2001) Leinweber D.J. and Madhavan A., 'Three Hundred Years of Stock Market Manipulations', *Journal of Investing,* Summer 2001

L'Habitant (2007) L'Habitant F.S., 'Handbook of hedge funds', *publisher John Wiley & Sons, Inc., Hoboken, NJ*

Li and Tsang (1999) Li J. and Tsang E.P.K., 'Investment decision making using FGP: a case study', *Evolutionary Computation, 1999. CEC 99. Proceedings of the 1999 Congress on,* vol: 2, p 1259, doi: 10.1109/CEC.1999.782584

Li and Tsang (1999a) Li J. and Tsang E.P.K., 'Improving Technical Analysis Predictions: An Application of Genetic Programming', *Proceedings of the Twelfth International Florida Artificial Intelligence Research Society Conference,* p 108-112

Libby, Mathieu, Robb (2002) Libby T., Mathieu R. and Robb S.W.G., 'Earnings Announcements and Information Asymmetry: An Intra-Day Analysis', *Contemporary Accounting Research,* vol:19 (3), p 449-472

Lien, Tse and Zhang (2002) Lien D., Tse Y.K. and Zhang X., 'Structural change and lead-lag relationship between the Nikkei spot index and futures price: a genetic programming approach', *Quantitative Finance,* vol:3 (2), p 136-144, doi: 10.1088/1469-7688/3/2/307

Lillo, Farmer and Mantegna (2003) Lillo F., Farmer J.D. and Mantegna R.N., 'Single Curve Collapse of the Price Impact Function for the New York Stock Exchange', *Working paper*

Lo and Wang (2000) Lo A. and Wang J., 'Trading Volume: Definition, Data Analysis, and Implication of Portfolio Theory', *Review of Financial Studies,* vol:13(2), p 257-300

Lo, MacKinlay and Zhang (2002) Lo A., MacKinlay C. and Zhang J., 'Econometric models of limit-order executions', *Journal of Financial Economics,* vol:65 (1), p 31-71, doi:10.1016/S0304-405X(02)00134-4

Longin and Solnik (2001) Longin F. and Solnik B., 'Extreme Correlation of International Equity Markets', *Journal of Finance,* vol:56 (2), p 649-676, doi:10.1111/0022-1082.00340

Longstaff, Mithal and Neis (2003) Longstaff F., Mithal S., and Neis E., 'The Credit-Default Swap Market: Is Credit Protection Priced Correctly?', *USC FBE Finance Seminar*

LSE (2006) 'Guide to Trading Services', *London Stock Exchange,* July 2006

LSE (2006a) 'SETSmm Evolution for success', *London Stock Exchange,* July 2006

Lyden (2007) Lyden S., 'Time of Day and Market Impact', *Journal of Trading,* Summer 2007

Lynch and Mendenhall (1997) Lynch A.W. and Mendenhall R.R., 'New Evidence on Stock Price Effects Associated with Changes in the S&P 500 Index', *Journal of Business,* vol:70 (3), doi:10.1086/209722

Lyons (2001) Lyons R., 'The Microstructure Approach to Exchange Rates.', *publisher MIT Press*

Ma, Wong and Sankar (2007) Ma I., Wong T. and Sankar T., 'Volatility forecasting using time series data mining and evolutionary computation techniques', *Genetic And Evolutionary Computation Conference archive Proceedings of the 9th annual conference on Genetic and evolutionary computation*

Madhavan (2000) Madhavan A., 'Market microstructure: A survey', *Journal of Financial Markets,* vol:3 (3), p 205-258, doi:10.1016/S1386-4181(00)00007-0

Madhavan (2002) Madhavan A., 'Market Microstructure: A Practitioner's Guide', *Financial Analysts Journal,* vol:58 (5), p 28-42, doi: 10.2469/faj.v58.n5.2466

Madhavan (2002a) Madhavan A., 'Index Reconstitution and Equity Returns', *ITG Inc. (www.itg.com)*

Madhavan (2002b) Madhavan A., 'Implementation of Hedge Fund Strategies', *Hedge Fund Strategies (Institutional Investor),* Fall 2002

Madhavan and Ming (2003) Madhavan A. and Ming K., 'The Hidden Costs of Index Rebalancing: A Case Study of the S&P 500 Composition Changes of July 19, 2002', *Journal of Investing,* Fall 2003

Madhavan and Smidt (1993) Madhavan A. and Smidt S., 'An Analysis of Changes in Specialist Quotes and Inventories.', *Journal of Finance,* vol:48 (5), p 1595–1628

Madhavan and Yang (2003) Madhavan A. and Yang J., 'Practical Risk Analysis for Portfolio Managers and Traders', *Journal of Portfolio Management,* vol:30 (1), p 73-85

Malkiel (2004) Malkiel B.G., 'A Random Walk Down Wall Street', *publisher WW Norton & Company*

Mariathasan and Bannister (2007) Mariathasan J. and Bannister M., 'A Market Perspective on the EuroMTS Government Bond Index Futures On Euronext.liffe', *Euronext publication*

Markose and Er (2000) Markose S. and Er H., 'The Black(1976) effect and cross market arbitrage in FTSE-100 index futures and options', *Economics Discussion Papers, University of Essex*

Markose, Malik and Ng (2007) Markose S., Malik A. and Ng W.L., 'Market micro-structure multi-agent simulator and London SETS', *CCFEA Summer School Presentation Sept 2007*

Markowitz (1952) Markowitz H., 'Portfolio Selection', *Journal of Finance,* vol:7 (1), p 77-91

Mase (2006) Mase B., 'The Impact of Changes in the FTSE 100 Index', *Financial Review,* vol:42 (3), p 461-484, doi:10.1111/j.1540-6288.2007.00179.x

Maslov and Mills (2001) Maslov S. and Mills M., 'Price fluctuations from the order book perspective-empirical facts and a simple model', *Physica A: Statistical Mechanics and its Applications,* vol:299 (1-2), p 234-246, doi:10.1016/S0378-4371(01)00301-6

McEachern (2007) McEachern C., 'Electronic Trading in Asia: the Pitfalls and Opportunities', *Advanced Trading (www.advancedtrading.com),* November 2007

McEachern (2008) McEachern C., 'Exclusive: Inside State Street's FICross', *Advanced Trading (www.advancedtrading.com),* August 2008

McIntyre (2006) McIntyre N., 'Sorting the wheat from the chaff', *FTMandate.com,* May 2006

Meese and Rogoff (1983) Meese R.A. and Rogoff K., 'Empirical Exchange Rate Models of the Seventies', *Journal of International Economics,* vol:14, p 3–24

Meissner and Kawano (2001) Meissner G. and Kawano N., 'Capturing the volatility smile of options on high-tech stocks-A combined GARCH-neural network approach', *Journal of Economics and Finance,* vol:25 (3), p 276-292, doi:10.1007/BF02745889

Mendelsohn (1993) Mendelsohn L., 'Preprocessing Data For Neural Networks', *Technical Analysis of Stocks & Commodities magazine (also on www.tradertech.com),* vol:11, p 416-420

Mengle (2007) Mengle D., 'Credit Derivatives: An Overview', *Economic Review- Federal Reserve Bank of Atlanta,* vol:92 (4), p 1-24

Menzly and Ozbas (2004) Menzly L. and Ozbas O., 'Cross-industry momentum', *AFA 2005 Philadelphia Meetings*

Middleton (2005) Middleton T., 'Understanding how algorithms work. Where does time slicing and smart order routing end and randomising your orders through complex algorithms begin?', *'Algorithmic Trading, A Buy-Side Handbook', 1st edition (2005), publisher The Trade (www.thetradenews.com)*

Middleton (2005a) Middleton T., 'Learning to use the technology tool', *FTMandate.com,* December 2005

Mitra (2006) Mitra S.K., 'Improving Accuracy of Option Price Estimation using Artificial Neural Networks', *Indian Institute of Capital Markets 9th Capital Markets Conference Paper*

Mittal (2008) Mittal H., 'Are You Playing in a Toxic Dark Pool? A Guide to Preventing Information Leakage', *ITG Inc. (www.itg.com),* June 2008

Mittal and Taur (2008) Mittal H. and Taur R., 'Maintaining Trade List Structure Across Dark Pools: The Right Aggregating Algorithm Makes all the Difference', *ITG Inc. (www.itg.com)*

Mittal and Wong (2008) Mittal H. and Wong J., 'Choosing the 'Right' Algorithm Can Minimize Trading Costs in Today's Volatile Markets', *ITG Inc. (www.itg.com),* November 2008

Monitor110 (2007) Website, *Monitor110.com*

Morgan (2007) Morgan J., 'Algos Explore New Space', *Waters magazine (www.watersonline.com),* November 2008

Morgan Stanley (2006) 'Exchange-Traded Funds Quarterly Report', *Morgan Stanley*

Morgan Stanley (2007) 'Morgan Stanley Electronic Trading Benchmark Execution Strategies', *Morgan Stanley (www.morganstanley.com)*

Moshiri and Foroutan (2004) Moshiri S. and Foroutan F., 'Testing for deterministic chaos in futures crude oil price; Does neural network lead to better forecast?', *Canadian Economics Association 2004 Annual Meeting*

MTS Group (2007) 'MTS Group Sees Strong Q1 Performance; Repo and BondVision Hit New Record Volumes', *Press release,* April 2007

Muchnik, Louzoun and Solomon (2006) Muchnik L., Louzoun Y. and Solomon S., 'Agent Based Simulation Design Principles - Applications to Stock Market', *Practical Fruits of Econophysics: Proceedings of The Third Nikkei Econophysics Symposium, publisher Springer-Verlag Berlin and Heidelberg GmbH & Co. KG,* p 183-188

Nakajima *et al.* (2004) Nakajima Y., Ono I., Sato H., Mori N., Kita H., Matsui H., Taniguchi K., Deguchi H., Terano T. and Shiozawa Y., 'Introducing Virtual Futures Market System "U-Mart"', *Working paper*

NASDAQ (2008) 'The NASDAQ Workstation', *NASDAQ (www.nasdaq.com)*

NASDAQ (2008a) 'Order Types and Routing Strategies Reference Guide', *NASDAQ*

Natenberg (1994) Natenberg S., 'Option volatility and pricing', *2nd edn, publisher McGraw-Hill/Irwin NY*

New York Fed (1998) 'U.S. Monetary Policy and Financial Markets: Ch 4 The Financial Markets', *New York Fed (www.newyorkfed.org)*

New York Fed (2009) 'Primary dealer transactions volume in U.S. Government and Federal Agency Securities', *New York Fed,* 11 October 2007

New York Times (1997) Wade N., 'Tests on mice block defense by cancer', *New York Times, November 27, 1997*

New York Times (1998) Kolata G., 'Hope in the lab: A special report; A cautious awe greets drugs that eradicate tumors in mice', *New York Times, May 3, 1998*

Nicoll (2004) Nicoll E., 'Reducing Transaction Costs and Recapturing Value for Your Plan', *Pension Observer Winter 2004*

Niemira and Zukowski (1998) Niemira M.P. and Zukowski G.F., 'Trading the fundamentals', *publisher McGraw-Hill, New York*

Norden and Weber (2005) Norden L. and Weber M., 'The Comovement of Credit Default Swap, Bond and Stock Markets: An Empirical Analysis', *forthcoming European Financial Management*

NRI (2007) 'Technical Assistance for Developing Bond Markets in Thailand Repo Market – Implications from foreign markets', *Nomura Research Institute*

NSX (2009) 'National Stock Exchange Historical ETF data', *www.nsx.com*

Nyholm (2002) Nyholm K., 'Estimating the Probability of Informed Trading', *Journal of Financial Research,* vol:25 (4), p 485-505, doi:10.1111/1475-6803.00033

NYSE (2006) 'Hybrid Market Training Program', *NYSE (www.nyse.com),* September 2006

NYSE (2009) 'Historical monthly volume', *New York Stock Exchange (www.nyse.com)*

NYSE Exchanges (2007) 'How much volume is hybrid', *NYSE Exchanges (exchanges.nyse.com)*

O'Connor (1999) O'Connor M.L., 'The Cross-Sectional Relationship Between Trading Costs and Lead/Lag Effects in Stock & Option Markets', *Financial Review,* vol:34 (4), p 95-117, doi:10.1111/j.1540-6288.1999.tb00471.x

Oppenheimer and Parry (2007) Oppenheimer S. and Parry T., 'Intelligent Backtesting: Gaining a competitive advantage in FX strategy development', *e -FOREX magazine,* Oct 2007

Ormoneit and Neuneier (1996) Ormoneit D. and Neuneier R., 'Experiments in predicting the German stock index DAX with density estimating neural networks.', *Computational Intelligence for Financial Engineering, 1996., Proceedings of the IEEE/IAFE 1996 Conference,* p 66-71, doi:10.1109/CIFER.1996.501825

Pagano and Padilla (2005) Pagano M. and Padilla A.J., 'The Economics of Cash Trading: An Overview', *Working paper*

Palmer *et al.* (1994) Palmer R.G., Arthur W.B., Holland J.H., LeBaron B. and Tayler P., 'Artificial Economic Life: A Simple Model of a Stockmarket', *Physica D,* vol:75, p 264–274

Pardo and Pascual (2006) Pardo A. and Pascual R., 'On the hidden side of liquidity', *Working paper*

Parlour (1998) Parlour C., 'Price dynamics in limit order markets', *Review of Financial Studies,* vol:11, p 789-816

Pascual and Veredas (2008) Pascual R. and Veredas D., 'What Pieces of Limit Order Book Information Matter in Explaining the Behavior of Limit-Order Traders and Market-Order Traders?', *Working paper*

Pasquariello (2007) Pasquariello P., 'Imperfect Competition, Information Heterogeneity, and Financial Contagion', *Review of Financial Studies,* vol:20, p 391-426, doi: 10.1093/rfs/hhl010.

Pensions & Investments (2003) Williams F., 'Trading cost analysis tools finally available for fixed-income world', *Pensions & Investments*

Perold (1988) Perold A., 'The implementation shortfall: paper versus reality', *Journal of Portfolio Management,* Spring 1988

Persaud (2001) Persaud A., 'Liquidity Black Holes', *Working paper*

Persaud (2006) Persaud A., 'Improving efficiency in the European government bond market', *ICAP and Intelligence Capital publication*

Phylaktis and Xia (2008) Phylaktis K. and Xia L., 'Equity Market Comovement and Contagion:A Sectoral Perspective', *Financial Management,* forthcoming

Pires and Marwala (2007) Pires M.M. and Marwala T., 'Option Pricing Using Bayesian Neural Networks', *Working paper*

Poon and Granger (2003) Poon S.H. and Granger C.W.J., 'Forecasting Volatility in Financial Markets: A Review', *Journal of Economic Literature,* vol: 41 (2), p 478-539, doi: 10.1257/002205103765762743

Potvin, Soriano and Vallée (2004) Potvin J.Y., Soriano P. and Vallée M., 'Generating trading rules on the stock markets with genetic programming', *Computers & Operations Research,* vol:31 (7), p 1033-1047, doi:10.1016/S0305-0548(03)00063-7

Qi and Sui (2007) Qi R. and Sui L., 'The Addition and Deletion Effects of the Standard & Poor's 500 Index on Option Markets', *2007 FMA Conf. (Orlando)*

QSG (2008) 'Study of NYFIX Millennium Trade Executions Shows Significant Reduction in Market Impact Across Market Sectors and Trading Strategies', *NYFIX Press release,* June 2008

Raberto et al. (2001) Raberto M., Cincotti S., Focardi S.M. and Marchesi M., 'Agent-based simulation of a financial market', *Physica A: Statistical Mechanics and its Applications,* vol:299 (1-2), p 319-327, doi:10.1016/S0378-4371(01)00312-0

Raberto et al. (2003) Raberto M., Cincotti S., Focardi S.M. and Marchesi M., 'Traders' Long-Run Wealth in an Artificial Financial Market', *Journal Computational Economics,* vol:22 (s2-3), p 255-272, doi:10.1023/A:1026146100090

Ranaldo (2004) Ranaldo A., 'Order aggressiveness in limit order book markets', *Journal of Financial Markets,* vol:7 (1), p 53-74, doi:10.1016/S1386-4181(02)00069-1

Ranaldo (2008) Ranaldo A., 'Intraday Market Dynamics Around Public Information Arrivals', *published in: Gregoriou G. and L'Habitant F.S. (eds): "Stock Market Liquidity: Implications for Market Microstructure and Asset Pricing", 2008, John Wiley and Sons*

Refenes and Holt (2001) Refenes A.P.N. and Holt W.T., 'Forecasting volatility with neural regression: A contribution to model adequacy', *Neural Networks,IEEE Transactions on,* vol:12 (4), p 850-864, doi:10.1109/72.935095

Refenes, Zapranis and Francis (1995) Refenes A.P.N., Zapranis A. and Francis G., 'Modeling stock returns in the framework of APT: a comparative study with regression models', *'Neural Networks in the Capital Markets',* ed. Refenes A., publisher John Wiley & Sons, p 101–125

Rime, Sarno and Sojli (2008) Rime D., Sarno L. and Sojli E., 'Exchange rate forecasting, order flow and macroeconomic information', *Working paper*

Rivero (2005) Rivero R., 'FIX and algorithmic trading', *FIX Global (www.fixglobal.com),* Vol 1 Issue 7 Q3 2005

Rosenblatt Securities (2007) Gawronski J., 'Is this Really Goodbye? And Why? An analysis of shrinking price improvement at the NYSE, its causes, the potential for a reversal, and other market quality and market structure observations', *Trading Talk, Rosenblatt Securities Inc. (www.rblt.com),* February 2007

Rosenblatt Securities (2007a) Gawronski J., 'The Decline and Fall of Displayed Markets??? Highlighting some recent trends in non-displayed liquidity pools (PART DEUX)', *Trading Talk, Rosenblatt Securities Inc. (www.rblt.com),* October 2007

Rosenblatt Securities (2008a) Schack J. and Gawronski J., 'Let there be light', *Trading Talk, Rosenblatt Securities Inc. (www.rblt.com),* December 2008

Rosenblatt Securities (2009) Schack J. and Gawronski J., 'Let there be light', *Trading Talk, Rosenblatt Securities Inc. (www.rblt.com),* May 2009

Safarik (2005) Safarik D., 'Fixed Income Meets the Black Box', *Advanced Trading (www.advancedtrading.com),* October 2005

Saperia and Gross (2008) Saperia N. and Gross J., 'Credit Event Auction Primer', *www.creditfixings.com*

Schittenkopf, Dorffner and Dockner (1998) Schittenkopf C., Dorffner G. and Dockner E.J., 'Volatility Predictions With Mixture Density Networks', *ICANN 98 – Proceedings of the 8th International Conference on artificial Neural Networks, L. Niklasson, M. Bodén and T. Ziemka, ed., Berlin,* p 929-934

Schittenkopf, Dorffner and Dockner (2000) Schittenkopf C., Dorffner G. and Dockner E.J., 'Forecasting time-dependent conditional densities: A semi-nonparametric neural network approach', *Journal of Forecasting,* vol:19 (4), p 355-374

Schmerken (2006) Schmerken I., 'Exchanges Gamble On Multi-Asset Trading', *Advanced Trading (www.advancedtrading.com),* January 2006

Schmerken (2008) Schmerken I., 'NYSE Says Good Bye to Specialists; Hello DMMs', *Advanced Trading (www.advancedtrading.com),* June 2008

Schmerken (2009) Schmerken I., 'Regulatory Push for Clearing Platforms in Credit Derivatives Could Pave the Way for E-Trading', *Advanced Trading (www.advancedtrading.com),* January 2009

Schwartz and Pagano (2005) Schwartz R. and Pagano M., 'On Exchange Consolidation and Competition', *A Comment Letter to the Competition Commission in Connection with the London Stock Exchange Inquiry*

Schwartz, Van Ness and Van Ness (2004) Schwartz A.L., Van Ness B.F. and Van Ness R.A., 'Clustering in the futures market: evidence from S&P 500 futures contracts', *Journal of Futures Markets,* vol:24 (5), p 413-428, doi:10.1002/fut.10129

Seo, Giampapa and Sycara (2002) Seo Y.W., Giampapa J. and Sycara K., 'Text Classification for Intelligent Portfolio Management', *Tech. report CMU-RI-TR-02-14, Robotics Institute, Carnegie Mellon University*

Shalen (2002) Shalen C., 'The Nitty-Gritty of CBOT DJIA Futures Index Arbitrage', *Chicago Board of Trade (www.cbot.com)*

Sherstov and Stone (2004) Sherstov A.A. and Stone P., 'Three Automated Stock-Trading Agents: A Comparative Study', *AAMAS 2004 Workshop on Agent Mediated Electronic Commerce VI*

Shiller (1989) Shiller R.J., 'Comovements in Stock Prices and Comovements in Dividends', *Journal of Finance Papers and Proceedings of the Forty-Eighth Annual Meeting of the American Finance Association, New York,* vol: 44 (3), p 719-729

SIFMA (2006) 'Fixed income e-commerce survey', *SIFMA (www.sifma.org)*

SIFMA (2007a) 'Securities Industry and Financial Markets Global Addendum 2007', *SIFMA (www.sifma.org)*

SIFMA (2008) 'Average Daily Trading Volume in the U.S. Bond Markets', *SIFMA (www.sifma.org)*

SIFMA (2008a) 'Research-Quarterly', *SIFMA (www.sifma.org),* September 2008

SIFMA (2008b) 'Outstanding Money Market Instruments', *SIFMA (www.sifma.org)*

SIFMA (2008c) 'U.S. Treasury Securities Outstanding', *SIFMA (www.sifma.org)*

Silvapulle and Granger (2001) Silvapulle P. and Granger C.W.J., 'Large returns, conditional correlation and portfolio diversification: a value-at-risk approach', *Quantitative Finance*, vol:1 (5), p 542-551, doi: 10.1080/713665877

SIN (2006a) Harris L.E., 'No End to Fragmentation', *Securities Industry News - Special Report Market Structure*

SIN (2007) Trombly M., 'Buy-Side-Driven Trading Takes Hold in Hong Kong', *Securities Industry News - Algorithmic Trading, April 2007*

SIN (2007a) Kite S., 'Two bond platforms, two approaches', *Securities Industry News, April 30 2007*

Sinclair (2008) Sinclair E., 'Volatility Trading', *publisher John Wiley & Sons, Inc., Hoboken, NJ*

Smith (1998) Smith S.N.P., 'Trading Applications of Genetic Programming', *Financial Engineering News,* Sep 1998, vol:6

Smith (2005) Smith H., 'ECNs: An uncertain future', *IBM: Building an Edge — the Financial Services newsletter,* vol:6 (9)

Sofianos (1990) Sofianos G., 'Index Arbitrage Profitability', *Journal of Derivatives,* vol:1 (1)

Sosvilla-Rivero and Rodríguez (2004) Sosvilla-Rivero S. and Rodríguez P.N., 'Linkages in international stock markets: Evidence from a classification procedure', *Working paper*

SPA (2008) Website, *Structured Products Association (www.structuredproducts.org)*

Steiner and Wittkemper (1995) Steiner M. and Wittkemper H.G., 'Neural Networks as an Alternative Stock Market Model', *'Neural Networks in the Capital Markets' ed. Refenes A., publisher John Wiley & Sons*

Stoll (1969) Stoll H.R., 'The Relationship Between Put and Call Option Prices', *Journal of Finance,* vol:24 (5), p 801-824

Stoll (2001) Stoll H.R., 'Market Microstructure', *Handbook of the Economics of Finance,* vol:1(1), p 553-604

Streichert (2002) Streichert F., 'Introduction to Evolutionary Algorithms', *Frankfurt MathFinance Workshop presentation*

SunGard (2006) 'SunGard's Loanet Centralized Order Routing Service Reaches Milestone for Daily Volume', *SunGard (www.sungard.com),* August 2006

Switzer, Varson and Zghidi (2000) Switzer L.N., Varson P.L. and Zghidi S., 'Standard and Poors depository receipts and the performance of the S&P 500 index futures market', *Journal of Futures Markets,* vol:20 (8), p 705-716

Tabb (2004) Tabb L., 'A New Market Structure for Bonds', *Finance Tech (www.financetech.com)*

TABB Group (2003) Tabb L., 'NYSE: Why the buy-side is crying for change', *TABB Group (www.tabbgroup.com)*

TABB Group (2006) Johnson J., 'Locating the Invisible: Aggregating Dark Book Liquidity', *TABB Group (www.tabbgroup.com)*

TABB Group (2007) Iati R., 'The FX market has become fragmented', *TABB Group (www.tabbgroup.com)*

TABB Group (2007b) Sussman A. and Simon M., 'European Institutional Equity Trading 2007: The Buy-Side Perspective', *TABB Group (www.tabbgroup.com)*

TABB Group (2007d) Nybo A., 'Exchange-Traded Equity Derivatives: The Buy-Side's Increasing Exposure', *TABB Group (www.tabbgroup.com)*

TABB Group (2007e) Berke L., 'FX Algorithms: Bringing Best Execution to the FX Markets', *TABB Group (www.tabbgroup.com)*

TABB Group (2008) Berke L., 'US Institutional Equity Trading: Crisis, Crossing and Competition', *TABB Group (www.tabbgroup.com)*

TABB Group (2009) Nybo A., 'US Options Trading 2009: Resilience in the Face of Crisis', *TABB Group (www.tabbgroup.com)*

Takeuchi (2005) Takeuchi A., 'Study of Impediments to Cross-border Bond Investment and Issuance in Asian Countries', *Asian Bonds Online (asianbondsonline.adb.org)*

Taniguchi (2003) Taniguchi T., 'Who lost MTS? The Electronic Trading Platform Killed By JGB', *GLOCOM (www.glocom.com)*, 6 November 2003

Tay and Cao (2001) Tay F. and Cao L., 'Application of support vector machines in financial time series forecasting', *Omega: The International Journal of Management Science*, vol:29(4), p 309-317, doi:10.1016/S0305-0483(01)00026-3

Taylor (1986) Taylor S., 'Modelling Financial Time Series', *publisher John Wiley & Sons*

TBMA (2005) 'European Bond Pricing Sources and Services: Implications for Price Transparency in the European Bond Market', *SIFMA (www.sifma.org)*

Tetlock, Saar-Tsechansky and Macskassy (2008) Tetlock P.C., Saar-Tsechansky M. and Macskassy S., 'More Than Words: Quantifying Language to Measure Firms' Fundamentals', *Journal of Finance*, vol:63 (3), p 1437-1467, doi: 10.1111/j.1540-6261.2008.01362.x

TextMap (2007) 'Relational network for Google', *TextMap (www.textmap.com)*

The Trade News (2008) 'Turquoise breaks through 5% market share barrier', *The Trade News (www.thetradenews.com)*, 7 November 2008

Theocharides (2006) Theocharides G., 'Contagion: Evidence from the Bond Market', *Working paper*

TheOptionsGuide.com (2007) 'Dividend Arbitrage', *TheOptionsGuide.com website*

Thiriet (2006) Thiriet O., 'Level best execution', *The Trade Magazine*, Issue 7 Jan-Mar 2006

Tiňo, Schittenkopf and Dorffner (2000) Tino P., Schittenkopf C. and Dorffner G., 'Temporal Pattern Recognition in Noisy Non-stationary Time Series Based on Quantization into Symbolic Streams: Lessons Learned from Financial Volatility Trading', *Working paper*

Traders Magazine (2007b) 'Traders Magazine Special Report: Algos 3.0 Developments in Algorithmic Trading.', *Traders Magazine (www.tradersmagazine.com)*

Tradeweb (2008) Website, *www.tradeweb.com*

TradingMarkets (2007) 'Singapore Exchange's target price raised to 20 SGD from 15 SGD - UBS Tuesday, October 09, 2007', *Trading Markets (www.tradingmarkets.com)*

Trombly (2007) Trombly M., 'Asia Report', *Waters magazine (www.watersonline.com)*, July 2007

Tsang et al. (2000) Tsang E.P.K., Li, J., Markose S., Er H., Salhi A. and Iori G., 'EDDIE In Financial Decision Making', *Journal of Management and Economics*, vol: 4 (4)

Tsang, Markose and Er (2005) Tsang E.P.K., Markose S. and Er H., 'Chance discovery in stock index option and futures arbitrage', *New Mathematics and Natural Computation.*, vol:1 (3), p 435-447

Tsibouris and Zeidenberg (1995) Tsibouris G. and Zeidenberg M., 'Testing the efficient markets hypothesis with gradient descent algorithms', *'Neural Networks in the Capital Markets', ed. Refenes A., publisher John Wiley and Sons*

Tucker (1991) Tucker A.L., 'Financial futures, options, and swaps', *publisher West Pub. Co St. Paul*

Tuttle (2003) Tuttle L., 'Hidden orders, trading costs and information', *2008 FMA European Conf. (Athens)*

Twain (1907) Twain M., 'Chapters from My Autobiography', *North American Review, No. DCXVIII., July 5, 1907*

U.S. DOA (2009) Website, *U.S. Department of Agriculture FATUS Commodity Aggregations (www.fas.usda.gov)*

U.S. DOT (2009) Website, *U.S. Department of Transport Fatality Analysis Reporting System (www-fars.nhtsa.dot.gov)*

Van Gestel et al. (2001) Van Gestel T., Suykens J.A.K., Baestaens D.E., Lambrechts A., Lanckriet G., Vandaele B., De Moor B. and Vandewalle J., 'Financial time series prediction using least squares support vectormachines within the evidence framework', *Neural Networks, IEEE Transactions on*, vol:12 (4), p 809-821, doi: 10.1109/72.935093

Vapnik (1995) Vapnik, V., 'The Nature of Statistical Learning Theory.', *publisher Springer, NY*

Veredas (2006) Veredas D., 'Macroeconomic surprises and short-term behaviour in bond futures', *Empirical Economics,* vol:30 (4), p 843-866, doi:10.1007/s00181-005-0002-y

Vidyamurthy (2004) Vidyamurthy G., 'Pairs Trading: Quantitative Methods and Analysis', *publisher John Wiley and Sons*

Wael (2008) Wael L., 'Adjustment of stock prices to earnings announcements: evidence from Euronext Paris', *Review of Accounting and Finance,* vol:7 (1), p 102-115, doi:10.1108/14757700810853879

Wagner (2006) Wagner W.H., 'Creating A Hierarchy of Trading Decisions', *Journal of Trading,* Winter 2006

Wagner and Edwards (1993) Wagner W.H. and Edwards M., 'Best execution', *Financial Analysts Journal,* vol:49 (1), p 65–71, doi: 10.2469/faj.v49.n1.65

Wagner and Glass (2001) Wagner W.H. and Glass S., 'What every plan sponsor needs to know about transaction costs', *Transaction Cost Guide, Institutional Investor Inc.,* p 9–16

Wang, Zu and Kuo (2006) Wang M.C., Zu L.P. and Kuo C.J., 'Anatomy of Bid-Ask Spread:Empirical Evidence from an Order Driven Market', *Money Macro and Finance (MMF) Research Group Conference 2006*

Wang, Zu and Kuo (2008) Wang M.C., Zu L.P. and Kuo C.J., 'The State of the Electronic Limit Order Book, Order Aggressiveness and Price Formation', *Asia-Pacific Journal of Financial Studies,* vol:37 (2), p 245-296

Wei and Zee (1998) Wei H.P. and Zee S., 'Interday variation in price volatility, volume and open interest in the market for foreign currency futures', *Journal of Research in Finance,* vol:1, p 6–27

WFE (2007) 'Focus', *World Federation of Exchanges (www.world-exchanges.org),* May 2007 No171

WFE (2007a) 'WFE Annual Report 2006', *World Federation of Exchanges (www.world-exchanges.org)*

WFE (2008) 'WFE Annual Report 2007', *World Federation of Exchanges (www.world-exchanges.org)*

WFE (2009) 'WFE Annual Report 2008', *World Federation of Exchanges (www.world-exchanges.org)*

White (1988) White H., 'Economic prediction using neural networks: the case of IBM daily stock returns', *Neural Networks, 1988., IEEE International Conference on,* vol:2, p 451-458, doi:10.1109/ICNN.1988.23959

Wiese (1930) Wiese R.F., 'Investing for True Value', *Barron's,* September 1930, p 5

Wikipedia (2006) 'Diversification (finance)', *Wikipedia (en.wikipedia.org)*

Wikipedia (2008) 'Nearest neighbor (pattern recognition)', *Wikipedia (en.wikipedia.org)*

Williams (1938) Williams J.B., 'The Theory of Investment Value', *publisher Harvard University Press*

WSJ (2004) Malik N.S., 'Currency Trading Is Moving From Brokers to Home Offices', *Wall Street Journal,* 25 November 2004

www.IndexArb.com (2007) Website, *www.indexarb.com*

Yang (2005) Yang J.W., 'Predicting Stock Price Movements: An Ordered Probit Analysis on the Australian Stock Market', *Working paper*

Yang and Jiu (2006) Yang J. and Jiu B., 'Algorithm Selection: A Quantitative Approach', *'Algorithmic Trading II', publisher Institutional Investor, New York*

Yao and Poh (1995) Yao J. and Poh H.L., 'Forecasting the KLSE index using neural networks', *Neural Networks, 1995. Proceedings., IEEE International Conference on,* vol: 2, p 1012-1017, doi:10.1109/ICNN.1995.487559

Yao and Tan (2000) Yao J. and Tan C.L., 'A case study on using neural networks to perform technical forecasting of forex', *Neurocomputing,* vol:34 (1), p 79-98, doi: 10.1016/S0925-2312(00)00300-3

Yao, Tan and Poh (1999) Yao J., Tan C.L. and Poh H.L., 'Neural networks for technical analysis: a study on KLCI', *International Journal of Theoretical and Applied Finance (IJTAF)*, vol:2 (2), p 221-241, doi: 10.1142/S0219024999000145

Yeo (2008) Yeo W.Y., 'Serial Correlation in the Limit Order Flow: Causes and Impact', *2008 FMA European Conf. (Prague)*

Yuan (2005) Yuan K., 'Asymmetric Price Movements and Borrowing Constraints: A Rational Expectations Equilibrium Model of Crisis, Contagion, and Confusion', *Journal of Finance*, vol:60 (1), p 379-411

Zemke (2002) Zemke S., 'On Developing a Financial Prediction System: Pitfalls and Possibilities', *Proceedings of DMLL-2002 Workshop at ICML-2002, Sydney, Australia*

Zhang and Zhou (2004) Zhang D. and Zhou L., 'Discovering golden nuggets: data mining in financial application', *Systems, Man, and Cybernetics, Part C: Applications and Reviews, IEEE Transactions on*, vol: 34 (4), p 513-522, doi:10.1109/TSMCC.2004.829279

Index

Made in the USA
Middletown, DE
22 November 2024

65186896R00329